Child Development
Individual, Family, and Society

Child Development
Individual, Family, and Society

NO GOL BOOKPLATES, OK
ULL

Alan Fogel
Purdue University

Gail Melson
Purdue University

West Publishing Company
St. Paul   New York   Los Angeles   San Francisco

Study Guide

A study guide has been prepared by Jeanne Karns to assist you in mastering concepts presented in this text. The study guide is available from your local bookstore under the title *Study Guide to Accompany Child Development: Individual, Family, and Society*. If you cannot locate it in the bookstore, ask your bookstore manager to order it for you.

Composition: Carlisle Graphics
Copyediting: Deborah Smith
Interior and Cover Design: Christy Butterfield
Artwork: Lee Ames & Zak, Ltd.
Cover Image: Used with permission of Grandma Moses Properties, Inc., and the White House Collections.

COPYRIGHT © 1988   By WEST PUBLISHING COMPANY
50 W. Kellogg Boulevard
P.O. Box 64526
St. Paul, MN 55164-1003

30114 004754662

Printed in the United States of America

Library of Congress Cataloging-in-Publication Data

Fogel, Alan.
  Child development

  Includes bibliographies and index.
    1. Child development.   I. Melson, Gail F.
II. Title. [DNLM: 1. Child Development.
WS 105 F655c]
RJ131.F6   1988   155.4   86-33948
ISBN 0-314-25869-8

Photo credits appear after the Index

To Jacqueline Fogel and Robert Melson

About the Authors

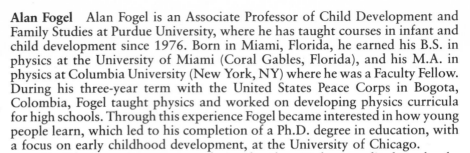

Alan Fogel   Alan Fogel is an Associate Professor of Child Development and Family Studies at Purdue University, where he has taught courses in infant and child development since 1976. Born in Miami, Florida, he earned his B.S. in physics at the University of Miami (Coral Gables, Florida), and his M.A. in physics at Columbia University (New York, NY) where he was a Faculty Fellow. During his three-year term with the United States Peace Corps in Bogota, Colombia, Fogel taught physics and worked on developing physics curricula for high schools. Through this experience Fogel became interested in how young people learn, which led to his completion of a Ph.D. degree in education, with a focus on early childhood development, at the University of Chicago.

Dr. Fogel is active as a researcher and author. He has co-edited two books on research in early child development: *Emotion and Early Interaction* (with Tiffany Field), and *Origins of Nurturance: Biological, Cultural and Develomental Perspectives on Caregiving* (with Gail F. Melson). He has also written an undergraduate text on infant development, *Infancy: Infant, Family and Society*. Fogel has published scholarly papers on development in infancy. These include studies of emotional development, social development in relation to parents and to peers, and on topics of infant development of concern to health care providers and early childhood educators. This work is published in *Child Development, Developmental Psychology, Infant Behavior and Development, Journal of Pediatric Psychology, International Journal of Behavioral Development,* and *Current Topics in Early Childhood Education.*

Fogel has been supported in his research through grants from the National Science Foundation, The National Institutes of Health, the National March of Dimes Foundation, and the United States Department of Agriculture. He is a member of the national research honor society, Sigma Xi. He has lectured widely in the United States, Europe, and in Japan, where he spent a year (1983–1984) as a senior research scholar under a Fulbright Fellowship. He is currently working on a comparison of infant social develoment between Japan and the United States.

Gail F. Melson   Gail Melson is an Associate Professor of Child Development and of Psychology at Purdue University. She received a B.A. *cum laude* from Harvard University in philosophy, an M.S. in psychology from Michigan State University, and a Ph.D. in developmental psychology from Michigan State University, where she held a NIMH predoctoral fellowship. For the past 15 years, she has taught undergraduate and graduate courses in child development, life-span development, and family relationships.

Dr. Melson's research centers on the social development of young children, and she has published studies on such topics as children's responses to infants, sex differences in personal space, communication between friends and non-friends, and children's understanding of social relationships. This work has appeared in such journals as *Child Development, Genetic Psychology Monographs, Sex Roles, Perceptual and Motor Skills,* and *Home Economics Research Journal.* Dr. Melson is the author of *Family and Environment: An Ecosystem Perspective* (Minneapolis, MN: Burgess Publishing Co., 1980) and co-editor of *The Origins of Nurturance: Developmental, Cultural, and Biological Perspectives of Caregiving* (Hillsdale, NJ: Erlbaum, 1986).

Dr. Melson also has a strong interest in cross-cultural development and in social policy implications of child development research. She received a Lilly Faculty Open Fellowship to study social policy from a cross-cultural perspective, and has been a visiting professor at Hebrew University in Jerusalem, Israel.

Outside the classroom and laboratory, Dr. Melson enjoys tennis, swimming, aerobics, and travel with her family, which includes husband Robert, a professor of political science, 19-year-old daughter Sara, and 16-year-old son Josh.

Brief Contents

Contents

Focus Boxes

In the past several decades, dramatic changes have taken place in the lives of children, their families, and the societies in which they live. Divorce, single parenthood, and remarriage have made the experiment of growing up more varied than ever before. The now normative pattern of all parents, mothers and fathers, in the workplace is fast replacing the model of a mother–childrearer, father–breadwinner. On the societal level, rapid technological change and economic interdependency have created a global village in which social change and dislocation rapidly reverberate.

These changes among others have moved the lives of children and their families from the periphery of public consciousness to the center of national debate over issues such as:

1. How should young children be cared for in an era when neither parent is available for full-time child care?
2. What are the effects of divorce, single parenthood, and remarriage on the developing child?
3. What is the best way to educate children to become productive citizens in a global economy?
4. Why does child abuse occur, and how can it be prevented?

Child Development: Individual, Family, and Society presents a comprehensive introduction to the study of child development. Major theoretical perspectives are linked to critically examined current research findings. However, this book goes beyond the common core of knowledge found in most texts in order to address current issues affecting children through an ecological systems perspective, a sensitivity to cultural differences, and explicit treatment of policy-related topics. Distinguishing features of the book include:

1. Chronological treatment of child development—infancy, early childhood, middle childhood, and adolescence. These divisions correspond to the major junctures in children's lives as they move into first experiences with peers and outside-the-home care (early childhood), to elementary school (middle childhood), and then to junior-senior high school and beginning college (adolescence).
2. Topical treatment of areas of development within each chronological period—physical, cognitive and social-emotional development.
3. An ecological systems orientation reflected by a "Connecting with Others" chapter for each developmental period examines development within the major contexts of family, school, and other children.

4. Extensive coverage of traditional theories with continued application of theory to research throughout.
5. In-depth examination of selected research studies as well as thorough coverage of research findings.
6. "Focus" sections on current policy, issues, and areas of risk/intervention affecting children.

Pedagogical Features of the Text

There is no more fascinating story than the account of how a unique individual develops from a fertilized ovum. *Child Development: Individual, Family, and Society* brings to instructors and students the most important classic and recent research and theory but in a way that preserves the sense of wonder and fascination that the story itself holds. A primary concern has been to share with students the excitement of studying child development as a scientific field of inquiry.
of the Text

Each chapter contains a number of specific pedagogical aids:

(1) *Opening quote:* Each chapter begins with a quotation to spark interest and set the tone for the topics to come. Opening selections are drawn from well-known observers of children, interesting historical sources, famous individuals reminiscences of childhood, or the words of children themselves, for example, John Stuart Mill and John Paul Sartre on their childhoods, Ann Frank's diary entries, Claude Brown's memories of growing up in Harlem, and the thoughts of a four-year-old interviewed by Jean Piaget.

(2) *Introduction and overview:* To help alert students to the main points of the chapter, the introduction that follows the opening quote identifies specific topics of the chapter and outlines the major themes that are explored.

(3) *Focus on Policy:* In each chapter, a "focus" box insert examines policy concerns related to children's development, for example, children's legal rights, bilingual education, the provision of education to handicapped children, and the regulation of television violence.

(4) *Focus on Issue:* Each chapter also contains a focus box insert examining an issue currently debated by child development professionals or the public at large. Examples include "test-tube babies," "latch-key" status and its effects on development, the causes and effects of childhood obesity, and sex-role development in single-parent families.

(5) *Focus on Risk/Intervention:* A third type of focus box insert found in each chapter examines an area of risk

to development and evaluates the most common interventions. Topics such as hyperactivity, learning problems, child abuse, social rejection by peers, and adolescent depression and suicide are covered.

(6) *Detailed examination of selected research studies:* Along with broad coverage of research findings, the student is encouraged to take a more detailed look at the approaches and methods of child development investigators. The logo indicates that an individual study will be described in greater detail. Studies selected for this more in-depth treatment may be "classics," excellent illustrations of a particular implication of theory, exemplars of a particular methodology, or recent examples of "cutting-edge" investigations.

(7) *Tables, figures and photographs:* Each chapter includes many tables and figures that present key information and illustrate important research findings. The extensive use of color photographs and graphics through the text enhances student interest by creating an engaging visual presentation.

(8) *Chapter summary:* Each chapter closes with a point-by-point summary to help students organize and master the material.

(9) *Recommended readings:* Following each chapter, a number of books recommended for further reading are described, with their major features outlined for the student.

(10) *Key terms and glossary index:* Important terms are italicized and carefully defined when they first appear. In addition, a complete glossary at the back of the book allows the student to easily reference new terms or concepts.

(11) *References:* Research and theory references are noted by author and date in American Psychological Association style in the body of the text, with a complete reference list provided.

Ancillaries

A number of ancillary materials makes *Child Development: Individual, Family, and Society* a complete learning and teaching package.

(1) *Instructor's Manual with Test Bank:* Jeanne Karnes and Linda Wark of Purdue University have developed an excellent instructor's manual and battery of test questions. The authors bring considerable experience in high school and college teaching as well as child development expertise to this carefully written manual, which includes for each chapter a description of chapter focus, a detailed chapter outline, learning objectives, and key terms. The extensive test bank includes multiple-choice, short answer and essay questions of various degrees of difficulty, organized by chapter.

(2) *Student Study Guide:* Professor Jeanne Karnes of Purdue University has written an outstanding student study guide which students may purchase. It includes a chapter outline, stressing key points, learning objectives, and key terms and concepts. Programmed self-study and sample test questions are also included.

(3) *Transparency masters:* Key tables and figures are reproduced from chapters and placed on transparency masters for instructors using overhead projectors. In addition, original supplementary material not found in the text but suitable for lecture presentation is also reproduced on transparency masters. The original material is keyed to chapter texts for ease of lecture organization.

Acknowledgements

We wish to gratefully acknowledge the unstinting help in manuscript preparation through endless retypings and revisions given us by Alice Smith, Phoebe Herr, and Kristen Hart. Special thanks to Dr. Robert Lewis and our colleagues at the Department of Child Development and Family Studies, Purdue University, for creating the supportive and collegial atmosphere that made the production of this book possible.

We wish to thank the following child development professionals who carefully reviewed portions of the manuscript. Their many comments, criticisms and suggestions substantially improved and informed the book:

Marvin Berkowitz	Elaine Justice	Bill Romoser
Theodore Bosack	Daniel Kaye	Shirley Rosenwasser
Jim Campbell	Daniel Kee	Helen Warren Ross
Debra Clark	Melvyn King	Toni Santmire
Robert Coon	Mary Kralj	Sherrie Shugarman
Barbara Davis	Larry Kurdek	Barbara Sommer
Jan Deissler	Linda Lavine	Michael Sosulski
Cathy Dent	Betty Marrs	Robert Stewart, Jr.
Dora Dien	David Moshman	Joyce Stines
Sandra Fiske	Faye Murphy	Francis Terrell
Robert Haaf	Gregory Reichhart	Ross Vasta
Jerry Harper	David Richards	F. L. Whaley
Bruce Hinrichs	Arthur Roberts	William Zachry
Mary Hood		

The editorial staff at West has contributed enormously to our efforts; in particular, the assistance of Laurie Bailey, Tamborah Moore and Kristen McCarthy is gratefully acknowledged. Our deepest appreciation goes to the "fairy godmother" of this book, Mary Schiller, editor at West Educational Publishing, who stimulated us to think about writing this book and then encouraged and guided its development over several years. While we alone take responsibility for any shortcomings the book may contain, the success of the text must be shared with her.

Alan Fogel
Gail F. Melson
Purdue University

PART I

Setting the Stage

CHAPTER 1

Introduction: The Developing Child in a Changing World

I *have thought a deal on 'Train up a child in the way he should go'. I have considered the New Testament precepts on the same subject; and I have endeavored to practice them . . . I recollected my being a child myself; how I behaved to my father and how he behaved to me . . . I took notice also of other families in the neighborhood, and attempted to derive some improvement from them. I laboured to preserve the love, esteem and affection of my children . . . I endeavored not to overburden them with work . . . I was especially determined to keep them from following any course of sin and from sinful companions . . . I made a practice of talking with my children, to instruct them to impress their minds . . . I then understood how unreasonable and cruel it was in parents to scold and beat their children for acting in such and such a manner; when they had taken no pains to instruct them that such actions were wrong.*

— Taylor, 1820, pp. 118–120; as
quoted in Pollack, 1983, pp. 156–157.

Developmental change is something we all take for granted. The fact that we grow and change is inseparable from our sense of self. Everyone is aware that children develop at a faster rate than do adults. If you know a child that you see only once or twice a year, it is always a surprise to note how that child has changed.

If you've ever had such an experience, you realized that the child had changed in some expected ways. As they get older, most children grow taller and fuller and become more knowledgeable and more aware of the world. There may also have been some aspects of the child's personality that remained: a streak of mischief, intelligence, or sensitivity to other people.

On the other hand, the child may have changed in ways that you never anticipated. He or she may have taken on new interests, outgrown an earlier stage of sullenness, or lost a particular trait that you once liked.

Have you ever wondered what causes people to change in some ways and remain the same in others? Perhaps you believe that people's characters are the result of experiences from early childhood, from the way their parents brought them up, or from some childhood handicap or disease. The quote at the beginning of this chapter shows that people have been pondering these questions for many years.

The Importance of Studying Child Development

If you've ever thought about any of the preceding, you probably have your own set of beliefs about the nature of human development. What you read in this book should push you to think more critically about those beliefs.

Why is this important?

All of us were—and in some ways still are—children. We are all endowed with a desire to understand our own childhood: where we came from, what we have been through, how we became the person we are today. What you learn in this book may help you to remember things from your own past that you might have forgotten. You may also come to understand certain aspects of your past that until now had been unclear to you.

This kind of self-searching is a normal and expected part of reading a book such as this one. Not only will you understand yourself better by the end of this book, but you should also be able to understand all children better by comparing your own experiences to theirs.

The better we understand the real reasons children grow and change, the better we can make decisions that affect children's lives. If you are, or plan to become, a parent or if you pursue a career working with children and their families (such as teaching, day care, nursing, medicine, counseling, or psychology), what you learn from this book will be an important foundation for your professional growth.

Even if you do not become a parent or if you choose a profession that is not directly concerned with children and families, many decisions that you will make in life will indirectly influence the welfare of children. If you become a supervisor or administrator, you will be setting policies that affect the lives of employees with children. Will you give your employees time off to take their children to the doctor or to see their child participate in a baseball game? Will you see your role as one of assisting your employees in raising a family, or will you merely consider your employees in relation to their contribution to the company?

Any time you vote in a public election, you are making a decision about children and families, since most public service offices deal in some way with families and children, from the local sheriff, the judge, the school board, and mayor, all the way up to state and national legislators, the governor, and the president. You'll see in this book how public policies made into law by legislators and decided upon by judges and law enforcement officers have a direct impact on children and families.

Finally, it is important to study child development simply for the purpose of gaining knowledge about an important and interesting aspect of nature. The development of human life—how we each become an individual and unique personality—is one of the great mysteries of science. The scientific study of human development can lead not only to practical information but also to the enrichment of our knowledge of the world. Just as the exploration of space or the probing of the atom has led to both practical and "pure" knowledge, so has the study of human development to which you will be introduced in this book.

What You Can Learn from This Book

You should get two basic ideas from this book:
1. Children develop through an orderly sequence of steps that lead from conception through maturity.
2. The scientific method can be applied to the developing child to separate fact from fiction in explaining the causes of differences between people that arise during development.

(1) *Development is ordered change.* Not all changes that we observe in children are developmental changes. A child can change from being happy to having a temper tantrum, but we wouldn't call such a change developmental, because the child soon changes back to the happy state.

Developmental changes are not reversible. Development has a direction that is always pointing ahead.

Developmental changes are not temporary. Such changes persist over relatively long periods: weeks, months, or years.

Developmental changes are not haphazard. Development occurs in an orderly sequence that is almost the same in all children. It is impossible, for example, to speak in sentences without first passing through a period of one-word speech.

Figure 1–1 shows a sequence related to the physical development of the lower limbs of the young child. The sequence is directional, since the child becomes increasingly competent with age. Each of the steps is persistent, because it lasts for a considerable period. In fact, children do not lose their earlier abilities as they gain their later ones. Finally, the sequence is orderly, since there is a logical progression of ability and since virtually every normal child progresses through these steps.

(2) *Explaining the formation of individual differences.* Human development is a complex process that cannot be reduced to a few simple explanations such as "She succeeded only because of her good looks," "Spare the rod and spoil the child," "It's their mother's fault; she never gave the kids enough attention," "It was the boy's fate to turn out this way."

Developmental researchers have tried to see if there is any truth to some of these frequently heard beliefs about the causes of child development. Consider the first one. You will read in Chapter 8, for example, that children who are physically attractive are often the most popular. This may seem desirable, but being popular may place demands on the child that his or her personality is not equipped to handle. In other words, being attractive has both risks and benefits.

Although some attractive children succeed, others do not. When you know one attractive person who has succeeded, it is tempting to attribute that success to attractiveness. But since not all attractive children succeed—and many unattractive children do succeed—other factors must be involved—perhaps intelligence, assertiveness, persistence, and good self-concept—that contribute to success. Chapter 8 discusses more about this issue.

With regard to the issue of discipline, research shows that physical punishment (rather than sparing the rod) is related to negative outcomes in children, especially if it is used persistently and without an understanding of the reasons for the child's behavior.

Understanding children's motives and points of view, clearly explaining the rules to children, setting limits that children can tolerate and understand, and forgiving children for "childish" mistakes not only are highly successful methods for assuring the child's compliance, but also help to build self-esteem and the use of intelligence for self-regulation. Discipline methods are discussed later in this chapter and in Chapters 7, 11, and 15.

The amount of time mothers spend with their children—often used to place blame or credit on the mother for the outcomes of childrearing—is not related to any measurable aspects of child behavior and development, as you will see in Chapters 7, 11, and 15. For example, there seem to be few differences between the children of working and nonworking mothers.

Research shows that there may even be some advantages to being the child of a working mother, including a sense of independence and a breaking down of sex-role stereotypes. This is because in dual wage-earner families, women share in earning income and many men share in childcare and household chores.

Little concrete evidence exists that fate explains child development. Child development researchers may not know all the reasons children turn out the

Figure 1–1

Sequence of Development for Lower Limb Movements

1. Crawling
2. Upright walking
3. Running and jumping
4. Organized games and sports

One goal of the developmentalist is to explain how differences between children develop. The preschool children shown here are the same age, but one can already distinguish between them. Besides the obvious differences in size and shape, behavioral and temperamental differences may be seen: Some are leaders and some followers, some shy and others outgoing, some are intent and serious while others are more excitable and lively.

way they do. The child development professional who cannot account for some aspect of a child's development is more likely to attribute it to the sheer complexity of development—the multiple and interacting causes and effects that lead to unpredictable outcomes—than to the idea of predeterminism.

How To Read This Book

Everyone—your grandmother, your teacher, the child development researchers whose work is reviewed in this book—has a unique view of child development. One's view of child development is shaped by one's childhood, one's store of knowledge about children, and one's direct experience with young children.

We, too, as the authors of this book, have a unique perspective on child development—a perspective that shaped the organization and contents of the book. In the following few pages, we share this perspective with you so that you can better understand how best to use this book to learn about children.

Ecological/Systems Perspective

We believe that children do not grow up in isolation. Although children spend some of their time alone, most of their life is centered around other people in the context of the family, friends, and school. An *ecological/systems perspective* means to consider the whole of the child's world as we seek to understand the causes of development.

You can think of ecological/systems perspective as a powerful zoom lens. When the lens is set at normal, we see the child in the family, the child in school, and the child playing with friends. When we zoom in for a closer view, we see the whole child, developing simultaneously in many areas: height, weight, thinking, emotions, and behavior. When we zoom out beyond the family and school, we see them as part of a neighborhood in which the child lives. Moving out to an even wider view, we can see that the family and school are contained in a complex society: a network of laws, historical precedents that have shaped society's beliefs, and supports as well as demands on the family and school. Even though the child does not directly experience the events taking place in the Supreme Court or at the parent's workplace, such events can and do shape the opportunities for that child in the course of development.

Infancy, Early Childhood, Middle Childhood, Adolescence

This book is arranged in chronological order. Rather than dealing with a particular topic such as physical development and reviewing in one chapter how children of different ages develop, each chapter in this book reviews a particular topic for one age group. The book thus has four chapters on physical development: one each on infancy, early childhood, middle childhood, and adolescence.

We believe that an ecological/systems perspective on children requires that you understand all the views from the zoom lens at the same time for the same age child. If you learn all of the concepts related to physical development from infancy to adolescence and then go back to learn about, say, emotional development, it is easy to lose track of how the ideas go together at any one age. We want you to understand babies or teenagers as whole people.

Our choice of age divisions is also guided by the ecological/systems perspective perspective. The terms *infancy, early childhood, middle childhood,* and *adolescence* correspond to the major changes in social relationships in families and schools during childhood. Thus early childhood is the preschool period, middle childhood covers the elementary school years, and adolescence refers to young people in junior and senior high school and early college.

Physical, Cognitive, Social, and Emotional Connections to Others

Within each of the four basic age units just discussed, we examine the views contained within our ecological/systems zoom lens. In the chapters and sections on physical, cognitive, social, and emotional development, we cover the close-up view of the whole child. In the sections and chapters on the "connections to others," we cover the wide-angle view of the child within the family, the school, and society.

Dividing the child into packages such as "physical development" or "cognitive development" does some injustice to the ecological/systems perspective. However, since our minds cannot comprehend all things at the same time, we have to separate these areas of the child conceptually before we can put the whole child back together.

We have tried to make this easier by providing references to other chapters where similar material is located. You don't have to read this book page by page, from start to finish. Some active skipping around will be necessary for you to integrate the material across the different chapters. Not only should you seek to put the whole infant or teenager back together conceptually, but you should also move among the major age units to be sure that you clearly understand what is different about each age period.

Focus on Research

The "facts" about child development reported in this book are based entirely on current research in this area. The facts change over time as research methods improve and better studies are made. The best approach to teaching about child development is to give you all the details about each research study so that you can see not only the scope but also the limitations of our knowledge about children.

Such a goal is impossible to meet because of the vast number of studies on children. In each chapter of this book we will be forced, because of space limitations, to summarize the results of research studies as we understand them. However, to give you a sense of how knowledge about children is acquired, we have chosen several research studies in each chapter on which we focus our zoom lens to provide a detailed description of the methods and findings. We choose to focus on a particular research study because it is illustrative of the typical research methods used in that area, and we believe our focus studies represent some of the best work in that area. When you see the symbol it means that we are about to focus in on one research study for a more complete description.

We feel that understanding the basics of child development research is so essential to our modern understanding of the young child that we have devoted an entire chapter (Chapter 3) to an explanation of research methods in child development. The chapter focuses on one research study that illustrates some of the important research methods. You'll be able to follow that study from conception through execution to interpretation.

Focus on Theory

Our ecological/systems perspective helps us to organize all of the information available about children. It helps us to put that information into a consistent conceptual framework so that our minds can comprehend the child as a whole. Researchers call such conceptual frameworks *theories*.

Even though we apply our ecological/systems theory of child development throughout this book, we are aware that there are other important theories that people use to understand children. We devote an entire chapter to defining and reviewing the major theories of child development (Chapter 2), and we apply these major theories in every chapter of the book. We attempt to weigh the evidence for and against particular theories and try to show why, in most cases, we keep returning to our ecological/systems perspective. Thus, even if you don't end up agreeing with us, we want you to have some alternative points of view that are as clearly articulated as our own.

Focus on Issue, Policy, and Risk/Intervention

Most of the topics in this book cover the traditional areas of child study that have been used in the field for decades. Child development researchers, however, are beginning to open up new areas of inquiry, such as the impact of hospitals on birthing practices, children's legal rights, the effects of working mothers on children, and the role of government intervention into matters of the family affecting child development.

Since many of these areas have been studied only in the past ten years, we cannot be sure how important they are or whether they will have a lasting effect on the field of child development. Thus, we are not yet ready to put this research into our textbook as a major subdivision carrying the same weight as, say, the physical development of the child.

This new research is, however, extremely informative to our ecological/systems view of children. Much of it covers applied topics such as health and nutrition not typically found in child development texts. To cover some of these potentially exciting new directions while doing justice to the traditional areas of child study, we have developed FOCUS sections, to be found in every chapter.

FOCUS ON ISSUE reviews current controversial topics in child development research, areas in which no conclusive answer is yet available or in which a current flurry of research activity exists. FOCUS ON POLICY speaks to the relationship between the child and society, such as the ways in which national and state legislation affects what children eat or what they see on television. FOCUS ON RISK/INTERVENTION deals with children who are sick, handicapped, or living in conditions such as poverty that are not conducive to healthy development. Such children are receiving increasing attention from child development professionals.

What To Expect from Each Chapter

Each chapter opens with a quotation, often the words of children, parents, and teachers, that sets the stage for the topic of the chapter. In addition to providing a comprehensive overview of current research, each chapter contains several sections focusing on single research studies, marked with Each of the words appearing in italics or boldface can be found in the glossary at the back of the book for easy reference when the same term is used in later chapters. Each chapter has three FOCUS sections: one each on ISSUE, POLICY, and RISK/INTERVENTION. Each chapter concludes with a point-by-point summary of the important findings and with a short list of recommended readings for further study.

The remainder of this chapter reviews the history of beliefs and practices related to children and describes the historical background for our modern scientific approaches to child development.

The History of Folk Beliefs About Childhood

The quote at the beginning of this chapter was written by John Taylor, a Baptist minister who lived from 1743 to 1819. Taylor kept a diary in which he discussed his work and family, including his six living children. He was a man of few words, making only a few short entries in his diary each year. It is interesting that he devoted so much of his writing to his children and his role as a parent (Pollack, 1983).

John Taylor's diary shows that Taylor did a good deal of thinking about his children—about the way to "train up the child" in accordance with the ideals and principles in which he strongly believed, about how to keep his children from sin while preserving their love and affection, and about understanding children as people and giving of his time to them.

The set of ideas that people have about childhood, childrearing, and parent-child relationships is referred to as a childrearing *belief system*. It includes ideas about the stages of growth and development of the child, the goals and methods of education, the role of the parent, the importance of health and well-being, methods of discipline, and the reasons for wanting a child. Belief systems are embodied in individual minds, but the quality of those beliefs is influenced by each person's own past history (for example, John Taylor's reflections on his own childhood), by the social context in which the person is living, and by the past history of that society.

This part of the chapter reviews the history of beliefs about children from ancient times until the twentieth century. Knowledge of the history of child development allows us to reject two myths about past times. One myth suggests that there was a Golden Age in the past in which parents were loving, their

The History of Services for Children in Families

In the past 100 years, public and private agencies have become increasingly active in the development of special services for children.

A *protective service* is a social service for children who are abused, neglected, or exploited in some way. This type of service has its nineteenth century origins in the Society for the Prevention of Cruelty to Children, which historically, was an outgrowth of animal protection societies. The Humane Society was founded to protect both children and animals (Zietz, 1969).

Currently, protective services are administered by state and local welfare departments. The social workers receive reports of abuse and neglect from police, schools, doctors, neighbors, and relatives. The child is considered to be the primary focus of intervention, but the parents usually receive the treatment, such as counseling, family support services, and, as a last resort, referral to family court to judge if the child should be removed from the home.

Recent efforts in child protective services involve preventive measures and community-based programs (Garbarino, 1982). Children in some communities are being taught to recognize the differences between normal affection from adults and physical contact that is abusive or sexually exploitative. Television programs and books are being developed to educate children about their bodies and their rights. This type of education may alert children from nonabusive families to recognize abuse in school and day care settings.

A current issue in protective services is the definition of the boundary between the public domain and the private domain of the family with regard to intervention to protect the child. Under what conditions can the state remove the child from the home? In cases where abuse is reported, it is the child who is the most informed witness. Studies are currently under way to assess the reliability of children's court testimony in such cases (see Chapter 11).

Supplementary child care outside the home for children who live in their own homes is called *day care service*. This includes day care centers, child development centers, nursery schools, day care homes, and Head Start programs. Day care homes are private homes in which the owner has a child care service for neighborhood children. Head Start is a federally funded preschool program that is geared to the needs of children from low-income families. Day care centers began in New York City in 1854 in an effort to provide for the children of working mothers and for children of the poor.

Nursery schools, providing preschool educational programs, were established in England by Margaret MacMillan and Grace Owen in 1909. In the United States, the first nursery schools were established as laboratories for research on child development and the training of college students majoring in home economics in the care of young children. The first U.S. nursery school was run by the Bureau of Educational Experiments in New York City in 1919. In 1922, Teacher's College of Columbia University in New York and the Merrill-Palmer Institute in Detroit established experimental nursery school programs. The National Association for the Education of Young Children was founded in 1926 (Zeitz, 1969).

Current controversies include the long-term effect on children of day care, of having a working mother, and of specific educational practices in the preschool. The potential mismatch between the typically child-centered preschool curriculum and the more task-centered curriculum of the public elementary school is a concern. The setting of minimum standards for class size and preschool teacher training has not been effectively resolved.

children obeyed them, and everyone lived in extended families and in communities that provided shelter and support. The other myth is that enlightened and loving parents are a recent invention, growing out of previous centuries of cruelty, ignorance, and abuse (Grubb & Lazerson, 1982).

At any given time in history, unfortunately, there have been children who suffer from abuse, neglect, poverty, and disease. There have also always been children who have been loved, living in stable and secure families and communities. Although we can document the historical continuity of belief systems referring to the inherent value of childhood and the goodness of children, no society at any time in history, including our own today, has been able to guarantee those birthrights to all its children.

Learning from History

A number of historians have suggested that until the last 100 years or so, there has been no concept of childhood in Western society. In writing about European childhood up until the twentieth century, these historians have claimed that the child was abused, ignored, and exploited by both parents and society (Aries, 1962; DeMause, 1974; Stone, 1977). In prior periods of history, a parent's only concern was for the survival of the child to make a productive contribution to the family. Childhood was seen as a biologically necessary prelude to adult life, "a state to be endured rather than enjoyed" (Tucker, 1976, p. 230).

Other historians have disagreed with these extreme views. Some have found evidence of parents who loved their children and viewed them as a pleasurable part of the family as early as A.D. 200 (Lyman, 1976). By the twelfth century there are "clear signs . . . of tenderness toward infants and small children, interest in the stages of development, awareness of their need for love" (McLaughlin, 1976, pp. 117–118).

Why should historians disagree so drastically over this matter? According to historian Linda Pollack's *Forgotten Children,* those who found negative attitudes toward children used *secondary sources,* such as medical advice books, religious sermons, paintings in which children were (or more often were not) depicted, fictional literature, philosophical writings (such as Aristotle, Plato, Locke, and Rousseau), and legislation. *Primary sources,* such as diaries, memoirs, and letters written by parents and sometimes by children themselves, have been used less frequently. When primary sources are studied, a much more favorable view of childhood emerges (Pollack, 1983).

The Ancient World.   Even within secondary sources, there is evidence that children were looked on favorably with love, kindness, and pleasure as early as three or four thousand years ago. Children's toys have been found from ancient Greece and Egypt, some homemade and others the products of specialized toy makers. Written descriptions of children's play and games exist from the period beginning two thousand years before the birth of Christ. Children imitated adult activities, using miniature soldiers and chariots, household furnishings, and dolls. Such toys can be seen today in museums in North America and Europe.

Formal education was present starting about six years of age among the ancient Greeks, Egyptians, Hebrews, and Chinese. The purpose of this education varied from country to country. In Greece children learned mathematics, athletics, and military skills; Egyptian education was more vocationally oriented to careers of priest, scribe, doctor, or artisan; in ancient Israel children learned basic subjects such as grammar, history, and geography from reading the holy book, or Torah (which has survived as part of the modern Old Testament).

The Greeks developed a view of life that placed importance on the development of the individual in both mind and body. The focus was on the fulfillment of each person's highest potentials. The Judeo-Christian tradition emphasized knowledge as a major goal of education. Each person should be

Schools have been in existence since the beginning of recorded history. Over 3,000 years ago this Greek boy stood rigidly reciting his lessons while his teacher reclined in a rather comfortable chair. His lesson from this teacher was in music. From other teachers he learned mathematics, literature and athletics. The Greeks were among the first to advocate what we now call a 'liberal arts' curriculum for the eduction of a well-rounded, informed citizen.

able to reach the highest possible state of knowledge or grace by an awareness of his or her own relationship to God and to the community. This belief placed importance on the individual's responsibility to him or herself first, and through that self-knowledge, to take responsibility for one's fellow man.

In China, education was based on the ideas of Confucius (551–479 B.C.) and his followers. Confucianism has three main points: man must find his place in nature without disturbing the harmonious workings of the universe; individuals can be improved through education; and the government's purpose is to serve the needs of its people. Education was used primarily to train government officials. The key concept of *harmony* means that humans should live with due respect for the natural world and its powers and processes. Harmony also refers to individual relations with others. Confucianism taught people to accept their place in nature and in the community and work to achieve a harmonious balance between the self and others (Loewe, 1966). Individual knowledge and fulfillment was supposed to grow out of one's involvement with and commitment to the group.

Throughout the ancient world, education was mainly for boys. In China, Greece, and Egypt it was reserved for upper classes, but not in Israel. Perhaps the first compulsory, universal education law (for boys, anyway) was established by the Israelite priest Joshua ben Gamala, 60 years before the birth of Christ (Greenleaf, 1978).

This suggests that by the second or first century B.C., an awareness existed—at least in some societies in the Middle East and in China and for certain educated subgroups within those societies—of the value of play in the early years, the inherent worth of children, the need for special care and training of children, and the role of adults in that process. The tradition of Confucianism in China and of Judaism in Israel revered the role of teacher. According to the Talmud, "a teacher should be venerated as much as God himself" (Greenleaf, 1978, p. 15), and teachers were accorded the highest social status throughout the ancient world.

The Middle Ages. In the Middle Ages (second to fourteenth centuries) Chinese awareness of childhood continued to grow. For example, Chinese writers dis-

?–10,000 B.C.	Food-gathering stage. Man lives in small tribal groupings.	1200–1500	Growth of European towns; the bubonic plague. Marco Polo goes to Asia. Islam spreads to Asia. Printing press is invented in Europe. Shoguns begin their rule of feudal Japan. The Americas are discovered by Europeans.
10,000–1500 B.C.	Man spreads to all corners of the world. Cities develop around 3000 B.C. in the Middle East and China.	1500–1700	Renaissance, followed by religious reformation and the rise of Protestantism in Europe. William Shakespeare writes; Galileo invents the telescope. East-West trade continues. The British come to India; the Taj Mahal is built. The Chinese population reaches 150 million around 1550. Christian missionaries in China and Japan. Japan is unified by Tokugawa Ieyasu and closes its borders to Westerners. French and British establish settlements in North America, the Spanish and Portuguese in South America.
1500–800 B.C.	The plow is invented; horses are used for work and travel. This is the time of Moses. Writing systems are developed in the Middle East and China.		
800–300 B.C.	Greek civilization reaches a high point. Buddhism begins in India, Confucianism in China.		
300 B.C. to A.D. 1	The Roman Empire expands from Northern Africa to northern Europe. The Great Wall of China is built. Worldwide trade routes are developed.	1700-1900	Newton's laws of motion published; steam engines invented; the French and American revolutions; classical music is established. Electricity, photography, science, art, and engineering make great strides. Classical theater develops in Japan and China. The Chinese population reaches 400 million by 1775, when the War of Independence takes place in the United States. In 1854, U.S. Naval Admiral Perry lands his fleet in Japan, precipitating the breakdown of feudalism and the modernization of Japan. Famine kills 12 million in India in 1880. In the United States, the Civil War ends in 1865, and the Indian Wars end 10 years later. Edison invents the light bulb in 1879; the first automobile is developed in 1892; the Wright brother's first powered air flight takes place 10 years later.
A.D. 1–300	Further Roman expansion. Paper and porcelain are invented in China.		
300–700	Christianity spreads. Mohammed founds the Islamic religion. Buddhism spreads through China and into Japan.		
700–1200	Viking civilization expands in the north. Feudalism spreads throughout Europe. The Venetians in northern Italy become world traders. The Crusades come to Palestine. The Chinese produce the first printed book, make paper money, and invent gunpowder.		

Figure 1–2

Summary of World Historical Events

cussed developmental changes in infancy. Qianjin Yaofang (middle of the seventh century) felt that smiling and vocalizing to people at about 60 days of age marked a major transition in the infant's life, as did the emergence of walking at about 360 days (Kojima, 1986). These milestones of development, by the way, occur at about the same ages with today's babies.

Wang Zhong-yang (thirteenth century) noted the age of 60 days as the beginnings of a sensitive period in infant development. Around the time of the birth of Christ in the west, Chinese writers suggested the need for a closeness and affection between parent and child and a need to recognize the child's readiness to learn. A seventeenth century Japanese writer interpreted the first century B.C. Chinese text *Liji* (*Record of Rituals*) to mean: "when training is premature, nothing is gained other than a great deal of work. Keep babies quiet, and do not stimulate them. Only after behavior emerges from inside can proper guidance begin" (Kojima, 1986, p. 44).

In Europe, the Middle Ages were difficult for all people, not just for children. The rapid settlement of Europe, the shift from farming and rural life to city life, and the decline of the great empires of the ancient world all contributed to an increase in poverty, disease, malnutrition, pollution, and

During the middle ages in Europe cities grew rapidly by attracting people from rural areas. Without modern systems of sanitation. health codes, and medicine, disease and poverty spread rapidly where the population was most dense. Children and the unborn—being the most vulnerable to disease and malnutrition—suffered high rates of casualty, deformity, and abuse.

ignorance. Infants and children died of disease and malnourishment in alarming numbers, and poor maternal nutrition and health probably contributed to the extremely high incidence of birth defects and deformities.

Christians called for the baptism of infants at birth to immediately protect their souls in case of early death. Children as well as mothers died during the childbirth or shortly thereafter, leaving a great many orphaned children and creating the fairy tales and fables related to parental loss and wicked stepmother figures (Greenleaf, 1978).

Children played and had toys, but fewer games and toys from the Middle Ages have survived than have those from ancient times. Education during this period was more oriented to service than to general enlightenment. Parents often sent children to the care of a tradesman or a nobleman, and the children spent many years in apprenticeship training. Children participated in the adult world of work and play. They took up gambling, fighting, and drinking at an early age (Greenleaf, 1978).

Does this mean that children were not loved or that no concern was shown when they became ill or died? Historians differ on this point. Since many members of the society were under considerable stress and in poor health, it is quite understandable that even potentially caring parents would neglect their children. Research on today's families and children shows consistently that children are at the most risk for disease, neglect, abuse, and exploitation when their parents are living in poverty with little or no personal or parental resources (Garbarino, 1982).

The Sixteenth to the Nineteenth Centuries: China and Japan. China possessed the longest continuous line of cultural stability in the history of the world. Since the time of Confucius until the nineteenth century when China came under the influence of Western nations, the imperial system of government and the Confucian ideals of education persisted with minor changes.

Although initially a derivative of Chinese culture, Japanese society began to develop its own identity during the period from the sixteenth to the nineteenth centuries. During much of this time, Japan was isolated from Western influence and developed under a feudal system with a warrior class (the *samurai*) and a peasant class whose fate was decided by the military leader (the *shogun*). By the middle of the eighteenth century, peasants, merchants, and artisans began to receive some of the educational benefits of the samurai class. For the most part, however, the family was the basic unit, and education took place in the home.

The Confucian idea of living in harmony with nature led to the widespread belief in Japan that children are inherently good, an idea that was late in coming to Europe by comparison. Japanese writings at the time of Rousseau expressed the belief that children need guidance, but that they have an autonomous ability to learn, especially through imitation (Kaibara, 1710/Kojima, 1986).

Confucianism's emphasis on the *way of doing things,* or *li,* as opposed to the end product or general principle, led to a Japanese emphasis on observational learning as the most effective teaching strategy. Children were required not to think as much as to follow carefully the movements and procedures of adult models. Because of the emphasis on interpersonal harmony, the learner was encouraged to question and understand the procedures. Teachers and parents did little overt discipline or reinforcement; they used moderate amounts of praise and punishment. The goal was for the child to learn the procedure autonomously through his own self-regulation and without creating the disharmony between parent and child brought about by punishment (Kojima, 1986).

In the middle of the nineteenth century, Japan opened its doors to the West, and its system of education became influenced by Western models. The adoption of universal, compulsory education for boys and girls regardless of social status began in the late nineteenth century at about the same time as in the United States.

The modern Japanese society is as complex as that of the West, and many of the social and physical structures that support children—schools, playgrounds, laws, social services, child development researchers, and practitioners—are well developed in Japan. Nevertheless, modern Japan has preserved some of the same principles of teaching and childrearing that were brought from China centuries ago.

The Sixteenth to the Nineteenth Centuries: Europe and North America. The period from the fourteenth to the sixteenth centuries in Europe is known as the Renaissance, or rebirth, of the art, education, and freedom experienced in parts of the ancient world. During this period, children were depicted in paintings and mentioned in literature, although in a highly stylized manner. Early representations of the Christ child, for example, depicted Christ with adultlike facial features and body proportions.

It is not clear, however, that these paintings represent parental belief systems. Using primary sources, Pollack (see Table 1–1) has reconstructed a view of everyday family life in the words of parents and their children, beginning in the sixteenth centuries in both England and North America. Admittedly, the 200 or more diarists she read came from the middle class. Child abuse and exploitation seem to have occurred in all historical eras, including our own, and in all social classes, although primarily at the lower end of the socioeconomic scale (Grubb & Lazerson, 1982).

The period from the seventeenth to the twentieth century was a time of great social change. European society was expanding the frontiers of mind,

Cultures differ in their beliefs about children's abilities and about the most appropriate means to educate children. Each culture also marks the important turning points of development in its own unique way. Children in Japan, for example, receive special blessing upon attaining the ages of 1, 3, and 5 years.

Table 1–1

ATTITUDES TOWARD CHILDREN: SIXTEENTH TO NINETEENTH CENTURIES IN ENGLAND AND NORTH AMERICA*

16th Century. An awareness came about that children pass through developmental stages, that they need to indulge in play and require care and protection, education and discipline. Parents gave affectionate advice through letters. Adolescents disagreed with their parents. Physical punishment was often used, but parents also sought other means of control, including advice and discussion. Some parents expressed dismay at their inability to control children, and others showed respect for the child's autonomy.

17th Century. Parents recognized childhood and indulged children. They had an awareness of the need to adapt education and advice to the level of understanding of the child. Fathers were not involved in day-to-day childcare but expressed a concern for their children's well-being and future. Parents expressed an inability to be as stern in real situations as they had intended, and many diarists expressed a realization of the limits of parental authority.

18th Century. For the first time in this century, childhood is referred to as a time of *innocence,* perhaps due to the work of Locke and Rousseau. Parents worried about their ability to shape their children's behavior in the long term, suggesting that they viewed children as having independent minds. Locke's (1694) views emphasized the importance of parental guidance for the successful development of the child. Only a small percentage of the texts refer to physical punishment. Writers tried to maintain a balance between severity and indulgence.

19th Century. The uncertainties of the times account for an increased *ambivalence* about parenthood. William Lucas (1804–1861), a Quaker brewer, wrote in his autobiography: "I feel at times much depressed from not being able to make myself so companionable as I ought to be with my children. . . . It is so difficult to put up with their extreme vivacity, and so difficult to remember what we once were at their age, and to make due allowance for it" (Pollack, 1983, p. 109). By the end of this century there is a drastic reduction of strictness. This coincides with the rise of "progressive" or "child-centered" education. Perhaps the adaptation to industrialization, the termination of the Civil War, and the free spirit of the westward movement in America contributed to these changes.

*(Adapted from Pollack, 1983)

space, and family life. A conception of the value of all human life and the need for children to be educated was emerging. Although the concept of education, schools, and parental responsibility had been around for a long time, this period in history is responsible for the notion of *universal* education, for all children, regardless of sex or social class.

A second social force was the expansion of the borders of Europe into the New World, the idea of personal freedom, and the desire for privacy. The American and French Revolutions in the eighteenth century represented the breakdown of traditional lines of authority and the establishment of democratic forms of government based on individual liberty. Instead of each person viewing him or herself as the king's subject, a mere extension of the royal order, democracy allowed each person to be an autonomous contributor to the public welfare.

The notions of public and private, in this sense, are fairly recent, and they extend into the very heart of the family. In earlier centuries, individuals derived their sense of self-worth from their role in the family. A person was defined by the kinds of relationships he or she had with others, especially the relationships with God, with society, and with other members of the family. People did not think of themselves as individuals outside of this network of relationships (Aries, 1962).

The notion of privacy also created the idea that the family was independent from other institutions in society and that parents' influence on children was superior to other influences. In American colonial communities, the welfare of children was considered the responsibility of the whole community. Ac-

The Future of Childhood

The basic laws of human growth and development have not changed for thousands of years. Society's conceptualization of the meaning of childhood and methods of childrearing has changed a great deal over that period of time.

As we've seen in this chapter, the concept of childhood that is held by members of a particular society is dependent upon cultural and historical factors. In many societies today, children perform labors that fit directly into the immediate needs and goals of the community, such as childcare (see Chapters 11 and 15), farm chores, and household tasks. In other societies, such as our own, children's lives are isolated from the adult community, as they spend most of their time in school.

Where the future of childhood lies is difficult to predict, since our ideas about the value and meaning of childhood experience are so dependent upon the culture. If present trends continue in the United States, for example, there will be an increased percentage of children who are malnourished and neglected as we move into the twenty-first century, the age at which children become economically independent of their parents will continue to rise, and because of increasing divorce rates fewer children can expect to live with their biological parents in the same household throughout their childhood years. A greater number of children will spend a greater proportion of time outside the home in the care of substitute caregivers. The graying of America, as the post-World War II baby boom generation ages, may take scarce government resources out of programs for children and into those for the elderly.

Social trends rarely remain stable enough to make predictions for more than a few years ahead. As one social tendency, such as the need for both parents to work, pushes children away from the family, another may arise to compensate for the potentially negative effects of such a change. We can see this in the rise of government attention in recent years to setting optimum standards for outside-the-home childcare and the certification of daycare teachers and facilities (Peters, 1980) and in the push for increased father involvement in family and childcare tasks.

Child abuse might continue to rise unabated were it not for the increased attention given to the problem by the news media surrounding the reported cases of child sexual and physical abuse in some daycare centers and in families. This attention has stirred public concern and put pressure on legislators and researchers to find ways of preventing child abuse. This forward-looking prevention effort has the possibility of changing the future for many children (Garbarino, 1985).

The problem is that predictions will change about where to get prevention funds, to which groups prevention is targeted, and which regions of the country are most likely to benefit, depending on other factors such as the economy. Evidence exists that child abuse rises in times of high unemployment (Garbarino, 1985).

In the sense we have described here, the child development professional—practitioner or researcher—should learn to read and follow the cultural indicators that may affect children in the future. Not only the economy, but issues such as women's rights, the distribution of family roles, and a wide range of social factors, can affect children (Suransky, 1982). Some developmentalists have suggested a return to the small communities of the past in which human life was valued and children were supervised by any number of concerned adults. In the high-tech, more densely populated world of the future, however, childhood is bound to take on new and unpredictable meanings.

cording to one account, ". . . town fathers and other public officials could enter homes to observe and correct family life. They could warn parents, publicly or privately, about too much or too little punishment, about inattention to religious instruction, unclean homes, and ill-kept children" (Grubb & Lazerson, 1982, p. 45). This kind of community intervention would not be tolerated in America today, where the state can intervene in the family only if it fails to behave responsibly to its children.

Table 1–2 summarizes some of the important historical milestones related to education, play, health, welfare and the legal rights of children in the nineteenth and twentieth centuries. Let us now turn to consider the development of some of the critical ideas that shaped our current conceptualization of childhood.

Table 1–2

*RECENT SOCIAL ADVANCES RELATING TO CHILDREN**

Education

Schools for young children were provided with public funds, and textbooks were introduced in Massachusetts about 1647. The Massachusetts 1827 education law provided America's first free, tax-supported, statewide school system.

In 1850, the best school system in the country was in Boston. It had 161 one-room, run-down schoolhouses that were barren except for the single-size desks for all ages of children. Negro salves were denied access to education. There were no laws regulating the training of teachers.

Frederick Froebel (1782–1852) developed the first kindergarten program in Germany, using toys, actions, play, and stories to teach. Kindergartens were started in the United States by German immigrants in the mid-1850s. Only later were they incorporated into the public schools.

The division of children into 12 grades by age beginning at age six was introduced by William Torrey Harris, a U.S. commissioner of education in 1870. In 1870, only 57 percent of the 5–17-year-olds were enrolled in school; only 2 percent graduated from high school.

Progressive education, led by John Dewey, advocated schools in which children could develop their own curiosity and creativity. Learning by doing and expressing oneself were favored over discipline and book learning. Furniture was designed to fit different ages; art and color were introduced; fishtanks and films were brought in; enrichment and field trips became established parts of the curriculum.

In 1954, the U.S. Supreme Court ruled that education should not be divided by race; racial integration was accomplished by the controversial busing of children across school district boundaries. Laws guaranteeing educational rights of handicapped children were also passed (All Handicapped Child Act, Public Law 94–142). By 1960, 82 percent of 5–17-year-olds were in school, and 65 percent graduated from high school.

Some groups have not yet been guaranteed an education. Included are children of migrant workers, children who are illegal immigrants or who are not citizens of the U.S., women who become pregnant, and students who choose to alter their dress or hair styles beyond the norm. Today almost 90 percent of children aged 5 to 17 attend school, and almost 80 percent graduate from high school in the United States.

Play

John Newberry published the first children's magazine, *The Lilliputian Magazine,* in 1751.

Manufactured toys began during the Industrial Revolution. The baby doll was introduced into Europe in 1825.

The first public playground was built in the city of Boston in 1885: a few heaps of sand dumped in a vacant lot. By 1915, over 430 cities had set aside well-planned playgrounds and parks in the United States.

The Teddy bear is introduced in 1903, based on a picture of U.S. President Theodore Roosevelt, after hunting in the Rocky Mountains, with a brown bear in the background.

Television for children was developed in the early years of the TV industry in the 1950s. Computers and computer games are the most recent innovations in the realm of children's play.

Health and Welfare

The first English language textbook on pediatrics was written in 1545. Most cures were based on home remedies and folk beliefs.

The first institution to take in dependent children (because of poverty and parental loss) began in 1727 in Louisiana. Charleston Orphan Home, in Charleston, S.C., was the first public orphanage, built in 1794.

*(Sources: Blank & Klig, 1982; Greenleaf, 1978; Zietz, 1969)

Table 1–2 (continued)

Health and Welfare (*continued*)

In the nineteenth century, pediatricians based their diagnoses and treatments on direct observations and experiments. Special children's and childbirth wards were opened in some hospitals, and the first hospitals devoted exclusively to children were opened around 1850.

During this same period, scientific studies were done on the composition of milk and its nutrients, and near the end of the nineteenth century, Louis Pasteur developed a process (called pasteurization) to destroy the disease-causing bacteria in cow's milk, making cow's milk the first safe substitute for human breast milk. Sterilization and anesthesia were developed, preventing many maternal and child deaths.

State Boards of Charity, established first in 1863, were the first government welfare institutions in the United States. Their role was to investigate abuses to children in orphanages and in factories and to provide adequate home care for children.

First White House conference related to child welfare, the Conference on the Care of Dependent Children, was held in 1909. It led to the development of minimum standards and licensing requirements for children's institutions, foster homes, and child welfare work. The Children's Bureau was created in 1912 to oversee this work.

The 1930 White House Conference on Child Health and Protection established minimum rights for handicapped children and indicated groups of children in special need, including children of Black, Mexican, Puerto Rican, or Native American parents. By 1934, all states except Alabama, Georgia, and South Carolina had enacted supportive legislation.

The Social Security Acts of the 1930s (amended in the 1960s) established the present welfare system, aid to dependent children, and financial and rehabilitation services for needy dependent children and their families.

European Philosophical Origins of Our Modern Views of Childhood

The idea of individuality was articulated in the writings of European philosophers during the eighteenth century. Although many writers discussed this idea, the most notable representatives were the Englishman John Locke (1682–1704) and the Frenchman Jean Jacques Rousseau (1712–1778). Locke represented a group of writers known as the *empiricists,* while Rousseau represented the so-called *romantics.*

Empiricists developed the idea that many human problems could be resolved by the process of reasoning: thinking about one's environment and life circumstances and taking the logical steps to change them. Empiricism means inquiry, observation, and logical analysis. Before Locke, people believed that their knowledge was given by God or the king. On the contrary, Locke suggested that all knowledge derived from direct sensation and that the individual could acquire through perception the necessary information to make rational choices. Locke's idea that people could use reason to be free was used by the writers of the U.S. Constitution in the formulation of the notions of liberty and personal freedom.

The purpose of education was, according to Locke, to prepare citizens for participation in a democracy by producing rational, independent thinkers from immature children. Locke believed that people did not develop according to some plan laid down by God. Rather, he believed that children at birth were open to experiences that could train and mold them into productive citizens. Locke felt that at birth children were like a blank sheet of paper, what he called a *tabula rasa* (Latin for blank slate), upon which parents and teachers could write in what they wished.

Jean Jacques Rousseau was the leading proponent of the philosophical view, called romanticism, *that emphasized the importance of feelings and direct experience for the young child. Children, according to Rousseau, should be spontaneous and learn by active involvement in a topic of their own interest.*

Legal Precedents That Have Changed the Quality of Life for Children

The specific mention of children in human rights legislation began to develop at a rapid pace in the nineteenth and twentieth centuries (see Table 1–2). In many cases, the new laws worked to the disadvantage of those children they were meant to protect. In the nineteenth century, the establishment of legal protection for children meant that separate laws be made for children. This coincided with the social movements designed to separate all "different" people—in poor houses, orphanages, mental institutions—and the rise of compulsory schooling that took children out of the everyday affairs of the family and into special institutions.

Greater protection for children coincided with increased restrictions on children's rights. Children were prohibited not only from alcohol and tobacco but also from many public places such as dance halls and skating rinks. Legally the child was considered a possession of the parent. Only in circumstances where the parents violate children's rights could the state step in to protect the child. This notion (*parens patriae*), still with us today in many areas of child rights, was part of English common law dating back to the fifteenth century.

In the late 1960s, a series of landmark court decisions changed the general pattern of restricting children. In February 1964, Jerry Gault, then 12 years old, was on probation in his home state of Arizona for the theft of a wallet. In June he was accused of making obscene phone calls to a neighborhood woman. While his parents were at work, and without their knowledge, Jerry was taken into custody. Neither Jerry nor his parents saw any written charges until two months later. When they did, there was no mention of the specific charges.

The Gaults went to a hearing to obtain the release of their son a week after the arrest. There was no written transcript, no sworn testimony, no statement of charges, and no explanation of why Jerry was released at that time. At another hearing on June 15, to which the Gaults were not asked to come, Jerry was committed to six years in the State Industrial School for making obscene phone calls, an offense that would have either put an adult in jail for less than a month or given the adult a small fine.

Since the Arizona state laws did not permit appeals in juvenile cases, the Gaults decided to appeal to the Arizona Supreme Court, which upheld the state laws. The Gaults appealed the case again, this time to the U.S. Supreme Court, whose decision in favor of the Gaults on May 15, 1967 (known as the *In re Gault* decision), has become a major landmark in children's rights.

The Supreme Court stated that the original juvenile court system was designed to protect children from excessive punishment, but children had lost some of their rights in the process. In its decision it stated that children should have the same rights as those given to adults by the Fourteenth Amendment to the Constitution: (1) the right to receive notice of charges, (2) the right to legal counsel, (3) the right to confront and cross-examine witnesses, (4) the privilege against self-incrimination, (5) the right to a transcript of the proceedings, and (6) the right of appeal (Zeitz, 1969). Although juveniles are not entitled to trial by jury, they at least presently have these other rights.

Another major decision ruling in favor of children's rights is *Levy* v. *Louisiana* (1968), which breaks down any distinctions between "legitimate" and "illegitimate" children, ruling that the parent's state of wedlock at the time of the birth is not the fault or burden of the child. In *Planned Parenthood of Central Missouri* v. *Danforth* (1976), minors were given the constitutional right to privacy. The decision itself granted the right of a child to seek an abortion without the consent of her parents.

However, some legislation has restricted children's rights. The sale of pornographic materials to children was restricted in 1968. *McKeiver* v. *Pennsylvania* (1971) affirmed that minors were not entitled to trial by jury. In 1976, the right of Amish parents to withdraw their children from school at age 14 was upheld, even though compulsory schooling laws prohibit withdrawal before 16 years. The school's right to use physical punishment was upheld in 1977, although the Supreme Court allowed suits for damages to remedy excess punishment.

A number of legal issues need to be settled. Parents still have many rights over children. Some are important for the protection of the child, but when parents abuse their authority with excessive punishment, there is no clear line at which the state can step in to protect the child (Ross, 1982; Melton & Russo, 1987).

Although the romantics agreed with Locke on the value of education, they felt that children bring something of their own into the world. The romantics believed children are not a *tabula rasa*, but are born with innocence and bring goodness into the world. They created the idea that childhood is a special and privileged time of one's life and that children should be allowed to flower on their own with minimal guidance.

One of the most influential books on education, Jean Jacques Rousseau's *Emile*, is about a tutor who devotes his life to a single child. Rather than corrupt the child with traditional education, the tutor takes Emile on long journeys during which Emile's true teacher is nature and the experiences of life. *Emile* was revolutionary because it emphasized the role of feelings and the enjoyment of childhood experience in the educational process (Greenleaf, 1978).

Nature or Nurture?

Without realizing it, Locke and Rousseau were taking positions that would carry through into the present time to organize our thinking about the causes of child development. Their ideas were given support as the natural sciences developed during the nineteenth century.

Charles Darwin's (1809–1882) studies of plants and animals in their natural environments led to the theory that all forms of life evolved over millions of years from single-celled organisms. Darwin's concept of *natural selection* means that species of plants and animals evolved because the individuals who survived long enough to reproduce (and pass their characteristics on to the next generation) possessed characteristics that made them adapt successfully to their environment. Over generations, species become better adapted to the environment. Darwin's theory placed human beings in the world of nature, and Darwin suggested that our complex abilities for feeling, language, and thought evolved by the same process as the wings of birds or the fur of mammals.

Francis Galton (1822–1911) set himself the task of understanding what made one person different from another. He believed that personality differences between people were partially inherited from one's parents by genetic transmission and were partially the result of environmental influences such as education. To show these inherited tendencies, he studied the similarities and differences between identical and fraternal twins. His studies were among the first to take explicit account of those aspects of a person's individuality that depend primarily on *nature* (inherited by genetic transmission) and those that depend on *nurture* (aspects of the environment such as nutrition, health, child-rearing, and education).

In the early part of the twentieth century, behavioral scientists took positions either on the side of *nurture* or on the side of *nature* as the primary force controlling individual differences in personality, skill, and psychopathology.

Arnold Lucius Gesell (1880–1961) fell into the *nature* tradition. Gesell thought that the orderly changes in development were specified by the genes. The genetic timetable for the emergence of new behaviors was called *maturation*. Gesell carefully measured changes in physical size and motor skill in infants and children. He pioneered the use of the one-way mirror to hide the observers and was the first to use film to record behavior.

Gesell's work was very popular with the general public, because he constructed a concept of the "average" child based on the ages at which most

John Locke, the founder of the empiricist *tradition*, emphasized the need for children to become rational thinkers. Education in his view was meant to teach the child how to evaluate experience in order to make logical and moral decisions that are not influenced by momentary swings of emotion.

Charles Darwin made a radical break with Western religious and social beliefs by suggesting that man's origin could be explained by rational, scientific principles. He observed similarities between the development of the human child and the young of other species, finding commonalities in birthing, nursing, attachment and weaning.

John Watson, following in the footsteps of John Locke, did experiments showing that children could be affected directly by their environment. By discovering the correct principles of teaching-learning, Watson believed that a child could be shaped into any kind of individual.

children typically advanced in specific skills. The idea of the average child was rooted in Gesell's belief that the genes controlled the timing of the major developmental milestones. In fact, the environment does have an effect on the timing of developmental change, and children do vary from the average times set out by Gesell. Parents, however, thought these average times were the most desirable times. Thus, if their child walked or talked earlier or later than Dr. Gesell said they should, parents became worried.

One of the major representatives of the *nurture* point of view was John B. Watson (1878–1958), who believed that children could be trained to do almost anything. In one of his studies, he made an extremely loud noise by banging a steel bar behind the head of a small child just as the child was about to touch a cuddly looking pet animal. After several times being startled by the noise, each time leading to the child's becoming extremely upset, the child learned to avoid any contact with the pet (Watson, 1928).

Despite the shocking nature of this experiment and the highly question-able ethics of creating such fears in small children, Watson's work had enor-mous influence on American child study and on the American family. Watson said that parents have the major responsibility for bringing up a healthy and well-mannered child. He encouraged parents not to kiss or hold their babies, because this would cause the children to be dependent on the parent rather than to explore their environment and become emotionally independent of the parents. As we now know, individual differences in children are the result of *both* genetic and environmental influences. Watson's ideas created unnecessary guilt for parents when they failed to maintain total control over the behavior and development of their children.

Watson's view was more consistent than Gesell's with the traditions developing in North America at this time. Waves of refugees from Europe made the United States and Canada a land of immigrants where one could make a new life and become self-reliant and in which all people regardless of race, creed, or color had the same opportunity to succeed. These people had to learn to take responsibility for themselves by shedding their past and adapting to the demands of the new environment. Thus, learning and doing, rather than inheritance, were the keys to success.

The nature versus nurture issue is still with us today, although in some-what changed form. Today we realize that both nature and nurture contribute to human development. The theories of child development that we have today try to explain the ways in which nature *interacts* with nurture to produce a unique individual. The next chapter discusses these theories and how they deal with the nature versus nurture issue.

Continuity versus Discontinuity

The nature versus nurture issue was not the only one that early develop-mentalists were debating. They also wondered whether development was a slow and gradual process or whether development occurred rapidly in spurts. A change that is slow and gradual is a developmental *continuity*, while change that occurs in spurts is called *discontinuous*.

In Watson's view, for example, developmental change is the slow and gradual increase of learned associations. What may appear to be spurts are the result of the combination of many small steps that had been previously learned.

Other developmentalists that we'll study in the next chapter, Jean Piaget and Sigmund Freud, thought that some periods of development were marked by slow and gradual change and that children at other times showed a sudden discontinuous shift to a higher level of functioning. The periods of slow, continuous change were called *stages*, while the discontinuous periods were called spurts or *stage shifts*.

During middle childhood, for example, children grow taller at a steady rate (continuity). At about the age of 11 for girls and 13 for boys, the rate of physical growth increases dramatically (discontinuity). The adolescent growth spurt lasts several years before the rate of growth begins to slow down again. During this growth spurt, the body's secondary sexual characteristics also develop and the child makes a rapid shift to reproductive maturity. Thus, the stage of middle childhood (called the latency stage by Freud and concrete operations by Piaget) is separated from the stage of adolescence (called the genital stage by Freud and formal operations by Piaget) by a much shorter stage shift period of rapid change.

The next chapter discusses how current theories of child development answer the question of developmental continuity versus discontinuity.

Chapter Summary

WHY IT IS IMPORTANT TO STUDY CHILD DEVELOPMENT
□ To help in understanding your own childhood.
□ To aid you in making informed decisions as a parent or a child care professional.
□ To make you an informed citizen when corporate or government policies are likely to affect children and families.
□ Because knowledge of the developmental process is valuable for its own sake.

WHAT YOU CAN LEARN FROM THIS BOOK
□ Child development is an orderly process. Developmental changes are directional and persistent and occur in an ordered sequence of steps.
□ The development of differences between people can be understood by a consistent application of the scientific method. We no longer need to rely on myths to explain development.

HOW TO READ THIS BOOK
□ The authors' theoretical orientation is to view the child in ecological/systems perspective, taking into account both the child and the wider world of the family, school, and society.
□ The text is organized into four age units: infancy, early childhood, middle childhood, and adolescence. The chapters in each of these units cover physical, cognitive, social, and emotional development, as well as the transaction in the wider world that affect the child both directly and indirectly.
□ Each chapter focuses on theory and research within the body of the chapter and contains special topics of current interest under the headings FOCUS ON ISSUE, FOCUS ON POLICY, and FOCUS ON RISK/INTERVENTION.

THE HISTORY OF BELIEFS ABOUT CHILDHOOD
□ The prevailing view of most social historians has emphasized the lack of a concept of childhood before the twentieth century. Recent studies of both Western and Eastern history have uncovered a sense of the continuity and stability of ideas about children across many centuries.
□ The Confucian ideals of harmony and of the natural goodness of the child persist even today in China and Japan, where harmonious interpersonal relationships and group activity are favored over independent self-seeking.

□ The Judeo-Christian and Greek beliefs related to personal fulfillment are found in the search for independence and self-awareness in today's Europe and North America.

□ Evidence exists that childhood was recognized as a separate and special stage of life and that parents loved their children and mourned their loss in all stages of human history. Children have also been abused and neglected in all stages of history.

□ The views of child development as being due to nature or nurture evolved out of European philosophical ideas and became translated into scientific theories in the nineteenth and twentieth centuries.

□ The modern view is that the development of individual uniqueness is a complex and changing interaction between organismic and environmental factors, in which both the child and the environment change in the process.

Recommended Readings

Azuma, H., & Stevenson, H. (eds.). (1986). *Child development and education in Japan*. New York: Academic Press. A collection of works by different authors on the history and culture of Japan as they affect children.

Greenleaf, P. (1978). *Children through the ages: A history of childhood*. New York: Barnes and Noble. An easy-to-read overview of childhood since ancient times. Many good illustrations.

Grubb, W. N., & Lazerson, M. (1982). *Broken promises*. New York: Basic Books. A well-documented review of the failures of society today to provide adequate protection for all its children.

Pollack, L. A. (1983). *Forgotten children*. London: Cambridge University Press. A collection and analysis of diaries written by parents and by children in the sixteenth through nineteenth centuries in America and England.

Suransky, V. P. (1982). *The erosion of childhood*. Chicago: University of Chicago Press. A look at day care from the child's eye to expose impatience, prejudice, and neglect in even well-managed centers. Contains sections on the history of childcare.

CHAPTER 2

Theories of Child Development

. . . those who are destitute of philosophy may be compared to prisoners in a cave, who are only able to look in one direction because they are bound, and who have a fire behind them and a wall in front. Between them and the wall there is nothing; all that they see are shadows of themselves, and of objects behind them, cast on the wall by the light of the fire. Inevitably they regard these shadows as real, and have no notion of the objects to which they are due. At last some man succeeds in escaping from the cave to the light of the sun; for the first time he sees real things, and becomes aware that he had hitherto been deceived by shadows.
— *Bertrand Russell, 1945, p. 125.*
describing Plato's analogy of the cave

Through this story, the ancient Greek philosopher Plato sought to illustrate what might happen when a person does not study and examine the world. Such persons who are "destitute of philosophy" will see only shadows of things, with no sense that realities exist beyond the shadows.

How does this story apply to child development? When we look only at the surface of the child—at the child's appearance and behavior—perhaps we see only the shadow of the real child. The "real" child lies unobserved behind the surface features that we can see directly. The real child is a complex network of feelings, thoughts, motivations, and physiological processes, none of which can be observed.

No one can observe the inner processes of another. We can see only the "shadows" of such processes. Developmental scientists as well as all people who are sensitive to the inner states of others are somewhere between the people locked inside Plato's cave and the man who managed to escape from the cave and see reality. We know a reality exists beyond the mere appearance and behavior of people, though we still cannot see that reality directly.

Defining Developmental Theory

A *theory* is a set of concepts that explain some feature of the observable world with structures, processes, or mechanisms presumed to exist but unable to be observed directly. A theory differs from the belief systems discussed in Chapter 1 in three important ways:

1. A theory helps us to describe a set of observations that are derived from scientific research, using accepted methods of knowledge acquisition and testing. (The next chapter discusses these methods.)
2. A theory is stated in general form so that it can explain that set of observations.
3. To predict future observations that may be obtained, a theory must go beyond the established set of observations.

A *developmental theory* is a theory, in the sense just defined, that tries to accomplish three basic goals (Miller, 1983):

1. Developmental theory describes the way in which children change over time in different aspects of functioning, such as behavior, thinking, feeling, and perceiving. For example, developmentalists seek to obtain clear descriptions of the sequence of motor development in infants, from turning over, to

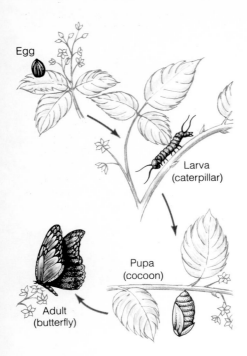

Figure 2—1

Discontinuous Developmental Changes of the Butterfly

crawling, to walking, to running. The changes from larva to cocoon to butterfly depicted in Figure 2-1 describe a developmental sequence.

2. Developmental theory seeks to understand the relationships between the different aspects of development. Developmentalists know that often many aspects of a child are changing simultaneously. Not only does the child grow taller, but motor skill improves, attention span lengthens, and thinking becomes more logical. In what ways do these different aspects affect each other in development? Do improvements in thinking help us pay attention longer, or is the reverse true? Similarly, the emergence of the butterfly cannot be explained by one single aspect, such as the growth of wings, but by a number of different features that are all changing together.

3. Developmental theory explains how and why children change during development. Simply describing the sequence of motor development in infants or the stages of butterfly development, does not help us understand the forces that move the individual from one phase to the next. Theories differ in how this is explained.

As we saw at the end of Chapter 1, developmentalists entered the twentieth century with a fundamental question about how developmental change proceeds from one phase to the next. Is the development of the child the result of the action of *nature* (the expression of the genes) or of *nurture* (the impact of the child's social and physical environment)? Developmentalists also puzzled over how to describe developmental change. Some thought human development progressed through a series of *discontinuous* stages, similar to the development of the butterfly in Figure 2-1. Others believed that such clearly defined stages did not exist for human children, that development was a slow *continuous* process of change.

This chapter discusses six modern theories of child development: ethological theory, psychoanalytic theory, cognitive-developmental theory, information processing theory, learning theory, and ecological systems theory. Each of these theories has a slightly different perspective with respect to the *nature* versus *nurture* issue as well as with respect to the *continuity* versus *discontinuity* issue. Tables 2-1, 2-2, 2-4, and 2-6 through 2-8 sum up each theory's position on these two issues along with the key concepts necessary to learn about each theory.

Modern Theories of Child Development

Ethological Theory

As we saw in Chapter 1, Charles Darwin's theory set the stage for thinking about the role of our genetic *nature* in the formation of individual characteristics. According to Darwin's theory, animal species evolve by *natural selection*. Each individual within the same species carries a slightly different set of genes that will create differences in their appearance and behavior in later life. Some of those individual characteristics will prove to be adaptive in a particular environment, and those individuals will survive and reproduce, passing their genes on to their children. The individuals without the needed characteristics will not survive, and their traits will be lost in future generations. Thus, the environment acts on natural genetic variations to *select* the fittest individuals (Darwin, 1859).

Following the ideas of Darwin, ethological theory assumes that all animal species, including humans, have a set of *species specific innate behaviors* that

The influence of the child's nature can be seen more clearly between identical twins than between fraternal twins, or between any other sibling pair. Even identical twins develop differences in appearance, behavior, and personality, suggesting that human development is a complex interaction of nature and nurture.

have evolved by natural selection over many generations. Behavior patterns that occur only in one species are called species specific. Examples are the barking of a dog, the speech of a human being, and the pecking of a chicken. Ethological theory assumes that the basic purpose of life is to survive by passing genes from one generation to the next and that the species specific innate behaviors help to guarantee that the individual is adapted to the needs of survival (see Table 2-1).

One of the most basic species specific innate behaviors that ensures the survival of young mammals is the close relationship between mother and infant. This relationship is ensured by different behaviors in each of the mammalian species. Mother cats lick and nuzzle their kittens; mother monkeys groom, cuddle, and carry their babies; and all mammals nurse their young. The infant emits certain species typical signals that allow the mother to recognize when the infant is in need of something, to help her recognize the baby as her own, and to endear the baby to the mother. These ties of endearment are known as *attachment bonds*.

Table 2—1

ETHOLOGICAL THEORY

Focuses On	Function of behavior related to survival.
Key Concepts	Natural selection, species specific behavior, attachment, sensitive period, imprinting.
Data Derived From	Observations of behavior in natural settings.
Nature Vs. Nurture	Innate behaviors are suited to learning from the environment in efficient ways.
Continuity Vs. Discontinuity	The form of change is not specified.

John Bowlby's (1969) theory of human attachment is a good example of the use of ethological theory to explain development. Bowlby suggested that newborn infants were innately tuned to be receptive to social stimulation, such as by quickly calming after being picked up. Infants have the innate ability to emit crying signals spontaneously when they are distressed. The cry serves to attract adults to come to the baby's aid. As the baby gets older and more aware of its social environment, the attachment relationship shifts from these innate signals to learned social signals, as when a frightened toddler yells, "Daddy, come here!"

Ethologists also believe that species have evolved a species specific way of learning about the environment to which they must adapt. In many species of animals, the young are biologically susceptible to acquiring a new behavior only during a limited period of time, known as a *sensitive period*, or a critical period.

An example of a sensitive period is the development of attachment in certain species of birds, such as geese. During a period of only a few hours— a period that occurs a few days after hatching—goslings are capable of learning about the characteristics of their mother. By following the mother around during this sensitive period, the goslings come to prefer their mother over other objects, and they will stay close to her after that period. This rapid learning of a preference for one object over another is called *imprinting*, which increases the goslings' chances of survival, keeping them near the food and shelter that the mother provides.

One of the major contributors to ethological theory, Konrad Lorenz, discovered that goslings could become imprinted on a variety of objects, including flashing lights, electric trains, and even to Lorenz himself, who caught the attention of his flock by walking near them for long periods, the whole time squatting and quacking. As he later wrote, "In the interest of science I submitted myself literally for hours on end to this ordeal" (Lorenz, 1952, p. 42).

Attempts to apply the sensitive period notion to human behavior have been less successful, because humans have a much longer and more flexible period (all of infancy and childhood, in some cases) during which they are susceptible to the acquisition of new behaviors. Chapter 5 explains that it is not necessary for human babies to be with their parents immediately after birth to become attached. On the other hand, the acquistion of attachment to someone usually is complete before the age of one year. Language is learned primarily before the age of three, as are the basic skills of motor coordination. Although these examples suggest that humans may have sensitive periods, such periods last years rather than hours.

Lest you think that ethology applies primarily to basic needs and behaviors that apply to all species, consider the application of ethology to understanding the cognitive development of children. According to the ethological view, intelligence has evolved to aid in the survival of the individual and the species. We would therefore expect intelligence to be used frequently to resolve everyday events that affect basic aspects of survival and access to resources.

Charlesworth (1979) found that in natural situations in the home, children devoted more time to solving the problem of how to get their mother to listen to their requests or to get around the mother's prohibitions than to solving problems related to their play with objects, such as in building a stable tower of blocks. Most studies of cognitive development are done in laboratories using tasks developed by researchers. Far fewer studies have looked at children's and adults' use of their intelligence in everyday situations.

The main contribution of ethology has been to focus our attention on the *function* of behavior, that is, on the way in which behavior contributes to making us better suited to exploit our natural surroundings effectively. We can understand more of children's behavior not only by placing the child in the context of the particular environment in which the child lives but also by looking at each child as one example of a larger history of species evolution. By comparing animals of different species and children living in different cultures, ethologists have discovered similarities of behavior that traverse these different groups and thus have better understood the differences between groups.

How do ethologists resolve the issue of whether *nature* or *nurture* is more important in explaining human development? They do not claim that all behavior is determined by the genes. Rather, they suggest that heredity provides certain behavioral abilities that are uniquely suited to the kind of environments in which humans typically will live. One ethologist (Freedman, 1974) suggested that behavior is 100 percent hereditary and 100 percent environmental, meaning that the individual's species heredity allows one to learn and adapt flexibly to the demands of living on this planet, to adjust to the nuances of group social relationships, and to bear and rear equally adaptive offspring.

On the issue of *continuity* versus *discontinuity* in development—whether development occurs gradually or in spurts or stages—ethological theory does not take a strong position. The sensitive period for attachment, for example, is a relatively discontinuous spurt of learning in birds, but a more gradual change in humans. Ethological theory does not provide us with a detailed description of the developmental process nor of the situations most likely to enhance or detract from normal development. Ethologists can provide little assistance in understanding the specific learning processes or experiences that might effectively guide parents and teachers in their work with children.

The focus of ethological theory is on behavior that is recognized as having universal survival value across species, such as attachment and aggression. Even here, it is difficult for ethologists to specify the exact origins in human history of behaviors such as attachment and problem solving. When scientists study evolutionary changes in the body's anatomy, they can use the concrete evidence of preserved fossils and bones. Because no such evidence exists about the evolution of crying and other vocalizations leading to attachment, we can only guess about what might have happened in our early social history as a species (Miller, 1983).

Psychoanalytic Theory

The first comprehensive theory of human personality development was that of Sigmund Freud (1856–1939). Freud's original intent was not the conceptualization of a developmental theory. While in medical practice in Vienna, Austria, Freud discovered that some symptoms of his adult patients—such as

Sigmund Freud was one of the first scholars to point out the role of early childhood experiences on the formation of the adult personality. He suggested that children develop through distinct stages of emotional and self-awareness. Each stage offered a new conflict for the child, a conflict whose resolution paved the way for the person's approach to similar conflict situations in later life.

headaches and dizziness—could not be traced to any physical problem in the body. Freud (1933 [1964]) suggested that such disorders come from a part of the mind he called the *unconscious*. The *conscious* part of the mind refers to mental processes controlling our thoughts, feelings, and actions of which we are aware, while the *unconscious* refers to mental processes that also influence thought, feeling, and action, but of which we are not aware.

Consciousness is like a searchlight that can be trained on only a small region of the self or the environment. Everything outside the beam of the searchlight cannot be seen, and some regions of the mind are hidden by psychological barriers so that the searchlight beam of consciousness cannot illuminate them.

The mental processes of the person, according to Freud, are made up of three basic structures: the id, the ego, and the superego (Freud, 1933 [1964]). The *id* is the collection of innate desires and needs possessed by all people. These needs include hunger, sleep, sex, love, and aggression. The id is regulated by the *pleasure principle,* the urge to meet these needs without delay whenever possible. The id acts in irrational and self-seeking ways. The hungry baby, for example, will scream until fed, with no sense of how this is affecting other people.

The *ego* is the self-regulatory aspect of the person. It includes the ability to tolerate frustration, to enjoy pleasure without becoming overwhelmed by it, and to think rationally. Unlike the id, the ego operates by means of the *reality principle* by which needs are not met immediately but are met after first evaluating alternative courses of action and selecting the one course that is most adaptive under the circumstances. In the initial stages of ego development, a hungry baby will be able to wait until mother can stop what she's doing or until the regular mealtime to eat.

The ego is like a coach who wants to win a basketball game but realizes that it is necessary to adapt the strengths and weaknesses of his team to those of the opposing team. The strong desire to win (the id) has to be balanced against the threat of the other team. When the coach has a good set of players and the other team is not too strong, a winning strategy can be worked out in a realistic manner (a well-functioning ego). But when the other team is too threatening, the coach tries to defend against an embarrassing loss.

Like the coach, Freud thought that the ego served the function of defense of the person in threatening situations. The *defense mechanisms* are unconscious distortions of one's feelings, perceptions, and thoughts for the purpose of reducing anxiety and psychological pain. Freud described several kinds of defense mechanisms. *Projection,* for example, is when a child denies that he or she has a troublesome thought or feeling by assuming that some other object or person has that feeling. A preschooler may feel jealous when her mother takes care of a new baby in the family. Instead of recognizing her own jealousy, the child would say that the baby is jealous of her. Another child's fear that someone will hurt him may be a projection of his own aggressive desires.

A second defense mechanism is *regression,* which is a kind of temporary developmental reversal. With the stress induced by a new brother or sister, a preschooler may show behavior typical of an earlier stage of development. She may cry more often, wet her pants or bed, or ask to be picked up and held like a baby.

One of the most common ego defense mechanisms is *repression,* by which anxiety-producing thoughts are pushed into the unconscious region of the mind. A child may conveniently forget a particularly disturbing incident that occurred while remembering other, more pleasant ones that occurred about the same time.

In some cases, defense mechanisms developed during childhood become the source of problems in adulthood. A person may fear social gatherings because as a child he was always ridiculed by peers. The ridicule was repressed, but the fear of social gatherings may remain. To cure similar symptoms in his patients, Freud worked with his patients to relive their childhoods in order to recall the long-forgotten situations that produced the original pain. His method of treatment, called *psychoanalysis,* (see Table 2-2) was to let a person's mind wander freely, creating spontaneous insights, called *free associations,* about one's past and present leading to the discovery of the repressed memories in the unconscious mind (Thomas, 1985).

The third structure of the mind, the *superego,* is that part of the ego most concerned with the rules and regulations of society. The superego is the person's conscience and is made up of parents' prohibitions, guilt feelings, and the standards and norms of acceptable behavior in the home, school, and playground. To continue with the analogy of the basketball game, the superego is like the crowd in the stands. It watches over both teams and the coach alike. The coach should be sportsmanlike and respectful to the other team and to his own players, whether winning or losing. The superego is the society "out there" that forces individuals to behave in orderly and socially acceptable ways.

According to Freud, development occurs in all three regions of the mind. The id develops through different phases of physical maturity, leading to the child's shifting awareness of pleasure and pain in different regions of the body (listed in Table 2-3). They represent the body's *erogenous* zones, the source of highly pleasurable stimulation. In addition, as the child's attention shifts to a new region of sensory awareness, the ego and superego develop to establish adaptive controls over the expression of impulses in those regions.

During the first period of development, which Freud called the *oral stage,* the region of the mouth is the most sensitive. At birth an infant has a host of uncontrolled and powerful desires. A hungry baby has no sense of social graces. The baby will scream in a demanding and insistent way until fed, and most small babies take in milk as if it were their first and last meal, attacking the nipple with voracious gulps and protesting loudly when interrupted.

Ego control is seen as the child develops the ability to wait for meals. In addition, as a result of the history of pleasure associated with the feeder, the child develops his or her first important and lasting emotional attachment. If the child's needs were met regularly and the development of ego controls accomplished gradually by sensitive caregiving, the infant would repress the oral urges toward the caregiver and should develop an emotionally secure and trusting attachment to the mother. If weaning is harsh or abrupt, the child will not be able to separate oral desires from a sense of security and trust. Excessive smoking, drinking, and eating in adults was thought by Freud to represent an oral personality who achieved a sense of security through oral means.

Focuses On	Emotions and needs, control of id impulses.	*Table 2—2*
Key Concepts	Id, ego, superego, conscious, unconscious, reality principle, pleasure principle, defense mechanisms, erogenous zones, Oedipal conflict, identification, identity crisis.	*PSYCHOANALYTIC THEORY*
Data Derived From	Psychotherapy interviews and self-analysis.	
Nature Vs. Nurture	Id desires and stages are determined by nature; the development of ego regulation is due to nurture.	
Continuity Vs. Discontinuity	Discontinuous stages.	

Table 2–3

PSYCHOANALYTIC STAGES OF DEVELOPMENT

Approximate Age	According to Freud	According to Erikson
0–1 1/2 years	*Oral stage*—Pleasure and experience gained from the mouth, sucking and biting.	*Trust vs. mistrust*—Development of expectancy of gratification or frustration.
1 1/2–3 years	*Anal stage*—Pleasure from anal region through elimination and retention.	*Autonomy vs. shame/doubt*—Self-assertiveness and self-control or uncertainty and shame.
3–6 years	*Phallic or Oedipal stage*—Interest in own genitals, desire to possess parent of opposite sex.	*Initiative vs. guilt*—Taking initiatives and a sense of purpose or guilt about independent activity.
6–11 years	*Latency stage*—No overt sexual desires, interest in learning new skills.	*Industry vs. inferiority*—Interest in learning and skill development or sense of inadequacy and loss of motivation.
Adolescence	*Genital stage*—Adult sexual desires and the establishment of sexual relationships.	*Identity vs. role confusion*—Perception of self as a unique individual, development of personal values, or confusion about identity and role in life.
Young adulthood		*Intimacy vs. isolation*—Emotional commitment to other people, lasting relationships, or sense of loneliness and isolation.
Adulthood and middle age		*Generativity vs. stagnation*—Investment in the world of work and childrearing or inactivity and purposelessness.
Old age		*Integrity vs. despair*—Acceptance of one's life as the only life one could live, acceptance of death, or despair over failures, losses, and mistakes.

During the *anal stage* the child becomes interested in waste materials produced by his or her own body. The child expresses pride over these productions and shows concern when these parts of his or her own body disappear down the toilet. Babies of this age may insist on walking around with a full diaper and resist efforts at toilet training.

Freud believed that this normal possessiveness created a conflict with the parents related to control of the child. During this stage, children act defiant, grab toys from others, and ignore parental prohibitions. If the parents respect the child's need to possess not only feces, but toys and people as well, and praise the child for his or her productions at the toilet and elsewhere, the child will develop a normal sense of self and respect for others. Harsh toilet training and severe discipline were believed to lead to a rigid and selfish anal personality.

During Freud's anal stage children become interested in the waste products of the body, and in establishing self-control over elimination of urine and feces. This child, still in the oral stage, has already become oriented to the toilet as a source of interest: the sound and feel of the moving water. Later, when he begins to feel the tug of strong sensations in the anal region, the toilet will take on new meaning and purpose.

During the *phallic stage*, the child becomes aware of the genital region and may experience some simple forms of pleasure when that region is self-stimulated, a normal occurrence during this period. Although the sensations from the genitals are not as powerful as they will be during the genital stage of adolescence, the phallic-stage child begins to develop a sense of gender identity. The young boy has sexual desire for his mother and wishes to exclude his father from the relationship. This is called the *Oedipal* conflict—named after Oedipus, a character from ancient Greek mythology who unwittingly married his mother and killed his father.

The boy during the phallic stage fears that his father will get revenge by cutting off the boy's penis. In most cases, boys repress these fears and longings and resolve the Oedipal conflict through identification with their father. *Identification*—taking on the father's beliefs and behaviors—is the beginning of the development of the superego in which the child learns self-control and the moral standards of the family.

The process of development in the phallic stage is somewhat different for the girl. The girl has sexual desires for the father, but she is not afraid of losing her penis. She thinks this has already occurred and secretly blames her mother for this loss. Since the fear of penis loss is not present in girls, Freud felt that this period is less intense for girls. Girls, like boys, resolve the conflict through repression of desires and feelings for the opposite-sex parent, and through identification with the same-sex parent. Unsuccessful resolution of Oedipal conflicts may lead to unrealistic expectations of members of the opposite sex, inability to become independent from parents, and lasting problems related to people in positions of authority.

During the *latency* stage, little happens with regard to the development of the erogenous zones. The child is presumed to have adaptively repressed the Oedipal conflict while waiting for the onset of the genital stage. The *genital stage* begins around the time of puberty and is associated with the development of mature sexuality and the formation of adult sexual relationships.

What is Freud's stand on the *nature* versus *nurture* issue? Like ethological theory, Freud's position is somewhere midway between nature and nurture. Although Freud believed that the stages of the child's id development were controlled by the physical maturation of the body and emerged according to a genetically controlled timetable, he insisted that the stages of ego and superego development were controlled by the social environment. The degree of appropriate self-regulation of the child's emotions was influenced largely by the parents' sensitivity versus insensitivity to the child's needs.

Freud's position on the issue of *continuity* versus *discontinuity* is that childhood is partitioned into the discontinuous stages outlined in Table 2-3. The body's spurts of physical maturation bring the child rapidly into a new stage, and it inevitably takes a number of years for the child to develop regulatory control over the id urges in each stage of development.

Freud's theory led to a concern by parents and educators for the child's emotional needs. Contrary to the position of Watson (refer to Chapter 1), Freud emphasized the need for babies to suck and to be held and for preschoolers to be possessive and messy. Play with clay, water and sand, mud, and fingerpaints was interpreted as a symbolic and acceptable means of understanding the body during the anal stage. Teachers learned about their importance as role models with whom the child could identify during the Oedipal and latency stages.

Another area of influence was in psychotherapy for both adults and children. Child psychotherapy was advanced greatly by Freud's daughter, Anna Freud (1895–1982), who developed *play therapy* in which children can represent their conflicts and feelings about others by means of playing with dolls and drawing pictures. Children often express angry and hostile feelings through such play—feelings that would be repressed when the children are with those people whom the dolls represent.

These influences of Freudian theory are with us today in virtually all aspects of family and social life and educational and therapeutic settings. Freud's theory has had less of an impact on scientific studies of development, because his concepts of mental life are too far removed from anything scientific studies can measure accurately. Developmentalists have failed to find a link between early feeding and later social adjustment. Rather, the person who spends the most time engaged in social interaction with the infant is more likely to be an object of the child's attachment than is the person who only feeds the baby (see Chapter 7).

One of the main problems of Freud's theory as an explanation of development is that it was meant to explain adult mental life. Because Freud never actually observed infants and children, it would be more accurate to describe his theory as a representation of childhood as remembered by adults.

Applying Theory to the Real World

The three focus sections of this chapter revolve around the central issue of applying theory to real-world problems. Theory achieves its power from its generality. By making statements that are simple, conceptual, and general, theory can make specific predictions to real situations.

The real world is messy by comparison. No real child develops exactly in the way that any one theory suggests. Even if we combined all of the theories (known as an *eclectic* approach), the complexity of the real-world situation would be beyond our capacities to explain.

Mission-oriented theory and research seek to apply theoretical concepts to real-world problems (Achenbach, 1978). Mission-oriented theory has two basic goals. One is to influence *social policy,* that is the laws and social structures that affect children and families. The other is to influence *intervention strategies,* that is, the therapeutic and educational curricula designed to improve the lives of children and families at risk.

Basic theory and research is more issue oriented and less applications oriented. its goal is to discover the universal processes of human development, and it is more closely linked to the other theories discussed in this chapter.

Given the large number of theories reviewed in this chapter, you may find it difficult to decide among them in thinking of an application to policy or to intervention. Because of the inherent complexity of child development, no one theory can account for all aspects of development and behavior. Thus, researchers and practitioners (educators, psychotherapists, and social workers) try to choose the theory or combine elements of theories in ways that best fit their particular application.

In spite of the great strides made in understanding child development in the past 50 years, the lack of a unified theory requires every professional to be familiar with many different approaches and to be creative in their application: choosing the theory and method to fit the problem at hand. There is no single best answer that fits all children in all situations. A wide variety of experiences with different children, balanced against a conceptual understanding of the diversity of theories of development, is the best guide to becoming an effective parent, teacher, or researcher.

A more recent adaptation of Freud's theory to child development was the work of Erik Erikson (1902–). Erikson studied with Anna Freud and later observed children and adults in different cultures and in a wide variety of circumstances. His stages of psychosocial development parallel those of Freud but add more detail, especially during adult development (refer to Table 2-3). In addition, Erikson showed how cultural differences influenced the kinds of responses that parents made to developmental changes in the child's awareness of the erogenous zones proposed by Freud. One culture, for example, may actively encourage all forms of oral expression, such as sucking, licking, biting, and chewing, for as long as the child wants to engage in them, while another culture may prohibit such activities at an early age. These cultural differences in response to expressions of the id lead, according to Erikson, to differences between cultures in adult personalities (Erikson, 1950).

Erikson saw each stage in the life cycle as a period of unique potential to learn and grow. In addition, each stage presented a unique risk and challenge. If the child meets that challenge, he or she can advance successfully. If not, the child will experience psychological problems associated with that stage (Erikson, 1950) (refer to Table 2-3).

Erikson's focus was on the formation of a sense of self. In adolescence, when children become aware of themselves as developing persons with the ability to take control of that development, they experience what Erikson called an *identity crisis*. During this period of identity crisis, young people attempt

Erik Erikson followed the outlines of Freud's theory, but placed more emphasis on the child's relationship to the family and society during each stage of emotional development. His concept of the adolescent identity crisis entered the mass media and popular culture as a useful way to describe the emotional conflicts of the teen years.

Jean Piaget was known for his theoretical contributions, and also for his empathic sensitivity with young children. During his interviews he was able to probe the full extent of the child's knowledge without asking leading questions, and all the while showing respect for the child as a person with unique ideas.

to gather information, explore new forms of experience, and try to integrate their current and former selves with their vision of their own roles in society.

Erikson's work has influenced the response of parents and schools to teenagers by recognizing the teen's need to understand the self and adjust to adult life. Today's junior and senior high school students learn what to expect about changes in their body, take courses in sexuality and human development, and are exposed to a wide variety of issues relating to values and ethics.

Cognitive-Developmental Theory of Jean Piaget

Another early developmental theorist was Jean Piaget (1896–1980) from Geneva, Switzerland. Piaget trained as an invertebrate biologist before he became interested in the study of human development. Biologists conceptualize development in terms of the individual's adaptation to the environment. *Adaptation* is a change in functioning that makes the individual better suited to survive in a particular environment.

One of Piaget's most important insights was that human intelligence is a form of adaptation to the environment. In this sense, Piaget's theory bears some similarity to ethological theory. Piaget believed that even small infants could act in intelligent ways, not by thinking, but by using their bodies to act on the environment to meet their own needs and goals (Piaget, 1950).

For Piaget, an infant learning to chew solid foods is developing an intelligent way of "knowing" the food. Piaget's view is that knowledge is not something static, an acquired body of information. Rather, knowledge is a *process*. To know something means to act on that thing. A specific pattern of action that operates on the environment to achieve a goal is called a *scheme*. Schemes can be either physical, as in chew*ing,* or mental, as in remember*ing* or think*ing.* The emphasis here is on the active engagement of the knower and what is to be known. Remembering is a kind of reenactment of the original action involved in the process of knowing.

Piaget reasoned that all complex forms of knowing develop out of simpler forms found in infants. Infants know the world through their motor schemes: sucking, chewing, reaching, looking, crawling, and touching. In the same way that an infant comes to know an object by turning it over, moving it around, and trying to fit it into other objects by action, mental schemes of thinking involve a kind of "interiorized" action by which we take new perceptions, ideas, and feelings, turn them around mentally, and try to fit them into other ideas that already exist in our minds (Piaget, 1952).

According to Piaget, schemes develop through the interaction between the individual and the environment. This interaction—called *adaptation*—occurs in two ways: assimilation and accommodation (see Table 2-4). *Assimilation* is the attempt to fit the environment into one's existing level of ability. It is the application of what one already knows or does to the current situation. *Accommodation* is the alteration of existing abilities to better fit the requirements of the task or environment. It occurs when assimilation does not result in an effective adaptation to the environment.

In reality, most actions involve both assimilation and accommodation, and it is often difficult to tell the two apart. Consider a baby drinking from a bottle. In most cases, the bottle is familiar and the baby, having sucked many times before, assimilates the bottle to the sucking scheme. On the other hand, there are minor variations from one feeding time to the next. Perhaps a slightly smaller or larger nipple is used, the rate of liquid flow is slower or faster, or

Table 2—4

COGNITIVE-DEVELOPMENTAL
THEORY OF PIAGET

Focuses On	Motor development, thought, language, action, and adaptation of skills to the environmental demands.
Key Concepts	Adaptation, assimilation, accommodation, schemes.
Data Derived From	Observations of children, open-ended interviews.
Nature Vs. Nurture	Assimilation and accommodation are given by nature; nurture determines the specific kinds of schemes developed through the child's own actions.
Continuity Vs. Discontinuity	Discontinuous stages but smooth transitions between them.

the liquid varies in temperature. Accommodation is the process by which the infant adapts to these minor variations.

Accommodation also plays a role in making developmental advances, as in the shift between drinking from a bottle to drinking from a cup. When babies first drink from a cup they try to assimilate the cup to bottle-feeding patterns. They will suck on the rim of the cup, will fail to hold the cup steady, and may turn the cup bottoms up like a bottle. Gradually, babies accommodate to the special characteristics of cup drinking.

Piaget divided childhood into a series of developmental stages (see Table 2-5). Each stage is defined by the type of knowing used by the child to adapt to the environment. Children progress through periods of knowing through direct action, through symbols and fantasies, through thinking and feeling, and through the logical reasoning process.

During the *sensorimotor stage* infants know the environment by means of their direct action on it. Memory, for example, is the ability to reenact the same pattern of behavior every time the baby returns to the same situation. By the end of the second year of life, infants develop the ability to represent actions by mental images and to move those images around mentally to compare them and make judgments. During the *preoperational* period, the child's ability to think has some important limitations. Children often focus on one aspect of a problem that is most salient and seem to forget other information that is equally important.

Table 2—5

COGNITIVE-DEVELOPMENTAL
STAGES OF CHILD
DEVELOPMENT

Approximate Age (Years)	Stage	Description
0—2	Sensorimotor	Infants learn through direct experience of the senses and by handling objects and moving them around. They do not understand that things exist outside their own actions.
2—6 or 7	Preoperational	Ability to form mental representations, language, thinking as internalized action but centered on the self's perspective; inability to think logically.
7—11 or 12	Concrete operational	Thinking takes the perspective of others and is logical with respect to concrete actions and objects, such as the rules of a game; inability to think about abstract things.
12—adult	Formal operational	Thinking about nonconcrete, abstract things, ability to solve word problems, to form a coherent system of thought relating many ideas, and to think about future possibility.

Most errors of logic are eliminated during the *concrete operational* period due to the child's continuing interactions with other people and the child's developing ability to adapt his or her own perspectives to those of others. In this stage, however, the child's thinking is limited to images that have direct physical counterparts. The stage of *formal operational* thinking heralds the emergence of the ability to think about abstract entities such as peace, justice, and love. Although concrete operational children can do complex arithmetic, they cannot do algebra, because the concept of "*x,* the unknown quantity" is too abstract for them. (We shall discuss each of these stages in more detail in the chapters on cognitive development throughout this book.)

What is Piaget's answer to the *nature* versus *nurture* issue? His theory is similar in many ways to both ethological and psychoanalytic theories in that he stresses the role of biological maturation on the child's development. Piaget's theory, however, sees the child as more of an active free agent than do the other theories.

Piaget does not go so far as to suggest, as did Freud and Darwin, that the child's stages of development are determined genetically. Piaget says that the ability to adapt is encoded in the genes as well as in certain physical characteristics of the child's body and brain. Given these basic inputs, the rest of development is the result of the child's own actions on the environment and interactions with other people. Thus, we can conclude that for Piaget both nature and nurture are important, but that nature provides rather open-ended specifications for development, leaving most of the outcome due to the interaction with the child's environment.

What about the *continuity* versus *discontinuity* issue for Piaget? A look at Table 2-5 suggests that Piaget theorized discontinuous developmental stage shifts between each of these periods. Piaget believed, however, that children shifted gradually from one stage to the next. Even though one could see differences between the developmental stages, Piaget felt that adaptation was a continuous, slow, and gradual process for each individual child. Nevertheless, Piaget is remembered best for his descriptions of those stages of cognitive development, and he did believe that children persisted in one stage for several years before moving to the next one.

Through knowledge of Piaget's stages of the development of thinking, curriculum planners have learned to create educational sequences that are adjusted to the levels of understanding of children at different ages. Subject matter is supposed to be introduced in grade levels that is consistent with the child's readiness to assimilate and to accommodate new information (Elkind, 1976).

Outside of action and thinking skills, however, Piaget's theory is of little help. Piaget was not concerned with individual differences, nor did he spend much time discussing emotional problems and emotional development. Although peers enter into his theory as sources of knowledge, Piaget does not tell us how to facilitate peer interactions or how to help children who cannot make friends. Furthermore, Piaget has little to say about broader social and environmental influences on development.

Information Processing Theory

Developments in science and technology in the 1940s and 1950s had a profound effect on psychologists. Machines were invented to communicate and to do mathematical calculations, processes that had been restricted to the human brain before this time. It was thought that computers could eventually be designed to simulate logical thinking and other more complex cognitive processes (Newell & Simon, 1961). Psychologists reasoned that like a computer, our brains receive and process information in a series of steps. *Information processing theory* envisions our complex cognitive processes as broken down into smaller subprocesses.

Let's consider what happens when a child tries to read the word *cat*. As a first step, the child must control *attention* well enough to concentrate on the word and nothing else around it. Next, the color and shape of the ink markings on the page must be entered into the brain by a process of *perception*. Perception includes not only the encoding of the image into nerve impulses but also the control of head direction and eye scanning movements that allow the entire word to be seen. Next, those squiggles of ink marks must be interpreted as a recognizable word, which involves a comparison of the immediate perception with some prior *memory* of visual images and word meanings. Having gotten this far, the next step is to relate these memories and perceptions to the appropriate *motor control* centers that activate speech (see Figure 2-2).

Developmentalists have been interested in when and how children acquire each of these separate subprocessing abilities that characterize adult thought. How do children learn perceptual strategies that allow them to filter out irrelevant information and recognize information that is important for the task at hand? How does a child develop effective strategies for remembering and for solving difficult problems?

Because information processing theory postulates that our minds process information in a series of steps or subprocesses, such as attention, perception, and memory, we also need a set of *control strategies* (see Table 2-6) that regulate the flow of information between the different subprocessing units. To continue our computer analogy, the separate subprocessing steps represent the computer's (or the brain's) hardware (the brain and the nervous and sensory systems). The subprocessing steps are represented by the boxes in Figure 2-2. The control strategies represent the computer's (the brain's) software (programs or schemes). Control processes are like computer programs that organize the flow of information between the various sections of the computer's different processing units. Control processes are represented by the arrows in Figure 2-2.

As they get older, children need to become aware of their own thinking processes to change them. This awareness of one's own thought process is called *metacognition*. By the fourth or fifth grade, for example, children become aware of the limitations of short-term memory. Children learn ways of remembering, such as rehearsing and writing things down, and methods of accessing information from long-term memory, such as recreating the original situation in their minds. These *mnemonic,* or memory, strategies reflect the development of metacognition (Miller, 1983). Returning to the computer analogy, metacognitive abilities are like being able to write your own computer

Focuses On	Sequential organization of mental processes.	
Key Concepts	Subprocessing steps, control strategies, metacognition.	
Data Derived From	Laboratory experiments on thinking and memory.	
Nature Vs. Nurture	The cognitive subprocesses are given by nature, and the control processes and metacognitions are developed through nurture.	
Continuity Vs. Discontinuity	Continuous, gradual development of information processing strategies.	

Table 2—6

INFORMATION PROCESSING THEORY

Figure 2–2

Subprocessing Steps and Control Strategies in Information Processing

A typical sequence begins with attention and ends with action, although an individual may go back over individual steps when perception, memory, or decision making fail.

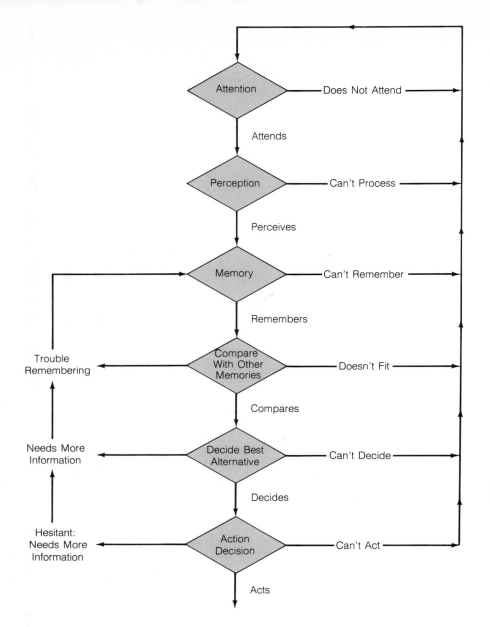

programs—to organize your brain's abilities in ways that best suit your adaptive needs.

It is this feature of human information processing—self-modification via metacognition—that machines cannot yet perform. Computers can only use the information processing steps and control strategies that are programmed by the human user: They cannot make up new ones as a result of experience. The field of *artificial intelligence* is a union of psychologists and computer scientists working to develop machines that have the characteristics of intelligent thinking.

Information processing theories seem to stand on the side of *nurture* rather than *nature* in explaining development. These theories suggest that the human is endowed genetically with certain basic mental hardware, but that

Theory and Social Policy

Child development theory has been applied to the development of social policies for children in a number of areas. Later in this book, we will be discussing some of these areas in more detail. For example, the effect of day care on children's development influences federal and state allocations for day care as well as state licensing requirements (Chapter 7). Research on the development of conceptual thinking in children leads to educational policies (Chapter 9). Laws affecting the amount of violence shown on television have been influenced by the study of the effects of TV violence on children (Chapter 10).

Although theory is stated in general and value-free terms, social policy is caught in a web of politics and conflicting values. Consider the issue of federal subsidies for day care services used by the children of working mothers.

Only psychoanalytic theory predicts that the mother should be the sole caregiver during the early years of the infant's life. Other theories suggest that children can learn from a variety of circumstances and that their development will not be sidetracked by exposure to more than one significant adult during the early years. Research has supported this position for most children, although some questions remain about the advisability of day care for children under the age of two (see Chapter 7).

The real world, however, is not swayed so easily by scientific theory and evidence (Melton & Russo, 1987). Until recently, day care was seen as something used only by disadvantaged families, those who could not bring up children on their own. This is the attitude of many Americans toward most social services for children and families.

Day care subsidies such as tax deductions and state-supported public day care for poor families have been available for some time, but the demand for day care subsidies has been made by the middle class only since the early 1980s. Is this because parents, legislators, and program planners have accepted the views of child development theories that children can thrive in day care? In part, this is true. Were it not for strong endorsements of day care by child development professionals, it would be harder to make a case for the value and benefits of day care. On the other hand, such endorsements had been available for some time before any action was taken.

The more important reason for day care subsidies seems to be economic. The proportion of children under age 10 is expected to increase in the next decade: part of a late twentieth century baby boom. It is estimated that in the last decade of this century, the rising costs of living and other factors will cause the percentage of children with working mothers to reach 53 percent for children under six and 81 percent for school-age children. Three and one-half million more children will thus need day care in 1990 than needed it in 1980 (Phillips, 1984).

What this increase means is a shift in public attitudes. Although day care was previously seen as a service for poor families, it is becoming viewed as being the right of every family. A shift in public values seems to coincide with an increasing amount of theory and research from the child development community about the development of children in the early years and the impact of day care on children and families. This convergence between public opinion, public demand, and scientific advocacy is what spurs social policy change (Peters, 1980; Phillips, 1984). A similar process occurred at the end of the nineteenth century as a skeptical public began to see the value of publicly supported compulsory education for all children. The need to educate immigrants in American ways and to give all children a basis for surviving in an increasingly complex technological society was combined with the public statements of professional educators to induce legislative change.

the software development is almost completely a function of experience acquired during development as one interacts with one's environment and adapts one's mental processing abilities to particular tasks. Information processing theory favors a position of developmental *continuity* as opposed to *discontinuity*. From this perspective, the child gradually acquires more efficient control strategies through continual transaction with the environment. Information processing theory does not accept that there are discontinuous stage shifts in thinking processes.

Modern computers do not develop, and the use of the computer as an analogy to human information processing does not give this theory an adequate explanation for development. Although information processing theorists have documented changes in information processing with age, they cannot completely explain how it happens.

Information processing theory, however, has been useful in designing curricula and intelligence tests that rely on children's real-world understandings. Furthermore, it has shifted the focus of education from memorizing facts to the development of metacognition: learning how to learn by developing memory and perceptual strategies.

Perhaps the most important application of information processing theory is in the treatment of learning disabilities. Diagnosticians can more effectively isolate that aspect of information processing that is impaired in a particular child, and treatment can be directed more specifically to the problem. Children that may have been diagnosed years ago as retarded or unteachable are today being treated for specific perceptual and motor disorders (Thomas, 1985).

Learning Theory

Piaget and the information processing theories were not the only ones to be concerned with the problem of how children adapt to the environment. This issue has been addressed in quite a different way by learning theorists. This section discusses three types of learning theory: classical conditioning, operant conditioning, and social learning.

Classical conditioning.   Watson's own ideas were influenced strongly by the research of the Russian physiologist, Ivan Pavlov (1849–1936), on learning in dogs. Pavlov worked with the salivation reflex in dogs that occurs when a hungry dog is given some food. Pavlov discovered that if he rang a bell every time a hungry dog was presented with some food, the dog eventually salivated at the sound of the bell, even in the absence of the food. This process, called *classical conditioning,* is shown in Figure 2-3.

In his experiments with dogs, Pavlov determined that the dog learned about the environment by a process of association between the bell and the food. Classical conditioning assumes that there must be an unconditioned stimulus that induces the behavior. The unconditioned response is usually some innate reflex, such as salivation in the presence of food. The conditioning process pairs the unconditioned stimulus with the conditioned stimulus so that the conditioned stimulus will now elicit the behavior.

Operant conditioning.   B. F. Skinner (1969), working with birds and small mammals, found it difficult to determine the unconditioned stimuli accounting for all the behavior of the animals. Skinner reasoned that although some behavior is *elicited* by unconditioned reflexes and conditioned stimuli, other behavior is simply *emitted* from the individual voluntarily and not in response to some innate reflex being triggered.

Skinner was not interested in the causes of the emitted behavior—the thoughts, motives, and feelings of the animals. He accepted the fact that each species of animal will have a different set of emitted behavior. In his experiments, he discovered that the rate of emitted behavior could be controlled by

B. F. Skinner found that behavior could be controlled by its consequences. His theory proposes specific methods that parents and teachers can use to teach discipline, correct problem behavior and teach skills. His theory has proven useful in a wide variety of educational settings.

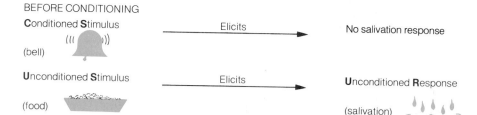

BEFORE CONDITIONING

Conditioned **S**timulus   Elicits   No salivation response

(bell)

Unconditioned **S**timulus   Elicits   **U**nconditioned **R**esponse

(food)   (salivation)

Figure 2–3

*Classical Conditioning and
Pavlov's Dog*

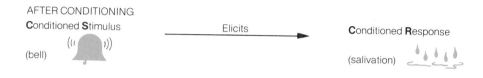

DURING CONDITIONING

Conditioned Stimulus (bell) is followed by presentation of Unconditioned
Stimulus (food), which elicits Unconditioned Response (salivation).

AFTER CONDITIONING

Conditioned **S**timulus   Elicits   **C**onditioned **R**esponse

(bell)   (salivation)

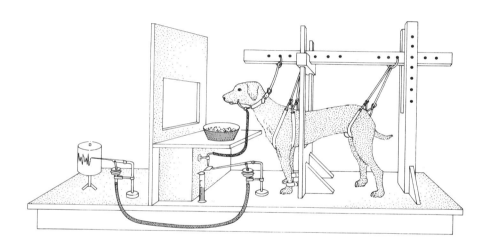

the *consequences* of the behavior, and he focused his theory on the kinds of
consequences that best controlled the emission of behavior.

In one experiment, a pigeon is put into a cage with no food tray. On the
side of the cage is a colored disk. One of the bird's emitted behaviors, pecking,
is applied to the floors and walls of the cage at random. When the pigeon
pecks the colored disk, however, a small bit of food falls into the cage. If this
happens often enough, the pigeon will peck the disk more frequently.

We could say that the pigeon has learned disk pecking to get food.
Actually, disk pecking has been selected from the pigeon's existing behaviors.
The pigeon now performs disk pecking more frequently than other kinds of
pecking. Controlling the consequences of an individual's action in such a way
as to change the frequency of occurrence of that action in the future is called
operant conditioning.

If the consequences of emitted behavior are rewarding to the animal, the
action will be repeated when the animal is in similar circumstances. Consequences that increase the frequency of actions are called *reinforcers*. Reinforcers

are rewarding to the individual in two ways: positive and negative. A *positive reinforcer* is a favorable consequence that increases the frequency of an action. If the frequency of a response is increased following the removal of an unfavorable or adverse event, the absence of such an event is a *negative reinforcer*.

Suppose a child performs a behavior that the parents desire, such as cleaning her room. Parental praise (positive reinforcement) after the child finishes cleaning the room will increase the likelihood that the child will clean the room in the future. On the other hand, suppose the parents find the child has not cleaned her room; they may scold her or withhold some special privileges. In such a case, the child who wishes to avoid being scolded (negative reinforcement) will be more likely to clean the room in the future. It is the absence of scolding that is negatively reinforcing, leading to an increase in the frequency of the desired behavior.

In some cases, the frequency of a behavior is decreased rather than increased. This, too, can happen in two different ways: by punishment and by extinction. A *punishment* is a consequence that decreases the frequency of the behavior it follows. For example, if scolding reduces the frequency of a child's aggressive acts against peers, then scolding is a punishment. Note that in this example, scolding works as a punishment to decrease the frequency of aggression. On the other hand, the absence of scolding (a negative reinforcement) may increase the frequency of friendly behavior.

Extinction is the process by which a response slowly decreases in frequency once it stops being reinforced. For example, suppose a child's aggressive behavior leads to the child's getting more attention from teachers. This attention acts as a positive reinforcer. Teachers may extinguish the aggression by ignoring the aggressor while attending to the victim.

Consequences of behavior may occur at different times following the behavior. The pattern of providing consequences in relation to behavior is called a *schedule of reinforcement*. A *continuous reinforcement* schedule provides a reinforcement every time the child emits a desired behavior. This type of schedule is most effective in the early stages of acquiring a new behavior. A *partial reinforcement schedule* is when the child is sometimes reinforced and sometimes not reinforced following a desired behavior. Usually, once a response has been learned, an occasional reinforcement is enough to guarantee its repetition. For most children, occasional praise is more effective than praise following every single instance of desired behavior.

Learning theory has been applied to education. In classrooms, for example, children learn to keep still and work for extended periods. Talking, moving, and wandering around are behaviors that teachers would like to eliminate. The role of the teacher is to arrange the schedules of reinforcement so that adaptive behavior is increased and undesirable behavior is decreased. This method of teaching is called *behavior modification* (Bijou, 1984).

Some learning can occur independently of other people. If you touch something hot and are burned, you will avoid touching that object in the future. In addition, classical conditioning can combine with operant conditioning to expand the scope of learning. The person who provides positive reinforcement in a specific situation may come to be seen by the child as more generally reinforcing: The child will look up to that person as a source of pleasure and as a role model.

Skinner's ideas were expanded into a developmental theory by Bijou and Baer (1965), who consider the child's past history and internal motivations as important elements in directing the emission of behavior. Although they recognize the adult's role in setting up reinforcements that control behavior, Bijou and Baer argue that a lot of learning is the result of internal processes.

As children get older, their own actions upon the environment change the environment. Because such change can be interpreted by the child as either a positive or a negative reinforcer, the child can control not only the frequency of emission of behavior but also the consequences of the behavior.

In Piaget's theory, the child is working toward a particular goal or is attempting to construct a more adaptive view of the environment. Learning theorists assume not that the child has a particular direction of growth but rather that growth is controlled by its consequences. It doesn't matter if the consequences are controlled by the self or by others (see Table 2–7).

Learning theory was elaborated further by incorporating the role of learning from other people. *Social learning theory* (Bandura, 1977) rejects the idea that all behavior is learned by controlling the consequences. Take the example of a baby going from babbling to speaking words. To create a recognizable word from babbling sounds by reinforcement, parents would have to reinforce all of the spontaneous emissions of sounds that resembled syllables. They would then have to reinforce the linking together of component syllables into words and phrases.

Bandura suggested that this method would take too long and be too difficult. He observed that entirely new behaviors can be learned almost immediately through *observational learning* by imitating the actions of another person. Sometimes imitation is reinforced, although sometimes people learn

Pretending to talk on the phone with family or friends is a frequent game of young children. This game illustrates that children learn by observing and imitating adult models. Imitation of this sort often begins in play situations before the child is ready to apply the learned behavior to making a real telephone call. Imitation also serves emotional development. By pretending to talk to her grandma who lives at some distance, it awakens the memories and feelings associated with that person.

Table 2—7

LEARNING THEORY

Focuses On	The acquisition of new behaviors.
Key Concepts	Classical conditioning, operant conditioning, reinforcers, punishment, extinction, schedule of reinforcement, observational and incidental learning, behavior modification.
Data Derived From	Observable behavior, laboratory experiments.
Nature Vs. Nurture	Developmental changes due almost entirely to nurture in the form of contingencies.
Continuity Vs. Discontinuity	Slow, gradual acquisition of behavior.

by imitation even if they do not perform the behavior immediately and if they are not motivated to learn the task at the time they see it modeled. This type of learning, called *incidental learning*, accounts for more general effects of role models beyond the specific task being learned.

Bandura also recognized the role of internal processes that lead a child to select a role model or to be influenced by particular kinds of reinforcers. Children need a minimal level of attention to the model and a motivation to learn from the model. Thus, the theory can be applied to television programming to make models more attractive to the children whom the show's producers are intending to reach.

Another difference between social learning theory and operant conditioning theory is the way in which the consequences of an act affect future performance. Bandura (1977) did not believe that consequences have an automatic, mechanical effect on the child. Children may see consequences and not act on them. They may observe the consequences of others' acts and think about their own behavior. For Bandura, consequences are sources of information that an intelligent child can use to develop self-regulation over behavior.

Learning theory has had a significant impact on education and in the relief of some children's psychological and behavior problems. Because learning theory focuses on the role of the immediate environment in controlling the child's behavior, it advocates the establishment of environmental conditions that encourage desirable behavior and the elimination of conditions that foster undesirable behavior (Kipnis, 1987).

The educational practice of breaking down complex learning tasks into small steps that the child can perform easily and get positive reinforcement for the accomplishment of is based on learning theory. Computer learning packages, in which the child gets immediate feedback for correct and incorrect answers without the negative sanctions of getting bad grades, are an innovation taken from learning theory (Thomas, 1985).

It should be clear by now where learning theory stands with regard to the *nature* versus *nurture* debate. The child is seen as a relatively passive individual who is subject to having behavior controlled by the kinds of consequences available in the environment. Learning theorists realize that each animal species is not equally trainable. Within a species, however, they tend to ignore individual differences that may be due to genetic variation. They will assume all humans are equally trainable using the right kinds of reinforcers.

Learning theory suggests that developmental change arises by small steps in which complex skills are built from simpler ones by a series of reinforcements. Thus, the learning theorists view developmental change as *continuous* rather than *discontinuous*.

Learning theory contributes little to the understanding of fundamentally human processes such as creativity, empathy, love, hope, and language development. Rather, learning theorists focus on basic processes that explain learning in all animals. Thus, they pay little attention to the role of hereditary factors, except to recognize that each species has a unique set of emitted behaviors.

Ecological Systems Theory

The psychologist Kurt Lewin (1890–1947) was one of the first to recognize that human behavior was determined by a wide range of influences. For example, a child's behavior in school may depend upon such things as the child's feeling of being liked or disliked by the teacher, how hungry the child is, whether the child is behind on his or her homework, how well a child does in a particular subject, and the anticipation of after-school social events (Lewin, 1942; Thomas, 1985).

Lewin's colleagues Roger W. Barker and H. F. Wright (1955) created the concept of *ecological psychology,* the study of the effect of the child's immediate surroundings on behavior (see also Chapter 3). For example, you can expect children to run and jump on the playground but not in the classroom. Children will not read books when they are riding a bike, but they may read at their desk at home or in the library.

Later, behavioral scientists began to refer to the complex relationship between the different environments and the different people within them as an ecological system. A *system* is a set of interdependent components in which each component affects all the others in an interdependent fashion. *Ecology* is the science of studying the complex interdependencies between all living things and their physical environment.

In the area of child development, systems thinking has been used in several ways. One is the study of the processes of exchange between people in social relationships within the family, such as parent-child relationships and sibling relationships (Furstenberg, 1985; Minuchin, 1985). This is called *social systems* or *family systems* theory. The other is the study of the effects on child development of the different systems in which the child is a member: the family, the school, the community, and the nation (Belsky, 1980; Bronfenbrenner, 1979). This is called *ecological systems* theory (see Table 2-8).

Social systems theory explicitly recognizes the relationship between the child and others as an important subject of study. The basic principle of this approach is that all members of a social group affect each other. Not only does the parent affect the child through childrearing practices, but the child affects the parent in turn. Different children will require different approaches. A baby who is fussy will elicit different responses from an adult than will a baby who is generally easy-going.

Parents and children affect each other developmentally as well. The adult must continually readjust and reassess his or her behavior and responses to the child as the child changes with development. The theory of Lev Semanovich

Focuses On	Complex environmental and social influences.
Key Concepts	System, ecology, micro-, meso-, exo-, and macrosystems.
Data Derived From	Observations of children in natural environments.
Nature Vs. Nurture	Nature and nurture interact in complex and dynamic ways throughout the life span.
Continuity Vs. Discontinuity	Form of change not specified.

Table 2–8

SYSTEMS THEORY

Vygotsky (1896–1934) was developed in Russia using the principles of Marxism-Leninism—that every individual is a member of a community and that all knowledge is socially constructed. Vygotsky, like Piaget, became known in the West through translations of his work that were done in the late 1960s. Vygotsky said that adults do not teach children directly. Rather, the child's own motivations to learn suggest to the adult how to guide the child. According to Vygotsky, when the child is uncertain about something, he or she is most susceptible to the guidance of the adult. In the process of working out his or her own problem, the child can observe the adult's behavior and thus learn the culturally accepted ways of doing things. Thus, parent and child learn from each other.

Taking a broader view of the effect of society on the child, Urie Bronfenbrenner's *ecological approach to human development* is "the study of the progressive, mutual accommodation, throughout the lifespan, between a growing human organism and the changing immediate environments in which it lives, as the process is affected by relations obtaining within and between those immediate settings, as well as the larger social contexts . . . in which the settings are embedded" (Bronfenbrenner, 1979).

Bronfenbrenner defines a nested set of systems in which the child takes part (see Figure 2-4). The *microsystem* is the relationship between the child and the immediate setting. Families, schools, peer groups, day care centers, and hospitals are microsystem settings. The *mesosystem* involves the interrelationships between the microsystems, such as the school-family relationship. The *exosystem* is the set of social institutions that affect each microsystem and mesosystem. The child is not a direct member of the exosystem, which includes the work place, the media, the government, and the economic system. The

Figure 2—4

Ecological Systems Theory

The child is contained within a nested system of social relationships and institutions. Except for microsystems, children are not direct participants in any of the other social systems that may affect their lives.

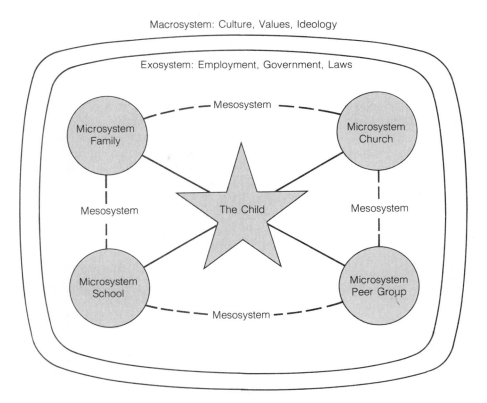

Theory and Intervention

Problems arise in the application of theory to the development of effective intervention programs for at-risk children. This book will discuss risk and intervention in areas such as hyperactivity (Chapter 9), child abuse and neglect (Chapter 11), learning disabilities (Chapter 13), bulimia (Chapter 16), and adolescent suicide (Chapter 17). In such cases, the application of theory to practice is often more direct than in the social policy area. This is because intervention programs may be designed and carried out by developmental researchers themselves. When brought into hospitals, schools, clinics, and family service agencies, intervention programs are used in the way they were originally designed, with minor modifications to fit local conditions.

Child development professionals—both researchers and practitioners—have more direct control over the design, implementation, and evaluation of intervention programs. However, the real world is still more complex than the theory can anticipate. For example, in the field of child abuse and neglect, developmentalists are beginning to use systems theories to explain the complexity of the phenomenon. It is now known that child abusers are not all disturbed personalities. There is a higher incidence of abuse in conditions of socioeconomic deprivation, in families with poor communication patterns, in homes in which the parents are unemployed, and in certain cultures where aggression and violence are accepted means of relieving frustrations (Belsky, 1980; Garbarino, 1982).

Systems theory predicts that the interventions for child abusers should focus not only on the abusers themselves but also on the community and social factors that create an atmosphere of abuse. Cultural attitudes toward violence might be changed by influential TV programs, federal programs can be made more sensitive to needs to preserve family ties in times of stress, and community agencies can work to improve informal and formal support systems for families in times of stress (Belsky, 1980; Cohn, 1983). The complexity of tying all these solutions into a comprehensive network of services, making sure some families don't "fall through the cracks," and working out the details of how such programs actually operate and who supports them is far beyond the ability of theory to predict or explain.

The result is that the actual design of programs combines some elements of theory and some elements of common sense and homespun remedies. If you want people to come to your carefully designed program, you have to know how to induce them and keep them there. Working through existing community organizations such as the YMCA, YWCA, and local church groups is one example of a practical element in getting intervention to work.

In the application to social policy, theory combines with public opinion and social conditions to create changes. In the application to intervention, theory combines with practical knowledge to speed implementation. In intervention, the best program is one that relies on the skills of both the researcher and the practitioner who will deliver the services to the target population.

macrosystem contains all the other systems as well as the generally held values, beliefs, and rules that regulate behavior among people within a culture.

What is the position of systems theories with regard to the *nature* versus *nurture* question? A systems theory would include the influence of both nature and nurture as equal contributors to the child's development. As we'll see in Chapter 4, systems theories provide the best explanation of prenatal development, because the genetic material contained in the fertilized ovum begins to interact with the ovum's physiological and chemical environment inside the pregnant woman's body. Thus, even from the beginning, the genes do not act in isolation, but rather they interact in systems fashion with each other and with their surroundings.

On the other hand, systems theories are not specific about whether development is *continuous* or *discontinuous*. Similar to ethological theory, systems theories have focused on finding some of the causes of child behavior and development and have paid less attention to the form of developmental change.

Systems theories are becoming useful in the study of a wide variety of situations that can affect children. For example, Bronfenbrenner has pointed out that an economic system that forces both parents to work, a work environment that gives little personal freedom for employees with children, and a society that does not foster the development of adequate child care, all conspire to undermine the values of family life and the amount of time parents have with their young children. Vygotsky and others have refocused developmental research to look not just at the child but at the parent-child interaction.

Systems theories have moved us away from thinking that each person is an isolated individual, a master of his or her own destiny. We can now see that everyone is linked to everyone else in complex ways. Systems theory concepts are still somewhat general, however. Although systems theory can focus our attention on the effects of the social environment on the child, little is known about the actual process of social transactions that best facilitate learning and development.

Chapter Summary

DEFINING DEVELOPMENTAL THEORY
□ Theory is defined in terms of its ability to organize and explain a set of observations gathered by the scientific method.
□ Developmental theory describes the sequence of change over age, attempts to understand the relationship between different aspects of development, and explains how children progress from one point in development to the next.
□ Developmental theories can be evaluated from the perspectives of nature versus nurture and continuity versus discontinuity.

MODERN DEVELOPMENTAL THEORIES
□ Ethological theory views development as a reflection of specific species typical patterns of behavior.
□ Psychoanalytic theory suggests that development is the result of the interaction between the child's desires and the adult's ability to help the child regulate those desires.
□ Piagetian theory views the child as an active participant in his or her own development while learning about the environment in the process of meeting goals.
□ Information processing theory breaks cognition into separate subprocesses and the flow of control between them.
□ Learning theory views the child as being controlled by the environmental consequences of his or her actions.
□ Systems theories suggest that the child is always an integral part of the social and physical environment and that development must be conceptualized as a function of the interactions between the child and the environment.

Recommended Readings

Bandura, A. L. (1977). *Social learning theory.* Englewood Cliffs, NJ: Prentice-Hall. A basic sourcebook on social learning theory.

Freud, S. (1949). *An outline of psychoanalysis.* New York: Norton. Requires some effort to read but gives a general overview of Freud's theory.

Erikson, E. (1950). *Childhood and society.* New York: Norton. One of the classic works on child development, beautifully written and fascinating to read.

Miller, P. H. (1983). *Theories of developmental psychology.* San Francisco: Freeman. An overview of the major theories of child development.

Piaget, J., & Inhelder, B. (1969). *The psychology of the child.* New York: Basic Books. A summary of Piaget's basic stages of child development.

Thomas, R. M. (1985). *Comparing theories of child development* (2nd ed.). Belmont, CA: Wadsworth. Overview of developmental theories with a good summary of historical influences.

CHAPTER 3

Studying the Child's Development

C hild (A girl, 4 years old): *Oh, the sun's moving. It's walking like us. Yes, it has little paws and we can't see them.*
Father: Where is it walking?
Child: *Why, on the sky. The sky's hard. It's made of clouds.*
   (The sun follows them while they walk)
   It's doing that for fun, to play a joke on us, like you when you smoke your pipe and play tricks on us.
Father: Why like me?
Child: *Like grown-ups.*
Father: Not like children?
Child: *No, it's having a joke like grown-ups.*
Father: But does it know we're here?
Child: *Of course it does, it can see us!*
(From Piaget, 1963, p. 252)

The preceding is a conversation that Jean Piaget had with one of his children during the early years of the child's development. It was an ordinary conversation that took place when the family was out for a walk one day. But this conversation was different from any of the others that might have taken place on that day between parents and their four-year-olds. First, it was later written down by the father alongside thousands of other conversations the father had with the same child during the preceding and subsequent years. Second, the conversations were interpreted by the father from the point of view of a theory of child development. The conversation was used as scientific data.

This chapter looks at how the scientific method has been applied to the understanding of child development. It covers the basics of research methods, starting with a brief history of child development research beginning in the eighteenth century.

Piaget was not the first person to observe children from a scientific perspective. Scholars in the eighteenth century began to record children's behavior and development in the form of detailed diaries. One of the earliest of the published diaries was written by the German philosopher, Dietrich Tiedemann (1748–1803). He described the development of his infant son in such areas as motor and language skills, thinking abilities, and social behaviors (see Figure 3-1).

Most of the diaries were written about an infant, usually the infant son of the author. For this reason, such diaries are called *baby biographies*. Other well-known baby biographies were written by William Preyer (1841–1897), who carried out some experiments on his son, and Charles Darwin (Kessen, 1965), whose theories of natural selection were discussed in Chapters 1 and 2.

Of the early diaries, the only one that was not about babies was written by the Swiss educator Johann Heinrich Pestalozzi (1746–1827). He studied the learning processes of his four-year-old son and used them to develop advice for parents and teachers about ways to observe children's behavior.

The diaries were limited in that they were based on the observations of only one child. The Belgian astronomer Adolphe Quatelet (1796–1874) was one of the first to gather data on many different people over a wide range of ages. His research concerned the developmental changes in heartbeat, muscle strength, height, mental illness, crime, suicide, and deliquency (Groffman, 1970).

Figure 3–1

*A sample page from the diary of
Dietrich Tiedemann, one of the baby
biographers of the nineteenth century.*

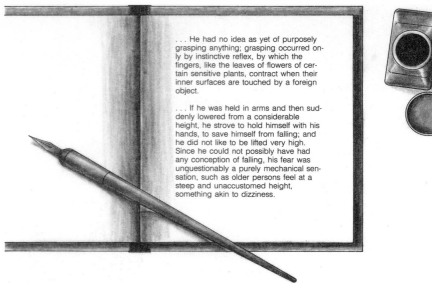

. . . He had no idea as yet of purposely grasping anything; grasping occurred only by instinctive reflex, by which the fingers, like the leaves of flowers of certain sensitive plants, contract when their inner surfaces are touched by a foreign object.

. . . If he was held in arms and then suddenly lowered from a considerable height, he strove to hold himself with his hands, to save himself from falling; and he did not like to be lifted very high. Since he could not possibly have had any conception of falling, his fear was unquestionably a purely mechanical sensation, such as older persons feel at a steep and unaccustomed height, something akin to dizziness.

Francis Galton (1822–1911) was already mentioned in relation to the issue of nature versus nurture (refer to Chapter 1). Galton was also a research pioneer. He studied hundreds of people at all ages. By comparing the differences between identical and fraternal twins, he developed a methodology for comparing the effects of genetics with the effects of the childrearing environment. He was one of the first to develop questionnaires, use statistics, and test a

*Johann Pestalozzi, a Swiss educator,
wrote extensively on the education of
pre-school children, and gave advice to
parents about the developmentally
appropriate needs of young children.*

person's intelligence (Rienert, 1979). His work was further elaborated by Alfred Binet (1857–1911), a French psychologist who refined the art of intelligence testing.

This chapter reviews some of the methods of developmental research that have been used in the twentieth century. The first section of the chapter applies some of the theories from Chapter 2 to develop researchable questions about children's behavior. The next sections of the chapter cover the basics of research design, assessment methods, and the interpretation of research.

From Theory to Research

Chapter 2 demonstrated that developmental theory serves to help us to understand the nature of developmental changes. This chapter shows how developmental research enables us to study how children behave at different ages and to gather data on what makes children change over time.

To help illustrate the use of research methods, we are going to take one research study as an example. Although no single study can illustrate all the research methods discussed in this chapter, the one we have chosen represents one of the more common methods of studying children. Furthermore, the study is one in which the authors clearly conceptualized their theoretical positions.

At what age should children be told about their adoption? Should parents continue to discuss adoption with the developing child, or is it better to say little beyond simply informing the child of the fact of adoption? The research study discussed in this chapter—based on a representative sample of single and multi-racial adoptive families—has some surprising answers about children's ability to understand adoption at different ages.

Finally, the study covers an important area that is rarely researched: the differences in development between adopted and nonadopted children.

It becomes a difficult problem for parents to reveal the fact of adoption to a child who was adopted during infancy. When should a child be told about the adoption? What should be said? How should parents respond to the questions that will continue to arise about adoption throughout the child's development?

Most adoption agencies recommend telling the child at an early age—between two and four years—at least in simple terms, and then providing more information as the child requests it. Typically, few guidelines about how to tell the child are provided by adoption agencies. This chapter reviews the methods and results of one research study (Brodzinsky, Singer, & Braff, 1984), which we'll call the Adoption Study, that attempted to address the question of when to reveal the child's adoptive status.

In this section, each of the six theories discussed in Chapter 2 will be applied to the problem of when children should be told about adoption and to how much children know about adoption.

Ethological Theory

This theory says that children will attend to those features of the environment that enhance their own survival and their ability to pass their own genes on to the next generation. Since reproduction is such an essential element in the evolution of the species, the ethological theory predicts that children will have a strong interest in the subject of reproduction, and hence both adopted and nonadopted children will seek knowledge about and show interest in adoption. This theory does not specify how age differences might affect children's understanding of adoption, however.

Psychoanalytic Theory

According to Freud, children will become interested in the relationship between their parents and in their own role in the family during the preschool years (Oedipal period), and it is at this time that children should be told about their adoptive status. Because of the explicit discussion of adoption brought on by the child's interest in family origins, children from adoptive families should gain more knowledge of the adoption process than should children from nonadoptive families.

Piagetian Theory

As the conversation at the beginning of the chapter demonstrates, preschoolers do not think logically. They tend to understand the world from their own perspective and would be likely to misinterpret or misunderstand their parents' discussion of adoption. During the concrete operational period, however, all children, whether adopted or not, should be able to understand adoption if described in concrete and specific ways. Understanding the abstract aspects of adoption, such as the legal implications and the ethical responsibilities of adoptive and biological parents regarding the child, would not be understood until the formal operational period.

Learning Theory

According to this theory, knowledge is acquired in gradual steps. If you break a complex concept into simpler components, teach the components individually, and then join them together, a child of any age could be trained to understand adoption if given enough repetition. Thus, adopted children should know more about adoption than should nonadopted children, because discussions about adoption will occur more frequently in the adopted child's home.

Systems Theory and Information Processing Theory

These theories can tell us little about the adoption questions. Neither theory has specified age differences in learning processes for children, and neither deals with the meaning adoption might have for the adopted child.

Of the theories that apply to the Adoption Study, only one, Piagetian theory, predicts that preschool children may not be able to understand the concept of adoption and that it therefore may be more appropriate to talk about the child's adoptive status in the early elementary school years. Although ethological theory does not specify an appropriate age, both psychoanalytic and learning theory suggest that children should be told about adoption during the preschool years, which is consistent with the advice given to parents by adoption agencies.

We'll complete our discussion of the results of the Adoption Study in the next sections of this chapter as we turn to the issue of how data on child development are gathered and interpreted using the scientific method. Understanding the basics of developmental research helps one to appreciate research findings as an intelligent "consumer."

Designing a Research Study

Approaches to Developmental Research

The most important distinguishing feature of developmental research is a concern with *change over time*. The Adoption Study looked at developmental changes in children's knowledge of adoption. The investigators selected children from five different age groups as shown in Table 3-1. Within each age group there were 20 adopted and 20 nonadopted children, making a total of 200 children.

Group	Age Range(yr.-mo.)	Average Age
1	4-0 to 5-11	5-4
2	6-0 to 7-11	6-10
3	8-0 to 9-11	8-10
4	10-0 to 11-11	10-10
5	12-0 to 13-11	12-7

(Brodzinsky, Singer, & Braff, *Child Development*, 1984, *55*, p. 870. ©The Society for Research in Child Development, Inc.)

Table 3—1

AGE GROUPS IN THE ADOPTION STUDY

The age range was selected because most of the developmental theories point to the preschool and elementary school years as being important for learning about adoption and because the theories differ in their predictions about the best age for telling children about adoption. Piaget's theory suggests that children can't really comprehend the concept of adoption until age seven, while other theories suggest that preschool-age children are capable of understanding adoption.

In the study of changes over time, developmental researchers can either follow the same group of children as they get older or study children of different ages at the same time. Each approach has advantages and disadvantages.

A *longitudinal study* is one in which the researcher follows the same group of children over a number of years. Children who are born in the same year form a *cohort,* or a group of same-age children. Most longitudinal studies follow a single cohort over time.

The Adoption Study looks at age differences in knowledge by comparing children of different ages at the same time. This kind of research is called a *cross-sectional study,* because the investigators have chosen a cross-section of the population of children who have reached a particular age when the study is done.

Cross-sectional studies are the most common in developmental research. Typically, investigators cannot afford to take the time to follow the same subjects from age 3 to age 12, as would be necessary to do the Adoption Study using a longitudinal approach. With cross-sectional research, one can get a general idea about age changes in a relatively short period of time.

Cross-sectional studies are helpful when it is not important to discover how a particular individual reached his or her ideas of adoption at age 12. One problem with cross-sectional research, however, is that we cannot always be sure that the children in each age group differ only by age.

The children in the Adoption Study were interviewed in 1983 (allowing one year for writing the study and getting it published). The three-year-olds in the study are taken from a cohort born in 1980; the thirteen-year-olds are from a cohort born in 1970. As we saw in Chapter 1, childrearing belief systems are subject to continual cultural change. If society's attitude toward adoption and toward when and how to tell children about adoption has changed over this ten-year period, it could be that the older children, aside from merely being older, are the product of a different set of attitudes and beliefs about adoption.

The only way to find out if the 1970 cohort is different from the 1980 cohort would be to follow, longitudinally, the children born in 1980 until they reach the age of 13. We would then be able to look for possible differences in knowledge about adoption between the 1970 cohort of 13-year-olds and the 1980 cohort of 13-year-olds. We could also test differences between 1970 three-year-olds and 1980 three-year-olds.

If no differences exist between the two groups of 13-year-olds (*cohort comparison*) and we do find differences between the 1970 thirteen-year-olds and the 1980 three-year-olds (*cross-sectional comparison*), we can be sure the differences are due to age. If, on the other hand, the two groups of 13-year-olds are actually different in their adoption knowledge (cohort comparison), the differences between the 1970 thirteen-year-olds and the 1980 three-year-olds (cross-sectional comparison) are partly due to age and partly due to cohort differences (see Figure 3–2).

It is unlikely that a major cultural shift in adoption beliefs occurred between 1970 and 1980. However, a wider age range, such as the 30- and 40-

Year	Cohort 1	Cohort 2

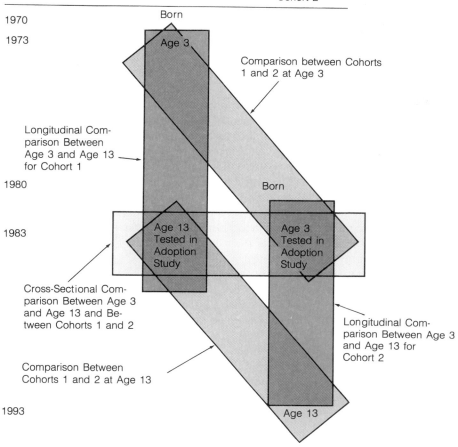

Figure 3–2

Cohort, Cross-Sectional, and Longitudinal Comparisons

Cohort comparisons use children of the same age, born in different years. Cross-sectional comparisons use children of different ages, tested in the same year. Longitudinal comparisons use the same children at different ages.

year spans found in studies of adult development, might lead to significant cultural differences between age groups. This problem is called a *cohort effect*, because each age group, or cohort of subjects, had a different cultural experience while growing up. Cohort effects have been found for political beliefs and sex-role stereotypes (see Chapter 17).

Even if the cohorts have basically the same cultural experiences while growing up, another potential problem with cross-sectional studies is called a time of measurement effect. A *time of measurement effect* occurs if the particular year you choose to do the study is unusual for one of the groups of children. Let's suppose that in 1983, junior high schools introduced a human development course required for all students and dropped the requirement the following year. Thus, 13-year-olds tested in 1983 may have more knowledge of adoption than would 13-year-olds tested in any other year.

Longitudinal studies are required when we want to see if early experiences of individuals contribute to their later development. For example, if we wanted to see whether differences in adoption knowledge of adolescents were due to how and when they were told about adoption, we would need to follow the same children from preschool until adolescence.

Longitudinal designs may also suffer from both cohort and time of measurement effects. If only one cohort of children is studied, we still do not know whether the developmental changes observed in that cohort would be different from the changes in some other cohort of children. For example, the adolescent identity crisis (see Chapter 17) is believed to be a developmental phase related to the postponement of adult responsibilities due to schooling. Since compulsory schooling for all adolescents has only begun in this century, earlier cohorts may not have experienced this developmental phase. Perhaps the best solution is to use a *cross-sequential study,* that is, to follow a number of different cohorts to do both cross-sectional and longitudinal comparisons. You will read about some research on adolescent development that used this approach in Chapter 17.

The danger of cohort and time of measurement effects is minimal in studies of young children, since the age range of developmental change is usually much shorter than the time periods over which social and cultural changes occur. In addition, younger children may be less susceptible to cultural influences than are adolescents and adults.

A more serious problem with longitudinal studies, and the main reason so few are carried out, is cost. Few researchers can find the research funds to sustain such long-term efforts. Furthermore, the changes in the technology of assessment procedures may make the methods chosen at the start of the study obsolete after a few years.

A final problem is *attrition,* the gradual loss of subjects as they grow tired of the study or move away. Not only does the number of subjects decrease, but the subjects who remain—because they are more committed or because they are repeatedly tested or observed—may be different from the general population.

Once we have chosen our basic developmental design—longitudinal or cross-sectional—what happens next? Most research is done to answer the question, Does X affect Y? (In the case of the Adoption Study, X = the child's age and Y = the child's understanding of the adoption situation.) The answer to this question is based on an analysis of differences between the children. If all the children had the same level of adoption knowledge at each age, there would be nothing of interest to study. Thus, researchers rely on variations between individuals.

Variables

X and Y are called variables. A *variable* is an attribute of the child or the child's environment that can be expected to vary from one child to the next or within the same child over time. Variables can be either independent or dependent.

An *independent variable* has three characteristics: (1) it is the variable manipulated by the experimenter, (2) it is the presumed cause of the experimental effects, and (3) it is the basis for predicting the experimental effects. A *dependent variable* has two characteristics: (1) it is the presumed effect of manipulating the independent variable, and (2) it is the effect that has been predicted.

An independent variable is independent because the investigator is free to use any level of the variable in an experimental situation. In the Adoption Study, the researchers chose the independent variable of age by deliberately selecting their age groups to fit the predictions of the different theories we examined. The independent variable of adoption status was selected to see if being adopted makes children more knowledgable about adoption. The independent variable is variable because it must have at least two different levels (values). The Adoption Study used five levels of age and two levels of adoption status (refer to Table 3-1).

A dependent variable is dependent because changes in its value are presumed to be a result of (to depend upon) the independent variable. The investigator deliberately chooses or manipulates the independent variable and observes the resulting changes in the dependent variable. Thus, in the Adoption Study, the level of the child's understanding of adoption is presumed to depend upon the child's age and adoption status.

Variables can be in the form of categories or in the form of a numerical value. For example, age can be expressed in either way. When children are classified into groups by age—such as preschool versus elementary school age—the age variable takes the form of a category. When the variable of age is expressed in years, it takes the form of a numerical value.

Basic Statistics About Variables

When a research study is done, researchers attempt to measure the variables for each of the subjects under investigation. The group of subjects included in any single research study is called a *sample*. To determine how the group as a whole scored on each of the variables, researchers use *statistics*, or summary scores that reveal how the average subject performed.

The scores for all the subjects in a sample can be made into a graph such as that shown in Figure 3-3. This graph, showing how many subjects received a particular score on a spelling test, is called the sample's *distribution*. Three measures of the sample can be computed: the mean, the median, and the mode. The *mean*, or average, is the sum of all of the scores divided by the total number of subjects. The *median* is the score of the subject whose score is exactly in the middle of the distribution. The *mode* is the score that is received by the largest number of children. These three measures are shown in Figure 3-3.

The Selection of the Sample

Developmental theories and hypotheses are generally presumed to be true of all children. Since it is not possible to actually study the hypothesis in the entire population of children, investigators select their sample of children to be *representative* of the larger population of children to which the investigator wishes the results to apply.

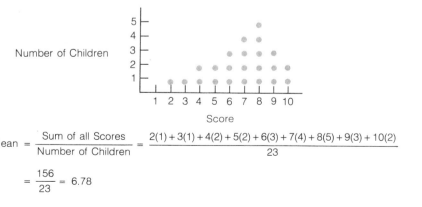

$$\text{Mean} = \frac{\text{Sum of all Scores}}{\text{Number of Children}} = \frac{2(1) + 3(1) + 4(2) + 5(2) + 6(3) + 7(4) + 8(5) + 9(3) + 10(2)}{23}$$

$$= \frac{156}{23} = 6.78$$

Median = Middle Score = 7 (The 12th Child in 23 Has a Score of 7)

Mode = Most Frequent Score = 8 (5 Children Got This Score, More Than Any Other Score)

Figure 3—3

Summary Statistics for a Spelling Test

To be representative of the North American population, research samples should contain a mixture of children from different racial and ethnic groups, as found in the Adoption Study sample.

In the adoption study, of the 100 nonadopted children, all were Caucasian, except one mulatto, three black, and five Oriental children. The 100 adopted children were all Caucasian except for five mulatto, six black, twelve Oriental, and six Latin-American children. Of the 29 non-Caucasian adopted children, 25 lived with Caucasian families. There were 102 girls and 98 boys. In addition, the families represented a range of socioeconomic levels. This ethnic, sex, and social class mix as well as the higher proportion of non-Caucasians in the adoption group is representative of the entire U.S. population.

Because of the cost and difficulty of doing longitudinal research on large samples of subjects, developmentalists have sometimes studied developmental change in a few carefully chosen subjects. This approach is called *case study*, or $N = 1$ (where N represents the number of subjects in a study) research.

The psychotherapy case studies of Freud, and Piaget's case studies of his own three children are examples of a case study approach. One of the authors of this book continues to study videotapes of the social interactions of two mother/infant pairs made between 1977 and 1978 in a laboratory playroom setting every week from the infants' birth to age one year (Fogel, 1981, 1982, 1985) (see Chapters 6 and 7).

Case studies are limited, since the subject sample is not representative of the larger population of children. The value of a case study is to discover processes of behavior and development that might have gone unnoticed when simpler measures are used on larger samples. The discovery of a new process can then be tested on a larger sample of subjects.

Cross-cultural research can be used effectively to test the generalizability of research findings. Some ways in which cross-cultural research has been used are to test the universality of a developmental process and to increase the range of variation to help explain differences in developmental outcomes.

The tests for the age at which children progress through Piaget's stages is an example of looking for human universals. Piaget believed that children progressed through stages of cognitive development without the influence of social and cultural factors. This has been found to be the case for the transition from preoperational to concrete operational thinking, but not necessarily for the transition to formal operational thinking, which depends on cultural factors (see Chapter 16) (Dasen, 1977).

The use of culture to increase variations in developmental settings has been used by Beatrice and John Whiting (1975) in their famous "Six Culture Study." The Whitings predicted, following social learning theory, that the development of children's social behavior would depend on social patterns of reinforcement of particular kinds of actions. For example, the Whitings studied cultures that differed in complexity. Complex cultures are those in which a high level of technology and a clear division of labor exist. Children in most complex cultures do not do many household tasks and spend most of their time away from the home in schools. In simpler cultures, children are trained to do many tasks around the home. People share chores, and specialization of roles is less developed.

The results showed that children from complex cultures, like our own, were more dependent on adults, more likely to seek attention from adults, and more dominant in social play with other children than were children from

In most countries of the world, children are given responsibility for certain chores, including farm work, cleaning, carrying and infant care.

simpler cultures. Children from simpler cultures, such as those living in small villages in Mexico and Africa, were more likely to act independently and responsibly in their chores, sought less attention from adults, and were more nurturant and responsible in their interactions with other children. Thus, the way the society is structured reinforces certain specific kinds of social behavior.

The generalizability of the Adoption Study will be limited to the social and cultural group from which that sample was taken. Other cultures may have different beliefs about adoption. For example, in some cultures, children whose parents cannot raise them will be sent to live with the family of a close relative, giving the child a greater sense of family ties and perhaps buffering the psychological impact of not growing up with one's biological parents.

Control Over the Research Setting

Most hypotheses in developmental research are of the form "Does *X* affect *Y*?" The type of control with which the researcher can manipulate *X* (the independent variable) and then observe the subsequent changes in *Y* (the dependent variable) is called an *experiment*. A *quasi-experiment* is one in which the researcher uses natural variations in the independent variable, such as age differences in the Adoption Study.

Experimental research always involves a comparison between a group that receives some kind of experimental treatment and one or more other groups that receive a different treatment or a no-treatment *control group*. The subjects should not be allowed to choose whether they are a member of the experimental or the control group. Rather, the researcher assigns the subjects to groups by a *random assignment* process and thus enhances the generalizability of the study. In random assignment studies, the flip of a coin determines whether subjects join the experimental or the control group. In this way, subject and researcher bias cannot enter into the group assignment process.

The problem with experimental research is that it cannot be used to study many aspects of human behavior and development, since we cannot manipulate the lives of people. In addition, even when we perform an experiment in which manipulation is ethically justified, we cannot always be sure that we have controlled all the important aspects of the situation.

Most of the important questions involving child development are not under the control of the researcher. Rather, we have to rely on comparing children in groups that arise because of natural conditions. A *quasi-experimental research study* is one in which the researcher does not manipulate the conditions that control the independent variables. The Adoption Study had two independent variables: adoption status and age.

Taking advantage of variation of the independent variable in the natural environment, the investigator can measure the dependent variable for the same subjects. For example, let's consider the relationship between age—one of the independent variables in the Adoption Study—and the dependent variable of adoption knowledge.

We can assess the relationship between the child's age and the level of the child's adoption knowledge by making a graph of age as a function of knowledge level. In Figure 3-4, the *Y* or vertical axis represents the knowledge level, and the *X* or horizontal axis is the child's age.

Three different types of possible relationships are shown in Figure 3-4. In Figure 3-4 (a), older children have the highest levels of adoption knowledge, and conversely younger children have lower levels of knowledge. By knowing the child's age, we can predict the child's level of knowledge from this graph.

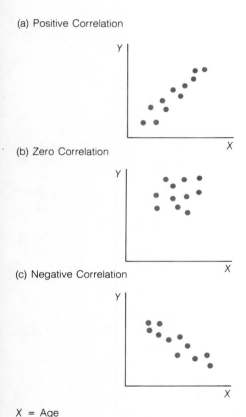

(a) Positive Correlation

(b) Zero Correlation

(c) Negative Correlation

X = Age

Y = Adoption Knowledge

Figure 3—4

Possible Relationships Between Two Variables

Each point on these graphs represents the data from one child. The coefficient of correlation tells how two variables are related for the entire group of subjects.

The Ethics of Research on Children

The ethical conduct of researchers who work with children is an issue that emerged after World War II with the discovery of horrible and inhumane experiments that Nazi physicians conducted on children who were prisoners in concentration camps. The Nuremberg Code, an official summary of the trials against these physicians and other war criminals for crimes against humanity, contained the first written guidelines for the protection of people who are subjects of research.

Between 1965 and 1973, guidelines were established in the United States by the Federal government for the protection of human subjects. These guidelines have been adopted by most research institutions in the United States. In addition, the American Psychological Association (1982) has published a similar set of ethical standards for the conduct of research and clinical practice in psychology.

The central issue in the guidelines is the subject's *informed consent* to participate in research. This means that the subject's participation in a research study is completely voluntary and takes place only after the subject has been fully informed about the nature of the research project. Some of the specific guidelines regulating research ethics are as follows (Keith-Spiegel, 1983):

1. A fair and understandable explanation of the research, its purpose, and the procedures to be followed must be given.
2. An understandable description of any risks, discomforts, and benefits that might be associated with participation must be provided.
3. There should be no coercion of subjects to participate.
4. The information obtained from the subjects should be confidential, and any legal limits to confidentiality should be explained.
5. The subject is free to obtain any information concerning the procedures at any time and has the right to be informed of the results of the research.
6. Subjects are free to withdraw from the study at any time.

Although these guidelines are clear and seem appropriate, they were designed primarily for research on adults. A number of important issues arise when the subjects of research are children. The very notion of informed consent is problematic. Children do not have the legal authority to enter into contracts, and their right to consent is usually decided by a parent or guardian. The ethical guidelines state clearly that the information provided should be understandable, although many adults will sign consent forms without fully understanding, even when the researcher has explained all the procedures (Cassileth, 1980). However, it is ethically wrong for an investigator to coerce a child into a research study if the child refuses to participate, even if parental consent has been granted.

Another problem related to research ethics is that of *deception*. Although most researchers do not wish to deceive subjects, all research involves a minimum amount of deception if the researcher is to keep the subject unaware of the hypotheses and the experimental condition. This is in conflict with the ethical guidelines concerning informing the subject about the procedures and proving information to the subject upon request. Generally, researchers are sensitive to these mild deceptions, and most studies include a debriefing session after the subject has completed all the procedures. At this session, the subject is told of the true nature of the study and given the opportunity to withdraw his or her data from the research study.

Balancing the rights of individual human subjects against the need of all people for more information on child development is a difficult ethical issue. Beyond the guidelines set by professional associations, every researcher has the responsibility to design studies of lasting value and to respect the rights and dignity of the individuals who grant their willing participation in this effort.

We would say that there is a direct relationship, or a *positive correlation*, between age and knowledge for this group of children.

In Figure 3-4 (b), some of the older children are high on adoption knowledge, while other older children are low on knowledge. Knowing the child's age, therefore, does not help you in making a prediction about the child's level of knowledge. For this group of children there is no relationship, or a *zero correlation*, between age and level of knowledge.

In Figure 3-4 (c), older children have the least knowledge about adoption, while younger children have the most. As in Figure 3-4 (a), we can predict one score from the other, but the relationship is an inverse one: as one variable increases, the other decreases. We would say there is an inverse relationship, or a *negative correlation* between the two variables.

The *coefficient of correlation* is a number ranging from $+1.00$ (a direct relationship) to -1.00 (an inverse relationship) that expresses the degree of relationship between two variables. A high (values close to $+1.00$ or to -1.00) correlation, whether positive or negative, does not mean that one of the variables is the cause of the other. It simply means that the two variables are related, although it doesn't tell us why or how they are related.

Let's suppose that the actual results of the Adoption Study reveal a direct relationship between age and level of knowledge. Does that mean that age is the cause of increased knowledge? Actually, age doesn't cause anything. Increased levels of knowledge may come about because of specific learning experience or because of cognitive changes due to maturation and experience. It is the experience, and not the age, that is the cause of changes in knowledge.

The choice of using an experimental or a quasi-experimental research design depends on the type of research question one has. Experimental methods are best for finding the causes of behavior, because the independent variable can be isolated from other sources of variation. When experiments are not methodologically or ethically feasible or when one wishes to study the child in natural surroundings, quasi-experimental methods are used.

Whether we are doing experimental or quasi-experimental research, we must consider the problem of how to measure the variables under study. You might have wondered how researchers could measure the child's level of adoption knowledge. The next section turns to the most common methods of assessment and measurement in developmental research.

Assessment Procedures

One of the most difficult problems of child development researchers is to decide how to determine a child's value on a particular variable. Researchers have devised several procedures for doing this: (1) observational methods, (2) automatic recording methods, and (3) testing methods. The choice of a particular method depends on the kind of variable one needs to assess in order to test a hypothesis.

Observational Methods

Observational methods are procedures for observing and recording children's ongoing behavior. They are especially effective for infants and young children for two reasons. First, young children are not as good as older children at taking tests. Second, young children are less likely than older children to be self-conscious about being observed.

Part of the conversation quoted at the beginning of this chapter was an observation of what a child said spontaneously while watching the sun "move." Piaget sometimes asked children specific questions designed to test their understanding of a particular situation. This approach—in which the researcher probes the child's knowledge as part of a natural conversation—is called the *clinical interview* method.

Piaget's clinical interview method was used in the Adoption Study to assess the child's comprehension of adoption. The questions used by the researchers are listed in Table 3-2. According to the researchers:

"It should be noted, however, that these questions served only as a guideline. The course of the interview was determined as much by the child's responses as by these specific questions. Furthermore, the interview was terminated following the first three questions if the child did not clearly differentiate between adoption and birth as alternative paths to parenthood." (Brodzinsky et al., 1984, p. 870).

Clinical interviews are relatively *open-ended;* that is, the researcher can write down whatever comes to mind or appears interesting to the subject. Although they may be helpful in the initial stages of studying an area of child development, open-ended methods are time-consuming and costly. Usually, researchers have specific questions and are looking for measures that are relatively easy to obtain.

Several procedures have been developed to make observational methods more efficient. The researcher tries to limit the scope of what is observed by defining in advance the types of behavior that will be recorded, called target behaviors. Let's suppose a researcher is interested in attachment behavior of infants to their mothers when an unfamiliar person approaches them. The researcher will attempt to define attachment in terms of specific child behaviors, such as approaching the mother, following the mother, and staying within arm's length of the mother. Attachment may also be expressed by verbal and vocal means, such as asking about the stranger, asking to be picked up or held, and crying.

Table 3—2

QUESTIONS ASKED DURING THE CLINICAL INTERVIEW IN THE ADOPTION STUDY

1. What does it mean to be a parent? Suppose two people want to become parents—a mommy and a daddy—what do they have to do?

2. Is there any other way of becoming a parent besides "making" a baby?

3. Let's suppose that a man and a woman wanted a baby and they decided to adopt one. What does this mean? What does adoption mean?

4. How do people go about adopting a baby? What do they have to do? Where do they have to go? What happens there?

5. Let's suppose a man and a woman decide to adopt a baby. Why do you think they would want to? Why do people adopt children?

6. If a man and a woman have already "made" children of their own, can they still adopt other children? Why would they want to?

7. What kind of child do people look for when they adopt someone?

8. Let's suppose that a child is being adopted. Where do you think the child would come from? What are the reasons that children are placed for adoption?

9. Suppose a man and a woman adopted a child. Is that child theirs forever? Can anyone ever take the child away? Why?

10. Let's suppose that an important decision had to be made for the child after the child had been adopted. Who should make that decision—the adoptive parents or the people who "made" the child? Why?

(Brodzinsky et al., *Child Development*, 1984, 55, p. 870. ©The Society for Research in Child Development, Inc.)

Videotape recordings of children's behavior allow researchers to stop, rewind and replay segments of tape, or to watch a segment in slow motion. Complex sequences of action can be better understood in this way. Researchers can also discuss differing interpretations of the same behavior.

Once the target behaviors have been chosen, the observer will be ready to record ongoing behavior. In some cases, investigators use pencil-and-paper methods. When one of the target behaviors is seen, it is checked off on a sheet of paper on which the target behaviors have been listed. In some cases, the observer will watch for a short time (for example, 30 seconds), take a break to record all of the target behaviors that were seen during that period, and observe for another 30 seconds. This method is called *time sampling*, since only short segments of time are chosen from the continuous stream of action.

Pencil-and-paper methods are difficult, because many different things are happening in real situations that are beyond the ability of an observer to see and record accurately. Recently, audio and video recording methods have improved the accuracy of observational data over pencil-and-paper methods. Once behavior is recorded on video tape, observers can replay certain segments until they get all the desired information. In addition, electronic devices called *event recorders* can be used to keep track of observations. Event recorders look like handheld calculators. Each key can represent a particular behavior. Because the event recorder has an internal clock, the observer can concentrate on the child and not on the time.

A final type of direct observation is called *trait rating*. Unlike the other observational methods in which some attempt is made to record the actual ongoing behavior of the child, in this method the observer watches the child's behavior in a particular situation and makes a judgment about the child's level of performance. The observer's *rating* of the child is usually made by selecting a level where the child seems to best fit on a rating scale.

In the Adoption Study, children's knowledge about adoption was observed during a clinical interview about adoption that took place in the child's home. After the interview, the children's responses were rated on a five-point scale, the levels of which corresponded to the complexity of the child's understanding of adoption (see Table 3-3).

Since rating involves a judgment about the child, different observers may rate the same child in slightly different ways depending upon their interpretation of the child's behavior. Nevertheless, ratings are effective when the variable of interest to the research cannot be equated with specific behaviors. Thus, although a child's attachment can be closely related to the amount of following the mother and asking to be picked up, the child's understanding of adoption can be inferred only after listening to the child discuss the issue from a number of different perspectives.

Automatic Recording Methods

Researchers have used the *automatic recording* of physiological activity of the body, such as heart rate, respiration rate, or brain wave recordings, to tap into psychological processes. These methods are especially effective in the study of infants who have relatively few means available for behavioral or verbal expression.

You will encounter research studies using different types of automatic recording methods in this book. Heart rate (HR) changes are recorded by small electrodes placed on the child's chest. They do not harm the child but pick up tiny electric currents under the skin that are created by the heart's movements. Gross motor activity has been recorded with a device called an *actometer*. It can be fixed to a child's clothing or to an infant's crib to record the number of shifts of position of the child.

Although automatic recording is free of observer bias and is relatively easy to do, researchers have to be careful in interpreting the meaning of the

Table 3—3

LEVEL OF ADOPTION KNOWLEDGE RATING SCALE

Level 0—Children exhibit no understanding of adoption.

Level 1—Children fail to differentiate between adoption and birth. Instead, they tend to fuse the two concepts together.

Level 2—Children clearly differentiate between adoption and birth as alternative paths to parenthood. They accept that the adoptive family relationship is permanent, but they do not understand why. At best they rely on a sense of faith ("my mother told me") or notions of possession ("the child belongs to the other parents now") to justify the permanent nature of the parent-child relationship.

Level 3—Children differentiate between adoption and birth but are unsure about the permanence of the adoptive parent-child relationship. Biological parents are seen as having the potential for reclaiming guardianship over the child at some future but unspecified time.

Level 4—Children's descriptions of the adoptive family are characterized by a quasi-legal sense of permanence. Specifically, they refer to "signing papers" or invoke some authority such as a judge, lawyer, doctor, or social worker who in some vague way "makes" the parent-child relationship permanent.

Level 5—The adoption relationship is now characterized as permanent, involving the legal transfer of rights and responsibilities for the child from the biological parents to the adoptive parents.

(Brodzinsky et al., *Child Development*, 1984, 55. ©The Society for Research in Child Development, Inc.)

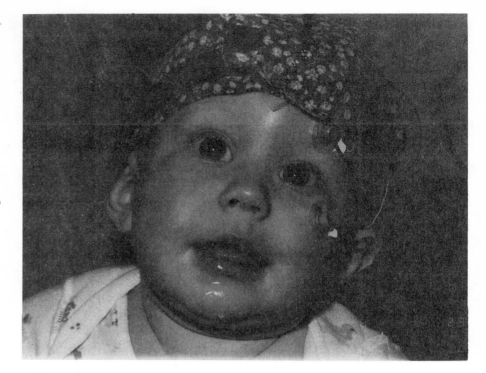

Brain activity creates small electrical currents that can be measured on the scalp by automatic recording devices. Researchers use this method to learn more about infant's information processing. The electrodes placed on the head do not hurt or shock the subject.

data obtained. Heart rate, for example, will increase when the subject is aroused, but it will also increase if the subject moves. In subjects older than infants, motor activity, and even heart rate, can be controlled voluntarily by the subject and thus may not be a good indicator of the subject's immediate, uncensored response (Achenbach, 1978). When used with other behavioral indicators, however, automatic physiological recording can be a valuable measurement method.

Testing Methods

Observation and automatic recording are by far the most popular methods of study for children under the age of seven. As children become more verbal and more skilled at reading and logical thinking, researchers have attempted to obtain information from children directly by administering *standardized tests.*

A type of standardized test with which everyone is familiar is the achievement test, which includes yearly achievement tests given in the public schools and the Scholastic Aptitude Test that most students entering college are asked to take. One's score on a standardized test is presumed to be an accurate representation of a person's characteristics or abilities. Generally, such scores are ranked compared to a *reference group* composed of all the other people taking the test to derive a percentile ranking score. Such tests are called normative tests, or *norm-referenced tests,* since each individual's score is compared with what is normal for the appropriate reference group.

Because of the ease of administration, testing methods are popular with researchers as well as with clinicians and educators, who need standardized assessments to create the most beneficial therapeutic and learning environments for children.

Standardized tests are limited in a number of important ways. Since most tests tap only a small number of a child's abilities, a child's score on a test should be used only as one piece of information about that child. It should be balanced with scores on other tests as well as with direct observations and interviews with the child and with those who know the child.

A greater problem is that tests leave little room for variation in the child's experience related to test performance. Standardized tests have been accused of favoring middle-class white North American children, who are used to test taking and who are familiar with the types of skills and vocabulary used in such tests. Children from other ethnic and income groups and children from different cultures all tend to score lower. The issue of cultural bias in intelligence testing is discussed in Chapter 13. Researchers, clinicians, and educators need to be aware of the limitations in testing procedures.

Errors in Assessing Children

Once researchers have chosen the variables and the assessment procedures in a research study, they need to convince themselves and others that these variables are accurate representations of the behaviors and concepts that they wish to measure. To do this, researchers must present evidence that they have taken into account most of the common sources of error in behavioral research. These sources of error are discussed under three headings: (1) reliability, (2) validity, and (3) unintended bias (discussed in the Focus on Issue section).

Reliability

Reliability is a measure of the consistency with which an assessment procedure is applied. When individuals make behavioral observations, their powers of observation and their judgments in ratings need to be checked. This is usually done by comparing the observation records of one observer with those of another well-trained observer.

Inter-observer reliability is the degree to which the variables derived from the observer records—frequencies and durations, for example—are consistently the same for different observers who independently record or rate exactly the same situation. Reliability checks are a way to make sure that the measuring instrument—the human observer—is seeing no more or less than what is intended.

In the Adoption Study, the variable of interest is the child's score on the five-point rating scale of adoption knowledge. Several different raters read the child's responses to the clinical interviews, and each rater scored the children on the five-point scale. When the ratings were compared across the different raters, they agreed exactly on the child's knowledge level for 170 of the 200 children interviewed. This is considered to be very good reliability.

Unintended Bias in Research Studies

Many problems can arise in the course of a research study that can affect the outcome. The subjects of the study may respond unfavorably to the research situation, and the researchers may not be aware of factors that influence the subjects outside of those that were measured. These factors can contribute to *unintended bias*.

Bias from the Subjects.

Sometimes the way in which a study is set up influences the subjects. For example, if the subjects of the Adoption Study interview are adolescents, they may try to guess what the researcher is really after and act in ways that fulfill their expectation of the research study. This type of problem, called *demand characteristics* of the situation, is more likely to occur in research on older children. The response of such children to the interview may also depend on such factors as the children's mood, how much the children feel they can trust the interviewer, and whether the children get to miss a class in order to participate.

One of the most famous examples of unintended bias is known as the *Hawthorne effect*. Researchers working in the Hawthorne plant of the Western Electric Company in the 1950s wanted to find out if variations in the working conditions could influence worker productivity. (Homans, 1958). The researchers chose a small group of employees as their test group. They found that every one of the changes introduced by the researchers increased productivity, and productivity of the group continued to increase even when the working conditions returned to normal.

It was later discovered through interviews with the employees that productivity increased because the members of this experimental group felt important and valued enough to be selected to participate in this special project. From this experience, researchers learned to introduce control groups in research designs.

To eliminate demand characteristics, it is important that subjects not be aware of the hypotheses of the study and that they be assigned to the experimental or the control group without knowledge of which group they belong to. In the Adoption Study, an experimental group of adopted children was compared with a control group of nonadopted children. Most of the children knew of their adoption status, but neither group of children or parents was aware of the researcher's hypotheses relating age and adoptive status to the level of adoption knowledge.

Bias from the Researchers.

Researchers spend a lot of time deciding on a problem for research, planning the study, and collecting the data. Most researchers have a particular theory or point of view that guides their research and hope to find evidence that is consistent with that theory. Thus, researchers have to be especially careful in protecting the research against themselves.

To eliminate both demand characteristics and researcher bias, not only the subjects but also the observers and raters in a research study should be unaware both of the study's hypotheses and of whether the subject currently being interviewed is a member of the experimental or the control group. Both the subjects and the observers should be "blind" to the hypotheses and to the experimental conditions, creating a *double blind* research study.

Even if observers are blind to the hypotheses and the group assignment of the children, there may be some factors that cannot be disguised. Observers will always be aware of the child's approximate age and the child's sex. Even if the observers are not aware that age and sex are important independent variables, they may nevertheless introduce their own cultural biases about age and sex differences.

Although there is no way to eliminate entirely the effects of bias in research, the best researchers work very hard to hold biases to a minimum. Often, biases are not discovered until other studies are done and after research results have already been published.

As a consumer of research, it is important to remember that no single research study can answer a question definitively. Research results acquire power from repeated studies whose findings relate to each other in a consistent and understandable way in relation to a well-articulated theory of child development. *Replication* is the repetition of the same research design and procedure in more than one sample of subjects.

Reliability is also an issue on standardized tests. In this case, reliability is the extent to which the same test gives a similar score to the same individual on repeated administrations. The correlation of test scores in a group between two administrations of the same test is called *test-retest reliability*.

Validity

Validity is the degree to which the procedure accurately measures what it was intended to measure (Achenbach, 1978). A measure is valid to the extent that it is correlated with other more standard measures of the same concept, called *criterion measures*. A criterion measure is a direct measure of what the assessment procedure is intended to measure. Thus, one would need to compare the observational measure of attachment (refer to p. 68, this chapter) with another measure that is directly related to attachment, such as a measure of the child's ability to use the mother as a source of comfort in times of stress (Ainsworth, Blehar, Waters, & Wall, 1978). Note that reliability is the test-retest correlation, while validity is the test-criterion measure correlation.

In situations such as the child's level of adoption knowledge, in which there is no accepted criterion measure with which to compare the current measure, validity becomes a complex and difficult issue. In this case, the validity of the measure cannot be established within a single research study. For example, in the Adoption Study, only age differences and differences between adopted and nonadopted children were studied. Other studies might look at the changes in the child's level of knowledge about adoption after the child is given an educational unit on adoption at different ages. To the extent that the five-point scale is related to age differences and to differences in educational experience related to adoption, researchers would say that the scale is a valid measure of adoption knowledge.

The Interpretation of Research

After collecting all the data from a carefully designed research study, the investigator must evaluate the results in relation to the hypotheses and theory that guided the study in the first place. Again, we'll illustrate the process by looking at the results of the Adoption Study. The main findings of this study are presented in Table 3-4. Note that the level of understanding of adoption is the highest for the oldest children. No important differences were found between boys and girls and between nonadopted and adopted children.

Only a small percentage of children under six have more than a level-2 understanding of adoption (refer to table 3-3). Such children often equate birth and adoption concepts. By the age of six, however, most of the children can tell the difference between birth and adoption as alternative forms of parenthood. They understand that adoption is permanent but do not understand why.

Between 8 and 11 years, children increase their understanding of adoption as well as their feeling of vulnerability. They worry about whether the biological

Table 3—4

NUMBER OF SUBJECTS WHO REACHED A PARTICULAR LEVEL OF ADOPTION KNOWLEDGE, CLASSIFIED BY AGE AND ADOPTION STATUS

Age and Status	Level of Understanding					
	0	1	2	3	4	5
4—5						
Adopted	6	5	8	1	0	0
Nonadopted	12	4	0	4	0	0
6—7						
Adopted	1	2	12	3	2	0
Nonadopted	4	1	7	7	1	0
8—9						
Adopted	0	0	10	5	4	1
Nonadopted	0	0	4	8	8	0
10—11						
Adopted	0	0	2	1	14	3
Nonadopted	0	0	0	4	9	7
12—13						
Adopted	0	0	1	2	7	10
Nonadopted	0	0	0	0	9	11

(Brodzinsky et al., *Child Development*, 1984, 55. © The Society for Research in Child Development, Inc.)

parent has the ability to come and reclaim the child. It is not until the age of 12 that children regain their certainty in the permanency of the adoption relationship and understand the legal basis of the transfer of parenting rights from the biological to the adoptive parents.

The authors note that the developmental changes in adoption knowledge are "closely tied to knowledge about birth and reproduction, family roles and relationships, values, interpersonal motives, and the functioning of societal institutions" (Brodzinsky et al., p. 877). In addition, there were few differences between adopted and nonadopted children in spite of the fact that adopted children are exposed to more information about adoption than are nonadopted children.

The investigators interpreted their findings as confirmation of Piaget's theory that the children's social understanding in general, and adoption understanding in particular, increased at ages related to the transitions to concrete and to formal operational thinking. Note that even though adopted children are exposed to more information about adoption, both groups had equal levels of knowledge. The authors suggest that adoption knowledge is not acquired by a process of gradual accumulation of facts, nor by modeling and reinforcement as hypothesized by Social Learning Theory, but rather because of more general cognitive changes.

With regard to the applied issue of when parents should tell their adopted children about adoption, the investigators believe that even if children are told during the preschool period, they are not likely to understand what they have been told. Telling the child early causes no harm, and if the parents continue to discuss the issue openly during the child's development, the child will continue to integrate his or her understanding of adoption into more general social understandings.

The problem is with those parents who tell the child early but do not continue discussing the issue. These parents assume that their preschoolers can understand adoption, and their later communication with their children

Applied Research

As discussed in the FOCUS sections of Chapter 2, policy makers and program implementers usually have a rather different set of priorities from those of child development researchers. Most researchers are trained to make their research questions fit the predictions of existing theories and to advance the cause of basic research.

A researcher who wishes to make a contribution to the way in which children are treated in the real world often tries to balance practical needs against the rigors of the scientific method. In many cases, however, the need people have for answers from researchers is not related to theories of child development. In addition, research in the real world must be done under less than ideal conditions that are often not under the control of the researcher.

An example of such problems is research on the delivery of day care services to preschoolage children. Using a basic theory approach, research comparing day care versus home-reared children is seen as a test of differences in developmental outcomes due to different childrearing environments.

Legislators need to have very different information (Phillips, 1984). If, for example, they establish licensing requirements that might drive up the cost of establishing a day care center, would the benefits to children in higher quality care exceed the costs to society of having fewer placements due to day care center closings? Will private for-profit day care centers work only to meet minimum requirements and fail to invest in providing the best possible environment?

Some evidence exists that parents base their choice of day care on the cost of the program and not on quality. Are there some reliable indicators of quality, such as staff-to-child ratios, teacher job satisfaction, and the stability of the play groups, that both parents and state officials could use to judge day care?

Legislators who are asked to provide tax benefits for day care for middle-income parents might want to know what those parents do if they cannot get day care. Does it affect the family's ability to earn an acceptable income? Does it leave the children at home unattended for long periods (so-called latch-key children)? Does the availability of day care increase the chances that people will remove themselves from welfare and obtain gainful employment?

Legislators especially want to know if day care is a good economic investment in the care of at-risk children of low-income families. Research suggests that low-income children who attend quality day care will have more success in school along with a lower drop-out rate and a higher employment rate than will low-income children who do not attend day care in the early years (Lazar & Darlington, 1982). We do not know whether day care helps to alleviate either child abuse or child health and nutrition problems.

If it could be shown that a relatively low cost "preventive" program such as day care will later save the government money on such high cost "treatment" programs as supplemental nutrition and health care for low-income families, day care funds will be more likely to be allocated. This kind of research is more difficult to do, and it requires methods perhaps more familiar to sociologists than to child developmentalists. Research leading to effective intervention strategies should address the real needs of people and policy makers and use the expertise of researchers from different fields.

"will be mediated by a false sense of security about the child's existing knowledge and adjustment. In turn, this may well lead to a premature termination of the disclosure process—a factor that presumably could place the child, and parents, at risk for future adjustment problems" (Brodzinsky et al., p. 877).

The concerns of children and teachers regarding daycare are often different from those of policymakers who are concerned about minimum requirements of health and safety, and about daycare's costs versus benefits to society.

Chapter Summary

FROM THEORY TO RESEARCH

□ The Adoption Study was introduced. Its purpose was to determine the age at which children best understand the concept of adoption and whether differences exist between adopted and nonadopted children in adoption knowledge.

□ Predictions were derived from psychoanalytic, Piagetian, learning, and ethological theories.

DESIGNING A RESEARCH STUDY

□ Developmental studies can be done either cross-sectionally or longitudinally, and each has advantages and limitations.

□ Cohort effects and time of measurement effects must be taken into account in long-term developmental studies with older children and adolescents.

□ Variables are classified as independent—potential causes—and as dependent—potential effects.

□ Three statistics measure a sample's average: the mean, the median, and the mode.

□ Sample selection depends on the theory and hypotheses of the study. Samples should be representative of the population.

□ Case studies can explore fine details of developmental processes.

□ Cross-cultural research increases the range of variation leading to more generalized explanations of developmental change.

□ Experimental methods allow the researcher control over the independent variables. They are difficult to carry out, and often ethical considerations prevent them from being done on humans.

□ Quasi-experimental methods employ naturally existing variations and depend on correlations to show relationships between variables. They cannot conclusively separate cause from effect.

□ The FOCUS ON POLICY section considered the ethical guidelines for research on children and showed the difficulty of getting informed consent from children or their parents.

ASSESSMENT PROCEDURES

□ Observational methods are procedures for recording the child's ongoing behavior.

□ Automatic methods use mechanical or electronic instruments to keep records of physiological and behavioral activity.

□ Testing methods are standardized assessments used for evaluation and diagnostic purposes.

ERRORS IN ASSESSING CHILDREN

□ Reliability measures the extent to which the subject will receive the same score on repeated assessments or between different observers.

□ Validity measures the degree to which the assessment captures the psychological or behavioral meaning behind a variable.

□ Unintended bias can arise because either the subjects or the experimenters are aware of the purpose of the research and alter their behavior in favor of a positive outcome. This is covered in FOCUS ON ISSUE.

THE INTERPRETATION OF RESEARCH

□ The Adoption Study results were consistent with Piaget's theory.

□ The FOCUS ON RISK/INTERVENTION discussed the differences between research questions generated by theoretically oriented researchers and those generated by policy-oriented researchers.

Recommended Readings

Bailey, K. (1982). *Methods of social research*. New York: Free Press. An introduction to research methods for the social and behavioral sciences that is appropriate for college level students. Presentation is comprehensive and clear.

Brodzinsky, D. M., Singer, L. M., & Braff, A. M. (1984). Children's understanding of adoption. *Child Development, 55*, 869–878. The original version of the Adoption Study, recommended for reading as you work through this chapter.

Bronfenbrenner, U. (1979). *The ecology of human development: Experiments by nature and design*. Cambridge, MA: Harvard University Press. An excellent discussion of the problems with laboratory research on children, with suggestions for bringing the developmental researcher into the real world of the child.

Melton, G. B., Koocher, G. P., & Saks, M. J. (1983). *Children's competence to consent.* New York: Plenum. Discusses the ethical issues of obtaining children's consent for research and also for medical treatment and hospitalization.

Minium, E. (1988). *Statistical reasoning in psychology and education,* 2nd Edition. New York: Wiley. A very clear presentation of introductory statistical concepts.

Piaget, J. (1965). *The moral development of the child.* New York: Free Press. One of the easiest to read of Piaget's books. It is difficult in places but presents a good sense of how Piaget used diary descriptions and the clinical interview method.

Whiting, B. B., & Whiting, J. W. M. (1975). *Children of six cultures: A psychocultural analysis.* Cambridge, MA: Harvard University Press. A classic study of cultural effects on children's behavior.

CHAPTER 4

Human Origins

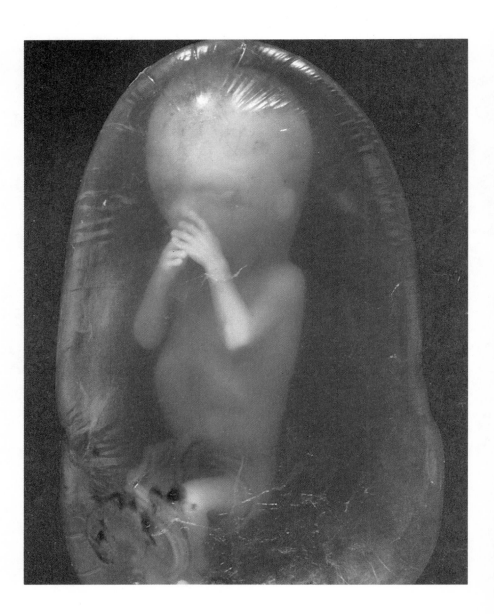

I think of it as being like the pictures in the book, curled up in a fetal position. But it is also filled with emotion for me, a feeling of warmth I have about it so that the image becomes very three-dimensional. It's very real for me in a way, real as a trip you'll take and you haven't taken yet, real in that it's already very much a part of our lives and has changed it somewhat already.

— A pregnant woman's words, from Leifer, 1980, p. 76.

The woman being quoted expresses an emotional tie to the new life that is growing within her body. Every individual is a link in a vast chain of living beings who sustain themselves by passing their biological heritage on to their offspring during reproduction.

This chapter looks at the beginnings of human development, reviews the process of conception and the ways in which genetic codes are transmitted between parents and offspring, looks at the effect of heredity on behavior and the formation of sex differences between individuals, covers the stages of prenatal development, and concludes with a look at the effects of pregnancy on the mother and the family.

Conception

Conception and Fertility

Conception is the union of a female *ovum* with a male *spermatozoon* (a single sperm cell) that usually occurs in the female Fallopian tube, the pathway from the ovary to the uterus (see Figure 4-1). Millions of male spermatozoa enter the vagina during sexual intercourse. Through their own swimming action and additionally propelled by the rhythmic action of the vaginal muscles, a small number of the spermatozoa will reach the Fallopian tubes. The passage takes a number of hours, and only the strongest of the spermatozoa can survive. If no ovum is encountered within 24 to 48 hours, all the sperm cells can be expected to die.

Fertilization is the process by which the ovum becomes impregnated with a spermatozoon, creating the conditions for continued growth. Fertilization of the ovum cannot occur without the combined action of hundreds of spermatozoa, which surround the ovum and trigger a chemical reaction that will eventually create an opening in the ovum's cell wall. Once a single sperm cell has entered, the cell wall automatically closes up. This fertilized ovum is known as a *zygote* and has the ability to attach itself to the uterine wall and begin to divide and grow.

Not all zygotes become implanted in the uterus: They may simply pass out as part of the menstrual flow. Others may become implanted for a period of weeks or months and then spontaneously become aborted. *Spontaneous abortion* refers to the involuntary expulsion of the zygote or embryo (the next stage of prenatal development), which usually occurs because of some abnormality that prevents normal growth. It is estimated that about 78 percent of all conceptions are spontaneously aborted in the early weeks of pregnancy (the mother may never realize that she was pregnant) and that this automatic

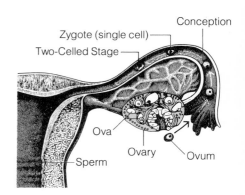

Conception — Zygote (single cell) — Two-Celled Stage — Ova — Ovary — Ovum — Sperm

Figure 4—1

Conception

One of the millions of sperm that entered the uterus has found and fertilized the ovum in the Fallopian tube, about an hour after intercourse. This union produces a zygote, a single cell which contains all the genes and chromosomes of the person-to-be.

Family Planning and Society

Large families such as the one shown here are not uncommon in third world nations. Family planning efforts often conflict with religious and traditional beliefs about procreation and desired family size.

Family planning is a good example of how large-scale social and cultural factors influence the decisions made within the family and how the moral, spiritual, and interpersonal climate within the family can affect those broader social values. This section takes a look at family planning programs in two overpopulated Asian countries—India and China—in order to study the interaction between society and family in more detail.

Family Planning in India

India is one of the most crowded nations on earth. Table 4-1 compares the population density (number of people per square mile) of India, China, and the United States as well as the annual percentage of increase in population. In India, a significant proportion of people are illiterate and live below poverty level with inadequate food, shelter, and clothing. Because the Indian culture has a strong commitment to maintaining a large family, people have actively resisted family planning efforts (Blaikie, 1975).

Family planners in India tried to make parents feel they were a part of a community effort to limit their families and stressed the value of small families. The Indian government, however, sensing the slow speed with which such re-education efforts were taking root, passed a law requiring compulsory sterilization for parents with more than two children who wished to con-

tinue receiving welfare benefits. The law was controversial, and it was repealed in 1977 after only two years of use. Today, after creating a wide network of family planning centers all over India, the rate of voluntary contraception has increased, with sterilization being the most popular choice after several children have been born (Blaikie, 1975).

Table 4—1

POPULATION STATISTICS FOR THREE LARGE NATIONS

	India	People's Republic of China	United States
Area (in millions of square miles)	1.2	3.7	3.5
1986 population (in millions)	785	1,050	241
Annual percentage of increase in population	2.9%	0.9%	0.9%
Population density (in number of people per square mile)	620	283	67

(From: *Information Please Almanac*, 1987.)

Family Planning in the People's Republic of China

In China, the family values were similar to those of India, but the key factor in reducing the number of births was to interpret family planning as one of the political goals of revolutionary communism. These goals included raising the standard of living of the rural people, equalizing status and income between social groups, and reducing the inequality between the sexes. Because of this, the leaders were able to formulate the following principle: Delay marriage until a late age and restrict each family to only one child. Not only does this reduce the birth rate, it also allows both men and women to contribute their younger years in service to the party and the country and to the ideals of hard work and equality (Taeuber & Orleans, 1965).

Today slogans appear on billboards throughout the Chinese nation. Some say "The People's Republic of China Forever," while others say "Carry Out Planned Childbirth," "For the Sake of the Fatherland's Four-Point Modernization, Marry Late and Reproduce Late," and "A Family of Three, Satisfied and Happy."

To add muscle to these words, the Chinese, like the Indians, have adopted a complex system of rewards to couples who comply. For example, a newly married couple in which the husband is 28 years old or older and the wife is at least 26 years old is able to get an 18-day honeymoon, while younger couples are granted only a three-day vacation. Elderly women in each village, called "granny police," are charged with counseling and disciplining women who wish to have a second child. As in India, the Chinese have opted for a program involving a balanced use of sterilization and conventional contraceptives; however, abortion rates are higher than in India (*New York Times,* May 12, 1985).

Conclusions

Family planning is a complex enterprise involving an awareness of people's needs and motives. Ideologies such as the status of women and children and belief systems favoring large families also contribute to population control measures. On the other hand, due to the pressing ecological demands on large societies to limit population against dwindling resources, governments often act decisively to limit population growth. Such actions may have major consequences for the structure of the family and for people's views of their own life and its meaning. Furthermore, political and religious ideologies can enter into the form of the government's decisions. Such ideologies may at times conflict with and at times complement those of individual family members.

Thus, family planning policy is illustrative of the principles of ecological systems theory (refer to Chapter 2). When the government feels the need to intervene in the basic relationships within the family, one can expect to see complex processes of mutual change and accommodation between family and society.

---

process is a natural method of reducing the number of abnormal births (Roberts & Lowe, 1978). A *miscarriage,* on the other hand, is the birth of a fetus (the third and final stage of prenatal development) before it can survive apart from the mother.

Spermatozoa and ova, the reproductive male and female cells, are known as *gametes.* Female gametes are present in immature form in the ovaries when a female child is born. They remain inactive until puberty begins the monthly menstrual cycle (see Chapter 16), during which one ovum will be released on its journey to the uterus. Adult females will ovulate about 350 to 400 times during their approximately 30 years of fertility. The beginning of puberty in boys starts the production of spermatozoa. About two million spermatozoa will be produced every day of a man's lifetime after puberty.

Heredity

The union of the spermatozoon and ovum produces a zygote that possesses a set of molecular messages that will direct the formation and development of a unique human being. This section discusses how these molecular messages are formed and how they play a role in the individual's development.

A Molecular View of Human Inheritance

The basic building blocks of cells are proteins. There are one thousand kinds of plant and animal proteins. From a chemical point of view, the problem of heredity is to produce a combination of proteins in the offspring similar to those in the parents.

The individual cell's solution to the problem of heredity is simply to divide itself in two. Each new cell inherits the same structure as the original cell. This happens because some molecules within the nucleus of each cell have the ability to copy themselves so that each new cell contains the exact same set of these copying molecules. The copying molecules are called deoxyribonucleic acids (or *DNA*) and are shaped like a long double spiral staircase (or double helix) of smaller molecular components.

Aside from DNA's ability to reproduce itself, the arrangement of the molecular components in the staircase is a kind of chemical code which, upon contact with the protoplasm surrounding the nucleus of the cell, has the potential to direct the formation of specific cell proteins. A segment of a DNA molecule that carries a unit of hereditary information is called a *gene*. Genes are usually arranged in long strings, like beads on a necklace, in a structure known as a *chromosome*.

In every cell in one's body, except for the gametes (more on this later), there are identical sets of 46 chromosomes, or about one million units of genetic information. In cases where genes and chromosomes need to be diagnosed for the presence of a disorder such as Down's syndrome (discussed later in the chapter), chromosomes can be seen under a microscope by using a special stain on a sample of cells. A photograph is taken of the chromosomes and is cut and arranged so that 23 matching pairs can be placed side-by-side for easy identification (see Figure 4-2). This method of arranging chromosomes is called *karotyping*.

Figure 4—2

Human Chromosome Pairs Before and After Karyotyping

Humans have twenty-three pairs of chromosomes, and in the karyotype the pairs have been matched. One member of each pair is from the mother and one from the father.

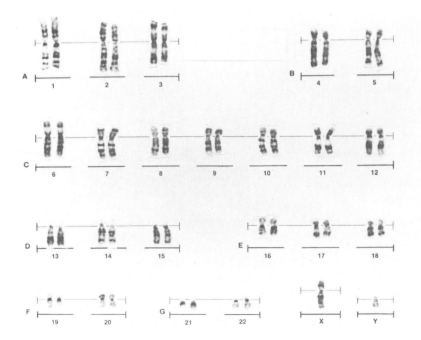

During the process of cell division, called *mitosis*, each of the 46 chromosomes makes a copy of itself, producing a total of 92 chromosomes within the cell just before it splits. When the cell actually divides, each daughter cell takes with it identical sets of 46 chromosomes.

Genotype and Phenotype

The genes contain the directions for the formation of the specialized cells and tissues of the body. The *genotype* of the individual is the set of chemical messages contained in DNA that direct the formation of specific proteins within each cell. The genotype is like a blueprint for building a house. The contractor must follow the blueprint, made only out of paper, and transform it into the wood, bricks, and mortar of a house. Similarly, during human development, the messages contained in the genotype are transformed into a wide variety of cell types—muscles, bones, nerves—to produce an individual organism. The organized collection of living cells, the functioning organism, is called the *phenotype*. The phenotype is analogous to the house built from the genotype of the blueprint.

Every cell in the body has exactly the same genes in its nucleus. How can it be then, that the same genotype residing in every cell will create the diverse tissues—muscle, blood, or organs—of the phenotype?

Research using nonhuman embryos has shown that as cells begin to divide in the early stages of development following fertilization, they form a small spherical cluster. Some of the cells will be on the outside of this sphere in contact with the mother's tissues, while other cells will be on the inside. The cells on the outside will thus experience a different chemical environment from those on the inside of the sphere.

The local chemical environment begins to send signals to the genes, telling some of them to "turn on" their action and some of them to "turn off" their action. Due to the differing chemical environments, one set of genes will be turned on in the center of the sphere, while another set of genes will be switched on at the surface.

Once genes begin acting, they create their own chemical messages, which cause further changes in the cells in that region. The cells begin to form into groups in which one kind of chemical process occurs within one group but not within another. Boundaries are formed between one group and another that prevent the transmission of chemical information between groups. These isolated and different chemical processes affect the gene expression within all the cells of that group, thus producing greater differences between the groups (Trevarthen, 1973). Thus, we have an example of ecological systems theory, in which the genes affect the cell and its environment, and the environment affects the cell and its genes.

Figure 4-3 shows how one kind of structure—a tube with holes—can be created. The cells on the outside (top) surface have active genes that make them more flexible, while cells on the inside (underneath) surface have active genes that make them contract. The result is the formation of a curved sheet of cells and eventually a tube such as the spinal cord of a human embryo.

In the example of the curved sheet, all the cells in one region, say the upper surface, behave alike: They all become flexible. Experiments with chick embryos have shown that if you take some cells from a part of the embryo that will eventually become skin tissue, for example, and transplant those cells to an area that will become, say, nervous tissue, these original skin cells will form into normal nerve cells (Spemann, 1938). This means that the environment of the cell can shape the development of that cell.

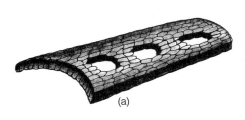

(a)

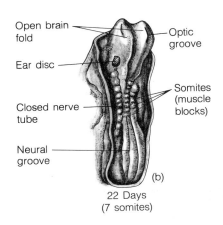

Open brain fold

Optic groove

Ear disc

Somites (muscle blocks)

Closed nerve tube

Neural groove

(b)

22 Days
(7 somites)

Figure 4–3

Creation of a Structure

(a) During the process of cell differentiation, some cells begin to create structures. The early formation of a tube with holes is shown. The cells become less elastic on one side and more elastic on the other, causing a sheet of cells to bend. Differential rigidity around the region of the holes can create spaces between cells.
(b) In the 22-day-old embryo, such a tube structure will eventually become the spinal cord and spine.
(From Trevarthen, 1980, in Developmental Psychology and Society, J. Sants, ed., by permission of Macmillan, London and Basingstoke.)

Test Tube Babies

Methods of Treating Infertility

About 15 percent of adults are not able to have children. In males, infertility is often the result of a low sperm count. There are not enough sperm to survive the journey to the Fallopian tubes and surround the ovum. In such cases, sperm can be collected from the father and injected into the uterus directly. This procedure is known as *artificial insemination*. In females, failure of the ovum to pass into the Fallopian tube may be due to a blockage, which can be removed surgically. If such methods do not solve the problem, a number of drugs are available that increase fertility in males and females. They often have unwanted side effects, however, such as the production of multiple births (twins, triplets, etc.), nor are these methods always effective.

In recent years, many couples have been given new hope of having their own child by the recent successes in the field of *in vitro* fertilization. In vitro means, literally, in glass, and children developed from eggs fertilized using this method are sometimes called test tube babies.

In this process, fertile ova are removed surgically from the mother's ovary and placed in a sterile glass dish, where one ovum can be fertilized by the father's sperm. The zygote is kept in the dish until it reaches eight cells in size—which takes about 48 hours—and is then inserted into the mother's uterus with the hope that it will attach itself—the part of the process that is most likely to fail. Although scientists feared that even 48 hours of development external to the mother's body might lead to serious deformities in the fetus, an increasing number of reports are being made from around the world of the birth of healthy test tube babies.

In vitro fertilization will not work if the mother has an abnormal uterine lining that cannot sustain the zygote or if she is not able to produce an ovum because of malfunctioning ovaries. A mother may also have potential genetic diseases that she does not want to risk passing on to her children. In such a case, the husband's sperm can be used to artificially inseminate another woman who provides a donor ovum. The fertilized ovum is then removed from the donor woman and transplanted into the uterus of the mother-to-be. The zygote is taken from the donor's uterus, in an *embryo transfer* technique that does not involve surgery and does not expose the zygote to an unnatural laboratory environment (Buster, 1984).

Dangers of In Vitro Fertilization and Embryo Transfer

Although the medical community has been able to eliminate the dangers of deformity, many people are now wondering where such a method might lead in the future. In 1932, Aldous Huxley wrote the novel *Brave New World,* which predicted a time in which artificial wombs produced babies under controlled conditions. The gametes were chosen for fertilization on the basis of desired characteristics, and the donors were not important. Children were reared in group nurseries and subjected to constant observation and propaganda, while adults, freed of their biological burden of childbearing, were able to pursue other endeavors more fully. Some people think that our present society is coming close to this prediction, made more than 50 years ago.

Another problem is a legal one. Once gametes are removed from the bodies of their donors, they are free to become implanted into any woman, not necessarily the mother. Who would legally "own" such a child, the donor or the woman who gives birth to the infant? Could low-income women be induced to "manufacture" the children of other couples in a kind of pregnancy prostitution? In what way would the environment and nutrition of the pregnant woman affect the development of the zygote from the donor couple? Who would be responsible for failures and for unhealthy or deformed births? Would the child be considered a legal heir to the donor or to the birth mother?

We don't yet have answers to these questions. The currently available methods, however, have allowed many parents who had given up hope to look forward to giving birth to a child of their own.

Relations Between the Genotype and the Phenotype

Some parts of the genotype contain messages that direct the formation of phenotypic characteristics in similar ways for all the individual members of the species. Phenotypes that tend to occur in a wide variety of environments with little or no inter-individual variation are said to be *canalized*. Canalized characteristics include the human body's structure and sense organs, human emotions, and the ability to use language and complex tools. However, many forms of human behavior are not highly canalized. The phenotype is determined strongly by the type of environment to which the genotype is exposed. Non-canalized characteristics include differences between people in height, weight, personality, and intelligence.

Genes may act alone to produce the phenotype, or they may act together. *Polygenic* expression occurs when several or many genes are responsible for a single phenotypic characteristic. Virtually all phenotypic characteristics, from hair color to behavior, are the result of complex polygenic interactions. Genes that act together to express a particular phenotypic characteristic are called *alleles*. Alleles are often found in similar positions on each member of a pair of chromosomes (see Figure 4-4).

Another pattern is called *plieotropy*, in which a single gene is responsible for a number of phenotypic characteristics. It is believed that Abraham Lincoln suffered from a genetic disorder called Marfan's syndrome that may produce a weakened heart, mild bone structure deformities, long fingers, and eye lens disorders. This disorder is caused by a single defective gene and is an example of plieotropic inheritance.

There is still a great deal we do not understand about how the genotype operates to create the phenotype. Modern developments of molecular biology will soon lead to the ability to modify human genes. The hope is that by modifying the genotype, we can create stronger bodies and even different kinds of behavior. Such principles of *genetic engineering* are currently being used to make new strains of plants and bacteria that are helpful in agriculture and in disease control for plants and animals. However, such advances in scientific knowledge may lead to unethical and dangerous tampering with the genes. Before such methods can be applied to humans for the goal of reducing pain and disease, we need to have a much better understanding of the specific relationship between the genotype and the phenotype. Because of the multiple transactions between the developing phenotype, the genotype, and the environment, there is some danger in tampering with even a single gene without knowing precisely how it contributes to behavior and development. The artificial modification of the genotype will be a major scientific and social issue in future generations.

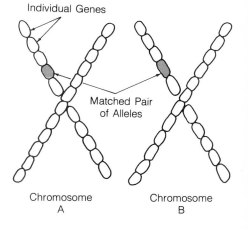

Figure 4—4

The Relative Position of Two Alleles in a Chromosome Pair

The Special Role of Sex in Heredity

Sexual reproduction evolved rather early in the history of life on the earth. The reason is rather simple. Self-reproducing individuals can make a copy only of themselves. When an offspring is produced from the combination of two individuals, a greater chance for diversity exists.

Why is diversity important? Based on Darwin's theory of evolution (refer to Chapters 1 and 2), the individuals who are the most adaptable in a particular environment will be those most likely to survive. Thus, by *natural selection,* the fittest individuals will pass their genes onto the next generation. If every individual had the same set of genes, even minor environmental fluctuations might wipe out the species. On the other hand, if a diversity of abilities and structures exists within a species, it increases the chance that some of the members will survive environmental challenges to pass on their genes to the next generation.

Human Sexual Reproduction in Comparative Perspective

Since sex differences have a genetic origin, the degree of male-female difference in physiology and in behavior will differ from species to species. The differences related to sex are called *sexual dimorphism*. Differences between the sexes in physiology and behavior have evolved to increase the chance that successful mating will occur.

With respect to dimorphism in physical size, males are usually larger than females, although the degree of relative difference depends upon the species. Our closest animal relatives are the primates: monkeys and apes. Monkeys are smaller than apes or humans, and there is little difference in size between the males and the females. Among the apes, the male gorilla is about twice the size of the female. In chimpanzees, the male is about 12 percent heavier than the female. In humans, men are 20 to 30 percent heavier than women, are stronger, and are faster runners. However, there is a large area of overlap in ability between the sexes, with some women outperforming some men (Mitchell, 1981).

Human sexual behavior is rather different from other species. In other mammals, including primates, for example, females are sexually receptive for only a short time during each reproductive cycle (such as a female dog in heat). Mating occurs over a relatively short period of time, and the female may be mounted by many males during this period. The human female has a longer time during which mating is possible, and humans engage in sexual intercourse considerably more often than their nearest species neighbors.

Humans tend to form pair bonds easily and maintain them over long periods. The close relationships between people that are based upon reproductive behavior—courting, mating, and childrearing—may be one of the foundations of our uniquely human ability to form complex societies and cultures. The pair bonds lead to family stability, and the relatively long period of parent-

In most animal species males and females differ in size, appearance and sometimes coloring. These differences are believed to enhance the attractiveness of each sex for the other, leading to successful mating.

child attachments in humans has no doubt contributed to the formation of our ability to communicate, think, and cooperate with others.

Sexual Reproduction and Genetic Variability

From a biological perspective, sexual reproduction is a remarkable process that must have taken millions of years to perfect. Since all cells in the human body are composed of 23 pairs of chromosomes (other species have a greater or fewer number of pairs), a simple union of male and female gametes would produce a large cell containing 46 pairs, or 92 chromosomes. To prevent this, sexual reproduction evolved in such a way that each of the gametes (ova and spermatozoa) contain only 23 chromosomes. Gametes do not have paired chromosomes. Each chromosome finds a paired mate in the process of fertilization with a gamete of the opposite sex.

The problem that evolution had to solve was the manner of creating cells with only half the usual number of chromosomes. The solution, which is the foundation of sexual reproduction in all species, is a process called *meiosis* (see Figure 4-5). A cell is selected from the tissues of the ovary or from the testes. This cell, like all the others in the human body, has 46 chromosomes in 23 pairs. Under the influence of the special environment of the ovary or testes, each of these cells can divide without making a copy of its chromosomes, as occurs during the usual process of mitosis. Thus, the daughter cells of meiotic cell division contain only 23 chromosomes each.

Genetic variability is created in two ways. First, each of the gametes resulting from meiosis possesses a slightly different collection of genes. Of

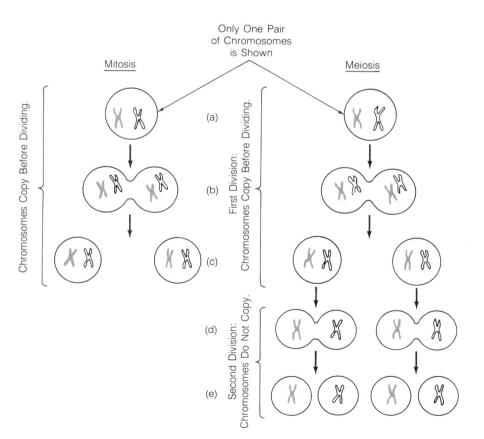

Figure 4–5

Comparison of Mitosis and Meiosis

course, the basic genes producing species-wide canalized traits will always exist in each gamete, but genes that control individual variations (such as hair and eye color) will be distributed among the gametes. Second, variability can occur during fertilization, since the zygote combines one of the many millions of different spermatozoa with only one ovum. Thus, even within the same mating pair, a large variety of genetically different offspring is possible.

Although children born from the same parents are likely to resemble one another, they are genetically unique individuals, since no two gametes from the same parent are identical in genetic composition. This is also true for fraternal or *dizygotic* twins, which form when two separate ova are fertilized in the same menstrual cycle. *Monozygotic* twins, however, are produced when a single fertilized ovum splits to form two zygotes. These two individuals will have identical genotypes. Monozygotic twins are often called identical twins, since they look and sometimes act alike. Dizygotic twins, although the same age, bear no more resemblance to each other than any other two children that might be produced by the same parents. In fact, dizygotic twins can be of opposite sexes.

Mechanisms of Heredity

In most cases, phenotypic patterns are determined by at least two genes, one from the mother and one from the father. Many such characteristics tend to produce a continuous range of variability in the offspring. Skin color is an example; it is likely to be somewhere between that of the mother and that of the father. In a racially mixed marriage, for example, one child may more closely resemble the skin color of one parent. But, if this couple had many children, they might produce many different skin colors that varied between that of the mother and that of the father.

Other characteristics are not continuously variable, such as eye color. The phenotypes can be, in most cases, either brown or blue, hazel or gray, but not in between. In this pattern of inheritance, one allele (refer to Figure 4-4) will be expressed to the exclusion of another. The expressed allele is said to be *dominant,* while the other is said to be *recessive.* Blue eye color, for example, is carried on a recessive allele. Two blue-eyed parents will always produce a blue-eyed child, but two brown-eyed parents could produce either a blue-eyed or a brown-eyed child, and similarly for a couple in which one parent is blue-eyed and the other is brown-eyed. In general, for a recessive allele to be expressed, the genotype must contain no dominant alleles (see Figure 4-6).

Sex Determination

Because sex is so fundamental to biological survival and reproduction, some sex differences in physiology and behavior are specified in the genotype. The biological basis of sex differences begins at conception. Of the 23 pairs of human chromosomes, one pair contains the genetic information that directs the formation of sex differences. As you will recall from the karotype illustration in Figure 4-2, each chromosome has a shape that looks like either the letter *X* or the letter *Y.* In the female, the twenty-third pair of chromosomes is composed of two *X*-shaped chromosomes, while in the male, this pair contains one *X*-shaped chromosome and one *Y*-shaped chromosome.

During meiosis, gametes are formed with 23 nonpaired chromosomes. In the ova, the twenty-third chromosome is always an *X;* in the spermatozoa, about half will have an *X* in the twenty-third place and half will have a *Y.* The

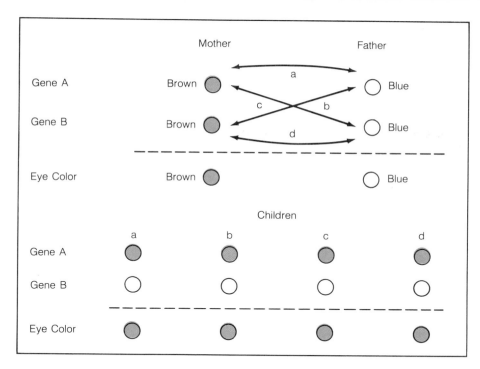

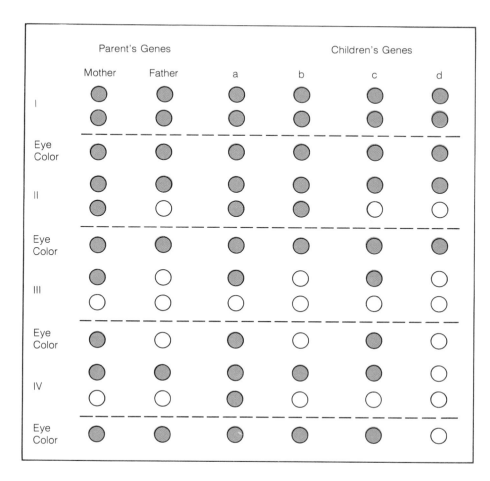

Figure 4-6

Dominant and Recessive Inheritance

(a) Inheritance of eye color from a brown-eyed mother and a blue-eyed father. Four possible combinations of mother's and father's genes are possible, as represented by the lines a, b, c, and d. Since brown is the dominant color, all the children will have brown eyes.

(b) Examples I and II show two other ways in which all the children will have brown eyes. In each case, all the children have at least one dominant brown-eyed gene. Four blue-eyed children will result if both parents have two blue-eyed genes. In example III, a blue-eyed father and a brown-eyed mother produce two blue-eyed and two brown-eyed children, because the father has two recessive genes. Compare this to example II, which also has a brown-eyed mother and a blue-eyed father. Example IV is the most curious. Both parents, although brown-eyed, have a one-in-four chance of producing a blue-eyed child, since they both carry a recessive gene.

sex of the zygote thus depends upon the composition of the particular spermatozoon that fertilized the ovum. Although it takes both a spermatozoon and an ovum to produce a zygote, the father's sperm determines the sex of the baby.

For reasons not fully understood, more males are conceived than females. By birth, there are slightly more males than females, about 105 males to every 100 females. This is known as the *sex ratio*. During the life span, however, more females survive at every age, causing the sex ratio to reverse over time. For example, at age 60, the sex ratio is about 70 males for every 100 females (McMillen, 1979).

As we have seen, the genes interact with the environment of the cell, and the cells interact with other cells and the general environment of the mother's body in ways that determine how the genes will be expressed. The same is true in the development of the sex organs, which do not appear until the third prenatal month. Before that time, both males-to-be and females-to-be have similar genital structures. A hormone called *testosterone* begins to be secreted in male fetuses, which induces the formation of the male sex organs.

Because females have two X chromosomes, they actually have more genes than males have. You can think of the male Y as an X that is missing one of its branches. For that reason, males and females will inherit some different characteristics related to those genes that are carried on the twenty-third pair of chromosomes. Differences in inheritance related to the sex chromosomes are described as *sex-linked*.

Sex-Linked Inheritance

Most of the sex-linked characteristics are carried on the extra part of the X chromosome that is not present in the Y. For this reason, one might think that women would have more sex-linked characteristics than would men; however, this is not the case. Some of the more well-known sex-linked characteristics of baldness, red-green color blindness, and a disorder of blood clotting processes leading to excessive bleeding, called *hemophilia,* occur primarily in males.

Each of these characteristics is caused by a recessive but defective allele carried on the X chromosome. If the recessive allele is paired with its dominant allele from another X chromosome, the dominant allele can override the influence of the defective recessive allele. A lack of baldness (normal hair density), a lack of color blindness (normal color vision), and a lack of hemophilia (normal clotting of the blood) requires at least one dominant allele to ensure the healthy development of the phenotype.

The female may inherit a recessive defective allele (for example, one that might lead to hemophilia) on one of her X chromosomes, but since the female's other X chromosome contains a dominant allele for blood clotting, hemophilia will not be expressed (see Figure 4-7). The same female, however, might pass her X chromosome, the one containing the recessive clotting allele, to her children. If the child is a male, he will have no corresponding dominant allele, since his Y chromosome inherited from his father is missing the section that might have contained the dominant allelic counterpart of the mother's recessive X. Thus, in the male, the recessive allele will be free to express itself (McClearn, 1970). In this manner, the female's extra genes cause some to be *carriers* of the disorder, while the male's lack of genes causes some to suffer from this disorder.

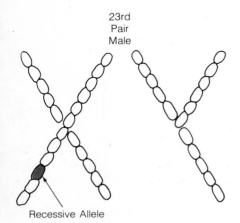

23rd
Pair
Male

Recessive Allele

23rd
Pair
Female

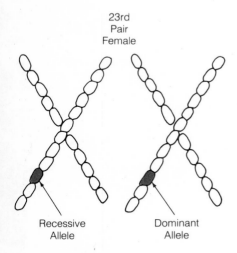

Recessive
Allele

Dominant
Allele

Figure 4—7

Sex-Linked Inheritance

The male Y chromosome is missing dominant alleles that are found on the lower left-hand branch of the female's X chromosome.

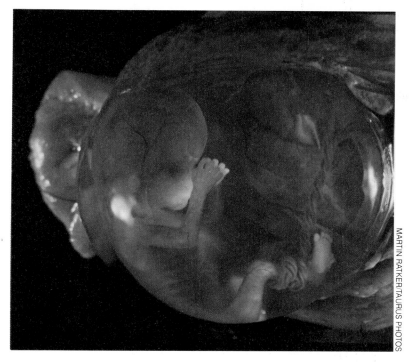

Prenatal development, 8 weeks gestational age.

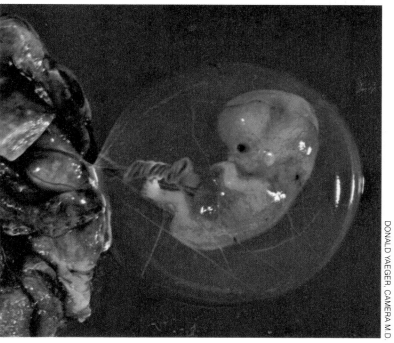

Prenatal development, 12 weeks gestational age.

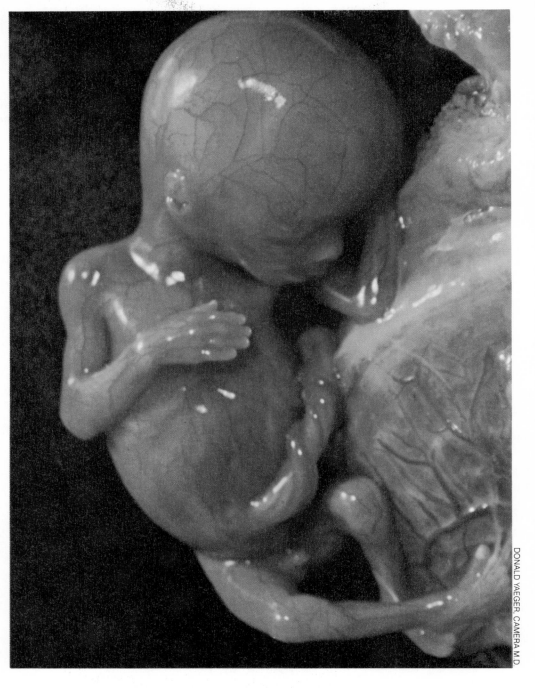

Prenatal development, 16 weeks gestational age.

Development Before Birth

The nine months of human *gestation,* or prenatal development, is the most mysterious phase of the human life cycle. In the past, many believed that the womb was a place of shelter and peace. All needs are taken care of, and one floats in a dreamy world of semiconsciousness, feeling only warmth and hearing only soft sounds. Many spend their adult lives searching for a way to recreate this state of serenity and comfort. Perhaps our concepts of heaven, Nirvana, paradise, and peace derive from a distant and intangible memory locked inside the early-formed parts of our brains and tissues.

Human gestation lasts about 38 weeks, but two weeks earlier or later is considered normal or *full-term* (see Chapter 5 for details about variations in gestational age). The first period lasts about two weeks, from the time of conception until the zygote is implanted in the uterine wall. This is called the *ovular period,* or the *period of the zygote.* After implantation occurs until the developing individual takes on distinctly human features—the vital organs form and the bones begin to harden or ossify—at about the eighth week, is known as the *embryonic period,* or the *period of organogenesis.* Organogenesis means the development of the organs of the body. After eight weeks, and until birth, the organism in the womb is referred to as a *fetus;* this period is termed the *fetal period* (Eichorn, 1970).

The Period of the Zygote

During the first three or four days, the zygote will divide into about 20 cells. Shortly thereafter, some of the cells begin to look different from others: The first kinds of cell differentiation have begun. At the end of the second week, structures known as the *embryonic disk,* the *yolk sac,* and the *amniotic sac* (see Figure 4-8) will have formed. Now the developing individual is called a *blastocyst,* and it will become implanted in the uterine wall during the third week. Only 1/125 of an inch long, the blastocyst induces the secretion of maternal hormones that will suppress menstruation. The hormone responsible for this is called *human chorionic gonadotropin,* or HCG, and it can be detected in the urine. The presence of HCG in the urine is the basis for the laboratory pregnancy test.

The Period of the Embryo

Of the three primitive structures of the blastocyst, further differentiation will occur. The embryonic disk will differentiate into three distinctive layers of cells as it becomes an embryo. The inner layer of cells is called the *endoderm.* Eventually the endoderm will become the digestive, urinary, and respiratory systems. Two outer layers are formed. The *mesoderm* becomes the muscles, bone, circulatory systems, and reproductive systems. The *ectoderm* becomes the central nervous system and brain, the sense organs, and the skin, hair, nails, and teeth.

The yolk sac manufactures blood cells and will later become part of the liver, spleen, and bone marrow, which all help to produce blood cells. The yolk sac is a transitional structure that all but disappears after the second month, the end of the embryo period.

The amniotic sac will persist throughout the pregnancy. It will gradually grow to cover the embryo and will contain the *amniotic fluid,* a watery sub-

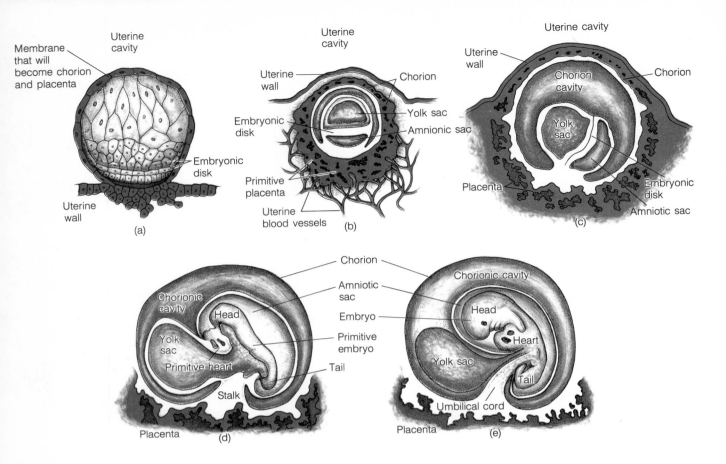

Figure 4-8

Early Stages of Prenatal Development

(a) Blastocyst stage: The fertilized egg (zygote) has made its way down the Fallopian tube and has undergone repeated cell division and multiplication on the way. It attaches to the uterine lining and begins to grow into the uterine wall in search of nutrients.
(b) and (c) Cell division and differentiation continue at a rapid pace, and specific structures begin to take shape. The developing organism is now a bulge on the uterine wall. (d) and (e) Embryo stage: Gradually the form of the embryo takes shape. By the end of the first month, the head and the arm and leg buds are visible, a primitive heart has started to pump, and other organs are beginning to develop. At this stage, the human embryo closely resembles the embryos of most other animals.

(From Mary J. Gander and Harry W. Gardiner. Child and Adolescent Development pp. 58–59. Copyright © 1981 by Mary J. Gander and Harry W. Gardiner. Reprinted by permission of Little, Brown and Company.)

stance that surrounds the embryo and fetus, serving to cushion the baby from shocks due to mother's movements and maintaining the baby at a constant temperature.

Surrounding these primitive structures is the placenta. This highly specialized organ forms the link between the embryo and the mother's body via the blood. Through the umbilical cord, the mother's blood can pass essential nutrients and oxygen to the fetus and remove the fetal wastes in the placenta. The mother's and embryo's blood never actually mix, but they can exchange nutrients and waste in the placenta. Between the placenta and the amniotic sac is a protective membrane called the *chorion*.

By the third week, one can see a head and a primitive circulatory and skeletal system. A week later there is a beating heart, but it does not have chambers. There are cavities for the ears, nose, and mouth, although no nervous tissue is connected yet to these structures. The head is large compared to the body, and there are limb buds present. Interestingly, at this age (30 to 40 days) the embryo, only 3 to 5 mm (1/5 in.) long, has a tail and structures that resemble fish gills (see Figure 4-9).

In the next two weeks the eyes, nose, lungs, and liver form and bones begin to appear. The gill structures change into the bones of the inner ear and neck. By six weeks, limbs are rapidly forming, and fingers and toes soon appear. By eight weeks, the total weight is about 2 grams (1/14 ounce), about half of which is head. The embryo has all its essential organs and looks basically human in form. Still there is no movement, nothing we could call behavior, except for the beating of the heart (see Table 4-2).

In some ways, the development of the embryo reflects the history of the evolution of life on earth: from one-celled organisms, to fish (the embryo does not breathe air and has gills), to reptiles (the embryo's tail), to mammals, and then to humans. Certainly, many of our body functions and structures are similar to those possessed by other species: The physiology of sensory, motor, digestive, and respiratory systems are similar in all land-dwelling, air-breathing animals.

For reasons that we don't fully understand, development produces some kinds of structures that can be called *transitional*. Such structures appear for a short time and then disappear. It is these transitional structures that give the embryo a more animal-like appearance at different times during the prenatal period. In the development of the embryonic hand, for example, a kind of webbed structure first forms, and then the cells of the web disappear, leaving fingers (see Figure 4-10).

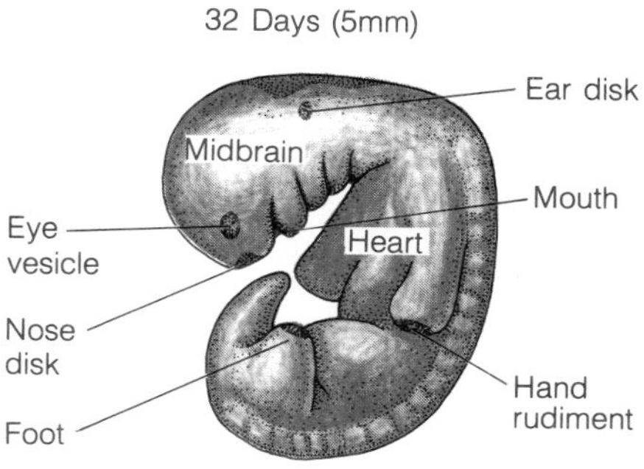

The Period of the Fetus

At the beginning of the third month, the genitals begin to form. In addition, recognizable behavior begins with movements such as limb motion, hand motion, facial expressions, swallowing, and urination. At the end of the third month, the fetus is three inches long and weighs about one-half ounce. In the fourth month a long, fine hair, *lanugo,* covers most of the body. This disappears just before or soon after birth. The coarser hair of the head appears in the fifth month. During this same period—the second *trimester,* or three-month-

Figure 4—9

Sensory Surfaces of a Human Embryo at Four Weeks

(From Trevarthen, 1980, in Developmental Psychology and Society, J. Sants, ed., by permission of Macmillan, London and Basingstoke.)

Table 4—2

PRENATAL BEHAVIOR

Age (weeks)	Behavior
8	Stroking mouth region produces flexion of upper torso and neck and extension of arms at the shoulder.
9	Some spontaneous movements. More of the whole body responds when mouth is stroked.
10½	Stroking palms of hands leads to partial closing of the fingers.
11	Other parts of face and arms become sensitive.
11½	Sensitive area spreads to upper chest.
12½	Specific reflexes appear: lip closing, swallowing, Babinski reflex (see Chapter 5), squinting.
14	Entire body is sensitive, with more specific reflexes such as rooting, grasping, finger closing.
15	Can maintain closure of the fingers (grasp) with muscle tightening, muscle strengthening.
16 to 18	Defined periods of activity and rest begin; movement of eye from central position.
19	Chest contractions begin but are not sustained. Grasping with hand appears.
25	Respiration is sustained for up to 24 hours. Eyelids open spontaneously, rapid eye movements occur, and Moro reflex appears (see Chapter 5).
27 to birth	Blink response to sound at 28 weeks, except for sucking at 29 weeks. Rhythmic brain waves appear. After this age, it becomes less easy to elicit reflexes in the fetus until the time of birth. Habituation begins at 30 weeks. After 36 weeks, eyes are inactive, as in deep sleep.

(From Birnholz & Farrell, 1984; Hooker, 1952; Trevarthen, 1973.)

44 Days

50 Days

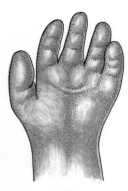

52 Days

period—the fetal skin becomes covered with a waxy protective substance, the *vernix caseosa.* During the second trimester, the finger and toe nails will form, as will adult teeth buds. Eyebrows and eyelashes appear in the seventh month.

During the first six months of gestation, the brain develops more rapidly than at any other time in life, primarily by cell division. After six months prenatally, new brain cells are formed, but at a slower rate, and the brain increases in the complexity of its connections between cells and in increased efficiency of intercellular communication (see also Chapter 8). Changes in the brain are illustrated in Figure 4-11.

Brain growth in the fetus suggests that learning in utero is possible; this has been confirmed in animal studies. Rat pups exposed to a lemony smell in utero preferred to suckle from mothers whose cages had the same lemony odor, even if those mothers were not their own (Pedersen, Williams, & Blass, 1982). Studies reviewed in Chapter 5 suggest that human newborns have similar kinds of odor preferences.

At six months, the fetus weighs 900 grams (about two pounds). Most babies cannot survive if they are born at this age. In a normal pregnancy, this is about the time that the mother can begin to feel the fetal movements and that the doctor can hear the fetal heartbeat with a stethoscope. During the last trimester, few new structures are formed. Subcutaneous fat tissue is formed to give the skin a smooth appearance and provide insulation. This contributes to a weight gain of about 2,500 grams (about five pounds) during this period. In general, the last trimester is a kind of dormant period in which the fetus seems to be preparing for birth (refer Table 4-2).

Figure 4–10

Development of the Embryonic Hand over a Period of About One Week

In the early stages of the development of the hand, it is completely covered by skin between the bones, similar to a duck's webbed feet (44 days). This skin gradually disappears (50 days) to yield 5 independent fingers.

Figure 4–11

Development of the Human Brain
Upper set: Human brains at the same scale of magnification.

Lower set: Development of the corpus callosum linking the hemispheres and of the cerebellum.

(From Trevarthen, 1980, in Developmental Psychology and Society, J. Sants, ed., by permission of Macmillan, London and Basingstoke.)

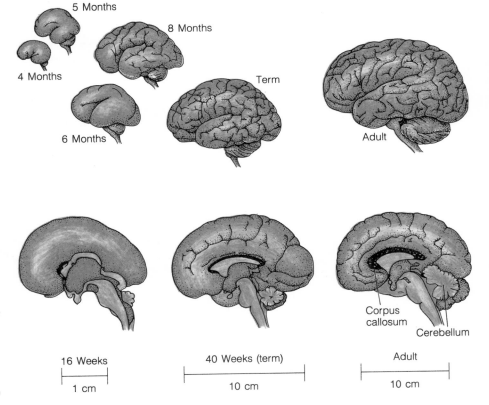

So far we have discussed the normal process of prenatal development. It is perhaps the period of the most rapid development in human life. For this reason, the unborn individual is the most susceptible to factors that can retard development. It is precisely at the time when growth occurs most rapidly that it can be led most easily off track. Indeed, most post-natal mortality, deformity, handicap, and disease can be traced to a prenatal origin (Kopp & Parmelee, 1979).

Prenatal Risk

In general, three sources of risk are present during the prenatal period: genetic disorders, chromosomal abnormalities, and environmental hazards. This section considers the causes and consequences of these problems.

Genetic Disorders

Genetic disorders can usually be recognized by studying the family *geneology,* the patterns of family inheritance over many generations. We have already mentioned a number of genetic disorders. *Sex-linked* disorders, such as color blindness and hemophilia, appear primarily in males, while some females are the carriers. Other disorders appearing in one or the other sex are also suspected of having a genetic cause. Examples are autism in males and depression and phobia in females after puberty (Schwarz, 1979).

Some genetic disorders are caused by a single recessive gene as in *Marfan's syndrome,* discussed earlier in relation to Abraham Lincoln. Although many genetic disorders are polygenic, most of the research has focused on single gene recessive disorders, since they are among the easiest to diagnose and study.

Another example of a single gene recessive disorder is *phenylketonuria* (PKU), in which an essential amino acid (phenylalanine) found in many kinds of foods cannot be properly metabolized. PKU is unique, since it can be treated by changing the child's environment. If the level of phenylalanine-containing foods is not reduced in early infancy for these individuals, nervous and mental deficits will develop. PKU, which occurs once in every 25,000 births, can be tested at birth, and parents can be counseled regarding their infant's diet (Levy, Karolkewicz, Houghton, & MacCready, 1970).

Some recessive allele disorders often occur within similar racial groups in which members are likely to intermarry and thus increase the chances of a double recessive allelic combination. Jewish couples who can trace their ancestry to European origins (Ashkenazic Jews) have one chance in 3600 of producing a baby with *Tay-Sachs disease,* an enzyme deficiency that brings a steady deterioration of mental and physical abilities and finally death before the age of five years. The baby becomes blind, then deaf, and then unable to swallow. Eventually muscle atrophy and paralysis set in (Silver, 1985). Fortunately, the disorder can be diagnosed by testing the amniotic fluid during pregnancy, and the parents can have their blood tested to determine if they are carriers of this recessive disorder.

Black babies have one chance in 400 of contracting *sickle cell anemia,* a disorder of the red blood cells, some of which are shaped like sickles. With overexertion, the cells tend to clump together and block off blood vessels. People afflicted with this disorder may have retarded growth, neurological disorders, or heart and kidney failure.

Preventing Birth Defects

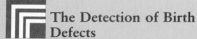 **The Detection of Birth Defects**

In recent years, a growing number of methods for diagnosing the presence of a potentially defective fetus have been developed. Generally, if a parent is considered to be at risk for a birth disorder, one of these methods can be recommended by the mother's physician. The fetus is considered at risk if the family has a history of genetic disease, if the parents are under 17 or over 35, or if the mother was exposed to a potentially dangerous substance during the early part of pregnancy. Parents who believe they might be at risk for a defective birth can receive *genetic counseling* to determine the best course of action.

Chromosomal abnormalities and some genetic disorders can be detected after the sixteenth week of gestation by *amniocentesis* (Nora and Fraser, 1974). With this procedure, a long, hollow needle is inserted into the uterus through the mother's abdominal wall. The fetal cells in the extracted amniotic fluid can be tested for disorders of the genes and chromosomes. The actual testing of the fetal cells is the most time consuming and expensive part of the process. No single test exists for all possible birth defects. Each type of gene requires a different detection procedure, and not all genetic abnormalities can be detected prenatally. Usually, genetic counseling can determine which specific disease is likely to be present, and the amniotic fluid can be tested for that disease. Fetal sex can also be determined, if the parents want this information.

Amniocentesis is done only when there is a case of risk, since about one in 200 mothers could have a spontaneous abortion as a result, and about two percent of fetuses could receive minor injuries from puncture wounds. The procedure is also limited by its relative lateness. Decisions to induce abortion if the fetus is found to be defective are more difficult to make after three and one-half months of pregnancy, and abortions carry a greater risk once the fetus is this old.

A safer procedure is *ultrasound,* in which high-frequency sound waves can be bounced off the fetus to reveal outlines of the body. Gross abnormalities can be detected, and sometimes ultrasound is used to help locate the position of the fetus during amniocentesis. Recently, ultrasound has been used to detect small movements, such as blinking, in response to a sound made outside the mother's abdomen. Lack of a blink response after 28 weeks (see Table 4-2) indicates a fetal abnormality. This use of ultrasound may provide a safer, earlier means of identifying problems (Birnholz & Farrell, 1984). The risks of ultrasound have not been determined.

Another recent advance in the detection of birth defects is *chorion biopsy,* or *chorionic villi sampling* (CVS). The cells of the chorion in early pregnancy are the same as the fetal cells, and they can be tested for the same range of disorders as in amniocentesis. The advantage of CVS is that it can be done during the first trimester, and it does not require puncturing the amniotic sac. Instead, a sample is collected by a catheter, or tube, inserted into the uterus via the cervix. Although this procedure appears to be safer than amniocentesis, it still requires a number of years of testing before it can be put into general use (*Science News,* 1984).

The Treatment of Birth Defects

Recently, a new branch of medicine has evolved in the hope of correcting defects while the fetus is still in the uterus. *Fetal medicine* has successfully treated some fetal vitamin deficiencies by giving the mother doses of the missing vitamin. In other situations, tubes have been inserted into the fetus to drain off excess fluid accumulations from the head before they can cause brain growth retardation. Although still in highly experimental stages, fetal medicine is currently the only alternative to the usual two other options: give birth to a defective infant or surgically terminate the pregnancy.

Table 4—3

ABNORMALITIES OF THE SEX
CHROMOSOMES

Disorder	Chromosome Pair	Abnormality	Symptom
Turner's Syndrome	23rd	Monosomy—X	Incomplete genital development, physical deformity, mental retardation.
Kleinfelter's Syndrome	23rd	Trisomy—XXY	A male with female characteristics, some mental retardation.
Trisomy X	23rd	Trisomy—XXX	A female with no genital malformation but has later problems with menstruation, and early menopause, mild retardation.
XYY Anomaly	23rd	Trisomy—XYY	A male with above average height, mild retardation, emotional problems.

(From Money, 1968; Rosenblith & Sims-Knight, 1985.)

The same gene that causes sickle cell anemia has a positive side effect, however. Carriers of the gene, as well as those who suffer from the disorder, are partially immunized against the deadly disease of malaria. The sickle cells are not good hosts for the malaria parasite that spends part of its cycle in the blood. Because of this malaria protection, the sickle cell trait has been maintained in the population.

Chromosomal Abnormality

Chromosomal abnormalities can be traced, in most instances, to the formation of gametes inside the ovaries and testes. During meiosis, as chromosomes split and recombine to increase variability, one gamete may end up with one too many chromosomes, leaving another gamete with too few. If a zygote is formed with one too many chromosomes, one of the resulting pairs of chromosomes will have an extra chromosome attached to it. This is called a *trisomy*. In the opposite case, one of the normally paired chromosomes will end up without a partner, which is called a *monosomy* (see Table 4-3).

Perhaps the most well known chromosomal disorder is called *trisomy 21,* a trisomy of the twenty-first pair, otherwise known as *Down's syndrome,* and characterized by short stature, flabbiness, cardiac and glandular abnormalities, a small mouth, mental retardation, and folds of skin over the eyes. This last trait has led to this disorder's being more commonly referred to as Mongolism. The risk of Down's syndrome increases for both very young (under 17) and older (over 35) mothers (see Table 4-4) and fathers (Arehart-Treichel,

Age of Mother	Proportion of Births
<30	1/1500
30—34	1/750
35—39	1/280
40—44	1/130
>45	1/65

(From Quienan, 1980.)

Table 4—4

RISK OF DOWN'S SYNDROME AS
A FUNCTION OF MATERNAL AGE

Children with Down's Syndrome can often lead enjoyable lives and share experiences with others around them. The emotional and social development of Down's children is more advanced than their cognitive development.

1979; Crowley, Gulati, Hayden, Lopez, & Dyer, 1979). It is thought that certain sex hormones present in the sex organs enhance the process of meiotic cell division. These sex hormones are at their highest level in both sexes between the ages of 17 and 35. A small percentage (four percent) of Down's syndrome cases are caused by a genetic disorder of the twenty-first chromosome, but most cases are due to spontaneous errors in meiosis.

Environmental Causes of Prenatal Risk

Perhaps the major source of prenatal risk comes from environmental factors, which, in many cases, can lead to deformities and disorders that are more severe than those caused by genetics or chromosomal irregularities. Before the mechanisms of genetics were well understood, people tried to explain the occurrence of birth defects and deformities on the basis of superstition. A mother might be told not to eat twisted or deformed plants, as it might lead to the creation of a child similarly shaped.

Today our understanding of birth defects is more scientific and less superstitious, but the scientific term for the study of the causes of birth defects—*teratology* from the Greek word *tera,* meaning monster—carries at least some traces of human history's past beliefs about defective births. Research on teratology helps to detect specific sources of risk, and the pregnant mother can learn to avoid exposure to potentially harmful situations. A list of proven or suspected sources of risk, called *teratogens,* is presented in Table 4-5.

Table 4—5

COMMON TERATOGENS

Factors Known to Cause Birth Defects in Humans	Factors Suspected of Causing Birth Defects in Humans	Factors Not Yet Proven But Potentially Dangerous
Drugs and chemicals		
Tranquilizers and hypnotics		
Thalidomide	LSD	
Barbiturates	Marijuana	
Anesthetics		
Narcotics (Heroin)		
Alcohol		
Stimulants		
Amphetamines	Caffeine	
Nicotine		
Analgesics		
Antibiotics		Aspirin
Streptomycin, tetracycline		
Hormones		
Other drugs		
Contraceptive foams and creams		Antihistamines
		Diuretics
		Antiallergens
		Antacids
Chemicals and radiation		
Mercury	Asbestos	Pollutants
	Lead	Cleaning fluids
	Agent Orange	Paints
	Pesticides	Cosmetics
	X-rays	Deodorants
Nuclear radiation		Additives and preservatives
		Microwaves
Foods		
Excessive amounts of vitamins (esp. A)		Dietary supplements
Poor nutrition		
Disease		
Rubella ⎫		
Influenza ⎬ Viral		
Smallpox ⎪		
Chicken pox ⎭		
Polio	Some vaccines	
Syphillis		
Toxoplasmosis		
Diabetes		
Hypertension		
Obesity		
Toxemia		
Maternal factors		
High stress		
RH incompatibility		
Age		
Multiple pregnancy		
Low SES		
Poor prenatal care		

(From Butler, 1974; Heinonen et al., 1976; Jones, 1975; Kopp & Parmelee, 1979; O'Brien & McManus, 1978; Rosenblith & Sims-Knight, 1985; Smith, 1978.)

Usually, the effect of a teratogen will depend on such factors as the amount of exposure and the time in pregnancy when the exposure occurred. About two-thirds of all birth defects are associated with exposure to teratogens during the first trimester of pregnancy (Heinonen, Sloane, & Shapiro, 1976). The period of greatest risk is the period of organogenesis. If exposure to a toxic agent occurs at a time when a particular organ or body part is undergoing its most rapid rate of development, a structural defect in that organ can occur. If the exposure occurs after the most rapid period, any defect would be in the form of a growth retardation (see Figure 4-12) (Kopp & Parmelee, 1979).

The problem is that during the period of organogenesis, a woman may not yet know that she is pregnant. Thus, anyone who suspects she is pregnant would be wise to avoid the potential teratogens listed in Table 4-5.

One of the best documented drug-induced problems was from *thalidomide,* a mild tranquilizer taken by women, especially in England, in the 1950s. Physicians later traced cases of heart defects and deformed or missing limbs to this drug. They discovered that the time in pregnancy during which a mother had taken the drug was related to the resulting deformity.

Some vaccines and viral diseases, especially a type of measles called *rubella,* have been proven to be harmful. If the mother has rubella during pregnancy, the infant is likely to suffer deafness, heart defects, mental retar-

Figure 4—12

Stages of prenatal development and birth defects

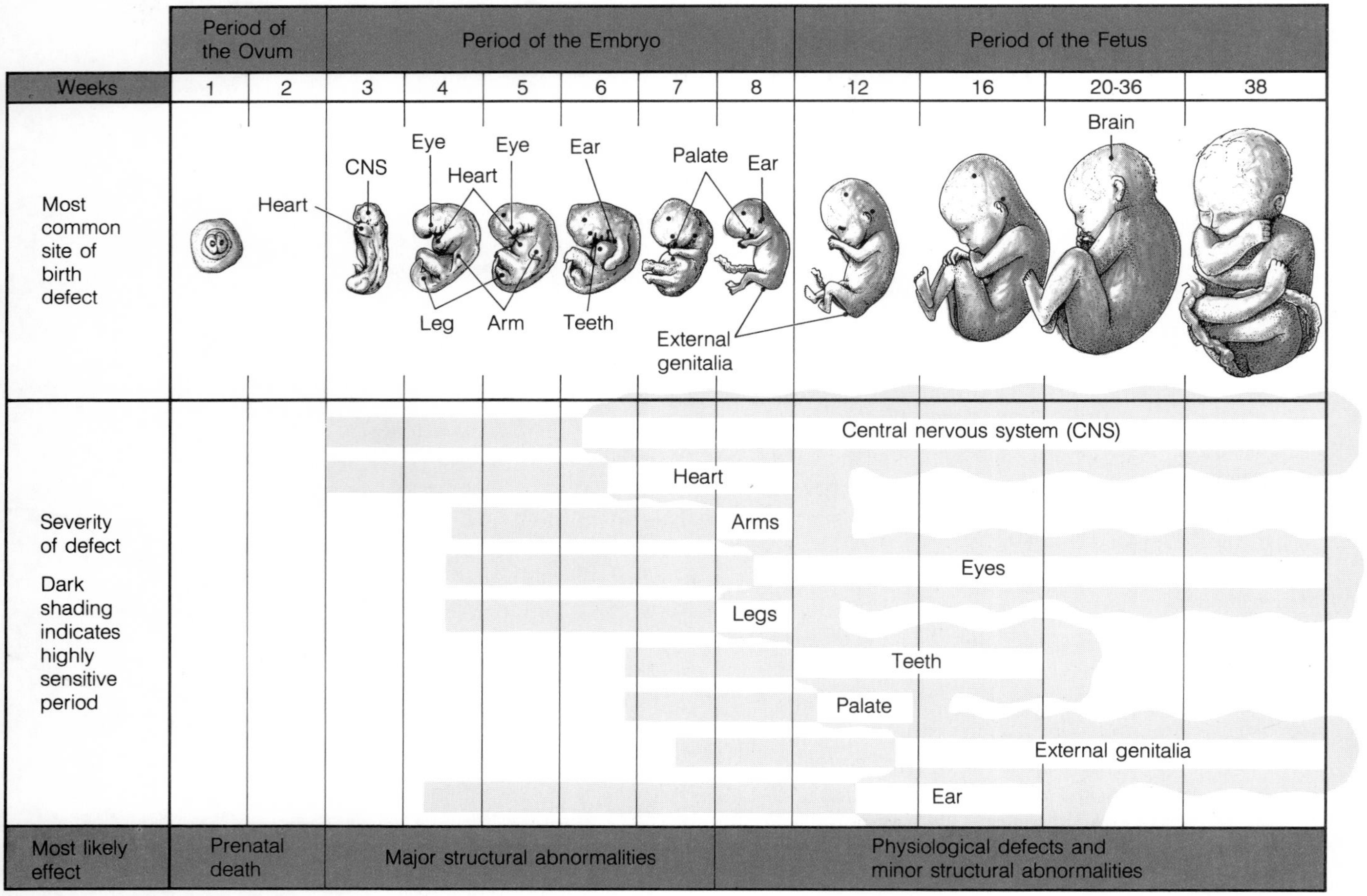

dation, eye problems, and defects of the immunological system (McIntosh, 1984). On the other hand, some research has shown that both mother and fetus can be effectively immunized against other viral diseases, such as tetanus, and researchers are looking for other types of prenatal immunizing agents (Gill et al., 1983).

Another source of birth defects comes from social conditions. It is well known that the risk of birth defects is higher in low-income mothers and in teenage pregnancies, with the primary disorder being low birth weight. Research has shown, however, that it is not the age or social class of the mother per se, but rather the problems associated with poor nutrition, high stress, poor medical care, and exposure to teratogens (Gunter & LaBarba, 1980; Phipps-Yonas, 1980). In fact, teenage pregnancy occurs disproportionately in lower-income groups (see Chapter 16) (Alan Guttmacher Institute, 1981). Some evidence exists, however, that chronic depression and anxiety due to severe stress can lead to a variety of obstetric complications and abnormal labors, but there is no conclusive evidence that maternal stress contributes to the formation of birth defects (Field & Widmayer, 1982; Rosenblith & Sims-Knight, 1985).

Heavy maternal alcohol consumption during pregnancy can cause *fetal alcohol syndrome* (FAS), producing infants with low birth weight, learning problems, small heads, abnormally spaced eyes, an underdeveloped jaw, and a flattened nose (Jones, 1975). Heavy smoking is also associated with physical and neurological defects in the newborn.

One of the current controversies in the field of teratology is related to the effects of moderate alcohol intake and smoking. Although babies born to moderate users of these drugs appear normal, they may have more subtle deficits that go undetected until later in childhood.

In one study (Streissguth, Martin, Barr, & Sandman, 1984), a total of 452 children whose mothers smoked or drank alcohol during pregnancy were tested at four years of age while performing an attentional task. The children had been diagnosed as normally developing and had none of the abnormalities associated with FAS. The task was similar to an arcade game in which one has to aim and shoot at targets as they pop up unexpectedly. The children were asked to press a button when they saw a kitten appear in the window of a drawing of a house. The researchers measured both reaction time when the children saw the kitten and the number of times the child failed to press the button when the kitten appeared.

The amount of alcohol consumed by the mothers during pregnancy ranged from zero to ten ounces per day. The researchers also measured maternal use of nicotine, caffeine, and other drugs during pregnancy. The results showed that there was a dose-response relationship between alcohol consumption during pregnancy and the children's attention to the target at four years of age. A *dose-response* relationship occurs when change in the amount of the drug consumed is directly correlated with changes in the dependent variable. The more alcohol consumed by the mother, the slower the reaction time to the kitten and the more failures to respond at all. The effect for one to two ounces per day was small, but it increased drastically for higher levels of consumption.

The effects of alcohol were independent of those due to nicotine and other drugs. Similarly, there was a dose-response relationship between smoking and the four-year-olds' attention, independent of alcohol consumption. Subtle effects on newborn behavior, such as smaller size, shorter gestation, placidity, and neuromotor control, have also been associated with moderate amounts of alcohol and smoking during pregnancy (Jacobson, Fein, Jacobson, Schwartz, & Dowler, 1984).

This research should caution pregnant women against even small to moderate amounts of smoking and drinking alcohol during pregnancy. However, there are some problems with these studies, since we know that correlation does not always mean a cause and effect relationship. First, not all women who drink or smoke will produce defective offspring. We need to know more about the characteristics of mother and child that protect the child against such effects. It could be that some children are more genetically susceptible to these effects than others. Second, most of the research has not measured pre-pregnancy drinking and smoking behavior. It could be that drinking and smoking before pregnancy may produce reproductive disorders and that a mother who begins using these drugs during pregnancy may not produce a defective child. We simply don't know, and more research is necessary in this area (Rosenblith & Sims-Knight, 1985).

Another problem in the study of teratology is that a large part of our modern environment is composed of potentially harmful chemicals, radiation, and pollutants. Industrial and agricultural chemicals, x-rays, and microwaves, though they may not be harmful to adults, may be harmful to the fetus. Because these things are part of the fabric of modern life, they are difficult to study scientifically and difficult for pregnant women to avoid.

Some people think that pregnant women should take no drugs unless absolutely necessary, avoid x-rays and microwaves, foods containing preservatives, colorings, and other additives, and contact with people who have viral diseases and other infections. This is probably good advice, to the extent that it is possible.

Pregnancy and the Parents

A view of prenatal development that considered only the fetus and its physiological interactions with the mother would be seriously lacking. During the gestation period, the pregnancy is being experienced and interpreted psychologically by each member of the family (refer to quote at the opening of the chapter). The kinds of feelings and concepts that are stirred up in each parent may determine the parents' reaction to the unborn child and initial contacts with the baby. Let's first consider the changes occurring in the pregnant mother.

Body Changes During Pregnancy

The first sign of pregnancy is usually the failure to menstruate. In some cases, however, a woman can menstruate for several months after conception. In other cases, failure to menstruate can be associated with other conditions—age, illness, or emotional stress, for example. Other symptoms that may be associated with pregnancy in the early stages are feelings of fullness or hypersensitivity of the breasts and so-called morning sickness. The latter affects about one-half of all women. Its symptoms are mild and transient feelings of nausea that may be related to biochemical changes taking place in the placenta and its interaction with maternal respiratory, circulatory, and eliminative systems. Some of the changes in the maternal circulatory system are shown in Figure 4-13.

Even though a pregnant woman may experience these physiological changes through physical symptoms, the only foolproof pregnancy test is a

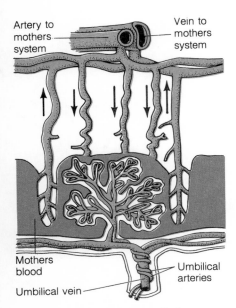

Artery to mothers system

Vein to mothers system

Mothers blood

Umbilical vein

Umbilical arteries

Placenta (cross section)

Figure 4—13

Changes in Maternal Circulatory System During Pregnancy

A detailed cross section of the placenta is shown here. Note that there are two portions of the placenta: the embryo's portion and the mother's and that they are interwoven. Those parts of the drawing that belong to the embryo are shown in black and grays, those of the mother are in color. The gray umbilical vein and arteries carry the embryo's blood, exchanging nutrients, wastes, and so on, with the mother's blood—but the two blood supplies do not come in direct contact.

laboratory urine test for HCG (refer to page xx, this chapter). Do-it-yourself pregnancy test kits, available in some stores, are not always reliable indicators.

Pregnancy brings changes in muscle tissues. The uterus grows from two ounces to two pounds, abdominal muscles increase in length by ten times, and the vagina increases in length and capacity. Hormones that provide nutrition to the fetus and prepare the mother's body for birth and lactation are secreted by the placenta as it is stimulated by the embryo. These hormones produce an increase in vaginal secretions that will assist in the birth process and provide a mild bacteriological effect. Because of such secretions, sexual intercourse during pregnancy may be more satisfying to some women than it was before pregnancy. In general, sexual intercourse during pregnancy is not harmful, although one should consult with her physician, since each individual is different, and intercourse late in pregnancy may not be advised. Physicians who care for women during pregnancy and deliver babies are called *obstetricians/gynecologists,* while physicians who care for the baby immediately after birth and throughout childhood are called *pediatricians.*

The breasts increase in size as fat tissue is replaced by mammary gland (milk-producing) tissue and an increased blood supply. After the fourth month of pregnancy, a clear, yellowish liquid, *colostrum,* which is high in proteins and antibodies and which forms the breast-fed infant's first nutrient after birth (see Chapter 5), is secreted. Breasts may change in their sensitivity to sexual stimulation, and couples should adjust their behavior according to these changes.

Because a woman's body must work harder to meet the nutritional and eliminative demands of the developing fetus, the heart, lungs, kidneys, intestines, and sweat glands must bear the extra load. Because of this, women may suffer from such problems as varicose veins, shortness of breath, and indigestion. In the later months, fatigue may occur easily. The severity of these symptoms depends upon a woman's body structure, nutrition, and physical and mental health.

Prenatal Nutrition

As one of our most important environmental resources, nutrition can affect the physical and psychological well-being of all persons (see Chapter 8). This is especially true during pregnancy, when a woman requires adequate nutritional input to maintain her physical well-being and to cope with the psychological effects of her bodily changes. In addition, nutritive intake is one of the environmental sources that can have an effect on the developing fetus.

For reasons not fully understood, the developing brain is the organ that is most susceptible to nutritional deficiencies (Brown, 1966; Diena, & Dellinger, 1969; Werner, 1979). As the previous section pointed out, the first six months of gestation is the period of the most rapid growth of new brain cells. Malnutrition of the mother during this period can have a significant impact on brain development, since the number of brain cells will never again increase as rapidly as during the prenatal period, even if proper nutrition is restored.

It is hard to define malnutrition, since the fetus may be able to use maternal stores of nutrients even if the mother's nutrient intake is low (Guthrie, 1979). However, such fetal dependency may permanently affect the mother's health. Calcium, contained in dairy products and some vegetables, is especially important, since the fetus will drain calcium deposits from the mother's teeth and bones, leading to possible dental problems unless the mother has sufficient calcium intake during pregnancy.

Mothers are advised to eat a balanced diet rather than rely on vitamin and mineral supplements that could damage the fetus. It is the balance of proper nutrients, rather than simple increases in caloric intake, that most benefits the fetus (National Academy of Sciences, 1975; Shank, 1970).

Pregnancy is not a good time to go on a diet. Although the average woman gains between 24 and 40 pounds, most or all of it consists of the weight of the baby plus the weight of the extra muscle and breast tissue. Typically in the year after pregnancy, most or all of this weight is lost.

Psychological Adaptation to Pregnancy

Research on the subject of adaptation to pregnancy has revealed two basic patterns. The first is that maternal feelings change, usually for the better, in the later stages of pregnancy compared to the earlier stages. The second is that each mother has her own characteristic reaction to being pregnant: There is no single type of psychological experience that always occurs during pregnancy.

Men can be important sources of emotional support as their partners experience the physical and psychological changes of pregnancy. During this period fatigue and doubt often co-exist with hope and exhilaration.

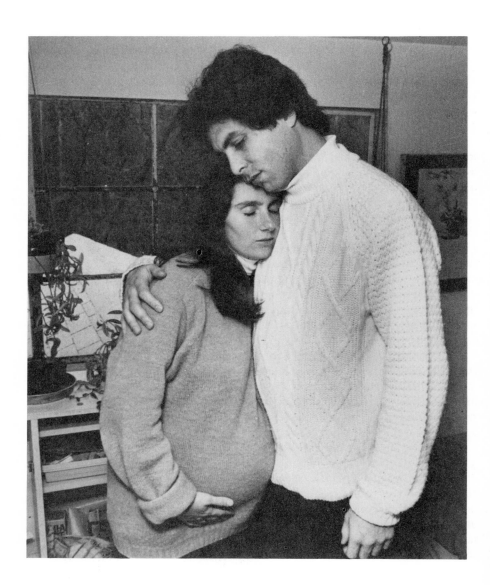

Pregnancy and childbirth make up a critical transition in adult life. Once an adult has a child of his or her own, it represents a kind of psychological break from one's own childhood (Rossi, 1968). Pregnancy often helps women to reestablish ties with their own mothers. The mother-daughter relationship may change, from one in which the daughter is still like a child to one in which the daughter develops a greater sense of identification with her own mother.

In response to the physical changes taking place in their bodies, most women are surprised at the amount of physical discomfort during the first trimester and think of their symptoms as a nuisance. In the second trimester, many women in North America become preoccupied with their weight gain. In our culture, a high value is placed on a slender body and female physical attractiveness. Even though some women enjoy the sense of being pregnant, most worry about their appearance in some way. Many women have a sense of losing control over their bodies; they feel conspicuous or embarrassed at times. Later in pregnancy, their increased size leads to feelings of awkwardness. In this condition, many women worry about their attractiveness to their husbands. As sexual intercourse decreases near the end of pregnancy, some women fear their husbands will abandon them in favor of more attractive women (Leifer, 1980).

One research study found a close relationship between prenatal attitudes and mental states and postnatal attitudes and behavior. The researcher classified mothers into three basic groups according to the nature of their adaptation to pregnancy and to childrearing: a high functioning group, a moderate functioning group, and a low functioning group (Leifer, 1980).

Mothers in the high functioning group maintained a satisfying relationship with their husband before birth, became involved with all aspects of their pregnancy, reacted to childbirth as a peak emotional experience, and later developed an intrinsically pleasurable relationship with the baby. Moderate functioning mothers showed both positive and negative feelings and were consistently ambivalent about becoming a parent. Mothers in this group often had their baby too early in their marriage, before they had fully made the personal decision of readiness to become a parent. Such mothers experienced the initial phases of childrearing as more stressful, but many successfully adapted and became comfortable with the parenting role.

The low functioning mothers were essentially unmotivated for motherhood. They typically had marriages with limited communication between spouses, had a negative or passive response to pregnancy, and had a similar reaction to the infant.

Because long-term follow-up studies are lacking, we cannot be sure how each of these mothers behaved as a parent. It could be that those mothers who are initially low functioning are able to rescue themselves from their difficulties, although they have a more difficult initial adaptation to parenthood than do mothers who are highly motivated to become a parent at the initiation of the pregnancy.

The Father's Adaptation to Pregnancy

Humans are the only species for which there is a concept of fatherhood. No other animals have the intellectual ability to link the fertilization of the ovum with a particular individual. It has been said that fatherhood is a cultural invention, meaning that the father's status is only what the culture defines it to be, and the father's role has been undergoing transition and redefinition for many years.

Although fathers do not have as strong a biological tie to the infant as do mothers, they have a strong psychological tie to the pregnancy and to the infant and mother. This may take the form of being interested in the childbirth process, taking time off from work to help the mother, going to prenatal classes, and attending the delivery. These actions on the part of men suggest that the men do not want to be left out of the parenting process. It also reveals a sense of value and respect for the importance of the woman's role in childbearing.

Anthropologists have noticed similar patterns of male behavior in societies where the woman's role is placed in high esteem. The acting out by males of the female role during pregnancy in a socially approved manner is termed *couvade* (Whiting, 1974). In our culture, this may include taking prenatal classes with the mother, doing the stretching and breathing exercises with her, and attending the childbirth.

As with mothers, wide individual differences exist in the male's response to the pregnancy. Some men see it as an indication of their potency, while others may feel threatened by a sense of bondage or by feelings of financial and psychological responsibility to mother and baby. Some men increase in their devotion to their wives, while others engage in extramarital sex or turn to physical abuse of their wives to blunt their own frustrations (Gelles, 1978).

Because fathers have a more tenuous biological tie with the fetus, their behavior can be influenced favorably by their wives. If men are made to feel important and are encouraged in their role as provider and psychological supporter of the wife and child, even those with little experience or initial desire to parent can learn to increase their attention and devotion to the needs of the family. Men can quickly become competent in providing childcare to infants (see Chapters 5 and 7). Although men approach childbearing and childrearing with different motives, desires, and intuitions than do women, they can have equal competence as parents, even during the prenatal period.

Chapter Summary

CONCEPTION
☐ Successful fertilization results in the formation of the zygote.

HEREDITY
☐ Molecules of DNA combine to form genes, which are linked into strings called chromosomes.
☐ Gene expression is a systems interaction between the genotype and the phenotype. The human species members' common characteristics are defined by canalization processes that have evolved by natural selection.
☐ Sexual dimorphism has evolved to allow for greater genetic diversity in offspring. Sex differences in size, structure, and behavior between male and female adults contribute to the attraction between the sexes that ensures continued mating and pair bonding needed to create children and families.
☐ The sex of the fetus is determined by an interaction between the genotype and the hormonal environment of the placenta.
☐ Sex-linked inheritance describes a process in which females are carriers of certain disorders while males display the symptoms.

DEVELOPMENT BEFORE BIRTH
☐ The period of the zygote represents the initial stages of cell differentiation and implantation in the uterine wall.

□ The period of the embryo leads to the development of most of the external human forms and all of the internal organs.

□ The period of the fetus contains the formation of the genitals, hair, weight gain, and beginnings of behavior.

PRENATAL RISK

□ Genetic disorders are those inherited from the parents in the genotype.

□ Chromosomal abnormalities refer to damage to the chromosomes or errors of genetic matching that occur during meiosis and fertilization.

□ Environmental causes of risk include pollutants, drugs, infectious disease, and radiation.

PREGNANCY IN THE FAMILY

□ The mother's body changes to adapt to the needs of the fetus.

□ Most parents successfully adapt to the woman's body changes as they prepare themselves for the birth of the child.

Recommended Readings

Blaikie, P. M. (1975). *Family planning in India*. New York: Holmes & Meier. A case study of the interaction between the individual, family, and society.

Fogel, A., & Melson, G. (1986). *Origins of nurturance*. Hillsdale, NJ: Erlbaum. Contains chapters on the transition to parenthood and the adaptation of parents to pregnancy.

Leifer, M. (1980). *Psychological effects of motherhood: A study of first pregnancy*. New York: Praeger. A report of a longitudinal research study on the adaptation to parenthood.

Mitchell, G. (1981). *Human sex differences: A primatologist's perspective*. New York: Van Nostrand Reinhold. A discussion of the evolution of sexual dimorphism in size and behavior.

Money, J. (1968). *Sex errors of the body: Dilemmas, education and counselling*. Baltimore: Johns Hopkins University Press. A discussion of the causes and consequences of prenatal errors of genital formation.

CHAPTER 5

Birth and the Newborn Infant

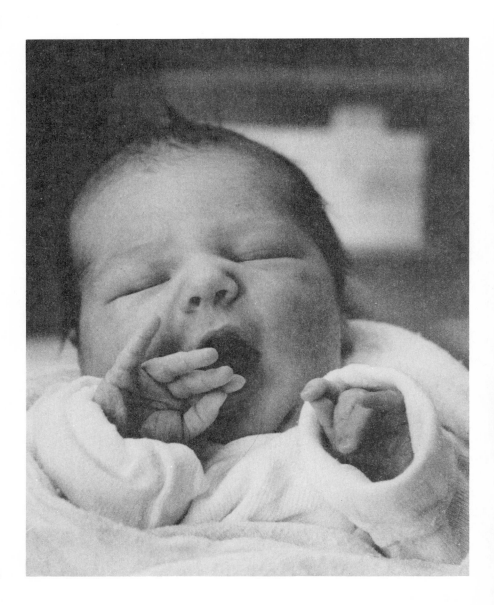

O f Mayan Indian descent, the Zinancantecan Indians live in a mountainous and remote region of Mexico. During labor and delivery no drugs are used. Instead of hospitals and doctors, the expectant mother receives support and encouragement from another woman, a midwife, who guides the mother until after the baby is born. When the birth is complete the newborn child is carefully placed near a fire while the midwife begins to pray for the Gods to look kindly upon the child. A long skirt made of heavy fabric is placed on infants of both sexes at this time, and will be worn all during the first year of life. The Zinancantecans believe that infants should be wrapped carefully in order to prevent the loss of their souls. The mother and infant are kept isolated during the first few weeks and months in order to prevent illness to the child and to protect against the invasion of evil spirits.

— adapted from Brazelton, 1972.

In the small villages of southern Italy, birth also occurs in the company of a midwife and without doctors, but generally in a hospital setting. Specially prepared ceremonial clothing, provided by the newborn's family, are the first garments the baby wears after birth. Here the similarity between Mexico and Italy seems to end, since within about 10 minutes after birth, the midwife escorts the new mother's entire extended family into the birthing room to give them all a chance to congratulate, kiss and touch both mother and infant, followed by a party of pastries and liquors for all those present. During the first weeks and months the mother is rarely left alone, and she will receive many visitors during this time. Most of her affairs are managed by her mother-in-law, who feeds the new mother special delicious and nourishing foods for up to one month after the birth. The baby usually sleeps in the same bed as the mother, or in a nearby cradle.

— adapted from Schreiber, 1977.

As we saw in Chapter 4, human development begins from the moment of conception and continues throughout the life span. From this broad perspective, birth is only one event in a continuous process of change. The importance of birth for the infant is the first exposure to a complex and rich environment of light, sound, and smell, an environment in which the newborn can begin to apply its vast potential for learning and growing. Birth also forces the infant into a series of changes in basic bodily functioning, including the transition from a condition of constant temperature to one of temperature changes and from an aquatic existence to life as an air-breathing organism.

For the family, the baby's birth provides the first look at the child that could only be imagined. It is also the beginning of a new set of responsibilities and joys in which this tiny human is destined to restructure the workings of the family and the experience of each family member. Because of what the

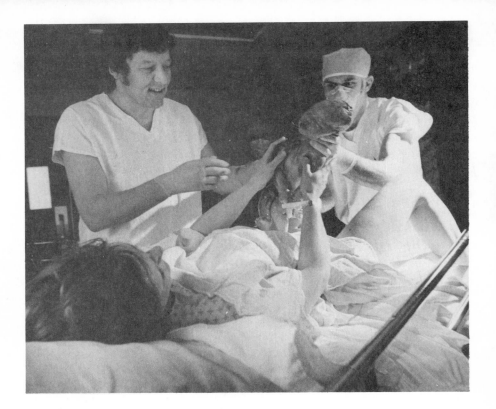

The birth of a baby is an intense emotional experience for those in attendance.

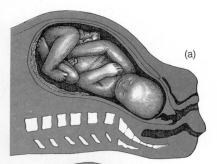

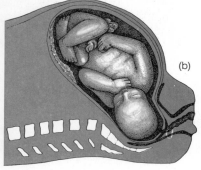

Figure 5–1

Birth Process: Stage 1 and Part of Stage 2

(a) End of the first stage of labor. Baby's head is moving through the cervix. (b) Transition. The baby's head is moving through the birth canal, the vagina. (c-e) The second stage of labor. The baby's head is moving through the opening of the vagina (c), it emerges completely (d), and the head is then turned so that the rest of the body slides out (e).

(From *In the Beginning: Development in the First Two Years,* by J. F. Rosenblith and J. E. Sims-Knight. Copyright © 1985 by Wadsworth, Inc. Reprinted by permission of Brooks/Cole Publishing Company, Monterey, California 93940.)

occasion of birth means to the family in the long run, rituals such as those just described have been created in every society. These rituals not only mark the occasion of the birth of a new human being but also serve to orient the family members to the tasks that lie ahead: the surprises, the troubles, and the pleasures of parenthood.

The Birth Process

The Last Month of Pregnancy

The events leading up to the birth as well as the birth itself require the participation of the muscles of the uterus, the abdomen, and the pelvis. Childbirth requires two basic muscle movements: contraction and relaxation. During the last month of pregnancy, the uterine muscles begin to move from time to time in a series of gentle contraction-relaxation cycles, called *Braxton-Hicks contractions,* or false labor. These gentle contractions have the effect of opening the *cervix,* the point of connection between the uterus and the vagina. By the time labor begins in earnest, the cervix will have opened about one or two centimeters (one-half to one inch).

Another change that usually occurs during the last month is the final adjustment of the fetus's position, ideally with the fetal head down and oriented toward the cervix (see Figure 5–1). About four percent of all births occur with the buttocks born first. Such births are called *breech* births, and they can sometimes lead to minor dislocations of limb joints. In a small percentage of cases, fetuses are oriented with their side toward the cervix, a *transverse* presentation. These cases usually require delivery by *Cesarean section*. In a Cesarean delivery, the fetus does not pass through the vagina but is delivered through a surgical opening in the abdominal wall. Cesarean deliveries are also used in some breech presentations, with some twin deliveries, for overly large babies, or if the fetus shows a sudden change in its life signs (called *fetal distress*).

The United States has had an increase in Cesarean deliveries in the past 30 years: About 16 percent of babies are delivered by Cesarean section. Perhaps this is because better prenatal care and nutrition has led to the development of larger fetuses. On the other hand, some controversy exists over whether obstetricians tend to overuse this method to get higher fees and avoid malpractice lawsuits in the event of a complication during a vaginal delivery. There is no way to prove this assertion, however.

The Stages of Labor

Based on averages from many mothers, babies are usually born about 280 days from the first day of the mother's last menstrual period, but very few births actually occur exactly on their predicted due date. The normal range is within two weeks—before or after—of the due date (Guttmacher, 1973).

A series of moderate contractions once every 10 or 20 minutes is usually a good sign that *labor* has begun. Labor is divided into three stages, as described in Table 5–1. The first stage, from the beginning of regular contractions to the full opening (about 10 cm.) of the cervix, can last from a few minutes to a few days (Guttmacher, 1973). This is the longest stage of labor.

For mothers who are giving birth for the first time, the average duration of the first stage is 8 to 14 hours. For mothers who have previously given birth, the first stage is usually a bit shorter, about six hours on the average (Danforth, 1977; Parfitt, 1977). Certainly, knowing the average time is no consolation for a mother who spends 20 or more hours, with little sleep, in the first stage. Fortunately the other two stages of labor, though more intense, last only an hour or so each.

Pain Control During Labor

One might think that labor pain is such a basic experience that humans would have found universally effective ways of dealing with it. On the contrary, a wide variety of ways to relieve pain exists, with seemingly no ideal way that is suitable to all situations.

Wide cultural variations exist. Some peoples, like the Laotians, the Navaho Indians, and the Cuna of Panama, soothe the pain with music while the Comanche and the Tewa Indian tribes apply heat to the abdomen. Some believe that the position of the mother's body is most important and encourage women to give birth in an upright position. The Taureg people of the Sahara give birth in a kneeling position, and most obstetric textbooks in the United States at the turn of this century recommended upright postures (Mead & Newton, 1967).

Until the early part of this century in North America and Europe, most births took place in the family's home, perhaps with a midwife in attendance and with little or no medication. Before that time, Judeo-Christian peoples believed that the pain of labor was each woman's punishment for Eve's sins. This seems to be due to a mistranslation of a phrase from the Bible regarding Eve: "In *sorrow* thou shall bring forth children" (Genesis 3:16). In 1849,

(continued)

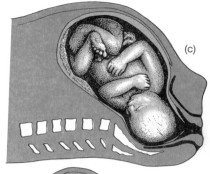
(c)

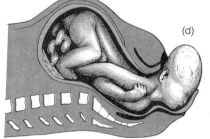
(d)

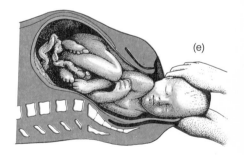
(e)

Figure 5–1

Table 5—1

THE STAGES OF LABOR

The First Stage

Early Effacement of cervical opening (softening of cervical tissue). Effacement is usually complete before the cervix begins to dilate (open), especially in a first pregnancy. The cervix dilates to approximately four centimeters. Contractions are relatively slow (every 10 to 20 minutes).

Active Beginning of regular contractions, about five minutes apart, each lasting about 45 seconds. The cervix dilates to five or six centimeters. Deep breathing is usually enough to handle the pain. This is the time to go to the hospital or call the doctor.

Transition The last two to three centimeters of dilation must be completed. Transition is the most difficult part of labor, where the contractions are stronger, longer, and closer together than at any other time—approximately 90 seconds long and 60 seconds apart. Deep breathing no longer works; panting is recommended. Fortunately, this phase is relatively brief, lasting at the most one hour.

The Second Stage

Early The infant's head appears at the vaginal opening in the early *second stage of labor.* Pushing the baby through the vagina is the main job. There is more time between contractions than in the transition phase.

Birth The baby is pushed over the pubic bone. Most of the pressure is relieved after the head has passed out of the vagina.

The Third Stage

The *third stage of labor* is the birth of the placenta, which must all come out to avoid hemorrhaging. This stage lasts no more than one hour.

(From Parfitt, 1977.)

James Young Simpson, the discoverer and a major proponent of chemical pain relief during childbirth, proposed that the Hebrew word originally translated as *sorrow,* should have been rendered as *labor* (Brackbill, 1979). With the growing acceptance of modern medical practices in the past 150 years, women no longer have to feel condemned to a painful childbirth.

Modern medicine has drugs for both *anesthesia* (loss of sensation) and *analgesia* (pain relief). Drugs can help to induce or to speed up labor, reduce discomfort, and help in muscle relaxation. Although all of the drugs in use have been proven safe and effective for the mother, some data suggest that most of these drugs can cross the placenta during labor and delivery and thus adversely affect the fetus (Brackbill, 1979). In general, drugs tend to make the fetus and the newborn drowsy and listless and may affect muscle tension and perception. In recent years, obstetricians are reducing dosages or finding drugs that do not affect the fetus as much.

Even the reduced levels of drugs used in modern obstetric practice can affect the newborn infant. One study looked at 62 vaginally delivered and 35 Cesarean section infants at 3 days and at 28 days after birth (Hollenbeck, Gewirtz, Sebris, & Scanlon, 1984). A *double-blind design* (refer to Chapter 3) was used in which the subjects were unaware that the researchers were looking for drug effects and the observers were unaware of how much medication the mother might have taken during labor and delivery.

Using an observational procedure, both mother-infant and father-infant interactions were scored for such behaviors as caregiving, kissing, imitating, smiling, touching, vocalizing, fussing, and feeding. Each infant was observed for 30 minutes at each age. In addition, observers used summary rating scales to score parental involvement, positive emotions, sensitivity, and appropriateness of parental response to infant.

Mothers who received higher doses of medication kissed their infants less, looked at them less, and touched them less but smiled at them more than did mothers with lower doses of medication. These results were found for both vaginal and Cesarean section mothers and for both 3-day and 28-day observations. Fewer differences were found for the fathers, although fathers of Cesarean section babies were somewhat more involved with the infant than were fathers of vaginally delivered infants.

These findings suggest that drugs continue to affect maternal behavior even one month following the birth. Fathers may be more involved with Cesarean-delivered infants because mothers receive somewhat more medication and take more time to recover from their surgery.

The research, however, remains somewhat inconclusive. A fetus who was already listless and lacking muscle tone might be harder to deliver and therefore require more pain control medication. In such case, the listlessness of the newborn would not be associated with the drug effects at all, and perhaps the mother's reduced responsiveness could be attributed to having a relatively less responsive baby.

Nevertheless, mothers and obstetricians might be cautioned to use drugs sparingly. For many mothers, drugs have an undesirable psychological side effect. The drug may make the mother drowsy or disoriented, resulting in her missing part of the excitement of giving birth and seeing her new baby for the first time (Affonso, 1977).

Alternatives to Chemical Pain Relief

Today, laboring women and their families have a wide range of alternatives from which to choose, and often they can select from a number of different methods that best suit their needs. Perhaps the most widely used is the *Lamaze method,* which employs a set of breathing patterns and posture shifts designed to help muscles relax and thus prevent pain from overly tight muscles (Karmel, 1959). Prenatal childbirth education can also be an effective preventive, since some research studies have found an association between lack of knowledge and negative attitudes towards the impending childbirth and the amount of pain felt during childbirth (Nettlebladt, Fagerstron, & Udderberg, 1976; Newton, 1972). Since the perception of pain is a subjective experience, it is difficult to do conclusive research about the effectiveness of these methods. Because of this, we offer them here as possible alternatives, no one of which has been proven to be effective for all women.

Social support during the labor and delivery has also been proposed as a means to ease pain. Women perceive labor and delivery as less painful if the husband is present (Davenport-Slack & Boylan, 1974; Nettlebladt et al., 1976), although it could be that women who are more likely to be able to endure childbirth pain are more likely to want their husbands to be present during this particularly intimate and stressful time.

Upright postures during birth have been found effective. However, we need to be cautious of the findings, because subjects are not randomly assigned to experimental and control groups: It is a matter of personal choice. It could be that women who elect to use upright postures are already predisposed to easier labors. It has been found, however, that the upright posture offers greater elasticity of the pelvis, more effective pushing in the second stage due to the

Figure 5—2

Birthing Chair

A modern birthing chair can be adjusted for both vertical and horizontal delivery positions according to the comfort of the mother.

(Adapted from *In the Beginning: Development in the First Two Years*, by J. F. Rosenblith and J. E. Sims-Knight. Copyright © 1985 by Wadsworth, Inc. Reprinted by permission of Brooks/Cole Publishing Company, Monterey, California 93940.)

assistance of gravity, shorter labor with less pain, better blood circulation to the fetus, and more active and alert infants (Carr, 1980). In one study the birthing chair was studied with 1800 women (see Figure 5—2). The Cesarean rate was only eight percent for this group, labors were shorter, and there was less need for episiotomy (Caldeyro-Barcia, 1981). An *episiotomy* is the surgical cutting of the perineum (the tissue between the vagina and the anus) that helps prevent the perineum from tearing. Episiotomies are done in 90 percent of deliveries in the United States (Banta, 1981).

Although alternative methods of childbirth are designed for pain relief in the mother, at least one method is designed to aid in the relief of discomfort to the fetus and newborn. In many hospitals, infants are born into the cold air, placed under bright lights, and exposed to harsh sounds. Frederick Leboyer (1975) suggested that delivery room lights be lowered and the room be insulated from loud noises. He recommended not spanking the baby, placing the newborn on the mother's warm abdomen until the cord could be cut, giving a gentle massage, and then gently placing the baby in a warm-water bath. Leboyer's claims that such procedures increase the newborn's alertness and relaxation have not been scientifically verified. Most studies reporting positive effects were biased by observers' clear preference for the method (e.g., Rappoport, 1976). A well-controlled study (Nelson et al., 1980) found no differences in alertness between Leboyer babies and non- Leboyer babies, nor were there any differences in developmental test scores between the two group at eight months. Furthermore, half of the Leboyer babies reacted to the warm-water bath with irritable crying. On the other hand, no negative side effects of Leboyer's procedure were observed.

Perinatal Risk and Mortality

Immediately after a baby is born, hospital staff check basic physical signs to determine the newborn's ability to survive on its own outside the mother's body and without the need for medical assistance. The newborn's ability to survive is called *viability*. Hospitals in most parts of the world use a standardized scoring system, known as the Apgar rating, named after its founder, Virginia Apgar (see Table 5—2). The baby is rated at one minute and again at five minutes after birth. A score of seven or better usually indicates that the

Table 5–2

THE APGAR RATING SCALE

Area	Score 0	Score 1	Score 2
Heart rate	Absent	Slow (<100)	Rapid (> 100)
Respiration	Absent	Irregular	Good, infant crying
Muscle tone	Flaccid	Weak	Strong, well flexed
Color	Blue, pale	Body pink, extremities blue	All pink
Reflex irritability:			
Nasal tickle	No response	Grimace	Cough, sneeze
Heel prick	No response	Mild response	Foot withdrawal, cry

(From Apgar, 1953.)

baby is in no immediate danger. A baby who rates less than four is in critical condition.

Although the vast majority of babies are born normal and healthy, 85 percent of the serious disorders and mortality of infants and young children can be traced to prenatal and perinatal complications (Kopp and Parmelee, 1979). The *perinatal* period usually refers to the time from about two weeks before to about two weeks after birth. As distinct from prenatal risk factors, perinatal risk is usually due to some of the following causes: problems in delivery (such as a breech presentation), neonatal infections, *asphyxia* (loss of oxygen to the fetus during the birth process), *hypoglycemia* (loss of blood sugar), cardiac and respiratory difficulties related to the transition to life outside the placenta, and low birth weight.

In one study, 103 infants were rated on the number of perinatal risk factors, such as those listed in the previous paragraph. The infants with the highest number of risk factors had the lowest Apgar scores and were relatively unresponsive. By six months, however, the perinatal risk score was not correlated with the infants' behavior and development (Molfese and Thompson, 1985). With adequate postnatal care—including nutrition and normal stimulation from caregivers—most babies have the ability to recover from perinatal complications (Sameroff & Chandler, 1974).

Low Birth Weight

Full-term births are those that have at least 37 weeks *gestational age* (time since the mother's last menstrual period). Full-term infants either can have a normal birth weight of at least 2,500 grams (about 5.5 pounds) or can weigh less and thus fall into the category of *small for gestational age,* or "small for dates," babies. *Preterm* births occur before 37 weeks gestational age. Preterm babies may have weights that are appropriate for their gestational age, or they may be small in relation to their gestational age. In either case, preterm babies always suffer from low birth weight.

About nine percent of all births in North America are considered preterm. In 1975, over 40 percent of preterm infants who survived developed severe mental and physical handicaps because of the inability of the hospital environment to supply the proper factors necessary to support development outside the uterus and placenta. Today the percentage of serious disorders is below 10 percent and continues to fall. In addition, smaller babies have a good prospect for survival (Kopp and Parmelee, 1979). Research shows that differ-

The Case of Baby Doe

On April 9, 1982, a severely ill baby was born in Bloomington, Indiana. The baby had Down's syndrome (refer to Chapter 4), a blocked esophagus, and possibly an enlarged heart. Given the multiple complications, doctors advised withholding treatment, because surgery would be difficult and the infant had a poor chance of survival. Even if the baby survived, it was felt that its life would be short and difficult for both the infant and the family. The parents agreed, as did two county judges who later ruled on what has come to be known as the case of Baby Doe. The county prosecutor felt that this was a case of criminal neglect and asked the Indiana State Supreme Court to intervene and issue an order to feed the baby.

This case and others like it have raised some very emotional issues regarding *euthanasia* for newborns. *Euthanasia* is the act of painlessly putting to death a person suffering from an incurable disease. In most cases, this means the withholding of drastic medical treatments in cases where death is inevitable and would only be prolonged by the treatments.

The case of Baby Doe was hotly debated by right-to-life advocates, by people who felt that newborns had a constitutional right to treatment even without their parents' consent, and by medical and parent groups who argued for the newborn's right to die peacefully in extreme cases and who thought that the quality of life was as important as the preservation of life.

As a result, the U.S. Senate in 1984 added an amendment to the Child Abuse and Prevention Act of 1974, under which the government provides aid to victims of abuse and neglect. Under this new amendment, the "withholding of medically indicated treatment from disabled infants with life-threatening conditions" would be considered a form of child abuse and neglect. The amendment, however, has three exceptions that justify the withholding of life-saving treatment:

1. The infant is chronically ill and irreversibly comatose.
2. The provision of such treatment would merely prolong dying, not be effective in ameliorating or correcting all of the infant's life-threatening conditions, or otherwise be futile in terms of the survival of the infant.
3. The provision of such treatment would be virtually futile in terms of the survival of the infant, and the treatment itself under such circumstances would be inhumane.

Although this piece of legislation satisfied a wide range of advocacy groups, it failed to be endorsed by the American Medical Association, because the amendment did not address the issue of quality of life (*Science News,* July 14, 1984). In other words, suppose that the infant would certainly survive a medical intervention and thus by law must be treated. But what if such infants are so deformed or handicapped that their prognosis would include a life of discomfort, pain, and severe restrictions on movement?

The case of Baby Doe illustrates that the best interests of the child at risk are not always so clear. Are some handicaps so extreme that the best intervention is not to intervene? Is survival—the preservation of life at all costs—the only justification for intervention? At what point do we consider the parents' rights? To what extent should the fact that a severely handicapped child can be an emotional and financial drain on the family be taken into account in quality of life decisions?

There are no easy answers to these questions. All we can say is that issues such as this—and elective abortion, as another example— seem to defy the ability of individuals and governments to establish clear guidelines for decision making.

ences between preterm and full-term babies in alertness and in social skills decline steadily over the first year of life (Crawford, 1982).

Interventions That Help Preterm Infants

Recently, researchers have developed ways to make the intensive care unit a more pleasant experience for premature babies while enhancing the babies'

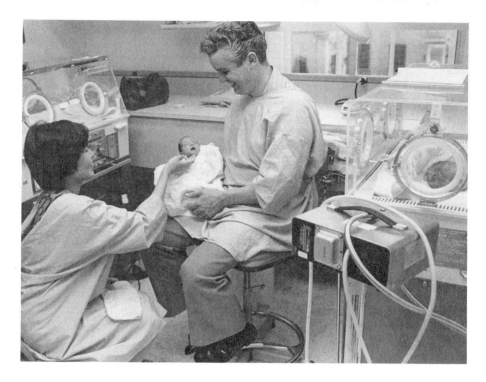

Modern neonatal intensive care units are responsible for the excellent developmental prognosis of premature and sick infants. The comprehensive treatment of the intensive care infants includes not only medical intervention, but also social interaction and physical therapy.

development. For example, since premature infants must be fed through tubes, they have no opportunity to suck. If they are given the chance to suck non-nutritively on a pacifier between their tube feedings, they have fewer medical complications and they sleep better (Anderson, Burroughs, & Measel, 1983; Woodson, Drinkwin, & Hamilton, 1985).

Inside their isolettes, the babies may have to lie on mattresses that feel hard because they have little fat tissue underneath their skin. Researchers at Stanford University have eased this by designing waterbeds for newborns. The beds are gently warmed, and the babies develop rounder, more naturally shaped heads. Some of the waterbeds are equipped with vibrators that gently rock the baby. The waterbeds help the premies (premature babies) to sleep better and breathe easier and make them more alert when they are awake than babies reared without the waterbed (Korner, 1979).

Gentle stroking of the premies' head and limbs and movement of the limbs have been shown to increase the babies' weight gain by 47 percent over nonstimulated babies who received the same amount of food. The stimulated babies were released from the hospital six days sooner on the average, saving an average hospital cost of $3,000 per infant. In addition, the stimulated babies had larger heads and fewer complications than did the nonstimulated babies (Field & Sostek, 1983).

Maternal visitation to the intensive care unit also increases stimulation for the baby and helps the mother by increasing her positive perceptions of the infant's ability to recover. Babies who were visited most often were released from the hospital sooner (Zeskind & Iacino, 1984).

Infant Mortality

Perhaps the leading cause of neonatal mortality is inadequate prenatal and perinatal care: Malnutrition, poor sanitation, and lack of physical stamina can lead to poor health in both the mother and the fetus. Table 5–3 shows the *mortality rate* (the percentage of deaths) for both mothers and infants. The table shows that higher mortality rates exist in relatively underdeveloped countries in which more people are living in poverty. Because of worldwide improvements in health care, the mortality rates are slowly declining, but many countries still fall behind the more advanced nations.

One of the reasons seems to be a lack of knowledge about how and when to feed infants. For example, infants need nutritional supplements beyond mother's milk after about six or seven months of age (see Chapter 6). In some African countries, women wait until the infant is 18 months old before weaning and then give the infant adult foods that are hard to chew and digest. Even if food is plentiful, this treatment would lead to malnutrition and death for many infants.

From an intervention perspective, more children would be saved by providing basic health education, clean water, and sanitation to parents than would be by sending large quantities of food (*Science News,* July 6, 1985). The United Nations has developed and tested a successful health education program called GOBI. *GOBI* stands for Growth charts, Oral rehydration, Breast-feeding, and Immunization (Werner, 1986). By comparing their child's development to standard growth charts, parents can detect failure to thrive. Oral rehydration—providing fluids—is the primary treatment for infantile diarrhea, one of the world's leading causes of infant death (Puffer & Serrano, 1973). Breast-feeding provides both adequate nourishment and natural immunization, which, when coupled with medical immunization procedures, significantly lowers mortality rates.

Even within a well-developed country like the United States, the effects of poverty are visible. Although infant and mother mortality have fallen for both whites and nonwhites in the United States, nonwhites were about 10 years behind whites in perinatal mortality rate in 1983 (*Information Please Almanac,* 1986). Nonwhites who are not living in poverty enjoy mortality rates comparable to the nonimpoverished whites, suggesting that the differences in white and nonwhite rates are related to socioeconomic factors and not to race.

Table 5–3

INFANT AND MATERNAL MORTALITY

Country	Maternal Mortality		Infant Mortality	
	1979	1982	1979	1983
Mexico	108.2[a]	91.8[f]	44.1[b]	53.0
United States	9.6[b]	9.2[e]	13.0	10.9
Canada	6.4[b]	1.9	11.9[b]	8.5
Venezuela	65.1[b]	—	33.1	39.0
Chile	66.0	52.4	37.9	21.1
Sweden	1.0	4.3	7.5	7.0
England	11.6	6.7	12.9	10.2
Egypt	84.8[c]	77.9[d]	73.5[b]	113.0
Singapore	20.2	4.7[f]	13.2	9.4
Japan	22.9	18.4	7.9	6.2

Less than one year of age. Maternal deaths per 100,000 live births: infant deaths per 1,000 live births
[a]1976   [d]1979
[b]1978   [e]1980
[c]1977   [f]1981
(From United Nations, Demographic Yearbook, 1980, 1984.)

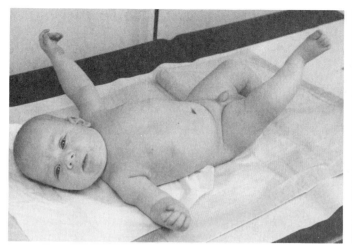
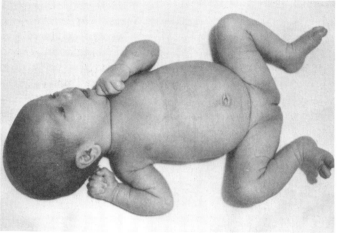

The Newborn's Appearance

Physical Appearance of the Newborn

After an emotionally absorbing birth experience, most parents think that their newborn is the most beautiful thing in the world. If you see a newborn that's not your own child, you may wonder how anyone could call that baby beautiful.

At birth, a baby's skin is wet with amniotic fluid and may have specks of white that look like cottage cheese—the remains of the vernix caseosa (refer to Chapter 4). Some babies have rather pale skin, while others' skin may be pink. Pink blotches may also show the effects of the pressure of the birth process on the skin. Some babies may have slightly yellowish skin, a condition known as *normal physiological jaundice,* resulting from a not-yet-balanced liver functioning. It is easily treated by placing the baby under special lamps.

A newborn's head is large compared to its body, with the head accounting for about one-fourth of the baby's total length. The baby cannot control its head, which must be cradled carefully when the baby is lifted. Usually, a newborn's legs are bowed, and its feet are bent so that the soles of the feet are almost parallel. To add to this rather ungainly portrait, the neonate (another word for newborn) has a very small neck, no chin, and a rather flattened nose. The shape of the head may be somewhat deformed, again the result of the pressures exerted on the newborn's body during birth. The baby's face and body may look wrinkled, since body fat does not begin to develop until after birth, although the cheeks have some fat, which is necessary for sucking. Most of these more unattractive features disappear after several weeks of age.

Babies may or may not have hair at birth. If they do, the hair might be not only on the head but also on the eyebrows and the back. This is the fetal lanugo (refer to Chapter 4) and is usually replaced by more permanent hair during the first few months. Almost all babies are born with smokey-blue eyes, and even black neonates have light skin and blue eyes for a short time. True eye color is not known for about six months, since pigments in the eyes and the skin need to be exposed to white light to develop further.

Because of the need for a flexible skull during birth, there are openings between the various bones of the skull called *fontanels* (see Figure 5–3). These spaces also allow for continued growth of the brain and do not fully close until about 18 months, about the age when new brain cells stop being formed.

The newborn has many more brain cells than does the adult. After birth, the brain actively selects the healthiest cells and those most adapted to the prenatal environment. The brain cells that remain increase in size and in the complexity of their interconnections. As new connections are made, the cells are covered with a substance called *myelin,* which protects and insulates the conductive pathways. Because of these processes, the brain of a one-year-old is almost double the size of the brain of a newborn (Tanner, 1970).

Physical Adjustments to Post-Natal Life

Newborns must assume responsibility for three basic survival mechanisms: breathing air, processing orally fed nutrients, and regulating body temperature. During the prenatal period, these three functions were carried out by the mother while the fetus floated freely in its temperature-controlled, nutrient-rich sphere. At birth, most babies are able to start immediately on the path of self-maintenance.

Air breathing does not require any kind of slapping or jarring to get started. Usually, the mere exposure to air is enough to induce respiration. Newborn breathing may seem a bit shallow and raspy at first, since the lungs are partially filled with mucous and amniotic fluid, which will take some weeks to become absorbed. Oxygen levels in the blood reach normal levels in about 30 hours.

Intake of nutrients is assured by the sucking reflex. Most newborns, however, lose a small amount of weight during the first few days of life. This is due in part to the excretion of the substance that was filling their bowels, called *meconium,* which is composed of amniotic fluid, mucous, and bits of skin and hair that were shed prenatally and ingested.

A second cause of weight loss for breast-fed infants is the excretion by the mother's breasts of colostrum (refer to Chapter 4) for several days before milk production begins in earnest. Colostrum helps to clear the meconium and has some ability to immunize the baby against bacterial infections.

Newborns and small infants have difficulty with temperature regulation. In general, babies should be dressed with the same number of layers worn by the adults around them, and they need to be exposed to both heat and cold to help them develop their ability to regulate their own body temperature, beginning at about one month of age.

Perceptual Abilities of the Newborn

Another aspect of adjustment to the new environment is the newborn's ability to perceive and react to various forms of stimulation. Newborns can see, hear, taste, smell, and feel, but their abilities in each of these areas are somewhat limited.

Vision.   Because of a relative immaturity of the nerve cells in the retina and in the optic nerve, a newborn's vision is somewhat blurry—about 20/400, improving to about 20/50 by six months. Excellent visual acuity is about 20/20, which babies reach at about eight months (Salapatek & Banks, 1978).

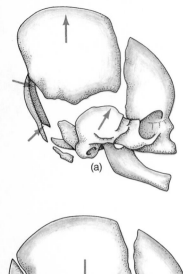
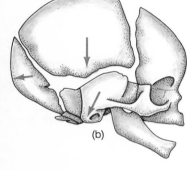

Figure 5–3

Skull of a Newborn

(a) Molding of the bones of the baby's head during passage through the birth canal. (b) By the third day of life the bones return to their normal position.

Newborns can move their heads and eyes in response to visual stimulation. They can follow the path of a moving object, provided it does not move too quickly, and they can adjust their focus to some extent according to the distance to the visual object. Newborns can adjust the openings of their pupils to regulate light intensity (pupillary reflex), but this too is somewhat slow (Kessen, Haith, & Salapatek, 1970; Salapatek & Banks, 1978).

Researchers have also been interested in whether a newborn can recognize particular shapes, such as its own mother's face. There are two ways of determining whether a baby can recognize a familiar person's face or whether the baby can tell the difference between two different expressions of the same face: visual preference and habituation.

In the *visual preference* procedure, an infant is given the opportunity to look both at the mother's face and at the face of an unfamiliar person. If the baby looks consistently longer at one or the other, it is concluded that the baby can tell the difference between the two. In the *habituation* procedure, a baby is shown, for example, slides of its mother's face repeatedly until it begins to look less and less at the same slide. The decrease in looking, or *fixation* time, to repeated presentations of the same stimulus is called habituation.

Once the baby has been habituated to the picture of the mother, the researcher shows the baby a slide of a different person. If there is no change in fixation time between the last presentation of the mother's picture and the presentation of the stranger, it is concluded that the baby probably did not notice the difference. If the baby looks at the stranger's picture longer, this *recovery* of visual fixation time indicates that the baby can recognize a difference between the two photos. Conversely the baby may be habituated to the stranger's picture, while the researchers look for recovery to the mother's picture.

In one study (Field, Cohen, Garcia, & Greenberg, 1984), newborn babies sat in an infant seat in front of a small window. An adult—either the mother of the baby or an unfamiliar woman—would open the window and look at the baby. Using a habituation procedure babies distinguished the mother from the stranger. Since this study used live adults, and the adult came very close to the babies (a newborn's visual acuity is rather poor), we can't rule out the possibility that the babies were using the mother's smell rather than vision to detect the difference.

This kind of research with small infants is very difficult. The babies should be in an alert and nonfussy state, which happens seldom at this age. Giving the baby a pacifier may calm a baby down, but sucking may alter the infant's visual and auditory information processing (Acredelo & Hake, 1982). Since only a small proportion of babies can maintain their attention during the entire experiment, this has led to the question: Can the results of studies from this select subgroup be generalized to the entire population of infants?

Audition. Since sound can penetrate the fetus's prenatal environment more readily than light can, many people believe that hearing is the newborn's primary channel of sensory perception. In addition, the bones of the middle ear are adult size at birth, and the auditory nerve between the ear and the brain is more mature at birth than the optic nerve (Eilers & Gavin, 1981). Newborns can turn their heads in the direction of a sound source, but like visual following, the head-turning response is rather slow and inaccurate. It is easier to get the baby to turn to a continuous sound than to an intermittent one (Muir & Field, 1979).

Newborns prefer sounds in the frequency range of an adult's voice, and they are most attracted to higher pitched sounds in that range (Kessen et al., 1970). When adults talk to babies, they have a tendency to raise the pitch of their voices, perhaps because they notice that the baby is more sensitive to the higher pitches, and the naturally higher pitch of a female's voice may give women a slight advantage in attracting the newborn's attention, at least as far as the use of the voice is concerned.

Odor. Smells such as those produced by vinegar, licorice, and alcohol are greeted by newborns with facial expressions resembling disgust and by turning away from the bad smell (Lipsitt, Engen, & Kaye, 1963). Breast-fed, but not bottle-fed, newborns can tell their mother's milk odor from that of another mother (MacFarlane, 1975; Russell, 1976). Breast-fed babies can also recognize their own mother's underarm odor compared to other women, although newborns do not recognize their father's odor (Cernoch & Porter, 1985). This is probably due to the close skin contact between mothers and breast-fed babies. Mothers, by the way, are quite good at recognizing their own baby by smell alone (Porter, Cernoch & McLaughlin, 1983).

Taste. At birth, babies can tell the difference between some kinds of tastes, but like their other senses, taste is not as sensitive as it will become later. Using an automatic "suck recorder" (see FOCUS ON ISSUE), it has been found that newborns will suck faster and will hold liquid in their mouth longer if the liquid is sweetened, although if the liquid is overly sweet, they will reject it. The most preferred concentrations of sugar in water are about the same for newborns as they are for adults (Crook, 1978; Crook & Lipsitt, 1976).

Newborns will make facial expressions that are consistent with what they are tasting. In response to a sweet taste, they roll the tongue and close the mouth (as if savoring the taste). In response to a bitter taste, newborns will turn their mouth corners down, wrinkle the nose, and purse the lips (Ganchrow, Steiner, & Daher, 1983).

Some evidence exists that newborns as well as older infants use their mouths also as a primary means of exploring the environment. In one study, newborns were given a series of nipples of different shapes. After each new nipple was put in the infant's mouth, the regular pattern of rhythmic sucking was disrupted. On the new nipple, infants sucked with irregular movements of the lips and tongue, as if exploring the novel shape of the nipple (Rochat, 1983). For newborns, it appears that oral stimulation relates as much to the sensation of touch as it does to the sensation of taste.

Touch. Touch is perhaps the newborn's most sensitive and most important sense. The sense of touch includes responses to heat and cold, pressure and pain. Touch can arouse a baby if it is calm and quiet a baby who is upset. Touch can trigger a host of automatic responses, called *reflexes,* that help the newborn to adjust to its environment.

In summary, newborns can perceive variations within each of the five senses. They can see, hear, taste, smell, and feel. In each case, however, the sensory systems have not fully matured. It takes several months or years before the senses become as sharp as those of an adult.

Can Newborns Recognize Their Mother's Voice?

Parents want to know when the baby can recognize them as different from other people. Since newborns can't describe their own perceptions, researchers have to be creative in designing methods to study them. The sucking response has been used in many studies of newborn perception.

A study by DeCasper and Fifer (1980) used newborn sucking to investigate the newborn's ability to recognize the voice of the mother over the voice of another female adult. Each adult was asked to read a segment from a Dr. Seuss story into a tape recorder. The infants listened to the recorded voices through a pair of headphones.

The newborn's response to the voices was measured using an automatic "suck recorder," a pacifier specially designed to convert the infant's squeezing of the nipple during sucking into electrical impulses that can be recorded on a graph. After the baby was comfortably settled in a soundproof room, sucking was recorded for five minutes, with no sound coming through the headphones. During this *baseline* response period, the experimenters calculated the median duration of the pauses between sucks.

During the next 20 minutes, the recorded voices of either the mother or the unfamiliar female were presented under the following conditions. If the baby sucked slowly (the pauses between sucks became longer than the median pause length), the recording of the mother's voice was played to the baby. If the baby sucked more rapidly (the pauses between sucks became shorter than the median pause length), the experimenters played the recorded voice of the unfamiliar female adult. At first, each baby was not aware of the relationship between their sucking and the voices they heard. Gradually, however, the babies began to suck more slowly to hear their mother's voice more often. This means that the babies could hear the difference and that they were capable of changing their behavior to select one voice over the other.

After five babies were studied in this way, another five were observed, only this time they had to suck faster to get the mother's voice and slower for the unfamiliar voice. In this study, eight of the ten infants were able to shift their pause duration in favor of hearing the mother's voice during the 20-minute test period.

One day later, four of the infants were retested so that the criterion for obtaining the mother's voice was reversed from the one they had the previous day (if on day one they had to slow down, on day two they had to speed up to hear the mother). All of the babies continued to suck in favor of hearing their own mother.

A second group of 16 infants was studied in a slightly different way. An audible tone was played in the background over the earphones. Half of the newborns were presented with their mother's voice if they sucked when the tone was heard, while half were presented with the mother's voice if they heard no tone. Again these newborns preferred to suck for the mother's voice.

The study shows that newborns can use sound for recognition. One of the most salient sounds the fetus hears is not the mother's voice, but her heartbeat. Using the same conditioned sucking method, it was found that newborns would change their sucking rate in the "correct" direction to hear a heartbeat sound (DeCasper & Sigafoos, 1983). This does not prove, however, that the babies recognized the heartbeat of their own mother.

In a more recent study, the same group of researchers (Panneton & DeCasper, 1986) asked pregnant women to sing the melody of "Mary Had a Little Lamb" two weeks before their due dates. After birth, the babies' preferences for "Mary Had a Little Lamb" over the song "Love Somebody" were tested using the conditioned sucking procedure. Not only could the newborns tell the difference between the two melodies, but they also preferred the song they had heard prenatally.

Newborn Behavior

Newborns arrive with a complex set of behavior patterns designed to set the stage, not only for basic survival but also for future cognitive, emotional, and social developments to which each human infant is heir.

Newborn behavior is classified into two phases: sleeping and waking. Each of these phases can be further subdivided according to the kinds of behavior patterns that can be seen (see Figure 5–4). These subpatterns, called *states of arousal,* are described in Table 5–4. Specific kinds of actions, such as feeding or following the movement or a sound or a visual object, can occur only in certain states of arousal but not in others. Newborn behavior is therefore said to be *state dependent.*

Following a moving object with the eyes occurs only during the awake states, but not during crying. Because muscular activity can compete with external stimulation for the infant's attention, an infant is more likely to follow a sight or a sound in the alert inactivity state than in the waking activity state. As infants gain better control over their attentional processes with age, attention becomes less state dependent and may even persist during crying.

In three-month-old infants, smiling occurs during waking states, but in the newborn, smiling occurs only during drowsy sleep states. Newborn smiles are tied to fluctuations in internal arousal levels that are seen only when other activity is absent. Such smiles are not related to gas, but we do not know whether or not they are associated with feelings of pleasure (Sroufe & Waters, 1976).

During sleep, newborns tend to startle more often (Huntington, Zeskind, & Weiseman, 1985). Startles seem to represent a spontaneous discharge of neural energy that occurs when the baby relaxes during sleep.

The Effect of the Environment on Newborn Behavior

Increasing Infant's Arousal.   Stimulation from the environment can make infants more alert and active. In one study, infants were given extra stimulation

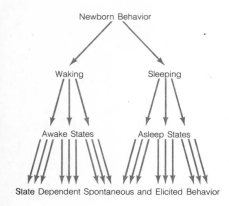

Figure 5–4

Newborns smile, but only during a drowsy sleep state. They can attend to visual and auditory stimulation, but their attention span is longer during the state of alert inactivity. We can expect to see different kinds of behavior, depending upon the infant's state of arousal, and upon whether the infant is in a sleep or waking state.

Table 5–4

NEWBORN STATES OF AROUSAL

State Name	Description
Regular sleep	Respiration is regular, eyes are closed and not moving, and the baby is relatively motionless.
Irregular sleep	Muscles are more tense than in regular sleep, the eyes may be still or move in jerky pattens called *rapid eye movements* (REMs), and breathing is irregular.
Periodic sleep	Spontaneous movements occur in rhythmic bursts, with periods of relative quiet between them—a combination of regular and irregular sleep.
Drowsiness	Opening and closing of the eyes, increased activity, more rapid and regular breathing, occasional smiling.
Alert inactivity	Eyes are open and the environment is being scanned; the body is still, but respiration is more rapid than in sleep.
Waking activity	Awake with body and limb movements, although infants are less likely to attend to external stimulation and focus their eyes less often than in alert inactivity.
Crying	Elevated activity and respiration rate, plus cry vocalization (newborns cry without tears).

by being rocked, held, and talked to more than a matched sample of control infants who received the usual amount of stimulation. The infants who were stimulated more were more visually attentive (White & Castle, 1964). This research failed, however, to determine which form of stimulation was the most important for increasing visual alertness. For example, the tactile stimulation derived from body contact with adults may be the principal cause of increased alertness. A second possibility is that changes in the infant's posture and body position during handling could cause the increase in alertness. It could be that babies who are lying down are more likely to fall asleep than babies who are upright or partially reclining. A final possibility is that the movement of the baby's body—called *vestibular-proprioceptive* stimulation—is the main cause of increased alertness.

Later research has shown that body contact does not contribute to alertness, although the second two factors do. For example, being held upright increases alertness (Frederickson & Brown, 1975; Gregg, Haffner, & Korner, 1976), and infants who are moved while being held become more alert than those who are merely held without being moved (Korner & Thoman, 1970). If you want to get a drowsy baby into an alert state, the best way is to hold the baby upright against your shoulder and bounce the baby up and down gently while walking slowly around the room.

Decreasing Infant's Arousal.   When a newborn is crying, it is rather helpless to stop itself. Many techniques have been devised by caregivers to assist an infant in calming itself down, such as feeding, swaddling, rocking, and singing to the baby. Do these methods have any effect?

In one study, infants were rocked at varying speeds and in varying positions. All forms of rocking seemed to help in calming the babies, but one kind worked better than any other. Infants were calmed the best when they were held upright and rocked intermittently by gentle bouncing rather than by continuous rocking. Another common method of rocking is to hold the baby in a reclining position and rock continuously. With this kind of rocking, babies not only calmed down but also went to sleep (Byrne & Horowitz, 1979).

What about singing? We mentioned before that high-pitched sounds increased a baby's attention. Research has shown, however, as you might expect, that low-pitched sounds are better for calming (Friedman & Jacobs, 1981; Hazelwood, 1977). Adult humming just so happens to be pitched at the level most appropriate to calming a newborn. In addition, if sounds are relatively loud (loud versus soft singing), and if the sound is continuous rather than intermittent, they increase the effectiveness of the sound for calming (Brackbill, 1970, 1975).

These findings represent general trends. For any individual baby, the caregiver may need some weeks or months to find just the right style of rocking, holding, singing, and humming that is most effective in calming the baby. In this sense, the results of research can only give some suggestions about what *might* work with a particular infant.

Reflexes

A *reflex* is a behavior that is started only by a specific kind of stimulation, such as stroking the infant's cheek or touching the palms. A reflexive behavior looks about the same each time it is started, and once the infant is exposed to the specific condition that starts the reflex action, the action must continue its course until the entire movement is executed. This means that an individual

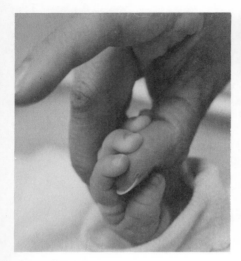
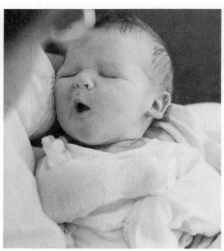
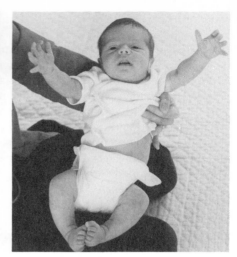

The grasp reflex; The rooting reflex; The Moro reflex.

who responds to something in a reflexive manner has no voluntary control over the starting and stopping of the behavior.

Table 5–5 lists the most common and most easily seen reflexes of newborn infants. Each infant will show a slightly different form of the same reflex behavior, and individual differences will exist in the degree of movement, the strength of the movement, and the kind of stimulation necessary to start the reflex. To take the *rooting* reflex as an example, some babies turn their heads by simply being touched on their cheek near the mouth, while others require gentle stroking of the cheek. Some babies turn their heads only part way, while others turn almost 90 degrees to the side and open their mouths, as if to anticipate the insertion of a nipple (Kessen et al., 1970).

A wide range of variation is considered normal. A noted lack of many reflexes or a lack of reflex responses on one side of the body can be evidence of brain or neurological disorders. Since most reflexes weaken and disappear after several months, persistence of neonatal reflexes beyond that time can be a diagnostic indicator of neurological malfunction. Some reflexes such as the blink response, are important protective mechanisms and remain throughout one's lifetime.

The Newborn Cry

Although crying may seem to be the main activity of newborns, infants cry, on the average, only about seven percent of the time. Even the fussiest baby cries only 22 percent of the time (Korner, Kraemer, Haffner, & Thoman, 1974). This can be wearing on a parent, however, since this figure means that the baby is crying well over half the time that it is awake.

Newborns have different types of crying patterns, which a parent can learn to recognize rather easily. When a baby is hungry or sleepy, the cry is a rather rhythmical alternation between sound and silence. When the baby has received a painful stimulus, the cry is less rhythmical. There is a long wail, followed by a long pause, then several short cries and pauses, followed by another long wail. Because the long silence gives the listener the feeling that the baby has stopped breathing, the sound of the pain cry creates a greater sense of urgency in the adult to respond to the baby (Wolff, 1966).

Table 5–5

NEWBORN REFLEXES

Body Part	Name	Description
Head and face	Head turning	Place baby face down on a mattress. Baby will turn head to side to free breathing passages.
	Rooting	Stroke baby's cheek gently near the mouth. Baby will turn head to the side that is being stroked.
	Sucking	Place a nipple-sized object in baby's mouth. Baby will start sucking movements.
	Defensive reaction	Cover the baby's nose and mouth with a cloth. Baby will turn head and move arms in an attempt to free breathing passages.
Arms	Tonic neck reflex	Turn the baby's head to one side or the other. The baby's arm will extend in the direction in which the head is turned, and the other arm will flex upward. This is also called the fencer's reflex.
	Moro reflex	Drop the baby's head slightly but abruptly. The baby's arms and legs will spread open and make an embracing movement, as if to grasp hold of something. This is a kind of startle reaction.
Hands	Palmer reflex	Lightly touch the baby's palm, and the fingers will clamp into a fist.
Torso	Swimmer's reflex	While baby is lying on its stomach, gently tap the back along the side and above the waist. The baby will twist its lower extremities toward the side that was touched.
	Crawling	Push against the soles of the baby's feet while the baby is lying on the stomach, and rudimentary crawling movements will result.
Legs	Standing reflex	Hold the baby gently under the arms while the feet touch a table. As you release support slowly, the baby will begin to show some resistance to the weight by stretching the muscles of the legs.
	Walking reflex	Hold the baby under the arms with the baby's feet touching a table and move the baby forward, keeping contact between table and feet. The baby will take "steps".
Feet	Plantar reflex	Similar to the palmer reflex. The toes will curl inward when the instep is lightly touched.
	Babinski reflex	Gently stroke the outer side of the bottom of the baby's foot. The toes will curl outward like a fan.

Research on adult responses to these different cries shows that adults can easily tell the differences. Furthermore, adults perceived the early phases of the pain cry (the long wail and pause) as more urgent than the later phases. On the other hand, the later phases of the hunger cry created a greater sense of urgency (Zeskind, Sale, Maio, Huntington, & Weiseman, 1985).

If it is true that the sound of the cry reflects something about the infant's immediate experiences, could it also be true that the cry sound might reflect a more serious underlying disorder? Some research has shown that minor birth complications and abnormalities could affect the sound of the cry. When a rubber band was gently snapped on their heels, infants born with more complications required harder snapping to begin the cry, had a shorter first cry sound, cried less overall, and cried with a higher pitch than did infants born with few complications (Zeskind & Lester, 1978; 1981). Many of these babies, however, gradually improved their condition over the weeks and months following birth, and their cries began to sound more normal. Thus, although an abnormal cry indicates the baby has a disorder, the disorder may be temporary.

Individual Differences in Newborn Behavior

One of the most fundamental questions that people ask is: How did I get this way? or What made me the way I am now? At least one part of the explanation of individual differences in human development may be that inborn personality traits are present at birth that continue to shape our responses to the environment throughout our lives.

Sex Differences at Birth

As we shall see in later chapters, one of the important debates today is whether observed sex differences in behavior in older children and adults are the result of inherited sex differences (nature) or the result of differences in education and opportunity offered to members of each sex (nurture). Studies of sex differences in newborn behavior have been used to investigate this issue.

In North American hospitals, where most of the research has been done, male infants are routinely circumcised on the second or third day after birth. This additional stress may cause transient behavior changes in males, making newborn sex difference studies invalid (Marshall, Stratton, Moore, & Boxerman, 1980). A second problem is that many of the observers in neonatal sex difference research were aware of the sex of the newborns before and during their observations. If we wish to study the human being before behavior becomes sex stereotyped, we must try to remove the observer's own sex biases from the outcomes of the research study.

Only a small number of studies exist in which newborns were observed before circumcision (or studies using uncircumcised males) and in which the observers were "blind" to the newborn's sex. These studies have shown that females tend to be more oral, that is, they show more smiling and mouth moving and are more likely to prefer sweet fluids than males. Males, on the other hand, are longer and heavier than females, are more likely to demonstrate more gross motor movement, are fussier and have a stronger grip strength than females. No consistent sex differences have been found in tactile sensitivity, sleeping and waking patterns, or feeding behavior (Feldman, Brody, & Miller 1980; Jacklin, Snow, & Maccoby, 1981; Korner, 1969; Osofsky & O'Connell, 1977; Phillips, King, & DuBois, 1978).

What do these results mean with regard to the roles of nature and nurture in sex differences? We know, for example, that during the birth process, maternal sex hormones are secreted in large amounts and partially absorbed by the infants. These sex hormones are likely to affect males and females differently. In addition, as we saw in Chapter 4, even prenatal sex differentiation is not completely determined by the genes but is a complex interaction between the fetus and the environment of the placenta. Thus, sex differences at birth may not reflect genetically controlled differences between the sexes but are the temporary result of the interaction between the individual and the environment.

Chapter 6 discusses in detail the lasting individual differences between infants. For now, however, it can be said that research has revealed few persistent individual differences. In more technical language, there is little *correlation* of behavior (refer to Chapter 3) between the newborn and the baby during later periods (Sameroff, 1978).

Some newborn assessment procedures are listed in Table 5–6. Although these procedures are valuable for diagnosing perinatal problems that may lead to conditions of risk, they are not very good at predicting long-term developmental progress. The tests are divided into three groups: screening, neurological, and behavioral. *Screening* assessments give an indication of the newborn's ability to survive. *Neurological* assessments test for problems in the newborn's central nervous system, such as major brain or spinal cord damage. *Behavioral* assessments look for the newborn's perceptual capacities and the time spent in each state.

In one of the more commonly used assessment procedures, the strength of the baby's reflexes is tested as well as the baby's ability to turn to light and sound stimulation, the relative amount of time the baby spends in different states, and the relative ease of transition from one state to the next (Self & Horowitz, 1979). It is the baby's scores on such items that are not stable (Isabella, Ward, & Belsky, 1985; Sameroff, 1978).

Recently, however, other kinds of newborn measures have shown a greater ability to predict later behavior. Newborn heart rate is one such measure. Newborns who have a highly rhythmic, regular heart rate have more positive developmental outcomes at 8 and 12 months (Fox & Porges, 1985). Activity level of newborns, measured by an automatic activity level monitor, is correlated with the same children's activity level as measured by an *actometer* (see Chapters 3 and 8) during the preschool period. The most active, vigorous neonates were also rated by their mothers as more likely to approach, rather than withdraw from, novel experiences during the preschool years (Korner et al., 1985).

Many parents firmly believe that their baby has a distinct personality. When mothers are asked to rate their babies' typical patterns of behavior and

Table 5–6

NEWBORN ASSESSMENT TESTS

Type of Test	Name of Test	Description of Test
Screening	Apgar	Heart rate, respiration, and other vital signs.
Neurological	Dubowitz Assessment of Gestational Age	Differentiation of small-for-dates, from appropriate weight for gestational age.
	Neurological Examination of Prechtl and Beintema	Test of reflexes, posture, and motor development.
Behavioral	Graham-Rosenblith Tests	Responses to physical objects, strength of grasp, and response to covering the nose and mouth.
	Brazelton Neonatal Assessment	Reflexes, responses to social and physical stimuli, response to covering nose and mouth, time spent in different states, and number of changes between states.

temperature, they report considerable stability over time (see Chapter 6). It could be that developmental scientists have not been very successful in designing an assessment procedure that captures the true essence of the infant's personality in the newborn period. It may also be that parents infer a persistence and a sameness to their infant's behavior that is not really present. The next section of this chapter looks at parental behavior and thought during the newborn period.

First Social Relationships

The fetus is able to survive and grow during the prenatal period because of its physiological tie to the mother. In the case of the newborn, that original biological link is no longer present. To ensure the continued survival of the infant, the human species has evolved a *behavioral system* of mutual interaction (refer to Chapter 2) by which the infant's needs are matched by the parents' ability to meet those needs.

As we mentioned in the discussion on crying, the infant's sounds have a predictable effect on any adult who hears them. In the same way, the sight of a newborn triggers protective responses in adults (Alley, 1983; Fullard & Reiling, 1976). Babies have physical characteristics that distinguish them from older individuals, and these characteristics are thought to make babies attractive to adults. A baby's limbs are shorter and heavier in proportion to their trunks than an adult's are. A baby's head is larger in relation to its body, and its forehead is more prominent. Compared with the rest of the face, a baby's eyes are larger and its cheeks are more rounded than in an adult. A baby usually has softer skin (or fur), and its sounds are higher pitched than those of older children or adults (Hess, 1970; Hildebrandt, 1979). These characteristics are referred to as *babyishness* (see Figure 5–5).

Effects of Newborns on Parents

In other mammal species, parents must learn about infant care on the job. In the course of millions of years of evolution, these species have developed certain behavioral signals to guide the early protection of the young soon after birth. For example, after her kittens are born, a mother cat will lie on her side to make her nipples available to them. Since the kittens are blind at birth, they establish an orientation to the mother's body by the mother's licking them. With this initial direction giving, the kittens have reflexes that make them open their mouths and search for a nipple upon contact with the mother's fur. The mother performs in such a way as to guide the kittens' searching-sucking behavior, and the kittens provide stimulation, such as their appearance, smell, and sound, that initiates the mother's responses toward them (Rosenblatt, 1972), thus creating a continuing behavioral system of interaction.

Humans have similar behavioral control mechanisms. For example, when human mothers nurse their newborns, the sight and sound of the infant orient the mother to provide nourishment. As the mother holds the infant and stimulates the baby's mouth region, the rooting reflex is activated (this is similar to the searching movements of the kittens). This reflex stimulates the mother to adjust the position of the nipple so that the infant will find it quickly. Once the nipple is in the infant's mouth, sucking movements begin. The action of the sucking then stimulates the *let down* response, with which the milk can be released from the breast. Sucking also stimulates the production of maternal

Figure 5–5

Babyishness Characteristics

In most species of animals, babies have larger heads and eyes and more rounded features than adults. These babyish characteristics are attractive to older children and adults, and they elicit protective responses.

The decision to breast feed or to bottle feed is best made on the basis of personal preferences. Aside from the heightened immunological properties of colostrum and breast milk over formula, few differences have been found in the physical, social or psychological development of infants fed by breast vs. bottle. A consistent and warm parent-child relationship is more important to infant development than the method of feeding.

hormones that produce more milk and encourage the contraction of the uterine muscles, necessary to prevent further bleeding after the birth (Cairns, 1979).

Because of our intelligence, language, and culture, we can override the biological signals if we see problems occurring, and we can look for alternative expressions of the infant's needs and goals if the ones we expect to see do not turn up. For example, even if a mother does not breast-feed, many of the same processes can still operate. The orientation of the mother and newborn to each other and the adjustments made by the mother according to the infant's on-going behavior would be the same. If the baby is bottle-fed, the stimulation of final contractions of the uterus as well as a rapid reduction of milk production is usually achieved by artificial doses of female hormones given to the new mother.

Is It Better to Breast-Feed or to Bottle-Feed a Newborn?

Currently in the United States, over half of all mothers breast-feed their babies. These mothers are mostly well-educated and middle-income. It was not always this way. In 1966, only 18 percent of mothers were breast-feeding, and in 1900, virtually all mothers breast-fed their babies (Guthrie, 1979). This kind of historical trend may have to do with what is fashionable and acceptable as childcare practice within a particular culture, since virtually all women can produce sufficient milk for their babies, regardless of breast size. The most important factor in breast-feeding success is the desire of the mother to do it (Guthrie, 1979). In many cases, sucking stimulation alone is all that is needed to start milk production, as evidenced by the ability of some women to nurse their adoptive infants (Hormann, 1977).

One of the main arguments in favor of breast-feeding is that the composition of breast milk, like the behavioral responses of the mother to the newborn or the biological adaptations of the placenta during pregnancy, is uniquely suited to the needs of the newborn. Cow's milk is higher in fat and protein and lower in lactose and carbohydrate than human milk. Cow's milk must be artificially altered to resemble the composition of human milk, since the human newborn cannot digest the complex fats and proteins that are suitable to the newborn calf. To that extent, humans can override nature in favor of bottle feeding.

On the other hand, human mothers produce a special substance called *colostrum* during the first few days after birth. This yellowish, clear liquid has been shown to retard the growth of certain kinds of bacteria and may serve as a powerful disease preventive and immunological agent for the newborn (Guthrie, 1979; Robinson, 1978). It is not known what long-term effects can occur if a baby does not receive colostrum, although there seem to be no long-term differences in the health of adults who were bottle-fed versus those who were breast-fed.

In general, research, both psychological and medical, has failed to turn up any strong negative effects of bottle feeding, so long as the proper formula is used and care is taken to properly sterilize the bottle, milk, and nipple. Bottle feeding of infants in underdeveloped countries has serious negative consequences, since mothers may add contaminated water sources to the formula milk and may not have the resources to sterilize the bottles and nipples. Companies that manufacture baby milk formulas have recently been criticized for unethically promoting the use of bottle feeding in areas of the world where this kind of health problem can occur.

Fathers and Newborn Infants

One of the advantages of bottle feeding is that someone other than the mother can feed the baby.

One research study used the bottle feeding of newborns by their fathers to see whether mothers were more sensitive than fathers to their babies. By observing how the fathers held and fed and talked to the babies, it was found that fathers were at least as active as mothers and sometimes showed even more social and affectionate behavior to the babies than did the mothers (Sawin and Parke, 1979). When lying next to their naked newborn, fathers touched the baby's fingers, toes, and limbs and then touched or rubbed the baby's trunk. This pattern of behavior seen on first contact with a newborn infant is just the same in fathers as it is in mothers (McDonald, 1978; Rodholm & Larsson, 1978).

If mothers and fathers seem equally sensitive to their newborns, you might wonder how new parents divide the time spent in childcare. In the vast majority of cases around the world, women are the primary caregivers of young infants. In North America, however, an increase in father involvement has taken place. Recent research has found that middle-class Caucasian-American fathers spend an average of three hours each day in childcare and play with their two-year-old infants (Easterbrooks & Goldberg, 1984).

Research shows that fathers often have the desire to share in the experience of parenting, but they need support from their wives and family to do this. Men who adjusted better to parenthood and spent more time in childcare tasks were found to have more knowledge about children and to have better relationships with their wives (Fein, 1976; Feldman & Nash, 1986; Wente & Crockenberg, 1976).

The effect of the wife on the husband's participation in childcare reflects the importance of the family as a system in which each member can support and influence the behavior of other members and their relationships to each other. A woman can influence the quality of the father-infant relationship, even if she does not directly participate in that relationship.

The same effect happens in the other direction. Mothers are more affectionate and interested in the newborn when fathers are directly involved in infant care (Sawin & Parke, 1979). It could be, however, that mothers who are the most affectionate and interested in their babies could also be the most adept at encouraging their husbands to participate in childrearing. Such mothers may have selected husbands who were already more affectionate. In any case, it is clear that the family operates as a system in the support of the developing newborn and infant.

In families with parents and a newborn, the relationships are somewhat unbalanced. Even though the parents have some ideas about their relationship to the infant as well as to each other, the newborn has no such conceptions. The view that newborns have a special sense, that they can feel the parents' happiness and tension, has no scientific evidence to support it. Most developmentalists would agree that newborns have no concept of their existence as separate individuals and that they have no awareness of their parents' psychological states. On the other hand, parents have some rather elaborate ideas about their babies, and parents respond to the birth and the transition to parenthood as both a physical and psychological experience.

The Experience of Being a New Parent

The transition to parenthood represents an important developmental change in the life of most adults. Chapter 7 discusses this change in detail. Here we will review one study that examined the mother's immediate responses to pregnancy and childbirth.

Because of the major impact on the life of an adult of giving birth, major psychological adjustments can be expected in the weeks before and in the weeks and months after the event. In one study, women were asked to report their feelings during pregnancy, labor, and the hospital stay as well as after returning home with their new babies. Two hundred women from Sydney, Australia were the subjects of this research. Most women reported positive feelings at all stages of the process, although anxieties and worries changed over time. Women reported feeling the most anxiety during pregnancy and labor, usually in the form of fears of death and mutilation. These feelings were reduced soon after the baby's birth (Westbrook, 1978).

After birth, women often feel brief episodes of mild depression or sudden episodes of crying without warning. In a sample of 129 women following childbirth, only 16 were severely depressed and only 15 experienced no unusual mood changes. Those who were severely depressed had had an incidence of psychiatric illness before the birth. The rest reported at least a few episodes of crying (Meares, Grimwalde, & Woods, 1976). These episodes have been called *postpartum blues,* and they seem to be relatively harmless and transient effects perhaps due to stress, excitement, and fatigue. In general, after birth, women and their husbands feel rather elated, their high feelings lasting several weeks and months (Murai, Murai, & Takahashi, 1978).

Birth Order Differences in Parent's Responses

Parents usually spend more time taking care of their first-born than they do of their later children (Kilbride, Johnson, & Streissguth, 1977). This could be true for a number of reasons. Mothers giving birth for the first time usually

Bonding: Fact or Myth

Since the rise in popularity of hospital deliveries in the early part of this century, childbirth and the first relations between a baby and a parent have undergone a progressive "medicalization." Recently, however, many families are opting for more natural childbirth, for a return to midwife-attended births unless there is a clear medical emergency, for home births, for early discharge from the hospital, and for a greater involvement with the whole family. Newborns are allowed to stay by their mothers' side for longer periods, and the hospital nursery, in which newborns were isolated from their mothers for observation, is becoming nearly obsolete.

These changes are the result of complaints by families and organized family advocate groups, such as LaLeche League, that wanted a return to more traditional childbirth methods. They argued, correctly, that most births are not medically pathological but are expressions of a normal female body function, which, in most cases, occurs with few complications. A second source of change was research that claimed to show the importance of contact between mother and infant during the first few minutes and hours after birth. Such early contact began to receive increasing scientific attention as being critical for the development of a healthy attachment relationship.

As mentioned earlier, when placed next to their naked newborns, mothers and fathers explore and touch the babies in a systematic manner; this experience has the effect of heightening a parent's initial interest in the baby. Some pediatricians who observed this situation felt that this initial exposure served to bond the parent to the infant and helped to provide the parent with a strong motive to nurture the baby.

These pediatricians exposed a group of lower-income black mothers to early contact with their babies and compared the babies' development with that of the babies of a group of mothers from the same social group who received routine hospital care in which the babies were separated from the mothers immediately after birth for periods of up to 24 hours. There were 28 first-time mothers, half of whom were assigned to one hour of extra contact at birth and another five hours of extra contact while in the hospital. Several months later, these mothers were more likely to maintain eye contact with their babies, and the babies had elevated scores on standardized intelligence tests at five years of age (Klaus, Jerauld, Kreger, McAlpine, Steffa, & Kennell, 1972).

Similar studies of middle-class infants have failed to find clear differences between groups of mothers and babies who received early and extra contact and groups that received routine care (Curry, 1979; Schaller, Carlsson, & Larsson, 1979). For fathers, also, long-term effects of early contact have not been substantiated. It appears that such long-term factors as orientation to the parenting role and the husband-wife relationship are better predictors of caregiving outcome than are early contact (Palkovitz, 1985).

Thus, the effect of giving a mother extra contact with her baby may be more important for mothers who are more at risk—mothers in poverty and under stress—than it is for healthy middle-class parents. The latter group will become attached to their babies even without early contact. Studies show that adopted infants also develop healthy and complete attachments to their parents—and their parents to them—in spite of their missing the early contact in the hospital (Singer et al., 1985).

This is a good example of how a scientific finding can be picked up by the public and used for policy change in spite of flaws in the research. In this case, the ending is a happy one. Even if early contact cannot be demonstrated to be a cure-all to improve parent-child relationships, it may help some mothers at risk. It is also clear that such early contact is emotionally satisfying, one of those thrilling moments in life that seem to transcend the everyday and make the sacrifices of parenthood seem worthwhile. We don't need a scientific study to see the importance of this kind of experience, and such experiences do not need lasting impact in order to justify them.

receive more obstetrical pain-relieving medication, leading to a more drugged and sluggish infant. Such a baby requires more time to feed and to get alert than does a baby who was born with less medication (Brown, Bakeman, Snyder, Frederickson, Morgan, & Hepler, 1975).

Other research has found that mothers of first-borns spend more time in shifting the infant's posture, talking to the infant, and stimulating the infant, while the first-born infants did less actual sucking during feeding sessions. By the end of the first week, however, no differences existed between first-time and later-time mothers. This could be explained either by a relative lack of skill in primiparous mothers or by a relatively more unresponsive first-born (Thoman, Leiderman, & Olson, 1972).

Sex of Infant and Parent's Response

In many cultures, male newborns are preferred over females. Males may be considered more valuable members of society or heirs to the family name. Young couples in North America today are likely to disavow any overt desire for one sex over another. In this age of relative equality between the sexes, modern parents-to-be generally respond to the question, "Do you want a boy or a girl?" with a few reasons why one or the other sex might be preferred, but usually end up by saying, "It really doesn't matter, as long as the baby is healthy."

Research studies, however, have found differences in parental behavior and attitudes toward each sex. In one study, males tended to be rubbed, touched, rocked, and kissed more than females (Brown et al., 1975) while female newborns were smiled at and talked to more (Thoman et al., 1972). In a study done in lower-middle-class suburban Boston, parents were asked to describe their newborn infants. Female newborns were more likely to be rated as little, cute, pretty, and resembling the mothers, while males were rated as larger, stronger, firmer, and more alert than females. These differences in ratings were found for both mothers and fathers, although fathers tended to emphasize the differences a bit more (Rubin et al., 1974).

As previously noted, relatively few behavior differences exist between male and female newborns, and virtually no physical differences exist in the length, weight, or Apgar scores of male and female newborns (Rubin, Provenzano, & Luria, 1974). It seems, therefore, that parental attitudes toward the sexes at birth are more dependent upon existing cultural stereotypes than on actual differences between male and female infants.

Because human development is so strongly shaped by family and cultural influences, our approach in later chapters tends to emphasize this dynamic interactional or systems theory of development. So far, we have seen that both prenatal and newborn behavior and development are not the simple result of nature or nurture but are the result of a continual process of transaction between a changing individual and a changing environment.

Chapter Summary

THE BIRTH PROCESS
☐ The mother's body begins to prepare for birth about one month before the due date.
☐ Labor is divided into three stages: initial contractions and dilation of the cervix, delivery of the baby, and delivery of the placenta.

□ Pain control by chemical means is beneficial but must be used carefully because of potentially harmful effects on the newborn and the mother.

□ The Lamaze method of relaxation and breathing and the upright position have been shown to enhance delivery outcomes. The Leboyer method has not received scientific confirmation.

PERINATAL RISK AND MORTALITY

□ If they are treated, most perinatal complications do not lead to long-term effects.

□ Premature infants have much better chances of survival now than they did even 10 years ago.

□ Infant mortality is primarily due to poor sanitation, poverty, and lack of education about infant care and nutrition.

THE NEWBORN'S APPEARANCE

□ The newborn's appearance is caused by the vestiges of prenatal life and the rigors of the birth process. Most of the features disappear in the first few months of life.

NEWBORN BEHAVIOR

□ The type of behavior displayed by a newborn depends on the current state of arousal.

□ Simple interventions such as holding, rocking, feeding, talking, and singing are highly effective in changing a baby's state of arousal, either making the baby more alert or calming the baby down.

□ Spontaneous behavior and reflex actions make up most of the newborn's repertoire of behavior.

INDIVIDUAL DIFFERENCES IN NEWBORN BEHAVIOR

□ Both sex and birth order differences have been found for newborns. In some cases, however, these differences may be due to differences in parental beliefs and handling of the infant.

□ Few aspects of newborn behavior persist into later years, although a rhythmic heart rate and newborn activity level remain stable over time.

FIRST SOCIAL RELATIONSHIPS

□ Newborns are linked to their parents through complex biological processes as well as social signals that are universally understood.

□ Parents are naturally attracted to the physical features of the infant.

□ Few long-term differences exist between breast-fed and bottle-fed infants.

□ Fathers can develop affectionate ties to their newborns if they invest the time in it.

THE EXPERIENCE OF BEING A NEW PARENT

□ New parents experience some psychological changes, which diminish within a few months.

□ Parents respond differently to their newborns depending on the birth order and sex of the baby.

Recommended Readings

Field, T., & Sostek, A. (1983). *Infants born at risk: Physiological, perceptual, and cognitive processes.* New York: Grune & Stratton. An excellent summary of recent approaches to risks and interventions in infancy.

Karmel, M. (1959). *Painless childbirth: Thank you Dr. Lamaze*. Philadelphia: Lippincott. An introduction to the Lamaze method and its historical background.

Osofsky, J. (1979). *Handbook of infant development*. New York: Wiley. Contains a number of chapters on birth and the newborn period.

Leboyer, F. (1975). *Birth without violence*. New York: Knopf. The original source on the Leboyer method of childbirth.

PART II

Infancy

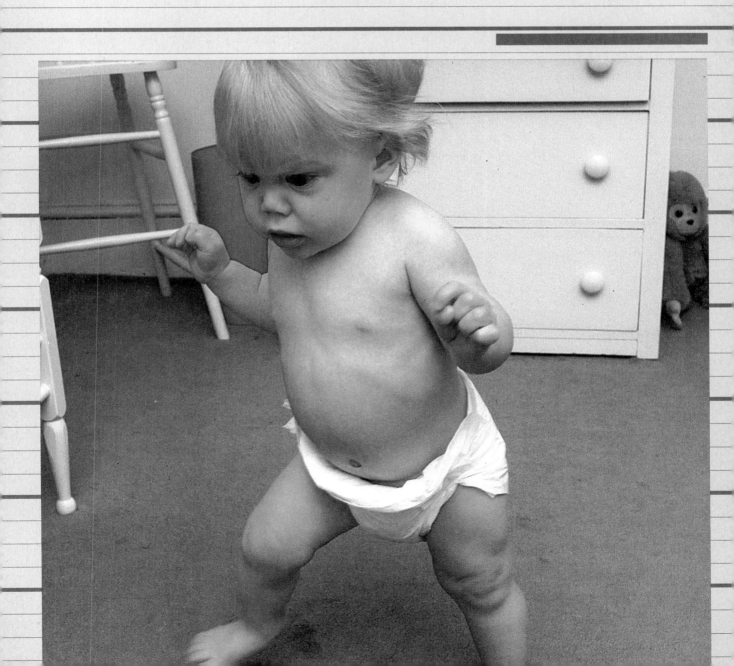

The First Two Years: The Process of Development

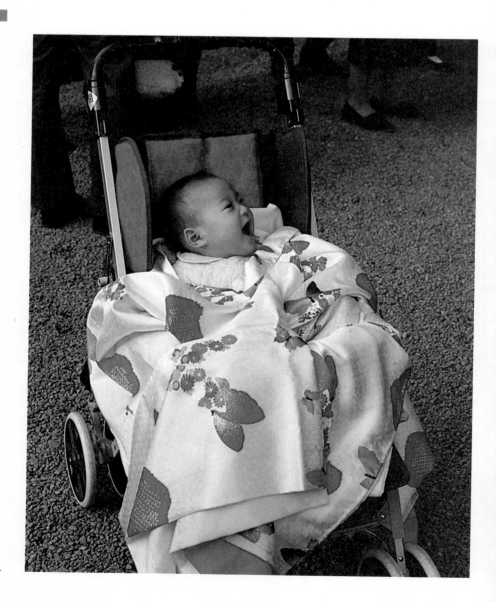

A *fter the surprising delight of birth other pleasures followed in their multitudes. Feeding, smiling, gazing. . . Comfortable holding and carrying; babies fitted so well against one and seemed to like it there so much, how could one not enjoy it oneself? And when they are a few months old, they lie and look around and wave and smile and undergo a constant gentle agitation, as though they were sea anemones, gently waving in some other element, delicately responding to currents we cannot feel.*

> — *Margaret Drabble,*
> *Novelist, 1973**

Infancy is perhaps the most mysterious part of the human life cycle. Unless you have had frequent opportunities to be in the company of infants, you might find it a bit threatening to be asked to pick up, hold, or interact with an infant. This is probably due to several factors. First, we have no memory of our own babyhood; second, babies cannot communicate verbally about their own view of the world; and finally, babies in our culture are kept somewhat isolated from older children and adults outside the family context.

This and the next chapter discuss some of the knowledge we have about babies. This chapter focuses on the basic processes of infant development: physical development, health, perceptual and cognitive development, and emotional and social development. Chapter 7 examines the contexts of the infant's world such as parents, peers, and infant day care.

Physical Development

Changes in Size and Shape

The newborn's head accounts for about one-fourth of the total body length, but by the end of the first two years of life, the toddler has developed proportions more like that of an adult. From an average total length of 50 cm (20 inches) at birth, two-year-olds grow to about 85 cm (34 inches), or about one-half of adult height. At birth, infants vary from 47 to 55 cm, while at two years, height can range from 83 to 94 cm (Eichorn, 1979).

At birth, babies weigh between 2½ and 4½ kg (between 5 and 9 lbs.), and at age two years, between 10½ and 15 kg (21 and 30 lbs.). Because the infant almost quadruples birth weight during the first two years, large quantities of milk must be consumed. It is no wonder that ingesting and excreting this volume of liquid takes up a good deal of the baby's time (Eichorn, 1979).

A baby's length is a good predictor of adult height. At three months, the correlation between length and height at 18 years is .50. The correlation between height at two years and height at 18 years is .70 (Kessen et al., 1970). In addition, the correlation of parental height and the child's height at age two and at age 18 is about .50 (Eichorn, 1979). This kind of regularity is remarkable. As we'll see later, few measures of behavior exist in the infant period that can predict later behavior (Kessen et al., 1970). Nor is infant weight such a good predictor of adult weight.

*"With All My Love, (signed) Mama," by Margaret Drabble, August 4, 1973 (Op-Ed). Copyright © 1973 by The New York Times Company. Reprinted by permission.

Figure 6—1

Development of Gross Motor Skills

The scale markings shown under each of the motor skills indicate the ages at which 25%, 50% and 90% of a normative sample of North American infants are able to perform that skill. Aside from the differences in age when the average infant (50% mark) reaches a particular skill, note that skills differ in the range of ages at which they are attained. Most babies learn to lift their head while prone over a 6 week period. Walking while holding on to furniture, on the other hand, could begin anytime during a 6 month period.

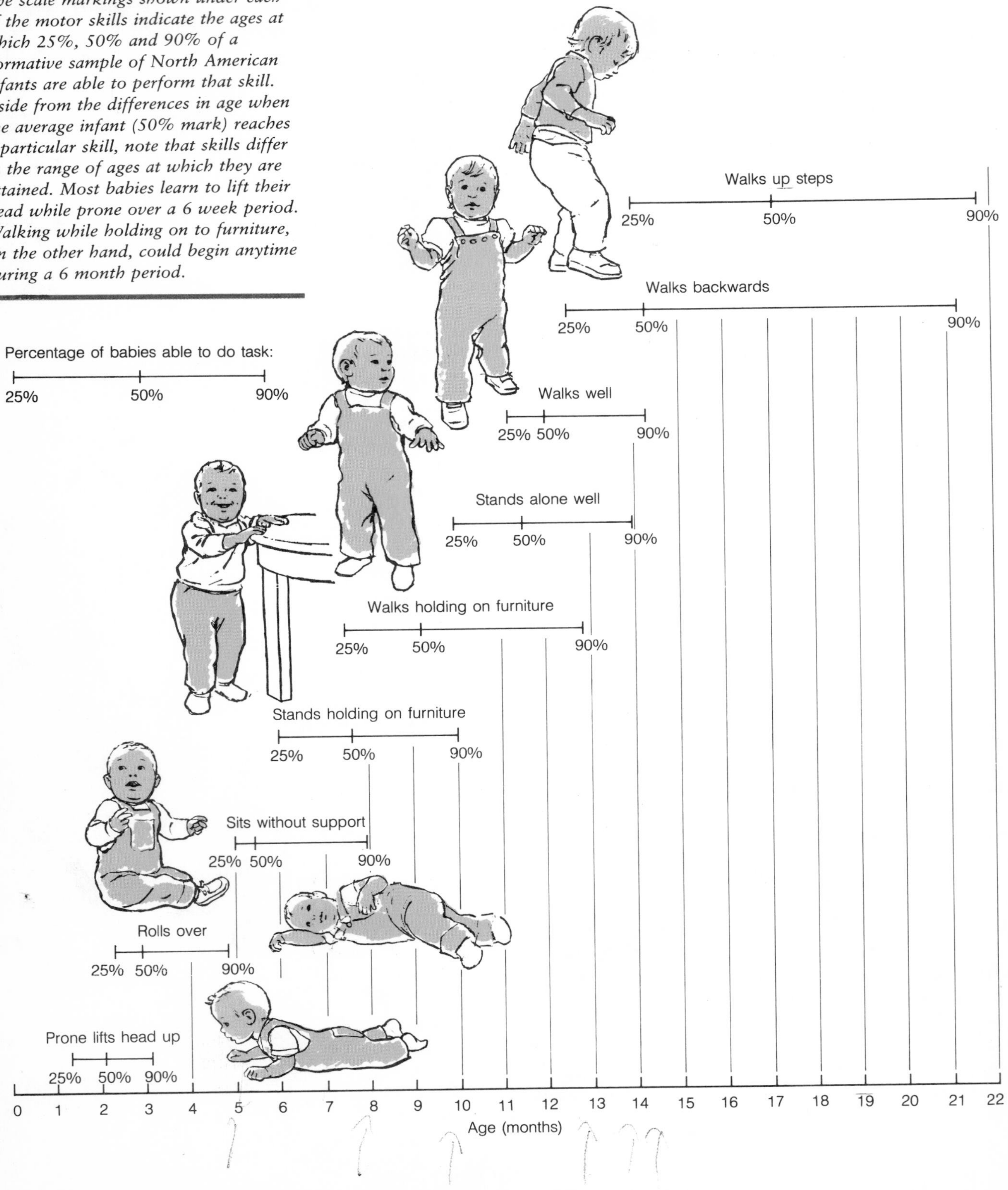

Percentage of babies able to do task:

25%   50%   90%

Walks up steps
25%   50%   90%

Walks backwards
25%   50%   90%

Walks well
25% 50%   90%

Stands alone well
25%   50%   90%

Walks holding on furniture
25%   50%   90%

Stands holding on furniture
25%   50%   90%

Sits without support
25% 50%   90%

Rolls over
25% 50%   90%

Prone lifts head up
25% 50% 90%

0   1   2   3   4   5   6   7   8   9   10   11   12   13   14   15   16   17   18   19   20   21   22

Age (months)

Although the infant's nervous system—the *receptor* organs of touch, taste, smell, hearing, and vision—is relatively mature at birth, the *effector* systems involving the bones and muscles are relatively immature. An infant's muscles are smaller and weaker than an adult's and contain a greater proportion of water. It takes several years for a baby to develop the muscle strength necessary for self support and for fine motor control (Eichorn, 1979).

The relationship between muscle strength and motor control was shown in a study of the developmental changes in the newborn stepping reflex (refer to Chapter 5). Stepping occurs when a baby's feet are allowed to gently touch a horizontal surface while the baby is supported under the arms. This reflex, along with most others, disappears between one and two months of age.

The study's investigators (Thelen, Fisher, & Ridley-Johnson, 1984) tied small weights around the thighs of one-month-olds who could still perform stepping. The amount of weight added was estimated to be the amount gained by each leg between one and two months of age. The weights had the effect of decreasing the stepping response. In another study, somewhat older infants who had already lost the stepping reflex were emersed to torso level in a tank of water (Thelen & Fisher, 1982). The babies began stepping as their feet touched the bottom of the tank.

These studies suggest that muscle strength develops more slowly than the increase in the weight of the legs. It takes almost a year—walking emerges at around 10 to 12 months—for the muscles to develop the strength to hold the baby's body upright and for spontaneous stepping to appear again. Because of the different rates of development of fat and muscle tissue, stepping disappears between two and ten months.

Basic Milestones of Motor Development

During their first two years of life, babies develop a wide variety of skills as they gain control over their muscles, gain in muscle size and strength, and increase their awareness of the world.

Developmentalists have created a wide variety of assessment procedures to document this growth of skill. Some of the more commonly used assessments and the areas they cover are listed in Table 6-1. After many infants have been tested with these procedures, developmentalists can begin to see how babies differ from each other in their rate of development of various skills. For any particular skill, such as making a tower of blocks, infants will master the skill over a range of ages. When the age ranges are grouped according to the proportion of babies that can be expected to "pass" a particular test item at a given age, we call this the *age norm* for that skill.

Figure 6-1 shows some of the important motor milestones in infancy, and Table 6-2 gives the age norms on the Denver Developmental Screening Test (DDST) for children between 0 and 6 years of age. Note that by age 15.5 months, for example, 25 percent of infants can be expected to make a tower of four cubes. By 2.2 years, we can expect 90 percent of infants to accomplish this feat: That means there is nearly a full year variation in the age at which this skill might be acquired.

One problem with assessment based on norms is that the norms are derived from the particular group of babies that were used as the *normative sample*. Often, this means white middle-class infants in North America. Growth

Table 6–1

COMMONLY USED INFANT DEVELOPMENT TESTS

Name of test	Areas of Competency Assessed
Gesell Scales (Gesell, 1925)	Motor behavior, language behavior, adaptive behavior, and personal-social behavior.
Bayley Scales of Infant Development (Bayley, 1969)	Motor area (gross body coordination) and mental area (adaptability, learning, sensory acuity, and fine motor coordination).
Denver Developmental Screening Test (Frankenburg, Dodd, Fandal, Kuzak, & Cohrs, 1975)	Personal-social behavior, fine motor-adaptive behavior, language behavior, and gross motor coordination.
Einstein Scales of Sensorimotor Development (Escalona & Corman, 1969)	Prehension, object permanence, and space (detour behavior and perspective taking).
Infant Psychological Development Scales (Uzgiris & Hunt, 1975)	Object permanence, development of means, development of imitation, development of causality, development of objects in space, and development of schemes for relating to objects.

rates may be different for infants of other ethnic, national, economic, and racial groupings. Ideally, the norms should be made for each of these different groups. If not, however, caution should be used in interpreting data from infants who are not members of the group from which the normative sample was drawn. In addition, as health care and nutrition improve over the years, new norms should be established periodically.

Although the assessment procedures in Table 6-1 are useful in establishing age norms for a population of infants, they are less reliable for *diagnostic* purposes; that is, a particular infant's score in the first year of life on one of these tests is not likely to predict that infant's later development (refer to Chapter 5) (Kessen et al., 1970; Sheehan, 1982; Yang, 1979).

Individual differences in motor development are due to both nurture and nature. Evidence for the contribution of nature comes from studies of twins in which identical twins were more likely than fraternal twins to reach particular milestones at the same time (Wilson and Harpring, 1972). On the other

Table 6–2

AGE NORMS FOR THE DENVER DEVELOPMENTAL SCREENING TEST

Item	Age at which a given percentage of the population passes an item			
	25%	50%	75%	90%
Grasps rattle	2.5 mo.	3.3 mo.	3.9 mo.	4.4 mo.
Lifts chest from prone position	2.0	3.0	3.5	4.3
Sits without support	4.8	5.5	6.5	7.8
Transfers cube hand to hand	4.7	5.6	6.6	7.5
Walks holding onto furniture	7.3	9.2	10.2	12.7
Makes pincer grasp of raisin	9.4	10.7	12.3	14.7
Drinks from a cup	10.0	11.7	14.4	16.5
Walks alone well	11.3	12.1	13.5	14.3
Makes a tower of four cubes	15.5	17.9	20.5	2.2 yr.
Walks up steps	14.0	17.0	21.0	22.0 mo.
Puts on shoes, not tied	20.1	22.3	2.6 yr.	3.0 yr.
Balances on one foot for one second	21.7	2.5 yr.	3.0	3.2
Copies a circle	2.2 yr.	2.6	2.9	3.3
Dresses alone	2.6	3.6	4.1	5.0

(From Frankenburg, Dodd, Fandal, Kuzak, & Cohrs, 1975)

hand, studies have shown a correlation between the amount of practice parents give infants in such skills as crawling and walking and the age at which those skills emerge. Babies in Africa walk earlier than those in other places, but the African cultures in which walking occurs the earliest, such as the Kipsigis of Kenya, have cultural beliefs that emphasize the importance of teaching this skill at an early age (Super, 1976).

If a baby suffers sensory impairment or is delayed in many different areas of functioning, tests of motor skills in the first year can be used effectively. Babies with Down's syndrome, for example, are slow to develop across all areas of the Denver Developmental Screening Test (Table 6-2) compared with normal infants, and by the second or third year, their development becomes completely arrested in certain areas. Some concern might be shown if a baby has significant delays beyond the age norms of the DDST in even a single area that could reveal a potential learning disability. In such cases, babies should be assessed by a pediatrician or at a developmental diagnostic clinic.

Health and Nutrition

The Effects of Nutrition on Development

Postnatal malnutrition has less severe consequences than does prenatal malnutrition. The effects of postnatal malnutrition often can be reversed once the child is placed on a proper diet, although it depends on the length and severity of the period of malnutrition as well as environmental factors, such as parental knowledge about infant care and availability of health resources (Dickerson, Merat, & Yusuf, 1982).

A number of research studies have been done in which nutritional supplementation has been given to undernourished mothers and their infants. These studies, done in Guatemala, Colombia, Taiwan, and New York City, show that a multiple intervention in which nutritional supplementation is backed up with parent education and health care is highly effective in enhancing the intellectual level of the children and in reducing learning disorders. Providing nutritional supplementation alone, without health care and education, has little effect on the children's development (Pollitt, Garza, & Leibel, 1984).

General Nutrition and the Development of Eating Skills

Under normal circumstances, foods of various kinds should be introduced to babies gradually over the first few years of life. There appears to be no nutritional need for solid foods until the beginning of the sixth month. Furthermore, the early introduction of solids does not help babies sleep through the night (Committee on Nutrition, American Academy of Pediatrics, 1981; Grunewaldt, Bates, & Guthrie, 1960).

Since solid foods are nutritionally inferior to milk for babies younger than six months, they will require proportionately more to satisfy the infant, leading in the short term to gastrointestinal upset in some cases and in the long run possibly to obesity. Feeding of solid foods too early has also been linked to the development of food allergies, food dislikes, and digestive malfunction (Guthrie, 1979; Robinson, 1978; Weir & Feldman, 1975).

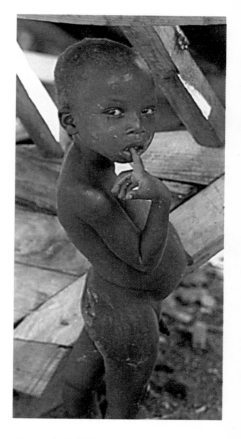

Distended abdomens with thin arms and legs are some of the physical characteristics of malnourishment in infants, toddlers and young children.

Society and Infant Health

The major threats to proper development are poverty, natural disasters, famine, and war, which breed disease through malnutrition and lack of sanitation. In many cases, political and territorial disputes have caused governments to withhold resources or block the shipment of aid and supplies to certain populations in a deliberate attempt to starve them into submission. These kinds of silent civil wars, which still continue, have claimed the lives of millions in Asia and Africa. Even those who manage to survive may be permanently impaired as adults due to failure to receive either basic or remediative health care and nutrition.

Health Programs in the United States

Political issues cloud the delivery of nutritional services in the United States as well, as can be seen in the decision-making process to increase or reduce Congressional appropriations for the Supplemental Feeding Program for Women, Infants, and Children (WIC). This program provides additional nutrition vouchers, over and above food stamps, for such items as milk, cheese, juice, cereal, eggs, and peanut butter, to women who fall below certain income standards and who are pregnant or who have an infant.

In January 1984, the U.S. General Accounting Office (GAO) released a report on all the evaluation studies of the WIC program:

"GAO found insufficient evidence for making any general or conclusive judgments about WIC's effectiveness overall. In a limited way, however, the information indicates the likelihood that WIC has modestly positive effects in some areas" (GAO/PEMD–84–4, 1984).

Although this was true overall, a closer reading of the report showed that many families received positive benefits from WIC. WIC increases birth weights up to 20 percent, especially for teenage and black women. The supplemental nutrition may also counteract to some extent the effects of the mother's smoking and drug use during pregnancy, decrease the incidence of anemia in infants, and enhance the mother's iron intake and weight gain during pregnancy. These findings held true especially if women stayed in the program at least six months before delivery. WIC, however, did not improve neonatal mortality rates.

The research was criticized in the GAO report because the studies lacked sufficient generality. For example, the studies showing positive effects may have been done only in one or two states. In other cases, women dropped out of the program before any benefit could be felt. Other studies may not have been adequately controlled or statistically analyzed. Many child advocates argued that the report was unnecessarily negative, and newspapers published editorials in favor of continuing the WIC program. Congress voted to maintain about the same levels of funding for the 1985 fiscal year. Although this was somewhat less than deemed necessary to meet increased demands, the program is assured to continue for some time.

Part of the reason for this seems to be that babies have not developed the proper enzymes to digest certain complex carbohydrates. In addition, a baby's chewing and swallowing skills have not matured before six months of age. Small infants suck milk, not by the kind of suction made by older children when sucking on a straw but by *expression* from the nipple. As the lips close around the nipple, the tongue is extended outward to squeeze the nipple against the roof of the mouth (Kessen, et al., 1970). When solid foods are first introduced, this tongue extension reflex still operates, which is why babies often expel more food than they ingest.

By six months, the baby has digestive enzymes, greater control over the mouth and tongue, greater saliva production to lubricate chewing and to create drooling until the baby can control the saliva in the mouth, and teeth pushing under the gums to provide a base for chewing.

What Is the Best Nutrition for Babies?

The U.S. Department of Agriculture, the Department of Health and Human Services, and the American Academy of Pediatrics recommend that *all* normal, full-term babies be breast-fed for the first four to six months (Committee on Nutrition, American Academy of Pediatrics, 1981; Gaull, Jensen, Rassin, & Malloy, 1981). These recommendations are controversial and may cause some concern to mothers who do not want to breast-feed about the possible health risks for formula-fed babies. Some mothers cannot breast-feed, perhaps because their babies require hospitalization during the first few months of life. Some manufacturers of infant formula have been criticized for advertising the benefits of formula milk in Third World countries in which the water used to dilute the formula milk may be contaminated with bacteria.

Breast milk is believed superior to formula milk for two reasons: immunologic and nutritional. The immunologic properties of human milk derive from a protein (called Secretory IgA, or SIgA) that coats the inner lining of the baby's intestines and acts to trap and destroy harmful bacteria. When infants gurgle and blow milk bubbles as they eat, SIgA enters the breathing passages and may even protect against respiratory diseases. Remarkably, the milk of a mother who is infected with a bacterial disease contains higher concentrations of SIgA that will be passed on to her baby. Research has shown that breast-fed infants have fewer diseases on the average than bottle-fed infants (Pollitt et al., 1984).

Although the immunologic properties of breast milk are well established, the nutritional and behavioral advantages have not been conclusively demonstrated. It is difficult to establish minimum nutritional requirements for an individual infant as well as to monitor the amount of milk taken by a breast-fed baby. In addition, longitudinal studies of growth rates for breast-fed and formula-fed babies may be inconclusive, because mothers who breast-feed longer may have higher milk outputs and produce nutritionally superior milk (Pollitt et al., 1984).

From a behavioral point of view, no conclusive differences have ever been found between breast-fed and formula-fed babies or between mother-infant interactions depending upon the method of feeding. Mothers who breast-feed may feel physical differences, since the baby is close to her skin, and we know that breast-fed infants are more likely than formula-fed infants to recognize their mother's smell (refer to Chapter 5). It is not clear, however, that these differences have any long-term consequences for infant development or for mother-infant attachments.

Mothers who feed by bottle can find other ways to establish physical closeness to their babies, such as during bathing. An infant who is not exposed directly to its mother's body odors is able to use sound and sight for maternal recognition. Thus, the parent-infant interaction system is flexible enough to adapt to a variety of feeding methods during the first months of life. Infants whose mothers cannot or choose not to breast-feed can still develop normally.

For a baby learning self-feeding skills, food can be a plaything as well as a source of nourishment.

Causes of Infant Mortality after the Newborn Period

Although many babies develop minor infections, even if they are breast-fed, a small number of infants develop fatal illnesses. Other babies die from accidents and maltreatment. If a baby is going to die after birth, the highest probability for such an occurrence is during the first 24 hours (refer to Chapter 5). For infants who survive beyond the first day of life, the odds of mortality are very low, about one infant per one thousand, or lower, depending on the health risks of the country in which the infant lives.

In most cases, deaths that occur after the first month of life can be called unexpected, since most of the fatal diseases of childhood have been eliminated in the more developed nations of the world by screening and vaccination programs. One particular form of unexpected infant death, sudden infant death syndrome, or SIDS, is discussed in FOCUS ON RISK/ INTERVENTION.

Typical causes of death during the first two years of life are accidents—automobile accidents or home accidents such as suffocation, burns, poisoning, and drowning—and homicide, including maltreatment, infanticide, sexual offenses, kidnapping, and parent-infant suicides (Hartmann & Molz, 1979). Over one thousand children under the age of five are killed each year in automobile accidents; only 8 percent of children under five are strapped into safety seats (Reisinger & Williams, 1982). In states where mandatory child restraint laws have been introduced, safety belts have virtually eliminated the risk of death and injury in automobile accidents (Associated Press, November, 1984).

The purpose of studying the causes of infant death and disease is ultimately to improve the quality of life for infants and their families. Aside from SIDS, which appears to be one of the last of the medically treatable major causes of death that have not been brought under control, infant health and well-being is largely a social and economic problem, an example of how the macrosystem of society—legal and economic constraints—affects the development of young children.

Perception

Chapter 5 discussed the sensitivity of each of the newborn's basic senses. *Sensation* has to do with the ability of each sense to detect information, and acuity is a measure of this ability. *Perception* is the process by which sensory information is organized and interpreted. For example, if you sit in the sun, you will have the sensation of warmth. When you interpret this sensation—as leading to a tan or as heat that makes you sweat and causes discomfort—you are perceiving the heat of the sun.

This difference is important for the study of infant development, since sensation is part of the newborn's physiological inheritance, but perception develops gradually through the interaction of the individual with the environment. Perception develops via two basic processes: (1) *sensory/neurophysiological,* in which the conduction pathways to and from each sense organ leading to the brain and the corresponding regions of the brain involved in sensory information processing develop, and (2) *perceptual/psychological,* in which the infant learns to remember and categorize sensory information into meaningful images and patterns.

Sudden Infant Death Syndrome

The most frequent cause of death during a baby's first year is not only unexpected but also unexplained. Known as sudden infant death syndrome (*SIDS*), or crib death, it claims thousands of infants' lives every year.

SIDS is usually diagnosed when parents discover that their baby has died, perhaps at night or during a nap, without apparent cause. Before SIDS received national attention several years ago, parents were often suspected of the murder of the baby. This usually unfounded implication, in addition to the shock, grief, and guilt that all parents feel after losing an infant (Drotar & Irvin, 1979; Helmrath & Steinitz, 1978; Markusen, Owen, Fulton, & Bendiksen, 1977) has led many to despair. Parents who need help and support in such cases can contact one of several groups organized by parents of SIDS victims, such as the National Foundation for Sudden Infant Death, Inc. (1501 Broadway, New York, NY 10036) or the International Council for Infant Survival (1515 Reistertown Road, Baltimore, MD 21208). Legal and medical information as well as advice on prevention for subsequent children born to such families can be obtained.

What Causes SIDS?

SIDS has many suspected causes, though none are conclusive. Since most crib deaths occur during sleep, some have been linked with suspected respiration problems. Many infants cease breathing for brief periods, called *apneic pauses*, especially during sleep. It could be that some infants do not have the ability to come out of these otherwise normal apneic pauses due to a failure of the respiratory control system. In addition, the repeated occurrence of prolonged apneic pauses and the subsequent loss of oxygen may itself cause a gradual weakening of the infant or subtle brain damage (Black, Steinschneider, & Sheehe, 1979; Lipsitt, 1979a).

Another suspected cause is *infant botulism*, a disease that affects the nervous system caused by a toxin found on some fruits and vegetables and often in honey (Marx, 1978). Thus, infants under 12 months should not be fed honey, and their food should be carefully washed.

Other suspected causes are heat stroke caused by overdressing (Stanton, Scott, & Downhan, 1980), vitamin deficiency, especially the B complex vitamin biotin, and hormonal imbalance (Chacon & Tildon, 1981). Currently, SIDS is considered to be a collection of multiple disorders with different causes. Unfortunately, it has eluded early detection efforts and has no cure.

Infants who have been deprived of oxygen in the perinatal period, have high apnea rates or hormonal imbalances, or have siblings who have succumbed to SIDS are now considered at risk for the disorder. Parents can use a home apnea monitor, which sets off an alarm when the infant stops breathing during sleep. Although this causes considerable anxiety in parents when first introduced, most parents feel it is beneficial (Cain, Kelly, & Shannon, 1980).

Theories of Perception

The process by which perception develops is a matter of some theoretical discussion. J. J. and E. J. Gibson believe that perception as well as sensation is determined primarily by nature. Since perception is so basic to survival, the Gibsons' theory of *ecological perception* suggests that there is no such thing as pure sensation. Whenever an individual senses something, that thing becomes immediately interpreted in terms of the individual's abilities to adapt to the environment (Gibson, 1966).

Related to this view is that of T. Bower (1974), who felt that newborns could interpret sensory information and act in adaptive ways. For example,

(a)

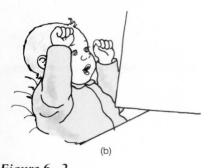

(b)

Figure 6–2

Response to a Large Looming Object
Even babies who have never seen a
looming object respond as if they
"know" the object will hit them. Is this
an innate response, or merely a
perceptual illusion?

suppose you see a friend on the opposite side of a small pond. To meet this person, the shortest path is directly across the water, but you choose to walk around the pond. On the other hand, if you had a boat, you might go directly across. Thus, your perception of each pathway to the other person depends on what kind of action you can perform. Without a boat, the longer route is perceived as the best path, but with a boat, the shorter route is perceived as the best path.

The alternative to the theory of ecological perception is based on Piaget's (1952) theory of sensorimotor development and D. O. Hebb's (1958) and Richard Held's (Held & Hein, 1963) *constructivist* theory of perceptual development. Piaget viewed perceptual development in the same way as motor and cognitive development: as an interaction between nature and nurture. Nature provides the infant's motivation to adapt and the processes of assimilation and accommodation (refer to Chapter 2). Using these adaptive processes, each child must slowly construct perception from sensation. According to Piaget, Hebb, and Held, sensation gradually leads to perception as the infant actively explores the environment and learns how sensations are related to motor actions and environmental responses.

In the example of the pond, Gibson's ecological perception theory would say that water and dry land are immediately interpreted as substances that support or do not support traveling, depending on the means of travel. If the road around the pond becomes muddy or slippery, one will walk more carefully. According to Gibson, such surfaces would be perceived immediately and without learning, since they are so important to human adaptation.

Piaget and the other constructivist theorists would say that unless you have had some experience with walking on different kinds of surfaces, you are not likely to interpret the differences as meaningful. Thus, a toddler who has never seen a slick or wet surface is likely to perceive it as a dry surface and will slip and slide on the first few attempts to cross it. For the constructivists, experience is essential for the development of perception.

What evidence exists for each of these views of perceptual development? Some of the first studies of infant perception suggested that infants had a built-in set of perceptual categories. For example, Fantz (1963), one of the first people to study perception in human infants, presented newborns with three drawings: a stylized face, a face in which the elements had been scrambled, and an oval shape containing equal amounts of black and white as the faces. He found that infants, even at birth, preferred the stylized face, and he reasoned that face perception was innate. Since, as we have seen, parents are essential for infant survival, this finding seems to fit into the Gibsons' theory.

Bower and his colleagues found that when a two-week-old baby saw an object projected on a screen that seemed to be approaching the baby on a collision course, the baby raised his arms and moved his head back. When the projected object seemed to move on a course that would miss the baby—to the right or the left—no such reaction was seen (Bower, Broughton, & Moore, 1970). This was interpreted as an in-born defensive reaction against the looming object (see Figure 6-2).

E. J. Gibson studied depth perception in 8- to 12-month-old infants. The ecological theory suggests that if you are moving and come to a steep dropoff, it is adaptive to feel fearful and to back away from the edge of the cliff. This was studied in infants using an apparatus called the "visual cliff" (Gibson &

Infants do not show fear of the visual cliff until the second half of the first year.(Photo courtesy of Richard Walk, whose granddaughter is pictured here.)

Walk, 1960). A dropoff of several feet is covered by a piece of clear glass so that the baby can see it but cannot fall over it. The babies were reluctant to cross the glass, even when their mothers were on the other side of the dropoff urging them to cross.

These three sets of findings—in the areas of facial form, looming object, and depth perception—seem to support the ecological perception view that innate perceptions exist for situations adaptive for survival: forming social relationships and avoiding impending collisions and falls. However, more recent research has led to alternative interpretations of these findings.

Following the work of Fantz on visual preference for facial forms, researchers began showing babies a wide variety of visual stimuli. In so doing, they discovered that newborns like to look at objects with a clear and sharp outline and not necessarily at faces (see Figure 6-3). When the original figures that Fantz used were reexamined, it was found that only in Fantz's stylized face was the outline distinctly separated from the internal features (Sherrod, 1979).

Other research on looming objects has shown that young infants will follow the top edge of a looming stimulus with their eyes. This is because the top edge is a sharp and clear outline, and the baby's eyes get hooked on this edge. As the object approaches, the top edge appears to move upward in the

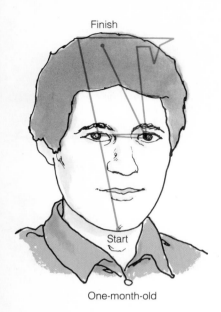

Finish

Start

One-month-old

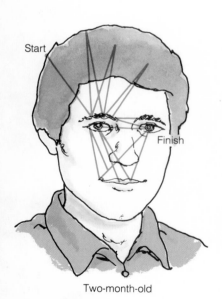

Start

Finish

Two-month-old

Figure 6—3

Facial Scanning Patterns

The superimposed lines show where a baby will look at a face. One-month-olds look mostly around the outside, while older babies look at the inner details, especially at the eyes.

infant's visual field, thus causing the baby to look at a steeper upward angle. The baby eventually loses control of the head, which falls backward, bringing the arms up with it (Yonas, Bechtold, Frankel, Gordon, McRoberts, Norcia, & Sternfels, 1977). This interpretation has been questioned in later studies, and more research is needed before we can decide conclusively what infants are actually perceiving in this situation.

Research on the visual cliff has been repeated with younger babies even before they could crawl. The researchers (Campos, Langer, & Krowitz, 1970; Schwarz, Campos, & Baisel, 1973) placed infants aged two, three, five, and nine months on the glass of the deep area of the apparatus while measuring their heart rates. Heart rate changes indicated that all the infants noticed a difference between the deep and shallow areas, but that only the nine-month-olds showed a fear and avoidance response to the deep side. A later study revealed that infants who had more experience in crawling around and those given additional practice in crawling developed fear of the visual cliff at an earlier age (Campos et al., 1978; 1981).

These more recent findings suggest that in all three areas—facial form, looming object, and depth perception—very young infants are able to perceive differences in shapes, movement, and depth. However, inborn perceptual abilities are not those predicted by the ecological theory. Rather than having an innate perception of adaptive aspects of the environment, people have an innate perception of the contrast between a line and its background or between brightness and darkness. The research further suggests that the perception of meaningful patterns, such as a face, depth, or a looming object, requires active experience with real objects in order to develop.

Perception, therefore, can be explained as a combination of both the ecological view of innate abilities and the constructivist view of the need for concrete experiences. Perceptual development is a process in which inborn preferences orient the infant to pay attention to particular aspects of the environment. This in turn allows the infant to gather and remember information about those things. Gradually, through repeated experiences with everyday objects, the infant begins to sort these initial images into psychologically meaningful shapes, patterns, and people.

Let's review some of the developmental changes in *vision* and *audition*, two of the most studied and therefore best known perceptual systems. We can presume that similar developments are taking place in the *tactile* (touch), *gustatory* (taste), and *olfactory* (smell) modes.

The Development of Vision

Between three and six months of age, the neurophysiological features of the visual system become almost adultlike. Visual acuity improves to about 20/50, the eyes can focus on objects at different distances (convergence and divergence) and can easily follow moving stimuli, and the pupils readily adjust to changes in light intensity (Kessen et al., 1970; Salapatek & Banks, 1978).

By three months, infants can scan objects to detect internal and external features. Younger infants get visually hooked on the outside edges of objects and may have difficulty breaking gaze contact. This lack of control over the direction of vision, called *obligatory attention*, leads to frustration and distress at times but is usually overcome by three months (Pipp & Giffen, 1981; Maurer & Salapatek, 1976). Although newborns can see in color, they can discern fewer colors than an adult can. By three months, babies can perceive the same set of hues that adults see (Bornstein, 1976).

The formation of meaningful visual images also begins at three months. One of the ways researchers have tried to demonstrate this is to see if babies can recognize and distinguish important features of their environment. At this age, the most important feature is the primary caregiver, usually the mother, and the baby spends a lot of time looking into the mother's face, cooing, and smiling.

By three or four months, there is no question that babies can visually differentiate between their mother compared to an unfamiliar female using both habituation and visual preference tests. The baby can even tell the difference between its father and a male stranger as well as between two unfamiliar people (Barrera & Maurer, 1981; Maurer & Heroux, 1980). By four months or earlier, babies can also recognize the difference between different expressions on the same face (Field, Woodson, Greenberg, & Cohen, 1982; Haviland & Lelwica, 1987; Nelson & Horowitz, 1983).

The Development of Hearing

Hearing, like vision, matures relatively rapidly. The bones of the middle ear are adult size at birth, and the external auditory canal (between the earlobe and the eardrum), the tympanic membrane (the eardrum), and the middle ear cavity all reach adult size by one year. The auditory nerve myelinization is nearly complete at birth (Eilers & Gavin, 1981).

Studies of auditory perception have used preference and habituation methods as well as conditioned sucking (refer to Chapter 5). Newborns can distinguish between sounds of different loudness, pitch, and duration (Leventhall & Lipsitt, 1964), and they prefer vowel sounds to consonants (Clarkson & Berg, 1983).

Babies under three months of age like to listen to sound in the frequency range of adult voices and in the range of notes found on a piano, and they prefer the higher pitched sounds. They like a wide band of frequencies (a piano chord) rather than a single note or tone, and they pay attention to sustained sounds rather than intermittent sounds (Eisenberg, 1976).

Between 6 and 12 months, infants can readily recognize melodies sung to them and can distinguish variations on a theme as well as different melodies (Chang & Trehub, 1977; Trehub, Bull, & Thorpe, 1984). One of the most remarkable abilities possessed by humans is language, and long before the baby utters the first true words, the ability to differentiate different vowel and consonant sounds by auditory perception develops.

The Perception of Speech Sounds

The basic sound units of a language—the vowels and consonants—are called *phonemes*. By using habituation methods, researchers have discovered that infants as young as one month can distinguish between two phonemes that are closely related, for example, between the sound "puh" and the sound "buh" (Eimas, Siqueland, Jusczyk, & Vigorito, 1971; Kuhl, 1981).

Some people have wondered if very small infants can distinguish between any pair of phonemes taken from any human language. If this were so, it would mean that newborns come into the world ready to hear and learn any language spoken around them. One might also predict that after several months or years of listening to only a single language, the ability to hear phonemes not present in that language would gradually disappear.

Several studies indicate that this might indeed occur. For example, African infants under six months were able to distinguish their native Kikuyu language phonemes as well as those found in English (Streeter, 1976). Babies born into Spanish-speaking homes could distinguish both Spanish and English before six months (Eilers, Gavin, & Wilson, 1979), but in this study, the babies in the English-speaking community had a hard time hearing the Spanish sounds. A more conclusive study followed babies until they were 12 months old from three language groups: English, Salish (a native Canadian language), and Hindi. Babies from each group were tested with phonemes from each language. The results showed that once the infants began producing sounds like those made in their own language—after 10 months of age or so—they rapidly lost the ability to detect cross-linguistic phonemic contrasts (Werker & Tees, 1984).

Intermodal Perception

One of the most important aspects of perception is the relationship between the different sense modalities. Suppose the lights went out in your house and you had to find your way between rooms by feeling the walls and furniture. In the past, you had navigated from room to room by sight alone, having never touched particular walls or furnishings. Yet you manage to find your way in the dark by touching things you had only seen before. The ability to do this relies on *intermodal* or *intersensory perception*, or the integration of different perceptual systems, in this case touch and sight.

The ecological perception theory suggests that infants are born with intermodal perception, which can be easily demonstrated by the newborn's head turning in the direction of a sound source. Sounds sometimes interfere with and sometimes enhance visual perception in newborns (Lawson & Turkewitz, 1980).

In one study, four-month-olds heard a series of sounds occurring at a regular or an irregular rhythm. They were later shown a puppet moving its mouth silently to either an irregular or a regular rhythm. They preferred to watch the puppet performing the rhythm that they had not heard (Mendelson & Ferland, 1982).

The infants in the sound and puppet study seemed to sense some quality (the rhythm) that was the same in both sound and sight sense modalities. It is quite likely that some sense modalities are integrated at birth and that further skill at recognizing similarities between modalities develops with age. For example, when you learn a tennis stroke, it is difficult to execute it skillfully merely by watching the instructor. It takes considerable practice to transfer the visual information (watching the instructor) into the tactual sensation (from your own attempts) of the ball hitting the strings in just the right way.

The constructivist approach to perception suggests that experience is essential in the acquisition of intermodal perception. Even though the senses may be linked innately in simple ways, it is not until near the end of the first year that babies are able to utilize intersensory information to achieve their goals.

In one research study (Ruff, 1984), 108 infants at ages 6, 9, and 12 months were observed playing with objects of different kinds. During the period from 6 to 12 months, there was a decrease in mouthing and an increase in fingering objects. To see whether babies actually gained information from fingering and mouthing, familiar objects were replaced by objects that had been changed in one element: texture, shape, or weight (see Figure 6-4).

Figure 6—4

In this study 3 sets of objects were used. Within each set there was a standard object, and then 3 other objects that differed from the standard, either by weight, texture, or shape.

(H. Ruff, *Developmental Psychology*, 1984, 20 p. 16. Copyright 1984 by the American Psychological Association. Reprinted by permission of the author.)

By the age of one year, exploration becomes more deliberate. Children use play to learn about the relationships between objects, such as the placement of the rings on the pole.

If the object's texture was changed, babies increased the amount of looking at and fingering of the object. If the object's shape was changed, looking and fingering also increased, but so did rotating the object and transferring it between the hands. Fingering the object seemed to be the primary means of getting information about texture, while transferring it between the hands was the means of getting information about shape. Weight changes did not affect exploration, and younger infants were not affected by weight or by shape changes. This means that by 12 months, intersensory perception can be used effectively as a way of knowing, understanding, and forming relationships between different aspects of the environment.

Cognition

Cognition refers to the individual's ability to use the environment in adaptive ways to meet needs and carry out goals and plans. In some cases, cognition is a mental process involving the manipulation of concepts and symbols in the mind. In other cases, cognition is a motor process in which the direct action on the environment is carried out in planned and controlled ways.

As we saw in Chapter 2, cognitive development in children has been explained by a number of different theories. This chapter first considers Piaget's theory (refer to Chapter 2) and then discusses information processing approaches to cognitive development in infancy. Piaget's cognitive-structural theory suggests that during the first two years of life, cognition can be seen in the baby's motor actions upon the environment. It is not until the end of the second year that children begin to use mental processes in order to adapt to their environment.

Piaget's Theory of Infant Sensorimotor Intelligence

Jean Piaget made clear that the behavior of small infants, although not conceptually based, was nevertheless *intelligent*. By this he meant that infants had ways of meeting their needs, of using their own and other resources in the environment, and of adapting those resources to the specific nature of the task at hand. This *sensorimotor intelligence* was embodied not in the mind but in the actions and movements that the baby made in direct interaction with its environment.

Table 6-3 shows how Piaget divided the first two years of life into sensorimotor stages.

Stage I: Reflexes. According to Piaget, the newborn reflexes—involuntary movements elicited by a specific stimulation (refer to Chapter 5)—are thought to be the first *schemes* (techniques for operating on the environment) of sensorimotor action. Piaget described how infants use simple reflexes to meet their needs. For example, the babies must adapt the sucking and the rooting reflexes to fit the typical manner in which they are fed. They must adjust their mouth shape according to the size, shape, and texture of the nipple being used.

Stage II: Primary circular reactions. After the first month of life, and through repeated use, the baby may begin to use reflex action in situations not directly related to their original purpose. This simple extension of reflex action to produce an interesting or pleasurable sensation is called a *primary*

Table 6—3

JEAN PIAGET'S STAGES OF
SENSORIMOTOR DEVELOPMENT

Approximate Age (months)	Stage	Description
0–1	I. Reflexes	Exercising innate motor patterns, such as sucking and crying.
1–4	II. Primary circular reactions	Repetition of behavior patterns that have been associated with interesting results using the baby's own body.
4–8	III. Secondary circular reactions	Beginning separation of means from ends, attention shifting from own body to object, purposeful action, coordination of sensory modalities, brief search behavior.
8–12	IV. Coordination of secondary circular reactions	Further separation of means from ends, intentional behavior, interest in qualities of objects, exploration, search for hidden objects, anticipation of events, tool use.
12–18	V. Tertiary circular reactions	Back-and-forth exchanges with environment, variations of means to produce desired ends, active experimentation to produce novel effects, systematic search for hidden objects, complex imitation.
18–24	VI. Invention of new means	Internalized thought and mental problem solving, symbolic representation, language, symbolic play, deferred imitation.

(From J. Piaget. *The Origins of Intelligence in Children.* New York: International Universities Press, 1952.)

circular reaction, an action that is discovered by chance through the exercise of a reflex and repeated in rapid succession. Thus, a baby may suck repeatedly in the absence of a nipple or, with a nipple in the mouth, will use its tongue or lips to explore the nipple's shape or texture without trying to get milk from the nipple.

The following is an example from Piaget's observations of one of his own three children. (Piaget records an infant's age in the following form: 0;2(26), which means 0 years, 2 months, 26 days.)

> . . . at 0;2(12) Lucienne, after coughing, recommences several times for fun and smiles. Laurent puffs out his breath, producing an indefinite sound. At 0;2(26) he reproduces the peals of his voice which ordinarily accompany his laughter, but without laughing and out of pure phonetic interest (Piaget, 1952, p. 79).

In this example, both babies repeat simple actions such as coughing and puffing, not because these reflexes are stimulated by a cold but purely for the fun of repeating the action.

Stage III. Secondary circular reactions. Primary circular reactions are repetitions of reflex actions, discovered by chance, that involve the infant's own body. *Secondary circular reactions* are similar to primary circular reactions, but they involve events and objects outside the baby's own body.

While kicking the side of her crib, a baby may discover that this action creates movement in an overhead mobile. She will continue to kick to get the mobile to move. The baby has no idea that her kicking caused the mobile to move, because she is not aware of the fact that the mobile is connected to the crib or even that her feet are touching the crib to make it move.

Laurent . . . at 0;4(21) has an object in his hands when, in order to distract him, I shake the hanging rattles which he is in the habit of striking. He then looks at the rattles without relinquishing his toy and outlines with his right hand the movement of "striking" (Piaget, 1952, p. 187).

Laurent understands the relationship between striking and getting the hanging rattles to shake, and he expects that by making the striking movement, he can get the rattles to shake without letting go of the toy.

Stage IV: Coordination of secondary circular reactions.   In the previous stages, the infant's actions are simple repetitions of previous results that were discovered by chance. In this stage, the infant becomes aware of goals and is able to use existing actions and combine them intelligently in order to reach a goal. This active goal-seeking behavior is called *intentionality.* Babies in this stage are able to understand that an object they see is the same one they are touching (intersensory perception). Thus, the baby combines information from various sense modalities to coordinate action and understanding.

At 0;8(8) Jacqueline tries to grasp her celluloid duck but I also grasp it at the same time she does. Then she firmly holds the toy in her right hand and pushes my hand away with her left (Piaget, 1954, p. 219).

During Piaget's stage IV, infants learn to find hidden objects. When this first happens, finding ordinary objects can be exciting for the child. Games like peek-a-boo take advantage of this developmental shift in cognitive ability. In the process of playing peek-a-boo infants can solidify their cognitive achievement while improving their social interactional skills.

Note that in this example, Jacqueline can coordinate the grasping scheme of one hand with the pushing scheme of the other hand.

Because of their ability to coordinate the different senses, babies know that a thing exists even when it can't be seen or heard. This is called *object permanence,* and infants get progressively better at retaining the images of objects and pursuing quests for missing objects over the next year or so. They will search for hidden objects and go around barriers to get them.

Stage V: Tertiary circular reactions. *Tertiary circular reactions* are repetitious actions, like primary and secondary circular reactions, but instead of discovering the relationship between action and effect by mere chance, the tertiary circular reaction involves intentional repeated attempts to explore the nature of the environment.

Instead of simply using a spoon to eat with, a baby using tertiary circular reactions discovers that the same spoon makes an interesting sound when banged on the table or cup or dropped to the ground from the highchair. In this stage, babies try out new skills or arrange objects in novel ways to reach their goals in what is called *trial and error* learning.

> At 0;10(11) Laurent . . . grasps in succession a celluloid swan, a box, etc., stretches out his arm and lets them fall. He distinctly varies the position of the fall. Sometimes he stretches out his arm vertically, sometimes he holds it obliquely, in front of or behind his eyes, etc. (Piaget, 1952, p. 269).

Here Laurent is using trial and error to discover the properties of a variety of objects as they fall from different positions. He repeats essentially the same action—dropping—with small variations in a guided, intentional manner.

Stage VI: Invention of new means. During this period, infants become able to do the same things mentally that before they had to do by trial-and-error experimentation. Instead of having to try out a series of possible actions in the solution of a problem, the two-year-old can conceptualize a series of possible solutions, conserving both time and energy, before actually trying one out.

In this stage, a very important one for the development of conceptual and logical thinking, the infant can represent one object with another object. A shell might become a cup or a boat; a block might be used as a car. This substitution of one object for another is called *symbolic representation.* In addition, the representation of the object can become divorced from any resemblance to the object, taking on a conventional rather than an idiosyncratic usage. A conventional symbol is called a *sign;* an example is the word *cup,* which as a string of sounds bears no resemblance to the actual cup. It is during this stage that infants begin to use and understand language.

> At 1;8(30) Jacqueline stroked her mother's hair, saying *kitty, kitty.* At 1;9(0) she saw a shell and said *cup.* . . . The next day, seeing the same shell she said *glass,* then *cup,* then *hat* and finally *boat in the water* (Piaget, 1963, p. 124).

From this description of Piaget's stages of sensorimotor development, one can see how a baby gradually progresses from picturing schemes based entirely on action, to having a growing mental picture of a world of permanent objects, and finally to acquiring the ability to form symbols and signs that are the basic units of the thinking process.

Information processing theories do not disagree with Piaget's basic descriptions of the sensorimotor period. They suggest, however, that mental processes occur even in very young infants in the form of memories and simple mental comparisons between the present and the past.

Information Processing Views of Infant Cognitive Development

The *information processing view* of cognitive development suggests that infants will evaluate new information by comparing it to prior knowledge and that the degree of difference between the old and the new information will determine how much attention the baby pays to the new information.

Information processing before 6 to 8 months.   According to Kagan (1971), infants between two and eight months of age prefer to look at objects or people that are a bit different from what they have already encountered. If newly presented stimuli are exactly the same as previously seen ones, the child does not look at them for long—a kind of habituation. Similarly, if the newly presented stimulus is totally different from previous experience, the baby will probably ignore it.

A newly presented stimulus that is slightly different or *moderately discrepant* will get the most attention. A moderate discrepancy might be a change in facial expression or a change from one face to another. Babies of this age like to watch adults who make animated and exaggerated facial movements and vocalizations, adults who make their social play a series of moderately discrepant stimuli.

To be able to compare the present object with a previously seen object, infants must have some kind of memory abilities early in life. This was demonstrated in a study on infant kicking. Three-month-old infants learned that they could move an overhead mobile by kicking with either the left or right leg. Without the baby's awareness, the experimenters tied a string to one or the other leg. They then waited until the baby discovered by chance (refer to Table 6-3, Stage III) that kicking that leg made the mobile move. This study used a *conjugate reinforcement* method, in which the amount of movement of the mobile was directly proportional to the amount of effort the baby put into the kick. Kicking more and kicking harder produced more movement of the mobile. This type of reinforcement appears to be especially conducive to babies in this stage of development.

After lots of practice that day, the same baby was returned to the same situation on another day. If the baby was brought back after 20 or more days, there was no memory of how to make the mobile move. However, after any interval less than 20 days, babies soon began to kick the same leg that produced the movement on the first day (Sullivan, Rovee-Collier, & Tynes, 1979).

This study shows that three-month-olds placed in a similar situation on repeated occasions will evoke a similar motor movement—a motor memory—in much the same way that opening a book to the page where you left off reading will help you evoke the mental memory of what you had previously read.

Information processing between 6 and 12 months.   The next important step in the development of information processing is for the baby to figure out how two different things are related to each other and to the baby's own actions. This could be the relationship between two objects, such as a cup and a spoon, or it could mean the relationship between two independent parts of the baby's own body—vision and touch, for example.

At about this same age, infants learn to relate two separate objects to each other. Rather than randomly combining the toys, the babies do such things as putting lids on pots, cups on saucers, and spoons in cups. This is called *relational play* (Fenson, Kagan, Kearsley, & Zelazo, 1976).

Object permanence also reflects an awareness of the relationship between one object and another (the object behind or under which the other object is hidden). Not only can babies of this age look under a cloth or a cup where they have seen someone hide an object, but they will also go around a barrier to get something, a skill called *detour ability*.

Researchers have disagreed about exactly when a baby develops object permanence. Some have suggested that infants can understand the relationship between objects well before stage IV but that they lack motor skills necessary to lift a cloth under which the object is hidden or to move around a barrier. Could infants at a younger age keep track of hidden objects with their eyes if no motor skills were required?

In a study by Bower, Broughton, & Moore (1970), 20-week-old infants watched a toy train moving back and forth on a straight track. A screen placed at the center of the track hid the train from view for a short time as it passed behind the screen. The researchers found that the babies would follow the train's movement with their eyes as the train moved from one side to the center of the track where the screen was placed. After the train disappeared behind the screen, the infants would look toward the opposite side of the screen as if to anticipate the reemergence of the train. Sometimes the investigators tried to trick the babies by making a different object appear on the other side of the screen where the train should have emerged. When this happened, the babies looked confused and stopped looking at the new object.

This study suggests that 20-week-olds have a concept of object permanence, about three to four months earlier than Piaget claimed. The same results might be explained in other ways, however. Muller & Aslin (1978), in a replication of the same procedure as Bower and his colleagues, found that babies failed to follow the movements of the object when the object went behind the screen just as often when the object remained the same as when it changed. They also found that some babies continued to move their eyes along the track even if the train stopped in plain view or if it stopped behind the screen and no other object reemerged. Thus, looking to the side of the screen where the train is likely to emerge may not be object permanence but a secondary circular reaction of repeating the same head movement.

Using 10- and 11-month-old infants who were still in stage III, Benson & Uzgiris (1985) were able to facilitate the transition to stage IV and object permanence by giving infants the opportunity to crawl around a box where an object was hidden. Infants who were carried around the same box did not make attempts to search for the object. This study confirms Piaget's theory that cognitive development is enhanced by the infant's own exploratory actions upon the environment.

This and other research suggests that Piaget's interpretations of an infant's cognitive abilities may be correct. In infancy research, however, the danger always exists that investigators have failed to find the best way for the baby to express what he or she "knows." It could be that using a response system other than head turning or lifting covers off objects would better illustrate how the infant processes information at younger ages.

Information processing in the second year.   It still takes some time—until the age of 15 to 18 months—for the skill of searching for missing objects to be perfected. For example, a 12-month-old will search for an object in one hiding place, but if you move the object to another place, even in plain view of the baby, the baby will look puzzled but will not search further.

Curiously, if an object is hidden behind an opaque barrier, the 12-month-old will retrieve it easier than if it is behind a transparent one (Lockman, 1984). The fact that the object can be seen makes the baby think that a direct reach through the barrier is the best way to get it. It takes another six months or so for babies to learn that looks can be deceiving.

The reasons for the infant's visual fixation time to stimuli also change at this age. Three-month-olds will rarely look at the scrambled face shown in Figure 6-5, because the face is too discrepant from their usual image of a face. After the age of ten months, babies look at the scrambled face for a longer time than they would the normal face, apparently because they are trying to figure out the relationship between the different parts of the face or between the scrambled face and something else they have seen. For example, when seeing this kind of face, a three-year-old might ask, "Who hit him in the nose?" or "Who that, mommy? A monster?" Kagan (1971) called these attempts to find relationships between different objects *hypotheses*.

Both Piagetian and information processing views have contributed a great deal to our knowledge about infant cognitive development. We now know that infants are alert, intelligent, and active learners from the beginning of life. Their transition from simple reflex action to intelligent thinking in just two years is one of the most remarkable developmental periods of the human life span.

Figure 6—5

Scrambled and Unscrambled Faces

During the first year babies prefer to look at the unscrambled face, while the reverse is true in the second year.

(*Change and Continuity in Infancy*, Kagan, J. Copyright © 1971. Reprinted by permission of John Wiley & Sons, Inc.)

Emotional Development: The Discovery of the Self

Infants take great delight in developing new skills and discovering new things through exploration. They can also get rather frustrated when they fail to understand things or when they are unable to carry out an intended act. In this sense, an infant's emotions are directly related to cognition.

At birth, infants have two basic emotional states: pleasure and displeasure. By the age of two years, the infant's emotional life is extremely complex: a world containing delight, fear, shame, anger, and anxiety. Where do these emotions come from? Why do they emerge gradually over the first two years rather than all at once at the time of birth?

Table 6-4 gives a summary of the kinds of emotions that babies develop and the approximate ages at which they can be expected to appear. These emotions have been organized under three groups: pleasure-joy, wariness-fear, rage-anger.

The Development of Pleasure-Joy

The development of new emotions appears to be tied to changes in cognitive development. The emotion of *pleasure,* for example, appears at about three

Month[a]	Pleasure-Joy	Wariness-Fear	Rage-Anger
0	Endogenous smile	Startle/pain	Distress due to covering the face,
		Obligatory attention	physical restraint,
1	Turning toward		extreme discomfort
2			
3	Pleasure		Rage (disappointment)
4			
	Delight Active laughter	Wariness	
5			
6			
7	Joy		Anger
8			
9		Fear (stranger aversion)	
10			
11			
12	Elation	Anxiety, immediate fear	Angry mood, petulance
18	Positive valuation of self affection	Shame	Defiance
24			Intentional hurting
36	Pride, love		Guilt

[a]The age specified is neither the first appearance of the affect in question nor its peak occurrence; it is the age when the literature suggests that the reaction is common.
(*Handbook of Infant Development,* Osofsky. Copyright © 1979. Reprinted by permission of John Wiley & Sons, Inc.)

months, after the infant is able to remember and recognize familiar stimuli. Babies of this age smile upon seeing their mothers or when they have created an expected effect on the environment. These are both cognitive achievements that occur in Piaget's sensorimotor stage II.

Research suggests that babies enjoy the feeling of recognizing the relationships between their own movements and the environment. This was demonstrated using mobiles that a three-month-old baby could learn to activate by pressing a small pillow with the head. As soon as the infants learned to establish the head press/mobile movement association, they smiled and cooed. Once they had learned how to do this, if the pillow acted in a capricious manner by inconsistently rewarding head presses with movements, the infants became frustrated and distressed (Watson, 1973).

By three or four months, babies come to establish these simple learned expectancies between their own behavior and the environment. The more consistent the relationship between environment and behavior, the more we can expect to see positive responses such as smiling. Between two and five months, the emotion of pleasure becomes more intense as babies develop an increasing sense of control. During five minutes of face-to-face play with their mother, each of two babies observed at weekly intervals increased the number of smiles per observation from two at two months to eight at three months to fifteen at five months on the average. One of the babies smiled 28 times in one five-minute session at five months (Fogel, 1982). These changes correspond with trends found in larger samples (Kaye & Fogel, 1980).

The beginning of the emotion of *delight* is seen in the expression of laughter. Babies first laugh at about four months of age when tickled or bounced. Because their laughter is tied to their understanding of relationships during stage III, they will laugh when they see their mother suck on a bottle or pacifier and when the baby tries to pull it out of the mother's mouth. At this age, caregivers and babies begin to play enjoyable games together (Sroufe, 1979).

By one year, infants can sustain their positive feelings beyond the simple joke of the kind just described. This kind of long-term positive mood state is called *elation*. Babies of this age will show off to get a laugh, and they will playfully exaggerate their expressions. They can show delight in their own achievements, especially as they develop the cognitive means to explore and gain mastery over the environment. They can also express affection for important people in their lives (Demos, 1982; Sroufe, 1979).

The final stage in the development of positive emotions is a sense of positive self-evaluation and a budding sense of *pride*. Now enjoyment is derived not merely from control or mastery but from having a sense of self in which a performance can be compared to a set of personal goals and standards. Pride differs from elation in mastery, because pride involves the feeling of "I did it," while mastery is the feeling "It's done" (Rheingold, Cook & Kolowitz, 1987).

The Development of Wariness—Fear

Babies at birth will show reactions of avoidance to adverse stimuli. For example, they will turn their heads from foul odors, and they will startle at loud noises, sudden movements, or looming objects. Although these reactions are automatic reflexes present at birth, *wariness* reflects a cognitive change occurring in Piaget's stage III. As the baby begins to detect regularities in the environment and to develop expectancies, things that cannot be initially understood create feelings of wariness. Babies may become quiet and stare at a strange person. When presented with a novel stimulus, they may knit their brows and become momentarily sober or look away (Bronson, 1972).

Such changes represent the infant's developing ability to control emotional reactions by *appraising* the situation before responding. This increased awareness of the environment, especially the development of object permanence and the ability to see relationship between things, leads at nine months to the development of *fear*. Babies of this age begin to show many fears that were not present before.

Acquired fears.   Fears acquired by a conditioned association between some object or thing and something painful or stressful are quite common. Examples are fear of particular people, of people wearing white coats (such as doctors), or of a dog's bark (Bronson, 1972). Specific types of acquired fears will differ among individuals.

Caregivers can help to attenuate acquired fears by showing the child a positive response in such situations. In one study, a noisy, flashing robot approached a year-old child. The child's mother, who was sitting nearby, was asked to make either a fearful face, a smiling face, or a neutral face. Infants were less likely to get upset if the mother posed a smile or neutral face (Klinnert, 1981). Known as *social referencing*, infants and young children often look to adult's reactions to help them figure out how to respond in ambiguous or fearful situations (Campos & Sternberg, 1981).

Fear of strangers.   Although infants of one year generally behave differently to strangers than to familiar people, not all infants develop adverse reactions to strangers, and those that do seem to be afraid of strangers only under certain conditions.

Babies are less likely to show fearful reactions to strangers if the strangers approach them slowly (Kaltenbach, Weinraub, & Fullard, 1980; Trause, 1977), if their mothers are present when the strangers approach (Eckerman & Whatley, 1975; Riccuiti, 1974), if they are with familiar caregivers (Fox, 1977), if the strangers are small people (including children) (Brooks & Lewis, 1976), if the strangers do not tower over the infants (Weinraub & Putney, 1978), and if they are in an unfamiliar setting such as a grocery store rather than a familiar setting such as their own home (Brookhart & Hock, 1976; Skarin, 1977).

You can reduce the baby's fear of strangers by asking the person to approach slowly, be sensitive to signs of wariness, and approach when the baby is with someone familiar. Because of the possibility of acquired fears, a baby may always be afraid of certain people because they remind the baby of some unpleasant past situation.

Separation. It was once thought that a baby's distress at being separated from the mother or from another familiar caregiver was due to a sense of loss of that particular person. Even two-month-olds have been shown to cry more after their mothers leave them than after being left by a stranger (Fogel, 1980). Recent findings show separation distress in infants is not always due to a sense of loss of a particular person but rather is due to being left alone without anyone else around.

Infants respond more positively to separation if they are left in the company of any other person, but especially if they are left by their mother or father with familiar people (such as grandmother, babysitter, or daycare provider (Riccuiti, 1974; Stayton, Ainsworth, & Main, 1973; Suwalsky & Klein, 1980), if they are left with toys or if they can see their mother in an adjoining room (Corter, 1977), and if they are left with their own pacifiers or blankets (Halonen & Passman, 1978; Hong & Townes, 1976). Babies who go to a new nursery school or a hospital are helped if accompanied by peer friends or by siblings (Field, Vega-Lahr, & Jagadish, 1984; Robertson & Robertson, 1971).

As babies enter their second year, they can cope with separation more easily. Instead of crying, they might search for their mother, try to alternate between frowning and pouting, or bite their lower lip to try to control the fear (Demos, 1982; Serifica, 1978; Sroufe, 1979).

As infants understand language and develop self-awareness toward the end of the second year, parents can help a baby prepare for separation by exchanging a few words of goodbye, explaining their absence, and giving a few instructions on what to do while they are away. Research has shown, however, that leave takings should not take longer than two or three minutes, after which the child starts to cling. Babies whose parents took only one or two minutes to say goodbye may have cried briefly as the mother left, but as soon as the mother was gone, the babies settled into a normal play pattern with the alternate caregiver. The longer the parent took to say good-bye, the harder it was for the baby to adjust to the separation (Field, Gewirtz, Cohen, Garcia, Greenberg, & Collins, 1984; Weinraub & Lewis, 1977).

By the age of 24 months, children will develop new kinds of fears related to their growing ability to think symbolically. A child might see a shadow in the dark as a lurking monster or expect fearful creatures to be hiding behind doors and refrigerators. Generally, such fears are real to the child, who is beginning to believe in the reality of the symbolic, fantasy creations that are newly forming in the mind.

The Development of Rage—Anger

This emotion begins with the baby's first cry (refer to Chapter 5). By age three months, as babies develop the expectations that lead to smiling, the failure of the environment to meet the previously established expectations can lead to the emotion of *disappointment*.

The emotion of *anger* arises between four and six months. Anger is the direct result of having one's motives disrupted. One study of infants' reactions to inoculations shows the transition from distress to anger. Two- and four-month-olds reacted to their shots with a pain cry and crying with tightly shut eyes. Seven-month-olds, however, responded with more angry expressions: crying with open, vigilant eyes (Izard, Hembree & Huebner, 1987). Anger usually results from the abrupt termination of pleasurable play or interaction.

The direct heir of this early anger is the emotion of *defiance*, seen in the aggressiveness of the two-year-old child during the stage of development popularly known as the "no" stage. The difference between defiance and anger is that the former is related to feelings that the self should not be restricted. Defiance, therefore, is a sign of the child's growing sense of personal autonomy and is related to the positive emotion of pride.

The Development of the Self

When a small baby looks in a mirror, there is a good chance that he sees another baby there. After 15 months of age, however, he sees himself in the mirror. How do we know this? If a red mark is put on the baby's forehead, 15-month-old and older infants will touch their own foreheads when seeing their image in the mirror. Younger babies will touch the mirror or not respond at all (Lewis & Brooks-Gunn, 1979).

Around the end of the second year, children begin to use words such as *I* and *mine*, indicating a clear sense of self versus others. What do these words mean to a baby? In one research study (Levine, 1983), 78 boys between the ages of 22 and 28 months were observed in a playroom with their peers. The children were also given some standard tests of self-definition such as the mirror recognition task and a test of the child's understanding of the personal pronouns "mine," "your," "I," and "me" (for example, the mother told her child to first "touch my nose" and then "touch your nose").

Children who scored the highest on the self-definition test were the most likely to label toys taken by peers with the word *mine*. In observing the peer interactions, the researcher discovered that saying "mine" rarely led to a conflict. It seemed that in saying "mine," the boys were attempting to understand the limits of the self rather than trying to lay claim over possessions, as in the following example:

Ted: My car, mine.
Mark: Mine.
Ted: Me.
Mark: Mine.
Ted: Me. No. No.

In this example (Levine, 1983, p. 548), Ted uses the word *me* to define his own body as well as his possessions. Rather than trying to regain a toy that Mark took, Ted is trying to define the toy as his. Mark can play with the car, so long as he knows it belongs to Ted (Levine, 1983).

Beginning around this time, the baby also learns words referring to inner states of the self. For example, a two-year-old might say "Head-ouch-cut" or

"I'm sad I popped it" (balloon) to explain inner states, or "Can't. Too hard" or "You need a stool to climb up" to explain the self's limitations and abilities (Bretherton, McNew, & Beeghly-Smith, 1981).

This kind of *self-awareness* is coupled with an awareness of the inner states of others and with the ability to function independently from mother and father in a wide variety of settings and tasks. The child also develops *self-control,* or the ability to regulate behavior, delay gratification, and tolerate periods of frustration (see Table 6-5). Both self-control and self-awareness are parts of a sense of personal autonomy that develops gradually over the first two years of life.

Communication and Language Development

The primary medium for interpersonal communication is verbal language. Indeed, it is through the use of language in interaction with other people that the child becomes aware of an autonomous self. Although its first words do not emerge until late in the first year of life, the baby begins to communicate at birth through *nonverbal communication* such as facial expression, cries and other sounds, and body movements.

The next chapter discusses how communication develops during social interactions in the first two years of life. The remainder of this chapter focuses

Table 6—5

CLAIRE KOPP'S DEVELOPMENTAL
PHASES OF SELF-REGULATION

Approximate Age (months)	Phase	Description
0 to 2½	Neurophysiological modulation	Activation of innate patterns of behavior and "automatic" modulation of arousal using sucking, sleeping, and habituating, culminating in stable periods of alertness.
3 to 9 and over	Sensorimotor modulation	Change of ongoing behavior in response to events in the environment, engaging in voluntary motor acts with awareness of the meaning of the situation, awareness of own actions.
12 to 18 and over	Control	Awareness of social demands of a situation; initiation, maintenance, and termination of physical acts; communication and compliance; self-monitoring of behavior. (Cognitive prerequisites are intentionality, goal-directed behavior, conscious awareness of action, memory of own behavior.)
24 and over	Self-control	Ability to delay behavior on request, to behave according to social expectations in the *absence* of external monitors (Cognitive prerequisites are representational thinking and recall memory, symbolic thinking, and a continuing sense of self-identity. Loss of control is evident in unusual or extreme situations, and few adaptive strategies are available to meet unexpected delays or problems.)
36 and over	Self-regulation	Flexible control processes that are responsive to changing situations, self-control strategies, conscious introspection.

(From C. B. Koop. Antecedents of Self-Regulation. A Developmental Perspective. *Developmental Psychology.* 1982.)

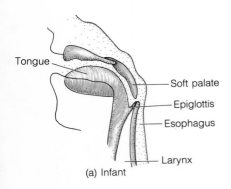

Tongue

Soft palate
Epiglottis
Esophagus

Larynx

(a) Infant

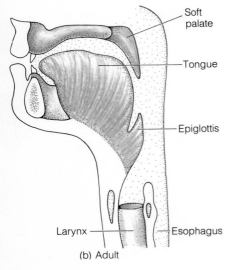

Soft palate

Tongue

Epiglottis

Larynx — Esophagus

(b) Adult

Figure 6—6

Comparison of Infant and Adult Vocal Tracts

(Reprinted by permission of the publisher from "Articulatory-Acoustic Perspectives on Speech Development," by R. D. Kent, in R. Stark (Ed.) *Language Development in Infancy and Early Childhood*, p. 109. Copyright 1981 by Elsevier Science Publishing Co., Inc.)

on vocalizations and gestures made by the baby, first prelinguistic and then linguistic.

Prelinguistic Communication

When asked about the first communicative sounds a baby makes, most people would mention crying. But what about the sounds made when burping, coughing, sneezing, and sighing? Parents respond to these sounds as well as to sounds related to bowel movements. Researchers have discovered that the first deliberate sounds a baby makes beginning at about age three months—called *cooing*—are nothing more than a recombination of the sounds that already were present in the "vegetative" noises just listed (Stark, 1978).

In cooing, babies seem to be singing. Vowel-type sounds are strung together as in "aaahhhh" or "ooooooooo," corresponding to Piaget's stage II. In stage III, infants begin to make new combinations of the cooing sounds, and new developments in the oral cavity allow for the production of consonants. Beginning at four months, the oral cavity and vocal tract begin to widen, and a piece of soft tissue (the epiglottis) that partially covered the larynx or wind pipe to prevent choking now moves up, allowing freer air flow, oral breathing (not efficient before this age, making it important to keep a small baby's nasal passages clear), and new sounds (see Figure 6-6) (Kent, 1981).

During the next few months, called the *vocal expansion* period, babies experiment with their ability to vary the direction of air flow, pitch, loudness, and abruptness of the sounds. A kind of vocal exploratory play called *babbling* emerges (Zlatin, 1973). Babbling sounds more like single syllables, for example, "ga-ga-ga-ga" or "buh-buh-buh-buh," than does cooing. It is no coincidence that babbling occurs during Piaget's stage III, secondary circular reactions. The sound produced is similar in nature to the baby's discovery by chance that he can move objects.

The use of gestures also undergoes developmental changes over the first year (see Figure 6-7). Pointing appears as a hand gesture in the first month, about the same time as facial expressions and vegetative vocalizations (Trevarthen 1977). By the second month, pointing tends to occur when the infant is in an attentive state, neither smiling nor crying (Fogel & Hannan, 1984; Hannan, 1982). At this age, the baby is not pointing in any particular direction; pointing seems to be a spontaneous expression of interest or attention. By six months, pointing is used to explore objects of interest by touching and tapping. It is not until nine months that pointing is intentionally used as a gesture. At this age, infants extend their arms and point their fingers toward an object or person (Fogel & Thelen, in press).

Near the end of the first year, infants begin to use pointing together with words to single out an object and to refer to the object while communicating with others. Sometime during the second year, they can combine words and gestures to make sentences that obey grammatical rules.

Explaining Language Development

Although it may seem logical for the child to progress from babbling to one-word speech to grammatical speech, developmentalists have puzzled long and hard over the process by which this change occurs.

Social learning theory. Certainly, children learn language in part by imitation and reinforcement. It is not necessary for a child to reproduce a word right after hearing it. Sometimes a child will say a word or phrase weeks or months after hearing it, in a process known as *deferred imitation*. By the process of *generalization*, children will also use the word in contexts and sentences other than those in which they originally heard it (Bandura, 1977; Bijou & Baer, 1965).

However, imitation, reinforcement, and generalization may explain the development of vocabulary, but not the *linguistic universals* of grammar common to all languages, such as subject, verb, and object. These latter properties have been explained using biological factors—that humans are born with a kind of brain that understands the environment in terms of the basic elements of actions and objects (Chomsky, 1975).

Ethological theories. These theories explain language by assuming the child has an innate mechanism for acquiring language. In McNeill's (1970) view, for example, children are believed to act like a language learning machine, or *language acquisition device* (LAD) (see Figure 6-8). Linguistic input is entered into the LAD, which contains some knowledge about word meanings and some innate grammatical structures that analyze words into parts of speech. The LAD then generates the linguistic output—the child's response—in grammatical form. The LAD is innately structured to recognize the linguistic universals of grammar and phrasing.

At 1–2 months
Spontaneous pointing.

At 6 months
Pointing used to explore objects.

At 9 months
Pointing intentionally used as a gesture.

Figure 6—7
Infant Pointing Patterns

McNeill's theory has its limitations. Although it can explain the existence of linguistic universals, it cannot explain why children take so long to develop grammar. One- and two-year-old children memorize certain word orderings. The concepts of subject, verb, and object do not emerge until the third year of life. It may be that children use words not as grammar but as means to an end, just as they would use any actions during stages V and VI of the sensorimotor period.

Cognitive theories.   Cognitive theories of language suggest that the first words are used as actions and obey the rules of action before they obey the rules of grammar. It has been found that stages of language development occur in parallel with stages of cognitive development. Research has shown that the beginnings of one-word speech occur during stage V, while the first word combinations develop during stage VI (Bates, 1979; Chapman, 1981; Corrigan, 1978).

Cognitive theories, while correct in identifying the link between cognition and language, tell us little about how language is acquired in real life. To do that, we have to look at the child's interactions with other people in the natural environment.

Ecological/systems theories.   It is obvious that childr___ ___t learn language by themselves. They speak to others to get ___ ___ addition, adults adjust their speech to fit the lev___ ___ interpret even poorly articulated speec___ ___ social system within a com___

    Childre___ ___te to achieve their own plan ___aying things correctly at firs ___yncratic. In other words, ch ___d action— to perform the f___

    Ecological s ___commu- nicate are made p___ ___can use the context and th ___child's idiosyncratic words ___ge devel- opment are not cooi ___n. Rather, they are achievement ___ning to take turns in a prelinguistic ___he object that the adult is looking a___ ___rstood by both the speaker and the list___

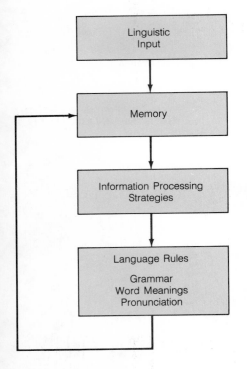

Figure 6—8
Theoretical Language Acquisition Device
(From McNeill, 1970.)

One Word Speech

Toward the end of the first year, babies begin to use sounds to communicate. At first, babies invent words to express things. One British boy, Nigel, used "nanana" to mean "give me that," "oh" to mean "that's interesting," and "mmmm" for "that tastes good" (Halliday, 1979). Another child used "mama" to mean "that tastes good" and "piti" to mean "that's interesting" (see Table 6—6).

These sounds are used in part as unique inventions of the child and in part because babies have some difficulty when first trying to imitate the words used by adults (Ferguson & Farwell, 1975). Adults who are familiar with the baby can often interpret the correct meaning of the word, because the baby's word may have the same number of syllables and the same intonation pattern

Table 6—6

THE FIRST SEVEN "WORDS" IN
ONE CHILD'S VOCABULARY

Utterance	Age (Months)	Meaning
eh	8	Said to people, distant objects, and toys.
dididi	9	Disapproval (loud) or comfort (soft).
mama	10	Refers to food; also means tastes good and hungry.
nenene	10	Scolding.
tt!	10	Used to call squirrels.
piti	10	Always used with interesting.
duh	10	Used with same g ongoing action.

(From *Speech Development of a Bilingual Child* b
Northwestern University Press.)

as the adult word (Menyuk & Bernho
to infer meaning, for example, by lool
or following the direction of the infa

We distinguish between *idiosyn*
and *conventional* uses—the words u:
Among the first conventional words ar
and *daddy*. Probably because it is :
speaks about daddy, babies usually
baby will use these words to refer t
the words will be applied to total strangers (Brooks-Gunn & Lewis, 1979).

The use of one word to apply to instances not typically included in the
adult's definition of that word is called *overextension*. A year-old baby may
use the word *car* to apply to all kinds of vehicles, such as trucks, planes, and
bicycles. Although it may appear that babies have trouble grasping the definition of the word *car* or the word *daddy*—similar to their lack of skill in
imitating adult sounds—this does not seem to be the reason that children
overextend word usage.

In one study (Nelson, Rescorla, Gruendel, & Benedict, 1978), the same
child who used the word *car* to talk about many different vehicles was able
to easily point out the correct vehicle when asked the question, "Where's the
truck?" Another child correctly identified strawberries when asked, but continued to call them "apples."

Two things are happening here. First of all, children's *comprehension*
skills are better than their *production* skills. Indeed, 13-month-olds can understand about 50 words, but they cannot speak 50 words until the age of
about 19 months. Also, children can pick up new words much faster at 19
months than at 13 months, sometimes after a single hearing (Oviatt, 1978).
The second thing that seems to be happening is that the child is using a single

Table 6—7

DEVELOPMENT OF
CONVENTIONALIZED
WORDS AND GRAMMAR

Age	Words	Grammar
9 to 12 months	Sensorimotor gestures	
12 to 18 months	Idiosyncratic words (symbols)	
19 to 24 months	Conventional words (signs)	Idiosyncratic word order
Over 24 months		Conventional word order

word to express several different meanings. A 13-month-old who says "apple" in reference to an apple is likely to mean "This is an apple" or "Give me some apple." The same child, when using "apple" to refer to a strawberry, may mean "This object is *like* an apple."

Because the child can recognize the strawberry when asked, it is unlikely that the child means "This object *is* an apple." This suggests that infants are using language to extend their understanding of the world. A strawberry is, in fact, like an apple in that both are red, round, and sweet. Overextensions, rather than being "mistakes" of usage, may reflect an intelligent attempt at category formation and a testing of the meaning and usage of words. Rather than try to correct the child's use of an overextension, research suggests that adults should merely respond with the correct adult word (Gruendel, 1977).

Using Sentences

In the next stage of language development, occurring around the second half of the second year of life and corresponding to Piaget's stage VI, children begin to combine words to make sentences. At first these sentences represent idiosyncratic word combinations that do not resemble adult grammatical sentences (see Table 6-8). The baby seems to learn some simple word orders and applies them in a fill-in-the-blanks fashion (Braine, 1976).

Table 6—8

EARLY TWO-WORD COMBINATIONS

Function	Formula	Example
Drawing attention to something	*see* + X *here* + X	see car here milk
Object's properties	*big/little* + X *hot* + X *old* + X	big house hot pipe old cookie
Possession	X + Y	doggy hole pig tail Kendall birthday
Plurality	number + X	two books
Recurrence	*more* + X *other* + X	more raisins other hand
Disappearance	*all gone* + X *all done* + X	all gone airplane all done juice
Negation	*no* + X *not* + X	no water not eat
Actor-action relations		sits doll sleeps baby Kendall break Mommy hit Kendall
Location	X + preposition	rock outside milk in there milk in cup
Request	*want* + X	want dessert want get down

(From M. Braine, *Monograph of the Society for Research in Child Development*, 1976, 164, p. 56. © The Society for Research in Child Development, Inc.)

To ask for something to happen again, English-speaking babies will use the simple formula "*more + X*" or "*other + X*," for example, "more milk" or "other toy." Similar patterns emerge in other languages (Slobin, 1970). In Germany, "more milk" comes out sounding like "mehr Milch," in Russia like "yesche moloka," and in Finland like "lisaa kakkua." Indeed, this type of speaking is so universal that we can see it in the first combinations of hand signs used by deaf children learning sign language (Dale, 1976).

These first sentences have been called *telegraphic speech*, because only a few words are spoken and because the words lack the grammatical refinements of older children. Telegraphic speech leaves out small words such as articles and prepositions, and it leaves out *inflections* (word endings such as *-ing*, *-'s*, and *-ed*).

Sometimes 18-month-olds speak what appear to be fully grammatical sentences, for example, "I don't want it" and "I don't know where it is." Researchers have found, however, that these phrases are poorly articulated and used almost as a single word. The same child cannot apply grammatical principles to different sentences (Nelson, 1981). The foregoing sentences are an example of *expressive speech*, which is usually found in social contexts and may have been imitated from the adult's "I dunno where it is" or "D'ya wanna go out?" This speech differs from *referential speech*, which is clearly articulated and refers primarily to specific objects rather than to actions or relations (see Table 6-9).

One of the basic requirements for the development of conventional grammar is the ability to use verbs, which is not acquired until the third year. Verb use is acquired later than noun use, because nouns refer to specific objects, while verbs tell about the relationship between tangible things, nontangible things such as actions, and abstract properties such as *to think* and *to feel*. Chapter 9 considers these developments as well as refinements such as plurals, verb tense, question asking, and pronunciation skills.

Chapter 7 considers the adult-infant interaction in more detail, demonstrating that social interaction in infancy contributes not only to language development but also to cognitive, motor, and emotional development. From the moment of birth, infants respond preferentially to social stimulation, prefering to look at faces and to listen to voices, for example. Chapter 7 discusses how these early social responses lead caregivers to help infants reach the developmental milestones discussed in this chapter.

Attribute	Referential Speech	Expressive Speech
Word type	Object names	Social routines
Part of speech	Nouns	Pronouns
Syntax	Single words	Phrases
Size of vocabulary	Large	Small
Content	Substantive	Relational
Production	Original	Imitative
Articulation	Clear	Mumbled
Situational	Referential	Interpersonal
Context	As in reading books	As in free social play

(From Nelson, 1981.)

Table 6—9

TWO STYLES OF WORD USE IN INFANCY

Chapter Summary

PHYSICAL DEVELOPMENT
- Infants grow about 14 inches during the first two years.
- Within age norms for motor development, wide variations exist that are considered normal.
- Assessment tests are better at establishing age norms than they are at diagnosing later problems.

HEALTH AND NUTRITION
- Undernourished infants are best served by a combination of nutritional supplements and parent education.
- Political, legal, and social barriers may impede the delivery of services to infants in need.
- Aside from the immunological properties of breast milk, both breast milk and formula milk provide adequate nutrition for infants under six months of age.
- Most infant deaths from accidents and poor health conditions are preventable. Sudden infant death syndrome is the leading cause of infant death for which there is no prevention or cure.

PERCEPTION
- Perception develops by a combination of neurophysiological changes and psychological improvements in information processing.
- Most aspects of vision and audition reach adult levels by six months of age. By three months, infants can recognize familiar faces and distinguish speech sounds.

COGNITION
- Piaget's theory of sensorimotor intelligence focuses on the transformation of simple reflex actions into intelligent goal-directed behavior and finally into thought processes.
- Information processing theories focus on the development of memory and the ability to compare current perceptions with those in memory. During the first two years, infants become able to compare multiple objects or ideas, using multiple sensory modalities.

EMOTIONAL DEVELOPMENT
- Emotions develop slowly and in relation to changes in cognition.
- Children become aware of themselves near the end of the second year of life when they can distinguish their own possessions from another's and control their own behavior and emotion.

COMMUNICATION AND LANGUAGE
- Communication begins at birth through nonverbal expressions and movements.
- Vocalization skills develop gradually over the first year before the first words are spoken.
- Theories of language emphasize the role of biological and social factors in the acquisition of language.
- Grammatical speech does not appear until the end of the second year.

Recommended Readings

Chomsky, N. (1975). *Reflections on language.* New York: Pantheon. A classic analysis of the biological approach to language development.

Lewis, M., & Brooks-Gunn, J. (1979). *Social cognition and the acquisition of self.* New York: Plenum. A review of studies of the development of self-awareness and self-understanding in infants.

Piaget, J. (1952). *The origins of intelligence in children.* New York: International Universities Press. Piaget, J. (1960). *The construction of reality in the child.* New York: Norton. Piaget, J. (1963). *Play, dreams and imitation in childhood.* New York: Norton. These three works are Piaget's studies of his own three children during their infancy period.

Stark, R. (1981). *Language behavior in infancy and early childhood.* New York: Elsevier. Contains research on prelinguistic and language development.

CHAPTER 7

The First Two Years: Connecting with Others

I remember the disappointment I felt when the pediatrician said that our two-year-old was in the fiftieth percentile on the growth charts as far as weight and height were concerned. Who wants to have the normal child? I resented the implication that my child could be average in any possible way. Certainly my children were destined to be above average. . . . Most of us are secretly worried that if the child is not special, then maybe we as parents are not. . . . If the child is little, you start talking about the joys of a "dainty" girl. If the baby is big, you pride yourself on having a "healthy" child. If the little heir is active, you describe him as "alert and intelligent." A quiet child becomes a "contented" child.

— *Angela Barron McBride,*
1973, pp. 65–67

Chapter 6 considered the growth and development of infants as if such processes happened without assistance. If you provide a baby with food and water, warmth and safety, and little else, what kind of person would result? People have tried to answer this question by depriving monkeys of their mothers and observing the abnormalities that result in their development.

Ethics have prohibited researchers from carrying out such studies on humans, but observations have been done on infants who have suffered natural deprivations of maternal care. In some orphanages, for example, children have received basic physical care but little attention and love from overworked staff. Infants observed in one such orphanage in Iran about 30 years ago were greatly retarded in their motor development, and fewer than 15 percent of them were walking by the age of three (Dennis, 1960). When these infants were provided with only 15 hours of social and physical stimulation (holding, talking, moving, playing) each month, their rate of development approached that of normal infants (Dennis & Sayegh, 1965).

This chapter takes a closer look at the specific features of how infants learn and grow in the company of other people. As the quote from Angela Barron McBride indicates, parents often interpret their observations of the baby in terms of their own needs, values, and expectations. Caregivers are people who themselves are developing, trying to reconcile their own needs with the responsibility of caring for a helpless infant. A baby is not merely a number on a growth chart but the object of intense love, the cause of fear and anxiety, and the impetus for the shaping of a new set of family rules, affections, and alliances.

This chapter also covers relationships outside the immediate family, concluding with a consideration of the long-term effects of experiences encountered during the infancy period and the extent to which early individual differences in temperament will continue to shape the personality of the older child and adult.

The First Relationships: Infants, Parents, and Siblings

Initial Physiological Regulations

The first few months of life are occupied with getting the infant's basic biological cycles into a regular and predictable pattern (refer to Chapters 5 and

6). Parents experience a lot of sleeplessness and fatigue during this period. By prolonging periods between feedings and by developing active and quiet times, a parent can help a baby to sleep less during the day and more at night (Sander, 1962). Occasional night wakings are common, however, even into the pre-school period (Richards, 1977). Following this early period in which mutual adjustments are based on physiological demands, the parent-infant interaction begins to focus more on behavioral, emotional, and cognitive aspects of infant development.

Reciprocal Exchange During Face-to-Face Play

At about two months of age, the baby becomes able to discern inner details of a face, spends more time looking into the mother's face and eyes, and smiles in recognition of the mother. Adults' response to these changes depends on the cultural context. In the Marquesas Islands of Polynesia in the South Pacific, three-month-olds are held on the lap facing away from the adult. Little mutual gazing takes place, and babies are rarely talked to or cuddled (Martini and Kirkpatrick, 1981). Navaho Indian mothers living in the Southwest of the United States will gaze for long periods at the baby's face while holding their three-month-old and may play by moving their hands and fingers in front of the baby's face to get the baby to follow their movements. These mothers, however, rarely talk to babies of this age (Callaghan, 1981).

In Caucasian peoples of North America and Europe, face-to-face play is an occasion for parents to show off a range of facial expressive and vocal acrobatics to the baby. When adults engage in such *baby talk,* they raise the overall pitch of their voice and include many tonal variations, producing a kind of sing-song speech (Stern, Spieker, & MacKain, 1982).

Eye-to-eye contact and the ability to respond to another person's smile are the foundations upon which most human interpersonal communication is based. By age 2 months, because of improvements in the infant's ability to perceive inner details of another's face, most infants are able to engage in responsive and lively face-to-face interactive play.

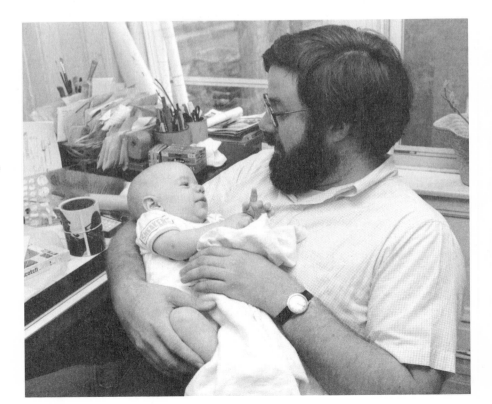

The speech in baby talk is highly repetitive compared with speech between adults, but each repetition makes a slight change over the previous statement. One mother, for example, was observed to say the following things in sequence: "*Hi . . . Hi* honey . . . *Hi* honey . . . *Ooh* . . . Ya gonna *ooh* . . . *Ya gonna* smile." Note how each statement repeats a theme and introduces a small variation. In addition to the verbal statements, nonverbal expressions show a similar *theme-and-variation* format. An adult may make a series of head nods punctuated by smiles and gentle touches (Stern, Beebe, Jaffee, & Bennett, 1977). These features of baby talk are believed to help the infant learn to perceive changes in sounds and expressions through repetition while maintaining interest through variation.

During face-to-face interaction with babies between two and five months of age, adults will notice that the baby displays predictable cycles of activity and pause. The baby may look at the adult for a few seconds, then turn away for a few more, and turn back to the adult. This "gaze-gaze away" cycle occurs because babies of this age do not have the ability to sustain their attention for long periods. When they look away it means they need a "time out" to regroup their attentional resources, and one should not prod babies into looking back before they are ready (Brazelton, Koslowski, & Main, 1974; Stern, 1974).

In a sample of 52 mothers and babies observed in face-to-face interaction at six weeks, the mother's facial expressiveness was very effective in holding a baby's attention if the baby was already looking at the mother when she became expressive. In only 18 percent of such cases, the baby looked away from the mother before the mother ended her facial expression (see Table 7–1) (Kaye and Fogel, 1980).

Table 7–1 also shows that if six-week-old babies are not looking at the mother, they are more likely to start looking if the mother is relatively unexpressive. For six-week-olds, the mother should be facially unexpressive to *get* the baby's attention and facially expressive in order to *maintain* attention. By six months, however, a baby is just as likely to look at or away from the mother during mother's facial activity or inactivity, suggesting that the older baby can take initiatives and sustain attention to mother regardless of the mother's state: The baby is becoming more of an equal social partner.

Initiative and Apprenticeship Through Games and Social Routines

Beginning at about six months, or during Piaget's sub-stage III, infants begin to take initiatives exploring their environment in systematic ways. They can

Table 7–1

PROBABILITY THAT THE INFANT WILL CHANGE GAZE DIRECTION DURING PERIODS IN WHICH THE MOTHER IS EITHER FACIALLY EXPRESSIVE OR FACIALLY NONEXPRESSIVE

Age Group	Infant is *not looking* at mother: Probability of changing to *looking at* mother		Infant is *looking at* mother: Probability of changing to *not looking at* mother	
	Mother Expressive	Mother Not Expressive	Mother Expressive	Mother Not Expressive
6 weeks	.30	.53	.18	.33
6 months	.41	.56	.55	.56

(From Kaye & Fogel, *Developmental Psychology, 16*, pp. 454–464. Copyright 1980 by the American Psychological Association. Reprinted/adapted by permission of the authors.)

integrate sensory information between two sense modalities, and they can relate two or more objects to each other. One of the main problems to solve in this period is how to coordinate attention to the parent and attention to objects of interest in the environment (Bakeman & Adamson, 1984).

Because the infant's skills are still incomplete, parents provide social supports by interpreting what they think the infant is trying to do and helping the infant carry out intended acts. Parents also set up challenges for the baby. Kenneth Kaye (1982) has referred to the infant as an *apprentice* in the rules and roles of society. In Kaye's theory, infants begin life with a set of inborn responses that draw adults to them (see Table 7–2).

At first, social interactions are structured primarily by adults. Gradually, however, the infant develops the ability to take initiatives and respond appropriately to others. By the age of six or eight months, infants learn to make their wishes known and realize that they can affect others by means of communication gestures rather than by direct action (Cohn & Tronick, 1987).

Because infants cannot clearly express their desires, adults try to interpret those desires and help the infants to carry them out, such as by retrieving an out-of-reach object. Adults also create new intentions by challenging the infant to reach a bit farther, providing displays the infant can try to imitate, and playing games that require the infant to learn the rules. In such cases, the infant is an apprentice, following the lead of the "master" and being given small and manageable tasks to work on. A parent's role is to break down complex tasks into subtasks that the infant can master easily and to facilitate the infant's attempt to assemble all the parts of the task. This is analogous to making a scaffold to provide temporary support while a building is in the process of construction; these caregiver behaviors have been called *scaffolding*.

Table 7–2

KENNETH KAYE'S STAGES OF
INDIVIDUAL DEVELOPMENT IN A
SOCIAL CONTEXT

Approximate Age (months)	Stage	Description
0 to 3 1/2	Shared Rhythms	Parents use the inborn regularity in infant behavior—cycles of sucking and attention arousal—to build an "as if" dialogue. Parents provide frames to help the infant regulate arousal and attention.
2 1/2 to 13	Shared Intentions	Sharing begins as a responsibility of the parents, who guess the infant's intentions and attribute meaning to the infant's behavior in a "he says" manner. Parents also serve as an auxiliary memory bank for the infant, possessing information useful to the infant's continued functioning.
8 to 24 and over	Shared memory	The infant can anticipate the parents' intentions and remember shared experiences. The infant learns what to expect of others and what others expect of him or her. The infant recognizes gestures and words but does not know that others understand them.
15 and over	Shared language	Self-consciousness and the consciousness that others have selves develops. Symbols are used. The infant projects his or her own view of reality into the minds of others and internalizes the perspective of others. The infant understands that the meaning of symbols is understood by both partners and therefore can participate in true dialogue.

(From Kaye, *The Mental and Social Life of Babies.* Chicago: University of Chicago Press, 1982.)

Toward the end of the first year, infants actively seek physical contact to alleviate distress or to establish attachment bonds when they are afraid or need assistance (Hay, 1980). One-year-olds will use the caregiver as an object of exploration by grabbing an ear or the nose, manipulating the adult's lips or a necklace, or pulling hair.

Although the need for physical contact is present throughout one's lifetime, cultures differ in how much contact is given as well as when and by whom it is given. Studies have shown that patterns of physical contact are related to *ecological factors:* the environment and the family system.

One of the most important environmental factors regulating physical contact between infants and parents is climate (Whiting, 1981). In warm climates all around the world, infants tend to be carried by caregivers (see Figure 7–1), kept in close physical contact during the day, and slept with at night. They are breast-fed for up to several years of age. Infants in cold climates, such as North America and Europe, tend to be separated physically at an early age in infant seats, and playpens, and they are carried in backpacks and pushed in strollers with little skin-to-skin contact. They sleep in cribs or cradles, apart from the parents. This is believed to be due to the need to wrap babies as protection from the cold, separating infant and adult by layers of protective clothing. It may be, too, that warmer climates present more dangers to crawling, curious babies such as insects and impurities in food and water (McSwain, 1981).

One of the most important aspects of parent-infant interaction after six months of age is play. In North America, infants and adults play games such as peekaboo, ball, give-and-take, point-and-name, patacake, and horsie (see Table 7–3). Games in North America occupy only about 10 percent of waking time for babies, with the rest of the time being taken up by solitary play, eating, and being cared for (Gustafson, Green, & West, 1979).

In other cultures, the proportion of playtime will vary, as will the types of games played. For example, Dutch and English mothers play about the same proportion of time with babies as in North America, and they all use verbalizations during game sequences. English mothers' games involve social exchanges and objects, like peekaboo, while the Dutch mothers play more physical games, including a lot of tickling and tossing (Snow, DeBlauw, & Van Roosmalen, 1979).

During the latter portion of the first year, as infants show evidence of understanding the words spoken to them, parents' speech to them changes (refer to Chapter 6). Speech to eight-month-olds is actually simpler than speech to four-month-olds (Davis, 1978; Sherrod, Crawley, Petersen, & Bennett, 1978). This is because by eight months, babies can understand some speech if it is made simple for them. This simplified speech is called "motherese," although fathers and other adults also use it (see Table 7–4). In addition to using motherese, adults use speech in play, making a cow "moo" or a dog "bark." They will describe object properties to infants, give pop quizzes ("What does the cow say?"), teach etiquette ("please" and "thank you"), and correct mistakes (West & Rheingold, 1978).

Verbal Interactions and Conversation

Within the context of a game, babies are learning the rules of grammar and conversation. Take, for example, the description of a peekaboo game as it develops between a mother and her 11-month-old daughter (Table 7–5). Note that the action of the game has clear rules: a sequencing of hiding and un-

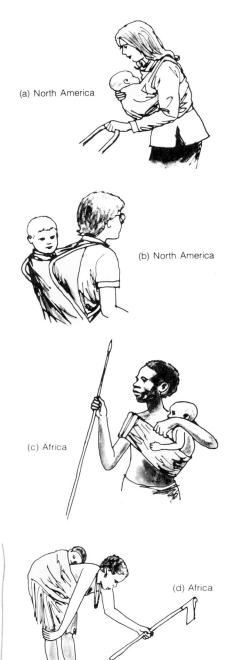

(a) North America

(b) North America

(c) Africa

(d) Africa

Figure 7–1

In warm climates infants spend more time in skin-to-skin contact with adults. Infants in cold climates must wear protective clothing making them more difficult to carry for long periods.

Table 7—3

CATALOGUE OF MOTHER-INFANT
GAMES

Name of Game	Game Description
Gonna get you:	Mother repeatedly tickles, grabs, jostles, or provides other tactual/kinesthetic stimulation to the infant. Often includes a repeated vocalization such as "I'm gonna get you" or "Ahhhhhhh-boom!" which terminates just as physical contact is made. (Active participation by an infant could include fleeing when approached or attempting to "get" the mother.)
Patacake:	Primary components are the mother's saying patacake and clapping or banging performed by either the mother or the infant. (Active participation by the infant would include beginning to clap only after the mother said "Patacake" or patting the mother's hands.)
Horsie:	Primary component is the mother's bouncing the infant, who is sitting on her knee or foot. The mother's verbalizations include "Want to play horsie?" or "Ride the horsie." (Active participation by the infant involves initiating the game or trying to prolong it by continuing to bounce after the mother has stopped.)
Peekaboo:	One member of the dyad is hidden and reappears. Hiding is typically accompanied by mother's calling to the child (if the mother is hidden) or by her asking, "Where's _____?" (if the child is hidden). Reappearance is typically accompanied by verbalizations such as "Peekaboo," "Peepeye," or "There he/she is!" (Mother may control all the hiding and uncovering, or the infant may actively perform some of these activities.)
Ball:	Involves the infant's repeatedly receiving and losing the ball. (Mother may hold up both ends of the game by tossing the ball to the infant and then taking it away, or the infant may actively participate by presenting or returning the ball to the mother.)
Vocal game:	Minimal requirement is that the mother be attempting to elicit a word or vocalization from the infant in expanded form, these interactions are verbal or vocal-verbal "conversations."
Build tower-knock down:	One member of the dyad builds a tower of blocks, and the other knocks the tower over. The sequence may be repeated many times. (Active participation by the infant is typically limited to knocking the towers down.)
Give and take:	Involves repeated giving and receiving of objects. Receiving by the mother is often accompanied by a carefully articulated "Thank you." Typically, the infant gives and the mother receives, although mother often returns the object to the infant.
Point and name:	One member of the dyad (usually the infant) repeatedly points to objects, each time waiting for a vocalization by the other (usually the mother, in the form of naming the object) before pointing to the next object. Pointing is sometimes accompanied by a questioning vocalization or by the query "What's this?"
Miscellaneous:	Any traditional infant game that occurs very infrequently at a particular age. Included are the game "Overboard," in which the mother repeatedly turns the infant upside down and says "Little girl overboard," and the game So big, in which the mother says "How big are you?" and the infant outstretches his arms while the mother says "So big." Also included are sequences with a toy telephone, in which the receiver is put to the infant's ear and the mother says "Hello," and interactions in which one or both members of the pair were waving or saying "Bye-Bye."

•Games are described here in complete form. Attempts to initiate these games were also included in the analyses.
(From Gustafson, Green, & West, 1979, p. 304. Reprinted by permission of Ablex Publishing Co.)

masking. Within the constraints of those rules, variations can take place. The person doing the hiding and unmasking can change, the signal for unmasking changes (and the baby makes a joke of using the cleaning tissue by saying "achoo" instead of "boo"), and the duration of the masking can be varied. In this way, rules of interaction such as taking turns are learned and used productively and creatively (Bruner, 1975).

By 18 months, parents and infants can do more than simply exchange objects or hiding/masking roles. They can participate in *cooperative play* in

Table 7—4

"MOTHERESE"—ADULTS' SPEECH TO CHILDREN

Characteristics	Differences from Speech to Adults
Speed	Half the speed.
Pitch	Higher pitch, more pitch contrast, ending sentences on a rising pitch, more whispering, more double stress (Example: "*Push* the *green* block").
Mean length of utterance (MLU)	Shorter.
Grammar	Simpler.
Vocabulary	Use of special words: bye-bye, peepee. Use of diminutives (doggie). More limited vocabulary. Unusual use or omission of pronouns (Example: "Where are mommy's eyes?" instead of "Where are my eyes?").
Semantic relations	More limited. Frequent use of statements about action ("Daddy's going away") or about object location ("The apple is in the basket").
Other characteristics	Frequent repetition and prompting the child with questions. Becomes more complex as child progresses.

(From Gleason & Weintraub, 1978, Adapted.)

which they work together to reach some joint goal (Hay, 1979), for example, one holding a cup while the other "pours" imaginary tea. Nonplay interactions, such as dressing, begin to take on a more cooperative character at this age.

Throughout the second year, adults continue to create social routines and help babies elaborate their communication and language skills through scaffolding procedures. In conversations, for example, adults make statements, ask questions, and lead the conversation by talking about things the child is able to discuss with one- or two-word utterances. The example of a mother and her two-year-old reading a picture book (see Table 7–6) illustrates this. During reading, adults give the names of pictures, ask for names using *what-* questions ("What's that?" and "What does the cow say?"), and ask for pointing by the child through *where-* questions ("Where's the cow?") (Ninio, 1983).

Some aspects of adult language correlate with individual differences in children's speech development. Others do not. Aspects of adult language that do correlate with children's advances are using simple noun phrases, repeating words and phrases, asking simple *what-* and *where-* questions, asking for information, asking the child to repeat an utterance, and asking permission

Table 7—5

PEEKABOO GAME

Age of Child	Rules of Game (M = Mother, C = Child)
11 months	M initiates game while drying C's hair after bath, covering baby's face with towel, saying *boo* twice on uncovering. Both laugh. Ten minutes later, C initiates, raising her petticoat over face and holding there until M says *boo*. Laughs and lowers petticoat. C repeats three times, M maintaining excitement by varying time to say *boo*, and C does not lower petticoat until signal *boo* is given.
11 months, 14 days	C has cleaning tissue in hand. Raises it in two hands to cover face, says *Achoo*, lowers it, and looks at M, both laughing. M does the same, saying *Achoo*.

(From Bruner, 1975.)

Table 7—6

CONVERSATION DURING
PICTURE BOOK READING

Mother	Child (Thirty Months)
1. (Points to a picture) What is that one?	
	2. Kitty cat
3. Well what is it?	
	4. Kitty cat
5. Well, I know there's a kitty in it; what's he in?	
	6. Huh?
7. What's he riding in?	
	8. Airplane
9. Right.	
	10. (turns page)

(From Kaye, *The Mental and Social Life of Babies*, 1982. p. 100. © The Society for Research in Child Development, Inc. Reprinted by permission of the publisher and the author.)

("Can I help?"). Simple verbal acknowledgement by the adult of children's statements—agreement with the child or partial repetition of the child's utterance—do not correlate with children's language level (Hoff-Ginsberg, 1986). These findings show that language development can be enhanced when adults ask children to produce new sentences, to think about their speech, and to clarify their meaning. The adult, therefore, should actively prod the child beyond the present language level to produce more precise and more complex speech (Rutter & Durkin, 1987).

Attachment and Affection in the Parent-Infant Relationship

Attachment refers to a lasting emotional tie between people such that the individual strives to maintain closeness to the object of attachment and acts to ensure that the relationship continues. The process by which infants develop lasting, affectionate emotional ties to adults over the first few years of life has been the subject of a great deal of scientific research. Before reviewing the findings of these studies, let's first look at some of the theoretical perspectives on how attachment develops.

Psychoanalytic theory suggests that attachment is the normal resolution of the oral stage of development (refer to Chapter 2). If the id's oral urges are gratified regularly during the first few months of life, the baby will develop the expectation that needs can be met and that distress will not continue for long without some relief.

After the baby is two or three months old, parents begin to notice that the baby's cry is a little less urgent when the baby is hungry or tired. At this time, psychoanalytic theory prescribes that the parent should wait a short time before responding to the baby. If the baby calms down, the parent has allowed the baby to meet this small crisis with his or her own resources. Not only do these minor frustrations lead the baby toward self-control, but they also make the baby aware of the person who is responsible for satisfying the oral needs. This awareness gradually expands into a dependency on that particular person and later into affection, attachment, and trust.

Learning theory has focused not on the feelings or concepts of the infant but on the behaviors observed when caregivers and infants are together. Caregivers seek positive reinforcements from their infants. For example, when parents pick up a baby, they expect the baby to become calm or to smile. When parents feed the baby, they expect the baby to coo and gurgle. When these positive reinforcements occur, the frequency of the same parental actions is increased on future occasions, which in turn reinforces the calming down, smiling, cooing, and gurgling of the baby. Learning theory, therefore, predicts that attachment behaviors develop by a complex process of mutual reinforcements (Cairns, 1979; Gewirtz, 1972).

Ethological theory suggests that adults have inherited some kinds of caregiving responses that are triggered in the presence of infants and young children and that infants are innately drawn to particular aspects of the caregiver.

In a classic study of the maternal-infant feedback system in infant monkeys (Harlow and Harlow, 1965), the babies were provided one "mother" made of wire mesh with a milk bottle attached and another "mother" of the same size made of wire covered with a soft cloth. The monkeys took food from the wire mother but spent almost all of the rest of their time with the softer mother substitute. In fearful situations, the monkeys clung to the soft mother and, when they got older, were even seen to carry the cloth mother around as a security object.

For monkeys, contrary to the predictions of psychoanalytic theory, physical contact with the mother is more important than food in the formation of attachments. Contrary to the predictions of learning theory, infant monkeys become attached to soft objects—an innate preference—and not to the object that gave positive reinforcement—the food-giving wire mother.

Studies of human infants in Great Britain (Schaffer & Emerson, 1964) have shown that the infants are most attached to the people who play and interact with them. Some babies who lived in extended families with many siblings and who had mothers who concentrated primarily on caretaking tasks such as feeding and diapering were less attached to the mother than to an aunt, uncle, or older sibling who spent the most time playing with the baby. This suggests that attachment in humans is based more on social interaction and communication than on feeding or physical contact as predicted by the psychoanalytic theory.

It was a dissatisfaction with the psychoanalytic and learning theory accounts of attachment that led John Bowlby (1969) to develop an ethological theory of attachment in humans. Bowlby suggested that mutual responsiveness and attraction between adults and infants resulted not because of mutual reinforcements but because physical appearance and behavior of adult and infant each innately attracts the other.

Such behaviors were discussed in Chapters 5 and 6. The newborn and small infants' physical appearance, called babyishness, elicits protective responses from adults. Babies also have a host of behaviors such as crying, sucking, smiling, looking at the caregiver preferentially, following the adult around, and becoming distressed when the adult leaves that have the net effect of orienting the caregiver to the infant and increasing the time that the infant spends in proximity to the caregiver (see Table 7–7).

As the infant develops cognitively, Bowlby suggests that attachment shifts from its reliance on innate responses to any adult, to the identification and recognition of a particular adult, to seeking that adult in an intentional, goal-oriented manner. The baby establishes a goal of maintaining proximity to the parent and uses information about the parent's present and past movements, the baby's locomotor skills, and current needs to keep the parent within view or to seek contact when needed.

By eight or nine months of age, infants begin to develop the same kinds of emotional feelings of closeness to the parents that the parents had felt for

In Harlow's research on attachment, monkeys are given substitute mothers with different characteristics. They prefer the soft and cuddly substitute over the substitute with the food.

Table 7–7

JOHN BOWLBY'S STAGES IN THE
DEVELOPMENT OF ATTACHMENT

Approximate Age (months)	Stage	Description
0 to 2 and over	Orientation to signals without discrimination of a figure.	The infant shows orientation to social stimuli—grasping, reaching, smiling, and babbling. The baby will cease to cry when picked up or when seeing a face. These behaviors increase when the baby is in proximity to a companion, although the baby cannot distinguish one person from another.
1 to 6 and over	Orientation to signals directed toward one or more discriminated figures.	Similar orientation behaviors as in the first stage appear, but they are markedly directed to the primary caregiver. Evidence of discrimination begins at one month for auditory and at two and a half months for visual stimuli.
6 to 30 and over	Maintenance of proximity to a discriminated figure by means of locomotion as well as signals.	The repertoire of responses to people increases to include following a departed mother, greeting her on return, and using her as a base for exploration. Strangers are treated with caution and may evoke alarm and withdrawal; others may be selected as additional attachment figures (for example, fathers).
24 to 48 and over	Formation of a goal-corrected partnership.	The child begins to acquire insight into the mother's feelings and goals, which leads to cooperative interaction and partnership.

(From J. Bowlby. *Attachment*. New York: Basic, 1969.)

Infants display behavior directed to other people such as smiling, gazing, cooing and cuddling. According to Bowlby, these simple behaviors have a powerful effect on the baby's social partners, causing the person being smiled or cooed at to draw closer, and to become affectionate and protective toward the infant. Even though infants are not able to walk, talk or feed themselves, they are not helpless, having been endowed with expressions that encourage other people to take care of them.

the infant since before the birth. We know this because infants of this age begin to display affectionate responses to the parents. During reunions after brief separations, one-year-olds feel genuinely happy to see the parent and may approach briefly for a hug or kiss (Sroufe, 1979). Infants will follow the parent and may be distressed at separation.

Bowlby's theory has been refined and expanded upon by others. Mary Ainsworth, who studied attachment in Uganda and North America (Ainsworth, 1979), suggests that there is a distinction between the *attachment system* (the network of feelings and cognitions related to the object of attachment) and *attachment behavior* (the overt signals such as crying and following that bring the parent and child in close proximity). She points out that each child's attachment system would be expressed through behavior in a unique way. For example, just because a baby does not get upset when his mother leaves does not indicate a lack of attachment. Rather, it may indicate the infant's relative feelings of security to carry on temporarily without the mother present.

Ainsworth believes that virtually all infants are attached to their parents but differ in the sense of security they feel in relation to the adult. The ease with which a distressed infant feels comforted by a caregiver is called the *quality of attachment*, which has three basic patterns: securely attached, insecurely attached-resistant, and insecurely attached-avoidant, (Ainsworth, Bell, & Stayton, 1971; Ainsworth et al., 1978).

Attachment quality is assessed in the Ainsworth Strange Situation Test in which infants are observed with their caregivers in an unfamiliar playroom (Ainsworth & Bell, 1970). The test consists of eight episodes:
1. Parent and infant are brought to the observation room by the observer.
2. Parent and infant play together for several minutes.
3. Parent and infant play with an unfamiliar adult.
4. The mother leaves the baby with the stranger for three minutes.
5. The stranger leaves, and the mother returns.
6. The mother leaves the baby alone.
7. The stranger returns without the mother.
8. The stranger leaves, and the mother is reunited with her baby.

An infant who is *securely attached* will seek comfort from the caregiver during the reunion (episode 8) and once comforted will return to independent play. Securely attached infants show interest in objects and the stranger and will get acquainted with the unfamiliar setting by making brief forays, always returning to the adult's side, and using the caregiver as a *secure base* from which to explore. Such infants will feel comfortable and secure in most situations.

There are two types of insecure attachments. *Insecurely attached-resistant* infants have a more difficult time feeling comfortable in a strange situation. They will vacillate between mother and an interesting object, but once near the object, they will not explore as freely as will securely attached infants. The resistant infant is more wary of strangers and tends to get more upset when the mother leaves the room. During the reunion, such infants show ambivalent responses to the mother, first approaching her and then pushing her away.

Insecurely attached-avoidant babies tend not to be upset when left with an unfamiliar person or in a strange setting. During the reunion episode, they may avoid approaching caregivers for comfort and may actively resist any attempts to be comforted by turning away and squirming to get down if picked up.

The Ainsworth Strange Situation Test and the three types of attachment quality by which infants can be classified have been shown to be highly reliable and valid. Test-retest reliability has been found in middle-class samples (Waters, 1978, 1983). This means that a baby who is classified as securely attached at one age will generally remain so at later ages. Those babies whose security classification changes over time come from homes in which there is a high level of social and economic stress, such as divorce, job changes, and poverty (Vaughn, Egeland, Sroufe, & Waters, 1979).

Stability of security classification does not mean that the children display the same kinds of behavior in the strange situation at different ages. Recall Ainsworth's distinction between the attachment system and attachment behavior. Sroufe and Waters have contributed to attachment theory by specifying the ways in which different kinds of behavior can be organized into a pattern that indicates a secure or an insecure attachment system (Sroufe, 1979; Sroufe & Waters, 1977). For example, in the study by Waters (1978), infants were observed in the Strange Situation test at 12 and 18 months. A baby may have been classified as avoidant at 12 months because he turned his head away from the mother when she picked him up, while at 18 months the same baby's avoidance might be expressed by arching his back and pushing away from the mother.

The validity of the Strange Situation test has been shown through correlations between the security classifications and other aspects of infant and parent behavior. For example, mothers of insecurely attached infants were inconsistent in their responses to the infants' cries and often ignored the infants' demands (Stayton et al., 1973). Infants who required less proximity and physical contact with the mother as they developed were classified as securely attached (Clarke-Stewart & Hevey, 1981).

The Ainsworth Strange Situation test has been criticized for being too subjective, since there is no direct correspondence between attachment behaviors and the attachment system. In addition, the test has not traveled well to other cultures. Usually, in North America, about two-thirds of the infants are classified as securely attached. This has not been true in other countries (see Table 7–8) (Grossman et al., 1985; Miyake et al., 1985; Sagi et al., 1985).

Takahashi (1986) has suggested that the Strange Situation test is too stressful for Japanese infants, who are rarely separated from their mothers and exposed to strangers during their first years of life. The higher percentage of resistant infants in the Japanese sample may be the result of an infant's becoming overstressed and thus resisting attempts by the mother for comforting. Thus, cultural differences in childrearing practices and culture specificity of the test may contribute to differences in outcome. More research is needed on this topic, however.

On the other hand, the reliability and validity studies have been conducted using double blind procedures, and the findings have been replicated in a wide variety of settings and samples. More controversy exists over the theory of attachment used by Ainsworth and her colleagues. In particular, the process by which secure and insecure attachments are developed is not well understood.

Table 7—8

PERCENTAGE OF INFANTS CLASSIFIED INTO THREE CATEGORIES OF SECURITY OF ATTACHMENT IN FOUR COUNTRIES

Country	Secure	Attachment Classification Resistant	Avoidant
Israel	37.5	50.0	12.5
Japan	72.0	28.0	0.0
United States	62.0	15.0	23.0
West Germany	32.7	12.2	49.0

(From Grossman et al., 1985; Miyake et al., 1985; Sagi et al., 1985)

What determines the quality of attachment at one year of age? There are two possible explanations: failure of the mother during the first year to create a warm and sensitive relationship with her baby, and behavior problems that reside in the child that no maternal response can alleviate.

Some studies have shown that the more responsive the mother is to the infant's needs at three months, such as during face-to-face play or in responding relatively soon to the infant's cries, the more likely the baby is to be securely attached at one year (Ainsworth et al., 1971; Belsky et al., 1984; Blehar, Leiberman, & Ainsworth, 1978; Grossman et al., 1985). Thus, unresponsive mothering can lead to anxious or avoidant attachment.

On the other hand, it is possible that a mother who has a fussy baby might respond to the baby less often simply because she has learned that her interventions are not always effective. Lack of security of attachment may therefore reflect an inborn inability to regulate distress and a heightened feeling of anxiety or wariness. The evidence for infant effects on adults is mixed, with some studies showing such effects and others not (Bretherton, 1985).

It is unlikely, however, that either the mother or the infant is the sole determiner of attachment quality. There are other cases, for example, in which three-month-olds cry more because their mothers are not responsive to their needs (Belsky, Rovine, & Taylor, 1984), thus setting up a negative cycle of infant fussiness countered by maternal insensitivity leading to a lack of security of attachment at one year.

Insecure attachments at 12 months were predicted by newborn fussiness, but only for those mothers who were not responsive to the infant's cries at three months and who had few opportunities for social support (Crockenberg, 1981). In addition, parents who are at risk for failures of attachment—teenage mothers, adoptive mothers, or single parents—can often inspire babies toward secure attachments. It is only when these parental risk factors are compounded by lack of support networks, poverty, or a history of psychiatric disorders that insecure attachments develop (Allen, Affleck, McGrade, & McQueeney, 1984; Brooks-Gunn & Furstenberg, 1986; Sameroff & Seifer, 1983; Singer, Brodzinsky, & Ramsay, 1985). Thus, insecure attachment can be explained by ecological systems theory as a complex combination of infant, parent, family, and social factors.

Attachment and Social Relationships

Once a child becomes securely attached, he or she is likely to remain that way, and this security will carry over into other social relationships and tasks. Infants who are assessed as more securely attached at one year show more sociability with strangers and greater competence in exploratory play at one and two years, and they are more socially competent with peers during the preschool years (Arend, Gove, & Sroufe, 1979; Slade, 1987).

Research has shown that infants can become attached to several people—mother, father, other family members, and substitute caregivers. Even when infants spend most of the day in the company of substitute care, such as on an Israeli kibbutz, they will show more positive responses when reunited with the mother after a brief separation than they will after a similar reunion with the *metapelet* (caregiver), and they can develop independent attachments with different substitute caregivers (Fox, 1977; Sagi et al., 1985).

Some of the earliest studies of attachment showed that infants were attached to their fathers, crying when the father left them and showing positive greeting when the father returned (Pederson & Robson, 1969; Schaffer & Emerson, 1964). Later studies of fathers and mothers in the Strange Situation test found few differences between mother and father attachment, although this seems to vary among families (Lamb et al., 1983). So long as infants are securely attached to at least one parent, they are less likely to be wary of strangers than are infants who have trouble approaching either parent in times of distress (Lamb, 1978a; Main & Weston, 1981).

The Emergence of Compliance

Once the baby settles into a secure attachment relationship, such security paves the way for the growth of autonomy and the development of the self. However, autonomy sometimes leads toddlers to be uncooperative, putting an emotional strain on the parent-infant relationship. At this age, caregivers begin to wonder how to gain control over the baby without losing the strong bond of mutual affection that has developed over the past two years.

How do parents behave to get their young children to comply with requests? The efforts parents make in this regard are called *control techniques;* the child's reaction is termed *compliance.* Compliance was studied in a laboratory situation with 24-month-olds by asking mothers to get their babies to play with each of the toys that the researchers had set out (Schaffer & Crook, 1979; 1980). Three types of compliance were discovered.

Orientation compliance means the mother could get the baby to look at a particular toy. Mothers could succeed in getting orientation compliance about 50 percent of the time on the first try, but all achieved it if they persisted. *Contact compliance* means getting the baby to touch the intended toy. First-time success occurred 33 percent of the time, and it was much more likely that the baby would touch the toy if he or she had already been looking at it as a result of either interest or prior orientation compliance. Manipulation of the toy in the appropriate manner was called *task compliance,* occurring on only 25 percent of the mothers' requests and usually only if the child was already looking at *and* touching the toy.

The message of this research is that you can get a baby to be compliant by timing your request to coincide with a behavior that is most likely to lead into the desired response. Thus, compliance is like adult-infant play in which the parent fits his or her behavior into the infant's existing ability. To some extent, to get a toddler to comply effectively, adults must comply with the toddler's needs and goals, at least for a short time, which is a kind of reciprocation of compliance (Parpal & Maccoby, 1985).

With two-year-olds, it helps to repeat requests and suggestions while trying to time the request to occur when the child is most likely to respond. Mothers are about as effective as fathers in controlling children of this age, but fathers tend to do more repetition of commands and requests (McLaughlin, 1983).

A final hint comes from a study by Holden (1983), who did unobtrusive observations of mothers and their two-year-olds in supermarkets. Mothers who took preventive measures, such as talking to the child or giving the child a bottle or something to eat while shopping, were less likely to have to scold their children for grabbing things off shelves or for creating a nuisance at the check-out counter. Thoughtful anticipation of the baby's most likely "mis"-

behavior and the provision of appropriate resources to help the baby maintain control of the situation, consistent with the apprenticeship theory of parent-infant interaction, seem to be the best kind of control techniques for caregivers of toddlers.

Sibling Relationships in Infancy

Research has shown that the middle-class North American mother typically prepares the older child or children for the birth of the new sibling while she is pregnant. In response to the news of a new baby, few toddlers expressed negative feelings: 47 percent were positive, and 40 percent were ambivalent (Nadelman & Begun, 1981). After birth, about half these children showed positive responses to the new baby. The others either were ambivalent or reverted to periods of babylike behavior such as following the mother, fussiness, demands for attention, or bed wetting (Nadelman & Begun, 1981; Rapaport, Rapaport, & Strelitz, 1977).

It seems that the toddlers are concerned about their own relationship to the mother and need reassurance that the attachment is still intact. If they do not receive this reassurance, negative reactions may develop (Dunn & Kendrick, 1981a). One of the best ways to lessen sibling rivalry is to avoid overindulging the first-born when a small baby. Research has shown that those toddlers whose mothers gave them lots of attention, played with them often, and issued few prohibitions when they were babies showed the fewest positive responses to the new baby and the most jealousy (Dunn & Kendrick, 1981b).

As the younger sibling develops language and motor skills that allow for an equal partnership between siblings, the internal dynamics of the family change in important ways. We can think of a family as a nested set of relationships and alliances (Vandell & Wilson, 1987). After the new baby is born, alliances may develop between the mother and the new baby and between the father and the older sibling. During disputes, parents may act as advocates and allies of one child or the other, or they may encourage the first-born to give in to some of the younger child's demands.

Sibling relationships change as children get older. A toddler's interest in a new baby may be replaced later with resentment as the baby begins to take a greater share of family resources: toys, space and parental time. Most sibling relationships are a mixture of both enjoyment and distress, play and conflict. The overall quality of sibling relationships depends in complex ways on the children's ages, sexes, and the quality of the parent-child relationship with each child individually and together.

Research on 49 families has shown that by the time they reach age two, older siblings are becoming sensitive to these family dynamics (Dunn and Munn, 1985). Using methods of direct observation of how family conflicts were initiated and resolved, it was found that two-year-olds showed a talent for learning how to annoy the younger sibling (for example, teasing, making disparaging remarks, showing a toy spider to a sibling who does not like spiders) and to enlist the help of the mother during sibling conflicts.

When the conflict involved the younger baby and the mother, the two-year-olds were extremely interested. They rarely laughed at their baby brother or sister in such conflicts and often came to the younger child's aid when he or she became distressed. Some of the strategies used by older siblings to diffuse the conflict between mother and younger sibling were, for example, repeating the sibling's action that the mother disliked, giving the sibling a similar object of the kind the mother had just taken away, prohibiting or "scolding" the mother for her punishment of the sibling, and comforting the sibling. These findings show that the family provides a situation in which the child becomes motivated to understand other people. In some cases, this means understanding how to annoy people, but it also means learning how to nurture and protect.

After language is acquired by the younger siblings, new alliances form. One type is a same-sex alliance: mother-daughter, father-son. Another is based on mutual interests and shared activities: One parent reads with the children, the other goes for walks with them. A final type is a same-generation alliance: parents versus children. According to the research of Kreppner, Paulsen, and Schuetze (1981), each child's sense of self is enhanced in this type of alliance. With the younger child as ally, the older child is able to develop a more objective view of the parents as separate individuals. Parents may begin to feel freer, and they become able to discuss openly their own needs as adults within the family context.

When the youngest child in the family reaches the end of infancy, parents can relax more and perhaps return to some of the priorities that were set before they became parents. Chapter 11 discusses further the topic of sibling relationships during the preschool period.

The Transition to Parenthood: Effects of Infants on Parents

Psychoanalytic Theory.   Because infants change so rapidly, parents seem relatively stable by comparison. The experience of being a parent can change an adult's sense of self and provide an outlet for an adult's need to be productive and to make a contribution to society. Erik Erikson (1950) called this the need for *generativity*. Child-bearing and childrearing are only one way to meet this need. Another way is in the world of work and careers. Many adults attempt to balance a desire to parent with a desire to work. In any case, including a baby in one's life is not an easy task for most new parents.

Ecological/systems theory also suggests that the parent-infant interaction is affected by all the other relationships within the family (Belsky, 1981), including both direct effects and mediated effects. *Direct effects* are those that occur as a result of social interactions with others. *Mediated effects* are those that occur as a result of interactions in which the infant is not a direct participant. Thus, for example, the quality of the mother-father relationship has been shown to affect the infant's attachment to the mother.

Pregnancy requires coping with physical changes and the uncertainty of the future as well as with marital and sexual changes. In the early months and years of the infant's life, parents must deal with a nearly total alteration of their lifestyle, lack of sleep, lack of time as a marital couple, and the needs of older siblings (refer to Chapter 4).

Predictors of Involvement in Childcare

A growing amount of research is emerging on how adults manage this transition, the prior factors that predict a successful transition, and the concurrent factors that sustain the parents' well-being. This research reveals that men and women derive different meanings from the experience and require different kinds of support to sustain them.

Although there are conflicting findings, when one compares results across research studies, a number of clear trends emerge. The amount and quality of childcare offered by the father seem to depend upon the father's relationship to the mother. Men who are more satisfied with their marriages, who believe that men and women should play important roles in childcare, and whose wives share similar sex-role attitudes will spend more time engaged in childcare. Amount of childcare by men is also predicted by the quality of the men's relationship with their own fathers (Belsky, Gilstrap, & Rovine, 1984; Feldman, Nash, & Aschenbrenner, 1983; Goldberg & Easterbrooks, 1984; McHale & Huston, 1984; Palkovitz, 1984). Women's involvement in childcare is less likely to be susceptible to such factors. Although the amount of time spent with infants is reduced if mothers work, the quality of interaction with their infants is about the same for working as for nonworking mothers (Stith & Davis, 1984).

It is notable that sex of infant is not an important predictor of childcare involvement during the infancy period for either mothers or fathers, and a parent's expressed sense of masculinity versus femininity is related inconsistently to childcare.

In general, a parent's ability to nurture an infant depends on the adult's personal resources such as a capacity for empathy and seeing the perspective of the infant, the pleasure derived from nurturing, and personality integration, that is, the adult's ability to tolerate anxiety and uncertainty, control hostile feelings, and effectively utilize external support networks such as friends, spouse, and other family members (Belsky, 1984; Heinicke, 1984; Kropp & Haynes, 1987). The latter—social support—is particularly important for parents who lack personal maturity or the knowledge and skills required to parent. Teenage mothers who live at home with their own mothers, for example, become more knowledgeable about infants and provide better quality care than do those who live alone (Brooks-Gunn & Furstenberg, 1985; Stevens, 1984).

On the other hand, some women who are abusive and neglect their children behave in similar ways to their friends and relatives. Thus, even when a potential support network exists, the mother's antisocial behavior leads to her alienation from sources of support and creates a negative cycle of child maltreatment and mother despair within the family and social system (Crittenden, 1985).

Parent support and parent education programs can be effective ways to help parents at risk for abuse and maltreatment. The most successful programs are those in which the staff is well trained and has a professional attitude toward its role as parent educator, those that help the mother develop a wide range of social and employment skills as well as parenting skills, those in which the program recognizes and incorporates the values of the parents' cultural or subcultural group, and those that have a clear conception of the process of adult development and change (Powell, 1984).

Differences in Mothers' and Fathers' Childcare Styles

The results of research on differences in childcare styles often conflict, due perhaps to the changes taking place in society about the amount and type of parenting roles acceptable for men and women. Studies done in the mid-70s reported closer physical ties and more sharing with infants of the same sex (Lewis & Weinraub, 1974; Weinraub & Frankel, 1977), although such effects have not been found for middle-class samples in recent research.

In the late 70s, research findings showed that mothers used more verbalization and toy play and held the babies more than did fathers, who used more physical/social play (Clarke-Stewart, 1978; Lamb, 1977). Fathers were found to play at higher levels of arousal and use more physical action (such as tossing the baby in the air) than were mothers (Yogman, Dixon, Tronick, Als, Adamson, Lester, & Brazelton, 1977). These differences were found even in families in which the father was the primary caregiver (Field, 1978). Another study found that the type of speech to babies was similar for mothers and fathers speaking individually to infants, but when all three were observed together, mothers did more talking (Golnikoff & Ames, 1979).

As more women with infants return to the work force, fathers will have increasing opportunities to share in the care of their young children. Research studies show most men are caring parents, and enjoy the time spent with their children.

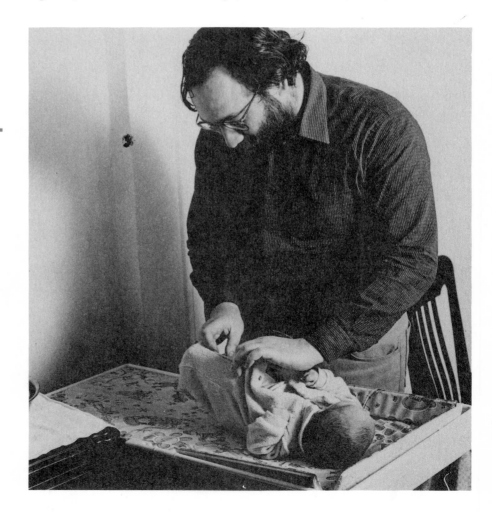

Research done in the early 80s found that mothers gave more social stimulation, caregiving, and affection than did fathers, and mothers were more responsive to infants' cues of interest and bids for attention than were fathers. These differences were true primarily for the first half year, and fewer mother-father differences were found in the second half-year (Belsky et al., 1984; Power, 1985). It seems that fathers take a more active role in parenting when the baby is older and more capable of independent play, when they are alone with the baby, and when the marriage and social/cultural norms provide support and encouragement for an active fathering role.

Some evidence exists that the father's involvement is important to the infant's development. For example, marital quality is related to the security of the child's attachment to mothers and fathers (Goldberg & Easterbrooks, 1984). In addition, the amount of support and empathy a husband provides for his wife seems to be a better predictor of toddler sensorimotor and attachment development than is the amount of time the father spends in childcare (Easterbrooks & Goldberg, 1984; Feldman et al., 1983). Similar results were obtained in Japan, where the role of the father during the infancy period is considerably less significant than it is in North America (Durrett, Otaki, & Richards, 1984).

These findings show that social support in the form of empathy for the parent's difficulties—from within or from outside the family—can have a powerful effect on the parent's success in that role and on the infant's development.

Relationships Outside the Immediate Family

Peers

A psychoanalytic view of early development suggests that infants first learn to regulate emotions in the mother-infant relationship. Systems theory suggests that infants learn the basic rules of social exchange and communication within the scaffolding framework of the parent-infant interaction. These views of early social development imply that an infant's response to and relationship with age-mates is a secondary relationship based on the skills and rules learned in the primary parent-infant relationship.

Research evidence only partly supports these views. Although it is true that some social and emotional regulations are learned when one is a social apprentice to an adult, the inherent equality of peer relationships seems to offer infants and young children the chance to take initiatives and to create their own unique games and social routines with someone at their own level (Hartup, 1979).

Even at age three months, infants will look at an age-mate for longer than at an adult and make more abrupt, excited movements to the peer (Fogel, 1979). Three-month-olds vocalize, reach, and squirm more to a peer than to their own mirror image (Field, 1979a). By six months, infants direct more looking and vocalizing and less touching at peers than at mothers (Vandell, 1980).

Between six and 12 months, peers become more involved in mutual play, including mutual touching, smiling, and gesturing (Eckerman & Whatley, 1977; Jacobson, 1981), which by one year evolves into mutual exchanges of tickling, touching, and laughing at each other (Ross & Goldman, 1977). Between 12 and 18 months, toys become integrated into peer play, such as giving and taking of objects and rolling and throwing balls back and forth, but interactions

Families of Infants with Long-Term Illnesses and Handicaps

The results of the research reported on determinants of parenting behavior and attitudes were taken from middle-class families with normal infants. When infants are born with some sort of disability, such as prematurity, deformities, Down's syndrome, or cerebral palsy, additional stress is placed on the family, and the parents may suffer a great deal.

Depending upon the severity of the handicap, family members may suffer chronic sorrow for themselves and for the handicapped infant. Family members may feel an initial rejection of the handicapped infant mostly because of fear and lack of knowledge of the condition, and many people find that their interpersonal relationships become strained (Blake, Stewart, & Turcan, 1975; Brooks-Gunn & Lewis, 1982). Families may also suffer strain from the extra visits to doctors and hospitals, the cost and time arranging for special equipment, and emotional swings from alternately wanting to abandon and wanting to overprotect the infant (Rapaport et al., 1977).

Handicapped infants may affect marriage stability as well, although this occurs in less than 10 percent of cases. Siblings experience disruptions in their lives and may receive less time from parents than children in families with normal infants. Vacations, family routines, and social times are all affected by the handicapped infants (Korn, Chess, & Fernandez, 1978).

Some aspects of the parent-infant relationship depend on the severity of the handicap. The mildest effects are seen in premature infants. Parents tend to overcompensate for the presumed deficit and provide additional indulgence and stimulation during the first year of life, which is the time when most preterms "catch up" to normal infants in their developmental assessment scores (Branchfeld, Goldberg, & Sloman, 1980; Crawford, 1982; Field, 1982).

At least one study found, however, that during the second year of life, mothers of preterms are less responsive to their infants than are mothers of normal infants (Barnard, Bee, & Hammond, 1984). Although these differences are small and perhaps not noticeable except when large groups of preterms are compared with normals, other research has shown that subtle but significant effects of prematurity may persist into early and middle childhood in areas of emotional maturity, language skill, and perceptual-motor functioning (Grigoroiu-Serbanescu,

1981; Taub, Goldstein, & Caputo, 1977). Significant improvements made in neonatal intensive care (refer to Chapter 5) may lessen the magnitude of these effects for infants being born today.

Down's syndrome (refer to Chapter 4) is another category of risk to the parent-infant interaction. Down's babies smile and vocalize less to parents than do normal infants (Berger & Cunningham, 1983; Rothbart & Hanson, 1983); in return, the parents smile and vocalize less at their Down's babies (Jones, 1977). A general lack of smiling and vocalizing characterizes other disorders, such as cerebral palsy and brain dysfunctions, creating risk for parent-infant attachment. On the other hand, Down's babies show no differences in activity level, amount of crying and soothability, and actually gaze for longer periods at their mothers (Rothbart & Hanson, 1983).

Research shows that if parents are educated about the nature of the disorder and if they make an effort to treat their infants as normal children with "special" problems, positive benefits result for the infants. Handicapped infants who received more social stimulation in the first year of life scored higher at age two on the Gesell Developmental Schedule, the Bayley Scales of Infant Development, and a language development assessment (Cohen & Beckwith, 1979).

quickly break down if one child fails to take his or her turn in the game, perhaps because of the absence of a scaffolding partner (Jacobson, 1981; Ross & Goldman, 1977; Vandell & Wilson, 1987).

During the second year of life, peer play becomes increasingly related to *situational constraints,* such as the presence of a third person, the child's familiarity with the peer, and the child's past experience with other peers. When 10- to 14-month-old children's mothers were present in a parent co-op nursery school, the children were less social and more negative to peers than when the mothers were out of the room (Field, 1979b). The mothers' presence caused more toy snatching and more crying. At this age, these responses may serve as signals to the mother of the infant's discontent about something rather than as a reflection of the infant's relationship to peers.

Familiarity has been shown to affect children as young as 12 months. Friends were more likely than nonfriends to touch and lean on each other, to initiate interactions with each other, and to show positive feelings towards each other (Lewis, Young, Brooks, & Michalson, 1975). In addition, toddlers with more peer experience are more active in peer encounters and show more complex social behavior with peers (Mueller & Brenner, 1977; Vandell, 1979).

It does not take children long to develop peer friendships, and even inexperienced toddlers can quickly develop peer interaction skills. Research suggests that children are drawn to each other from an early age, and in spite of real limitations in the ability to structure and maintain social interaction, peer interaction contributes something important to the toddler's social skills.

By the end of the second year of life, toddlers spend more time with their peers even if the mother is present and make fewer bids for maternal attention when a peer is present than when they are alone with mother. If, however, the mother has a friend at the house and the infant does not, the child is more demanding of the mother's attention than when mother and infant are alone (Rubenstein, Howes, & Pedersen, 1982). This kind of jealousy reflects the still immature social and perspective-taking skills of the toddler.

Alternative Caregivers

The number of employed mothers with infants has significantly increased over the past few years. Using a representative sample of 55,000 households in the United States, it was found that 33 percent of mothers with children under one year of age were employed in 1982 compared to only 24 percent in 1977. Almost half of the mothers whose youngest child is under four years of age were employed in 1982 (Klein, 1985).

Many people are concerned about the kind of care their baby will receive in group care settings and about whether the amount of time away from the baby will weaken the mother-infant attachment relationship.

In one research study using six-month-old infants, the responses of 10 nonemployed full-time mothers to their babies were compared with those of 10 employed mothers who had children in group care and with 10 substitute caregivers in group care environments. No differences were found between employed and nonemployed mothers in social stimulation, contingent responding to the baby, and display of positive emotions, and both groups of mothers were higher on these measures than were the substitute caregivers. The latter finding seems to be due to the larger number of children cared for by the substitute caregivers rather than to any lack of competency in childcare on their part (Stith & Davis, 1984). There were no differences between the groups of infants in their Bayley scores.

A number of research studies have shown that group care experience does not disrupt the mother-infant attachment. Infants tend to choose their mothers over the caregiver when given a choice between the two in a stressful situation (Kagan, Kearsley, & Zelazo, 1978; Portnoy & Simmons, 1978; Ra-

Effects of Separation from Mother in Infant Monkeys: A Model for Humans?

Because the environments of human infants are complex and involve many variations in living arrangements, nutrition, number of primary caregivers, type of alternative care, etc., it is impossible to isolate the effects of the separation alone without doing experimental studies. Since the patterns of attachment and responses to short-term separations—distress, following, lack of interest in exploration—are similar in humans and other primate species (Bowlby, 1969; Hinde, 1974), one group of researchers attempted to recreate in rhesus monkeys patterns of mother-infant separation that were roughly similar to those of human infants in a day care situation (Suomi, Mineka, & DeLizio, 1983).

The subjects of this study were eight infant rhesus monkeys and their mothers, four of whom were in the separation group and four in the non-separation control group. The infants and mothers of both groups lived in their home cages undisturbed until the first separation. At age 14 weeks, the infants were separated from the mothers from Monday until Friday. The procedure was continued for eight weeks with four days separation and three days of reunion. After this period, the infants remained in the home cage with the mothers for six weeks. Then came another eight weeks' separation and reunion cycle, followed by another six weeks of nonseparation in the home cage.

When the subjects were 43 weeks old, both the separation and the control groups were separated from their mothers for 30 weeks. All four of the separation infants lived together in one cage, while the four control infants lived together in another cage. After 25 weeks of living in the peer group, all the subjects were given a social preference test. The infant's own mother was presented along with other adult females and then again with the infant's peer group members.

The study found that in response to each of the four-day separations, infants showed the reaction to separation that is typical of rhesus monkeys: protest cries, self-clasping, reduction of exploratory play, and passivity-despair. However, the intensity of the protest response declined over the repeated separations, and few infants displayed the passivity-despair response.

The repeated separations had a marked effect on the infants' development of independence compared to the control group. When reunited with their mothers, infants clung to them more than just before the separation and more than the levels of clinging found in the control group. Separated infants were also somewhat slower to develop locomotor and social responses. However, few differences existed in the interactions with peers between the separation and control groups.

Seven months after they were separated from their mothers to live in the peer group, the infants were given the social preference tests. Infants in the separation group tended to avoid approaching their mothers. Control infants tended to avoid the unfamiliar females and did not ignore their mothers when in the company of peers.

These findings are surprising, because during the period of regular reunions, the infants showed increased clinging and other attachment behavior to the mothers. It may be that avoidant reactions similar to those observed in human infants develop as a means of coping with the repeated separations and the feelings of conflict or distrust of the mother (Main, 1981).

Even though the infants in this study seemed to "get used" to the repeated separations and showed little despair, they showed heightened anxiety during reunions with the mother and avoided their mothers later in the social preference tests. Thus, the effects of repeated separations from mother may be *masked* in some settings and more visible in others.

No easy comparison can be made between different species, especially since during the regular separations the human infants would never be left alone as were the rhesus monkeys. Nevertheless, the results of the study suggest that there may be some long-term effects of mother-infant separation in humans and that researchers and caregivers alike should be alert to possible disturbances in children's behavior.

After parents return to the work force, a baby will typically spend part of the time in a group care setting. Research shows that well-managed and well-funded facilities for infants and pre-school children can be healthy and stimulating environments for children. The United States has been slow, however, to establish minimum standards for group care of infants. Such standards would guarantee that all children have the opportunity to benefit from a high quality group care experience.

gozin, 1980). Indeed, infants seem capable of forming multiple attachments while still preserving a special place for parents in their lives. In addition, group care does not have a negative effect on social and cognitive development, and it may even enhance development for some groups of infants because of the extra stimulation provided, especially from peers (Kagan et al., 1978; Clarke-Stewart, 1982; Rubenstein, Howes, & Boyle, 1981).

The problem with some of these research studies on the effects of group care is that they have been done primarily in well-managed and well-funded day care centers and day care homes. We cannot say what the effects of day care might be in situations in which the child encounters lack of adequate stimulation or neglectful and abusive conditions. In such situations, it may be difficult to isolate the effects of the day care situation from the effects of separation from the mother.

The discussion on the effects of group care on long-term development of infants raises a more general issue: How do different kinds of experiences in the infancy period affect the potential for future behavioral and psychological development of the child? To what extent is the infancy period responsible for the creation of individual differences in our personalities and intelligence? We turn to these questions in the final section of this chapter.

Day Care Regulation

No national standards or any enforceable laws currently exist to regulate the kind of outside-the-home care received by infants and young children. Large day care centers are regulated by licensure laws, which vary from state to state, but licensed day care facilities account for only 17 percent of the three million children under the age of 14 who spend at least ten hours per week in out of home care. The majority of group care takes place in nonlicensed, family-run day care homes. At highest risk are lower-income black children, who are overrepresented in day care (28 percent in day care compared to 17 percent of blacks in the total U.S. population). Day care homes in low-income areas are likely to take in more children than they can handle in order to increase their earnings (Klein, 1985; Nelson, 1982; Ruopp & Travers, 1982; Slaughter, 1980).

One problem in the creation of new day care facilities by private organizations is that most families in which both mother and father are working cannot afford to place a child in a day care center, the cost of which might be as much as 20 percent of their income. It is unlikely that in the next decade free, publicly funded day care will be provided for anyone other than poor, handicapped, or abused children. Although some parents can claim a personal income tax credit for day care, the credit does not cover the costs (Morgan, 1983).

According to Diana Slaughter (1980), there are three reasons for the lack of a coherent policy on day care for infants and children. First is the myth that the modern family can be independent and self-sufficient. Even though research on children and families has revealed that the welfare of people depends upon a complex network of social support, many Americans believe that social policy legislation in general infringes on the rights of the family to make its own choices. This distrust of social policy legislation does not occur in other advanced nations. Israel, Japan, and Sweden, for example, all have model legal and social systems that explicitly protect the rights of women and provide for the health and welfare of people from infancy to old age. These countries view such policies as the right of all citizens, regardless of income.

The second reason offered by Slaughter is the fragmentation of social services that exist for families, especially for lower-income families. Services, when they exist, are scattered among many different agencies, while efforts to streamline the system typically meet with strong political opposition. Consistent guidelines for day care, called the *Federal Interagency Day Care Requirements* (FIDCR), were formulated in 1968. Although they have been revised over the years, they were never implemented in legislation because of political controversies about which agency could best administer them. The FIDCR's search for an administrative home finally succumbed to Federal budget cuts in the 1981 Reagan administration.

The third reason for failure to implement day care legislation is a public disaffection for behavioral science research. Beause of public complaints about a small number of social science research projects, all other projects are tainted by association. Public attention in recent years has shifted to matters of personal well-being—interest rates, employment, threat of nuclear war, and budget deficits—and many feel that social programs of the federal government, including social science research, are luxuries with which we can easily dispense.

A recent rash of discoveries of sexual and mental abuse of middle-income children in group care settings (see Chapter 11) (Associated Press, October, 1984) may serve to redirect attention to the issue of day care regulation. People are beginning to see that establishing professional credentials for day care staff, minimum wage requirements, and government supervision and subsidy for all group care are necessary to protect the rights of all children.

The Long-Term Effects of the Infancy Period

Why is it that some children become more competent, more intelligent, or more outgoing than others? Developmentalists have separated some of the causes of individual variation into two basic categories: organismic factors and environmental factors. *Organismic factors* are the dimensions of the individual's basic organic/biological composition, including heredity, sex, perinatal factors, temperament, and developmental level. *Environmental factors* are those experiences that contribute to individual differences, including both the social and physical environments.

Organismic factors are similar to the effects of nature, while environmental factors correspond to the effects of nurture (refer to Chapters 1 and 2). The research reviewed in this section shows that child development outcomes are a complex combination of both organismic and environmental factors.

Environmental Effects on Organismic Factors

Prenatal and Perinatal Factors. Chapter 4 discussed the role of heredity and the prenatal environment in human development. It appears that even during the prenatal period, the environment interacts with the genes and chromosomes to produce a wide variety of cells, even though each of the cells has the same set of genes.

In the case of contact between mother and infant right after birth, we learned in Chapter 5 that normal mother-infant attachments could develop even for babies who had been hospitalized for long periods due to prematurity or other perinatal problems. Now we are asking whether perinatal problems—oxygen deprivation, prematurity, low birth weight, etc.—are critical factors in the formation of lasting developmental deficits in infants.

Research has shown that lasting deficits from such problems can be alleviated by a supportive environment. In a study using a multiracial, multiclass sample of 670 children from the Hawaiian island of Kauai, the incidence of perinatal problems was similar in all races and social classes, about 13 percent with moderate and 3 percent with severe complications. However, group membership predicted how well the children recovered from the complication. By the age of ten, lower scores on school achievement and intelligence tests were better predicted by social class than by perinatal complications. This means that environmental factors that persist over long periods have more effect on development in the long term than do birth complications (Werner, Bierman, & French, 1971).

Other research studies have supported the view that infants take longer to recover from perinatal problems in stressful environments where parents are lacking in social and economic support (Crockenberg, 1981; Sameroff & Chandler, 1975; Waters, Vaughn, & Egeland, 1980). Furthermore, individual differences in newborn behavior among normal newborns do not correlate with measures of behavior in the school years (Bell, Weller, & Waldrop, 1971).

It appears that certain kinds of environments can compensate for individual variation in perinatal factors. Some have suggested that infants are buffered against difficulties encountered during early life and that given an appropriately stimulating environment, most babies (barring severe disorders) are *self-righting*, meaning that they have the ability to maintain their development on a proper course.

Temperament.   Similar organism-environment interactions have been found for early differences in temperament among infants. *Temperament* refers to

Infants differ temperamentally in their intensity of reaction to the environment. This baby squeals and shows a delighted expression in response to a toy. Another baby's reaction may be more subtle and low key.

lasting individual differences in emotional expressiveness and general responsiveness to the environment.

How is temperament assessed? Many researchers have used parents as informed sources. The parents are asked to rate such characteristics as fussiness, cooperativeness, and responsiveness to efforts made by caregivers. These ratings are then classified into scores on such dimensions as activity level, adaptability, and quality of mood. Babies may also receive an overall classification of easy or difficult (see Table 7–9).

Table 7–9

TEMPERAMENTAL CHARACTERISTICS CRUCIAL IN CLASSIFYING CHILDREN AS EASY OR DIFFICULT*

Temperamental Quality	2 Months	2 Years
Activity level	Does not move when being dressed or during sleep.	Enjoys quiet play with puzzles. Can listen to records for hours.
	Moves often in sleep. Wriggles when diaper is changed.	Climbs furniture. Explores. Gets in and out of bed while being put to sleep.
Rhythmicity	Has been on four-hour feeding schedule since birth. Regular bowel movement.	Eats a big lunch each day. Always has a snack before bedtime.
	Awakes at a different time each morning. Size of feedings varies.	Nap time changes from day to day. Toilet training is difficult because bowel movement is unpredictable.
Approach/withdrawal	Smiles and licks washcloth. Has always liked bottle.	Slept well the first time he stayed overnight at grandparents' house.
	Rejected cereal the first time. Cries when strangers appear.	Avoids strange children in the playground. Whimpers first time at beach. Will not go into water.
Adaptability	Was passive during first bath, now enjoys bathing. Smiles at nurse.	Obeys quickly. Stayed contentedly with grandparents for a week.
	Still startled by sudden, sharp noises. Resists diapering.	Cries and screams each time hair is cut. Disobeys persistently.
Intensity of reaction	Does not cry when diapers are wet. Whimpers instead of crying when hungry.	When another child hit her, she looked surprised, did not hit back.
	Cries when diapers are wet. Rejects food vigorously when satisfied.	Yells if he feels excitement or delight. Cries loudly if a toy is taken away.
Quality of mood	Smacks lips when first tasting new food. Smiles at parents.	Plays with sister; laughs and giggles. Smiles when he succeeds in putting shoes on.
	Fusses after nursing. Cries when carriage is rocked.	Cries and squirms when given haircut. Cries when mother leaves.

(From Thomas, Chess, & Birch, 1970.)

*Colored rows highlight temperamental ratings and behaviors for easy children; uncolored rows describe difficult children.

One problem with parent ratings of infant temperament arises when the same parent comes up with different ratings of the same infant if asked to complete the ratings every six months. In other words, temperament measures lack test-retest reliability (Goldsmith & Gottesman, 1981; Hubert, Wachs, Peters-Martin, & Gandour, 1982).

With regard to validity, temperament ratings have been correlated with observed behavior in some studies. Infants who were rated as distractable by their parents at two weeks of age had lower scores on the Brazelton Neonatal Assessment Scale at one week and lower scores on the Bayley at ten weeks (Sostek & Anders, 1977). Infants who were rated as more difficult had cries that were rated by independent observers as more irritating and urgent (Lounsbury & Bates, 1982), and children who were rated as more intense by mothers had a faster tempo of play and were less likely to be distracted (Wenckstern, Weizmann, & Leenaars, 1984).

On the other hand, difficult temperament ratings were found in another study to be unrelated to Bayley scores or observations of infant behavior (Daniels, Plomin, & Greenhalgh, 1984). In addition, several studies found that maternal ratings of infant temperament were better correlated with maternal factors, such as personality and level of emotional stress, than with infant factors (Bates, Freeland, & Lounsbury, 1979; Sameroff, Seifer, & Elias, 1982).

Behavioral measures of temperament also have had limited success in predicting later behavior. For example, 117 infants were observed responding to unfamiliar stimuli in two different laboratory settings at 21 months and again at 31 months. Observations were made on their heart rate, respiration, and behavioral inhibition. Consistency of responding existed between the two laboratory sessions at the same age but not between the two ages. However, when the ten most inhibited and ten least inhibited infants were analyzed separately, a moderate correlation existed between the two ages (Garcia-Coll, Kagan, & Reznick, 1984).

Although measurement problems are an important factor, it seems likely that temperament, taken by itself, is not stable over the long term for most infants. Infants who are difficult or inhibited or outgoing during the first months and years of life are not likely to remain so in later life.

Based on the results just reviewed, we might be tempted to say that regardless of organismic factors, the environment can sustain and shape behavior in limitless ways. We could, if such a theory were true, literally create any kind of person we wished, simply by structuring a suitable environment. The environment, however, does not operate the same way on all infants. It seems that environmental factors interact with organismic factors to determine individual differences in human development.

The Effect of Organismic Factors on Environmental Influences

In one research study (Peters-Martin & Wachs, 1984) mothers' ratings of infant temperament were assessed at one, six, and twelve months. At these same ages, the researchers made ratings of the infants' home environment on such dimensions as organization, noise level, stimulus variety, and the provision of age-appropriate play materials. Temperament ratings were stable between one and six months and between six and twelve months, but not between one and twelve months. Thus, the mothers' ratings are consistent in the short term but not in the long term.

More interesting, however, was the finding that infants whose mothers rated them as active in the first six months scored higher on the Infant Psychological Development Scales (IPDS) at twelve months (refer to Chapter 6) if their homes were rated as organized. The correlation between the IPDS score and the organization of the home was not found for infants rated as inactive temperamentally. This means that the effect of the environment may be *mediated* by the infant's early temperamental disposition. Only active infants will be affected by the organization of the home (Peters-Martin & Wachs, 1984).

Similar findings have been reported for sex differences. Although girls do not outscore boys in assessments of infant development, girls seem to thrive in environments that may be detrimental to a boy's development and vice versa. For example, boys reared in homes with a high level of noise and overcrowding had significantly lower scores on the IPDS than did boys in calmer environments. Noise and overcrowding had no effect on girls. Girls' cognitive development, on the other hand, is enhanced by stimulus variety, such as rooms decorated with different shapes and colors. Stimulus variety has little effect on boys' cognitive development. Thus, the environments most conducive to a boy's development are relatively stress-free (that is, boys are more susceptible than girls to stress, even in infancy), while girls do well if their homes contain a variety of colors and shapes and a range of objects to play with and look at (Wachs & Gruen, 1982).

These results can be explained by a concept of *environmental specificity;* that is, specific aspects of the environment act more readily on certain types of infants than on others. Another aspect of the environmental specificity notion is that specific types of environments affect certain types of skills in all infants. For example, it has been found that exploratory play skills in the second and third years are enhanced by providing responsive toys, such as mobiles and pull toys, in the first year. An organized environment and the provision of age-appropriate play materials are the best predictors of the ability to invent new means and to plan effective strategies (Wachs & Gruen, 1982).

The responsiveness of the caregiver to the infant has been shown to affect specific developmental outcomes, especially communication, language, and social skills (Arend et al., 1979; Clarke-Stewart, VanderStoep, & Killian, 1979; Pastor, 1981). The way in which caregivers respond to babies is specific to the baby's age. Higher scores on infant assessments in the second year of life are associated with adults' tactile and vestibular stimulation under three months of age, vocalization and emotional involvement between three and 24 months, and a lack of restrictiveness and provision of opportunities to interact with other people in the third year (Bradley, Caldwell, & Elardo, 1979; Carew, 1980; Feiring & Lewis, 1981).

It is important to provide the best possible environment for infants. Even though the infant's characteristics may not remain stable, appropriate and responsive stimulation from the environment is essential for the maintenance of universal patterns of infant growth and development. Experience in infancy is important, not because it may lead to long-term benefits, but because it helps the baby into the next stage of short-term growth and enhances the quality and enjoyment of the baby's and the family's life at that time and place.

Responsive toys (those that make a noise or appear different when touched or manipulated) provided during an infant's first year of life can enhance exploratory play in the second and third years.

Chapter Summary

THE FIRST RELATIONSHIPS

□ During the infant's first three months, the interaction between infant and adult is concerned with feeding and the regulation of basic biological cycles such as sleeping and waking.

□ For the next three months, adults and infants engage in social play without objects which includes exchanging smiles, gazes, and vocalizations. Parents tend to adjust their behavior to fit the spontaneous behavior of the infant.

□ In the social apprentice period, beginning at six months, adults and infants develop and elaborate on games and other routines, such as peekaboo and give-and-take, in which the infant learns how to take turns, make initiatives, and effectively use vocal and manual gestures to communicate.

□ At the beginning of the second year, language is learned by the infant's participation in verbal interaction and conversation, which the adult continues to scaffold (by asking leading questions and interpreting the infant's incomplete responses) well into the preschool period.

□ The infant's attachment to the adult becomes more adultlike at the end of the first year, at which time individual differences in the security of attachment are observed. The origins of these differences may be partly due to the sensitivity of the early adult-infant interaction and partly due to infant temperament.

☐ Infant compliance in the second year depends in large measure on the adult's ability to couch requests of the infant in a social context in which the infant is most likely to comply. Preventive measures are also helpful. Infants at this age cannot be expected to obey most verbal commands.

☐ Although most toddlers are not negative to infant siblings, they may ignore them or show disruptive behavior. Parents have to work hard to ensure that both children have the attention they need and instruct the older child in how to respond effectively to a baby.

☐ Older children can learn nurturant responses and moral norms, while younger children use their older brothers and sisters as leaders and guides.

THE TRANSITION TO PARENTHOOD

☐ The parents' involvement in childcare is predicted by different factors for men and women. Men require more social support, especially in the form of a good marital relationship.

☐ Men tend to play more actively with their babies, although styles of play are subject to changes in cultural norms. We can expect more men to take on nurturing roles in the future.

☐ A good prognosis exists for handicapped infants when parents are highly involved in caregiving and social interaction.

RELATIONSHIPS OUTSIDE THE IMMEDIATE FAMILY

☐ Relationship skills with peers generally parallel those found in adult-infant interaction. Although peer play in infancy often breaks down quickly because of a lack of scaffolding to maintain the interaction, some evidence exists that the equality of peer relationships is an important factor in promoting normal social development.

☐ Alternative caregivers can be as sensitive as the child's parents so long as they do not have to care for too many infants at the same time. There is no evidence that the child suffers cognitive or emotional deficits from alternative care so long as the quality of care is good, although studies of monkeys indicate some subtle effects of long-term separation.

☐ Government red tape has limited the extent to which effective regulations have been drafted to ensure quality day care for all children.

LONG-TERM EFFECTS OF THE INFANCY PERIOD

☐ Sensitive early care can compensate for a number of developmental difficulties, and experience during infancy does not automatically determine later outcomes.

☐ Organismic factors, taken alone, and environmental factors, taken alone, do not predict later outcomes. Only when specific environments are matched with specific infant characteristics can we understand the effects of infant experiences.

Recommended Readings

Bowlby, J. (1969). *Attachment*. New York: Basic Books. The classic work on attachment between mother and infant.

Dunn, J., & Kendrick, C. (1982). *Siblings: Love, envy and understanding.* Cambridge, MA: Harvard University Press. An easy-to-read review of the research on sibling interactions in infancy.

Schaffer, R. (1977). *Mothering.* Cambridge, MA: Harvard University Press. Discussion of the functions of mothering and parenting during the infancy period.

Stern, D. (1977). *The first relationship: Infant and mother.* Cambridge, MA: Harvard University Press. Shows how infants learn about themselves and their emotions through interactions with their mothers.

PART III

Early Childhood

CHAPTER 8

Early Childhood: Physical and Motor Development

*J*ohn is two years old today. He stands just 31 inches (80 centimeters) tall and weighs in at 29 lbs (13 kg). From an adult perspective, his body seems top-heavy. On his short, chunky legs, he runs and climbs swiftly, if often unsteadily. John's girth is made wider by the diapers and rubber pants he sports under his corduroys, a testament to his uncertain struggle with the "potty". When John isn't trying out his legs (and his father says "his wings"), he loves to manipulate small objects. His pudgy fingers wrap around his miniature cars lovingly, as he makes them go "hrrm". Another favorite activity is "playing artist". Sitting under his mother's drafting table, John clutches a thick crayon and scribbles away.

On this same day, in another city, a boy named Marc is turning six years old. At 45 inches (115 cm) in height and 48 lbs (22 kg.) in weight, he is over 60% taller and heavier than John. His body proportions are different as well, with longer limbs relative to head and torso. Today, Marc "graduates" from his tricycle to what he excitedly describes as "a real bicycle, just like the big kids"; that is, if you don't pay attention to the small training wheels at the back.

Marc is not only a budding cyclist; he scales the biggest jungle gym with confidence, negotiates a series of complicated buttons and zippers each morning, ties his shoelaces, in short, performs routinely what would be feats of manual dexterity for John's less nimble fingers. He's been printing his name now for more than a year and can copy almost all the letters, although many are reversed and writing seems just as natural right to left as in the other direction. Marc loves to draw, too; his productions are filled with elaborate designs and detailed people, houses and objects.

John and Marc, the children described above, are both average examples of physical and motor development at two and six years of age. Although it is often helpful to have a mental picture of the "average" child at a particular developmental period, we must keep in mind that individual rates of development vary widely. This chapter examines the general pattern and individual variation in physical development during the preschool years.

Changes in Size and Shape

General Trends

As the descriptions of John and Marc indicate, substantial changes in size, shape, and body proportions are occurring during the preschool years. However, compared to the dramatic transformations of the first two years, the growth rate has slowed. Children grow twice as fast from the first to the third

Figure 8—1(a)

*Boys: 2 to 18 Years Physical Growth Percentiles**

(Adapted from: Hamill P.V.V., Drizd T.A., Johnson C.L., Reed R.B., Roche A.F., Moore W.M.: Physical growth: National Center for Health Statistics percentiles. AM. J. CLIN. NUTR. 32:607-629, 1979. Data from the National Center for Health Statistics (NCHS) Hyattsville, Maryland. © 1982 Ross Laboratories.)

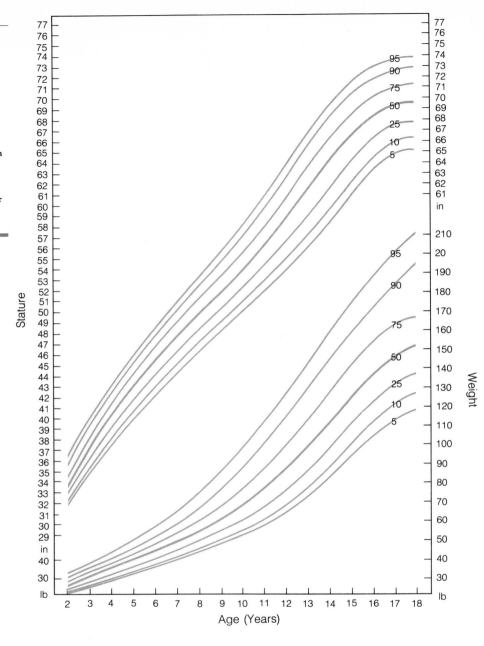

year as they do from the third to the sixth year (Cratty, 1979). Differences in heights of children tend to remain moderately stable during the preschool years. The correlation between a child's height at age one and at age five is between .4 and .5. Thus, children big for their age at the beginning of the preschool period are likely to be relatively large four years later. Although boys and girls develop at approximately the same rate, girls tend to be slightly shorter and lighter than boys.

Reporting averages in height, weight, and rate of growth at different ages obscures the wide individual variation in growth that occurs among children of the same age. To take this wide range of growth into account, heights and

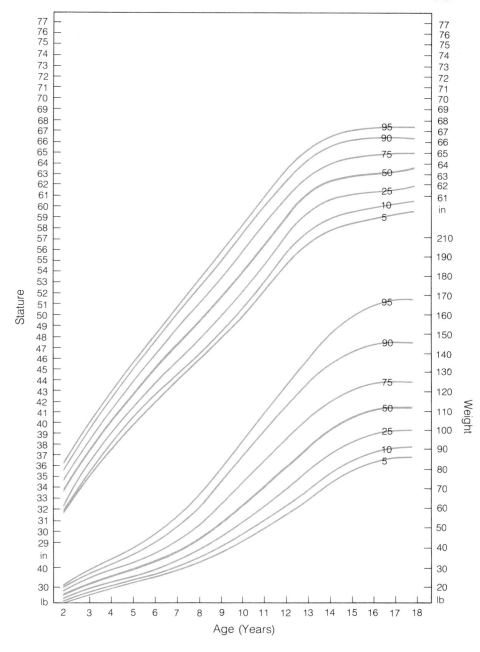

Figure 8–1(b)

Girls: 2 to 18 Years Physical Growth Percentiles*

(Adapted from: Hamill P.V.V., Drizd T.A., Johnson C.L., Reed R.B., Roche A.F., Moore W.M.: Physical growth: National Center for Health Statistics percentiles. AM. J. CLIN. NUTR. 32: 607-629, 1979. Data from the National Center for Health Statistics (NCHS) Hyattsville, Maryland. © 1982 Ross Laboratories.)

weights at different ages are reported in terms of *percentiles*. For example, children whose height is at the 50th percentile are average; half of the children their age are shorter, and half are taller. A child whose height is at the 25th percentile is taller than 25 percent of his peers but shorter than 75 percent of them, while a child at the 75th percentile is taller than 75 percent of other children of the same age and shorter than 25 percent of them. Heights or weights within the 25th to 75th percentile range are considered normal. The growth charts used by many pediatricians in North America to plot the height and weight of boys and girls in terms of these percentiles are shown in Figure 8–1(a) and (b).

Children whose physical growth is outside the normal range may none-theless be developing without problems. Since growth rates for children from different ethnic groups vary considerably, it is important that a child's growth be compared to those of the same cultural group. Thus, a Chinese child whose height is at the 50th percentile as compared to other Chinese children would be almost four inches (10 centimeters) shorter than a white American child (Meredith, 1978). If the Chinese child's height were compared to the heights of same-age American children, one might conclude mistakenly that the child was developing poorly.

The height gain of the preschool years is principally in length of legs. Two-year-old John, described in the chapter opening, is top heavy compared to Marc. By age six, leg length is about half that of the entire body length, a proportion that will remain fairly stable throughout development.

As height increases and body proportions change, cartilage turns to bone. The rate of *ossification*, or hardening of the bones, determines the bone age or skeletal maturity of the child (see Chapter 12). By comparing bone age to chronological age, growth problems can sometimes be detected. If a child is too tall or too short for his or her skeletal maturity, it indicates a possible disturbance in growth (Lowry, 1978). For example, a tall five-year-old whose bone age is four has grown more quickly than has the bone structure, while an equally tall five-year-old with a bone age of five is experiencing appropriate growth.

Other internal changes are taking place. In both boys and girls, infant fatty tissue is gradually being replaced by muscle, although girls retain slightly more fatty tissue than do boys. The large muscles of the legs and arms develop faster than the small muscles that control fine motor skills, such as drawing and sewing. This is why the three-year-old who can race around corners with the screeching precision of the Road Runner has trouble keeping a firm grip on a pencil (Cratty, 1979).

Mastering activities like swinging, which requires complex coordination of legs, arms and body movements, brings a sense of accomplishment to the young child.

Along with muscular strength and speed, *motor coordination* is also developing. This refers to the skills involved in coordinating physical movements. Through active play, young children are learning to channel strength and speed into smooth, accurate movements. Children of this age love to climb, run, and jump. As they stop and start and switch directions, children are mastering the ability to regulate their behavior. These gains in self-regulation in movement are part of a general trend toward greater self-control in all areas of development. The major milestones of motor development from age two to age six are summarized in Table 8–1.

What Helps Children Control Motor Activity?

The mechanisms that enable preschoolers to achieve self-regulation of movement are nicely illustrated in a study (Balamore & Wozniak, 1984) that observed 110 three- and four-year-olds in two situations involving self-regulation of movement. In one situation, the children were asked to hammer down some pegs four—and only four—times. In the second situation, they were asked to hammer down first a red peg, then a green one, and finally a yellow peg from a hammering board containing six different colored pegs. For each task, first the child was given the instructions and allowed to try. If unsuccessful, an adult demonstrated while repeating the instructions. The children were also encouraged to repeat the correct verbal sequence aloud themselves—saying "one, two, three, four" and "red, green, yellow"—as they pounded the pegs. Finally, each child was asked to carry out each task silently.

Most of the preschoolers observed could not successfully carry out these tasks silently. Only when children spoke to themselves could they regulate their own movements. For example, some children, on raising their arm to pound for the fifth time but saying "four," stopped the motion in midflight. Other children about to pound a green peg, hearing themselves say "red," inhibited the motion and reorganized their pounding sequence.

Table 8–1

MILESTONES OF MOTOR DEVELOPMENT DURING EARLY CHILDHOOD

Approximate Time of Appearance	Selected Behaviors
2 years	Walking rhythm stabilizes and becomes even Jumps crudely with two-foot takeoff Will throw small ball 4–5 ft True running appears Can walk sideward and backward
3 years	Can walk a line, heel to toe, 10 ft long Can hop from two to three steps, on preferred foot Will walk balance beam for short distances Can throw a ball about 10 ft
4 years	Running with good form, leg-arm coordination apparent, can walk a line around periphery of a circle Skillful jumping is apparent Can walk balance beam
5 years	Can broad-jump from 2–3 ft Can hop 50 ft in about 11 seconds Can balance on one foot for 4–6 seconds Can catch large playground ball bounced to him or her

(From Bryant J. Cratty, *Perceptual and Motor Development in Infants and Children.* © 1979, pp. 97, 222. Reprinted by permission of Prentice-Hall, Englewood Cliffs, NJ)

The importance of *verbal organizers* for learning complex motor skills is illustrated by the fact that children who had already successfully performed the tasks while verbalizing started to make errors when asked to do the tasks silently. This study shows how the child's developing language can be used to help organize new motor skills.

Lev Vygotsky (1962) and A. R. Luria (1980) have shown that initially, verbal organizers are most effective when the child speaks out loud while acting. Later, children *internalize* verbal cues, guiding their behavior by speaking to themselves (Tinsley and Waters, 1982). Children learn by doing, although they sometimes learn better by doing *and* saying. This study shows that young children need to think out loud to help themselves develop muscular coordination. In this sense, the physical development of the brain is extremely important, since this part of the body is the organizing center for all other psychomotor changes.

Brain Development

The brain is the most essential organ of the body, since it regulates behavior and life support and controls the process and timing of development of the rest of the body. The most basic parts of the human brain—those that control the sensory receptors, motor movements, and emotional processes—have similarities to the brains of other species of animals living today, including reptiles and other mammals (MacLean, 1984). Our advanced cognitive functions, however, are found only in human brains.

The adult brain is made of about 200 billion cells, called *neurons,* designed to receive information and issue commands to the muscles and organs of the body (see Figure 8–2). Communication is accomplished by chemical

Figure 8–2

Brain Cells

(From Teyler and Chiaia, *A Child's Brain* (M. Frank, Ed.), Haworth Press, New York, 1984.)

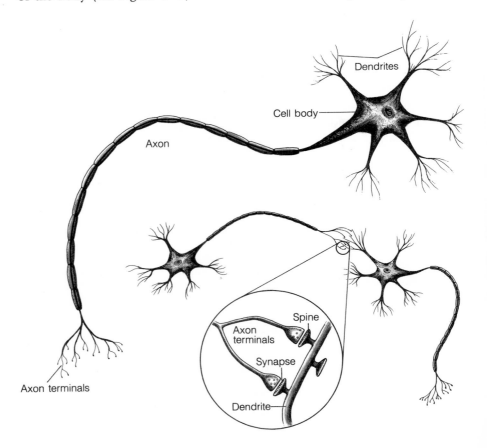

neurotransmitters secreted from the cell's *axon*, which may extend long distances from the cell body (Teyler & Chiaia, 1984.) The axons of the transmitting cell connect to the *dendrites* of the receiving cell at junctions called *synapses*. The number of dendrites and synapses plays a role in the efficiency of the brain's communication processes. The basic parts of the human brain are illustrated in Figure 8–3 and described in Table 8–2.

After birth, the brain grows rapidly. Its weight at birth is 25 percent of adult weight, at six months it is 50 percent, at two and one-half years it is 75 percent. By age ten years, the brain weighs 95 percent of its adult weight. Following the cephalo-caudal growth trend of development (refer to Chapter 5), at birth the rest of the body is only five percent of adult weight, and at ten years, only 50 percent (Tanner, 1970).

The central nervous system continues to develop well into early childhood. Although new brain cells are no longer formed after the second year of life, brain cells continue to grow in size and complexity, adding to the weight of the brain (Epstein, 1978). Specifically, the dendrites of the neurons lengthen and form more branches. In addition, the axons of the neuron, along which impulses travel, lengthen and thicken. Finally, *myelin sheaths*—fatty layers encasing the axons of many neurons—continue to form during the preschool years in a process called *myelinization*. As a neuron is sheathed in myelin, it is able to function more quickly and efficiently (Tanner, 1978).

How does this translate into the outward visible behavior of the child? As areas of the brain are myelinated, the behaviors they control show rapid development. For example, as the neurons of the visual system are myelinated,

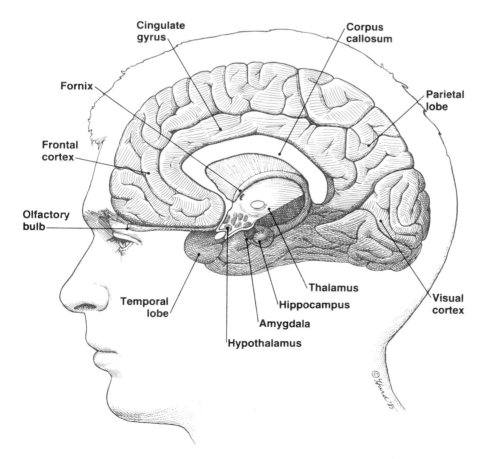

Figure 8–3

Basic Parts of Human Brain

(Illustration by Jane Hurd 1985)

Table 8–2

BASIC PARTS OF THE BRAIN

Name of Part	Description
Olfactory bulb	This structure contains about 2,000 small globular masses or *glomeruli* that contain the first synapse in the pathway sensitive to smell.
Frontal cortex	This area is essential for higher order thought processes, such as abstract thought and reasoning.
Fornix	An important connection between the *hippocampus* (see below) and an area called the *mammilary bodies,* which play a role in emotion and memory.
Cingulate gyrus	An area of the *limbic system* involved in emotional reactions.
Limbic system	A rim of structures in the cortex where a large number of circuits relating to different functions come together. It is thought to play a key role in the cognitive arousal of emotion and in memory processes.
Corpus callosum	A pathway of 200 million nerve fibers connecting the right and left hemispheres, or halves, of the brain.
Parietal lobe	The primary receiving area for bodily sensations and spatial perception.
Visual cortex	The primary receiving area for visual information.
Thalamus	The main relaying and integrating center for sensory information.
Hippocampus	A structure in the limbic system concerned with emotional reactions and memory stage.
Amygdala	A limbic system structure that controls emotional reactions and the processing of smells and is believed to have a role in memory processes.
Hypothalamus	A structure that controls arousal and emotional states and regulates food intake, water balance, body temperature, and sexual activity. It keeps the internal system of the body in balance in a process called *homeostasis.*
Temporal lobe	The primary receiving area for auditory information and visual recognition.

(From *APA Monitor,* September 1985.)

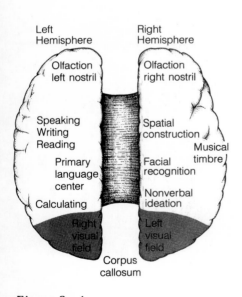

Figure 8–4

Brain Lateralization

As a result of brain lateralization, different tasks are performed better by one hemisphere of the brain than the other.

visual capacities improve. Most preschoolers are far-sighted; that is, they see more accurately at a distance than they do up close, and they have difficulty scanning small objects, such as printed words on a page. By age six, however, improved visual acuity allows most children to focus and scan more accurately (Vurpillot, 1968). Similarly, the ability to localize sounds continues to improve during the preschool years, paralleling the myelinization of the auditory system. The disintegration of myelin causes motor and sensory impairments in the incurable disease of *multiple sclerosis.*

The brain is not only growing in size and overall complexity but is also becoming more specialized. The brain is organized into right and left halves, or *hemispheres,* separated by the *corpus callosum* (see Figure 8–4). It is known that in right-handed individuals, the left side of the brain is responsible for analytic and linguistic function and the right side for spatial perception, facial recognition, and perception of musical and other nonlinguistic sounds. In addition, the left hemisphere controls the right half of the visual field, while the right hemisphere controls the left half of the visual field (Lenneberg, 1969). This specialization of function is called *brain lateralization.*

The Measurement of Brain Lateralization

Since we cannot easily peer into a young child's brain, how do we know that the right hemisphere is the center for the perception of emotion or that the left hemisphere is the site for language? A procedure called *dichotic listening*, which presents different material to the right and left ear through special earphones, has been used to study brain lateralization. For example, if the right hemisphere of the brain is controlling emotional expression, emotionally toned materials (such as "I love you") presented to the *left* ear should be heard more readily than the same material presented to the right ear only. Similarly, a preference for hearing neutral language (such as a list of numbers) with the right ear should exist if the left hemisphere is the center of language.

Experiments using dichotic listening have shown right hemisphere specialization for emotion and left hemisphere specialization for language to be well established in right-handed children (and right hemisphere specialization in left-handed children) by kindergarten age (Saxby & Bryden, 1984; Subirana, 1969). Other methods (Saxby & Bryden, 1985) find that children recognize facial expressions of different emotions more accurately using the left eye (right hemisphere) and letters of the alphabet using the right eye (left hemisphere). These studies conclude that lateralization of brain function is essentially complete by the time children enter school (Bryden & Saxby, 1985; Bryden, 1982).

Others argue that the processing of language may occur in both sides of the brain up to adolescence. Thus, right-handed children who have experienced damage to the left side of the brain usually can relearn to speak. Areas in the right hemisphere take over the language function. However, among adolescents and adults, damage to the left side of the brain results in permanent impairment (Lenneberg, 1970; Dawson, et al, 1986).

The Development of Handedness

Preference for the right or left hand is linked to growing specialization of the hemispheres of the brain. In infancy, preferences for right or left hand tend to be unstable. For example, Caplan and Kinsbourne (1976) found that although most four-month-old infants held a rattle longer with their right hands, for individual infants, preferences shifted over time, and at times no preference was shown.

By age three, stable hand preferences emerge, and they are well established by age five (Hardyck & Petinovich, 1977; Ramsay, 1979). For example, in one survey of 512 four-year-olds in Melbourne, Australia, 88 percent were classified as right-handed, eight percent as left-handed, and four percent as exhibiting no hand preference (Tan, 1985). Other studies find a similar pattern. A British investigation in which preschoolers were observed painting at an easel found that 84 percent of the children showed a right-hand preference, 11 percent a left-hand preference, and five percent no preference (Connolly & Elliott, 1972).

Traditionally, many people thought that left-handedness was, if not a handicap, at least a disadvantage in a "right-handed world." It was suggested that left-handed children were more likely than other children to have cognitive or perceptual-motor problems (Porac & Coren, 1981; Hallahan & Kaufman, 1977). However, these findings were based on assessments of children who already had motor or learning problems. More recent investigations of normal children find no differences between right-handed and left-handed children (Tan, 1985). Thus, there is no reason that parents or teachers should try to discourage a child's preference for using the left hand to hold a crayon or throw a ball. Since there is a

This child is using the "oblique palmar grip"—see Figure 8–6—which makes painting, drawing and writing difficult. With practice and physical maturation, more adult-like grips will be preferred.

genetic predisposition toward handedness, trying to switch the child is likely to be a frustrating experience for both child and adult.

Children who exhibit no consistent hand preference by age five may be experiencing problems in motor development. Several investigations have found that these children score somewhat lower on tests of gross motor activity, such as coordinating movements of legs and arms, and of fine motor activity, such as cutting with scissors or drawing with a crayon (Kaufman et al., 1978; Tan, 1985).

In summary, increasing evidence of handedness, brain lateralization, and self-regulation of movement characterizes the preschool years. In general, children's physical growth during this time shows two major patterns; differentiation and coordination. As body parts and movements become more specialized, a major challenge for the child is coordinating them.

Influences on Growth

Thus far, we have outlined broad growth patterns common to children of this period. However, no two children grow in precisely the same way. Many factors

Malnutrition and Growth

In countries where malnutrition is widespread, retarded growth, as reflected in diminished height for age, is common (Pollitt & Thompson, 1977). In fact, the association between shortened stature and malnutrition is so reliable that some studies use height for age as a measure of nutritional status (Cravioto, 1968).

Diminished height and retarded skeletal development are not the only possible effects of inadequate nutrition. When an infant's diet does not provide sufficient protein or enough calories to fuel the body's needs, the disease *marasmus* can result, causing the baby to stop growing, become weaker, take on a wrinkled appearance, and eventually die (Winick, 1976). Another deadly disorder, often called by one of its African names, *kwashiorkor*, can result from lack of protein in the diet even when sufficient calories are consumed:

> The children affected [by kwashiorkor] are nearly always not only small for their age, with hair and skin of a pale color, but also exhibit feet and legs swollen from an accumulation of excess fluid. Those more severely ill may have hair of any color to greyish-white, very pale skin, and swelling of the legs, thighs, hands, and face. In the most advanced state the hair is so loosely embedded that it can be pulled out in tufts without causing pain; the eyes may be closed with swelling, which occurs in nearly every part of the body, and the skin may break down as though it had been burnt. As this stage the child appears to be desperately unhappy or sunk in apathy. He resists any interference, even feeding (WHO, 1963).

In many countries, improvements in nutrition and general environmental conditions have significantly reduced the incidence of death from kwashiorkor and marasmus (Gomez, Ramox-Galvan, Frank, Cravioto, Chavex and Vasques, 1956). However, despite the higher survival rate, chronic malnutrition remains the world's number one health problem. In 1975, 82 percent of all the world's children under 15—1.2 *billion*—lived in less developed countries where the majority were growing up under impoverished economic circumstances (Barney, 1980). It has been estimated that 70 percent of all preschool-age children in developing countries are malnourished (Keppel, 1968). Even such estimates are probably too low, since many areas lack vital statistics or medical personnel who could keep accurate records.

Nutritional deficiencies threatening optimal growth are not restricted to developing countries. Among U.S. children aged six to twelve, 12 to 16 percent are estimated to have vitamin C deficiency and 30 percent are thought to have vitamin A deficiency. In addition, one-third of all children in the United States are estimated to have anemia severe enough to require medical care (Owen & Lippman, 1977). Recent attention has been drawn to the problem of *silent malnutrition* among poor children in technologically advanced countries. This refers to caloric intake adequate enough to prevent the swollen bellies and falling hair of kwashiorkor but deficient in nutrients essential for full growth. Children suffering from silent malnutrition are somewhat short and slight for their age and more prone to infection and disease.

Considerable debate has taken place about the extent of such silent malnutrition, which is difficult to document precisely. People also disagree about the extent to which increases or decreases in food assistance programs, such as Food Stamps or the Federal School Lunch program, affect the nutritional status of poor children.

Malnutrition not only can prevent children from reaching their full genetic potential in terms of physical size but also, depending upon its timing and severity, may have adverse effects on brain development and mental functioning. Since brain growth continues through the second year of life, malnutrition during the prenatal period and in the early years can delay neural cell growth (Dyson and Jones, 1976) and slow down the rate of myelinization. Observations of severely undernourished children show them to be apathetic, avoiding new situations, easily distracted, and having difficulty persisting at frustrating tasks (Barrett, Radke-Yarrow & Klein, 1982).

Because their apathy and withdrawal extend to other people as well as to learning tasks, malnourished children have problems not only in learning but also in establishing social ties. Indeed, some investigators believe that malnutrition damages development most severely in the social-emotional area. The inability to respond to others, particularly to the child's caretakers, sets up a vicious circle of withdrawal by the child and rejection by the caretaker (Barrett et al., 1982; Lester, 1979). Because malnutrition, withdrawal, and rejection tend to occur together, researchers find it difficult to isolate any single cause. Rather, malnutrition is part of a complex system of negative influences, each of which worsens the others.

affect patterns of physical development. Examination of the factors affecting individual patterns of growth illustrates the interplay between nature (genetic factors) and nurture (environmental sources of influence). In the absence of disease, nutritional deficiencies, or hormonal disorders, variations in height, weight, body proportions, and growth rate are largely due to the influence of the genes. However, we cannot hope to separate out genetic from environmental influences on growth and assign a percentage of influence to each, because all children's genetic potential is expressed within specific environments.

One way to understand the *interaction* between genetic and environmental sources of influences is to imagine a child's physical growth as a path laid down by the genes. Poor nutrition and health, for example, may act as obstructions preventing the child from a full traverse of the path. Because of the interplay of maturational and environmental influences, it is impossible to know precisely a child's genetically determined height. However, when there are optimal environmental conditions supporting growth, one may hypothesize that the height reached is close to the child's genetic potential.

Catch-up Growth

It is possible for children whose growth has been impeded by illness or malnutrition to experience a rapid increase in growth once the problem has passed, a process called *catch-up growth*. Recall our analogy of the genetic contribution to growth as a path. If you deflect the child from the path (by illness, malnutrition, etc.), the child will tend to return to the path (catch-up growth) once the obstacle is removed (Tanner, 1970). For example, Tanner reports the case of a boy who, because of a thyroid deficiency, stopped growing completely between ages 7 and 12. (Thyroid is a hormone essential to normal growth.) At age 12, the boy began taking thyroid supplements, and within eight months, his growth rate was over twice the average for boys of his age. By age 16, his skeletal age was 14, only two years behind his normally growing peers, and by age 20 he had caught up completely to his estimated height under favorable environmental and health conditions (Prader, Tanner, & von Harnack, 1963).

The operation of catch-up growth depends on the timing, length, and severity of the environmental obstacle to growth. For example, high caloric supplements given to malnourished Guatemalan children from birth to two years of age predicted improved development at age six, but the same level of supplementation given from ages two to four showed no later improvement (Barrett et al., 1982). In general, the earlier, the longer lasting, and the more severe the malnutrition, the more difficult it is to fully catch up later on, even when optimal nutrition is restored.

Since malnutrition and other health hazards can retard physical growth, overall long-term improvements in the environment should result in increases in the average height of children.

Secular Changes in Physical Growth

Although malnutrition remains a serious problem in many poor countries, general improvements in nutrition and health conditions in developed nations have resulted in *secular changes* in physical growth rates of children living in those countries. This is the term used by biologists to refer to changes in growth in a population over a relatively short period of time (tens or hundreds of years), too short to be attributed to species evolution by natural selection.

Childhood Obesity: Causes and Consequences

Because being slender is emphasized as an ideal in North American culture, the term *obesity* is often used imprecisely. Being obese is not the same as being overweight but actually refers to the proportion of *adiposity*, or fat cells, in the body. The most common method for assessing obesity is to pinch the skin on the back of the arm muscle midway between the elbow and the shoulder (an area called the *triceps skinfold*) with calipers to get an estimate of the amount of body fat that lies immediately under the skin surface. According to this method, it has been estimated that about 5 to 16 percent of all North American children are considered obese (Neumann, 1977; Mayer, 1968).

Negative Consequences of Childhood Obesity

Many obese children are markedly less physically active than their peers. Even when observed doing physical exercise, they expend a fraction of the energy that other children do. Evidence also exists that obese children are likely to be socially rejected by other children and by adults, particularly as they enter school (Richardson, Goodman, Hastorf & Dornbusch, 1961, Staffieri, 1967). Such rejection often leads a child to withdraw further from activity and social life, compounding the problem (Mayer, 1975).

Does Childhood Obesity Predict Adult Obesity?

Those who argue that childhood obesity is predictive of adult obesity point out that adipose or fat cells are manufactured primarily during three periods: prenatally, during the first two years after birth, and during puberty. Once produced, adipose cells cannot be eliminated but can only be reduced in size. For this reason, children who produce excess fat cells during early childhood (or early adolescence) will find it difficult to maintain an appropriate weight (Hirsch, 1975).

Overweight infants and toddlers are more likely to be overweight during the elementary school years (Neyzi, Saner, Alp, Binyildiz, Yazici-oghu, Emre & Gurson, 1976), and childhood obesity at age six is predictive of adolescent and adult obesity (Abraham & Nordsieck, 1960; Abraham, Collins & Nordsieck, 1971; Zack, Harlan, Leaverton & Cornoni-Huntley, 1979). However, many children with excessive fat cells do not become obese adults. Other factors, both genetic and environmental, play a role in determining obesity, both during childhood and in later years (Roche, 1981).

Causes of Childhood Obesity

The role of a genetic component is suggested by studies showing that identical twins (who share the same genetic makeup) are more similar with respect to amount of body fat than are fraternal twins or siblings (Mayer, 1968). In addition, a study comparing the weight and adiposity of adopted children with both their biological and their adoptive parents found a closer resemblance between biologically related parents and children (Stunkard, Sørensen, Harris, Teasdale, Chakraborty, Schull, & Schulsinger, 1986).

Environmental determinants of obesity have also been identified (Lebow, 1984). A major environmental factor is degree of physical activity and exertion. Overweight and excessive eating do not appear to be the major causes of the high fat content in the bodies of obese children. Rather, young children with problems of obesity have been observed as extremely sedentary and generally inactive (Mayer 1968, 1975).

Marital tension has been found in many families with an obese infant or preschooler (Bruch, 1973). In addition, parents, often the mother, may be overprotective of the child. This may occur either because the child was once sickly or for other reasons. In any event, often the parents both restrict the child's freedom to move around independently and feed the child excessively, as the following case study shows:

> This child was born during the depression years, after his father had lost his job and his parents had taken a position as a "couple" in another household. The mother felt she had to keep the baby quiet and would feed him whenever he cried, much against her conviction that a child should not be stuffed with food. He became monstrously fat, weighing 42 lbs. at one year. The father was so disgusted with his son's grotesque appearance that he wouldn't pay attention to him. . . . As soon as the family

had reestablished their own household, [the father] took an active interest in the boy, played with him, and encouraged him in sports and other activities. The mother permitted him a free choice of food, neither restricting it nor prompting him to eat more than he took . . . At the age of 10, he was a good athlete, his weight was within normal range, and he had no problems at all about eating (Bruch, 1973, p. 67).

This illustrates that the most effective treatments of obesity in children usually involve the entire family. Although obese children are at risk for adult obesity, it is not inevitable. As the foregoing case study illustrates, when parents encourage physical activity and feed the child appropriately, obesity can be overcome (LeBow, 1984).

Marked and rapid increases in height for age, body size, and rates of maturation have occurred in many developed countries over the past century. For example, as Figure 8−5 shows, a white North American six-year-old boy in 1960 was, on the average, ten cm (4 in.) taller than his counterpart in 1880 (Meredith, 1963). The impression you've probably had from looking over old family albums—that subsequent generations seem to be taller and bigger—reflects the fact that improved nutrition and health conditions have been associated with average increased stature. As such improvements enable most children to reach their estimated genetic potential, further improvements in the environment fail to be matched by increases in stature, and secular changes in growth level off (Roche, 1979).

Historically, improvements in nutrition have generally occurred together with reductions in infectious diseases, improved sanitation, and more adequate housing. All these factors are part of an environmental system supporting optimal growth. Thus, it is unwarranted to attribute secular changes in growth rates to changes in diet alone. However, adequate nutrition is clearly an important component of an environment that supports optimal physical growth.

Other Environmental Hazards

Despite the improvements in environmental conditions that have resulted in secular changes in growth, some environmental hazards may have actually increased in recent times. With industrialization, exposure to chemical toxins, lead, PCB, and other pollutants in air, water, and soil continue to pose risks to the health and growth of young children. The development of nuclear power and nuclear weapons increases the possibility of nuclear accidents with devastating consequences for children and adults over many generations.

The consequences of lead contamination have received the most attention from investigators (Needleman, 1984). Children who live near roads and hence are exposed to lead fuel emissions, who live in cities rather than rural areas, or who live near factories using lead products are more likely to have elevated levels of lead in their blood (Fine, Thomas, Subs, Cohnberg & Flasher, 1972). However, because lead exposure tends to be more frequent among poor children, the effects of lead are difficult to separate from other environmental factors such as poor nutrition, inadequate housing, and family instability.

However, the results of several studies that have carefully controlled these confounding factors suggest that absorption of lead into the body is related to deficits in both cognitive and social functioning. Needleman and his associates (Needleman, Gunnoe, Leviton, Reed, Peresie, Maher & Barrett, 1979; Needleman, 1984) found that six-to-seven-year-olds with high lead content in their baby teeth had lower IQ scores and slower reaction time after other factors were controlled than did those with low lead levels. When observed

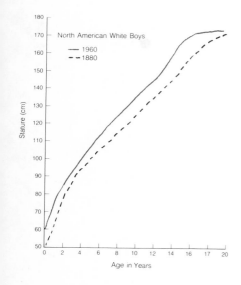

Figure 8−5

Stature in North American White Boys in 1880 and 1960, Compiled from Many Sources

(Based on synthesis of Meredith, 1963 in Monograph of the Society for Research in Child Development by A. Roche, 1979, No. 179, p. 8. © Society for Research in Child Development, Inc.)

Inner city poor children are particularly vulnerable to the environmental hazards of lead poisoning, pollution and substandard housing conditions.

four years later in the classroom, children with high lead absorption were concentrating less well on academic tasks. Similarly, in a study by Shaheen (1984), 18 preschoolers with a past history of lead poisoning showed deficient performance on several cognitive/motor measures as compared with matched controls.

Additional questions for research remain. The long-term effects of lead and other pollutants on cognitive and social functioning need to be documented. In addition, children exposed to the same amounts of lead have been found to differ in their rates of absorption of the toxin into the body (Harvey, 1984). It is likely that the effects of lead exposure interact with other environmental factors, such as poverty and family stress, to make some children more vulnerable than others.

Individual Differences in Physical Growth

As we've seen, the interaction of genetic and environmental influences causes variations in size, shape, and rate of development. In a healthy population of children, some will be markedly taller and heavier than others. Because their growth rates are faster, they will also look more physically mature. Adults have many expectations about optimal growth and appearance of children, and their views affect children in numerous ways.

Effects of Variations in Size

Relatively large children are often treated as being more socially and cognitively advanced. This has some basis in fact; children whose physical maturation is accelerated are also likely to be somewhat advanced in language development and IQ (Garn, 1966; Tanner, 1968). Adults and other peers may treat such children as more grown-up because they really seem to be. It could also be that this differential treatment may help produce the more rapid development of such children.

Children who are small for their age may be treated differently from other children; both adults and other children may be more likely to baby and protect relatively small children. The smallest child in a nursery school class may sometimes be relegated to the role of baby when children play house. Although preschoolers may enjoy occasionally trying on the role of baby—after all, they lived it not too long before—they need to experience competence and independence, too. Children who are particularly small for their age may be less likely to be given opportunities to show the full range of their abilities.

Effects of Variations in Physical Attractiveness

In every culture, ideals of physical attractiveness are communicated to children and, from a very early age, affect how parents and others respond to children. Even at birth, some infants are perceived as more attractive than others, and adults tend to attribute to these attractive infants more competence than they do to less attractive babies (Stephan & Langlois, 1984). By the preschool years, physically attractive children tend to be more popular with their peers. When shown photographs of unfamiliar children whom adults had previously rated as attractive or unattractive, preschoolers judged the attractive children to be more likeable, smarter, friendlier and less mean than the unattractive children. Preschool girls, in particular, seem to take attractiveness into account in their likes and dislikes of other children (Langlois & Stephan, 1977; Langlois & Vaughn, 1982; Vaughn & Langlois, 1983).

Physically attractive children like these tend to be perceived by both adults and children as more cognitively and socially competent than unattractive children.

Physically attractive children get preferential treatment from adults also. Because of stereotypes about appropriate physical growth differences for boys and girls, tall, husky girls and small, delicate boys do not fit traditional images, and adults may try to change the appearance of these children. Even teachers rate physically attractive children more favorably than they do their less attractive peers (Langlois & Stephan, 1984).

Are attractive children preferred because they behave differently? We noted previously that children who are tall and large for their age are also somewhat more advanced in general maturity. Similarly, it is possible that children judged as physically attractive by others have certain social skills that make them preferred. Perhaps because attractive children were treated *as if* they were more competent from infancy, their cognitive and social development was enhanced, and thus, by the preschool years, both peers and adults prefer them because of their skills. On the other hand, the continued operation of cultural stereotypes could be the reason for preferential treatment of physically attractive children.

 Why Are Physically Attractive Children Preferred?

To unravel the relationship between what children attribute to attractive peers—known as *behavioral attributions*—and the actual behavior of attractive children, Judith Langlois and Chris Downs (1979) observed the play of 64 three- to five-year-olds varying in physical attractiveness as rated by unfamiliar adults. They found that despite the fact that children perceive attractive peers as more friendly, there were no differences between attractive and unattractive children in positive social behaviors. However, among the five-year-old children, more hitting and other kinds of aggression took place among pairs that included an unattractive child.

In Langlois' words, her findings suggest that:

> . . . expectations for attractive and unattractive children may set a self-fulfilling prophecy into motion: unattractive children may be labeled as such and learn over time the stereotypes and behaviors associated with unattractiveness. Consequently, older children may exhibit aggressive behaviors consistent with this labeling and behave in accordance with others' expectations of them." (Langlois & Downs, 1979, p. 416).

Research on physical attractiveness and its impact on children shows how beliefs about physical appearance can shape behavior.

What children do with their developing bodies has important consequences for other aspects of development. As the preschooler's body changes in size and shape, coordination is improving and manual dexterity is increasing. Very few preschoolers develop coordination, flexibility, and strength through formal sports training or structured fitness programs. Instead, motor skills are most likely to develop in the context of play, discussed in detail in Chapter 11.

The Development of Motor Skills

If we observe children playing at a nursery school or day care center, we might see them climbing on jungle gyms, going down slides, building with blocks, molding with clay, looking at books, or putting together puzzles. Although such play can be incorporated into fantasy play, as when a jungle gym becomes a space ship for two "astronauts," it often simply expresses the sheer joy of movement itself. *Large muscle* activities such as running, climbing, jumping, and skipping are also common. These large muscle activities are important in developing motor skills and in enabling a child to fully explore the environment.

Rough-and-Tumble Play

An interesting kind of large muscle play is called *rough-and-tumble* play, a pattern of play among nursery school children characterized by pushing, shoving, chasing, and hitting and accompanied by wide-mouthed laughs and shouts. Although such behavior might appear aggressive to some observers, Nick Blurton Jones, a British ethologist, demonstrated that the children themselves did not view rough-and-tumble play as aggressive at all. What he called "true aggression" or "agonistic behavior" was characterized by close-mouthed stares and still bodies just preceding hits or shoves (Blurton Jones, 1977).

Vigorous physical activity, like rough-and-tumble play, is most likely to occur when ample space is provided for children's play. Research suggests that when play space is restricted, the incidence of rough-and-tumble play decreases (Smith & Connolly, 1976).

Sex Differences in Physical Activity

If you watch preschoolers on a playground and look for rough-and-tumble play, you are more likely to find boys rather than girls engaged in this kind of activity. In studies conducted in the United States and England, sex differences in activity level in general (Eaton & Enns, 1983; Eaton & Enns, 1986), and rough-and-tumble play in particular, have been found (DiPietro, 1981; Eaton & Keats, 1982). Preschool boys tend to play more actively than girls. The make-believe play of boys is more likely to occur out in the playground with running, jumping, and wrestling, while that of girls is more apt to be indoors and sedentary (Pulaski, 1970; Sanders & Harper, 1976). Since both boys and girls tend to play more energetically when with other children than when alone, boys in groups tend to be the most physically active of all children observed in a preschool classroom.

Preschool boys also are more likely than preschool girls to explore and take risks in a new environment. For example, in a study observing boys and girls at a zoo, boys were more likely than girls to pet and feed animals or climb a steep river embankment (Ginsburg & Miller, 1982). Given these sex differences in risk taking, it is perhaps not surprising that boys have significantly more accidents requiring emergency treatment than do girls throughout childhood (Mannheimer & Mellinger, 1967; Rivara, 1982). Boys also are five to nine times more likely than girls to be identified as *hyperactive* (Ross and Ross, 1982). (See FOCUS ON RISK/INTERVENTION, Chapter 9.) Observations of children outside classrooms in other cultures, however, do not always confirm the same pattern of sex differences. In a survey of six other cultures, Whiting and Edwards (1973) failed to find any greater preference for rough-and-tumble play among boys than among girls. It is possible that in the United States, as opposed to other countries, adults may encourage physical activity and risk taking more among boys than girls, or other factors may be involved.

Measuring Activity Level

A common problem with research on sex differences in behavior is that observers who record the physical activity of boys and girls are themselves some-

Although most preschoolers enjoy rough and tumble play at times, boys are thought more likely to engage in this type of play.

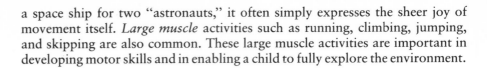

times subject to sex-stereotyped perceptions and may be more apt to notice the roughhousing of boys because they expect sex differences in these behaviors. To counteract this problem, the *actometer* has been developed as a mechanical means of measuring activity level in children (refer to Chapter 3). The actometer is a self-winding wristwatch modified to record movement rather than time. Typically, it is strapped to the child's arm or leg for a fixed interval and the "time" elapsed on the watch is used as a measure of motor activity (Johnson, 1971; Halverson and Waldrop, 1973; Buss, Block & Block, 1980). Since studies using actometer readings indicate that preschool boys are on the average more physically active than preschool girls, we know that this sex difference is not merely "in the eye of the beholder" (Eaton, 1983).

Why do boys tend to play more actively and rougher than girls? Perhaps they are stimulated by others, especially parents, to engage in more physical activity. We saw in Chapter 7 that fathers have been observed to play more physical games, such as tossing the baby in the air, with male infants than with female infants (Power & Parke, 1980). In general, parents provide boys with more toy trucks, sports equipment, and other materials that encourage activity than they do for girls (Rheingold & Cook, 1975). Boys' independent exploration is also more likely to be encouraged than that of girls (Block, 1983).

The Importance of Developing Motor Skills

Physical activity helps to bridge the gap between "knowing that" and "knowing how" (Bruner, 1972). Children generally understand the correct way to perform some action long before they have the skill to execute it themselves. For example, a two-year-old may know that to make a tricycle move, you must push the pedals with your feet. However, without practice, this knowledge will remain useless. Children who are more awkward and uncoordinated than their peers often lack self-confidence and may be hesitant to try new physical activities. Thus, they are likely to miss out on learning experiences that more active explorers of their surroundings absorb. For example, one study found that children who walked by themselves to a location could later remember it better than could children who had been led by an adult (Feldman & Acredolo, 1979).

 ### Exploration and Learning

A study by Nancy Hazen (1982) demonstrated even more clearly the advantages of active exploration for learning about a new environment. Hazen first observed a group of 64 two- to four-year-olds in a "touch and see" room of a museum of natural history. The children were allowed to touch and manipulate the objects on display, such as bones, stuffed animals, and furs. As the children wandered about, observers noted the amount of exploration and whether it was self-guided or guided by a parent. Later, in the preschool, the same children were shown a large three-room playhouse and taught a specific route through it. After each child knew the way, he or she was asked to reverse the route, find a detour, and then find a second, new route to the goal. Half the children were allowed to explore the playhouse freely before learning any routes through it, and half were not given this free play time.

Hazen found that children who were active, self-guided explorers at the museum also actively explored the playhouse when given the opportunity. Active explorers were also better able to reverse routes and learn detours and new routes than were the more passive explorers. Interestingly, Hazen found that it is not the amount a child moves around in a new place, but the *way* exploration occurs—actively or passively—that affects spatial learning.

Mainstreaming Handicapped Children

How best to help young children with physical, emotional, or mental handicaps has long been the subject of controversy. Until the 1960s, it was common to provide separate classes for handicapped children. Gradually, however, the courts began to view the segregation of handicapped children from other children as a separate and unequal system of education. Judicial rulings emphasized that separate special education classes reinforced the labeling of handicapped children as "different" (Turnbull, 1982).

Based on these findings, Public Law (P.L.) 94–142 was passed by the U.S. Congress in 1977. It set out the policy that:

(1) to the maximum extent appropriate, handicapped children, including children in public and private institutions or other care facilities, be educated with children who are not handicapped, and (2) that special classes, separate schooling or other removal of handicapped children from the regular educational environment occur only when the nature or severity of the handicap is such that education in regular classes with the use of supplemental aids and services cannot be achieved satisfactorily (*Federal Register*, August 23, 1977, p. 42497).

The law specified that handicapped children should enjoy the *least restrictive environment* possible by integrating them with nonhandicapped children. Such integration has become known as *mainstreaming*.

The mainstreaming of handicapped children became policy not only because segregation based on handicap was perceived as unfair but also because positive benefits of mainstreaming were predicted.

First, mainstreaming was thought to help handicapped children to learn social and developmental skills by observing and imitating nonhandicapped children. It was hoped that such early experiences would better prepare handicapped children to later join regular classes in elementary school. Second, advocates of mainstreaming felt that exposure to handicapped children would teach other children greater sensitivity to individual differences and make all children more accepting of one another.

How has mainstreaming affected both handicapped and nonhandicapped preschoolers? Ann Turnbull (1982), in a review of evidence concerning the effects of mainstreaming, concluded that there is some support for the claim that when handicapped children are mainstreamed into regular classrooms, they imitate the generally more advanced play of their nonhandicapped peers. Moreover, nonhandicapped children adjust their

Why is this so? Probably active exploration involves more attention to aspects of the environment, since the child is responsible for finding the way. When a child relies on others, such vigilance is not necessary. The child who is used to active exploration probably develops strategies for representing spaces and remembering important features of them. The passive explorer, lacking these strategies, is more likely to get lost when trying to explore on his or her own. This may lead to discouragement and avoidance of exploration the next time. Thus, it is likely that active exploration and self-confidence are related. In this way, self-guided activity enhances not only spatial learning but also other kinds of learning.

Handicapped Children

The benefits of independent activity are denied to many physically handicapped children. Observations of the play of handicapped preschoolers often report that their play is less active, varied, or imaginative than the play of nonhandicapped children (Wills, 1972). Physically handicapping conditions make children dependent upon parents, peers, and other adults. As the Hazen study showed, it is not activity alone that promotes children's learning but the self-guided quality of the activity. Handicapping conditions such as blindness, deafness, or cerebral palsy require a specially designed play environment to encourage the handicapped child's independent movement.

language to the developmental level of their listeners, and such adjustments help to modify the inappropriate verbalizations of some handicapped children.

In the absence of careful longitudinal research comparing handicapped children who have experienced mainstreaming with those who have been in segregated preschools, we do not have conclusive proof that mainstreaming better prepares handicapped preschoolers to compete successfully in regular elementary classrooms. However, since compensatory preschool experiences for children disadvantaged by poverty have documented benefits during the early school years, it is plausible that long-term benefits of preschool mainstreaming may be found.

Effects on Nonhandicapped Children

Preschool children are aware of handicaps and tend to have rejecting attitudes toward children with them. In mainstreamed classes, nonhandicapped children have been observed to stay closer to other nonhandicapped peers, choose nonhandicapped children for games, and prefer to sit next to nonhandicapped children during class activities. When only a handicapped child is available for play, nonhandicapped children often choose to play alone (Porter, Ramsey, Tremblay, Iaccobo & Crawley, 1978; Cavallaro & Porter, 1980; Peterson & Haralick, 1977).

These findings illustrate that when handicapped children are physically present in the same classroom with other children, they are not necessarily integrated into social activities. Because of this, special programs have been developed to increase the social acceptance of handicapped preschoolers. Components of such programs include the following: (1) Activities, such as dramatic play, painting, carpentry, and water play, designed to give handicapped children an opportu-

nity to observe and practice social skills. (2) For children identified as severely deficient in language or social skills, more specific individual training in how to join a group of children and how to respond appropriately to others. Observations of children's play in such programs found that compared with children in regular mainstreamed classrooms, nonhandicapped children played much more often with their handicapped peers. In addition, when only a handicapped child was available for play, nonhandicapped children were less likely to choose to play alone (Odom, Jenkins, Speltz & Deklyen, 1982). This research indicates that specific programming to encourage the social integration of handicapped with nonhandicapped preschoolers may be an effective way of achieving the goals of mainstreaming.

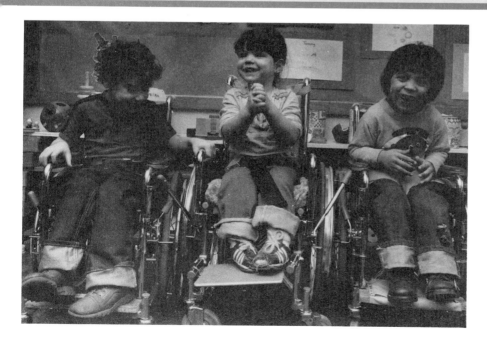

The environment of handicapped preschoolers needs special modification. For instance, toy shelves are placed at "wheelchair" height for easy access and to encourage independent functioning.

Small Muscle Activities

Another kind of play involves *small muscle* activities, such as drawing. Many kinds of small muscle play activities, such as stacking blocks, putting together puzzles, and drawing, involve the child in the use of patterns and sequences. Small muscle play activities also develop the eye-hand coordination and muscle dexterity that later will be important for reading and writing. An essential part of these skills is the ability to handle tools like pencils and pens.

Have you noticed the thick crayons and paintbrushes provided to children in child care centers? Practice with tools of this size and shape helps preschoolers to gradually strengthen hand muscles and coordinate them. As children practice gripping paintbrushes, crayons, and scaled-down hammers, their ability to use these tools improves.

Connolly and Elliott, two British ethologists, have observed how preschoolers grip paintbrushes when painting at an easel (1972). In 75 percent of their observations, they noted that the children used an adult precision grip, illustrated in Figure 8−6 (a). This is the grip that is most appropriate for writing. The remainder of the time, grips such as those in Figure 8−6 (b), (c), and (d) were used. These grips, though appropriate for using other tools, make small muscle activities such as painting or writing more difficult. With practice, preschoolers gradually become more adept at fitting the appropriate hand grip to the tool they are using.

Figure 8−6

Grips of Paintbrushes Used by Preschoolers
(From N. Blurton Jones (Ed.), *Ethological Studies of Child Behavior*, © 1972, Cambridge University Press. Adapted with permission of Cambridge University Press.)

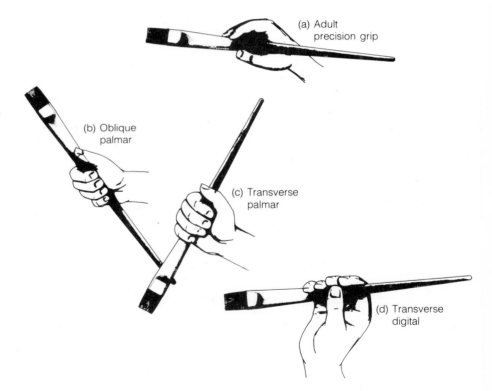

(a) Adult precision grip

(b) Oblique palmar

(c) Transverse palmar

(d) Transverse digital

Children's Drawing

The drawings and paintings of children have long fascinated adults, who tend to see in them the "true" expression of creativity, unfettered by conventional ways of seeing things. Many a parent who proudly displayed the colorful splashes of paint produced by his or her four-year-old "Picasso" feels disappointed by the unimaginative stick figures the same child later produces in third-grade art class.

Because preschoolers' art seems so much more expressive than their verbal productions, adults also tend to see in drawings clues to the child's emotional inner life. In this view, the child who draws himself as a tiny figure next to towering adults may be depicting feelings of vulnerability, while the child who draws people without arms could be revealing a distorted body image.

Although a sensitive clinician can often better understand a child's emotional concerns by examining drawings, one must be careful about overinterpreting children's art. Many aspects of preschoolers' drawings may reflect no more than limitations in motor skill and a growing mastery of how to organize simple shapes on paper, (Golomb, 1974; Freeman, 1980).

We can understand many things about the development of preschoolers' drawings by viewing them in terms of stages in the creation of patterned, organized forms. The first stage of drawing is scribbles, which later develop into simple shapes, such as circles or rectangles. A favorite shape of many children is the sun shape. Children then link together several shapes into a few preferred combinations, which gradually are adapted to represent objects, animals, and people.

At each stage, children incorporate the preferred shapes of an earlier period (Kellogg, 1969, 1979; Goodnow, 1977). By using the same few shapes over and over again to stand for many different things, the child is not showing a confused perception of reality but is discovering a concept, learning that many different things can be represented by a single symbol. When shapes are combined, they are not combined randomly but follow certain implicit principles.

The following are some of the "rules" preschoolers seem to use in their drawings:

(1) Don't overlap parts.
(2) Always place figures perpendicular to the horizontal axis.
(3) Follow a preferred sequence (e.g., draw from the top to the bottom or from right to left).

These rules sometimes produce odd-looking figures, as the drawing in Figure 8–7 illustrates. Because the child who made the drawing began each figure by drawing the face, she had little room left at the bottom of the page to draw the rest of the body.

In summary, we feel children's drawings can be understood as "visible thinking" and "visible concept formation" as well as "visible emotion" or "visible creativity." Indeed, preschool children can be a delight to observe because they are so up front about their thoughts and feelings. They think and feel expressively through action, drawing, and private speech. The next chapters take a closer look at the thoughts and feelings characteristic of early childhood.

Figure 8—7

Big head in relation to torso size is commonplace in children's drawings.

Chapter Summary

PHYSICAL GROWTH

☐ During the preschool years, changes in height, weight, and body proportions occur, although the growth rate has slowed since infancy. Brain cells grow in size and complexity, and the two hemispheres of the brain become specialized in function. Handedness develops in most children.

☐ Growth is influenced by both genetic and environmental factors. Inadequate nutrition can retard normal growth and impair both mental and social responsiveness. If malnutrition is not too severe or too early in development, catch-up growth is possible. Environmental pollutants, such as lead, have been shown to adversely affect cognitive and social functioning.

☐ Among well-nourished children, individual differences in size and appearance can be associated with differences in how children are treated by others. Physically attractive children are generally better liked by both peers and adults.

DEVELOPMENT OF MOTOR SKILLS

☐ Motor skills are practiced and consolidated through play. Large-muscle play involves running, jumping, climbing and skipping, activities that use the entire body. In some cultures boys tend to engage more in physically active, rough-and-tumble play than do girls. In general, however, boys and girls have more similarities than differences in their play.

☐ Independent exploration helps children learn about their environment and gives them self-confidence. Handicapped children need supportive environments that allow them the maximum independent movement.

☐ Small muscle coordination is developed through play activities such as drawing. Children's drawings pass through stages from scribbles to elaborate, realistic shapes.

Recommended Readings

Bruch, H. (1973). *Eating disorders*. New York: Basic Books. A therapist who has treated children suffering from obesity and other eating disorders analyzes the dynamics underlying these problems. Good examples from case studies.

Goodnow, J. (1977). *Children drawing*. Cambridge, MA: Harvard University Press. A slim but incisive overview of theory and research concerning the development of children's art. Engaging illustrations.

Lowry, G. H. (1978). *Growth and development of children* (7th ed.). Chicago: Year Book Medical Publishers. A detailed description of physical growth at various stages of development.

Tanner, J. (1978). *From foetus into man: Physical growth from conception to maturity*. London: Open Books. An authority on physical development provides a comprehensive overview with useful charts and tables.

The Young Child: Cognitive Development

I have no remembrance of the time when I began to learn Greek, I have been told that it was when I was three years old. My earliest recollection on that subject is that of committing to memory what my father termed Vocables, being lists of common Greek words with their signification in English, which he wrote for me on cards. Of grammar, until some years later, I learned no more than the inflexions of the nouns and verbs, but after a course of Vocables, proceeded at once to translation; and I faintly remember going through Aesop's fables, the first Greek book I read.

> — *From the autobiography of John Stuart Mill,*
> *English philosopher, 1806–1873.*
> *Mill, 1960, pp. 3–4.*

Accounts of prodigies like John Stuart Mill, the English philosopher just quoted, show us the outer limits of young children's abilities to learn. Although very few children or parents can be expected to tackle learning as Mill and his father did, the rapid cognitive strides of more typical young children remain impressive. Preschool children sometimes seem like sponges, soaking up knowledge about the often confusing world around them. They tug on pant legs and pull on skirts and keep asking "Why?"

As they develop, young children attempt to make sense of the world in their own terms. They develop explanations and go about solving problems in ways that are qualitatively different from those used by both younger and older children.

In this chapter, we'll attempt to get inside the heads of preschoolers. To help answer the question, How do preschoolers think?, Jean Piaget will be our first guide. Piaget's theory of the stages of cognitive growth common to all children has been the most influential (and most often challenged) model of how thought processes develop. (Refer to Chapter 2 for more detail.)

We will also examine another, more recent view of the cognitive development, the *information processing* approach (introduced in Chapter 2), which stresses how the components common to all thought—perception, attention, memory, etc.—gradually become better organized to notice, interpret, and store information. Finally, we'll explore what makes children different from one another rather than what they all have in common. This focus on *individual differences* stresses the many ways in which parents, teachers, and others affect the child's thinking and learning as well as the contributions made by the child's own characteristics.

Preoperational Thought

Although he was careful not to attach specific ages to stages of cognitive development, Piaget described the period from about age two to age six or seven as the *stage of preoperational thought*. In general, Piaget was interested primarily in describing how children develop the capacity for logical thought. By "preoperational," he meant "before the ability to perform logical mental operations."

By observing children at play and presenting them with ingeniously constructed tasks, Piaget was able to demonstrate the principal characteristics of preoperational thought. His description of this stage emphasizes more what children *cannot* do rather than their accomplishments. Perhaps it is because Piaget was so impressed with the rapid strides in thinking made during the first two years and again around age seven that the preoperational period appeared in comparison a time of relative dormancy.

Before we examine more closely Piaget's characterization of the difficulties in thinking with which the preoperational child has to contend, let's take a look at the positive gains of this period compared with the sensorimotor stage (refer to chapter 6).

Achievements of Preoperational Thought

Perhaps the key achievement gained by preoperational thought is *symbolic representation*, the ability to represent people, places, and ideas as symbols. A *symbol* bears some resemblance to the thing signified. For example, a road sign with a curved line symbolizes the fact that the road ahead is curved. In contrast, a *sign,* such as the word *cat,* is arbitrary and has no resemblance to its referent. During the preoperational period, both symbols and signs are evident in many aspects of children's behavior.

Deferred Imitation.   Several hours after watching her father shave, Inez takes a block and, making a "zzzz" sound, uses it to "shave" her face. Such imitation occurring long after observation implies a mental representation of "father shaving" which the child stored in memory and later retrieved.

Symbolic Play.   Inez's behavior can also be viewed as an example of symbolic play, in which a block stands for a razor. During the preschool years, play becomes increasingly symbolic (see Chapter 11). At first, objects closely resembling the real thing are employed. Gradually, children feel free to invent

The ability to use symbols is evident in preschool play. While children enjoy playing with child-size replicas of adult objects, like the doctor's kit and helmet shown here, they can also make use of sticks, blocks, almost anything, to create a pretend reality.

symbols and signs that have nothing in common with the objects they represent. Through symbolic representation, play during the preoperational period becomes less tied to the mimicking of reality.

3 *Mental Images.* The emergence of symbolic representation means that the child is able to entertain mental images of absent people, places, and things and to think about them. Recall the discussion in Chapter 6 of separation anxiety among toddlers. The anxiety engendered by separation from a parent is reduced when the child becomes capable of mentally representing the absent parent and understanding that absence does not mean disappearance. In many other ways, the preoperational child's use of mental images vastly expands the child's ability to think about events beyond the present.

4 *Language.* Perhaps the clearest evidence of symbolic representation lies in the development of spoken language. After all, words are signs for the objects and actions they represent. Chapter 10 takes a detailed look at the development of language during the preschool years. Let's now pause to appreciate how language allows for the internalization of action. With language, children can perform mental operations instead of overt ones. Language speeds up the rate at which experience can take place; the child can experience something by simply imagining it.

In summary, symbolic representation, as seen in deferred imitation, symbolic play, mental images, and language, is the source of many positive gains in thinking ability shown by the preoperational child. Another cognitive ability that evolves during the preoperational period, according to Piaget, is the concept of *identity*, the understanding that the nature of an object remains constant even when irrelevant aspects of its appearance are altered. The following research study illustrates how understanding of identity develops.

 A Black Cat Named Maynard

In an ingenious experiment, DeVries (1969) showed 64 three- to six-year-old children a black cat named Maynard (see Figure 9-1). She then placed a realistic mask of the head of a dog or a rabbit over the cat (Maynard was trained to sit still) and asked, "What is this animal now?" Finally, she removed the mask and again asked the child about the animal's identity. An analysis of the children's answers identified six levels of identity understanding occurring during this time. As shown in Table 9-1, with increasing age, more children gave higher level responses.

Limits of Preoperational Thinking

In spite of gains in identity understanding and symbol use, preoperational thinking is deficient in many ways.

Egocentrism. The inability to understand the world except from one's own point of view is called *egocentrism*. Although egocentric thinking can occur at any age (Elkind, 1967), Piaget described the preoperational child as naturally limited by this "me" perspective. When a three-year-old eagerly picks out a toy truck for Daddy's birthday or brings a favorite blanket to comfort a distressed adult, the child is showing the inability to consider other perspectives. This happens not because of selfishness or unwillingness, but because of limitations to thinking.

(a) Maynard the cat.

(b) Cat masked as dog, side view.

(c) Cat masked as rabbit.

Figure 9—1

Cat Used in Administering Live Form of Generic Identity Interview.

(Adapted from DeVries (1969).)

Table 9—1

STAGES IN THE ACQUISITION OF
THE CONCEPT OF IDENTITY

Stage	Description
1	No evidence of identity; Maynard's identity changes whenever mask is put on or removed.
2	Child predicts identity will not change; Maynard's appearance changes, but when mask is put on or removed, child states Maynard has been transformed into another animal.
3	Child states that Maynard has not changed physically when mask is put on or removed but believes that Maynard has changed identity.
4	Child believes that Maynard is still the same after masking transformations but that his name has changed.
5	Child believes that Maynard is still the same after mask is put on or removed but still thinks a possibility exists that Maynard's identity might change under magical circumstances.
6	Child believes that Maynard's identity cannot change when a mask is placed on or taken off the animal.

Source: DeVries, 1969.

Figure 9—2
Piaget's Three-Mountains Task

Piaget demonstrated egocentrism in his classic three-mountains experiment, depicted in Figure 9-2. After walking around a table with a three-dimensional display of toy mountains, the child is seated looking at the mountains from one side, while a doll is placed "looking" at the mountains from the other side. The child is asked to select the photograph (from a set of 10) that shows how the mountains would appear to the doll. Four-year-olds had no awareness that the doll would see the mountains differently. Six-year-olds did have this awareness, but still did not choose the correct perspective. Only by age nine was there complete ability to select the doll's perspective.

Centration. The major limitation underlying egocentrism, Piaget believed, was *centration,* the centering or concentrating on only one aspect of a situation. He contrasted this to *decentration,* or *compensation,* in which multiple perspectives can be taken into account at once. Piaget argued that in general, preschoolers have difficulty simultaneously considering multiple elements and the relations among them. This underlying problem produced not only egocentric thinking but also other mistakes in preoperational thought processes.

Cause-and-Effect Reasoning. Because preschoolers center on one aspect of a situation at a time, they are likely to consider events in isolation and to have trouble grasping how one event causes another. For example, when watching a television program interrupted by commercials, preschool children have difficulty linking events shown before and after the breaks. They tend to see the part where "the bad guy kills people" and the part where "the bad guy gets caught" as unrelated (Anderson, Alwitt, Lorch & Levin, 1979).

When preoperational children do identify cause-and-effect sequences, they are often incorrect, because they use *transductive reasoning,* which links two specific events that occur close together. Suppose it rained on the first day of nursery school. A preschooler might interpret this to mean that school started *because* it rained.

Another difficulty in understanding cause and effect comes more directly from egocentrism. Young children tend to explain events out of their own experiences. For example, when parents quarrel, a preschooler may feel that it is because the child has done something wrong. Natural phenomena are often understood in egocentric terms as well. A preschooler may explain, "It rained so I could wear my new boots" or "Flowers have colors so they're fun to pick."

A final difficulty that preoperational thinkers have in understanding causalty is *finalism,* the belief that every event must have a specifiable cause and that nothing happens by chance (Brainerd 1978). Thus, preschoolers wear the patience of adults with their endless questions beginning with "Why?"

Animism and Artificialism. Piaget noted that preschoolers tended to explain the behavior of natural phenomena, inanimate objects, or mechanical devices as though they were alive, a belief called *animism.* For example, the child believes that the room is lonely when it is empty, the moon is hiding when it is behind a cloud, and trees feel cold when the child does. Because preschoolers are alive, they ascribe life to all things.

Related to animism is *artificialism,* the belief that everything that exists has been created by humans or by divine plan. Thus, Piaget reports that preschoolers believe that "mountains grow because stones have been manufactured and then planted; and lakes have been hollowed out" (1967, p. 28). This stems from a failure to distinguish between physical and psychological causes.

Reasoning Problems—Making Inferences. Suppose you were to give a four-year-old this problem: "Sarah is older than Jennifer, and Jennifer is older than John. Who is older, Sarah or John?" Preschool children are often perplexed by such questions and are just as likely to answer "John" as "Sarah." Questions of this type, which require one to make a logical deduction, tap *inferential reasoning.* Piaget felt that preoperational children did poorly on such problems because they would center on individual elements and fail to consider the relations among them.

Classifying. Centration also makes it difficult for preoperational children to understand that people and objects can be classified in more than one way. For example, a collie can be considered a dog, a mammal, and an animal, in a hierarchy of subordinate and superordinate categories. To assess classification, Piaget and his colleagues showed children a set of seven toy dogs. Four of the dogs were collies, one was a German shepherd, one a poodle, and one an Irish setter. After the children showed that they understood the names of each breed and that all were dogs, they were asked: "Are there more collies or more dogs?" The answer invariably was, "More collies" (Inhelder & Piaget, 1964). Preoperational thinkers had difficulty understanding how superordinate categories ("dog") and subordinate categories ("collie") were related.

Children in the preoperational stage also tend to group objects together differently than do older children. Suppose we show a preschool child a variety of objects of different sizes and colors, like those in Figure 9-3, and ask, "Which things go together?" Instead of consistently using specific dimensions to group the objects—all the squares or all the red shapes go together—preschoolers are likely to use inconsistent and shifting categories, putting some objects together because they are near each other, or putting squares and circles together "because you can make a man out of them." This is an example of *syncretic reasoning,* idiosyncratically connecting unrelated ideas or elements into a whole.

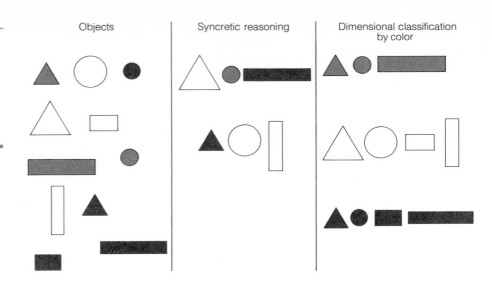

Figure 9-3

Ways of Classifying Objects

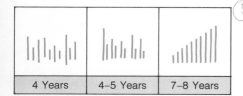

4 Years	4-5 Years	7-8 Years

Figure 9-4

Seriation

Between the ages of four and six, children have difficulty reordering a series. After age seven, they are able to correctly solve the seriation problem.

Seriation. Seriation refers to the ordering of items from largest to smallest or smallest to largest. Understanding seriation is an important component of quantitative thinking. Four- to five-year-old children, when given sticks of differing lengths and asked to select the smallest stick, then the next larger and to place it adjacent to the first, then the next larger, etc., until all the sticks have been ordered, are unable to complete the task successfully. In the late preoperational period (five to six years), children can order the sticks but only after considerable effort and frequent errors. With the emergence of concrete operations, around the age of seven, children usually complete the task easily (Piaget, 1952). (See Figure 9-4.)

Conservation. Piaget defined _conservation_ as understanding the invariance of certain properties, such as number, length, surface, and quantity in spite of apparent changes in objects. In a series of important experiments, Piaget showed that because of centration, preoperational thinkers have difficulty grasping the conservation of liquid, volume, length, mass, and number. Suppose we want to find out if a particular preschooler can conserve the volume of a liquid. Following Piaget's method, we first show the child two identical beakers, each filled with exactly the same amount of liquid. We make sure that the child has no difficulty in seeing that the beakers contain the same amount. Now, as the child watches, we pour the contents of one beaker into a taller, thinner container. Then we ask, "Do the two beakers have equal amounts of water, or does one contain more than the other?" The child will now say that the tall, thin container has more water than the shorter beaker (or that the shorter beaker has more). Perhaps, with some exasperation, we point out that we did not add or take away any water when we poured from one beaker into a differently shaped one. Nevertheless, the child will persist in claiming that now the beakers contain different amounts of water.

A similar pattern occurs in other tests of conservation. For example, to assess conservation of mass, Piaget showed children two identical lumps of clay. Then he rolled out one lump into a long, skinny "snake." Again, preoperational thinkers reported that the long, thin shape now contained more (or less) clay. In the conservation of number task, children were shown two rows of beads. After they were satisfied that each row contained exactly the same number of beads, the spaces between the beads of one row were increased. Nonconserving children would report that the longer row contained more beads.

Table 9-2 summarizes the major tests of conservation and the ages at which conservation is usually attained.

Why Preoperational Thinkers Don't Conserve. (Because children are centering on only one aspect of what they observe, such as changes in water level, shape, or line length, they are not able to understand that despite these perceptual changes, underlying properties such as amount, mass, or number do not vary. In effect, to conserve, children must learn to ignore the evidence of their senses and remember certain principles or logical operations. This is difficult for preoperational thinkers who are held captive by their perceptions of the immediate situation.) In the conservation of water task, the child's attention is drawn to the changed level of the water in a differently shaped beaker. An eight-year-old who has made the transition from preoperational

Table 9—2

CONSERVATION TASKS INVESTIGATED BY PIAGET

Task	Procedure	Age Acquired*
Conservation of substance	Two identical balls of clay are presented. Child admits they have equal amounts. The shape of one ball is changed. The child is asked whether the two balls still contain the same amount of clay.	6–7 years
Conservation of length	Two parallel sticks are shown to the child who admits they are equally long. One of the sticks is moved. The child is asked if the sticks are still the same length.	6–7 years
Conservation of number	Two rows, each containing the same number of beads, are placed in one-to-one correspondence. The spaces between the beads in one of the rows are changed. The child is asked whether each row still has the same number of beads.	6–7 years
Conservation of liquids	Two identical beakers are filled to the same level with liquid. The child sees that they contain the same amount. The liquid from one beaker is poured into a differently shaped beaker (so that the water level changes). The child is asked if the beakers still contain the same amount of liquids.	6–7 years
Conservation of Volume	Two glasses of water with equal balls of clay inside them are shown to the child. One of the balls is changed in shape. The child is asked if each piece of clay still displaces the same volume of water.	9–10 years
Conservation of area	The same number of small squares are placed in the upper left corner on two identical sheets of cardboard. The child sees that the same amount of space is remaining on each sheet. On one sheet, the squares are scattered. The child is asked if the same amount of space remains on each sheet.	9–10 years

*Note: *Approximate* age ranges are noted. Piaget recognized that individual children differ in the rate at which they acquire conservation, but the sequence is always invariant (i.e., conservation of area always comes later than conservation of length, number, and liquid). Adapted from Dworetsky (1984).

Piaget in the Preschool Classroom

Piaget was interested in going beyond a theoretical understanding of how young children develop the ability to think logically. He believed that educational policy and practice would benefit from implementing his ideas.

Piaget cautioned teachers to avoid traditional instruction in which a group lesson is given with a specific sequence of material to transmit and advised them to instead create a stimulating environment for children to explore. Concrete experiences in the context of play were recommended as best for learning during the preschool years. Piaget urged teachers to take into account each child's readiness and interest and to remember that preoperational language and thought are qualitatively different from those of older children and adults.

These guidelines have been the basis for all Piagetian curricula for preschoolers. In this sense, different programs share the same general philosophy. However, each program differs somewhat in emphasis. To illustrate this, let's examine three major implementations of Piagetian educational philosophy, each associated with the names of their founders: the Lavatelli, Weikart, and Kamii and DeVries programs.

The Lavatelli Early Childhood Curriculum

After studying with Piaget in Geneva, Lavatelli developed a preschool curriculum organized around three themes: (1) classification; (2) number, space, and measurement;

and (3) seriation. For each theme, a series of short activities is designed for teachers to use with small groups of five to six children. During each activity, the teacher uses questions to prod the children's thinking about each theme.

For example, one classification activity consists of the teacher making a string of beads and inviting the children to copy the string. At first, a simple string of beads of one color and size is constructed. The teacher then introduces more complex patterns, alternating colors, sizes, and shapes of beads. During the activity, instructions such as "Find all the beads that are alike" are given. As the children string beads, the teacher stimulates their thinking by saying, "Tell me what you're doing. Why did you choose that one?" In this way, the activities are thought to help preschoolers understand classification principles (Lavatelli, 1977).

The Weikart Cognitively Oriented Curriculum

Somewhat less structured than the Lavatelli curriculum is the program developed by David Weikart and his associates which emphasizes creating a stimulating environment through the use of *interest centers,* different sections of a large, open space where materials are provided for the child to sort, compare, and combine. Teachers ask questions and demonstrate activities in the interest centers, but unlike the Lavatelli curriculum, children rather than teachers initiate activities.

The Kamii and DeVries Approach

Even less structured than the Weikart program is the approach advocated by Kamii and DeVries, who feel that any attempts to teach children logical

operations such as classification through questions or demonstrations are misguided. Instead, they believe that the best way to foster cognitive growth is simply by providing an environment encouraging social interaction, curiosity, exploration, and play (Kamii & DeVries, 1974).

Evaluation

Do Piagetian-inspired programs help preschool children attain concrete operations more readily than do other curricula? Among Piagetian programs themselves, do children in Lavatelli, Weikart, or Kamii and DeVries learn differently? The lack of extensive evaluation makes it hard to give definite answers to these questions. However, the comparisons that have been made among programs suggest few real differences in impact on children. Weikart compared his program to two others, a traditional nursery school and a structured language-training program. Children in all three programs showed impressive gains in IQ and language ability as well as in emotional and social development (Weikart, 1973). Similarly, in a three-year evaluation of a Kamii and DeVries approach, children in both that program and a traditional nursery school showed similar progress on Piagetian tasks of classification, seriation, inferential reasoning, and conservation (Bingham-Newman, Saunders, & Hooper, 1976).

The indications are that good preschool programs, whatever their specific philosophical bent, are beneficial for young children. The common features of good programs include a consistent daily routine, a stimulating environment geared to the child's ability and interests, ample opportunity for social play, and responsive teachers (Lawton & Hooper, 1978).

thought to the stage of concrete operations is able to take account of the fact that because no water has been added or taken away, the same amount must be present when poured into a new container, no matter how differently shaped.

Another problem preschoolers typically have with conservation is understanding the *reversibility* of operations. Suppose that you are asked to explain the conservation of liquid in this two-beaker problem. You might answer, "Imagine reversing the process and pouring the water back into the original container; it *has* to be the same amount." It is just this imaginary reversal of an operation that stumps preoperational thinkers.

Despite Piaget's influence on both developmental theory and educational practice, his views of young children's cognitive development have been seriously challenged.

Can Conservation Be Taught to Preschoolers?

Piaget argued that preoperational thinking was a natural and universal stage on the way to logical thinking, which developed gradually in the context of play and exploration, not through adult instruction. He felt that as children played, they encountered many situations that challenged their ideas and produced *disequilibrium* or cognitive conflict. In efforts to understand these situations, children would gradually modify their thinking or, to use Piaget's term, *accommodate* to this new information. Some researchers, however, have challenged Piaget's contention that adults cannot teach preschoolers conservation.

 ## Training Preschoolers to Conserve

Reasoning that attending to irrelevant aspects of the problem was the source of children's conservation mistakes, Rochel Gelman (1969) devised a strategy for teaching five-year-olds how to conserve number by showing them sets of three items related to number and length. In each case, two of the items in the set were identical in number (or length), while the third was different. For example (see Figure 9-5), two rows of five chips and one row of three chips were shown with the three chips spread out to the length of the row of five. For each set, the children were rewarded for picking out the rows that were the same or different in number. Two other groups of children were also tested. One group received the same training but were given no feedback on whether their responses were correct, and a second group—a control group—received no instruction but were tested with toys to make sure they knew the meaning of *same* and *different*.

Tests for conservation of number a day after training indicated that only children who received instruction and feedback showed evidence of learning; correct responses rose from chance level to 95 percent. Even when tested two weeks later on conservation tasks for which they had received no training—conservation of liquid quantity and mass—effects of instruction, although less dramatic, were maintained. Moreover, these children were able to give explanations for their answers even though they had been told only whether their responses were correct or incorrect.

Does this mean that Piaget was wrong and preschool children can be easily trained to understand conservation? Not necessarily. Perhaps the five-year-olds in Gelman's study already had acquired through experience an understanding of conservation, and training simply helped them to express a skill they already had. Researchers who repeated Gelman's training procedures with four-year-olds found that half the children failed to give correct answers after

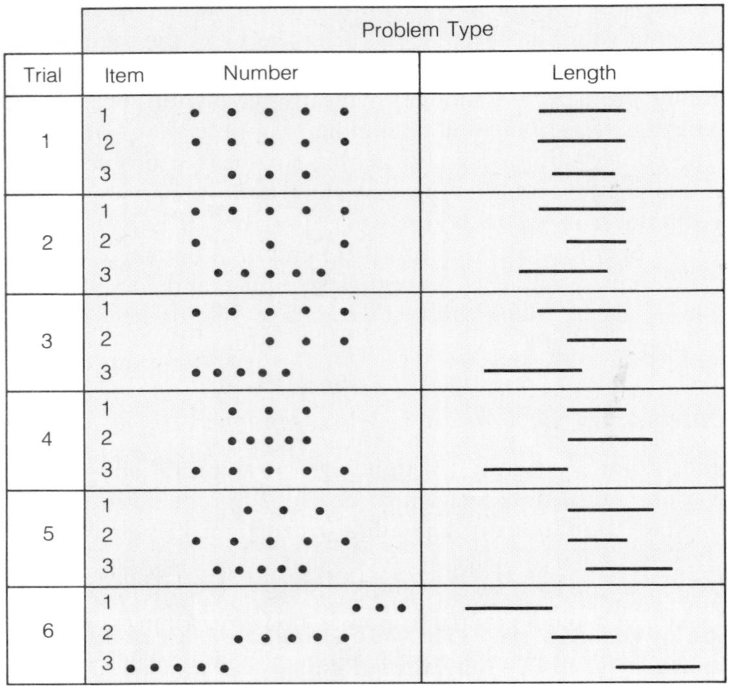

Figure 9–5

These sets of chips and sticks are examples of the groups of items that Rochel Gelman (1969) used in training children to discriminate number and length.

(From R. Gelman, *Journal of Experimental Child Psychology*, 1969, Vol. 7. Reprinted with the permission of Academic Press.)

Which Two Are the Same?

training and none of the children could explain the principle behind conservation (Vadham & Smothergill, 1977; Larsen, 1977). Moreover, in tests of conservation of number using larger sets of objects than Gelman had employed, preschoolers fail to show conservation understanding (Halford & Boyle, 1985).

Rather than teach children to ignore irrelevant aspects, some training procedures focus on reversibility (Imagine pouring the water back) (Sigel, Roeper, & Hooper, 1968) or on identity (It's still the *same* water when we pour it from a tall, thin container into a short one) (Field, 1981; Acredolo & Acredolo, 1979). Four-year-olds who received identity training could solve conservation problems up to five months after the end of training (Field, 1981). Other procedures have tried to induce cognitive conflict in nonconservers by having them pretend to conserve (the experimenter tells them the correct answer) or by having nonconserving children discuss conservation problems with older children (Silverman & Stone, 1972). Although we cannot be sure that such strategies actually produce internal conflict in the nonconservers, children generally do show improvements in conservation ability as a result of them (Murray, Ames, & Botwin, 1977; Murray, 1983; Ames & Murray, 1982).

Although this issue is still controversial, it seems as though demonstration, practice, and explanation are most effective with older preschoolers, like the five-year-olds in Gelman's study, who may be transitional conservers—already showing some, though not consistent, evidence of understanding the concept. However, training studies with younger children challenge Piaget's claim that instruction is useless in promoting understanding of conservation (Brainerd, 1978).

Other Criticisms of Piaget

Many feel that the Piagetian tasks used to assess not only conservation but also classification, cause and effect, seriation, and egocentrism were needlessly difficult and complex and thus do not provide a true indication of preschoolers' abilities. For example, in the three-mountains experiment (refer to Figure 9-2), children have to select the perspective the doll would "see" from two-dimensional photographs after they study a three-dimensional model. Preschool-age children have difficulty mentally rotating a scene (Huttenlocher & Presson, 1979), matching what they see to a picture (Gzesh & Surber, 1985), or detecting patterns or structures in pictures rather than in the real world (Gibson & Spelke, 1983). Moreover, preschoolers may be more skilled at making judgments about familiar objects, such as toy animals, than about mountains of different sizes. In a modification of the three-mountains experiment, Helen Borke (1975) allowed three-year-olds to rotate the displays on a turntable to show the doll's "perspective," and she also tested the children with displays of toy people, animals, and buildings. Under these conditions, 80 percent of the children gave correct responses.

Other evidence supports the idea that when children can actively move materials around in a perspective-taking task, they show less evidence of egocentrism (Flavell, Shipstead, & Croft, 1978). For example, three-year-olds can correctly perform the task of positioning dolls in a game of hide-and-seek and putting one doll behind a barrier so that two other dolls can "see it," even when the perspective of the dolls would be different from their own (Hobson, 1981).

Other researchers (Bryant & Trabasso, 1971) have argued that many Piagetian tests make excessive demands on the *memory* capacities of preschoolers. They do poorly not because they fail to understand the logic of the task, but simply because they can't remember all of it. For example, consider the problem we discussed earlier demonstrating preoperational thinkers' difficulty with inferential reasoning: "Sarah is older than Jennifer, and Jennifer is older than John. Who is older, Sarah or John?" Bryant and Trabasso (1971) showed that preschoolers failed this problem because they usually forgot the first part by the time they heard the last part. By training the children on each pair of relations until they were securely remembered, Bryant and Trabasso demonstrated that preschoolers could solve problems involving inferential reasoning almost as well as adults could.

In addition to their overall level of difficulty, some of the problems Piaget devised may have used *language* too difficult for preschoolers. Most Piagetian tasks require comprehension of terms related to absolute and relative quantity—*more, same, older than*—terms that are difficult for preschoolers to understand (for more about language during the preschool period, see Chapter 10).

This was demonstrated in the Bryant & Trabasso study, in which inferential reasoning problems were modified as follows:

"Sarah is older than Jennifer; Jennifer is younger than Sarah.
Jennifer is older than John; John is younger than Jennifer.
Who is older, Sarah or John?"

The use of two comparatives—*older, younger*—instead of one (*older*) apparently enabled the preschoolers in the study to answer correctly. The researchers argued that this was because, in the absence of a matching comparative (*younger*), preschoolers understood the word *older* to mean *old*. For them, the meaning of the problem was something like this:

"Sarah is old; Jennifer is not old.
"Jennifer is old; John is not old."

Because this encoded contradictory information—Jennifer is both old and not old—the preschoolers had difficulty answering the question (Riley &

Thought and Language

Does language determine or reflect cognitive development? *Reflect* asserts Piaget. *Determine* counters Jerome Bruner. In many respects, Bruner and Piaget hold similar views of how children's thinking develops. Both proposed stage theories describing a significant transition occurring around age seven in the ability to use logical operations to solve concrete problems.

Bruner, whose studies of children's thinking were conducted at Harvard, believed that language provides a very powerful system of symbols, the use of which allows children to grasp logical operations. He felt that preoperational thinkers store information primarily as visual images. Around age seven, they gradually shift to store information as symbols, such as words (Bruner, Olver, & Greenfield, 1966). This transition is called the *encoding shift hypothesis* (Kail & Hagen, 1982) because of the change in which children encode or store information.

Bruner (1964) illustrated the role of language in cognitive development in the following study: He first taught conservation of liquid quantity to a group of four- to seven-year-olds who had previously shown an inability to conserve. In his procedure, a screen covered the glasses so that the children could not see the changed water level when the water from the tall, thin glass was poured into a wide glass container. Half the four-year-olds, 90 percent of the five-year-olds, and all the six- to seven-year-olds gave correct answers and justified their responses with reasons such as, "It's still the same water." When the children were later retested with the screen removed, none of the four-year-olds could solve the conservation problem, but most of the older children continued to show evidence of conservation understanding, even though they now could see the change in level when liquid was poured from the thin beaker to a wider one.

Bruner attributed the gains made by the five- to seven-year-olds in his study to the encoding shift hypothesis. Rather than rely on visual cues, these children were able to employ an "internal verbal formula that shielded them from the overpowering [visual] appearances" (1964, p. 7).

Let's apply Bruner's thesis to another Piagetian task: classification. As discussed earlier, preoperational children tend to classify objects globally or using syncretic reasoning rather than along specific dimensions that might distinguish them (refer to Figure 9-3 and accompanying text). Bruner's interpretation of this would be that global classification occurs because preschoolers perceive objects in terms of visual images. As they learn the meaning and application of terms like *size, color,* and *shape* and other dimensions, they become able to classify objects along these dimensions. Thus, as language improves, so does classification skill.

Piaget's view of how language and thought are related is quite different:

Linguistic progress is not responsible for logical or operational progress. It is rather the other way around. The logical or operational level is likely to be responsible for a more sophisticated language level (1972, p. 14).

Thus, Piaget viewed language, like memory, as a reflection of underlying cognitive operations that develop out of the child's actions on the environment and reactions to it. Piaget argued that the preoperational child who does not understand the logical operation of reversibility and hence cannot understand how the volume of a liquid is conserved will not understand that the following two sentences have the same meaning: "John hit the ball." "The ball was hit by John."

The relation between language and thought remains a thorny issue. Like memory, language is a component of cognitive functioning and not really separable from it. A child's understanding of the terms used in tests of logical operations clearly affects ability to perform. In this way, thinking is constrained by level of language development. On the other hand, linguistic concepts may emerge as a result of earlier assimilation and accommodation experiences. For example, children may come to understand that the word *older* must imply *younger* only after they have mastered the underlying logical operation of reversibility.

Preschoolers like the girl shown here can simplify their language, adapt their behavior and use appropriate toys to interact with toddlers and infants. This is evidence that they can understand perspectives other than their own.

Trabasso, 1974). Findings such as these suggest that when children understand the correct meaning of key terms in Piagetian tasks, they may be able to perform the logical operations tested by these tasks.

Piaget has been criticized not only for using unfamiliar, difficult tasks to assess preschoolers' thought but also for paying insufficient attention to evidence that preschoolers are often *not* egocentric in their behavior. Researchers have been accumulating such evidence in recent years. For example, Shatz and Gelman (1973) asked a group of four-year-olds to explain how a toy worked either to another four-year-old or to a two-year-old. When speaking to younger children, the four-year-olds modified their language, simplifying it to fit the level of the toddler. This implies that these preschoolers were aware that *from the perspective of the younger child,* their explanations would be too complex.

In another study (Mossler, Marvin, & Greenberg, 1976), 60 percent of the four-year-olds and 85 percent of the five-year-olds realized that their mothers could not know the details of a film previously seen only by the children. Preschoolers are aware that a white card would look pink to someone wearing rose-colored glasses (Liben, 1978). Finally, to show another person a picture, even children under three will turn the picture away from themselves toward the other person (Lempers, Flavell, & Flavell, 1977).

It's clear that children in the preoperational stage of thought often show that they are sensitive to the needs and perspectives of others. Because of his rather narrow focus on how children acquire logical operations, Piaget paid scant attention to the ways in which preschoolers take account of the perspectives and feelings of others in their everyday lives. (It's also true that older children and adults can often be egocentric in their thinking.) In general, performance on the rather difficult Piagetian tasks often underestimates young children's competence.

Mounting evidence that young children's thought processes are more complex and variable than Piaget had suggested has led many researchers to wrestle more directly with the factors that bring about changes in thinking. Rather than describe cognitive development in terms of qualitatively different stages of thought, the information processing approach focuses on the gradual development of perception, attention, memory, and problem-solving strategies.

Information Processing Theories

The Development of Attention

Attention is fundamentally important because it determines the sources of information that will be considered. As Rochel Gelman's work showed, one reason preoperational children have trouble understanding conservation is that they pay attention to irrelevant aspects of the problem. In general, as children develop, their attention becomes more *selective*. Preschool-age children can be distracted more than older children and have more difficulty, when they *are* paying attention, concentrating on the relevant or distinctive features of a problem.

An experiment by Smith, Kemler, and Aronfreed (1975) nicely illustrates these attentional difficulties. In this study, 27 kindergarten, second-grade and fifth-grade children were shown a series of stick figures and asked to judge which pairs were identical. As they did this, one of three different distractions varying in similarity to the task were presented. Children heard tones (most dissimilar), saw a border around the stick figures (intermediate), or saw one figure in red and another in green (most similar). The results showed that no matter what the distraction, older children were more accurate than younger ones. The kindergarten children were more distracted by the tones and borders than by the differently colored figures, while the reverse was true of the older children. This is probably because the older children were better able to focus their attention on the task and so were more distracted by features that were similar to the ones they were looking for. The attention of the younger children, on the other hand, was more divided; hence, these children were more easily distracted by noises.

Sesame Street, the popular children's television program, features an exercise called "One of these things is not like the other" (see Figure 9-6). By being presented with four almost identical pictures and having their attention drawn to those features that make one picture different from the other three, children are helped to develop the capacity to attend to relevant dimensions of a problem.

Figure 9—6

Example of Sesame Street *Exercise,* "One of These Things Is Not Like the Others"

Incidental Learning

Have you ever studied material for a test and found you remembered irrelevant details such as the color of a photograph? Such *incidental learning* occurs when despite a focus of attention on one task, we take in additional information unrelated to that task. Since this information may be useful in another context, incidental learning can be a valuable source of knowledge.

If preschoolers have more difficulty than older children in focusing their attention, wouldn't they be better incidental learners? The evidence suggests they are not. For example, three- and six-year-old children were told to find a key in a box that would unlock another box with a treasure. The box that contained the key also contained several objects unrelated to obtaining the reward. Later, when shown a group of objects, the six-year-olds were better able to identify those they had seen in the box (Stevenson, 1954).

It may seem paradoxical that preschoolers are both more able to be distracted and less skilled at incidental learning. Although we don't have a precise explanation for this, one hypothesis is that as children develop cognitively, their ability to process information becomes more efficient. Thus, even though older children pay less attention than younger children to distractions, they learn more incidentally (Lane & Pearson, 1982).

An ingenious study documented the development of more efficient attention with the use of a camera to record the eye movements of children as they scan objects (Vurpillot & Ball, 1979). Children age four to nine were observed as they examined pairs of drawings of houses (see Figure 9-7) in order to judge which pairs were the same. The most efficient strategy for this task is to compare each window of one house with the corresponding window of the other (upper left in house A with upper left in house B, etc.). Films of the eye movements of the children showed that none of the four-year-olds did this, while most of the six-year-olds and almost all the nine-year-olds used the efficient information processing method.

The factors underlying attention during the preschool years are complex. Although individual children vary greatly in attention span and activity level, physical maturation enables most children to sit still for longer periods and focus their attention. Motivation also plays a role. The same child who can sit for hours in rapt attention to the television screen may drift off when an adult decides it's time to teach numbers. For a few children, sustaining attention may be extremely difficult, and such children may show little improvement with age.

Figure 9—7

Sample of the Drawings Used by Vurpillot and Ball (1979): A Pair of Identical Houses, and a Pair of Different Houses

(From E. Vurpillot, *Journal of Experimental Child Psychology*, 1968, Vol. 6. Reprinted with permission of the Academic Press.)

Over the preschool years, children gradually become able to sustain and focus their attention on tasks for longer periods.

The Development of Perception

One reason young children may not focus their attention on the relevant or distinctive features of a problem may be that they do not *perceive* these features as distinct or separate. Obviously, if children do not perceive objects in terms of specific dimensions, such as size, color, and length, they will have difficulty paying attention to these dimensions.

Suppose a child is given pictures of squares of differing sizes and colors and asked to put the pictures that "go together" into one pile. If the child sorts the pictures so that all squares of a certain size go together, regardless of color, (or all squares of the same color, regardless of size), the child is perceiving specific dimensions—size and color. However, suppose the child puts together a 2″ light yellow square, a 2.5″ yellow/orange square, and a 1.75″ yellow/brown square. This child is sorting on the basis of overall *similarity,* globally instead of dimensionally. In studies using this method, preschool and kindergarten children generally sort globally, children in the early elementary grades show evidence of some, but not consistent, sorting by dimensions, and sixth-graders consistently sort on the basis of specific dimensions (Shepp & Swartz, 1976; Smith & Kemler, 1977; Aschkenasy & Odom, 1982).

These research findings suggest that preschoolers do not *spontaneously* perceive separate dimensions of an object, although with training, their ability to focus on specific dimensions improves (Ward, 1980). This may be one reason that they have difficulty in attending to the relevant aspects of a problem and are easily distracted.

An important way that information processing becomes more efficient with age involves the use of memory. To complete the task shown in Figure 9-7, children had to remember which windows they had already examined and whether the windows had been judged to be the same or different.

Memory

As Table 9-3 shows, memory actually encompasses a number of complex, interrelated processes. Not all these processes develop at the same rate. In some aspects of memory, preschoolers are quite proficient. *Recognition* memory for simple objects is nearly as good among preschoolers as it is for adults. If preschool children are shown a stack of, say, 80 pictures and one week later are shown a stack of 120 pictures that include some of the original pictures, they will be highly accurate in recognizing the previously seen pictures (Kail, 1979).

Table 9—3

PROCESSES INVOLVED IN MEMORY

Process	Definition
Encoding	Placing information into memory.
Rehearsal	The use of repetition to make information less likely to be forgotten.
Search	Techniques used to scan memory to find information.
Clustering	The way information is sorted and organized in memory.
Elaboration	Associating one bit of information with another to facilitate recall.
Retrieval	The ability to take information out of memory.
Recognition	The ability to distinguish new from familiar information.
Recall	The ability to reproduce previously experienced information.
Metamemory	Awareness of and knowledge about one's own memory processes.

Memory for the location of objects in familiar environments is another well-developed skill. For example, when different objects in a familiar environment such as the home or classroom are hidden behind screens and children are asked to aim a tube at the places where these objects had been previously seen, children below six years of age are only slightly less accurate than fifth graders or adults (Hardwick, McIntyre, & Pick, 1976).

In memory tasks requiring search, rehearsal, clustering, and elaboration of information, preschool children perform differently and less efficiently than older children and adults. Suppose you are shown a list of objects to remember. Looking at the list in Table 9-4, the first thing you will probably notice is that some of the objects are foods, some are clothing, and some are animals. By organizing the information into categories, something you probably can't help doing, your recall will be improved.

When preschool children are given a task like the one in Table 9-4, they do more poorly than older children, because they do not use categories spontaneously to organize information for later recall. In fact, children do not use categories in the same way as adults do to memorize information until around the age of ten (Lange, 1979; Kail & Hagen, 1982).

Although five-year-olds may be taught to use categories to improve their memory, the benefits of such training do not last very long (Moely, Olson, Halwes, & Flavell, 1969). Preschoolers and kindergarten children who have had training in the use of categories to aid memory drop this strategy soon after the training is discontinued.

A similar pattern occurs with the strategy of *rehearsal*. If you have a list of names to remember, you will probably repeat the names to yourself over and over, rehearsing them for later recall. Although it may seem like an obvious memory strategy, preschoolers do not use it spontaneously.

One of the earliest studies to demonstrate the rehearsal strategy was conducted by John Flavell, a pioneer investigator of memory development, and his colleagues. They showed 60 five-, seven-, and ten-year-olds seven pictures and then asked them to remember a subset of two to five pictures. To test their memory, the children were asked to recite aloud which pictures were in the subset either immediately after seeing them or after a 15-second delay. During the task, an experimenter trained in lip reading watched each child to determine if the key pictures were being rehearsed. Only 10 percent of the five-year-olds used rehearsal as a memory strategy, but 60 percent of

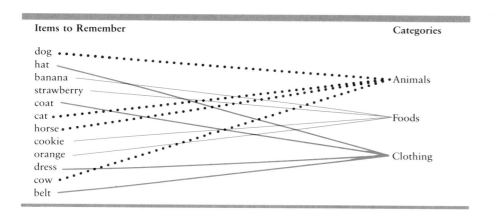

Items to Remember   **Categories**

dog
hat
banana
strawberry
coat
cat
horse
cookie
orange
dress
cow
belt

Animals
Foods
Clothing

Table 9—4

THE USE OF CATEGORIES TO AID RECALL: AN ILLUSTRATION

Hyperactivity

Although the term suggests a motor disorder, many researchers feel that hyperactivity is best characterized in terms of deficits in attention, visual search, and other strategies used to organize and process information (Douglas & Peters, 1979). Thus, the technical term for this problem is *Attention Deficit Disorder with Hyperactivity (ADD/H)* (American Psychiatric Association, 1980). Hyperactive children tend to approach problem solving impulsively. They have difficulty organizing and sustaining their attention for very long and do more poorly in tasks that require memory strategies. Their short attention span puts them at a disadvantage in learning situations. As demands to sit still and pay attention increase in the school years,

children who are hyperactive are likely to experience continued failure and come to see themselves as people who *cannot* learn.

Once thought of as a very rare disorder, hyperactivity is now the most common problem requiring treatment among school-age children and is increasingly reported during the preschool years. Some experts estimate that from 3 to 15 percent of all school-age children are diagnosed as hyperactive (Sandoval, Lambert, & Sassone, 1980; Swanson & Kinsbourne, 1979).

Causes and Treatments

It was once believed that some subtle form of brain damage was responsible, but research has failed to substantiate this claim. Some believe that hyperactivity is a form of allergic reaction to the chemical salicylate, found in food additives, such as artificial colors and flavors as well as in certain foods themselves,

such as tomatoes, oranges, almonds and berries (Feingold, 1974). Although some parents of hyperactive children attest to the effectiveness of special diets, carefully controlled research has provided little evidence to support the idea (Weiss, 1982).

A variety of environmental pollutants, such as lead, have been indirectly linked to hyperactivity. One study showed that children with serious learning problems had significantly higher levels of lead and cadmium in their bodies than did children in a control group (Pihl & Parkes, 1977). Children from poor innercity neighborhoods with dilapidated buildings with peeling lead paint are particularly vulnerable to toxic poisoning.

Another view is that hyperactivity is caused by some as yet unknown chemical imbalance in the nervous system and hence can best be treated by drugs. The most common drugs used to reduce the activ-

the seven-year-olds and 85 percent of the ten-year-olds did so (Flavell, Beach, & Chinsky, 1966).

Rehearsal, like category use, can be taught to preschool children, but after training is discontinued, the children stop using the technique (Keeney, Cannizzo, & Flavell, 1967). In summary, before the age of seven, children generally do not use rehearsal or other mnemonics (memory aids) spontaneously, although they can be trained to do so for a short period.

Relation Between Memory and Cognition

Seven is also the age commonly associated with the transition from preoperational thought to the stage of concrete operations. This raises the question of how memory and other cognitive skills are related. Piaget would answer in this way: The ability to perform logical operations is basic. Memory abilities reflect a child's level of thinking but do not determine it.

Piaget and his collaborator, Barbel Inhelder, demonstrated this point in a study of seriation (1973). They showed 63 three- to eight-year-old children ten sticks, ordered from shortest to longest, and asked them to study the array in preparation for a memory test. One week later, the children drew what they had seen from memory. As expected, three- to four-year-olds drew sticks of more or less equal length, four- to five-year-olds drew some

ity level of children diagnosed as hyperactive are amphetamines, such as Ritalin. Paradoxically, these stimulants, which increase activity in most people, seem to have the effect of depressing activity in hyperactive children.

Although the most widely used method of treating hyperactivity, drug treatments remain controversial. As many as 30 to 40 percent of hyperactive children do not respond well to drugs. Fairly high dosages are required, creating the danger of overdose and negative side effects (Swanson & Kinsbourne, 1979). The most serious drawback is the fact that medications do not produce any long-term improvement (Wallander & Hubert, 1985). Thus, hyperactive children are faced with the prospect of indefinite dependence on stimulants.

As a reaction against drug treatments, some researchers have sought other ways to help hyperactive children sustain their attention longer and approach problems in a more reflective manner. One promising direction is *cognitive training methods*. Hyperactive children are taught, as one researcher put it, to "stop, look, and listen" by observing models, rewarding themselves for appropriate behavior, and verbalizing as they tackle each step of a problem (Douglas, Parry, Martin, & Gaston, 1976). Although the long-term effectiveness of these methods is not known (Urbain & Kendall, 1980), more sustained attention and social adjustment in the classroom have been found (Kauffman & Hallahan, 1979).

The fact that hyperactive children can learn to modify their behavior raises doubts about the biochemical origins of the disorder. Some researchers believe that hyperactivity is a problem not of the child but of an unresponsive environment. Schools may demand too much of a child with a short attention span and provide too few opportunities for vigorous physical exercise. Rather than individualize the curriculum for the child's needs, teachers may too readily apply the label of hyperactive to a child who is hard to handle.

The problem with interpreting hyperactivity in terms of unresponsive environments is that it ignores the fact that a child's behavior is always the result of interaction with the environment. We suggest that hyperactivity can be best understood as a "mismatch" between the demands of the environment and a child's capacities to sustain attention and inhibit impulsiveness. Teachers can adjust their demands on children's attention to take account of individual differences. However, children who have severe difficulty in maintaining attention will still need help to cope with the demands of formal schooling.

longer and some shorter but several of equal length, and six- to seven-year-olds drew the sticks correctly.

Piaget and Inhelder came back to the same children six to eight months later and asked them to draw the set of sticks once again. Nearly 75 percent of all the children drew *more* accurately than before, although a longer time had elapsed for them to remember the original array. Contrary to the common sense expectation that memory would deteriorate with time, it actually improved.

Piaget and Inhelder explained their results in terms of the children's advancement in cognitive operations during the six- to eight-month interval. The children's recently acquired understanding of ordered relations gave them a powerful new tool for remembering items involving seriation.

Other researchers, such as Trabasso, whose research was discussed earlier, disagree with Piaget. Trabasso feels that by improving the ability to remember the components of a Piagetian task, the children's performance subsequently will be improved.

We believe both views have merit. Memory is a very important component of cognition and cannot be readily separated from it. It is likely that memory skills both help a child perform logical operations and reflect the child's level of thinking (Kail, 1979). As we have seen, before children acquire logical operations their memory is relatively poor. But what they remember is not haphazard; they do use some memory strategies, though not the ones common to older children and adults.

The birthday party is a familiar script for preschoolers. Events or objects that occur in the context of such a script can be more easily remembered than items on a list.

Script-Based Memory.   Young children generally learn information in the context of action. For example, a ball is first known as something to throw, catch, roll, and bounce. Children continue to acquire information as part of daily events. During a trip to the grocery store, a child may learn what an avocado is; at the zoo, the child may learn the word *giraffe.* Such familiar events become represented in the child's mind as what some researchers call *scripts* (Schank & Abelson, 1977) and others call *generalized event structures* (Nelson, 1978), or sequences of familiar events.

Preschool children are more likely to recall information that is embedded in scripts and to use scripts rather than categories as a way of organizing information for later recall. Thus, if we were to tell preschoolers a story in which a dog grabbed a woman's hat and then stole a child's cookie, the items "dog," "hat," and "cookie" from the list in Table 9-4 would be more likely to be remembered together because the story script had helped the child cluster these items in memory (Nelson, 1978; McCartney & Nelson, 1981; Mistry, 1983).

Most of the tests of memory used by researchers—presenting lists to memorize or pictures to match with words—are quite distant from the everyday concerns of young children. Because preschoolers can't use stories or events as scripts to organize their memory in these tests, their performance is quite inept.

When preschoolers' memory for past events is assessed at home in the course of conversation, their ability to recall looks more impressive. For example, in one study, an experimenter played with three- and four-year-olds for two hours in their homes. During play, questions about past events (Have you ever been to the zoo? What did you do last Christmas?) were inserted. On the average, 25 past events were recalled during the two-hour period. (Parents were able to confirm that most of the memories were accurate.) Even three-year-olds were able to store and retrieve long-term memories, since most of the events recalled had happened more than one month previously. When these same children were asked to recall a list of objects, they did more poorly (Todd & Perlmutter, 1980).

Although scripts continue to play some role as an organizing strategy for memory throughout life, they are gradually replaced in importance by category-based organization, rehearsal, and other memory strategies. In addition, during the school years, children become more aware of the memory demands of different problems, and they become able to select memory strategies suitable for different tasks. This awareness, called *metamemory,* is discussed in Chapter 13.

The exact nature of preschoolers' memory has important practical implications. Can young children's memories be trusted to report experiences of sexual and physical abuse accurately? Can the account of a preschooler who has witnessed a crime be relied upon? Although these issues are not yet resolved (Browne & Finkelhor, 1986), continuing research on the development of memory will help us answer these questions.

To sum up, the information processing approach to cognitive development in the preschool years emphasizes how the basic processes of perception, attention, and memory gradually become more efficient and better organized. Although not a stage theory, the information processing approach does not really contradict Piaget's description of preoperational thought. Both assign importance to the role of experience, and both present evidence that short-term training in cognitive skills has limited payoff. Both would agree that experience must be assimilated or understood by the child before it can enhance thinking. Both focus on the processes of cognitive development that are universally shared rather than on individual differences among children.

The approaches differ, however, in their emphasis. While Piaget stressed the qualitative changes associated with the transition from one stage of cognitive development to the next, the information processing approach focuses on the underlying processes common to all stages. Because the information processing model breaks down a complex learning task into its components, more emphasis is placed on the role of training in these components as an aid to cognitive development. Finally, the information processing view stresses how characteristics of a problem—its complexity, difficulty, and familiarity—can affect the way children perceive, attend to, and remember it.

Neither Piagetian theory nor the information processing approach has paid much attention to individual differences in children's thinking. If we want to know more about how and why the thinking of individual preschoolers differs, we need to examine other sources of evidence.

Individual Differences

Environmental Influences

Piaget emphasized how intelligence grows out of a child's active exploration of the environment and depends on both the opportunities for discovery provided by the environment and the conceptual tools the child already possesses. This suggests that the amount of appropriate stimulation in an environment together with the degree of encouragement of exploration will be associated with delays or advances in the acquisition of logical operations.

Such an environment contains materials that are neither too complex nor too simple for the child but pose manageable challenges. Materials such as a set of cups of differing sizes or a pile of beads of several colors and shapes provide opportunities to learn such concepts as reversibility, seriation, and classification. Research evidence also supports the view that parents who provide materials that stimulate children to think and explore are facilitating their children's intellectual development (Bradley et al., 1977).

To determine just what aspects of the home environment are most beneficial to the development of young children's reasoning, Bettye Caldwell and her associates devised a measure called the Home Observation for Measurement of the Environment (HOME) Scale. Based on both observations and interviews, the scale assesses the quality of stimulation available to the child in the home. Six areas are measured:
1. Emotional and verbal responsivity of the mother.
2. Avoidance of restriction and punishment.
3. Organization of the environment.
4. Provision of appropriate play materials.
5. Maternal involvement with the child.
6. Opportunity for variety in daily stimulation.

Let's take a closer look at one of these areas: organization of the environment, which taps such aspects of the home as regularity of substitute care, extent to which the child regularly leaves home, the safety of the play environment, and the availability of a special place for the child to keep toys. Note that in this area, as in the entire HOME scale, physical aspects of the home are entwined with social and emotional aspects. This recognizes that for the young child, the physical setting is experienced through relationships.

HOME assessments made when children are 12 months old predict scores on intelligence tests and measures of language ability at age three. Moreover, different aspects of the home environment are associated with cognitive advancement at different ages. For example, scores on the subscale "organization of the environment" during the first two years predict intelligence test scores at age three but not at age four and one-half. This suggests that children under three need a parent to structure their environment. At somewhat older ages, they can begin to organize their environment for themselves, and other aspects of the home, such as maternal responsiveness, involvement, and lack of restriction, become more significant (Elardo & Bradley, 1981; Gottfried & Gottfried, 1984).

Research using the HOME instrument illustrates that young children's cognitive growth is optimally enhanced when both parental warmth and encouragement of mastery are present. However, we should remember that measures of the home environment are not independent of parental intelligence, which has a substantial genetic component. Hence, a strong association between a stimulating home environment and a child's intelligence may not be due to environmental factors alone (Zimmerman, 1981).

Another way environment can encourage a child's mastery is suggested by Vygotsky's theory of cognitive development (refer to Chapter 2), which emphasizes that learning takes place in the context of social interaction. Warm, accepting parents have children who show evidence of cognitive competence (Bretherton, 1985).

In some studies, warmth and acceptance are measured by parental attitudes toward the child. In others, a parent's behavior is observed.

For example, Norma Radin (1971) observed both black and white lower-class mothers interacting with their children at home. Maternal warmth was defined as the mother's use of physical or verbal reinforcement (hugs or praise), her involving the child in decisions, and her sensitivity to the child's needs by anticipating the child's requests or feelings.

Radin administered standard intelligence tests to the children before and at the conclusion of preschool. She found that preschoolers whose mothers had displayed more warmth toward them at home scored higher on intelligence tests before school began, gained more in intelligence during the school year, and were more motivated to achieve and identify with the teacher.

In general, paternal warmth, coupled with involvement in the child's activities, also promotes cognitive growth (Lamb, 1981). However, the effect appears to be stronger for boys than for girls (Radin, 1981). One reason for this may be that young sons are more likely than daughters to identify strongly with their fathers and hence may be more affected by their behavior. Another possibility is that some fathers may send mixed messages to their daughters about the desirability of achievement and intellectual growth (Radin, 1981; Epstein & Radin, 1975; Lynn, 1976). Indeed, there is evidence that fathers express more concern about the cognitive advancement of sons than of daughters (Aberle & Naegele, 1962; Hoffman, 1977). Observational studies of fathers teaching preschoolers indicate a greater emphasis on cognitive aspects of the situation when teaching sons and more stress on interpersonal aspects of the situation when teaching daughters (Block, Block, & Harrington, 1974).

A note of caution, however. Most of the studies relating parental warmth to preschool cognitive growth are correlational. As discussed in Chapter 3, correlations by themselves cannot tell us about cause and effect. The fact that parental warmth is associated with a child's achievement *may* mean that warmth is causing the child to develop intellectually. It is also possible that because bright, alert, and curious children are a joy for parents to have, such children may evoke positive behavior from their parents. Although variations in their environments can influence preschoolers' cognitive development, individual differences in children also make an important contribution to development.

Cognitive Styles

Individual differences in children's perception and attention when they solve problems are called *cognitive style*. Two major cognitive styles—field independence-dependence and reflection-impulsivity—have been identified and studied in young children.

The *field independence-dependence* cognitive style refers to a child's ability to perceive a part separate from a complex whole. A sample item from a test used to assess field independence-dependence in preschoolers is shown in Figure 9-8. Twenty-seven pictures like the one in the figure are shown, and in each picture, the child must locate a simple shape embedded in the figure. Children who have little difficulty with this task and tend to perceive an element as independent of its perceptual field are termed "field independent" in style. Children who tend to see the picture as a whole and hence have trouble finding the embedded shape are considered to be "field dependent."

What implications does field independence have for learning? Many of the measures of attention and memory used with young children require the children to pick out specific aspects of complex visual arrays. (The almost identical houses in Figure 9-7 are a good example.) Children who are field independent will have greater facility in such tasks.

Beyond the research laboratory, skill in picking out distinctive elements of a complex whole is critical for many learning situations. One of the most important for young children is learning to discriminate first letters and then words. To see the difference between *ball* and *fall*, a child must identify a difference in one letter shape.

The consequences of having a field independent or field dependent cognitive style appear to go beyond learning situations. Evidence exists that field independent children are more autonomous and independent, while field dependent children appear to be more socially oriented (Witken, Dyk, Paterson, Goodenough, & Karp, 1962). In observations of preschool play, for example, field independent children prefer to play with objects, while those rated as field dependent seek out other children (Coates, Lord, & Jakabovics, 1975; Jennings, 1975). Field dependent preschoolers, when observed during infancy, seek more emotional reassurance from mothers than do field independent children (Moskowitz, Dreyer, & Kronsberg, 1981). This suggests that children may process information best when the task is suited to their cognitive style. Field dependent children may pay relatively more attention to material dealing with people, while field independent children are likely to be more responsive to nonsocial stimuli (Kogan, 1976).

The *reflection-impulsivity* cognitive style, sometimes called *conceptual* or *cognitive tempo*, refers to the extent to which the child delays response while searching for the correct alternative when uncertain about the answer (Kogan, 1983). To get a clearer idea of what this means, let's look at how reflection-impulsivity is actually measured.

Figure 9—8

Sample Item from the Coates Preschool Embedded Figures Test, with Simple Figure Shown at Upper Right

(Reproduced by special permission of the publisher, Consulting Psychologists Press, Inc., from the Preschool Embedded Figures Test by Susan Coates © 1972.)

In the Matching Familiar Figures Test (MFFT), the child is shown a drawing of a familiar object (the standard) and six drawings of similar objects, like those in Figure 9-9, and asked to select the drawing that matches the standard. The amount of time the child spends examining each alternative before making a choice and the number of errors made determine how reflective or impulsive the child is judged to be (Kagan, 1965).

Children with a reflective style are good at attention to detail and analyzing a complex problem into its components, while those who are more impulsive in style focus on the problem as a whole. In this respect, reflection-impulsivity is similar to field independence-dependence. Both cognitive styles tap the degree to which a child is likely to break down a complex whole into its parts to solve a problem (Zelniker & Jeffrey, 1976).

In general, children become somewhat more reflective with age (Salkind & Nelson, 1980). However, preschoolers who score high on reflection in tasks such as the MFFT use more advanced visual scanning procedures than do their peers. Reflectives are able to delay their responses long enough to examine all the evidence and hence make more confident, less error prone responses. Impulsives, on the other hand, blurt out their first answer, failing to examine all the alternatives in their hurry to come up with a solution. These differences tend to persist as the children become older (Messer, 1976; Messer & Brodzinsky, 1981).

Variations in cognitive style have implications beyond specific information processing skills. Formal education emphasizes the analytic approach, not the global approach, to problems. It is thus not surprising perhaps that preschool children with reflective cognitive styles do better in many learning

Figure 9—9

Sample Items from MFFT

(© 1965 by Rand McNally and Company Editor J. D. Krumboltz.)

(a) Match teddy bear standard at top with identical figure from six sample drawings.

(b) Match tree standard at top with identical figure from six sample drawings.

situations and continue to excel when they enter formal schooling (Messer, 1976). For example, reflective children learn conservation, perspective-taking, and memory tasks earlier than their more impulsive peers (Barstis & Ford, 1977; Brodzinsky, 1980, 1982).

Although more reflective children have an advantage in school-related tasks, there are situations, such as action-oriented skills, sports, and professions such as air traffic controller, in which rapid decision making is more optimal. In such situations, more impulsive individuals may actually perform better than their reflective peers. Parents and teachers should be encouraged to orient children toward activities that best suit their style of response. Nevertheless, the advantage reflective children have in school learning tasks tends to improve such children's self-confidence and self-esteem, with effects spilling over into many aspects of the child's life. For example, reflective children have been judged to be more attentive, less aggressive, and more concerned about making errors than impulsive children (Kagan & Kogan, 1970; Messer, 1970; Campbell, 1973; Wapner & Connor, 1986).

In an investigation of 100 middle-class four- to five-year-olds, personality characteristics as rated by nursery school teachers were compared for reflective and impulsive children, based on performance on the MFFT. The authors described the reflective children as "comparatively competent, resourceful, empathic, interpersonally attractive children—they were more socially perceptive, brighter, more reasonable, more approachable individuals. The [impulsives], on the other hand, appear to be relatively vulnerable, poorly defended, demanding, overly sensitive and brittle children—they are more lacking in self-confidence, more likely to feel discriminated against, tend to be more rigid, and are less happy" (Block, et al., 1974, p. 626).

Given the significance of differences in cognitive style for children's overall well-being, we need to ask how such differences come about in the first place and how they might be modified. One suggestion is that cognitive style differences can be traced to individual differences in infant temperament. (For more on the subject of infant temperament, refer to Chapter 6.) For example, Jerome Kagan, who first called attention to reflection-impulsivity as a cognitive style, has found that compared to reflectives, boys who are classified as impulsives at 27 months of age were more quickly bored by novel stimuli at four months of age, had a faster tempo of play at eight months, and were more restless at thirteen months (1971). This suggests that cognitive style may be at least in part genetically determined, although Kagan's findings may also be explained by early environmental experiences.

Another view traces cognitive style differences to experiences children have with success and failure and the expectations they build up about their performance. Perhaps parents who communicate to their children high expectations for performance in a warm, accepting manner promote in the children both self-confidence and concern over performing well. Such a child would feel able to properly complete a task like the MFFT but would be sufficiently concerned about possible errors to use reflective strategies.

Some evidence exists to support this view, at least for field independence-dependence cognitive style. For example, a study of adopted children and their adoptive mothers in the Netherlands found that mothers who were rated on the basis of interviews as encouraging their child's competence and independence had more field independent children than did other mothers (Claeys & DeBoeck, 1976). And a study of Chicano mothers and their five-year-olds found that mothers who were more likely to punish or restrain their children while trying to teach them how to make a Tinkertoy construction had children who were more field dependent than the children of non-punishing mothers (Laosa, 1980). Finally, fathers who use physical punishment and verbal aggression tend to have more field dependent sons (Dyk & Witkin, 1965). It is possible that inappropriate punishment and restraint may discourage the young child's independence and foster dependence upon the parent instead. This dependence may drain the child of confidence in his or her own ability, thereby discouraging attention to detail and causing possible errors in problem-solving tasks.

Influences on cognitive style can now be summarized. Although some genetically determined predisposition toward perceiving analytically or globally may exist, there is considerable evidence that parents and school experiences affect how young children will approach learning situations. In general, parents who in the context of warmth and acceptance encourage their children to master problems on their own are promoting cognitive growth.

Chapter Summary

PREOPERATIONAL THOUGHT (PIAGET)
- Preschoolers develop the ability to use symbols, as seen in deferred imitation, symbolic play, and language, and the concept of identity becomes better understood.
- Limitations of thinking include egocentrism, transductive reasoning, cause-and-effect reasoning, syncretic reasoning, finalism, artificialism, and animism. Preoperational thinkers have difficulty understanding multiple classification and seriation and are unable to understand how liquid quantity, weight, number, or mass is conserved when its appearance changes.
- Underlying these limitations is the tendency of preschoolers to center on only one aspect of a problem and to fail to understand the reversibility of operations.
- Piaget's methods have been challenged as too complex for preschoolers' abilities. Efforts at training children on conservation and other tasks have been successful, particularly with older preschoolers.

INFORMATION PROCESSING THEORIES
- Preschoolers' attention gradually becomes more selective with age, but preschoolers are more able to be distracted than older children.
- Preschoolers tend to perceive objects globally rather than in terms of specific dimensions.
- Preschoolers do not use specific strategies to scan or remember objects, and they are less aware of what memory or problem-solving techniques should be used in different situations.

INDIVIDUAL DIFFERENCES
- Two dimensions of family environments—warmth/acceptance and encouragement of mastery—acting together, appear to enhance young children's cognitive growth.
- Cognitive style differences among children have also been identified, specifically reflectivity-impulsivity and field independence/field dependence. Field independent children and reflective children use information processing strategies that help them be more successful in school tasks than field dependent or impulsive children.

Recommended Readings

Brainerd, C. J. (1978). *Piaget's theory of intelligence.* Englewood Cliffs, NJ: Prentice-Hall. A detailed description of each of the stages of Piaget's theory of cognitive development, with discussion of research that expands and revises the theory.

Saunders, R., and Bingham-Newman, A. (1984). *Piagetian perspectives for preschoolers: A thinking book for teachers.* Englewood Cliffs, NJ: Prentice-Hall. Application of Piagetian principles to curriculum planning and evaluation. An excellent resource for early childhood educators.

Flavell, J. H. (1977). *Cognitive Development.* Englewood Cliffs, NJ: Prentice-Hall. A prominent authority on the development of cognitive processes, such as memory, reviews research and theory on cognitive development from infancy through adolescence. A well-written, accessible account.

Kail, R. (1979). *The development of memory in children.* San Francisco: W. H. Freeman & Co. A clearly written, authoritative account of research on memory processes in children by an active researcher in the field.

8,9, 10,11, 12,16

CHAPTER 10

The Young Child: Social and Emotional Development

I was a good child: I found my role so becoming that I did not step out of it. Actually, my father's early retirement had left me with a most incomplete "Oedipus complex." No Superego, granted. But no aggressiveness either. My mother was mine; no one challenged my peaceful possession of her. I knew nothing of violence and hatred; I was spared the hard apprenticeship of jealousy. . . . I am adored, hence I am adorable. What could be more simple, since the world is well-made? I am told that I am good-looking, I believe it. . . . I know my worth.

—Sartre, 1964, pp. 26–27.

These reflections were made by the famous French philosopher, novelist, and playwright, Jean Paul Sartre, when he was 60 years old. In his autobiography, *The Words,* he examined the significant turning points of his early childhood that contributed to his eventual identity as a writer. In this quote, he describes his ideas and feelings about himself at the age of five, his fledgling sense of individuality, his range of emotions, and his sense of family relationships.

This chapter, also, will explore these themes, examining how the cognitive skills of preschoolers are applied to the understanding of themselves and others, what we call "the thinking self." It will also explore "the feeling self," the emotions that preschoolers feel and their awareness of their own emotional life. These changes in understanding and feeling about the self and others are part of the process of developing a sense of a personal, separate self and of one's place in the social world.

At the same time that children are becoming more individual, they are learning to fit in and deepen their relationships with others. They must learn to regulate their behavior and inhibit their impulses to adapt to the demands of their family and of their society. The section "Fitting In" examines the development of language and communication skills, prosocial behaviors, self-control, and the regulation of aggression.

The Thinking Self

The Self-Concept

By age three, most children have a sense of an invisible inner self that cannot be seen directly by others. This self-awareness is different from that of older children, however, as Table 10-1 shows. Preschoolers often are unaware of how others may see them. For example, a three-year-old grabbing a coveted toy from another child is likely to be startled if this action provokes crying. As preschoolers begin to realize that their behavior evokes reactions in others, they become more self-aware and behave in ways that anticipate the responses of others. Thus, a six-year-old wanting a toy in the possession of another child might suggest a trade or a "turn" with the toy. By early adolescence, children achieve sophisticated levels of self-awareness, able to see themselves simultaneously as others see them and as they see themselves.

Preschoolers' ideas about themselves tend to focus on activities more than physical characteristics or abstract psychological qualities (Broughton, 1978; Secord & Peevers, 1974). In a study by Keller, Ford, and Meacham

Table 10—1

STAGES IN THE DEVELOPMENT
OF SELF-AWARENESS

Level	Age In Years	Description
0	Birth—3	No difference between perspective of self and other.
1	3—7	Knows others feel differently but no understanding that they observe how self feels.
2	7—12	Appreciates that others know how self could be feeling.
3	10—15	Observes self as actor ("I") and as object ("me") simultaneously.
4	15+	Aware of unconscious processes in self and others.

(From Selman, 1980.)

(1978), three- to five-year-olds were asked to say ten things about themselves and to complete the following sentences: "I am a _____. I am a boy/girl who _____." In both cases, more than half the children responded with action statements such as "I help Mommy," "I play ball". Finally, when asked to choose which of two types of statements they would rather have written about themselves—"Johnny has blue eyes," "Johnny combs his hair"—the children strongly preferred the latter action statements. This thinking about oneself in terms of action reflects the important role physical activity plays for young children (Bannister & Agnew, 1977).

Compared with older children, preschoolers have self-concepts that are frequently changing and sometimes contradictory. One day, a child may boast, "I'm strong, I can lift this block" but will be unruffled when in the next few minutes she can't. Young children also tend to view themselves and others in all-or-nothing terms—*smart* or *dumb, pretty* or *ugly*. They have trouble understanding more subtle shadings of characteristics. Particularly difficult is the idea that opposing characteristics can sometimes be combined in a person, for example, that someone could be smart in some ways but "dumb" in others, or both happy and sad at the same time (Harter, 1983).

Preschoolers are also beginning to make judgments about how competent they are at learning tasks, social relations, and physical activities (Harter and Pike, 1984). These judgments, however, are likely to be confused with wishes to be competent. With increasing age, children gradually become more accurate in assessing their skills in relation to others (see Chapter 14) (Harter, 1982).

Preschoolers' Understanding of Age Differences

Because every culture emphasizes distinctions between people based on age and gender differences, many of the earliest differences that children notice refer to age and gender.

By age two, many children begin to use age categories such as *baby, little boy, big girl, man,* and *old woman* to distinguish between people of different ages (see Figure 10-1). As these terms suggest, young children generally confuse size with age. They also frequently use kinship terms, such as *grandma* (for an elderly woman) or *daddy* (for an adult male), to categorize people. Not surprisingly, older preschoolers are able to make more age discriminations than are younger children, particularly among adults of different ages.

By asking 84 preschoolers to sort a set of photographs of individuals ranging in age from one to 70 years, Carolyn Edwards (1984) determined that young children tend to call anyone under two years of age "baby," those between two and six years, "little children," between 6 and 14, "big children,"

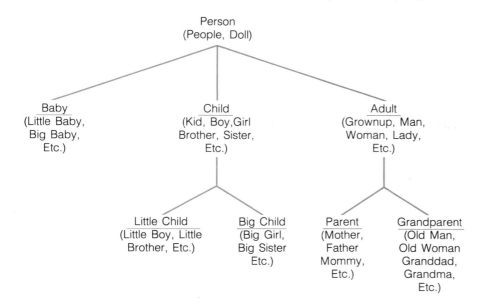

Figure 10—1

Age Labels Used by Preschoolers

(From C. Edwards, *Child Development*, 1984, 55, p. 445. © The Society for Research in Child Development, Inc. Reprinted by permission of the author.)

from 14 to 50, "mother/father," and older than 50, "grandmother/grandfather." Preschoolers also label *themselves* in terms of age categories, as *little boy, little girl,* or *big boy, big girl.* Interestingly, in Edwards' study (1984), half the four-year-olds interviewed identified themselves as "big" not "little" children.

From the beginning, the age distinctions that preschoolers make are paralleled by distinctions in gender—*boy, girl, man, woman.* Although age distinctions are an important way of categorizing people and defining the self, little research is available to tell us how age awareness continues to develop. In contrast to the topic of age awareness, the development of gender understanding has been intensively studied.

The Development of Gender Understanding

Research (Slaby & Frey, 1975) suggests that children go through stages in their understanding of *gender,* identity as a biological male or female (see Table 10-2). The first stage, *gender labeling,* occurs at about 18 to 24 months when children readily label themselves and others as male or female. However, they don't understand that such labels are stable. For example, they do not understand that a boy will grow up to be a man, not a woman, or that when a boy was a baby, he must have been a baby boy. Even after the second stage, *gender stability,* has been achieved at around age three, preschool children still think

Stage	Age Attained	Characteristics
Labeling	18–24 months	Can label sex of self and others.
Stability	3 years	Understands that self has been and will remain male or female.
Constancy	5–7 years	Understands that gender is unaffected by changes in motives or modifications in outward appearance.

(From Slaby & Frey, 1975.)

Table 10—2

STAGES IN THE DEVELOPMENT OF GENDER UNDERSTANDING

*gender level,
" stability
" constancy*

that gender can be changed by changing aspects of outer appearance, such as clothing or hair length. When asked, "If a boy puts on a dress, can he become a girl?," most four-year-olds would say *yes* (Gelman, Collman, & Maccoby, 1986). However, by age seven, children achieve *gender constancy,* understanding that gender is permanent, stable over time, and constant despite variations in outward appearance or behavior (Kohlberg, 1966; Guardo & Bohan, 1971). Children develop a sense of their own gender constancy before they appreciate that another child's gender is also constant (Gouze & Nadelman, 1980). Not until age nine, however, can children properly explain why gender remains constant when outward appearance changes (Wehren & DeLisi, 1983).

We can better appreciate preschool children's difficulties with gender understanding by recalling some of the characteristics of preoperational thought discussed in Chapter 9. Seeing yourself as others see you requires perspective-taking or decentering abilities that are not well developed during the preoperational period. The concept of identity as unchanged despite variations in appearance evolves gradually over the preschool years. Thus, a study directly comparing children's ability to conserve physical properties with their ability to understand gender constancy found that the conservation of physical properties was usually achieved before that of gender (Marcus & Overton, 1978).

With their developing understanding of gender, young children also develop ideas about the ways in which males and females are supposed to behave. These ideas, called *sex-role concepts* or *sex-role stereotypes,* appear at the beginning of the preschool period (Kuhn, Nash, & Brucken, 1978) and are quite rigid by age five to seven (Eisenberg, Tryon, & Cameron, 1984). We

During the preschool period play reflects a growing awareness of sex-role stereotypes.

once overheard a four-year-old insist, "Ladies can't wear pants, they only wear dresses," while her mother, wearing her customary pair of jeans, stood next to her with a puzzled expression.

Young children's behavior reflects their intense interest in male-female differences as well as their stereotyped ideas about them. Preschoolers, particularly boys, gravitate toward same-sex playmates, play with "boy" versus "girl" toys, such as trucks and dolls, and even actively discourage each other from nonstereotyped behavior (Ruble, Boggiano, Feldman, & Loeble, 1981; Fagot, 1977; Smetana & Letourneau, 1984).

Theories of Sex-Role Development

Learning theory explains sex role stereotypes primarily in terms of the reinforcement children experience for behaving in ways that their culture defines as gender appropriate. For example, when a whimpering four-year-old boy is told, "Big boys don't cry," or when a three-year-old girl gets approving comments for "looking so pretty and ladylike," ideas and behaviors about sex-role differences are reinforced. Boys have been observed to exhibit more *sex-typed behavior,* reflecting culturally approved masculine versus feminine behavior, than have girls. For example, male toddlers in a day care center played almost 60 percent of the time with "boy" toys but only 20 percent of the time with "girl" toys, while girls played more equally with both "boy" and "girl" toys (O'Brien, Huston, & Risley, 1983). This may be because parents, other adults, and peers are more rewarding of boys' sex-typed behavior and more punishing of "feminine" behavior (Fagot, 1977; Langlois & Down, 1980; Lamb, Easterbrooks, & Holden, 1980). A "tomboy" may be tolerated, but a "sissy" is less acceptable.

Social learning approaches emphasize the way children learn about sex roles from observing adult and peer models. For example, five- and six-year-old girls who saw female cartoon figures behaving in nontraditional ways later showed less conventional attitudes toward sex roles (Davidson, Yasuma, & Tower, 1979).

Psychoanalytic theory stresses how, during the preschool years, children wish to possess the opposite-sex parent exclusively and hence feel rivalry toward their same-sex parent. (Have you ever heard a four-year-old boy solemnly proclaim, "When I grow up, I'm going to marry Mommy."?) Since the child also loves both parents, it produces an internal conflict in the child—the *Oedipal complex* for boys and the *Electra complex* for girls—which is resolved by the child's identification with the same-sex parent (see Chapters 2 and 11).

Although the environmental factors emphasized by learning theory, social learning theory, and psychoanalytic theory are important in sex-role development, there is reason to believe that environmental influences alone cannot fully explain children's sex-role development.

First, the stages of gender understanding seem to apply universally to children. The same sequence, at approximately the same time, emerges for children in non-Western traditional rural cultures where the lives of males and females are distinctively different from early childhood, as well as for children in urban industrialized centers where male-female differences in appearance and behavior are less pronounced (Munroe, Shuimin, & Munroe, 1984). Second, preschool-age children often exhibit more stereotyped ideas about male-female differences than they experience in their environments, and there is no direct relationship between parental reinforcements or modeling and children's sex-typed behaviors. Boys' masculinity is unrelated to the masculinity of their

Preschoolers' "dress-up" can be a way of learning gender role identity.
(Source: Sendak)

fathers, while girls' femininity does not parallel that of their mothers (Hetherington, 1965, 1967)

A *cognitive* explanation for sex-role development, while recognizing the role of environmental factors, suggests that as children develop ideas about the stability and constancy of gender, they also learn about the culturally prescribed behaviors and activities associated with their own as well as the opposite gender (Thompson, 1975; Damon, 1977). As a result of these cognitive advances in understanding gender and sex roles, preschoolers begin to adopt behaviors and preferences that they see as consistent with their gender identity. Because they are in the process of sorting out for themselves the differences between males and females, they develop simple hypotheses about sex roles—for example, "Men wear pants, women wear dresses"—that overlook a considerably more complex reality. Gradually, such simple ideas are modified, and children develop a more differentiated view of sex-role behaviors (Kohlberg, 1966).

Cognitive and Environmental Factors in Sex-Role Development

The interplay of cognitive and environmental variables, such as parental influence, is nicely illustrated in a study by Marsha Weinraub and her colleagues, who assessed gender understanding, play with sex-typed toys, and awareness of sex stereotypes in 71 two- to three-year-old children (Weinraub, Clemens, Sockloff, Ethridge, Gracely, & Myers, 1984). Each child was observed in a playroom containing a variety of sex-typed and neutral toys, and the toys the child chose to play with were noted. To measure gender understanding and awareness of sex-role stereotypes, each child was shown pictures of males and females, of sex-stereotyped adult activities, such as ironing and car repair, and of children's toys and was asked to put each picture into either a box for "men and boys" or one for "ladies and girls." When this task was completed, the child was given his or her own picture and asked to place it in one of the two boxes. The children were also asked questions about themselves and each picture. Finally, each child's verbal intelligence was measured by the Peabody Picture Vocabulary Test, and information was collected about parental sex-role attitudes and behaviors.

As shown in Figure 10-2, by age three, the majority of children consistently sorted male and female pictures separately and indicated awareness of their own gender identity. Awareness of sex-role stereotypes in adult tasks (e.g., cooking as "female," car repair as "male") and in adult possessions (e.g., iron as "female," shovel as "male") also increased dramatically during the third year of life. The study found that gender understanding, awareness of self-role stereotypes, and sex-typed behavior all tended to develop together. Thus, children who responded to the question "Who are you?" with "a girl" or "a boy" also exhibited more sex-typed toy play than did other children.

Although almost all children showed this developmental pattern, there was considerable individual variation. Children scoring higher on the intelligence test were more aware of male-female stereotypes, suggesting that cognitive influences on sex-role development were operating. In addition, environmental factors played a role. Children whose fathers had traditional attitudes about sex roles and who reported that they engaged in "masculine" but not "feminine" tasks showed more evidence of gender understanding than did children with less traditional fathers. Finally, children of mothers employed outside the home were less aware of the sex stereotyping of toys than were children of full-time homemakers.

Single-Parent Families and Children's Sex Role Development

The psychoanalytic view implies that the presence of both parents is necessary for boys and girls to develop appropriate sex roles. Currently, over 20 percent of all children in the United States—or over ten million—live in single-parent homes. Among lower-class black families, a majority of children are growing up in single-parent families (Glick & Norton, 1978). Over 90 percent of all single-parent families are headed by women. Because fathers are more concerned than mothers about sex-typed behavior and because both boys and girls appear to be more influenced by fathers than by mothers in developing a sex-role identity (Cashion, 1982), there is concern that young children in father-absent homes may not develop an appropriate sense of themselves as male or female.

Studies of Father Absence

Beginning in the 1940s, studies were carried out to examine the sex-role development of boys in father-absent and father-present homes. Despite the fact that psychoanalytic theory emphasized the importance of both parents for the sex-role development of girls as well as of boys, almost no attention was paid to the experiences of preschool girls in father-absent homes.

In general, these early studies found that preschool boys from father-absent homes differed from those where fathers were present primarily in the amount of aggression and sex stereotyping of their toy play. In some studies, the father-absent boys were less aggressive (Sears, 1951; Bach, 1946), while in others, they showed more aggression, a pattern the investigators called "compensatory masculinity" (Lynn & Sawrey, 1959).

The effects of father absence were particularly marked if separation occurred when the son was a preschooler. For example, several studies reported that boys separated from their fathers before age five engaged less in stereotyped masculine behavior—less aggression, less physical contact games—at nine to twelve years of age than did boys who experienced later father absence (Hetherington, 1967; Biller, 1969; Biller & Bahm, 1971).

More recent studies indicate that preschool boys may be more adversely affected by divorce than are young girls; boys show more behavior disturbance toward their mothers, peers, and teachers (Hetherington, Cox, & Cox, 1982) (See FOCUS ON RISK/INTERVENTION in Chapter 11). Moreover, based on a study of middle-class six- to eleven-year-olds, boys showed higher self-esteem and better social adjustment when in the custody of their fathers, while girls fared better with their mothers (Warshak & Santrock, 1979; Santrock, Warshak, & Elliott, 1982).

The results of the studies seem to confirm the predictions of psychoanalytic theory that the absence of a father as a source of identification for boys would impair a boy's adoption of a masculine identity. However, many findings are difficult to interpret because of flaws in the studies, which failed to take into account such variables as the age of the child at separation from the father, the duration of father absence, the availability of other males as potential role models, and the amount of contact the child might have had with his father after separation (Biller, 1981). Findings based on middle-class white samples may not apply to lower-class black families, a greater proportion of which are headed by the mother.

Most researchers now feel that children in single-parent homes can develop gender understanding, ideas about sex roles, and sex-typed behaviors in much the same way as do children in two-parent homes, particularly when adult male role models are available and the mother communicates a positive image of the absent father (Radin, 1981; Lamb, 1981). Mothers who speak positively about absent fathers to their sons have children with more appropriate sex-role identification, better self-concepts, and fewer behavior problems than do mothers who portray the father negatively (Kopf, 1970). The availability of other male figures, such as stepfathers, older brothers, or male peers, seems to result in more traditional masculine sex-role behavior (Biller, 1981; Huston, 1983). Organizations such as Big Brother are available for those mothers who feel that their boys lack adult male role models. As an increasing percentage of young children spend at least part of their developing years in a single-parent, usually female-headed household, continued attention will be paid to developmental issues raised by this family form.

Figure 10–2

Development of Gender Labeling and Sex-Role Awareness in the Third Year of Life

(From M. Weinraub et al., *Child Development*, 1984, *55*, pp. 1493–1503. Reprinted by permission of the author.)

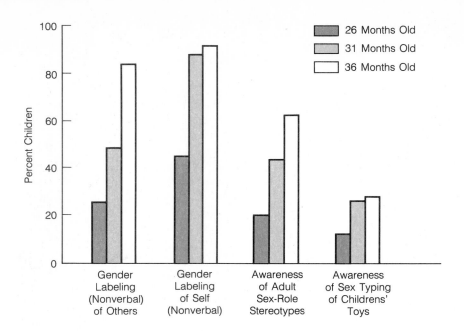

The Feeling Self

Emotional Development

During the preschool years, children begin to see themselves and others in terms of age categories, gender differences, and other characteristics. These ideas not only are descriptive labels, but also are accompanied by feelings and emotions.

Emotional experiences refer to the feelings children have in relation to persons, events, or ideas. Most investigators of emotion concur that humans universally experience a relatively small number of basic emotions—enjoyment, interest, excitement, fear, sadness, disgust, shame, and anger (Ekman, Friesen, & Ellsworth, 1972; Izard, 1971; Tomkins, 1962). By age three, children can experience all of these basic emotions. Perhaps because of this, most research has been devoted to the emotional development of infants and toddlers, with little attention given to children over age three (Fogel, 1980). Most of our knowledge concerning emotions during the preschool years comes from observations conducted in the 1920s and 1930s of young children in nursery school. These observations indicate that in general, preschoolers are more expressive than older children or adults. Young children use more of their bodies—arms, legs, torso—to express an emotion, whereas older children rely on fine motor movements of the face and body. Older children also become more capable of modifying or hiding their emotions, for example, appearing indifferent when feeling upset (see Chapter 14) (Fogel, 1980). The expression of specific emotions, such as fear, anger, distress, and enjoyment, also undergoes change during the preschool years (Cole, 1986).

Fear.   Overt expressions of fear—momentary stoppage of breath, screaming, stiffening of the body, whitening of the face—are observed less frequently in children over age three than in infants or toddlers (Fogel, 1980). However, preschool children may have nightmares, "see" monsters under the bed, or

Sudden changes of appearance in familiar people (such as those caused by Halloween costumes) may produce fear, surprise or delight in preschoolers.

become frightened by sudden changes in the appearance of familiar things. Because young children have difficulty understanding that transformations in appearance do not change identity, they can become alarmed when their own or another's appearance alters suddenly. This is why getting a haircut or seeing Halloween masks may frighten young children. Parents can help children cope with such fears by preparing them for changes and by avoiding masks or costumes if they alarm the child.

One of the earliest studies of young children's fears was conducted in 1935 by Jersild and Holmes, who designed eight laboratory situations to study fear in children from ages two to five. The youngest children were most afraid of animals (a large dog and a snake), falling off dark high boards, strange people, and loud, unexpected sounds. Fear of the dark and being left alone were more frequent among three- to four-year-olds than any other age group, and girls in general exhibited more fear than did boys.

Few, more recent, investigations of young children's fears exist. One by Draper and James (1983) asked parents of 600 preschoolers what, if anything, their children were afraid of. Interestingly, the same categories found by Jersild and Holmes were reported by these parents. However, girls were not reported as more fearful than boys.

Since so few investigations of young children's fears exist, we are left with many questions. Do parents' reports of their children's fear agree with observed fearfulness? Are there sex differences in the nature or intensity of

(a) Fear

(b) Happiness

(c) Anger

Figure 10—3

Preschoolers Can Readily Identify These Basic Emotions

(From P. Ekman, ed., *Darwin and Facial Expression*, © 1973. Reprinted by permission of the author and Academic Press.)

fears? Are there cohort differences in the expression of fear; that is, do children or parents of different generations (1930s versus 1980s) differ in the fears they display or report? We hope additional research will begin to fill in the many gaps in our knowledge of this subject.

Distress and Enjoyment.   In general, preschoolers cry less and laugh more frequently than younger children. Based on observational studies of children in nursery school, crying occurs about five times per month, on the average, while laughing occurs about two to four times per hour (Charlesworth & Kreutzer, 1973). Expressions of both distress and enjoyment are used as social signals, since they occur primarily in interaction with others. For example, preschoolers tend to return other children's happy expressions, ignore or leave children who act angry or sad, and show concern when another child bears a hurt expression (Denham, 1986). Beyond this, we know relatively little about other important aspects of emotional expressions of distress and enjoyment, for example, the use of crying to manipulate others, "pretend" crying and laughing as part of play, awareness of norms concerning crying, or the relationship between emotional expression and intelligence or social competence.

Some general characteristics of preschoolers' emotional expression are understood. Preschoolers tend to focus on one emotion at a time, their emotions fluctuate, and they often experience either-or extremes of emotion (Harter, 1983). For example, a four-year-old may yell at a parent "I hate you!" one moment and be all smiles the next (while the parent is still recovering from the shock). Adults often misinterpret such outbursts because they assume that preschoolers mean the same thing as they do when they use the language of emotions. However, children's awareness of their (and others') emotions and their ability to label emotional states is also just developing.

Preschoolers' Awareness of Emotions

Finding words for feelings is difficult; one must become aware of vague and fluctuating inner states and learn to apply appropriate verbal labels to them. Understanding the emotions of others is even more challenging, since we can't directly know another person's inner feelings. Instead, we learn to judge others' behavior, facial expression, and language as external cues to their emotions. The ability to both become aware of our internal life and decode the subtle cues expressed by others continues to develop throughout life.

During the preschool years, children show some awareness of their own and others' emotions. For example, by age three, children can understand and respond to questions about feelings (Lewis & Michaelson, 1983). Moreover, the basic emotions are accurately labeled as soon as the appropriate words are learned (Denham, 1986). Thus, most three-year-olds will readily say the face depicted in Figure 10-3(a) is "afraid," the one in 10-3(b) is "happy," and the one in 10-3(c) is "mad" (Ekman, 1973).

However, preschoolers do not always understand that their feelings originate from inside the self and are likely to blame their emotions on external events or persons (Wolman, Lewis, & King, 1971). Moreover, they are better able to recognize pure forms of single emotions—feeling angry, feeling sad— than they are more subtle blends of emotions—feeling angry and sad at the same time (Harter and Buddin, 1983). Young children also have difficulty understanding such emotions as shame, a sense of injustice, or the feelings aroused by patriotism or ideology (Gnepp, McKee & Domanic, 1987).

Cognitive Development and Emotion

It has been suggested that these difficulties come about because understanding of feelings is affected by level of cognitive functioning. A study by Carroll and Steward (1984) demonstrates this. They administered three classification tasks and two conservation tasks to a group of 30 four- to five-year-olds and a group of 30 eight- to nine-year-olds. From individual interviews about feelings, each child's understanding of having more than one feeling at a time, changing feelings, and hiding feelings was determined. A significant positive correlation (+.78) between cognitive level and understanding of feelings was found. (A perfect association would be 1.00.) In other words, children functioning at the preoperational level, regardless of age or intelligence, were less likely than those at the level of concrete operations to interpret feelings as being based on internal states, as being multiple, complex, and changing, and as being able to be hidden. Other studies find that children who can take the perspective of another are more adept at recognizing others' emotions (Denham, 1986).

Although cognitive limitations do affect preschoolers' understanding of their own and others' feelings, we should not exaggerate such limits. Although preschoolers are not as adept as older children at understanding emotions, they can show surprising sophistication. In one study (Gnepp & Gould, 1985), preschoolers, second graders, and adults were shown some pictures of children with unexpected facial expressions. For example, in one picture, a smiling girl is about to get an inoculation; in another picture, a sad-looking boy is being given a birthday party with cake and presents. Gnepp hypothesized that if preschoolers were behaving egocentrically, they would read into the situations their own probable emotions and disregard the facial cues of the depicted children. However, if preschoolers were sensitive to the emotions of others, even when they would conflict with their own feelings in similar situations, the facial cues would be most important.

Most young children in the study responded accurately to the facial cues, although they did not do so as often as older children and adults. In a follow-up study, Gnepp & Gould (1985) even found that half the preschoolers were aware of the conflicting cues and tried to reconcile them with explanations ("He's sad at his birthday party, because he hates birthday parties.") These results suggest that many preschoolers are capable of *empathy,* the vicarious sharing of another's emotion, because they can infer how others are feeling, even when these feelings would be different from their own (Hoffman, 1978, 1984). However, since nearly half the preschoolers in Gnepp's studies had trouble with such tasks, we need to find out why different children at the same developmental level vary.

Individual Differences in Emotional Understanding

Little support has been found for any biologically based individual differences in awareness of others' emotions. Although many people believe that girls show more social sensitivity and caring than do boys, research does not find any consistent sex differences (Maccoby & Jacklin, 1974; Eisenberg & Lennon, 1983).

More promising has been the search for specific environmental experiences to explain individual differences in understanding the feelings of others. Parents and other adults who help children label their own and others' inner states—"You must be sad because your goldfish died"—appear to promote awareness of feelings, although there is relatively little research in this area.

An important way that children come to understand how others feel is through play with other children. When preschoolers make believe with others—*social fantasy play* or *social role taking* to researchers—they practice placing themselves in different roles, experiencing different perspectives and feelings. Connolly and Doyle (1984) observed how much social fantasy play preschoolers engaged in and asked the teachers to rate the children's social skills and popularity. Each child was then told illustrated stories and asked to talk about the feelings of the characters. For example, in one story, one child's bag of candy is taken by another. The results showed that social fantasy play, social skills, and ability to understand others' feelings were all related.

But does social fantasy play really cause children to be more aware of feelings? Couldn't children who are already socially sensitive gravitate toward fantasy play, an activity that uses their skills? Although such an interpretation of Connolly and Doyle's results is plausible, other studies show that children given the opportunity for social fantasy play show subsequent improvements in awareness of others' feelings (Burns & Brainerd, 1979).

Emotions and Personality

The varied influences on emotional expression and the understanding of others' emotions combine to produce distinct individual differences among children. The typical emotional states of particular children is an important part of what we mean by *personality*. Personality is the consistent manner in which an individual behaves. It is a product of the complex interaction of biological factors—such as temperament—with environmental influences. The role emotions play in giving a child's personality its distinctive character is illustrated by the following descriptions of three children observed by Michael Lewis and Linda Michaelson (1983):

> B was observed almost always to be in the company of other children and to play a variety of games. His predominant facial expression was smiling. B appeared to be happy and sociable.
> G, on the other hand, was seen part of the time to be playing alone although most often she was in the company of another child. G tended to play with few toys and G's play was characterized by throwing things about rather than by sharing. G's facial expression was one of sadness and anger. G was characterized by the observers as a rather angry child who was often found fighting with peers and resisting the teacher's requests.
> L played alone. Her play was usually low-keyed and quiet. She was often seen with her head lowered and on several occasions was observed on her teacher's lap crying. The observers described L as sad and afraid.

These three different profiles indicate that broad individual differences exist in the way children express emotions, understand their own and others' emotional states, and use emotions to communicate socially. The determinants of these individual differences are complex and as yet imperfectly understood (Goldsmith & Gottesman, 1981).

We have seen that during the preschool years, children experience a wide range of emotions and are becoming aware of these feelings both in themselves and in others. This ability enables preschool children to have a sense of empathy, thereby vicariously sharing another's feelings.

Fitting In

Both the "thinking self" and the "feeling self" are ways that the young child becomes more of a distinct, separate individual. At the same time, children are deepening and expanding their ties to others. They are becoming more able to participate effectively in interactions with others, adapt themselves to the demands of society, and control and regulate their own behavior so that it fits in to the social world of which they are a part. This section focuses on four areas: the development of language and communication; the development of positive social behaviors such as caring, sharing, and helping; the development of children's self-control; and the inhibition of negative behaviors such as aggression.

Development of Language

Chapter 6 examined theories of language and milestones in language development during the first two years. Language skills continue to develop rapidly during the preschool years.

Vocabulary. Average vocabulary increases dramatically during the preschool years, from under 400 words at age two to over 2,500 at age six. At each age, children understand many more words (*receptive vocabulary*) than they can use in conversation (*productive vocabulary*). Although there are wide individual differences in vocabulary size at each age, the rate of increase is similar for most children (Cratty, 1979; Moskowitz, 1978).

Preschoolers often pick up and use words they hear around them, even though they may not understand those words. They also tend to have a *literal understanding* of word meaning, not comprehending that the same word can be used in different ways. For example, a young child may believe that underworld criminals live below the earth. Since adults often use indirect expressions for events they are uncomfortable about, explanations to children about death as going to sleep or about sexual intercourse as loving and kissing a lot only further confuse literal-minded preschoolers.

Grammar. By age two, children begin to speak in three-word sentences. English-speaking children begin to use the subject-verb-object (SVO) form characteristic of adult sentences: "Daddy give juice," "Mommy get ball." *Inflections* also begin to appear (Dale, 1976). Inflections are *morphemes* (or meaningful units of language) that are added to words to indicate changes of meaning, for example *-ed* (past tense), *'s* (possession), and *s* (plural).

Jean Berko Gleason (1958) used an ingenious method to determine the extent to which young children regularly use English inflections. She used nonsense words to depict strange animals and people doing odd actions. For example, she showed children a drawing of one of the animals, saying, "This is a wug," then pointed to a second picture and said, "Now there are two _____." (See Figure 10-4.) Five- and six-year-olds consistently added inflections in an appropriate manner, indicating plural—*two wugs*—, past tense—*he ricked yesterday*—, the third person singular present—*he ricks every day*—, and the possessive—*the bik's hat*. This tendency to add suffixes to nonsense words indicated that the children were abstracting rules for using grammatical morphemes and applying them consistently.

This is a Wug.

Now there is another one.

There are two of them.

There are two _____.

Figure 10—4

A Method for Determining Preschoolers' Use of Inflections

(From J. Berko, *Word*, 1958, Vol. 14, p. 154. Reprinted by permission of the International Linguistic Association.)

Research by Roger Brown (1973) has illuminated the process by which these grammatical morphemes are acquired over a period of time. In a classic study of language acquisition in young children, Brown collected language samples from three children, Adam, Eve, and Sara, for several hours each month. Adam and Sara were studied from age 18 months until four years of age, Eve until she was 28 months old.

As Figure 10-5 shows, there were wide individual differences in the average number of morphemes (called *mean length of utterance* or *MLU*) in each child's speech at different ages. For example, Eve's MLU at 24 months was similar to Sara's and Adam's at age 42 months. Despite these individual differences, grammatical inflections were acquired *in the same order* by each of the children. Brown recorded every occurrence of each grammatical morpheme in the speech samples of Adam, Eve, and Sara, and when the children used a morpheme in at least 90 percent of the contexts when an adult would have used it, it was considered to be acquired. As Table 10-3 shows, the first inflection to appear was the suffix *-ing* to indicate present action, as in "I going." Next appeared the prepositions *in* and *on*. Following that, the plural *s* began to be used. Finally, irregular past tenses, such as *went*, were added, and the possessive

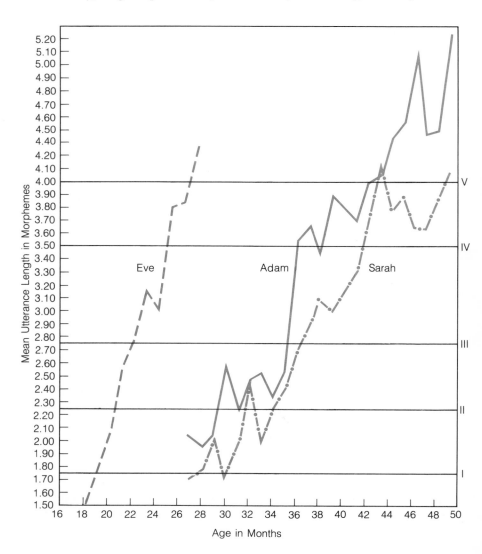

Figure 10—5

Average Length of Utterance in Morphemes at Different Ages for Three Children (Roman Numerals Indicate Stages of Development)

Table 10–3

FOURTEEN SUFFIXES AND
FUNCTION WORDS IN ENGLISH

Form	Meaning	Example
1. Present progressive: **-ing**	Ongoing process	He is sitt*ing* down.
2. Preposition: **in**	Containment	The mouse is *in* the box.
3. Preposition: **on**	Support	The book is *on* the table.
4. Plural: **-s**	Number	The dog*s* ran away.
5. Past irregular: e.g., **went**	Earlier in time relative to time of speaking	The boy *went* home.
6. Possessive: **-'s**	Possession	The girl*'s* dog is big.
7. Uncontractible copula **be**: e.g., **are, was**	Number; earlier in time	*Are* they boys or girls? *Was* that a dog?
8. Articles: **the, a**	Definite/indefinite	He has *a* book.
9. Past regular: **-ed**	Earlier in time	He jump*ed* the stream.
10. Third person regular: **-s**	Number; earlier in time	She run*s* fast.
11. Third person irregular: e.g., **has, does**	Number; earlier in time	*Does* the dog bark?
12. Uncontractible auxiliary **be**: e.g., **is, were**	Number; earlier in time; ongoing process	*Is* he running? *Were* they at home?
13. Contractible copula **be**: e.g., **-'s, -'re**	Number; earlier in time	That*'s* a spaniel.
14. Contractible auxiliary **be**: e.g., **-'s, -'re**	Number; earlier in time; ongoing process	They*'re* running very slowly.

(Based on R. Brown, *A First Language: The Early Stages*, 1973, © Harvard University Press, and adapted by H. H. and E. V. Clark, *Psychology and Language*, 1977, © Harcourt Brace Jovanovich, Inc. Reprinted by permission of Harvard University Press and Harcourt Brace Jovanovich.)

's appeared. Studies examining the speech samples of larger numbers of children have found the same sequence (De Villiers & de Villiers, 1973).

Overregularization.   As children begin to apply these grammatical morphemes in a rulelike fashion, they *overregularize* the rule. Overregularization is the application of a regular rule to an irregular case. For example, to form the past tense, they add *-ed* to the end of all verbs, including irregular forms, saying "they goed," "it comed," and "he hitted the ball." Parents may be surprised to hear a child who had used *went* and *came* appropriately suddenly begin to make mistakes in forming the past tense. This is because the earlier usage reflected imitation or rote repetition, while now the child is attempting to apply a grammatical rule. At first, the rule is applied in every instance, but gradually, exceptions are learned. However, even elementary school-age children sometimes have difficulty with irregular verbs.

Other aspects of grammar, such as negatives and questions, are also acquired in a systematic stagelike fashion. At each stage, the child appears to be using a set of grammatical rules; these rules are gradually modified to approximate adult usage.

Negatives.   During the first two years, children may express negation by shaking the head, frowning, gesturing, or using the word *no* alone. At the one- and two-word stages, negation often is expressed by words such as *bye-bye, all gone,* and *off,* as well as by *no* or *not* (refer to Chapter 6) (Clark & Clark, 1977).

Klima and Bellugi (1966) identified three stages in the acquisition of negatives based on analysis of speech samples of three children over a period of 16 months after they had reached the two-word stage (see Table 10-4). In stage 1, *no* or *not* is added at the beginning or end of a two-word utterance to express negation. In stage 2, children begin to incorporate negatives into their sentences and use *can't* and *don't,* although these terms are understood as units rather than as contractions of *cannot* and *do not.* Some stage 1 negatives, such as *no pinch me,* continue to be used. By stage 3, negatives are always incorporated into the utterance, and children understand that *don't* can be analyzed into *do not.* Children in this stage appear to have mastered the essentials of the adult use of negatives, although they still make mistakes, for example, saying *I not crying* rather than *I'm not crying.* Finally, use of *no one* and *nothing* is not fully understood, resulting in double negatives such as *no one didn't come in* (Clark & Clark, 1977). Similar sequences in the acquisition of negation have been found for other languages, such as Italian and German (McNeill, 1968).

Questions.   The stages children go through in the acquisition of interrogative sentences are roughly parallel to the stages for negatives (see Table 10-5) (Clark & Clark, 1977). At first, questions are indicated by a rising

Table 10—4

NEGATIVES IN CHILDREN'S SPEECH

First Stage	Second Stage	Third Stage
No. . .wipe finger	No pinch me	Paul can't have one
Not. . .fit	Book say no	This can't stick
No the sun shining	No square. . .is clown	I didn't did it
No mitten	I can't catch you	You don't want some supper
No sit there	You can't dance	I didn't caught it
Wear mitten no	I don't sit on Cromer's coffee	Paul didn't laugh
Not a teddy bear!	I don't know his name	I gave him some so he won't cry
No fall!	Don't bite me yet	Donna won't let go
	Don't wait for me . . . come in	No, I don't have a book
	That no O, that blue	That was not me
	That no fish school	I isn't. . .I not sad
	There no squirrels	This not ice cream
	He no bite you	They not hot
	I no want envelope	Paul not tired
		It's not cold
		I not crying
		He not taking the walls down
		Don't put the two wings on
		Don't kick my box
		I not see you anymore
		I not hurt him
		Ask me if I not made mistake

(Based on Klima & Bellugi, 1966, and adapted by H. H. and E. V. Clark, *Psychology and Language,* © 1977. Reprinted by permission of Harcourt Brace Jovanovich, Inc.)

Table 10—5

CHILDREN'S QUESTIONS

First Stage	Second Stage	Third Stage
Fraser water?	See my doggie?	Does lions walk?
See hole?	Dat black too?	Oh, did I caught it?
Sit chair?	You want eat?	Are you going to make it with me?
No ear?	I have it?	Will you help me?
What(s) that?	You can't fix it?	Can I have a piece of paper?
What cowboy doing?	This can't write a flower?	Can't it be a bigger truck?
Where Ann pencil?	Where baby Sarah rattle?	Can't you work this thing?
Where Mama boot?	Where me sleep?	Can't you get it?
Where kitty?	What book name?	Where small trailer he should pull?
Where horse go?	What me think?	Where the other Joe will drive?
Where milk go?	What the dollie have?	Where my spoon goed?
Who that?	What soldier marching?	What I did yesterday?
	Why?	What he can ride in?
	Why you smiling?	What did you doed?
	Why not?	Sue, what you have in your mouth?
	Why not me sleeping?	Why he don't know how to pretend?
	Why not me drink it?	Why kitty can't stand up?
		Why the Christmas tree going?
		Which way they should go?
		How he can be a doctor?
		How they can't talk?
		How that opened?

(Based on Klima & Bellugi, 1966, and adapted by H. H. and E. V. Clark, *Psychology and Language,* © 1977. Reprinted by permission of Harcourt Brace Jovanovich, Inc.)

pitch at the end of a statement, accompanied by an intent look at the adult. *Where* and *what* are also used, but as with negatives, they are tacked on to the beginning of two-word utterances. At this stage, children seem to understand *where* questions primarily, responding irrelevantly to *what* questions from parents (Klima and Bellugi, 1966; Ervin-Tripp, 1970). Thus, it is not surprising that *where* questions comprised 80 percent of the questions put to Adam, Eve, and Sara by their parents (Brown, Cazden, & Bellugi-Klima, 1969).

In stage 2, children's questions are more complex. *Why* questions are now asked, and a greater variety of verbs are employed. However, children omit forms of *be* as in *What book name?* for *What is the book's name?* By stage 3, subject and verb are inverted in questions like *Will you help me?*, but children still have problems with verb forms, as in *Did I caught it?* Positive questions are less complex and are acquired earlier than negative questions, which require the child to both invert subject and verb and insert the negative, as the following example illustrates (Bellugi, 1971):

Adult: Adam, ask the [puppet] what she'll do next.
Adam: What *will you do* now?
Adult: Adam, ask the [puppet] why she can't sit down.
Adam: Why *you can't sit* down?

Other Grammatical Forms.   At about age two to three, children begin to link ideas together with *and* to form *compound sentences* such as *John put on his coat, and his Mommy opened the door. Relative clauses* such as *See the ball that I got* also appear. When children construct compound sentences, they tend to avoid relative clauses that break up the main clause (Clark & Clark, 1977). For example, in one study (Slobin & Welsh, 1973), a child aged two years, four months, when asked to repeat sentences such as *The owl who eats candy runs fast*, said, *Owl eat a candy and he run fast.*

Young children find it easier to understand and produce complex sentences that mirror the actual sequence of events. Eve Clark (1971) asked three- to five-year-old children to act out the following sentences using toys: (a) *The boy patted the dog before he kicked the rock* and (b) *Before the boy kicked the rock, he patted the dog.* Sentence (a), where order of mention followed order of occurrence was much easier for the children to enact than sentence (b).

In summary, acquisition of syntax or grammar during the preschool years follows an orderly, stagelike progression. Although different children move through the stages at different rates, the sequence remains the same. At each stage, children's grammar follows a set of rules that may be abstracted from their speech, suggesting that the acquisition of grammar depends less on environmental influences than on innate factors.

Influences on Language

Chapter 6 examined the learning theory hypothesis that imitation or reinforcement of speech could explain the beginnings of language in the toddler. Although the way mothers and other caregivers talk to children has been shown to affect children's speech, the child's active role in extracting linguistic information from the environment is significant. Environmental influences are important in the sense that they provide children with many examples of speech to use as "raw materials" from which to extract rules.

We can illustrate this by returning to Roger Brown's investigation of Adam, Eve, and Sara (Figure 10-5). In addition to noting the appearance of various grammatical inflections in the speech of each child, Brown recorded the mothers' use of these inflections. If children are imitating adult language, they should acquire those forms that they hear most frequently. However, there was no correspondence between the order in which Adam and Eve acquired various inflections and the frequency with which they heard them from their mothers (Bellugi, 1964). Children have to hear a particular grammatical construction before they can acquire it, but the frequency with which they hear it is not related to its speed of acquisition.

The Development of Pronunciation

The same gradual approximation to adultlike forms that we have seen in the development of grammar is also evident in the development of pronunciation. Up until the age of two, children often pronounce two- and three-syllable words as one-syllable, and they have difficulty producing certain speech sounds, such as the *f* in *fish*, the *s* in *suit*, or the *y* in *yellow* (Ingram, 1976; Smith, 1973). In the next stage, two- and three-syllable words will be attempted, but unstressed syllables are often omitted, and there continues to be difficulty with certain consonants; for example, *telephone* may come out as *dewibun* or *tomato* as *mado* (Smith, 1973; Clark & Clark, 1977).

One way in which toddlers and young children gradually approximate adult pronunciation is through word play and bedtime "monologues." In samples of the language of young children talking to themselves and playing with other children, we can see children practicing particular classes of consonants (Weir, 1962, 1966; Chukovsky, 1963, Cazden, 1974). For example, in the following, a child named David is practicing the *r* sound in *story* (Weir, 1966, p. 163):

"Stoly/stoly here/ want a stoly/ Dave, stoly/ story, story/ story's de hat/ story's de big hat/ story's a hat"

The child has a powerful impetus to speak more distinctly—the need to be understood. Language is a matter not only of acquiring increasingly complex grammatical forms but also of using language for social purposes. *Communicative competence* refers to achieving desired goals through use of language, for example to get a desired toy, make a friend, or keep a parent nearby (Hymes, 1971).

The Development of Communicative Competence

Let's look at two conversations, both recorded by Catherine Garvey and Robert Hogan (1973) and shown in Table 10-6. Note in comparing the two conversations, C and D actually respond to the meaning of what the other child had previously said, more so than A and B (the researchers did not reveal the children's names). C and D are engaging in a real interchange of ideas as one child speaks and the other responds. As Table 10-7 shows, young children in their speech show considerable evidence of responsivity to their partners (Garvey & Hogan, 1973; Garvey, 1975) which increases over the preschool period.

Another feature more evident in the conversation between C and D than in that between A and B is *turn taking*. This occurs when one child alternates

Table 10-6

TWO CONVERSATIONS OF PRESCHOOLERS

Speaker	Speech
A	My group got shot. Did your group ever get shot?
B	No.
A	Well, mine did.
B (A does)	Will you put this hammer in (tool belt) for me?
B (A moves away, picks up toy snake)	Thank you. I'll take it now. Oh, the phone's ringing. Hello?
A	A snake can kill you.
C	If I grow up my voice will change and when you grow up your voice will change. My mom told me. Did your mommy tell you?
D	No, your mommy's wrong. My voice, I don't want it to change. Oh, well.
C	Oh well, we'll stay little, right?
D	What?
C	We'll stay little.
D	No, I don't want to. I *want* my voice to change. I don't care if it changes.
C	*I* care.

(Adapted from Garvey & Hogan, *Child Development*, 1973. © The Society for Research in Child Development, Inc. Reprinted by permission of authors.)

Table 10—7

CONVERSATIONAL TURNS IN
PAIRS OF PRESCHOOL-AGE
CHILDREN

Number of Turns	Percent of Pairs Observed	
	3.5–4.5 yrs.	4.5–5 yrs.
4	83%	92%
6	50%	92%
8	33%	58%
12 or more	16%	42%

(Adapted from Garvey & Hogan, *Child Development*, 1973. © The Society for Research in Child Development, Inc. Reprinted by permission of authors.)

with the other in "taking the floor," thereby developing a kind of communicative reciprocity. Turn taking involves attention to nonverbal as well as verbal cues to determine when one speaker has finished or wants to begin a turn. By age three, children rarely speak simultaneously (Garvey, 1984). Lois Bloom and her colleagues (Bloom, Rocissano, & Hood, 1976) found that although three-year-olds, in contrast to two-year-olds, could sustain a topic with an adult through successive turns, they seldom responded for more than two turns. By contrast, Garvey's analysis of peer verbalizations found longer turn taking to be common, in one case, up to 21 turns. Thus, the ability to take successive turns in conversation appears to vary with the situation.

In addition to responsivity and turn taking, other aspects of communicative competence, such as exchanging information, asking for clarification (Revelle, Wellman, & Karabenick, 1985), resolving conflict, and finding areas of agreement (Gottman, 1983), also develop during the preschool years (see Table 10-8).

Another aspect of communicative competence is *code switching*, or the ability to modify language to adapt to the perceived needs of one's listener. In Chapter 9, we mentioned a study by Shatz and Gelman showing that four-year-olds speak differently—with shorter sentences and simpler vocabulary—to two-year-olds than they do to peers. In addition to demonstrating that

Table 10—8

ASPECTS OF COMMUNICATIVE
COMPETENCE

Aspect	Definition	Example
Connectedness	Is responsive, in focus.	A: "I'm having hamburger for dinner. B: "I'm having hotdog."
Communicative clarity	Requests clarification; responds to requests with clarification.	A: "Hand me the truck." B: "Which one?" A: "The red one."
Information exchange	Asks for and gives information.	A: "You know what?" B: "No, what" A: "You can come to my house."
Common ground	Finds areas of agreement, similarity.	A: "My dolly's going to sleep, right?" B: "Right."
Conflict resolution	Complies to demands.	A: "Let's play chase now." B: "OK."
Self-disclosure	Expresses feelings.	A: "I'm sad, 'cause my grandma went away." B: "My grandma's far, too."
Joke/Fantasy Sharing	Reciprocates jokes, fantasy, gossip.	A: "He's a dum-de-dum-dum." B: "He's a double dum-de-dum-dum." (laughs)

(From Garvey, 1977; Garvey & Hogan, 1973; Gottman, 1983.)

preschoolers are less egocentric than had been previously assumed, these findings indicate that *code switching* is well established by age four. Not only do preschoolers adjust their speech to younger children, but they also speak distinctively to babies, using the speech styles called baby talk and motherese (see Chapter 6) (Gleason, 1973; Sachs & Devin, 1976).

Bilingualism

Perhaps the most dramatic evidence of preschoolers' abilities to fine tune their communication to different situations is *bilingualism,* the speaking and comprehension of two languages. Many people believe that children who are taught two languages simultaneously or who speak one language at home and another language outside the home will experience difficulties in communicating in either language. They worry that one language will interfere with the other, that children will mix up the two languages in their speech, and that the children's language development in general will be delayed.

Early studies of bilingualism seemed to confirm this view (Jones, 1960). However, these investigations did not take into account differences in socioeconomic status; many of the families with bilingual children were poorer than families with *monolingual* (one-language) children. More carefully designed research indicates that the process of language acquisition appears to be similar for both monolingual and bilingual children, and little evidence exists that bilingual preschoolers become confused and mix up languages (Grosjean, 1982). Instead, they seem to use one language with speakers of that language and the second in interactions with speakers of the other language (Bergman, 1976; Lindholm, 1980). Even when the same individuals speak two different languages with the child, the size of the child's vocabulary in each language is not affected (Doyle, Champagne, & Segalowitz, 1978).

For many young children growing up in a bilingual environment, both languages are not equally emphasized. For example, the children may speak Spanish exclusively at home and in their neighborhood while being exposed to English only during the hours they are at nursery school. When this occurs, there is some evidence of interference from the dominant language. For example, the child may insert a Spanish word for an English one that has not yet been acquired (Segalowitz, 1981). However, there is no evidence that this

Bilingual classrooms enable children to develop and maintain language skills in both languages.

has any long-term effect on language or cognitive development (McLaughlin, 1977, 1978).

Although their capacities for communicative competence are impressive, preschoolers do not necessarily show these capacities in their actual performance. As previously noted, children may look like more competent turn takers in some situations than in others.

Influences on Communicative Competence

During the preschool years, social experience—play with other children and speaking with adults—helps children develop conversational and other language skills. For example, children who are friends with one another have been shown to use more complex and reciprocal language than do children who are acquaintances (Gottman, 1983). Moreover, experiences with friends appear to spill over into other situations. When meeting an unfamiliar child, children who already have friends show more skill at breaking the ice with suggestions for play and questions about the other child than do children who don't have friends.

Evidence also exists that the types of social exchanges young children have with adults have an effect on the quality of their language. For example, middle-class mothers have been observed to use *elaborated* language with their children, that is, more complex sentences that contain more morphemes and more explanation. Lower-class mothers' speech was more *restricted*, using simpler sentences and involving more commands (Hess & Shipman, 1967). These differences have been mirrored in the language development of their children, although we do not know the precise mechanisms by which mothers are influencing their children's language.

More recent research documents that the language of caregivers in daycare centers may also influence language development (McCartney, 1984). Kathleen McCartney observed the language of caregivers toward 146 children in nine day care centers on the island of Bermuda. She found that the use of commands such as "stop that" was negatively related to language development, while caregivers' statements that gave or received information, for example, "The puzzle is in the box," were positively related to language

When toddlers and preschoolers "read" a storybook with an adult, they can learn new words, practice simple turn-taking, and anticipate familiar sequences of words.

Childhood Autism

We've chosen to include a discussion of the nature and treatment of autism in this chapter, not because it is a common disorder among preschoolers—it is estimated at 1:2200 live births (Coleman & Rimland, 1976)—but because it involves severe disturbances in both of the major developments highlighted in this chapter: the development of a personal identity and the deepening of relations with others.

The Nature of Autism

In 1906, a Swiss psychiatrist, Eugene Bleuler, coined the term *autism* to describe the disordered thought he observed in many of his adult psychotic patients. (Bleuler also gave us the word *schizophrenia*.) The first person to apply the term *autism* to children, however, was Leo Kanner, a child psychiatrist at Johns Hopkins University, in 1943.

Kanner's patients were children who had little awareness of others, who seemed preoccupied with physical objects rather than people, and who had a strong need to maintain sameness. Many of these children had speech delays and some were mute, although at times they appeared to understand language well. Speech disorders such as *echolalia*, the tendency to repeat speech sounds, also characterized the children. Behavior problems, such as temper tantrums, self-destructive behavior, repetitive body movements such as rocking, and disturbances of sleeping and eating, were common (Kanner, 1943).

Since Kanner first identified the disorder, many investigators have studied childhood autism. Despite this, a precise definition of autism is still difficult, because the behaviors appear in varying combinations and severity in different children diagnosed as autistic. In addition, terms such as *childhood psychosis* and *childhood schizophrenia* are sometimes used to refer to the symptoms of autism. Thus, it is most accurate to think of autism as a loose complex of behaviors, not all of which appear in every child with the disorder.

One of the most upsetting aspects of the autistic child's behavior is lack of social responsiveness, as this mother of an autistic child relates:

> I would talk to him and he didn't talk back and I didn't really know whether he understood, you know? My God, doesn't he understand or doesn't he hear—because he had the habit, if he wanted to ignore me he just would ignore me and there was no way for me to tell whether he didn't hear or just didn't understand (Mack & Webster, 1980, p. 32).

The Causes of Autism

Unfortunately, no one knows exactly why autism occurs. Some children show disturbances in their behavior during infancy, but most children are diagnosed in the third year of life (Ritvo, 1976). One theory, advanced by psychoanalytically oriented investigators (Lennard, Beauliue, & Embry, 1965; Goldfarb, Levy, & Meyers, 1972), suggests that a deficient mother-child relationship or a disordered family communication style can cause autism. However, most of the evidence supporting this idea can be interpreted as a family's coping *response* to having an autistic child rather than a cause of the problem.

Most people now believe that autism stems from an as yet unidentified malfunctioning of the child's central nervous system (Ritvo, 1976). In particular, some investigators believe that autism results from an impairment in the ability to integrate complex stimuli (Schreibman & Koegel, 1982). That is, autistic children can perceive individual sounds or visual stimuli in isolation, but when confronted with a complex combination, such as that presented by a talking human face, they cannot process the information.

Treatments for Autism

The most common treatment for autism, *behavior modification,* relies on the principles of *operant conditioning* to increase the frequency of desired behaviors, such as speech, and to decrease the frequency of negative behaviors, such as repetitive rocking of the body. The therapist tries to get the child to look at the adult by immediately rewarding the child, perhaps with a favorite food, following any look, even a momentary glance. Once the child is looking at the therapist, the child is rewarded for imitating speech sounds. Gradually, sounds are combined into words and words into sentences. This process is called *shaping,* the rewarding of successive approximations to the desired behavior (Lovaas, 1977).

Behavior modification techniques have been quite successful in increasing speech and social responsiveness and in decreasing negative behaviors. However, most of the effects are not long lasting. For example, in a four-year followup of 51 out of 54 autistic children who received intensive behavior modification to increase their communication, most of the children were still severely impaired (Mack & Webster, 1980). The treatment of childhood autism remains a difficult challenge.

skills. In addition, aspects of the center predicted language development and communicative competence. Well-organized centers with low noise levels where adult-child interaction was encouraged were associated with linguistic advancement. This study suggests that high quality day care experiences may promote children's language development.

Prosocial Behavior

Parents want their children not only to communicate effectively with others but also to show the positive social behaviors we associate with being fully human: helping, sharing, giving to those in need, and cooperating. These positive behaviors, called *prosocial behaviors,* also develop during the preschool period.

Theories of Prosocial Behavior

One view links arousal of emotion or empathy with the tendency to behave prosocially (Aronfreed, 1968, 1970; Hoffman, 1984). As we have discussed, young children can feel empathy at others' distress. It seems logical that children who show the most empathy would be those most likely to engage in prosocial behaviors, though this has not been supported by research (Radke-Yarrow, Zahn-Waxler, & Chapman, 1983).

Cognitive theorists reason that even when their empathy is aroused, preschoolers may not be able to help others because of cognitive limitations that can prevent them from understanding that the need for help exists or knowing the appropriate ways to help (Bar-Tal, 1976). In support of this view, several studies have found that the more egocentric a child is, the less likely the child will donate boxes of candy to "poor children" in laboratory experiments (Rubin & Schneider, 1973; Emler & Rushton, 1974; Rushton, 1975) or express concern for a hurt adult or sad child (Denham, 1986).

A study by Ruth Pearl (1985) illustrates the cognitive difficulties preschoolers may have in determining others' need for help. She showed 64 four-year-olds and 64 third-graders some short film segments of children having difficulty doing various things, such as opening the lid of a cookie jar. In some film segments, the child's problem was clearly depicted; for example, a boy struggling to remove the lid says: "Rats, the lid's stuck." In other segments, the nature of the problem is more ambiguous: The boy attempts to remove the lid, gives up, and stares at the jar.

All the preschoolers suggested ways to help and offered other positive responses when the film depicted clear cues concerning the need for help. However, when the cues for help were unclear, only 68 percent of the preschoolers could think of ways to help. The eight- to nine-year-olds were not affected by the clarity of cues; 93 percent of them suggested ways of helping in both the clear and ambiguous cue conditions. Although this study did not observe helping behavior, other research supports the idea that children will behave more prosocially when they understand how and in what situations to help, share, or cooperate (Bar-tal, Raviv, & Goldberg, 1982).

Learning theory emphasizes the environmental influences that may promote or discourage prosocial responding. Although there are occasions on which young children act *altruistically*—motivated not by self-interest but only by the desire to benefit another—most prosocial behavior is not selfless (Eisenberg & Hand, 1979). For example, Eisenberg and her colleagues (Eisenberg,

Pasternack, Cameron, & Tryon, 1984) observed 44 four-year-olds during play over a nine-week period. These children responded to requests from others for help or sharing 80 percent of the time they were asked to, while spontaneous prosocial behaviors occurred much less frequently. When asked about the reasons for sharing, the children explained their actions in practical terms— "He needed some scissors to cut, so I brought them."—or as a way to facilitate play—"I gave him the apron, so we could play house."—and rarely as a way to alleviate another's distress. In another study (Birch & Billman, 1986), preschoolers' sharing of food during snack time was observed; most children shared only when asked and when they had been shared with previously.

These observations are supported by laboratory experiments showing the positive effects of reinforcement and modeling on prosocial behavior (Doland & Adelberg, 1967; Hartup & Coates, 1967; Staub, 1971). For example, in one study, preschoolers who saw a "Lassie" episode of a boy helping a dog were later more likely to help puppies who appeared to be in distress than to continue playing a board game. Children who saw a neutral TV program were not more likely to exhibit such helping behavior (Sprafkin, Liebert, & Poulos, 1975). Watching television programs such as *Mister Roger's Neighborhood* that emphasize sharing with, helping, and understanding others has been shown to increase preschoolers' helpfulness, provided that the prosocial themes are reinforced through storybooks and puppet play (Fredrich & Stein, 1975).

A *systems* or *ecological* perspective emphasizes familial and cultural influences on prosocial behavior. Experiments showing that brief exposures to a generous or helpful model modify children's behavior suggest that more prolonged exposure to parental and other models will have even greater effects. Preschoolers who have warm relationships with their parents are more likely to behave generously in laboratory experiments (Rutherford & Mussen, 1968), and parents' altruistic values have been related to children's tendencies to behave altruistically (Hoffman, 1975).

The influence of culture is illustrated in the observations of John and Beatrice Whiting (1975) of 134 children between the ages of three and eleven years in farming communities of six cultures: Philippines, Kenya, Mexico, India, New England, and Okinawa. Observers who were thoroughly familiar with each culture followed the children around for several months, noting their behaviors and interactions in a variety of settings: house, yard, school, and other public places. They found that children from the Philippines, Kenya, and Mexico were significantly more prosocial toward others than were children from the other societies (see Table 10-9).

The cultures with a higher incidence of prosocial behavior among children also regularly assigned household tasks to children and put them in charge of caring for younger siblings. Moreover, within these cultures, first-borns were more prosocial than last-born or only children.

The Whitings and others (Staub, 1971, 1974; Maccoby, 1980) reason that caretaking responsibilities accustom children to helping by creating the *norm of social responsibility* or the expectation that they should help. (Caretaking experience also probably made the children more knowledgeable about ways to help and more confident about their abilities as helpers.) In these ways, a cultural emphasis on older children caring for younger ones promotes the development of prosocial behaviors.

In summary, prosocial behavior is complexly determined. Cognitive factors, social reinforcement and modeling, and familial and cultural influences all play a role.

The Development of Self-Control

A common situation preschoolers face is having to wait for things they want immediately. The cookie that gleams so enticingly has to be "saved" for dessert; the bike that another child is using won't be available until his or her turn is up.

While learning to delay is initially a demand others make on the child, in time, most children come to choose to pass up immediate satisfaction of their desires in favor of reaching more long-term goals. Preschool-age children already understand that it is worthwhile delaying immediate gratification if

Table 10—9

MEDIAN SCORES FOR PROSOCIAL
BEHAVIOR* OF CHILDREN FROM
SIX CULTURES

Culture	Score (positive scores = more prosocial)
India	−1.04
New England (U.S.A.)	−0.75
Okinawa (Japan)	−0.24
Philippines	+0.48
Mexico	+0.54
Kenya	+1.14

*Prosocial behavior is defined here as offers help, offers support, and makes responsible suggestions. (Adapted from B. B. Whiting & J. W. M. Whiting, *Children of Six Cultures*, 1975. Reprinted by permission of Harvard University Press.)

In many cultures older children are given responsibility for the care of infants and toddlers.

better rewards can be obtained later. However, although they know it is worth the wait, they have much more difficulty than older children overcoming temptation.

Harriet and Walter Mischel (1983) have conducted several important experiments to identify the difficulties young children have with self-control. In their research, a child is seated in a chair at a table with a bell and an inverted cake pan. The experimenter lifts the pan, revealing three marshmallows—two grouped together and one separate. The experimenter explains that he has to go out of the room for a while but can be summoned back sooner by the bell. The child is given a choice: eat one marshmallow if the child rings the bell or two if the child can wait until the experimenter returns. Although almost all preschoolers observed in this situation preferred to wait to have two marshmallows instead of one, they had more difficulty than older children in coping with delaying gratification. When the Mischels investigated the techniques that help children (and adults) resist temptations such as marshmallows, four strategies were identified:

1. Distract attention from the reward.
2. Take the reward out of view.
3. Don't think about the reward.
4. If you have to think about or see the reward, concentrate on the waiting (by saying such things as "I am waiting for the marshmallows") and not on the eating (thinking about how good the marshmallows will taste).

The last technique illustrates how language can be used to help control behavior (Luria, 1980; Vygotsky, 1962; Balamore & Wolzniak, 1984).

When the preschool children were questioned about what they do to help them wait, they were much less likely than older children to engage in any of these strategies and had little awareness of ways to make the waiting easier. As Figure 10-6 shows, not until age five do the majority of children begin to choose to cover the marshmallows from view or think "waiting" thoughts rather than "eating" thoughts (Mischel, 1974; Mischel & Mischel, 1983).

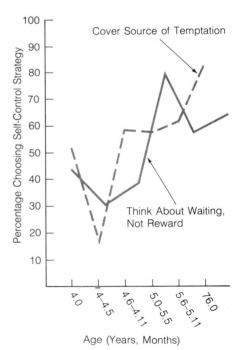

Figure 10—6

DEVELOPMENT OF SELF-CONTROL STRATEGIES TO DELAY GRATIFICATION

(From Mischel and Mischel, 1983. © The Society for Research in Child Development, Inc.)

Thus, because young children have difficulty knowing the best way to resist temptation, they need help from adults in creating situations so that they can successfully delay immediate gratification.

The Control of Aggression

Another aspect of self-control is the ability to inhibit inappropriate and harmful behaviors. Just as preschoolers are less skilled than older children in delaying immediate gratification, they are also less able to control their aggressive behavior.

Aggressive behaviors are those that cause harm or injury to others. Many researchers distinguish between *instrumental aggression,* which is used to achieve a goal, and *hostile aggression,* directed at harming specific persons (Brodzinsky, 1979; Tieger, 1980). Examples of instrumental aggression include quarreling over possession of toys and pushing another out of one's way, while hostile aggression includes hitting, knocking down, and criticizing or ridiculing others.

Both forms of aggression increase from the toddler period through the preschool years, as children play more frequently together and are forced to deal with conflicting demands for toys and the need to take turns. In the early preschool years, most aggression consists of hitting or pushing, but as language skills develop, verbal aggression ("You're a dummy!" "You're yucky!") becomes more frequent (Hartup, 1974). Young children initially lack effective strategies for dealing with such difficult situations; by age six to seven, however, aggressive behavior, particularly physical instrumental aggression, has decreased markedly for most children.

Resolving conflict: Sackin and Thelen (1984) observed 20 five-year-olds in several day care centers. Each child was observed for a total of five hours over a 7- to 12-week period as they played outside. Most of the conflicts children experienced ended when one child "won," the other "lost," and the two separated, but in 26 percent of the conflicts, the two children were able to resolve their disagreements peacefully. For example, one child might apologize to the other or suggest ways the two might cooperate and both have what they want. The investigators found that in 88 percent of the conflicts that were resolved by such peaceful means, children tended not to separate but to remain together playing. Such nonaggressive ways of dealing with conflict gradually increase in frequency as children become older.

Individual Differences in Aggression

In most studies, preschool boys are rated as more aggressive, particularly for physical aggression, than girls (Maccoby & Jacklin, 1980; Barrett, 1979). For example, in the study by Sackin and Thelen, discussed above, 73 percent of all observed conflicts between pairs of children involved boys. However, in most studies, the magnitude of the mean difference in aggression between males and females is not large (Tieger, 1980). A recent analysis of studies reporting sex differences in aggression concluded that only seven percent of the variation among individuals could be explained by their gender and that in general, boys and girls were more likely to be similar in aggression than different (Hyde, 1984).

This suggests that other influences on aggression are likely to be important. Although in the past, aggression has been viewed as an unlearned reaction to frustration or as a natural trait, most researchers currently believe that aggression is learned. According to this view, children who observe others behaving aggressively are more likely to imitate such aggression, particularly if the models are rewarded (Eron, 1980). Parents who use physical punishment, especially if used inconsistently, have more aggressive children (Patterson, 1982). Learning theorists believe that children whose own aggression is rewarded or left unpunished will be likely to continue this kind of behavior and to generalize it to other situations (Huesmann, Eron, Lefkowitz, & Walder, 1984).

Television Violence and Aggression

The emphasis on aggression as a learned response has led to considerable concern about young children's exposure to television violence. Laboratory experiments have demonstrated that exposure to filmed aggressive models can increase children's subsequent aggressive behavior, particularly if the model is not punished for the aggressive acts (Parke & Slaby, 1983).

Preschool children may be especially vulnerable to televised violence because they have more difficulty than older children distinguishing between reality and fantasy (Collins, 1983). The cartoon shows aimed at young children have a higher rate of physical violence than any other type of televised entertainment (Stein & Friedrich, 1975). Moreover, in many shows watched by young children, both heroes and villains behave violently, and aggressive acts are seldom immediately punished. Because of their cognitive limitations, preschoolers often have difficulty integrating earlier segments of a program from later ones, particularly if they are separated by commercial breaks. Thus, in cases where the "bad guy" gets caught in the end, young children may fail to connect it to the violence they viewed earlier in the program (Calvert, Huston, Watkins, & Wright, 1981).

Long-Term Effects of Viewing Television Violence.

In a series of large-scale, carefully conducted studies researchers have shown a clear relationship between television violence viewing in early childhood and aggression in both childhood and the adult years (Lefkowitz, Eron, Walder, & Huesmann, 1977; Eron & Huesmann, 1984; Eron, Walder, & Lefkowitz, 1971). In one study of over 500 third graders, boys who were heavy viewers of television violence—as compared to light viewers—were rated by their peers as more aggressive, were more aggressive at age 19, and at age 30 were more likely to use violence against their wives, have convictions for drunken driving, use physical punishment against their children, and be convicted for criminal offenses (Eron & Huesmann, 1984).

Another three-year investigation of 758 children from the Chicago area, half first graders and half third graders, demonstrated that heavy viewers of TV violence were more likely to believe that TV portrayals were realistic and that violent TV heroes were admirable. This distorted view of social reality has been found in other investigations as well (Gerbner & Gross, 1976; Singer & Singer, 1981).

Some critics (Cook, 1983) and many people in the television industry have argued that TV violence does not cause aggression in children but that already aggressive children gravitate to television violence. However, the work of Eron and Huesmann indicates that ratings of aggression in early childhood do not predict later television violence viewing, while extent of violence watching does predict later aggression (Eron & Huesmann, 1984). Once violence viewing engenders aggression, a circular process is set up: the more aggressive child seeks out more television violence, which in turn promotes still more aggression.

The "small screen" can exert a major influence on preschool children's ideas about the world. (Source: M. Sendak)

Regulating Television Violence

Public interest and concern have focused on the problem of television violence and its possible impact on children ever since television became widespread in American households. Hundreds of studies have documented how viewing violence affects children's behavior, particularly children's aggression and their tolerance for others' aggression. This FOCUS section looks at the relation between our knowledge of the link between television violence and children's behavior and the efforts to regulate television violence.

Congressional Hearings
In 1952, the first congressional hearing on television violence was held by the House Committee on Interstate and Foreign Commerce. Over the next decade, the Senate Committee on the Judiciary held a number of hearings on the same topic. The general tone was one of criticism of television as an excessively violent medium that promoted delinquent behavior (*Television and Behavior*, 1982). For example, one analysis of television content in 1954 counted an average of 11 threats or acts of violence per hour and suggested that the rate of violence depicted on the screen was increasing most rapidly in programs beamed at children (Remmers, 1954).

Governmental Commissions
Further attention was focused on television violence by two govern- mental commissions: the National Commission on the Causes and Prevention of Violence and the Surgeon General's Scientific Advisory Committee on Television and Social Behavior. The commissions' reports, issued in the early 1970s, concluded that evidence from both laboratory and field studies suggested that viewing violence on television might promote aggressive behavior in children.

Both the congressional inquiries and the governmental commissions increased public awareness of the problem of television violence and stimulated many additional studies designed to unravel the violence/aggression link. At the same time, the governmental reports generated controversy among scientists who charged that the cautious language of the reports could be interpreted as either supporting or challenging an association between television violence and aggression (*Television and Behavior*, 1982).

Citizens' Groups
Increasing public concern about the high incidence of violence on television led to the formation of such groups as Action for Children's Television that lobby for better quality programming for children. Other groups voiced their dismay over television violence. In the mid-1970s, the American Medical Association adopted a resolution asking broadcasters to reduce the amount of violence on television, while the National Parent-Teacher Association held public forums throughout the country and the National Committee for Broadcasting called advertisers in to account for programs with violent content (*Television and Behavior*, 1982).

Efforts at Regulation
The upshot of all this unrest was a move by the Federal Communications Commission, the agency that regulates all television stations, to restrict the amount of violence on television during hours when children were most likely to be watching. This period, known as family viewing hours, was subsequently challenged successfully in the courts by writers and broadcasters who argued that it was a violation of their First Amendment right of free speech. Nevertheless, the networks agreed to continue the family-time concept voluntarily.

Those who monitor television content report that in the years since the television networks adopted family time, television violence has decreased slightly in evening programming shown before 9 p.m. However, violence on children's weekend programs continues to be very high (*Television and Behavior*, 1982); 93 percent contain violent acts, presented at a rate of 17.6 per hour (Gerbner, Gross, Morgan, & Signorelli, 1980).

Regulating television violence remains a complex and controversial issue. Many people disagree about how violence should be defined and how it should be measured. Furthermore, exactly how violence affects children continues to be debated, although few researchers now claim that overall it has no effects. Finally, the best way to curb violent programming without infringing on other rights remains a thorny issue. As one government report concluded, "Television remains a violent medium" (*Television and Behavior*, 1982, p. 37).

Reducing the Impact of Television Violence.   Teaching children to distinguish televised depictions of violence from reality can help to break the TV violence/aggression link. An intervention program with children who were frequent viewers of television violence emphasized that the behaviors of television characters did not represent real life, that special effects were used to give the illusion that characters were performing highly aggressive acts, and that it is better to use other means to solve problems. Four months after the program, participants continued to be heavy viewers of TV violence, but they were significantly less aggressive than heavy viewers who had not experienced the intervention (Huesmann, Eron, Klein, Brice, & Fischer, 1983). This suggests that adults who help children interpret television content, express approval or disapproval of what is seen, and who help the young child cognitively integrate program material can lessen the adverse impact of television violence (Collins, Sobol, & Westby, 1981).

Chapter Summary

THE THINKING SELF

☐ During the preschool years, children are becoming distinct individuals in many ways. They are developing a self-concept and ideas about how they are similar to and different from others.

☐ Children begin to understand age and gender distinctions and gradually come to appreciate that gender is a stable and consistent attribute. Along with this understanding comes an interest in sex differences and an increase in sex-stereotyped behavior, such as playing with "girl" versus "boy" toys and joining sex-segregated play groups.

THE FEELING SELF

☐ Preschoolers develop feelings about their self-worth or self-esteem along with ideas about their characteristics. Consistent individual differences are evident in children's emotional lives and in the way children respond to different situations.

☐ Preschool children increasingly develop the ability to understand and share in the feelings of others, even when those feelings would be different from their own in similar circumstances. This development makes empathy with others possible.

FITTING IN

☐ In addition to increasing their vocabulary, children acquire grammatical and syntactic rules of language. Stages occur in the acquisition of grammatical inflections, negations, questions, and complex sentences, with the child's language structure gradually approximating adult usage.

☐ The tools of language gradually become coordinated into communicative competence, whereby children become able to carry on conversations, take turns, make requests, and in other ways use language as a social instrument.

☐ The ability to respond to others' needs is evident in children's prosocial behaviors, such as helping, sharing with, and giving to others. These behaviors are more likely when children feel expected to be prosocial and when they understand how to help or share effectively.

☐ The development of self-control is another important way in which preschoolers become more able to adapt to their environment. Although young children recognize the value of delaying immediate rewards for long-term goals, they still have difficulty resisting temptation. Gradually, children develop strategies that resolve their internal conflict and permit them to successfully delay immediate gratification.

□ Another aspect of self-control is the inhibition of aggression. Physical and verbal aggression increase from early childhood, but over the preschool years, most children learn ways of resolving conflicts with others. Variations in children's levels of aggression exist and studies have suggested a possible link between television violence and aggressive behavior.

Recommended Readings

Damon, W. (1983). *Social and personality development: Infancy through adolescence*. New York: W. W. Norton. An excellent overview of theory and research on the development of social understanding and social behavior by an expert on the topic.

Clark, H. H., and Clark, E. V. (1977). *Psychology and language: An introduction to psycholinguistics*. New York: Harcourt Brace Jovanovich. Comprehensive treatment of language development with extensive illustrations of language samples of children of various ages.

Selman, R. (1980). *The growth of interpersonal understanding*. New York: Academic Press. Based on extensive clinical interviews, an account of the stages of development of awareness of self and others by a prominent theorist on the subject.

Lefkowitz, M., Eron, L., Walder, L., and Huesmann, L. R. (1977). *Growing up to be violent: A longitudinal study of the development of aggression*. New York: Pergamon Press. An opportunity to read more about television and other influences on the development of aggression. Written by the team of researchers who have documented most carefully the television violence/aggression link.

CHAPTER 11

The Young Child:
Connecting with Others

S ara: (age 7) is busy building a "ship" of blocks in the living room.

Josh: (age 4) her younger brother: What's ya doing? Can I play?

Sara: This is a ship and I'm Captain and you can be the sailor.

Josh: I want to be Captain!

Sara: No, I'm Captain.

Josh: Mom, Sara won't let me be Captain! Not fair! No fair!

Sara: Okay, you can be Captain. But then I'll have a turn being Captain.

Josh: Oh boy! . . . What's a Captain?

Josh: I'm not going to be your friend, Tony. You're talking mean to me so I'm not going to be your friend.

Tony: You're talking mean to me.

Josh: You calling me names—Bloody Boy, Fire Boy.

Tony: Well, You're not letting me and David play by ourselves.

— Rubin, 1980.

Preschoolers can be delightful, exasperating, and absorbing companions often within the same ten minutes! Although ties to parents remain most important, young children are venturing out beyond the family. Many young children are spending part or most of their day outside the home under the supervision of other caregivers. Their experiences allow them to establish relationships with other adults and with other children. Often, school experiences provide the first opportunity to play regularly with peers, to become part of a group, and as the second quote illustrates, to make friends. Finally, young children also come into contact with younger and older children, often in informal neighborhood play groups. These three interrelated "worlds" of family, school, and other children are the focus of this chapter. (Chapters 15 and 17 discuss the effects of these "worlds" on the school-age child and on the adolescent.)

We'll look first at the family, focusing on parent-child relations, sibling relations, and some special topics related to young children's development within the family—divorce, parental work roles, and child abuse.

The second "world" of early childhood—that of other children outside the family—includes children's experiences in peer groups as well as with somewhat older and younger children. We'll examine the topics of social acceptance and the development of friendships. The final section evaluates the major school programs currently existing to provide part-day or full-day care and their impact on the child.

Family

Parent-Child Relationships: Socialization

Socialization refers to the transmission of values, attitudes, and behavior from one individual to another. In every society, parents seek to pass on their ways of thinking and acting to their young children. Most parents hope that their children will grow up to be well-functioning adult members of their culture and parents recognize, particularly during the early years of childhood, that they bear major responsibility for this childrearing task.

Of course, children are also socialized by peers, by other adults, and in our own culture, by media such as television. Nearly everywhere, however, parents remain the most important socializing agents during early childhood. In particular, as we saw in Chapter 10, this period of development is a time when children are learning a great deal about (and parents are focusing on) how to behave in socially acceptable ways and how to coordinate one's own desires with the needs of others. In the process of achieving these socialization goals, parents frequently have to find ways to modify their young children's behavior, through discipline or by other means. *Parenting techniques* or *styles* are the strategies that parents use to modify and regulate their children's behavior.

The following section describes parent-child relationships in the preschool years in terms of socialization and parenting techniques and compares four theoretical views of the socialization process and their implications for parenting (see Table 11–1).

Psychoanalytic Theory. Freud (1949) described socialization as an outgrowth of the emotional attachment the young child feels toward both parents. He viewed the preschool years as a time when the more diffuse sexual energy

Table 11–1

THEORIES OF SOCIALIZATION AND IMPLICATIONS FOR PARENTING

Theory	Process	Outcome	Implications
Psychoanalytic	Oedipal/Electra complex.	Identification with same-sex parent and internalization of parental vaues and sex role.	Two-parent family needed; different process for boys and girls; father both warm and dominant; mother warm.
Learning	Reinforcement; observation of parental models.	Adoption of rewarded behaviors; imitation of modeled behaviors.	Reinforcement should be minimally sufficient; parental praise to encourage behavior, consistent discipline to discourage behavior; perception of parent as warm, powerful, and skilled increases modeling.
Cognitive	Child understanding of parental goals and behavior; child affects parent.	Compliance with parent; adoption of parental goals as own.	Clear, consistent parenting adapted to child's cognitive level and to situation.
Systems	Mutual influence between parent and child; all relations in family affect one another; involvements of child and parent outside family also important.	Adoption of parental goals in context of family system change.	Awareness of multiple influences; effects of system change on parenting noted.

of the infant and toddler becomes centered around the genitals as a source of pleasure. This leads to the *Oedipal complex,* which is resolved when the male child gives up the fantasy of having the opposite-sex parent for himself and identifies with the same-sex parent, adopting that parent's attitudes, values, and characteristic behaviors (refer to Chapter 2).

The son's goal is to be more attractive to his mother and to maintain the positive affection of his father. In taking on the father's characteristics, the son *internalizes* them, or makes them his own. No longer does the child behave in certain ways only when the parents are there to enforce compliance, but the child is now capable of resisting temptation, feeling guilty after wrongdoing, and feeling responsible for appropriate behavior. Thus, the young boy's moral understanding is an important outcome of identification with the father. In addition, as we saw in Chapter 10, according to this theory, identification with the father also leads to the adoption of a masculine sex-role identity.

Freud posited a parallel process of conflict and resolution for girls, called the *Electra complex.* Like boys, preschool girls develop a desire to possess their opposite-sex parent. They, too, become aware that they cannot realize their fantasy and so identify with their mother, internalizing her characteristics and adopting a feminine sex-role identity. However, the psychoanalytic treatment of the process of identification in girls was considerably less satisfactory than the account of the Oedipal conflict. First, because, as Freud saw it, girls are originally attached to their mothers, they experience a deepening identification with their mothers, not a switch from one object of identification to another. Second, because mothers were not viewed as threatening and powerful to the girl, the motivation for giving up the fantasy of possessing the father was never made clear.

The awkwardness of Freud's account of the Electra conflict led him to conclude that compared to boys, girls experience less internal conflict, identify with the same-sex parent more weakly, internalize values less strongly, and hence have a weaker moral understanding. This view has been strongly challenged by later writers on moral development, such as Carol Gilligan (1982), who argue that females develop a different, more relationship-oriented sense of morality than do males as a result of their differing early experiences (see Chapter 14).

Erik Erikson's adaptation of the psychoanalytic approach deemphasized the Oedipal/Electra conflict and emphasized instead the development of a sense of identity. He considered the preschool period to be a time of *initiative versus guilt.* The parents' role was to socialize the child in ways that supported a sense of initiative through mastery of motor coordination, language, and fantasy play. Guilt could arise in the child if the parents overly inhibited the child's behavior, belittled fantasy play, or failed to respond to questions (Thomas, 1985).

Critique of Psychoanalytic Theory. The cross-cultural evidence for the Oedipal/Electra complex is weak. Children growing up in households with multiple caregivers develop attachments to those caregivers and not only to the mother and father. The mother-father-child triangle assumed by psychoanalytic theory does not fit the family structures typical of many non-Western cultures (see Table 11–4) (Whiting & Whiting, 1975).

Some researchers have also suggested that even within Western societies, psychoanalytic descriptions of socialization may not be accurate. Rather than there being a pattern of boys identifying with fathers and girls with mothers, there is evidence (Hetherington, 1967) that young children identify with both

Parents are perceived as powerful and rewarding models by preschool-age children.

parents and are especially influenced by the parent they perceive as dominant in the household. Finally, Erikson's description of the preschool period as a time of initiative versus guilt has been criticized as being overly vague and difficult to translate into testable hypotheses concerning parental and child behaviors (Thomas, 1985).

Learning Theory. This view applies general principles of learning to parents' socialization of young children and does not assume that any special relationship or conflict is necessary (refer to Chapter 2). Young children become socialized by parents who are the most frequent reinforcers and modelers of the child's behavior (Bandura, Ross, & Ross, 1963; Bandura, 1969, 1971). In general, children imitate the behavior of models they observe frequently and who are nurturant, powerful, skillful, and themselves rewarded. Since parents are likely to have these characteristics (at least in the eyes of their young children), parents are attractive models.

Critique of Learning Theory.   Although young children (along with people of all ages) are responsive to reinforcements and modeling, the effects are not always what parents might intend. For example, research on the use of physical punishment shows that although it may succeed in modifying the child's behavior while the parent is present, the change does not persist when the parent is absent. Moreover, since physical punishment is itself a form of aggression, it appears to teach the child aggressive responses (Martin, 1975).

Using positive reinforcement, such as praise, turns out to be a complicated parenting technique as well. When children are very frequently praised, they may become so accustomed to it that praise loses its ability to change behavior. For example, one study found that young children who experience very frequent praise at home did not respond to praise when it was used to reinforce learning in a laboratory task (Stevenson, 1965).

In general, children seem to be most motivated when they do not feel externally controlled, either by positive reinforcement, punishment, or close monitoring. This fits in well with what we know about young children's need to feel autonomous; it also encourages children to reward or punish themselves when parents are absent (Lepper, 1982).

These criticisms of a learning theory approach don't mean that parents should stop praising their children or stop trying to discourage inappropriate behaviors. It does mean, however, that reinforcement is most effective when sparingly applied. The *principle of minimally sufficient control* (Maccoby & Martin, 1983) refers to effective discipline that gives the child as much of a feeling of self-control as possible. For example, a preschooler might be given the choice of which of two kinds of vegetables to eat at dinner rather than being told "You must eat these peas" or being promised dessert if the child finishes them.

Cognitive Theory.   This approach emphasizes the child's understanding of parental goals and techniques as determinants of socialization (Maccoby, 1984). Thus, as preschoolers become more able to consider the perspective of others, parents increasingly can reason with the child and appeal to his or her understanding and feelings ("Look how you made him cry when you pushed him.")

Cognitive theory also stresses that many characteristics of the child affect how parents behave. Depending on the child's level of understanding, personality, temperament, etc., parents are likely to behave in different ways. In this view, parents are often responding *to* the child and the particular situation rather than behaving in accordance with consistent techniques of parenting (Bell, 1979).

According to cognitive theory, parenting techniques that take into account the child's level of understanding will be most effective. Flexibly adapting to the needs of the situation makes more sense than adopting a particular parenting style. Thus, sitting down and reasoning with a child would be a poor way of stopping a preschooler who is about to dash in front of oncoming traffic.

Critique of Cognitive Theory.   Differences in understanding are only a limited explanation for individual variations in parent-child relations. Children may understand what parents expect and still not want to comply. Factors such as needs, motivations, and the social context must be taken into account.

Systems Theory.   This theory stresses that the way parents socialize their children will be affected by the marital relationship, the relations the parents

When parents and children know supportive individuals in their neighborhood, such as police officers, teachers, firefighters or mail carriers, the parent-child relationship is enhanced.

have with the other children in the family, and sibling ties (Lerner & Spanier, 1978). The wider environment, from the family's neighborhood to the larger culture, also affects the family. The parent-child relationship is likely to be affected by such ecological variables as the extent of *social support* (individuals the parents can turn to for various kinds of assistance) (Crittenden, 1985), neighborhood quality (Garbarino & Sherman, 1980), availability of social services, and cultural values. In turn, characteristics of the parents may help modify these environmental effects. For example, parents who lack social skills may find it difficult to maintain supportive contacts, while those with little education may not be knowledgeable about or aware of how to use community services (Garbarino, 1985).

Critique of Systems Theory. Because the systems perspective stresses the complexity of the mutual influences within the family system and between the family and its ecological setting, it yields few specific implications for parenting techniques. Rather, it cautions parents to be aware of how their socialization of the child is affected not only by the child himself or herself but also by all the other relationships within the family and between the family and the external environment.

Although each theory of parent-child socialization—psychoanalytic, learning, cognitive, and systems—has important limitations, each identifies significant components of the socialization process. Psychoanalytic theory emphasizes the emotional quality of the parent-child relationship; learning theory, the role of parents as reinforcers and models; cognitive theory, the child's understanding; and systems theory, the mutual influence family members have on each other. Let's now compare these implications of theory with the research findings on parenting techniques.

Parenting Techniques

Although most of the research directly focused on parenting techniques has been *atheoretical* (not derived from any theory), two dimensions emerge consistently. One dimension refers to the affective quality of parent-child relations, while the second dimension refers to the parent's degree of involvement with and control of the child. For example, Earl Schaefer (1959) described parenting techniques in terms of combinations of these two dimensions, which he termed *love-hostility* and *autonomy-control.* (Other researchers have used slightly different terminology, for example, warmth-hostility and restrictiveness-permissiveness [Becker, 1964].)

Based on extensive interviews, Schaefer rated mothers (fathers were not studied) as *democratic* if they were highly affectionate with their children and also encouraged them to be independent and try new things (high autonomy). Although the children were not allowed complete freedom, these mothers kept rule enforcement to a minimum. Schaefer labeled as *overprotective,* mothers who were rated as high on love and high on control. These mothers coupled their frequent expressions of affection for the child with many restrictions. A combination of autonomy and hostility was called *neglecting* and referred to a pattern of low affection with few attempts to modify the child's behavior, while mothers who were both controlling and hostile were termed *authoritarian-dictatorial.*

Schaefer's observations of the children of mothers exhibiting these parenting styles suggested that preschoolers of democratic mothers were active, assertive, and cooperative, while preschoolers of mothers exhibiting neglecting, overprotective, or authoritarian-dictatorial patterns were either very conforming to adults or uncooperative and aggressive.

Parenting Styles and Child Competence

The most extensive investigation of how parenting techniques are related to preschoolers' behaviors was conducted by Diana Baumrind (1967, 1973, 1977), who built on and expanded Schaefer's approach. Baumrind asked what parenting techniques would be associated with *instrumentally competent* preschoolers, that is, children who were friendly, cooperative, independent, self-controlled, achievement-oriented, and energetic. To answer this question, she observed a group of 95 preschoolers and rated the quality of their peer play.

Through interviews and observations of the children's mothers and fathers, four major dimensions of parenting were identified: control, clarity of communication, maturity demands, and nurturance. *Control* and *nurturance* were similar to the dimensions of autonomy-control and love-hostility identified by Schaefer. *Clarity of communication* referred to the degree to which the parent asked the child's opinion and explained the reasons for decisions or discipline affecting the child. *Maturity demands* were defined as the parents' expectations for their children to perform up to their highest potential.

Just as Schaefer felt parenting could be best described not in terms of single dimensions but in terms of combinations of dimensions, so too did

Baumrind describe parenting styles as *combinations* of control, nurturance, clarity of communication, and maturity demands. As Figure 11–1 shows, the *authoritarian* parenting style, similar to Schaefer's authoritarian-dictatorial style, was high in control and low in nurturance. In addition, parents exhibiting this style did not solicit the child's opinion but did make high maturity demands. Parents who used a *permissive* approach were low in control and high in nurturance and often asked the child's opinion but did not demand much. A third style, *authoritative,* combined high control, high nurturance, high clarity of communication, and high maturity demands. Finally, a small group of parents were labeled *harmonious,* because issues of control rarely seemed to come up. These parents had control of their children, and their interactions had the quality of harmony, reciprocity, and equality.

Baumrind found a relationship between parenting style and instrumental competence in the preschoolers. Parents who tended to use an authoritative or harmonious style had children who were friendly, cooperative, independent, achieving, and full of vitality. On the other hand, children of authoritarian parents were withdrawn, shy among their peers, and less energetic. Boys were more hostile and aggressive than their peers. Interestingly, children of permissive parents also exhibited a lack of instrumental competence. Baumrind (1973) interpreted this in terms of the parents' providing a challenging yet supportive environment for the child. High nurturance and clear communication gives the preschooler a continued sense of positive attachment to the parent, while

Figure 11–1

Profile of Composite Parent Dimension Scores for Each Pattern [SRSO = Laboratory observation; HVSA = Home visit observation]

(From Baumrind, *Genetic Psychology Monographs,* Vol. 75, p. 73 Figure 2, 1967. Reprinted with permission of the Helen Dwight Reid Educational Foundation, 4000 Albermarle NW, Washington, DC 20016. Owner of copyright, 1967, Reid Foundation.)

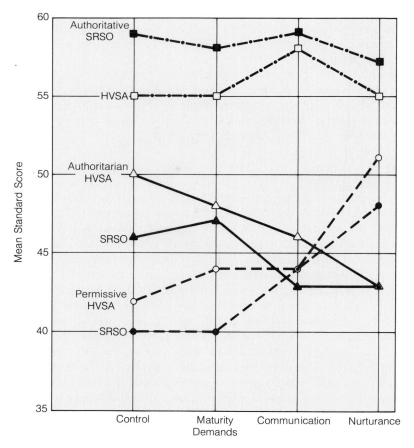

high maturity demands and control encourage the child to be independent and achieving.

Psychoanalytic theory and learning theory, although describing the process of socialization quite differently, both lead to predictions concerning parenting techniques that are compatible with Baumrind's results. Psychoanalytic theory sees the combination of warmth and control as helping the child resolve the Oedipal conflict, since these characteristics would predispose the child to both love and perceive the parent as powerful. In learning theory terms, the authoritative parent could be viewed as a rewarding and powerful model.

Cognitive theory and systems theory views of socialization have, however, challenged the interpretation that authoritative parenting *causes* instrumental competence in preschoolers (Bell, 1968; Bell & Harper, 1977), arguing that parents are likely to respond to a friendly, cooperative, and independent child with greater warmth, reasoning, and maturity demands than if they are confronted with a withdrawn or hostile child. Also, parents' cognitions about different socialization situations are likely to influence parenting behaviors, suggesting that parents are less consistent in the ways they treat their young children than Baumrind's typology would suggest.

In a study by Grusec and Kuczynski (1980), 40 mothers of children ages four to eight years were asked to respond to 12 different situations of child misbehavior, such as a child taking money from the mother's purse, ignoring calls to dinner, ignoring warnings of danger, and hurting others physically or psychologically (by calling names).

Instead of showing a consistent pattern, the responses varied by situation. For example, mothers reported they would be more likely to use an authoritative approach when psychological harm had been done to others than in situations where the child's immediate compliance was important (taking hand away from a hot stove). Moreover, mothers reported that rather than exhibiting a consistent parenting style, they used multiple techniques and adjusted their behavior to that of the child. As Table 11–2 indicates, eight different disciplinary techniques were mentioned by over half the mothers.

To determine if mothers would actually behave as they reported, Kuczynski (1984) observed 64 mothers and their four-year-old children. Half the mothers were told that they should get their child to complete a task sorting forks and spoons, but only in the mother's presence, while the other mothers were told that their child's compliance would be assessed later in the mother's absence. Detailed observations of all the mothers with their children showed that when these parents wanted their children to comply in their absence, they were more nurturant and used more reasoning and explanations. Mothers aiming only for short-term compliance gave more commands, threats, and demands for attention. Interestingly, all children, regardless of the mother's goal, were more compliant and worked more diligently at the task both in their mother's presence and, later, in her absence if the mother used reasoning and not commands or threats.

These studies show that parents vary in their parenting techniques, depending upon the child and the parent's appraisal of the situation, a finding that supports cognitive theory and systems theory. However, the results of Kuczynski's observational study (1984) also provide support for Baumrind's view that across a variety of situations, authoritative parenting is a more successful strategy than more authoritarian means for getting children's cooperation.

Table 11–2

DISCIPLINE TECHNIQUES IN ORDER OF SELF-REPORTED USAGE

Description	Percent of Mothers Using	Total Frequency of Usage
Power assertion—withdrawal of privileges	95	117
Matter-of-fact induction; description of rules or consequences of behavior; statement of norms	95	113
Power assertion—forced performance of appropriate behavior; forced compliance with request	95	103
Other-oriented induction; description of physical or emotional consequences for others, including mother	80	57
Power assertion—verbal; threats, yells, commands, shame	72	57
Power assertion—physical; physical punishment	68	76
Social or physical isolation; for example, sent to room, withdrawal of love verbally or by physical separation from mother	63	40
No reaction; disobedience ignored	58	39
Child diverted to an acceptable behavior	48	25
Simple request for compliance	23	11

(From Grusec & Kuczynski, *Developmental Psychology*, 16, p. 4. Copyright 1980 by the American Psychological Association. Reprinted by permission of the authors.)

A final criticism of the authoritative parenting-child competence link we'd like to mention comes from cross-cultural studies of parenting (Whiting and Whiting, 1975; LeVine, 1977). Many observations of childrearing in rural, nonindustrialized societies note that parents often spend little time with their young children, rarely communicate democratically with them, seldom praise them, and often assert parental power to enforce rules. Although this is clearly not authoritative parenting, children in these cultures generally grow up to be competent, self-controlled adults. This suggests that instrumental competence is a *culture specific* term, whose meaning varies with the particular context in which the child is growing up, and that the parenting techniques associated with competence in different cultures are likely to vary. For example, parental values in many African and other non-Western cultures stress the interdependence of individuals within the community rather than individual independence and achievement. In such cultures, the instrumentally competent child is one who is cooperative, obedient, and respectful of others (LeVine, 1977). These findings are consonant with the emphasis of systems theory on the cultural context of parent-child relations.

In Western industrialized societies, however, the implications of theories of socialization and the results of research investigating different parenting styles concur that authoritative parenting is associated with positive child characteristics. The theories disagree in explaining the process underlying this association. We suggest that authoritative parenting both encourages competence in the preschooler and is, in turn, affected by the child's own characteristics. Although we need to be sensitive to the ways in which children contribute to their own socialization, we should not exaggerate their influence and assume that parental behavior has little impact. Parents, after all, have explicit goals for their children, strategies for achieving these goals, and societal support for their role as childrearers.

Child Abuse

The parents in Baumrind's study whose socialization style was authoritarian were not abusing their children. Although definitions of child abuse vary, they commonly refer to behaviors that intentionally harm the child physically or psychologically. Sexual abuse is a particularly damaging form of abuse (Browne & Finkelhor, 1986) and refers to any use of the child's body for an adult's sexual gratification, ranging from stroking or fondling to sexual intercourse (Burgess, Groth, Holmstrom, & Sgroi, 1978).

It is estimated that each year, over 500,000 children are beaten, burned, sexually abused, or otherwise harmed by their parents, although precise figures are not available. Most people agree that the rate of child abuse probably has not escalated in recent years; rather, greater public attention and concern has increased our awareness of the problem.

Characteristics of Abusive Parents

Despite popular belief that abuse occurs only in poor families or among emotionally disturbed individuals, abusive parents are found in all social classes and are no more likely to be mentally ill than nonabusive parents (Gil, 1970). In comparison with nonabusers, these parents are more likely to be immature and socially isolated and have low self-esteem (Gil, 1970; Egeland, Breitenbucher, & Rosenberg, 1980). Often they are misinformed about normal patterns of child develop-

ment and thus have unrealistic expectations about what their children can be expected to do. For example, they may expect a 12-month-old infant to be toilet trained and a three-year-old to make her own supper. In addition, they expect a young child to provide them with nurture, rather than see nurturing as a parental responsibility. Finally, many parents who abuse report that they themselves were victims of abuse as children (Steele & Pollack, 1968; deLissovoy, 1973; Bee, Disbrow, Johnson-Crowley, & Barnard, 1981).

Characteristics of the Abused Child

Not all young children are equally likely to be victims of abuse, even in families where abuse is occurring. The abused child is often reported to be difficult to manage, excessively crying, aggressive, restless, and irritable. Infants who pose exceptionally heavy burdens on their parents, because of low birth weight or other reasons, are more at risk for later abuse than "easier" babies (Gil, 1971; Parke & Collmer, 1975). When an at-risk parent (with the characteristics listed above) cares for such an at-risk child, the chances of abuse further increase.

Characteristics of the Setting

In addition to parent and child characteristics, child abuse has been identified as part of a larger family pattern of violence. Spouse abuse may also be occurring, and siblings may be behaving destructively toward one another (Steinmetz & Straus, 1974). In such families, violence is often perceived as the way to solve problems (Baer, 1984).

Beyond the family, qualities of the neighborhood and of the larger culture can affect abuse. Neighborhoods that are unstable and physically deteriorated and that lack child care or support services for families tend to have higher rates of child abuse (Garbarino & Sherman, 1980). Moreover, cultures that accept physical punishment of children, tolerate a high level of violence among adults, and provide many sexually stimulating media images may create conditions that make child abuse more likely (Parke & Collmer, 1975). For example, Sweden, which has a child abuse rate far below that of the United States, recently outlawed spanking, even by the child's parents.

Combating Child Abuse

Child abuse is a crime, and following the passage of the Child Abuse Prevention and Treatment Act of 1974, each state enacted laws that require suspected child abuse to be reported. When child abuse is found, group and individual counseling with parents is usually used to help parents learn alternative problem-solving methods and develop supportive social contacts. Support groups such as Parents Anonymous, modeled after Alcoholics Anonymous (AA), have been successful. "Crisis nurseries" or other substitute care arrangements may give overburdened parents respite from the 24-hour demands of parenting.

Intervention, such as play therapy, for the child victim is necessary in most cases. Since young children are deeply attached to and dependent upon their abusive parents, permanently removing the child from the home is usually a last resort.

Family Structures: Effects on the Child

When you picture a family, you probably see a mother, a father, and one or two children (perhaps with the family dog or cat in the background). Because our mental images of family are influenced by both our own childhood experiences and by media portrayals, it's easy to forget that family forms differ in many ways. Rather than having one picture, we need a whole album of portraits to capture the diversity that currently exists in family life.

Differences in family forms, or *structure,* have been studied most intensively by anthropologists, the most famous of whom were Margaret Mead, Ruth Benedict, and, more recently, John and Beatrice Whiting (refer to Chapters 3, 10). They pointed out that some cultures are characterized by *polygynous* family structures, in which husbands may have several wives. This often means that several wives of the same husband cooperate in childrearing, and the father may rarely see the child in the early years.

Another important difference in family structure studied by anthropologists concerns where a husband and wife live after marriage. Western industrialized societies are *neolocal;* that is, newly formed couples are expected to establish an independent household (although financial or other circumstances may prevent them from doing so). However, in *matrilocal* cultures, newlyweds are expected to live with the wife's family, while in *patrilocal* cultures, residence with the husband's family is the norm.

These differences in where families live are often paralleled by differences in how descent is figured. Cultures whose members trace their lineage through their mothers, taking on their mother's names, are called *matrilineal,* while cultures where descent is determined through the fathers are termed *patrilineal.* Variations in family structure in different cultures are summarized in Table 11–3.

Cultural distinctions have many implications for young children's experiences within the family. In matrilocal, matrilineal families, mothers, aunts, and grandmothers are likely to be a more important part of the young child's family world than in patrilocal, patrilineal families. Later in the chapter, and in our discussions of the family life of older children (Chapters 15 and 17), we will return to these cultural variations in family structure, but for the time

In some cultures, grandparents, cousins, aunts and uncles may live in the same household with the child. In such circumstances, children form multiple attachments, and parent-child interaction is markedly different from that occuring in Western nuclear families.

Table 11—3

EXAMPLES OF DIFFERENT FAMILY STRUCTURES

Structural Characteristics	Brief Definition
Patterns of residence	
Neolocal	Married couple establishes residence independent of parents.
Patrilocal	Married couple lives with husband's family.
Matrilocal	Married couple lives with wife's family.
Bilocal	Married couple lives with either the husband's or the wife's family.
Household composition	
Nuclear	Independent family unit of one husband, one wife, and their children.
Extended	Two or more married couples and their children.
Types of approved marriages	
Monogamy	Union of one man with one woman.
Polyandry	Union of one woman with two or more men.
Polygymy	Union of one man with two or more women.

(From Sahlins, 1968; Murdock, 1959.)

being, keep in mind that many conclusions about parent-child and sibling relations are based on research conducted on the Western family form, which is based on neolocal, nuclear family structures.

Focusing on these broad cultural differences may give the impression that within a culture, families basically share the same structure. However, in recent decades, many changes in family life have occurred in North America, and there is increasing diversity within our own culture. A rising divorce rate, coupled with greater acceptance of childrearing outside of marriage, has meant that many young children are living in single-parent homes, almost always with their mothers (Chapters 10 and 15). And since approximately 80 percent of those who divorce eventually remarry, another family form becoming increasingly common is that of the *reconstituted* or *blended* family, in which previously divorced adults, often with children of their own, form a new household. Such families can be large, complex networks of relationships. Young children may be growing up with a parent, stepparent, siblings, and stepsiblings, while still maintaining ties with a noncustodial parent. Although we know remarkably little about the effects of blended families on young children (Santrock et al., 1982), more research has focused on single parenting after divorce.

 The Effects of Divorce on the Preschool Child

The most comprehensive research in this area was a two-year investigation of the impact of divorce and maternal custody on a group of 50 white, middle-class preschoolers conducted by E. Mavis Hetherington and her colleagues (Hetherington et al., 1978, 1979a, 1979b, 1982). Unlike the investigations of parenting we've examined thus far, this study is based on systems theory. In addition, it is an excellent model of a *multimethod, multimeasure* approach, using a variety of measures rather than only one or two.

Similar to the studies of Schaefer and Baumrind, parents were interviewed (fathers and mothers separately) to assess parenting techniques. In addition, information was collected about their relationship with the ex-spouse, family organization, economic stress, availability of economic and psychological support outside the family, and different aspects of the parents' personalities. Parents were asked to keep a diary for three days, indicating for each half hour their activities and their feelings at the time. Each parent and child was observed in both free play and structured situations.

Parents were asked to rate their children's behaviors, each child was observed during free play and during structured activities in nursery school, and teacher ratings of the child's behavior were obtained. Measures of the child's cognitive functioning, sex-role development, and acceptance by peers were collected. Each of these child and parent assessments was repeated three times: two months, one year, and two years after the divorce, and the results were compared with the responses of a control group of similar families who did not experience divorce.

Divorced parents made fewer maturity demands, communicated less well, and were less affectionate and more inconsistent in discipline than were the nondivorced parents, and this pattern was especially marked for divorced mothers interacting with their preschool sons. These mothers, attempting to control their children, behaved in an authoritarian fashion, while the noncustodial divorced fathers behaved permissively. This pattern was observed two months after divorce, was most pronounced one year later, and gradually moderated two years after the divorce. By that time, both mothers and fathers were behaving toward their children in a more authoritative manner.

Observations and ratings of the children's behavior indicated that the children became increasingly disruptive, aggressive, and dependent during the year following divorce. Boys particularly gave their mothers a hard time, and Hetherington reports some divorced mothers describing their relationship with their sons as "declared war," "a struggle for survival," and "like getting bitten to death by ducks" (Hetherington, 1982, p. 258). As with the parents' behavior, children were most negative one year after the divorce, and by two years later had markedly improved in behavior.

Consistent with systems theory, Hetherington's analysis does not conclude that poor parenting by divorced parents *causes* these negative child behaviors. Nor does she believe that parents are reacting solely to their children's misbehavior. Rather, she argues that both parents and children are mutually affecting one another in a vicious circle. For example, a mother's authoritarian attempts to get compliance from her son trigger hostility, which in turn leads the mother to be more coercive.

Hetherington's findings provide some support for the psychoanalytic view that preschool boys need a father in the home with whom to identify. (The noncustodial fathers in the study were seldom available to their children.) Another interpretation, based on systems theory, is that young boys may be vulnerable to stress generally, since Hetherington also found that boys were affected more adversely by marital conflict in nondivorced families (refer to Chapter 7).

Other research on the reaction of preschoolers to divorce suggests that cognitive limitations may make it difficult for young boys and girls to understand what is happening to the family. In interviews conducted with 60 middle-class children from California at the time of divorce and again one year later, Wallerstein and Kelly (1980) found that preschoolers were likely to blame themselves for the breakup of the marriage.

Adjusting to Divorce.   Research suggests a number of factors (summarized in Table 11–4) that seem to help families of young children weather the crisis of divorce and ultimately improve parent-child relations. As suggested by sys-

The majority of mothers of young children now juggle the demands of parenting and employment outside the home.

Table 11–4

FACTORS ASSOCIATED WITH
POSITIVE ADJUSTMENT TO
DIVORCE

Factor	Primarily Affects
Father's prior participation in child care and household during marriage.	Father
Mother's employment.	Mother
Mother does not begin employment during separation/divorce period.	Children
Establishment of new intimate relationship.	Mother and father
Low conflict with ex-spouse.	All family members
High paternal availability.	Children, especially sons
Authoritative parenting, especially by mother.	Children
Organized, predictable, and responsive school environment.	Children
Support in childrearing approach from ex-spouse.	Parent-child relationship
Supportive relationship with others outside the family, especially grandparents.	All family members
Positive relationship with stepfather in cases of remarriage.	Sons

(From Hetherington, Cox, & Cox, 1982.)

tems theory, many aspects of the family, including the relationship between the parents, economic stress, and relations with grandparents and others outside the family, affect the quality of parenting after divorce.

One important change in the family system that often occurs following divorce is *maternal employment*. Since only about 30 percent of divorced mothers regularly receive the full child support payments they are awarded, the vast majority of single parents are economically responsible for their children (U.S. Census Bureau, 1981). In addition, in recent decades, many mothers in nondivorced families have been taking jobs outside the home (Norton & Moorman, 1987).

Sibling Relations

The systems perspective we've applied to the impact of divorce and maternal employment on the young child suggests that all the relationships within the family mutually affect one another (refer to Chapter 7). This means that we cannot understand socialization completely without also considering sibling relations.

As every older brother or sister knows, the advent of a sibling changes many aspects of the parent-child relationship. Perhaps the most obvious change is the decrease in parental attention and time experienced by the first-born. This can produce feelings of jealousy and anger in a preschooler as well as in a toddler (refer to Chapter 7); it's not unusual for a four-year-old to demand that mommy "take the baby back." Thus, in one observational study of preschoolers with their younger siblings, conflict between mother and first-born was most likely when the mother was feeding and playing with the baby (Kendrick & Dunn, 1980). When the same families were observed 14 months later, quarrels between siblings were most likely when the mother behaved differently toward the siblings (Kendrick & Dunn, 1982).

Dunn and Kendrick (1982) found that when mothers drew the first-born into discussion of the baby as a person with feelings, wants, and needs for whom they could both take responsibility, the siblings were observed to play in a more friendly, positive way 14 months later. These discussions, begun

How Does Maternal Employment Affect Parent–Child Relations and Child Development?

Let's begin by looking at some of the changes in the family system that generally occur when mothers of young children are employed. The most obvious change perhaps is that in non-divorced families, dual employment enhances the economic resources of the family, with full-time employed mothers contributing about 40 percent of the family income (Hayghe, 1979).

At the same time, employed mothers are less available to perform the homemaking and child care tasks of a full-time home-maker. Since most families are unable to hire someone to perform these tasks, a division of labor must be worked out. However, most studies find little difference between dual-employed and other families. For example, one investigation of time use reported that husbands of employed women spent approximately 15 minutes more per week on family work than did husbands of homemakers (Pleck & Rustad, 1980).

The result for many employed mothers is *role overload,* a condition in which stress is felt from multiple responsibilities. One such responsibility is finding adequate child care. For many parents, this is a difficult problem, and it is not unusual for them to piece together a variety of substitute care arrangements to cover their working hours (Lein, 1979).

Awareness of these stresses has led some people to caution against maternal employment, at least during infancy and the preschool years (White, 1975; Fraiberg, 1977). However, available research does not indicate any clear pattern of effects on children. Many factors influence the impact of maternal employment on young children.

Quality of substitute child care is one important factor. When that care is consistent, warm, and encouraging of the child's development—in short, having the qualities of authoritative parenting—no adverse consequences of maternal employment have been found. Indeed, it has been suggested that children from economically or psychologically stressed homes may benefit from the opportunity to interact with peers and responsive adults in a supportive setting (Gordon, 1984).

The mother's attitude toward her roles as mother and worker is also important. Satisfaction with role, whether full-time homemaker or employed person, not the role itself, has been related to effective parenting (Hoffman, 1979). It is likely that the mother's positive and negative feelings about what she is doing are communicated in many ways to the young child. Similarly, when husbands are supportive and helpful, mothers feel less role overload and more satisfaction, and this affects the quality of their interactions with their children (Pederson, Anderson, & Cain, 1977).

The timing of changes in employment status are likely to affect the child and the entire family. When any major change in family routine is made, many adjustments are required and it is not unusual for young children to experience some stress. For example, they may revert to more babyish behavior for a while until they become used to the new routine. If a mother begins employment at the same time that the young child is coping with other major changes, such as divorce or a move, the adjustment is likely to be particularly difficult. Thus, in Hetherington's study of divorce, mother-child relations were poorest in families where the mother began employment soon after the divorce but were unaffected in families where the mother had been employed all along (Hetherington et al., 1982).

Interestingly, maternal employment has not been related to any decline in amount of time most mothers spend with children. This seems to be because employed mothers decrease their sleep and leisure activities to maintain the same level of involvement with their children and participation in household work.

Because many factors are acting together to affect the child, generalizations about the effects of maternal employment should be made with caution. In addition, many studies on the effects of maternal employment were conducted several decades ago, when employment by mothers of young children was unusual. Finally, very little information is available on long-term effects of maternal employment during the child's infancy and preschool years. Meanwhile, employment outside the home is a fact of life for millions of single-parent and dual-parent families.

when the mother was pregnant, helped the child to prepare for the advent of a new family member and encouraged the first-born to adopt more mature, independent behaviors, something that helps parents who suddenly have to cope with both a helpless infant and a young child (Dunn, 1983).

Although we often tend to think of young siblings as jealous and fighting, systematic observations of sibling pairs in the home show that preschoolers, after initially adjusting to the presence of an infant, soon develop a strong attachment to their young sibling, and an intense, complex relationship between them soon develops. To be sure, this relationship has elements of rivalry, but it is an oversimplification to characterize it in these terms alone (refer to Chapter 7.)

Siblings show both intense positive and negative emotions toward one another. Judy Dunn, whose observations of sibling relations in early childhood were described earlier, sums up the relationship in this way:

> Toward their siblings, children under 4 years of age can and do act as comforters, teachers, devious manipulative bullies, or sensitive companions entering the play world of the other. And this range of different roles, the very aspects of the sibling relationship that make it difficult to characterize in simple dimensions, demonstrates the wide range of capabilities that even two-year-olds possess (1983, p. 807).

Siblings are important individuals to each other in part because they spend a lot of time in each other's company. For example, in a study of 54 two-child families in London, Lawson and Ingleby (1974) found that by the time the younger child was one year of age, siblings were spending as much time with each other as with their mothers and far more time than with their fathers.

In many cultures, siblings spend more time in each other's company than they do with anyone else, including their mothers (Whiting & Whiting, 1975). This is because, in many non-Western societies, older children, especially girls, are expected to care for their younger siblings while their mothers are working (Weisner & Gallimore, 1977). Even in our own culture, where caring for young siblings is not a regular expectation, older siblings often comfort, reassure, monitor, and teach their younger brothers and sisters. For example, in Stewart's (1983) observations of 54 sibling pairs, over half the four-year-olds were successful in comforting and reassuring their younger siblings who were dis-

During the early years, brothers and sisters are "best enemies" . . . and best friends!
(Source: Sendak)

tressed by separation from their mother. When a stranger entered the room after the mother had left, the younger children moved closer to their older siblings, using them as a secure base from which to then direct friendly overtures to the stranger.

Other observations of preschoolers with their younger siblings (Pepler, 1981) find numerous examples of teaching as part of the sibling relationship. Older siblings demonstrated how to use a toy and how to play a game, taught words, and helped the younger siblings practice physical skills such as climbing.

The Only Child

The extensive influence that siblings have on one another raises the possibility that only children may be missing out on important socializing experiences. For example, in a study conducted in China, comparing 180 children with siblings to only children of the same age, sex, and family background, the only children were rated by their classmates as more self-centered, less cooperative, less popular, and less persistent (Tiao, Ti, & Ting, 1986). Although some American research also identifies only children as less popular and less friendly (Miller & Maruyana, 1976), Toni Falbo (1984) in a review of research on only children concludes that such children do not differ from other children in self-esteem or mental health and may even exhibit higher competencies in social skills and academic achievement. In general, the effect of sibling status itself is difficult to determine, since parents of only children may differ in systematic ways.

Peers

In North America and in other industrialized societies, most of preschoolers' experience with other children outside the family takes place with *peers*, that is, children of approximately the same age and developmental level. Still, neighborhoods and gatherings of relatives provide some opportunity for *mixed-age* interaction with both younger and older children. In nonindustrialized cultures, mixed-age interactions are more common than peer interaction (Konner, 1975).

The Nature of Play

When preschoolers get together, they play. However, no consensus exists about how to define play. This is not surprising considering the diverse activities— contests, games, fantasy, reverie, sports, dramatics, constructions—that are considered "play." It has been suggested that play is best defined not by any particular activities, but by the manner in which activities are carried out. In this view, *play* is any spontaneous, pleasurable activity (Bruner, 1972; Garvey, 1977; Rubin, Fein, & Vandenberg, 1983).

Some researchers have distinguished *exploration* from play. Exploration refers to the determination of the properties of a novel object or environment, as if the child were asking, "What is this?" For example, a child might turn an unfamiliar toy slowly, perhaps shaking it or poking it. As the child becomes more familiar with the toy, exploration shifts to play as the child uses a more relaxed, flexible manipulation of the object. The child's goal now is, "What can I do with this?" Corinne Hutt, a British psychologist, has shown that subtle physiological changes occur as children shift from exploring a novel object to playing with it (1979). Heartbeats are less variable during exploration than during play.

Varieties of Play

Piaget (1963) described a developmental progression during the preschool years in the kinds of play most likely to occur. The child first engages mainly in *practice play,* where after a skill has been acquired, it is repeated with "deliberate complications." An example of this is a child going down a slide. At first, the child goes down warily, careful to go down the "right" way, feet first. Once the slide has been mastered, the child delights in going down backwards or head first. According to Piaget, the pleasure of practice play comes from a sense of control over self and environment.

Out of practice play develops *symbolic play* (also called *fantasy play*). Three types are identified. In *object fantasy play,* the child uses play materials to represent some imaginary thing. The slide becomes a mountain to climb and roll down. In *person fantasy play,* the child pretends to be someone else, like a mountain climber. When children coordinate such pretend activities with others, it is called *social pretend play* or *sociodramatic play* and usually involves the assumption and coordination of different roles. For example, when children play house, one may take the role of mommy, one of daddy, and one of baby. Children playing in this way indicate they are aware of the make-believe nature of their play and can step in and out of a role. Thus, if the child playing daddy suddenly develops an interest in cuddling a soft blanket, the other two role players might protest, "You can't do that! You're still the daddy!" Another characteristic of social pretend play is the development of a common theme. As the children coordinate roles to play house, each child contributes to the resulting "script." If the blanket cuddler doesn't want to resume the role of daddy, she might say, "No, it's my turn to be baby. You be daddy now." In this way, social play also involves developing rules for social interaction, such as *turn taking* (refer to Chapter 10) (Garvey, 1974, 1977; Damon, 1983).

According to Piaget, the final stage in the development of play is the emergence of *games with rules* during the early school years. Here, play is

Examples of solitary, parallel and associative play may be observed in this playground scene.

governed by formal, relatively inflexible rules, involves some competition, and may produce some anxiety. For example, in a game like hide-and-seek, the rules require the seeker to count to some number, say 100, before beginning a search. Another rule requires the hiders to elude the seeker and reach "home" before being tagged. When preschoolers are included in this game, they usually have trouble following the rules. Naturally, they can't count to 100, but they also often give away their hiding place by calling out to the seeker.

Another influential stage theory of play was advanced by Mildred Parten in 1932. She focused on the development of interpersonal responsiveness among children as they played. Parten viewed preschoolers as progressing from unoccupied behavior through the stages of solitary, parallel, associative, and cooperative play. In *solitary play,* the child plays alone. In *parallel play,* other children are close by and engage in similar behavior but do not affect one another. In *associative play,* children play together and adapt their behavior to others but do not assume different and complementary roles. Only in *cooperative play* is the behavior of children coordinated around a common goal.

The stage theories of Parten and of Piaget are compared in Table 11–5. Both theories view increasingly complex forms of play emerging from simpler forms. It is true that social play appears later than both parallel and practice play, and with age, play that involves interaction among children increases while noninteractive play declines (Johnson & Ershler, 1981). Social play, involving role coordination, pretend activities, development of a common theme, and turn taking, increases in frequency during the preschool years (Parten, 1932, Smith & Connelly, 1972; Rubin & Maioni, 1975; Rubin & Pepler, 1980). For example, in Parten's observations of 42 children between two and five years of age, social play occurred only 3 percent of the time in the play of children under three years of age, 22 percent of the time among three- to four-year-olds, and 26 percent of the time among four- to five-year-olds.

Table 11–5

STAGE THEORIES OF PLAY: PIAGET AND PARTEN

	STAGE OF PLAY	DESCRIPTION
PIAGET	Practice play	Repeated movements to consolidate, perfect, or elaborate a skill. Example: Going down a slide.
	Symbolic play	Play in which one thing stands for another. Example: Playing house.
	Games with rules	Play involving rules and competition between individuals or groups. Example: Hide-and-seek.
PARTEN	Solitary play	Child plays alone. Example: Child sits alone in sandbox and fills pail with sand.
	Parallel play	Play in close proximity to other children but without interaction. Example: Two children sit next to each other in a sandbox, each filling a pail.
	Associative play	Children respond to each other during play but maintain separate goals. Example: Two children talk to each other while playing with sand in a sandbox.
	Cooperative play	Play is organized around joint activities. Example: Two children work together to build a sand castle.

Parten's results, along with more recent studies, show that although social play becomes increasingly frequent over the preschool years, it still takes up only a small part of young children's time with peers. Although Parten, Piaget, and others (Sponseller & Jaworski, 1979; Tizard, Philps, & Plewis, 1976; Hendrick, 1975) interpreted solitary, parallel, and practice play as relatively immature, other research suggests they are alternate forms that fulfill different functions for the child (Rubin, 1982). For example, solitary play with objects may aid in developing problem-solving skills (Moore, Everston, & Brophy, 1974). In summary, preschoolers' play usually is a mixture of different types of play (Krasnor & Pepler, 1980).

The Role of Play in Development

"Make-believe" can be a way of mastering fears.
(Source: Sendak)

Psychoanalytic Theory.   From a psychoanalytic perspective, play provides young children with the opportunity to act out conflicts and fears in a safe environment. Thus, boys experiencing an Oedipal rivalry with their father can express aggressive impulses without fear of punishment. Fear of abandonment can be experienced and overcome in small, manageable doses in the game of hide-and-seek. This view of social play has given rise to techniques of *play therapy*, in which young children who have experienced a trauma, such as child abuse, are encouraged to express their feelings with dolls and other materials.

Psychoanalytic theory also emphasizes that the pretend themes of fantasy play allow the young child to satisfy unrealized desires and to overcome frustrations. For example, by playing house, children can take on in fantasy the parental roles that, in reality, they are coming to realize they are not ready to assume. Finally, because play is constructed by the children themselves and not imposed by others, it provides opportunities to build self-esteem. Children can construct play episodes that are within their capacities and that show off their strengths.

Learning Theory.   This view stresses that play can provide an excellent opportunity for children to reinforce each other's behavior. A good example of this is preschoolers' reinforcement of sex-typed behaviors. Over the preschool years, children increasingly play with same-sex peers (La Freniere, Strayer, & Gauthier, 1984), and generally more positive exchanges and less conflict occur in same-sex play than in mixed-sex peer play (Langlois, Gottfried, & Seay, 1973; Jacklin & Maccoby, 1978; Lamb & Roopnarine, 1979).

Between ages three and five, peers increasingly give positive reinforcement for "appropriate" sex-role behaviors and negative reinforcement for "inappropriate" behaviors (Lamb & Roopnarine, 1979). How this happens is illustrated in a study by Roopnarine (1984), in which the free play of 54 three- to four-year-olds was observed. Roopnarine defined as male-typed activities play with vehicles, ball games, hammering, and building with blocks, while female-typed activities were considered art, doll play, and pretend kitchen activities. A category of neutral activities (for example, puzzles) was also defined. An observer recorded each child's activity as well as the responses of peers immediately following it as positive if others laughed, smiled, imitated, or joined in, and as negative if the other children criticized the child, tried to change the activity, or left the child. As shown in Table 11–6, among three-year-olds, girls were most likely to get a positive response from their peers

Table 11-6

PERCENTAGE OF
OBSERVATIONS IN WHICH
TARGET CHILD RECEIVED
POSITIVE RESPONSES FROM
PEERS

Behaviors	Three-Year-Olds		Four-Year-Olds	
	Boys	Girls	Boys	Girls
Male-typed	18	18	47	18
Female-typed	11	47	6	36
Neutral	26	33	12	31

(From J. L. Roopnarine, *Child Development*, 1984, 55, p. 1081. © The Society for Research in Child Development.)

when they engaged in female-typed activities, but boys were not systematically reinforced for sex-appropriate behaviors. By age four, however, both boys and girls were being differentially reinforced by their peers to play in ways that reflect sex-role stereotypes. Other research shows that peers reinforce a wide range of other behaviors, such as cooperation, helping, and aggression (Lamb et al., 1980).

Social learning theorists emphasize that social play provides many opportunities for children to observe their peers as models and to imitate them. Children seem attracted to models that are perceived to be like them in important ways, as same-age, same-sex peers are. Moreover, imitation of peers is thought to be a good source of learning, because less advanced children can learn more from observing moderately more advanced models (peers) than from watching models whose behavior is much more advanced (adults). This is because children cannot readily imitate behavior that is too dramatically different from their own repertoire of skills (Piaget, 1951).

Indeed, preschoolers quite frequently imitate each other during play. Abramovitch & Grusec (1978) observed two preschool classes over a period of several weeks and found 14.6 and 11.8 imitations per hour on the average, compared to approximately five per hour in the early elementary grades and less than two per hour by grade six.

Support also exists for the prediction of social learning theory that in the course of play, peer imitation results in increased learning. In one study (Morrison and Kuhn, 1983), 102 preschoolers were observed playing individually with some building blocks, and the complexity of their constructions was rated. Groups of four children with varying levels of skill at this task were then observed playing together with the same materials. Children who watched and imitated their somewhat more advanced peers made more complex constructions, while those who did not imitate at all or who imitated less advanced peers showed no improvement.

Cognitive Theory. The significance of social play for cognitive theorists lies in the frequent opportunities it provides to assume different roles and experience different perspectives. Cognitive theorists see social play as a natural training ground for decreasing egocentrism, prompting awareness of the feelings of others, and providing opportunities for creativity, empathy and prosocial behavior (Zahn-Waxler, Iannotti, & Chapman, 1982). Although children with already developed perspective-taking and empathic skills may gravitate to social play where they can use these abilities (Hartup, 1983), there is evidence that social play, particularly social fantasy play, promotes interpersonal understanding (refer to Chapter 10) (Selman, 1976), enhanced problem-solving (Sylra, Bruner, & Genova, 1976; Vandenberg, 1980) and creative thinking in young children (Dansky & Silverman, 1973, 1975).

In summary, three major theories of development—psychoanalytic, learning, and cognitive—agree that social play with peers is beneficial for young children. Psychoanalytic theory emphasizes the opportunities provided to act out and master feelings, learning theory stresses the acquisition of behaviors through peer reinforcement and modeling, and cognitive theory describes advances in understanding from role playing.

Because of the developmental significance of social play from a variety of perspectives, there is concern about young children who lack this experience. Although the majority of children between three and five years of age participate regularly in some kind of peer group, some children are sought out by others and are frequently involved in social play while others are ignored or actively rejected by their peers.

Peer Acceptance

One way to determine how well a child is accepted would be to observe a group of preschoolers over a period of time and note which children were usually found playing alone versus playing with others. Although this method is used (Mize, 1984), it is not sufficient, since the reasons for the children's behavior are not clear. To determine how other children in a group feel about each other, researchers usually assess a child's *sociometric status* or social acceptance in a group by asking each child to name or choose from a set of pictures those children they most like or dislike to play with. Using such a procedure, Craig Peery (1979) identified two dimensions of sociometric status: impact and preference. *Impact,* measured by adding up all the times a child was mentioned by classmates, positively or negatively, refers to how noticed the child is by peers. *Preference,* measured by subtracting the negative mentions from the positive ones, refers to how liked the child is. Combinations of these two dimensions resulted in four sociometric statuses, as shown in Table 11–7.

Popular children were mentioned frequently and positively by their peers, while rejected children were also frequently mentioned, though usually negatively. By contrast, isolated or neglected children were seldom mentioned by their classmates, but when they were, it was negatively. Amiable children similarly received little mention, but most of it was positive. These distinctions in sociometric status suggest that two groups of children—the rejected and the neglected—are being shut out from the benefits of social play, but in differing ways.

Is rejection or neglect by peers a lasting problem? Preschoolers' relations with peers are less stable than are older children's, and fluctuations in sociometric status do occur, especially when children are just getting acquainted. Although assessments of stability vary with the particular method used to measure sociometric status and with the length of interval between assessments, in general, children's sociometric status stays about the same over time. For

Preference	Impact	
	High	Low
Positive	Popular	Amiable
Negative	Rejected	Isolated or neglected

(From C. Peery, *Child Development*, 1979, *50*, p. 1232. © The Society for Research in Child Development.)

Table 11–7

FOUR SOCIOMETRIC STATUSES FOUND IN PRESCHOOL PEER GROUPS

example, in one study, when preschoolers' sociometric status was measured every four weeks, there was a positive correlation between weeks of .74–.81 (Asher, Singleton, Tinsley, & Hymel, 1979). Thus, there is reason to believe that young children who are rejected or ignored by their peers experience this as an enduring problem.

To some extent, sociometric status has been associated with physical attractiveness and ethnic background (Langlois & Stephan, 1977), with children perceived as attractive (according to adult standards) and ethnically similar being more popular. Other research has found differences in behavior among children varying in sociometric status. Popular children are more friendly and socially skilled than others, while rejected children, though friendly, often use more antisocial, inappropriate ways of interacting, such as getting another child's attention by breaking his or her toy (Masters & Furman, 1981). Children who are isolated or neglected make fewer friendly overtures to other children; rather, they are often seen hovering on the outskirts of groups, watching.

Do these differences in social behavior cause a child's social standing among peers, or are they a result of sociometric status itself? Although research on preschoolers provides only correlations between behaviors and peer acceptance, studies of elementary school-age children suggest that lack of social skills contributes to peer rejection (see Chapter 15).

Friendship

Sociometric status is a measure of the child's social standing within a group. Regardless of the child's level of acceptance, friendships may still form between individual pairs of children. *Friendship* refers to children's mutual preference for one another. It is a kind of attachment that two children feel for each other and is characterized by strong positive feelings. Thus, young children who are rejected or ignored by most of their peers may still have one or two friends.

Although certain characteristics of friendship endure throughout the life span, the meaning of friendship changes with development, and preschoolers'

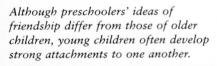

Although preschoolers' ideas of friendship differ from those of older children, young children often develop strong attachments to one another.

friendships are not the same as those of older children. We can illustrate this by looking at young children's concept of friendship.

Interviewer: Why is Caleb your friend?
Tony: Because I like him.
Interviewer: And why do you like him?
Tony: Because he's my friend.
Interviewer: And why is he your friend?
Tony (speaking each word distinctly, with a tone of mild disgust at the interviewer's obvious deafness):
Because . . . I . . . choosed . . . him . . . for . . . my . . . friend (Rubin, 1980, p. 34).

Preschoolers like Tony have difficulty articulating what they mean by *friend*, although they use the term and show stable mutual preferences that we adults would call friendship. When they do mention reasons, they are apt to see friends in terms of common activities, play preferences, or simply propinquity ("We're friends because she sits next to me.") (Hayes, 1978; Rubin, 1980; Furman & Bierman, 1983).

Despite the fact that preschoolers show little understanding of the idea of friendship in adult terms, when playing with friends, young children exhibit more prosocial behaviors such as sharing (Gottman & Parkhurst, 1980; Furman & Masters, 1980; Masters & Furman, 1981), play longer, engage in more complex and social play (Howes, 1984), and show more communicative competence (refer to Chapter 10) (Gottman, 1983) than they do when playing with nonfriends. Thus, having a friend appears to provide children with many opportunities to benefit from social play experiences.

Mixed-Age Groups

Rather than being characterized by the social play we've described as part of peer interaction, mixed-age groups are more often characterized by what might be called "teaching-learning" or "leading-following" play. When preschoolers play with younger children, they simplify their language and behavior (Shatz & Gelman, 1973), demonstrate skills, direct and monitor behavior, and thus resemble older siblings more than they do their peers. When playing with older children, preschoolers watch, imitate, seek help, and follow more than they do with peers. Another difference between peer and mixed-age groups involving young children is that the latter are less likely to be of the same sex (Harkness & Super, 1983).

Melvin Konner (1975), an anthropologist who has observed African children's play in mixed-age groups, feels that such groups promote development in several ways. First, by providing children the opportunity to practice caretaking and teaching toward younger children, they may encourage nurturance, perspective taking, empathy, and prosocial behavior (Fogel & Melson, 1986). At the same time, Konner believes that they provide valuable practice for future adult parenting roles.

Some support for this view comes from the six cultures study discussed in Chapters 3 and 10. In each of the six cultures, the types of behaviors children directed to younger children (infants and toddlers), peers, and adults were compared. As shown in Table 11–8, children behaved more nurturantly toward younger children than they did toward peers or adults.

Table 11–8

PERCENTAGES OF DIFFERENT
TYPES OF BEHAVIOR DIRECTED
TO INFANTS, PEERS, AND ADULTS
IN SIX CULTURES

Infants		Peers		Adults	
Nurturant	40	Sociable	28	Intimate-dependent	36
Aggressive	21	Aggressive	24	Sociable	23
Prosocial	18	Prosocial	17	Dominant-dependent	16
Sociable	14	Dominant-dependent	12	Nurturant	12
Dominant-dependent	5	Nurturant	11	Prosocial	8
Intimate-dependent	2	Intimate-dependent	7	Aggressive	5

(From B. B. Whiting & J. W. M. Whiting, *Children of Six Cultures*, 1975, Table 30. Reprinted by permission of Harvard University Press.)

Some evidence also exists that play with younger children may be especially helpful for those children who are experiencing difficulties with their peers. In a study by Furman, Rahe, & Hartup (1979), socially isolated preschoolers were observed with their peers after having 10 special play sessions with children one to two years younger than themselves. Compared with other social isolates who had no special sessions or a group who played with same-age children, those who had experienced the mixed-age "therapy" later significantly increased their peer interaction, as shown in Figure 11–2. It appears that play with younger children gave these socially isolated preschoolers more opportunities to take leadership roles and behave in a more socially assertive manner. These experiences rubbed off on the children's later play with peers.

By observing and imitating somewhat older children, younger participants of the group are exposed to more skilled models than peers but not so advanced as adults, a situation Piaget (1952) and others see as conducive to learning. In Konner's eyes, the mixed-age group is the ideal setting for promoting developmental growth, and Konner is concerned that our society and most other Western industrialized nations, by grouping children with their peers from an early age, neglect this context (Konner, 1975). Since little research has been done on the developmental significance of play in mixed-age groups, additional research is needed before we can evaluate Konner's ideas.

Up to now, we've been discussing the "worlds" of family and of other children as though they exist in isolation. Of course, this is not the case. Ecological systems theory emphasizes how the young child's participation in each of these contexts is related.

Influence of the Parent-Child Relationship on Peer Relations

Since in almost all cases—the Israeli *kibbutz* is a possible exception—young children form attachments to their parents before they develop ties to other children outside the family, it is reasonable to suppose that the quality of parent-child relations might affect adjustment to peers. Indeed, studies comparing infants' attachment to their mothers with their later peer relations as preschoolers supports this prediction (Lieberman, 1977; Waters, Wippman, & Sroufe, 1979). For example, in one study, 15-month-old infants were rated as "securely" or "anxiously" attached to their mothers from videotapes of the pairs in the "strange situation" (refer to Chapter 7). When the same children

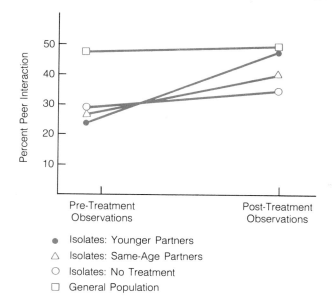

Figure 11—2

Effects of Play with Younger Children on Peer Interaction

(From: Furman, Rahe, & Hartup, *Child Development*, 1979, *50*, p. 918. © The Society for Research in Child Development. Reprinted by permission of author.)

were between three and four years of age, they were observed for five weeks during free play in the nursery school by observers who did not know the quality of their earlier attachment. Those who as infants had been securely attached to their mothers were more socially active toward peers, more sought out by other children, more sympathetic to peer distress, and generally more responsive toward others than were those children who as infants had been observed as anxiously attached (Waters et al., 1979).

Although an early supportive relationship with parents seems to help children get off to a good start with peers, it doesn't inoculate them against any future problems. Following parental divorce, preschoolers, especially boys, show more aggression, dependency, and whining in their peer play and are more likely to be rejected by playmates. This illustrates that family stresses may spill over into the child's relations with other children.

School

Most investigators have tended to assume that the flow of influence is mostly one-way—from parents to peers. However, research on the impact of early educational settings—preschools and day care programs—almost all of which are composed along peer group lines, suggests that when preschoolers' home environments are disadvantaged, experiences in peer group settings may affect children's relations with parents and their development more generally. This section examines programs for the young child and their effects.

Many infants and toddlers spend some time regularly being cared for by adults who are not their parents. By the third year, many young children begin to spend time in an early educational environment, or preschool. In North America, the majority of children three to five years of age are enrolled in a preschool program of some kind. In some other countries, preschool experience is more widespread and begins even earlier. For example, in France, the majority of all two-year-olds are enrolled in *crèche* (literally, cradle), or preschool (Kamerman & Kahn, 1981).

Parents place their children in preschool for a variety of reasons. They may want their child to be able to play with peers, to prepare for regular school, or to be cared for while the parents work. Because of these different goals, many different preschools have been developed. In some, children attend only two to three hours, several times a week, while in others, they may spend a full day. In addition to variations in time, a great variety of programs exist. Day care may range from an informal arrangement with a relative or friend to a *day care center,* where several adults care for a large number of children. Day care centers are licensed to meet minimum federal and state standards, while most home day care providers are not (refer to Chapter 7).

Some programs are designed primarily to provide substitute care for young children whose parents both work. Others exist to provide cognitive stimulation and to prepare children to cope successfully with the demands of later formal schooling. Still others focus on providing opportunities for peer play. The major preschool programs in North America are described in the following paragraphs.

Montessori

In the early 1900s, Maria Montessori developed a preschool curriculum to cognitively stimulate Italian slum children. Since then, this cognitively oriented program has been adopted in many countries. The focus is on each child working individually with a specially trained teacher on tasks that sharpen the senses and teach basic academic skills, such as letter recognition and counting. Special materials are designed to help young children learn. For example, letter recognition is taught by having children fit large wooden letters into matching

Many preschool programs provide cognitive stimulation through teacher-guided activities.

slots on a letter board. Such materials help the child visually and tactilely experience correct and incorrect responses rather than relying on teacher re-inforcement. In this fashion, the child progresses through a series of increasingly complex learning materials. The Montessori program is based on the assumption that young children are naturally curious and interested in learning and that their cognitive development can be fostered by structured tasks and the guidance of a specially trained teacher. Thus, any preschool advertising itself as Montessori must have teachers trained and certified by the Montessori association.

Bereiter-Englemann

The Bereiter-Englemann program is another cognitively oriented curriculum, also originally designed for disadvantaged children. However, unlike Montessori, it is based on learning theory principles. The emphasis is on learning basic concepts and on developing behavior patterns that will aid in later school adjustment. Thus, teachers often drill children in small groups, praising correct answers and pointing out incorrect answers. They encourage attention, concentration, and persistence at tasks and keep distractions to a minimum.

Developmental

Many preschools that parents are likely to encounter define themselves as traditional or developmental. This usually means that the program emphasizes social and emotional as well as cognitive development. Moreover, the curriculum is likely to reflect the belief than an enriched environment, containing many interesting toys and activities, and opportunities for unstructured free play will best stimulate children's creativity and learning. The emphasis is on tailoring the curriculum to the individual needs of different children, rather than providing a single structure. Most of these programs also include some teacher-led small group activities, such as singing or story telling, which help the children coordinate their behavior with a group and learn to atttend to a teacher. In general, however, the role of the teacher in such programs is less that of reinforcer or communicator of information than of a guide, helping the child to explore the environment and become positively involved with other children.

Piagetian

Many preschool programs incorporate aspects of Piaget's theory of cognitive development. For example, the emphasis of developmental programs on the child's learning through peer play and that of Montessori programs on active learning reflect Piagetian ideas. However, some programs are based more explicitly on Piagetian principles and include specific play materials to stimulate conservation of number, volume, weight, etc. (refer to FOCUS ON POLICY, Chapter 10).

The Effects of Preschool Experience

The role of preschools became increasingly important as evidence emerged in the 1960s that disadvantaged children, particularly poor minority children, were already significantly behind their peers in measures of cognitive achievement by the time they entered first grade and fell increasingly behind with each

Compensatory Education for Disadvantaged Preschoolers

 A major effort to provide preschool experiences to poor children was begun in the 1960s with *Project Head Start*. Initially, low-income young children were enrolled for a summer of enriched preschool experience, and this was soon extended to a full year. The hope was that the cognitive stimulation and peer play experiences provided in Head Start would counteract the disadvantages of poverty and put poor children on an equal footing with their more affluent peers when they entered first grade.

First reports from Head Start indicated success. At the end of the program, participants showed signif-

icant intellectual and social gains over other poor children who lacked this experience. However, a follow-up study of Head Start graduates several years later yielded more discouraging conclusions (Cicirelli, 1969). Gains made by participation in Head Start were not maintained, and by grade three, the IQs of children who had experienced enriched preschool did not differ from other disadvantaged youngsters. It appeared that the success story of compensatory preschool education was illusory.

In reaction, some argued that preschool compensatory education was ineffective and wasteful of taxpayers' money. Others claimed that preschool alone was too little, too late to make an impact on victims of poverty and that compensatory education must be continued through the elementary years if it is to have lasting effects. Still others claimed that Project Head Start was improperly evaluated. For example,

a variety of programs was implemented under the Head Start umbrella, and little research was undertaken to assess which programs worked best for which children. Finally, the use of IQ changes as the major index of success or failure of Head Start was attacked as culturally biased (see Chapter 13) and as ignoring many other important benefits compensatory education might bring.

These arguments spurred a number of developments. First, to maintain the gains of Head Start through the early grades, *Project Follow-Through* was established in 1967 to continue enrichment experiences for disadvantaged elementary school children and to provide such children and their families a variety of social, medical, and nutritional services. Additional evaluation studies were conducted, this time examining broader outcome measures, including changes in self-concept, cooperation, independence,

successive year. Moreover, observations of lower-class children with their mothers (Bee et al., 1969) showed that the children were less verbal and more impulsive and the mothers were more controlling and disapproving than their middle-class counterparts (refer to Chapter 10).

Such evidence led to the development of federally funded early educational interventions to give disadvantaged children a head start in their schooling and to compensate for what was seen as a less cognitively stimulating home environment (see FOCUS ON POLICY).

Chapter Summary

PARENT-CHILD RELATIONS

☐ Family relationships, particularly parent-child relationships remain primary in the early years. One goal parents in different family structures share is the socialization of their child—the transmission of parental values, attitudes, and desired behaviors.

☐ Four theories of parent-child socialization—psychoanalytic, learning, cognitive, and systems—have implications for effective parenting styles or techniques.

achievement motivation, and family aspirations (Stallings, 1974). In addition, an effort was made to look at different program characteristics and how they might affect different groups of children.

One such study (Lazar and Darlington, 1982) followed over 3500 disadvantaged children who had participated in 12 different compensatory preschool programs through the elementary school grades. Although none of the programs were funded under Head Start, each was designed to permit careful evaluation of a variety of outcomes and to assess how different program characteristics might affect different children.

The results of this study were considerably more optimistic than the original Head Start evaluation. Children who had experienced a compensatory preschool program were much less likely than other poor children to be having difficulty in elementary school. For example,

25 percent of the preschool graduates were referred to special education classes or held back a year, compared to 44 percent of a matched group of disadvantaged children without preschool. Moreover, the effects of the preschool experience resulted in higher achievement scores in reading and math and in higher IQ scores three to four years later.

When the preschool graduates were in their early teens, they gave more achievement-related answers to the question, Tell me something you're proud of about yourself, than comparable youngsters who had not attended preschool. Mothers whose children had benefited from preschool were more satisfied five years later with their children's educational progress and expressed higher aspirations for their children's future than did mothers of comparable children who had not attended preschool. Perhaps most important was the finding that these

extended benefits of preschool experience were true for a variety of programs and for different children, both boys and girls, most needy and least needy.

Each of the 12 programs showing these benefits was a specially designed, high-quality educational experience, emphasizing cognitive stimulation and a close teacher-child relationship. In most programs, the teacher child ratio was 1 to 5, considerably higher than typical preschools or day care centers. Although such programs represent a high initial investment of funds, analyses of the money saved in later decreased need for special education, later increased earnings by participants, etc., indicate that high-quality preschool intervention programs give an average return of 248 percent on every dollar invested (Schweinhart & Weikart, 1979; Berrueta-Clement, Schweinhart, Barnett, Epstein, & Weikart, 1984.)

□ Research directly examining parenting styles suggests that competent preschoolers are most likely to have parents who are authoritative, a parenting style that combines warmth, firm control, clear communication, and the encouragement of independence.

SIBLINGS
□ After a period of adjustment to a new sibling, young children form close relationships of mutual attachment.
□ Siblings show considerable empathy, prosocial behavior, teaching, and support as well as rivalry and anger.

PEERS
□ Play, the activity in which preschool peers engage most frequently, is distinct from exploration.
□ Stages of play have been identified by Piaget and by Parten.
□ Peer social play, with its opportunities for fantasy, turn taking, and role playing, is considered developmentally significant by a number of theories.
□ There is concern about preschoolers who are not well accepted by their peers and not included in such play.
□ Sociometric status, which includes popularity, rejection, or isolation, is fairly stable. Rejection and isolation are often accompanied by deficits in social skills.

□ An outcome of play with peers is the development of first friendships.

□ Although preschoolers have only a rudimentary understanding of the concept of friend, they show patterns in their behavior of mutual attachment and enjoyment.

□ Play with friends is more complex, more communicatively competent, and more socially skillful than is play with nonfriends.

MIXED-AGE GROUPS

□ Young children often play with older and younger children, particularly in non-Western societies.

□ Mixed-age play is more often characterized by "teaching" and "learning" than is peer play, and there is evidence that mixed-age play may benefit older children, particularly those having difficulties with peers.

SCHOOL

□ Montessori, Bereiter-Englemann, Developmental, and Piagetian are some of the major preschool programs.

□ A number of issues exist that are related to early childhood education as compensatory education.

Recommended Readings

Maccoby, E. (1980). *Social development: Parent-child relations and personality development*. New York: Harcourt, Brace, Jovanovich. A readable yet comprehensive discussion of the role of parent-child relations in the child's individual development. Chapters devoted to attachment, parenting styles, and the effects of the child on the parent. Written by a leading authority on the subject.

Rubin, Z. (1980). *Children's friendships*. Cambridge, MA: Harvard University Press. An engaging account of the development of children's ideas about friendships and their behaviors with friends. Liberally sprinkled with firsthand reports of preschoolers and older children.

Kamerman, S., and Hayes, C. (eds.) (1982). *Families that work: Children in a changing world*. Washington, D.C.: National Academy Press. A review of research related to maternal employment and its effects on children.

Wallerstein, J. and Kelly, J. (1980). *Surviving the breakup: How children and parents cope with divorce*. New York: Basic Books. A detailed report of the results of an influential study of how divorce affects preschoolers and older children.

Garvey, C. (1977). *Play*. Cambridge, MA: Harvard University Press. A brief, readable account of theories and developmental significance of play, particularly during the preschool years. Good examples.

PART IV

Middle Childhood

CHAPTER 12

Physical Development

"*C* an Phil beat you up?"
      "Yeah, Phil can, but I can beat up Sam."
"Bet you can't beat up Frank!"
"Well, well. . . .we're about the same in beatin' up."

These two ten-year-old boys whom we overheard discussing themselves and their friends were not particularly aggressive children. Fascinated by the strength of their growing bodies, they enjoyed testing their physical abilities in playful wrestling matches, which they referred to as "beating up."

Physical changes take on new meaning for children during the middle years. Cognitive growth, changes in self-awareness, and more time with peers (discussed in Chapters 13, 14, and 15) combine to enable children to compare their physical characteristics with others. Other children are questioning if they are as pretty as others or can run as fast. In this way, the development of physical characteristics and motor skills produces psychological consequences. Some children build confidence in their abilities, while others develop feelings of self-consciousness and inferiority.

Besides their psychological consequences, physical and motor development are important in another way. Many Americans have become more conscious of the need to maintain a healthful life style in order to reduce the risks of serious illness and improve the quality of life during adulthood. Although individuals are capable of change at any point in the life cycle, it is easier to maintain healthful habits if they are established during childhood.

This chapter explores two major themes: 1) changes in physical characteristics and motor skills during middle childhood and their psychological consequences and 2) the development of habits related to nutrition, exercise, accident prevention, and other components of a healthful life style. (Chapter 16 discusses smoking, alcohol abuse, and drug abuse, which are also discussed briefly later in this chapter.) This chapter also examines the development of children's ideas about health and illness which are important in determining the habits children are likely to form.

Changes in Size and Shape

Physical Maturation

As shown in Figure 12–1, growth rates for both boys and girls are not as rapid during middle childhood as they are during both earlier and later periods. The percentage by which growth increases—referred to as the "percent increment" in Figure 12–1—steadily declines from infancy through age nine for girls and through ages 12 to 13 for boys. In general, growth rates for both height and weight are relatively smooth during the middle years; that is, most children grow at a slow, steady pace from one year to the next, gaining on the average five to six percent of total height each year between ages 6 and 12 (Shonkoff, 1984; Williams & Stith, 1980).

As we noted in Chapter 8, although changes in height and weight are the most visible, the best indicator of physical growth is *skeletal maturity* or *bone age*, which is measured by the extent of hardening of the bones (called *ossification*). The lengthening of arms and legs as the child grows is caused by

Figure 12—1

Relative Growth Rate

(From Bauer and Bayley, *Growth Diagnosis*, © 1959. Reprinted by permission of The University of Chicago Press.)

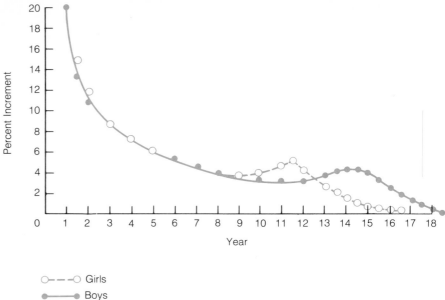

growth regions in the bones called *epiphyses*. Scientists measure the rate at which these growth regions harden to assess physical maturation. The onset of puberty (see Chapter 16) is better predicted by a child's bone age than by age in years (Shonkoff, 1984). Height is correlated closely with rate of ossification of the epiphyses. When the epiphyses completely harden in late adolescence, adult height is achieved.

The brain, skull, eyes, and ears grow even more slowly than body height or weight. Most of the growth in the head occurs prenatally and in infancy, following the cephalocaudal (top to bottom) direction. By age five, the child's head already has attained 91 percent of its adult size. The sex organs are formed prenatally and grow little before the onset of puberty (Tanner, 1970). On the other hand, the lymph system grows more rapidly during middle childhood than at any other time. (The lymph system is a network of vessels carrying lymph or tissue fluid from tissues into veins.) This pattern of different parts of the body reaching maturity at different times is called *asynchronous growth*, illustrated in Figure 12—2.

Changes in Shape

Because of asynchronous growth, the body contours of children gradually change during middle childhood. For example, at age five, the surface area of the child's head accounts for 13 percent of total body surface, while that of an adult is 8 percent. Thus, as they grow, children gradually look less top-heavy as their lower body grows at a more rapid rate than the head (Williams & Stith, 1980).

Other changes in shape also occur. The forehead becomes somewhat flattened, the nose grows larger, the arms and legs become more slender, the shoulder line becomes squarer, the abdomen flattens, and the waistline is more defined. These changes in body proportions occur in similar fashion for both boys and girls. However, as puberty begins, girls' hips and boys' shoulders widen, and sex differences in body proportions begin to be marked (see Chapter 16).

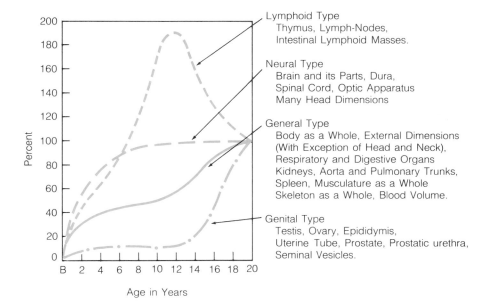

Lymphoid Type
Thymus, Lymph-Nodes,
Intestinal Lymphoid Masses.

Neural Type
Brain and its Parts, Dura,
Spinal Cord, Optic Apparatus
Many Head Dimensions

General Type
Body as a Whole, External Dimensions
(With Exception of Head and Neck),
Respiratory and Digestive Organs
Kidneys, Aorta and Pulmonary Trunks,
Spleen, Musculature as a Whole
Skeleton as a Whole, Blood Volume.

Genital Type
Testis, Ovary, Epididymis,
Uterine Tube, Prostate, Prostatic urethra,
Seminal Vesicles.

Figure 12–2

Graph of Major Types of Postnatal Growth of Body

The several curves are drawn to a common scale by computing their values at successive ages in terms of their total postnatal increments (to 20 years).

(From Harris et al., *The Measurement of Man.* Minneapolis: University of Minnesota Press. © 1930, by the University of Minnesota.)

One of the most visible body changes during the middle years is the loss of *deciduous* or *baby teeth.* Around age five or six, the first baby teeth begin to loosen and drop out, and by age twelve, 20 will have been lost to the "tooth fairy." Meanwhile, the first permanent teeth begin to appear in their place, and this process continues until age 18 or 20. During this time, children may experience temporary speech impediments such as lisping or have difficulty eating.

Many parents are unaware of the importance of proper care of the deciduous teeth by regular brushing and avoiding high-sugar foods. Even though they eventually drop out, these baby teeth provide spaces for the permanent teeth. If the baby teeth are neglected, poor alignment of the permanent teeth can occur, interfering with eating, speech, and appearance (Williams & Stith, 1980).

Individual Variation

Both genetic and environmental factors—nature and nurture—interact to produce individual differences in skeletal maturity as well as growth of the different organ systems of the body. Heredity accounts for some individual differences; children of relatively tall, large parents will tend to be taller and larger than their peers. However, in studies comparing parental physical dimensions with children's physical growth, parent-child resemblance is only moderate, with correlations around +.30 being typical (Garn, 1966; Kagan & Moss, 1959). Even this modest relationship may not be due entirely to heredity but to similarities in the environments of parents and children, for example, similar diets.

The importance of environmental factors such as nutrition has been well documented. As we've seen in Chapter 8, improvements in nutrition among a population will result in overall increases in height and weight. Nutrition can mask the effects of heredity; that is, a child with inadequate nutrition whose genes predispose him or her to be relatively tall may not grow to full height, while another child with "short" genes but more adequate nutrition may actually grow taller. Optimal nutrition allows the effects of heredity to be more visible.

Both genetic and environmental influences combine to produce ethnic differences in height and weight, as shown in Figure 12–3. Sex differences in physical maturation also exist. If you look back at Figure 12–1, you'll notice that the average growth rate of boys and girls in body height is virtually identical until nine years of age. From ages 9 until 12, girls grow on the average more rapidly than do boys, and this difference is most marked at approximately age 11. During middle childhood, girls mature physically about 20 percent faster than do boys, as measured by skeletal maturity (Sinclair, 1978). During the latter part of middle childhood, strength differences favoring boys appear (Malina, 1982). These sex differences also interact with environmental factors such as nutrition and heredity. As a result of all these influences, wide individual differences in height and size are found during middle childhood. A particular seven-year-old girl may be taller and heavier than a ten-year-old boy.

Development of Motor Skills

Developmental Trends

Along with changing in height and body weight, children are developing new abilities to use their growing bodies. As shown in Table 12–1, both boys and

While the rate of growth during the elementary school years is slower than during earlier or later periods, considerable changes in size and shape occur from ages 6 to 12.

Figure 12–3

The Relation of Mean Standing Height and Mean Body Weight among Contemporary Groups of Eight-Year-Old Children

(From Meredith, *Monographs*, 1969, Vol. 34. © the Society for Research in Child Development, Inc.)

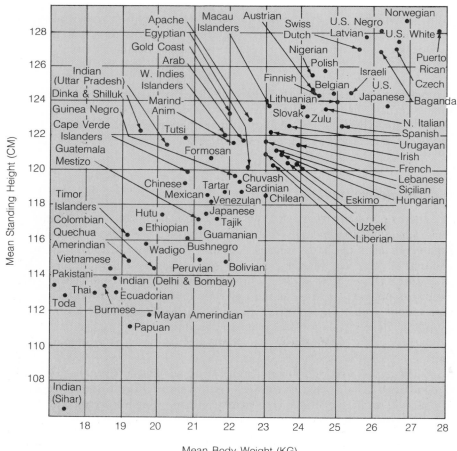

Table 12—1

EMERGENCE OF GROSS MOTOR SKILLS AGES 6–12

Age	Selected Behaviors
6 years	Girls superior in movement accuracy; boys superior in forceful, less complex acts.
	Skipping acquired.
	Throwing with proper weight shift and step.
7 years	One-footed balancing without vision becomes possible.
	Can walk 2-inch-wide balance beams.
	Can hop and jump accurately into small squares.
	Can execute accurate jumping-jack exercise.
8 years	12 pounds pressure on grip strength by both sexes.
	The number of games participated in by both sexes greatest at this age.
	Can engage in alternate rhythmical hopping in 2-2, 2-3, or 3-3 pattern.
	Girls can throw a small ball 40 feet.
9 years	Girls can vertical jump 8½ inches and boys 10 inches over their standing height-plus-reach.
	Boys can run 16½ feet per second.
	Boys can throw a small ball 70 feet.
10 years	Can judge and intercept pathways of small balls thrown from a distance.
	Girls can run 17 feet per second.
11 years	Standing broad jump of 5 feet possible for boys, 6 inches less for girls.
12 years	Standing high jump of 3 feet possible.

(From Cratty, Bryant J., *Perceptual and Motor Development in Infants and Children*, © 1979, p. 222. Reprinted by permission of Prentice-Hall, Englewood Cliffs, New Jersey.)

girls become more skilled in many aspects of motor behavior during middle childhood. They can run faster, throw farther, balance better, and jump farther. In general, their bodies become stronger, eye-hand coordination improves, and movements become more flexible and accurate with advancing age. *Reaction time*—the speed with which the child responds to an object such as a thrown ball with a response, such as catching—improves, and children's strength at gripping objects increases with age (Cratty, 1979).

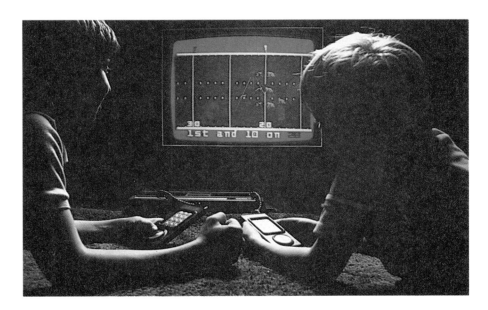

Some elementary schoolage children become exceptionally proficient at the fine motor skills and eye-hand coordination needed for video game prowess.

6yr. old's

12yr. old's

Figure 12–4

Comparison of Two Homemade Valentines As Illustration of Age Differences in Fine Motor Skill

The development of fine motor skills is evident when we look at differences in the writing and drawing of children from first grade until adolescence. Compare the crudely printed "I love you" of a six-year-old's homemade valentine to the smoothly flowing "Roses are red . . ." of a 12-year-old's more elaborate creation to get an idea of the changes in fine motor skill during middle childhood (see Figure 12–4). With increasing age, children become able to adjust their grip on writing tools such as pencils, pens, and paintbrushes and, through improved eye-hand coordination, to control the movements of finger muscles more precisely. These developments make possible not just the ability to make neater valentine cards but also mastery of musical instruments such as the piano or violin, acquisition of skills such as knitting, sewing, and model construction, and video game prowess.

Sex Differences

Although both boys and girls improve with age, sex differences are found in some motor skills. As you can see in Figure 12–5, on the average, from ages six to eleven, boys can throw a ball farther than can girls, and the gap between boys' and girls' throwing skill widens with age, even though girls as well as boys improve as they get older (Keogh & Sugden, 1985).

Girls excel at other motor skills. For example, the results of a study measuring how fast children could hop 50 feet on one leg found rapid im-

Figure 12–5

Performance Changes with Age in Throwing for Distance for Boys and Girls, Ages 7 to 17, Based on Composite Mean Values

(From Keogh & Bugden, *Movement Skill Development*. Copyright © 1985 by Macmillan Publishing Company. Reprinted by permission of the publisher.)

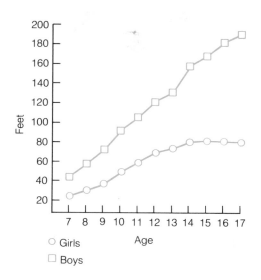

Sex differences in motor skill, such as boys' greater running speed, may be due to sex differences in preferences for various physical activities.

provement in speed for both boys and girls between ages five and seven and gradual improvement continuing from seven to eleven years of age. However, as shown in Figure 12–6, girls showed greater agility at this motor skill at most ages (Keogh & Sugden, 1985).

In general, boys excel at motor skills involving strength in the arms and legs, while girls show greater ability in tasks involving rhythmic and accurate motor agility, such as hopping or skipping (Cratty, 1979). Table 12–1 provides an overview of the motor skills emerging for both boys and girls from ages six through twelve.

What are some of the reasons for these sex differences? One factor is differences in the rate of physical maturation between the sexes. Another, perhaps more important, factor is the different activities that boys and girls prefer during middle childhood. In one study of the game preferences of 132 boys and 161 girls from ages six through twelve, girls named hopscotch, jump rope, and dodge ball as their favorite activities, while boys named football, bowling, and other ball games as their favorites (Cratty, 1979). Thus, more girls appear to be spending time practicing skills involving agility and precise

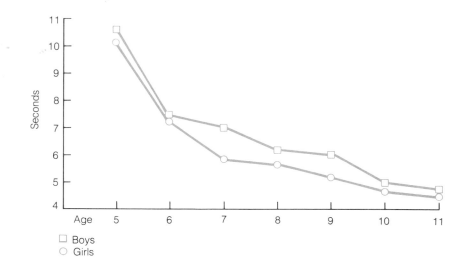

Figure 12–6

50 Hop Median Scores, Boys and Girls Ages 5 through 11

(From Keogh, *Motor Performance of Elementary School Children*, 1965. Reprinted by permission of author.)

movement, while boys tend to play games involving more throwing, catching, and running.

One should be cautious about interpreting evidence of sex differences in motor skills during middle childhood. First, reports of average differences may obscure wide individual variation in skills. Second, many of the studies documenting sex differences were conducted in the 1930s to 1970s. In recent years, there has been greater encouragement of girls' participation in sports and games such as soccer and basketball where running and ball handling skills are emphasized. Similarly, there is increased participation of boys in activities such as gymnastics and dance, which stress flexibility, agility, and precise movement. A more recent study (Hall & Lee, 1984) finds no sex differences in a range of motor skills among third-grade to fifth-grade participants in a coed physical education program.

Other Individual Differences

Simply knowing that a child is male or female will not tell us much about the child's level of motor skill. Some boys and girls become very proficient in many areas of motor performance, showing superior strength, agility, speed, reaction time, balance, and flexibility. Other children become expert at particular sports and games, such as ball throwing and catching or rope skipping, but are not particularly good at other activities. They may have difficulty in fine motor skills involved in writing or drawing but may do well in the coordination of large muscles in outdoor play activities. Still other children have great difficulty mastering the motor skills most commonly shown by children of their age.

According to one estimate (Cratty, 1979), from 8 to 15 percent of all schoolchildren have motor abilities that are less than adequate for their age. Many of these children are experiencing maturational lags that will disappear with time. Others are thought to have minimal neurological problems that interfere with coordination of body movements. Still others may avoid exercise and vigorous activity because they are overweight (refer to Chapter 8) or for other reasons.

Psychological Consequences of Motor Skill

Children who have difficulty mastering the fine motor skills involved in writing, printing, and painting may experience problems at school and may begin to feel less competent cognitively (Denckla, 1984), while those who excel at running, jumping rope, playing ball games, and other school sports are likely to be more popular with their classmates and more self-confident about their abilities (Harter, 1982).

Just as motor skill has been linked to social success, clumsiness has been associated with social difficulties. In an interview study, 111 boys diagnosed as clumsy on tests of motor coordination stated more often than other children that "other boys did not like them" and "made fun" of them and that they were "sad most of the time." (Cratty, 1979).

Helping Children with Motor Problems

Because motor skill has far-reaching consequences for many aspects of the child's development, specialists who work with children experiencing motor problems have developed treatment programs that help such children acquire needed skills. An example of such a treatment approach is described as follows:

Explanation of the diagnosis and level of motor impairment. . .should be reported to the parents and if the child is over the age of 10 years, to the child also. . .Then a priority list should be made of *which* activities should be worked upon with practice and special assistance, and which ones should be circumvented. Surely, when the child is motivated, overlearning (meaning practice in a benignly supportive environment without embarrassment) should be the method of choice. . . Children are often relieved to find out that their problem is "only motor coordination" because this is so widely regarded as independent of intellectual capacity. (Children have many fears as to whether they are really intellectually below normal or are really bad children who are not trying hard enough.) This freedom from the "stupid or bad" characterization is in itself a fringe benefit of correct diagnosis of clumsy children. (Denckla, 1984, pp. 253–254)

Injury, Illness, and Handicaps

Normal physical growth and the development of motor skills depend upon adequate physical health. Middle childhood is a period during which childhood illnesses are less frequent and less severe than during infancy and early childhood. Risks to health from smoking and alcohol and drug abuse as well as from automobile accidents are greater during adolescence (see Chapter 16). Nonetheless, during middle childhood, there is wide individual variation in physical health. Some children suffer from chronic diseases, such as asthma or diabetes. Handicapping conditions may limit physical activity, impair the development of motor skills, and cause psychological and emotional problems. Children may suffer injury through accidents. Others, although not experiencing illness, handicap, or injury, have established habits that may put them at risk for later disease.

Injury

Although during middle childhood, injuries due to accidents or violence are less likely than at earlier or later developmental periods (Butler, Starfield, & Stenmark, 1984), accidents are not uncommon. In a national survey of middle childhood, 20 percent of all children reported having experienced a serious accident at some point in their lives, with three percent reporting the accident within the past year (Zill, 1983). Moreover, accidents and violence are the leading cause of death among children ages five to fourteen, accounting for 51 percent of all deaths in 1978 (Butler et al., 1984). In fact, since the 1930s, there has been a steady increase in the percentage of all deaths during middle childhood attributable to accidents and violence, as Figure 12–7 illustrates.

It may seem paradoxical that during middle childhood, children are less likely to suffer fatal injuries than during other developmental periods, but when death occurs, it is most likely to come from injuries due to accidents or violence. This is because over this century, infectious disease, once the most common cause of fatality in childhood, has been dramatically reduced, leaving other risks such as accidents to account for proportionally more deaths. Childhood injuries are most likely to be caused by motor vehicles, water accidents and fire (Williams & Stith, 1980). Thousands of children are injured through neglect or abuse, and approximately 2,000 children die annually in the United

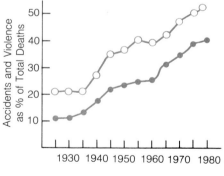

Figure 12–7

Death Rate from Accidents and Violence As Percentage of Death Rate from All Causes (Deaths/100,000 Resident Population) by Age

(From Select Panel for the Promotion of Child Health, 1981.)

Competitive Sports During Middle Childhood

Because of the social prestige of sports and the intense interest in sports activities shown by many peers and adults, children have been entering competitive sports—as members of teams and as individual participants—at ever younger ages. The effects of intense physical training and competition at young ages are being debated among developmentalists as well as parents, educators, sports professionals, and medical personnel. The serious competitor spends many hours each week practicing and training, extensive travel to competitions is usually involved, and the psychological pressures of competition can be intense.

Possible physiological effects are also of concern. For example, the muscles during middle childhood grow rapidly in length and breadth, whereas the heart grows more slowly during this period and is smaller in relation to the body than at any other period of life (Williams & Stith, 1980). This raises the possibility that intense physical activity over long periods of time may be taxing on the heart if the child does not have adequate periods of rest.

Vern Seefeldt, at the Institute for the Study of Youth Sports at Michigan State University, has been trying to determine the physical and psychological effects of long-term strenuous exercise. In 1983, he began studying approximately 50 runners, swimmers, wrestlers, and ice hockey players ages nine to sixteen, all serious competitors. The physical effects of competitively running long distances and participating in other strenuous sports activities are monitored regularly. In addition, psychological effects are assessed by having each child keep daily records of thoughts and concerns.

For most children studied, no adverse physical effects have thus far been documented. Some physical benefits of long-distance running have been found; the athletes' hearts and lungs worked more efficiently than did those of children who did not exercise regularly. In addition, the highly active children had proportionally less fat and more lean tissue in their bodies than did their more sedentary peers (Seefeldt, as reported in Curnutte, 1985). However, other studies caution that certain competitive sports activities such as baseball pitching or tackle football may risk injury to the joints of the elbow, shoulder, knee, and ankle, the parts of a growing body most vulnerable to physical stresses (Larson & McMahan, 1966).

In terms of psychological effects, Seefeldt's investigations find that based on self-reports, most of the young athletes cope well with the pressures of competition. He notes, however, "Running long distances may not hurt children now, but we take a cautious view of what is happening and what may happen in the future. Training and racing should be stopped or curtailed when a child is injured or exploited in any way" (Seefeldt, as reported in Curnutte, 1985).

Other studies (Scanlan & Passer, 1978; Martens, 1978; Simon & Martens, 1979; Martens, 1986) using physiological measures of anxiety such as elevated heart rate and galvanic skin response as well as paper-and-pencil tests conclude that although most children are not adversely affected by sports competition, some problems can occur. Children who are uncertain about their own abilities, about making the team, or about the outcome of a competition are more likely than others to become anxious.

One potential problem for young athletes occurs when parents become overinvolved in their child's sports competitions. Such parents can become "managers" of their children's "careers"; in speaking about the child's activities, these parents are so identified with the child that they talk as if they too are competing. Here is a father of a seven-year-old competitive runner:

> We're kind of peaking her now as far as age-group records go. She'll be 8 on Nov. 16, and with the cool fall weather, this is the time of year when she will run her best. We're going to try and get the third best time, which is 77:57. But we really don't go for records. We go for individual victories in races (Curnutte, 1985).

Such intense parental involvement in the child's competitive activities might make the child reluctant to express fatigue, lack of interest, or injury for fear of disappointing the parent. The young athlete may feel pressured to maintain a high level of competition, even when interests change and the sport is no longer as enjoyable. The parent may endorse ever-increasing time spent in training and competing, taking the child away from other school and social activities. Although competitive sports can be an exciting and rewarding experience for talented youngsters, parents and educators need to be sensitive to the dangers of pushing too hard.

States from child abuse (refer to FOCUS ON RISK/INTERVENTION in Chapter 11). Some children appear to be accident-prone, having multiple episodes of injury. In general, boys are more likely than girls to have accidents, perhaps reflecting their greater risk taking and exploration (refer to Chapter 8).

For both boys and girls, aspects of the family have been linked to the likelihood of childhood accidents. Systems theory (refer to Chapter 2) emphasizes that family functioning may make a child more vulnerable to accident or disease. For example, children from families experiencing severe marital conflict are more likely than children from less conflicted homes to have repeated accidents (Plionis, 1977). This may be because marital conflict may result in inadequate supervision of children, and the family environment may not be kept free of hazards. In addition, marital conflict itself is highly stressful to children (Zill, 1983), and there is evidence, discussed later in this chapter, linking stress to both accidents and illness. On the other hand, many aspects of the family, such as an orderly environment and good parent-child communication, may protect or buffer the child from injury.

Illness

In the United States and other industrialized nations, the communicable diseases of childhood, such as measles, mumps, rubella (also known as German measles), and chicken pox, diminish during middle childhood. Immunization, proper nutrition, and adequate rest and exercise help children resist infectious diseases. However, many children are not fully protected against infectious disease. According to one estimate, 20 percent of American children under age 13 are not adequately immunized against diphtheria, tetanus, and whooping cough, and 35 percent have not received measles and rubella vaccines (Williams & Stith, 1980). In many less developed parts of the world, rates of immunization are much lower, and many young children succumb to infectious diseases.

Although chronic illnesses afflict a relatively small number of children, they can have serious consequences for the entire family. At the same time, aspects of the family system, along with characteristics of the child, will influence how a child copes with the disease. To illustrate, we'll consider two of the more common chronic diseases of middle childhood: diabetes and asthma.

Diabetes affects 1.43 per 1,000 children, with the incidence most frequent between ages five and eleven (Calnan & Peckham, 1977; Eiser, 1985). In childhood diabetes (called *juvenile-onset diabetes*), the pancreas does not produce *insulin*, a substance essential in breaking down food into energy the body can use. As a result, the child may experience excessive hunger, thirst, weakness, and weight loss. Once diabetes is diagnosed, it can be controlled with daily injections of insulin. The amount of insulin needed each day must be assessed by regular analysis of urine and blood samples. In addition, special diets are often prescribed. Thus, diabetes involves many changes in daily life for the child and the child's family.

Although a serious, potentially life-threatening disease, diabetes can be controlled so that the child can lead a normal life. No differences in the cognitive or social development of diabetic children as compared with those without diabetes have been found (Eiser, 1985). However, long-term health complications are more likely, and they increase in frequency the longer the individual has had the disease.

Like all chronic illnesses, diabetes disrupts family life. Parents must face the fact that their child has a serious disease that must be managed carefully. The family's diet must be modified. The regimen of urine testing, blood monitoring, and daily injections of insulin must be monitored, and the parents must decide how much the child can manage these tasks alone. Finally, parents and other family members understandably are anxious about the child's current health and possible later complications.

Some children and families cope well with the demands of diabetes, while others have considerable difficulty. Research suggests that in families that cope well, the child's diabetes is openly discussed, and the parents tend to emphasize what is normal about the child's life while still adhering to the treatment program. In families that have difficulty coping with the child's disease, feelings are not openly expressed, the family avoids conflict, and the child and other family members are overprotected (Koski, 1969; Garner & Thompson, 1974; Minuchin, Baker, Rosman, Leibman, Milman, & Todd, 1975).

Asthma is a chronic illness characterized by intermittent episodes of wheezing and shortness of breath. It is relatively common during middle childhood, affecting two to five percent of all children (Kuzemko, 1980). Asthma appears to be caused by both a predisposition in the child and the presence of substances, such as pollens, dust, animal hair, or certain food products, such as milk or eggs, to which the child is allergic. Although asthmatic children are thought to be more neurotic, anxious, or insecure, little research exists to support this view (Eiser, 1985).

Asthma attacks are frightening for both child and parent. Seeing a child gasp for breath is likely to alarm any parent, and the threat of future attacks is likely to be stressful for the entire family (Eiser, 1985). There is evidence that the family system can influence the frequency and severity of asthma in some children. For example, when asthmatic children are removed from their homes to hospitals or boarding schools, many of them become symptom-free, only to develop asthma again upon returning home. This apparently is not due to the greater absence of *allergens* (substances to which the child is allergic) outside the home, since in one study, asthmatic children whose hospitalized rooms were sprayed with dust collected from their homes remained symptom-free (Long, Lamont, Whipple, Bandler, Blom, Burgin, & Jessner, 1958; Eiser, 1985).

In one study (Boyce, Jensen, Cassel, Collier, Smith, & Ramey, 1977) of the family factors associated with asthma, 58 children between the ages of one and eleven years were observed over a period of 12 months. They were checked for respiratory illness several times a week, and each incident of illness was rated for severity. At the end of the year, each family was interviewed about their daily routines and about any life changes that might have occurred within the family. In families experiencing high levels of change, children took longer to recover from respiratory illness once they got it but were not likely to have more frequent illnesses. Those families with many changes and many household routines had children who became more severely ill than did children from other families (Boyce et al., 1977). These findings parallel the results of studies of other physical ailments as well as of psychological problems and accidents in documenting a relationship between changes in the child's and family's life over a period of time and subsequent illness and stress.

Life Change and Illness

In the Boyce et al. (1977) study just described, each family was presented with a list of possible changes (see Table 12–2). Changes presumed to be especially

Experience	Score
Death of a parent	91
Divorce of parents	84
Marital separation of parents	78
Acquiring a visible deformity	69
Death of brother or sister	68
Jail sentence of parent for one year or more	67
Marriage of parent to stepparent	65
Hospitalization of yourself (child)	62
Becoming involved with drugs or alcohol	61
Having a visible congenital deformity	60
Hospitalization of parent (serious illness)	55
Death of a close friend (child's friend)	53
Failure of a year in school	53
Discovery of being an adopted child	52
Increase in number of arguments between parents	51
Birth or adoption of a brother or sister	50
Increase in number of arguments with parents	47
Suspension from school	46
Beginning first grade	46
Change to a different school	46
Change of father's occupation requiring increased absence from home	45
Jail sentence of parent for 30 days or less	44
Mother beginning to work	44
Hospitalization of brother or sister	41
Addition of third adult to family (e.g., grandparent)	41
Outstanding personal achievement	39
Loss of job by a parent	38
Death of a grandparent	38
Pregnancy in unwed teenage sister	36
Brother or sister leaving home	36
Change in parents' financial status	29
Decrease in number of arguments with parents	27
Decrease in number of arguments between parents	25
Becoming a full-fledged member of a church/synagogue	25

(Reprinted with permission from *Journal of Psychosomatic Research*, vol. 16, Coddington, pp. 9–10, 1972, Pergamon Press, Ltd.)

Table 12–2

RECENT LIFE CHANGES
AND THEIR SEVERITY
FOR ELEMENTARY SCHOOL-
AGE CHILDREN

disruptive to the child are given more weight than others. For example, the death of a parent is rated "91" and the divorce of parents, "84," while a change in parents' financial status is rated "29." Note, too, that both positive and negative changes are viewed as potentially disruptive, although positive changes are considered to be less stressful than negative ones. Thus, "decrease in number of arguments between parents" is rated as "25" in severity, while "increase in number of arguments between parents" gets a rating of "51."

Using this instrument, a total score of life changes over a particular period can be obtained. (Similar scales have been devised for college students and older adults.) A number of studies have found that the higher a person's life-changes score, the more likely he or she is to experience physical and mental illness, accidents, or other stresses (Holmes & Rahe, 1967).

Why has this relationship been found? Theories relating life changes to stress suggest that change occurring in the life of a child and that child's family requires new ways of behaving and thinking (Melson, 1980). Each adaptation to a new situation calls for energy; mental and physical resources are mobilized to meet the demands of the new situation. As changes accumulate, there is less and less time between new situations for the body and mind to recover. As a result, the person becomes vulnerable to illness or accident.

In the Boyce study, household routines—set times for meals, bedtime, and awakening; specific tasks for individuals at fixed times; and schedules for daily activities set by parents—combined with life changes to aggravate asthma in the children. When families are experiencing high levels of change, they may need to become more flexible in their behavior. Many routines, however, place additional demands for specific behaviors on the child and other family members and thus make flexibility more difficult.

This research helps us understand more about the process by which the family system may affect the child's coping with ill health. The absence of additional multiple stresses coupled with high flexibility of the family system appears to help children cope with chronic disease and may even affect the severity of their illness (Pratt, 1973; Mechanic, 1980).

We should not conclude, however, that all illness has negative effects on children. Arthur Parmalee (1986) has suggested that the common colds, runny noses, and upset stomachs that are so much a part of growing up may have a number of beneficial consequences for development:

1. They may help the child's development of a sense of self through experiencing disruptions and restorations of usual feelings and behavior, for example, by having a mild fever and then recovering from it.
2. They may help the child distinguish between physical and other causes of emotional changes, for example, between feeling "bad" because parents are leaving and feeling "bad" because of an earache.
3. When family members and other children fall ill, the child can observe and participate in caring for others, thus promoting prosocial development.

Handicaps

According to one estimate (Williams & Stith, 1980), over two million children under age 14 are living with long-term disabilities of some kind, including defects in the arms or legs; speech, hearing, and visual impairments; and conditions that retard normal growth. Some disabilities are relatively mild and may not be easily visible; others, such as cerebral palsy, are severe and result in multiple impairments.

Because physical handicaps often restrict physical activity and mark children as visibly different from their peers, they can have negative effects on children's self-esteem and social acceptance. In one study, 107 handicapped children ages nine to eleven were interviewed while they attended a summer camp for both handicapped and nonhandicapped youngsters. When asked to describe themselves, 40 percent of the handicapped boys (compared to 15 percent of the nonhandicapped) spoke negatively about their own physical abilities. In general, the children with disabilities spoke more frequently about social isolation, lack of confidence, and general negative feelings about themselves than did the other children (Richardson, Hastorf, & Dornbusch, 1964). Research also indicates that handicapped children are less well accepted than other children by their peers (Richardson & Royce, 1968). In general, the more severe and visible the handicap, the more children have been found to suffer adverse psychological and social effects.

Although handicapped children are at risk for the development of psychological problems, they can be helped in many ways. Systems theory suggests that the manner in which parents and siblings accept the handicap and interpret it to the child will affect self-esteem. Some families react with overprotection,

Children in the Hospital

Admission to a hospital is a potentially stressful event for any adult; for a child, it can be very frightening. Hospital buildings are large and intimidating; the child may feel easily lost amid a maze of corridors. Many strange adults, clad in unfamiliar uniforms and often carrying forbidding-looking equipment, move in and out of the child's view. The child must sleep in a strange bed, eat unfamiliar food, and wear novel clothing. All daily routines are interrupted, and the child may be awakened during the night for medical procedures. Added to this, the child is likely to be separated from parents, siblings, and friends, and his or her schooling may be disrupted.

Among the possible detrimental consequences of hospitalization, an observer noted:

> Children cry, whine or scream; they cling tenaciously to their parents; they eat or sleep poorly; they struggle against treatment and resist taking medications; they are tense and fearful; they become silent, sad and withdrawn. They may show an increase in regressive or compulsive behavior, they may become disruptive of their environment, or even themselves (Gellert, 1958, p. 171).

Although such distress is most likely among children between ages six months and four years, older children who are experiencing other stresses in their lives, such as starting school or adjusting to the arrival of a new sibling, and those who are highly dependent upon their mothers also may become upset (Stacey, Dearden, Pill, & Robinson, 1970).

It has been estimated that by age seven years, 45 percent of all children in Great Britain had been hospitalized at least once (Davie, Butler, & Goldstein, 1972). In the United States, poor children are more likely than middle-class children to be hospitalized. Because of stresses in their environment, poor children are more likely than more affluent youngsters to be ill and suffer accidents. Poor children also are less likely to have regular, preventive care from a physician outside the hospital context (Butler et al., 1984).

Helping Children Adjust to Hospitalization

Greater awareness of the adverse effects of hospitalization on children has led to changes in many hospitals. Unrestricted visiting of the sick child by parents is now encouraged, and many hospitals have established parent-child units so that a parent can stay overnight with the child. The hospital environment is made as familiar to the child as possible. Where medically feasible, the child is encouraged to bring a few favorite toys, is allowed to wear personal clothing, and is given familiar foods. *Child-life specialists* are hired by hospital pediatric units to help children and their families adjust to hospitalization.

When hospitalization can be anticipated, children who have information about what to expect and have their fears addressed experience less subsequent distress. Parents, who are usually anxious themselves, often have difficulty adequately preparing their children for this experience. For example, in one study, 100 children were asked what their parents had told them about why they were coming to the hospital (Goffman, Buckman, & Schade, 1957). Twenty-six percent had been told nothing, 22 percent had been given vague reasons, and 27 percent had learned about the impending hospitalization from overhearing their parents. Only one-quarter of the children had received adequate information from their parents. Thus, hospital personnel need to take an active part in helping to prepare children for hospitalization.

Preparation for the hospitalization of a child is done in a variety of ways. Preadmission tours are available in some hospitals. Children able to read can get written material acquainting them with the hospital and with the medical procedures they will be experiencing. Some hospitals use videotapes or home visits by a nurse or child-life specialist. Preschool and school-age children have been found to benefit from *play therapy*. For example, puppets representing doctor, nurse, child, and parent are used by the child-life specialist to convey information about the hospital and about medical procedures the child may undergo, such as receiving general anesthesia.

Helping Parents

Parents often need help in coping with their own anxieties and fears. In addition, parents can be more effective than any other adults in helping the child adjust to the hospital experience. Because of this, *parent education* programs have been developed by some hospitals to help parents better prepare themselves and their child for hospitalization.

In summary, although there is now widespread recognition that children and their parents need special help in adjusting to hospitalization, one survey of the U. S. hospitals found that only 33 percent provided any type of preparation for children and their families (Azarnoff & Woody, 1981).

A variety of supportive individuals and the presence of familiar objects can help children adjust to hospitalization and medical procedures.

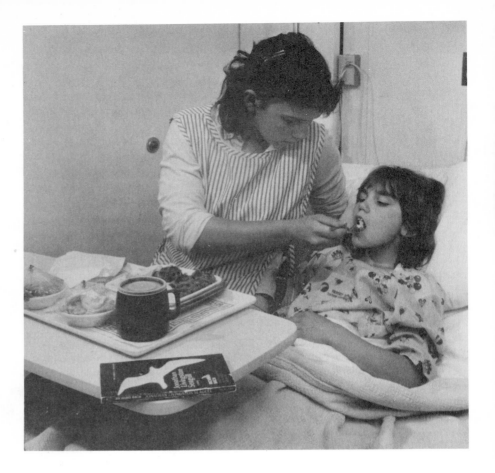

limiting the child's freedom to explore up to his or her physical capacities and restricting the child's social contacts. Others behave in an overindulgent fashion, giving the child less responsibility, placing few limits on behavior, and tolerating unacceptable behavior, often at the expense of other children in the family (Richardson, 1969). Parents who realistically accept the handicapped child's limitations but encourage independent activity and enforce standards of conduct similar to those used with other children enhance the optimal development of their handicapped child.

Note that in the earlier discussion of the impact of diabetes on children, a similar pattern of family behavior was associated with positive adjustment. In general, research on different risks to health yields a similar conclusion with regard to the importance of the family system in determining how seriously children are affected and how well they cope with the health risk once they have it.

Establishing a Healthful Life Style

To improve the well-being of children, understanding how to prevent illness and injury is very important. This section examines how beliefs and attitudes about health and illness develop during middle childhood and looks at evidence that children are acquiring attitudes and habits associated with a healthful life style.

In the past decade, evidence has been accumulating that the way in which people live has an important effect upon their health. A survey of over 400 leaders in the fields of medicine and social science concluded the following:

> The heaviest burdens of illness in the United States today are related to aspects of individual behavior, especially long-term patterns of behavior often referred to as "lifestyle." As much as 50 percent of mortality from the 10 leading causes of death in the United States can be traced to lifestyle (Hamburg, Elliott, & Parron, 1982, p. 1).

Because of this link between life style and health, increased attention has been paid to educating the public about health maintenance and illness prevention.

Some recent writers have described North American culture as being in the midst of a fitness revolution. Almost every adult knows that diet and exercise are related to health, and everyone is increasingly aware of the risks associated with smoking and alcohol and drug abuse. The result of public health education has been a prescription for what might be called a "healthful life style." Although many of us are aware of this prescription, we may not be taking our medicine regularly.

What do children understand about the link between behavior and health? What do they know about the causes of illness and the way their bodies work? Cognitive/developmental theory suggests that as children make the transition from preoperational to concrete operational thought around age seven (see Chapters 9 and 13), their ability to understand how the body works and what causes health and illness changes qualitatively. These changing beliefs can influence behavior. For example, children might eat properly if they understand the role nutrition plays in maintaining health.

Reinforcement and modeling also play a role. For example, a child who gets high-sugar "treats" as a reward or who is discouraged from physical exercise because "you might hurt yourself" is likely to develop beliefs that sweets and lack of exercise are "good" and may tailor behavior to fit these beliefs.

The family system is an important influence in maintaining children's healthful development.

Understanding How the Body Works

Figure 12–8 is a drawing by a seven-year-old of the inside of the body. The picture of a body with "blood and bones enerywhere" and chicken, chips, and ice-cream floating around in the middle is fairly typical of the depictions of children of that age (Eiser & Patterson, 1983).

Knowledge about how the body works increases with age. For example, Eiser and Patterson (1983) asked children ages six to twelve which parts of the body were involved in eating. The youngest children viewed the mouth and teeth as the only body parts involved in eating, while children age eight to ten years included the stomach. The oldest children mentioned the bladder as involved in removing waste food and also mentioned that food was transformed and circulated around the body as blood. A similar pattern was found when responses about body parts involved in swimming were analyzed. The youngest children saw arms and legs as the only body parts used, while some 9-year-olds and most of the 12-year-olds mentioned the lungs and brain as also involved. The results of this study and others (Johnson & Wellman, 1982) indicate that with advancing age, children not only can name more body parts but also have a greater understanding of how these parts are interrelated.

Understanding Health and Illness

Bibace and Walsh (1980, 1981) interviewed 24 children at each of three age levels: four years, seven years, and eleven years, asking them the questions listed in Table 12–3. Based on the children's answers, three broad stages of understanding were identified—prelogical, concrete logical, and formal logical—corresponding to the stages of cognitive development described by Piaget (see Chapters 5, 9, and 13). Within each stage, two substages were described. Table 12–4 summarizes these stages and gives examples of the different types of responses typical of each.

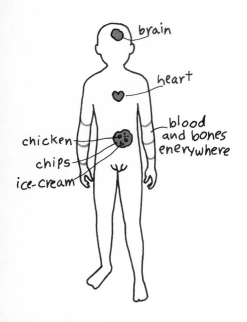

Figure 12–8

Drawing of the Inside of the Body by a Seven-Year-Old

(From Eiser, *The Psychology of Childhood Illness.* New York: Springer-Verlag, 1985. Reprinted by permission of publisher.)

Table 12–3

QUESTIONS ASKED OF CHILDREN CONCERNING HEALTH AND ILLNESS

Question

1. What does it mean to be healthy?
2. Do you remember anyone who was not healthy? What was wrong? How did he get sick? How did he get better?
3. Were you ever sick? How did you get sick? How did you get better?
4. What is the worst sickness to have? Why? What is the best sickness to have? Why?
5. What happens to people when they are sick?
6. What is a cold? How do people get colds? Where do colds come from? What makes colds go away?
7. What are measles? How do people get measles? What makes measles get better?
8. What is a heart attack? Why do people get heart attacks?
9. What is cancer?
10. What is a headache? Why do people get headaches?
11. Have you ever had a pain? Where? What is pain? Why does it come?
12. What are germs? What do they look like? Can you draw germs? Where do they come from?

(From Bibace and Walsh, 1980.)

Table 12—4

STAGES IN CHILDREN'S
UNDERSTANDING OF HEALTH
AND ILLNESS

Stage	Characteristic	Example
Prelogical (2–6 years)		
Phenomenism	Cause of illness an external and unrelated phenomenon.	"How do people get colds?" "From trees."
Contagion	Cause of illness in objects or people near but not touching the child.	"How do people get colds?" "When someone else gets near you." "How?" "I don't know—by magic I think."
Concrete-logical (7–10 years)		
Contamination	Cause of illness a person or action that is harmful through physical contact.	"What is a cold?" "It's like in the wintertime. . .You're outside without a hat and you start sneezing. Your head would get cold—the cold would touch it—and then it would go all over your body."
Internalization	Illness within the body but cause external. External cause linked to illness through process of internalization, e.g., inhaling or swallowing.	"How do you catch cold?" "By breathing in germs that get in your blood."
Formal-logical (11 + years)		
Physiological	Source of illness as malfunctioning of internal organs.	"What is a heart attack?" "The valves of the heart close and the blood won't go to the heart."
Psychophysiological	Awareness that thoughts or feelings may effect illness.	"How do you catch cold?" "There are many reasons. If you're depressed and don't take care of yourself, you could be more vulnerable to infection."

(From Bibace & Walsh, 1980, 1981.)

The first stage, *prelogical*, corresponds to Piaget's description of preoperational thinking (refer to Chapter 9). Children at this stage tend to explain illness, like other aspects of their world, in terms of specific, irreversible events, and they center their attention on single aspects of an event rather than on the whole. In the substage *phenomenism*, children believe that illness is caused by a single dramatic event associated with it. A child may say that the wind made her sick or that a heart attack is "when you fall on your back." Children at this stage are apt to believe that illness can be caused by bad feelings or as punishment for doing something wrong.

The next substage, *contagion*, is characterized by a belief that illness is caused by physical closeness but not necessarily by contact with something, for example, the belief that one can catch cold by walking near a person with a cold. Children thinking at this level often confuse the causes of illness and of accidents, describing both in terms of contagion (Jordan & O'Grady, 1982).

The second broad stage of understanding of illness is called *concrete-logical* and corresponds to Piaget's description of the period of concrete operational thought (see Chapter 13). During this stage, the child begins to distinguish between factors within and outside the body. In the substage *con-*

tamination, children interpret illness as caused by the physical contact of a contaminating agent with the body, for example, getting measles by rubbing against a person who has them. In the substage *internalization*, the child begins to realize that contaminants must be taken inside the body for infection to occur. During this period, the child also begins to view illness as potentially irreversible, understanding that some diseases are curable and preventable, while others are not.

The third stage, *formal logical*, corresponds to Piaget's description of the period of formal operations which emerges about age 11 (see Chapter 16). At this time, the child develops the capacity to reason logically and hypothetically and is no longer bound by what is observed. These new abilities permit an understanding of internal body functioning and the multiple causes of illness. In the *physiological* substage, illness is explained in terms of physiological mechanisms; for example, the blockage of a heart valve may cause a heart attack. In the *psychophysiological* substage, the adolescent recognizes that many factors may be involved in causing illness, including personal habits and attitudes. Reasoning at this stage involves a more realistic appraisal of vulnerability to illness; before age 11, many children fail to recognize their vulnerability to disease (Jordan & O'Grady, 1982).

In the interview study conducted by Bibace and Walsh (1981), most preschoolers gave stage 1 or prelogical explanations for illness: 54 percent gave contagion explanations and 38 percent gave contamination explanations. Many of the seven-year-olds also used contamination explanations (63 percent), but 29 percent of them also gave reasons based on internalization. Among the 11-year-olds, explanations were mainly in terms of internalization (54 percent) or physiological (34 percent) categories. Thus, with advancing age, children generally develop more accurate understanding of the causes of illness.

Interestingly, children who have a chronic illness, such as diabetes or heart disease, are not more knowledgeable than other children about the causes of illness (Eiser, 1985). Instead, the child's cognitive maturity appears to be the most important influence on the understanding of illness. These findings provide support for cognitive/developmental theory in explaining age changes in knowledge about illness (refer to the Adoption Study in Chapter 3).

Along with developing ideas about illness, children are developing beliefs about what health is and what behaviors promote it. In one interview study (Eiser, Patterson, & Eiser, 1983) 20 children at each of four age levels—six, eight, nine, and eleven years—were interviewed about what it meant to be healthy. As you can see from Table 12–5, the results show that with advancing age, children more often recognize the role of diet, exercise, resistance to infection, and avoidance of smoking.

Table 12–5

UNDERSTANDING OF CONCEPT OF HEALTH DURING MIDDLE CHILDHOOD

Concept	Percent responding at age (years)			
	6	8	9	11
Not being ill	10	35	10	45
Eating good food	10	45	45	60
Taking exercise	0	55	70	65
Being strong, fit, full of energy	10	20	65	70
Resistant to infection	0	0	5	5
Not smoking	5	0	10	5

(Adapted from Eiser et al., *Child: Care, Health and Development*. Oxford, England: Blackwell Scientific Publications, Ltd., 1983. Reprinted by permission of publisher.)

When we take an overview of findings concerning children's understanding of health and illness, we find increased awareness with advancing age of the components of a healthful life style. However, lack of research prevents us from pinpointing the causes of this change in understanding.

The following sections take a look at evidence concerning health-related behaviors during middle childhood, search the evidence for clues that such behaviors are affected by cognitive understanding and health-related beliefs, as cognitive/developmental theory would suggest, and look for evidence that environmental influences, such as reinforcement and modeling, are operating.

Physical Exercise

The benefits to adults of a regular program of vigorous physical activity in preventing heart disease are well documented (Thomas, Lee, Franks, & Paffenbarger, 1981). Also, evidence is accumulating that physical fitness promotes emotional well-being. Because of these findings, the development of physical fitness in school-age children and the promotion of physical exercise are important issues.

Although we think of middle childhood as a time of physical exuberance and activity, children during this period may be less fit than we assume. Only one out of three schoolchildren participates in a daily program of physical education (Select Panel for the Promotion of Child Health, 1981). Moreover, as defined by the standards of the President's Council on Physical Fitness and Sports (1977), one out of every six children 10 to 17 years of age was classified as physically underdeveloped.

Over middle childhood and into adolescence, physical activity generally decreases with increasing age (Shonkoff, 1984). As children grow older, the emphasis of many school systems on competitive sports may foster physical fitness mainly for the athletically gifted or early maturers. Other children may spend increasingly more time on the sidelines as spectators and less time engaging in vigorous physical exercise themselves (Martens, 1986).

Despite popular enjoyment of organized sports, participation in regular physical activity declines during the elementary school years.

In spite of the rather discouraging statistics concerning physical fitness among school-age children, there is reason for optimism about the future. Greater public awareness of the benefits of physical exercise are stimulating more programs for children. Involvement in sports activities has increased in recent years for both boys and girls (Shonkoff, 1984). Physical exercise such as running, swimming, and biking, which can be maintained throughout life, are increasing in popularity among children as well as adults.

More research is needed to determine the optimal levels of physical exercise for children of different ages. In addition, little evidence exists concerning the determinants of level of physical exercise. The role of opportunities and encouragement is suggested by findings that with changing attitudes toward girls' participation in sports and federally mandated school support for female athletic programs, girls have increased their participation in youth sports programs over recent decades (Seefeldt & Gould, 1980). In a study of 60 elementary school and high school students who dropped out of organized school sports activities, the majority of children cited an overemphasis on winning, personal lack of success, and lack of playing time; none mentioned changes in beliefs about exercise or sports activities (Orlick & Botterill, 1975).

Nutrition

In addition to physical fitness, an important component of a healthful life style is nutrition. Diets high in saturated fats, sodium, and sugar have been associated with greater risk of disease, particularly cardiovascular or heart disease, cancer, and diabetes. Diets high in carbohydrates that include generous servings of whole grains and fresh fruits and vegetables have been linked to lower incidence of these serious illnesses (U. S. Select Committee on Nutrition and Human Needs, 1977).

Although the public has become more aware of the role of nutrition in preventing serious disease and promoting well-being, nutritional surveys still find the diets of most North Americans high in those foods suspected of being injurious to one's health and deficient in those foods beneficial for good health (Surgeon General, 1979). So-called convenience foods and fast-food restaurants have gained in popularity in recent years. Increasingly, families are eating a substantial portion of their meals outside the home. In most cases, fast food is high in fat, sodium, and sugar and deficient in whole grains, fresh fruits, and fresh vegetables.

Surveys of the eating habits of school-age children in North America find that the typical diet of these children is high in saturated fat, sugar, and salt. One study reported that on the average, one-third of the children's total daily calories came from nutritionally poor snacks and fast-food items (Berenson, Frank, Hunter, Srinivasan, Voors, & Webber, 1982).

Such a diet can contribute to some immediate health problems. The high sugar content leads to tooth decay and cavities. According to one estimate, five-year-olds have an average of 2.2 decayed or filled teeth. Among children aged six to eleven years, 55 percent have one or more decayed, missing, or filled teeth, and a third have two or more such teeth (Kovar & Meny, 1981). Excess calories, coupled with insufficient exercise, are a principal factor associated with obesity in childhood (refer to FOCUS ON ISSUE in Chapter 8).

Long-range health problems are also a concern. Once established over many years during childhood, eating habits can be difficult to change in adulthood. However, some experts caution that we still lack conclusive evidence that nutritional or other health-related habits acquired in childhood remain

Nutrition Programs for Schoolchildren

Children who live in poverty or whose family lives are stressed may come to school without having eaten breakfast, and the food they consume at school may be the only full meal of their day. Because of this, government programs to ensure adequate nutrition for schoolchildren have been developed.

In 1946, the National School Lunch Act was passed, establishing a national school lunch program "to safeguard the health and well-being of the nation's children, and to encourage the domestic consumption of nutritious agricultural commodities and other food." This program, along with other nutrition programs for schoolchildren, is administered by the U. S. Department of Agriculture, which subsidizes all school systems, private as well as public, to serve school lunches. Depending upon parental income, children pay full or reduced fee or receive the meal at no cost. Thus, in 1980, children from a family of four with an income of $8,949 were eligible for a free school lunch each day, while children from similar families earning $14,000 per year paid a reduced fee (Pollitt et al., 1984).

The school lunch program is designed to provide one-third of the child's daily nutritional needs. The government provides guidelines to school systems prescribing daily portions of various food groups for children of different ages. Each year since its inception, the program has grown in size. In its first year, approximately 6.5 million children were served; by 1979, almost 22 million children were receiving school lunches (Longen, 1981). In 1966, the school breakfast program was added to provide a hot breakfast at school to children from low-income families and to those who traveled long distances to school. These groups of children were found to be most likely to begin their school day without a meal. Like the school lunch program, the breakfast program is available to all schools. In 1980, approximately one-third of all schools participated; within these schools, 24 percent of the children received breakfast (Pollitt et al., 1984).

School food programs have apparently helped to ensure more adequate nutrition for all youngsters. We must say "apparently," because systematic evaluation of the impact of the school lunch or breakfast programs has not been conducted. Yet, statistics on the number of children using these programs indicate that each year more children are receiving at least part of their nutritional requirements at school.

stable through adolescence and into adulthood (Pollitt et al., 1984). Others urge that because of potential health risks in adulthood, health education programs for school-age children should be expanded (Butler et al., 1984).

Although the nature of children's eating habits and the possible health problems such habits may pose are becoming better understood, relatively little is known concerning the determinants of children's diets. Children's beliefs and knowledge about nutrition appear to have limited impact upon children's behavior (Peterson, Jeffrey, Bridgwater, & Dawson, 1984).

What about the effect of models, through the food preferences of parents, other children, and, especially, television advertising? The commercial messages on children's programs focus on high-sugar foods of little nutritional value. One study found that 68 percent of all commercials on children's television programs were for food: one-quarter for high-sugar cereals, one-quarter for candy and sweets, ten percent for fast-food restaurants, and eight percent for snacks. Very few programs advertised foods that could be considered healthful. Many of the foods of low nutritional value were advertised by attractive child models (National Science Foundation, 1977).

The fact that children are exposed to many media messages promoting foods of little nutritional value and that their diets are relatively high in such foods does not, however, necessarily show that observational learning determines children's nutritional habits. High-sugar foods may simply be more available for children and their families. Studies are lacking that directly document the impact of models on nutritional habits.

Elementary school-age and younger children's diets are primarily controlled by such children's families. From a family systems point of view, parental characteristics such as education, income, and knowledge concerning nutrition might have an effect on children's eating habits. Evidence exists that in families with preschoolers, income and mothers' nutritional knowledge are associated with the quality of the children's diets (Sims & Morris, 1974). Moreover, among school-age children, general health status is associated with both family income and maternal education (Butler et al., 1984). Many poor children do not have access to a well-balanced, adequate diet.

Alcohol Abuse, Drug Abuse, and Smoking

Because teenagers are much more likely than younger children to abuse alcohol and drugs and to smoke, these risks to health are discussed in detail in Chapter 16. However, we want to mention here some alarming statistics indicating that middle childhood is increasingly a time of experimentation with alcohol, drugs, and cigarettes. For example, a 1985 survey of over 44,000 children throughout the United States found that a third of all sixth graders reported trying beer or wine, and almost 10 percent had tried hard liquor. By contrast, among the twelfth graders interviewed in the survey, 14.5 percent reported that they had tried beer or wine when they had been in the sixth grade, and 6.8 percent said they had tried hard liquor at that time (National Parents' Resource Institute for Drug Education, reported in Brody, 1985). These results, together with similar downward trends in the ages at which smoking and drug use begin, suggest that experimentation with alcohol, drugs, and cigarettes is occurring in middle childhood more frequently today than in the past.

Smoking and alcohol or drug consumption are reported to begin at earlier ages than has been true in the past.

The determinants of the change are still poorly understood. Do school-children who use alcohol, drugs, or cigarettes do so because they believe that these substances are not really harmful? Are children influenced by observing older children, admired adults, and media figures, who make alcohol, drug, and cigarette use seem "cool"? Might particular family characteristics, such as level of parental supervision of children's activities, be associated with alcohol, drug, or cigarette use?

Answering these questions is important, because education, prevention, and intervention programs might be targeted differently depending upon the determinants of alcohol, drug, and cigarette use. For example, if beliefs about these substances underlie behavior, programs might emphasize information about their harmful effects. However, if modeling is an important determinant, efforts might be intensified to discourage admired media figures from being shown consuming alcohol or using other harmful substances. On the other hand, if aspects of the family system are important, programs should be aimed at parents as well as their children. While research continues into the causes of alcohol, drug, and cigarette use during middle childhood, perhaps all three approaches should be utilized.

Type A Behavior Pattern

We've seen that during middle childhood, behaviors are being acquired that are related to adult risk factors associated with exercise, diet, and substance abuse. In addition, researchers have identified certain behavior patterns that may be related to disease. In particular, they have studied a constellation of behaviors called *Type A behavior pattern* in relation to heart disease.

In 1959, two researchers specializing in heart disease, Friedman and Rosenman, described a pattern of behavior in adults that, they argued, increased the risk of heart attack. Called *Type A behavior pattern*, or *coronary-prone behavior pattern*, it consists of extreme competitiveness, hostility, impatience, time urgency, and striving for the achievement of poorly defined goals. "The individual exists in a chronic struggle to obtain an unlimited number of things in the shortest possible time, or against the efforts of others or obstacles" (Lawler & Allen, 1984). Individuals who did not exhibit this behavior pattern were called *Type B*.

Since it was first identified, extensive research has confirmed that adults who show a Type A behavior pattern increase their risk of heart attack, even when other risk factors, such as diet, exercise, and smoking, are controlled. In addition, Type A behaviors increase the risk of having repeated attacks, of *hypertension* or high blood pressure, and of *atherosclerosis* or hardening of the arteries (Matteson & Ivancevich, 1980).

Because of the multiple risks associated with the Type A behavior pattern, some developmentalists have been asking whether it can be identified before adulthood. They reason that stable behavior patterns are likely to begin in childhood. If the sources of Type A behaviors could be identified early, many potential heart attacks could be prevented by helping children modify behavior patterns that put them at risk (Lawler & Allen, 1984).

Several tests for measuring Type A behaviors in children have been developed. One, the Hunter-Wolf type A measure, asks children to rate themselves on questions such as, "I am easygoing—I am hard driving" (Wolf, Sklov, Wenzl, Hunter, & Berenson, 1982). Another measure, called MYTH, asks an adult who knows the child well—usually the child's teacher—to rate the child on such items as "This child can sit still long" and "This child gets irritated easily"

(Matthews & Angulo, 1980). Still other assessments observe the child's aggressiveness, competitiveness, impatience, frustration, and anger during structured tasks such as puzzle completion (Bortner & Rosenman, 1967).

Using these measures, several studies have documented behavioral differences between children classified as Type A or Type B. For example, in one study of fourth and sixth graders, children were told to hold a weight but were not told for how long. Type A children held the weight for 50 percent longer than Type B children, showing the need to achieve at a poorly defined task (Carver, Coleman, & Glass, 1976). In another study, fourth-grade children were given a task to come up with as many responses as they could within a particular time period. In some cases, they were told a score they should try to attain; in other cases, no desired score was given. All children were free to compare their scores to those of a group of other children. (Actually, fictitious scores were provided.) Children classified as Type A persisted in comparing their scores with the top fictitious score, even when they were told what score they should aim for. Type B children, on the other hand, compared their responses to those of other children only when no standard was provided (Matthews & Siegel, 1983). In other words, Type A children showed achievement striving even in inappropriate circumstances.

Some evidence also exists that Type A and Type B children differ in their physiological responding, although relatively few studies have been conducted. In one investigation, researchers measured changes in heart rate and blood pressure in a group of 42 eleven- to twelve-year-olds as they engaged in several competitive tasks (Lawler, Allen, Critcher, & Standard, 1981). As Table 12–6 shows, children classified as Type A increased their blood pressure and heart rate more than did those classified as Type B while completing the tasks.

These results should be viewed with caution, however. Other research on differences in Type A and Type B physiological responding has revealed no differences or hard-to-interpret results (Lawler & Allen, 1984). More research is needed documenting how children with Type A and Type B patterns of behavior differ (Vega-Lahr & Field, 1986).

The real question is whether children who show Type A symptoms actually run a greater risk of later heart disease. Only longitudinal studies following into adulthood a group of children classified as Type A or Type B will be able to answer this question. We do know, however, that these patterns become increasingly stable during middle childhood.

In one study, 633 children in kindergarten through grade six were rated by their teachers using the MYTH measure of Type A behavior. Then, one year later, when the children had advanced a grade, their new teachers rated them. At all grade levels, there was considerable stability in scores (the average correlation was +.55), and the older children had more stable scores over the one-year period than did the younger ones (Matthews & Avis, 1983). These findings suggest that Type A behavior patterns may begin

Table 12–6

CHANGES IN BLOOD PRESSURE AND HEART RATE IN CHILDREN CLASSIFIED AS HAVING TYPE A OR TYPE B BEHAVIOR PATTERNS

Behavior Pattern	Blood Pressure	Heart Rate
Type A	8.6	10.1
Type B	2.3	4.0

(Adapted from Lawler & Allen, *Progress in Pediatric Psychology*, Burns and Lavigne, eds., © 1984, Table 5–2. Reprinted by permission of author.)

to develop as a stable trait during middle childhood, putting some children at risk for later heart disease.

The emerging research on Type A behavior patterns in childhood has led to suggestions concerning ways of aiding children who show this risk factor. Helping children set manageable goals, develop priorities, and work out plans for achieving goals can help relieve the sense of time urgency and impatience characteristic of Type A behavior. Others advocate that relaxation training be taught to children with Type A patterns (Lawler & Allen, 1984).

In summary, we've examined some of the major components of a healthful life style, one that reduces the risks of major illness and enhances feelings of well-being. The building blocks of such a life style begin to be laid down during middle childhood and even before, as children develop habits related to diet, exercise, alcohol consumption, and behavior patterns. Such habits may endure through adolescence and into adulthood and ultimately contribute to either increased health or increased risk of disease, although only longitudinal studies will demonstrate this conclusively.

Chapter Summary

CHANGES IN SIZE AND SHAPE

□ Physical growth is less rapid during middle childhood than during infancy or adolescence, with a slow but steady increase in height and weight.

□ Some parts of the body grow more rapidly than body height and weight; others grow more slowly. This results in a pattern of uneven or asynchronous growth and produces changes in body contours.

□ Sex differences begin to appear around age nine or ten when girls begin a growth spurt and start to develop secondary sex characteristics. The influences of heredity and environment, particularly nutrition, interact to produce wide individual variations in height and weight among children of the same age.

DEVELOPMENT OF MOTOR SKILLS

□ Girls are usually more adept at skills involving precise movement, agility, and balance, while boys excel at skills involving speed, strength, and ball handling. Such sex differences may be diminishing, however, as girls and boys participate in similar sports and games.

INJURY, ILLNESS, AND HANDICAPS

□ The danger of illness from childhood infectious disease is lower during middle childhood than during infancy and early childhood, but lack of adequate immunization is still a problem for many children.

□ As family systems theory points out, chronic illnesses such as diabetes and asthma as well as handicaps place special demands upon the child's family. At the same time, the family is an important support in helping the child cope with illness.

ESTABLISHING A HEALTHFUL LIFE STYLE

□ Cognitive/developmental theory emphasizes that children's understanding of health and illness will be an important influence on how children respond to illness and how they behave to prevent it. During middle childhood, knowledge about how the body works, what causes illness, and what promotes health increases. These changes in knowledge appear to be due to broad changes in cognitive understanding rather than to direct experience with specific illnesses.

□ Children's health habits often lag behind children's understanding. Many children do not engage in vigorous exercise on a regular basis; diets are often high in sugar, fat, and salt; and alcohol and drug abuse and smoking are beginning at increasingly early ages.

□ A risk factor among adults in the development of heart disease, Type A behavior pattern—a predisposition toward impatience, aggression, and extreme competitiveness—has been identified during middle childhood. It appears to be a fairly stable characteristic of some children who show many of the same characteristics as Type A adults. Although, in the absence of longitudinal research, we do not know if Type A children will be more likely to have heart disease as adults, the existing evidence suggests that intervention programs emphasizing goal setting and relaxation may be beneficial for these children.

Recommended Readings

Eiser, C. (1985). *The psychology of childhood illness*. New York: Springer-Verlag. A comprehensive recent review of research on children's understanding of health and illness, children's responses to hospitalization, and the effect of various illnesses on the psychological adjustment of the child and the child's family.

Stevenson, H., and Siegel, A. (eds.). (1984). *Child development research and social policy*. Chicago: University of Chicago Press. A collection of excellent review articles on such topics as child health, child nutrition, and handicapping conditions. Focuses on the links between current research findings and social policy.

CHAPTER 13

Cognitive Development

Interviewer: Can one put a violet in the box of flowers (without changing the label)?

Per: Yes, a violet is also a flower.

Interviewer: Can I put one of these flowers (a tulip) in the box?

Per: Yes, it's a flower like the violet.

Interviewer: Can one make a bigger bunch with all the flowers or with all the violets?

Per: It's the same thing, violets are flowers aren't they?

Interviewer: Suppose I pick all the violets, will there be any flowers left?

Per: Oh yes, there will still be tulips, roses, and other flowers.

— *Adapted from Inhelder and Piaget, 1964, p. 107.*

The preceding is an excerpt from an interview conducted by Piaget with an eight-year-old Swiss boy named Per. The questions were carefully constructed to reveal the structure of Per's thought, in particular, Per's ability to think logically. Per's answers revealed that Per understood that the category of "flowers" was greater than the category of "tulips" or "violets."

Through such interviews, Piaget and his colleagues demonstrated important changes in cognitive thinking taking place during a child's middle years, from approximately age six until age twelve. For many children around the world, these are also the school years, a period when children enter formal schooling and acquire many of the skills needed to become successful members of their society.

Our discussion of cognitive development emphasizes two broad themes. One theme stresses the processes of cognitive development that children share in common during their middle years. Following the approach taken in discussing cognitive development during infancy (Chapter 6) and early childhood (Chapter 9), we focus here on Piaget's theory of cognitive development and on the information processing approach.

The second theme of this chapter highlights how children become increasingly different from one another in cognitive behavior and development and traces the major influences on individual differences. We consider the meaning of individual variation in intelligence, the tests that have been developed to assess individual differences, the factors that influence performance on intelligence tests, and the relation between intelligence test scores and other indexes of cognitive development or achievement. The chapter also considers creativity and giftedness.

The Stage of Concrete Operations

Piaget viewed ages five to seven years as an important transition period in children's cognitive growth. He argued that around this time, a qualitative shift, called by others the *5-to-7 shift* (White, 1965), occurs in the child's ability to organize information logically, classify and order information, and coordinate information from several sources. Piaget argued that although children during this transitional period often show evidence of an ability to solve conservation or classification problems, they do not understand why their answers

In the stage of concrete operations, children understand the principles of reversibility and identity and can apply them to concrete problems.

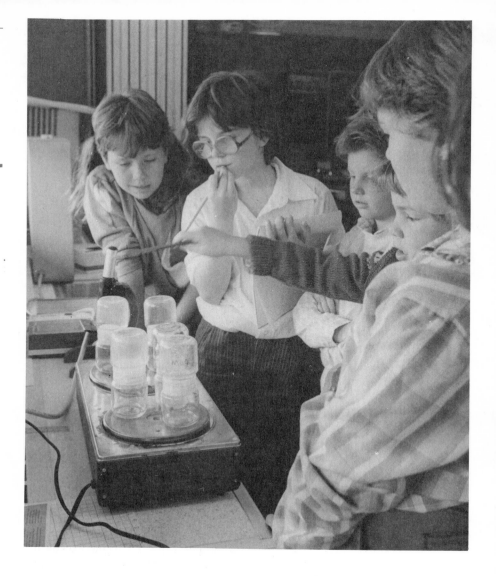

are correct, because they haven't yet grasped the logical principles underlying such problems.

By ages seven to eight, however, the *stage of concrete operations* has been reached, during which most children can reason about concrete problems, that is, objects and events they can perceive. These new reasoning skills are evident in the child's ability to solve problems involving conservation, classification, seriation, number concepts, and cause and effect.

Conservation

In contrast to the preoperational child, children in the stage of concrete operations understand that when a ball of clay is rolled into the shape of a snake, the amount of clay is unchanged. When water is poured from a tall, thin container into a shorter, wider one, children understand that the quantity of liquid is conserved (does not change). And when a row of objects, such as pennies, is lengthened by increasing the spaces between the objects, children grasp that the number of objects stays the same.

Moreover, concrete operational thinkers can explain their answers in terms of the principles of *reversibility* ("I could roll the clay back into a ball, and it would be the same" and "If I pour the water back, I will have the same amount") and *identity* ("It's still the same water"). The ability to understand conservation problems also indicates that the child's thinking has shifted from *centration,* centering on only one dimension of the problem—the change in shape or row length—to *decentration* or *relativism,* simultaneously considering two or more aspects of the problem.

Horizontal Decalage

Piaget predicted that children would master conservation problems in the following sequence: number, quantity, weight, and volume (refer to Table 9–1) (Piaget and Inhelder, 1969). He called such chronological variation in the emergence of different kinds of conservation understanding *horizontal decalage.*

To test this prediction, Ina Uzigiris (1964) administered four tests of quantity conservation, four tests of weight conservation, and four tests of volume conservation to children in grades one through six. If these forms of conservation are acquired in the predicted order, the children should fall into one of four groups: those who fail all three tests, those who understand quantity conservation only, those who pass both quantity and weight but fail volume conservation, and those who pass all three conservation tests. In support of this prediction, 93 percent of the children could be classified into one of these four groups. Although Uzigiris' tests did not include one for number conservation, other research (Brainerd & Brainerd, 1972; Gruen & Vore, 1972) confirms that it is acquired before conservation of quantity.

Piaget suggested that horizontal decalage occurs because some conservation tasks require more abstract reasoning than others. Thus, because the concept of weight must be inferred while quantity can be directly seen, children who understand that a ball of clay rolled into a snake shape does not lose or gain quantity will still not understand that the weight of the clay also does not change.

Another reason some researchers think horizontal decalage occurs is the different experiences children have with materials. For example, children might conserve number before weight because in their daily lives they are more likely to have opportunities to compare number rather than weights of objects (Zimmerman & Lanaro, 1974).

Classification

The principles of reversibility, decentration, and identity also enable children in the stage of concrete operations to solve classification problems. Unlike preoperational thinkers, who are more likely to use idiosyncratic, shifting categories to sort objects, children in the stage of concrete operations can consistently sort objects by such specified dimensions as shape, size, and color. However, *multiple classification* problems are more difficult and involve simultaneously sorting objects on two dimensions, such as shape and color (see Figure 13–1).

Another more difficult type of classification problem involves *class inclusion reasoning,* the understanding that a class always must be smaller than any larger class in which it is contained. Thus, there must be more flowers than violets (refer to the interview segment that opens this chapter), more animals than dogs, more humans than children. Piaget believed that children

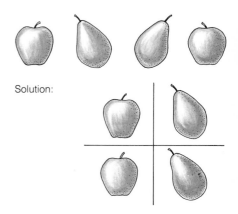

Solution:

Figure 13–1

Illustration of a Multiple Classification Problem

understood multiple classification and class inclusion later than simple classification (Brainerd, 1978).

Seriation

Piaget describes several stages through which the child must progress before achieving the ability to understand seriation problems, which involve ordering a set of objects along a dimension, for example, placing ten sticks of varying lengths in order from smallest to longest. As we saw in Chapter 9, preoperational children usually pick out the shortest and longest of a set of sticks but confuse the order of sticks of intermediate lengths. Children in the 5-to-7 shift tend to shuffle the intermediate length sticks by trial and error until they finally get them right. Children using concrete operational thought are able to systematically order the sticks by selecting the smallest, then the smallest of those remaining, and so on. When given a second set of sticks to integrate into the first series, the children are able to insert these sticks in the appropriate order (Piaget & Inhelder, 1969).

Knowing how to solve seriation problems implies the acquisition of another basic principle, *transitivity*, or *inferential reasoning*. For example, if stick A is longer than stick B, and stick B is longer than stick C, then stick A must be longer than stick C. Concrete operational thinkers—who can solve seriation problems—understand that A is longer than C without directly comparing the sticks as preoperational thinkers do (Acredolo & Horobin, 1987).

Development of the Concept of Number

Related to the ability to order a series of objects from smallest to largest is the development of the concept of number. It may seem surprising that this is achieved in the concrete operational period and not earlier, since even very young children use numbers. A preschooler, when asked how old he or she is, may proudly hold up three fingers and say "Three." Exposure to programs such as *Sesame Street* has made many young children more adept at counting than earlier generations of preschoolers were.

A child can count without understanding the concept of number; for example, a three-year-old might count his or her fingers twice. Concrete operational thinkers not only can use numbers in isolation, but, more importantly, also can employ them to count objects. Children in this stage understand that they must count each object in a group once—not skipping any—and only once—not repeating—called the *Rule of One-to-One Correspondence* (Gelman & Baillargeon, 1983). They also understand that when the tenth object is counted, that object is the tenth in a series and the total number of counted objects is ten. Finally, the concept of number includes understanding what "more than," "less than," and "equal to" mean (Flavell, 1977).

Cause and Effect

The more decentered thinking of the stage of concrete operations allows children to develop explanations that derive from their observations and enables understanding that motivations and desires do not necessarily cause events. It also permits children to distinguish between events that are reversible (as in conservation problems) and those that are irreversible or are chance occurrences.

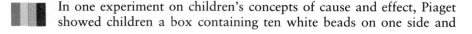 In one experiment on children's concepts of cause and effect, Piaget showed children a box containing ten white beads on one side and

ten black beads on the other, grouped in little compartments. As the box was rocked, the beads gradually began to mix. Each child was asked if, by further rocking, the beads could return to their original positions. Preschool-age children felt the beads would unmix themselves or, in Piaget's words "trade places with the whites in a kind of regular and rhythmic square dance" (Piaget and Inhelder, 1969, p. 113). However, children who had achieved concrete operational thought were aware that whatever caused the beads to mix was not reversible.

We can see the development of the concept of irreversibility—that certain events cannot be reversed or undone—in children's changing conception of death from the preschool period through middle childhood. Children younger than five often think that death is not final, that the dead have gone away or can wake up. They also fail to understand that death means the end of all life functions: They often answer "yes" to questions like "Can a dead person feel?" and "If someone died, could he still breathe?" Finally, preschoolers do not grasp that death is universal, that all living things, including themselves, eventually die. The realization of death as irreversible, devoid of life functions, and universal occurs for most children by age seven (Speece & Brent, 1984).

During the concrete operational period, children understand death to be final and irreversible.

Implications of Concrete Operational Skills

It's no coincidence that around the time that concrete operational thought is achieved, children become capable of understanding word games and humor based on double meanings (Shultz and Horibe, 1974). Elementary school-children delight in puns like the following: "Why is a rabbit dumb?" "Because he's hare-brained!" Such jokes require the child to decenter from the obvious meaning of a word to a nonobvious meaning and to consider these two meanings at the same time.

Classification and ordering skills also open up new ways of thinking about oneself in relation to others. Although preschoolers often will answer the question "Who is the best at drawing (singing, dancing)?" with "Me!", older children begin to compare themselves more realistically to others and to classify themselves and others ("Who's the smartest in the class? Who's the next smartest?") (see Chapter 14). They also show increased understanding of how individuals can occupy multiple and reciprocal roles, for example, how a woman can simultaneously be a mother to her son and a daughter to her own father (Watson, 1981).

Concrete operational thought underlies the acquisition of academic skills that are emphasized during the early school years. For example, addition and subtraction depend upon the ability to understand one-to-one correspondence, seriation (knowing that 253 is one greater than 252), and reversibility (knowing that the operation $2 + 3 = 5$ can be reversed by the operation $5 - 3 = 2$).

In summary, during the period of concrete operations, from approximately ages 7 to 11 or 12, gradual increases take place in the ability to think about and manipulate concrete objects and events. Although children during this time show that they understand reversibility/irreversibility, relativism, transitivity, and identity, they cannot apply these concepts to hypothetical or imaginary events. This may seem surprising, since we've seen that even preschoolers can invent imaginary social relations during fantasy play. The difference is that although young children can generate hypothetical ideas, they cannot apply logical operations to them. Thus, not until the emergence of formal operations around age 12 can the child begin to think systematically about an imaginary society and what social relations might be like there.

Limitations of Piaget's Theory

The development of concrete operational thinking has been a useful way to describe a number of important changes that take place in children's thinking beginning around age seven. However, as noted earlier (refer to Chapters 3 and 9), Piaget's theory has been criticized for underestimating children's capacities to acquire concrete operations because of the difficulty and unfamiliarity of many of the tasks used. For example, in one study using familiar objects such as clothing, furniture, or vehicles, children as young as three years of age could sort them into categories in a simple classification task, and about half of the five- to six-year-olds could successfully sort in terms of superordinate (for example "animal") and subordinate categories ("dog," "cat," "horse"), a class-inclusion reasoning task (Rosch, Mervis, Gray, Johnson, & Boyes-Braem, 1976).

In other studies, modifications of the language used to question children in tests of class-inclusion reasoning have been employed. For example, instead of asking, "Are there more violets or more flowers?" (as Piaget had done), language is used to highlight the difference between the subclass (violets) and the larger class (flowers): "Are there more violets or more of *all* the flowers?" (Siegel, McCabe, Brand, & Matthews, 1978). Other studies have used "family," "pile," or "group" to call attention to the larger class (Markman, 1973; Markman & Siebert, 1976, McGarrigle, Grieve, & Hughes, 1978). Using this technique, children as young as three and four years of age have shown evidence of class inclusion reasoning (Siegal et al., 1978).

Information Processing Approach

Other criticisms refer to the issue of whether children's cognitive development is continuous or stagelike (refer to Chapters 1 and 2) (Fischer & Bullock, 1984; Kuhn, 1984; Flavell, 1982). The view of cognitive development as continuous—the information processing approach—stresses the gradual development of the processes used to attend to, perceive, remember, and manipulate information in order to solve problems.

The Development of Attention

During middle childhood, children become more able to direct their attention to those elements of a problem that will help them find a solution. Thus, they can look for the slight differences that distinguish one letter from another or that tell them that $7 + 3 = ?$ is a problem in addition not subtraction.

Evidence exists that older children use attention more selectively than do preschoolers, are increasingly able to ignore distractions, and can shift their attention in a flexible and adaptive way.

In a study by Higgins and Turnure (1984), 72 preschoolers, 72 second graders, and 72 sixth graders were given a set of visual discrimination tasks under quiet, low noise, and high noise conditions. The tasks involved presenting a series of picture pairs and learning to pick out the "right" picture. Half the tasks were judged to be easy for each grade level, half to be difficult. Distractibility was measured by how often and long each child glanced away while learning the tasks.

The results, presented in Table 13–1, show that preschoolers made more errors, on both easy and difficult tasks, when more noise distraction was present. Second graders followed much the same pattern, but sixth graders showed a dramatic reversal: They actually made fewer mistakes the louder the

		Distraction Level	
Grade	Quiet	Low Noise	High Noise
Preschool			
Easy task	5.5	9.0	11.5
Hard task	31.9	35.5	41.2
Second grade			
Easy task	4.6	5.3	9.5
Hard task	26.8	36.1	31.7
Sixth grade			
Easy task	11.7	7.5	6.8
Hard task	40.6	34.7	31.8

(Adapted from Higgins & Turnure, *Child Development*, 1984, *55*, Table 1. © The Society for Research in Child Development, Inc.)

Table 13–1

MEAN ERRORS ON LEARNING TASK UNDER DIFFERENT LEVELS OF DISTRACTION

music was played. Although distraction caused the younger children to glance away from the task and hence make more errors, only the sixth graders reacted to loud noise by hunkering down to the task, glancing away less, and concentrating their attention. With age, children become not only less distractible but also more adept at directing their attention selectively when solving a problem, for example, by paying more attention to the difficult than to the easy parts.

Research illustrating this developmental change observed the study strategies of first graders, third graders, and college students, 15 in each group (Masur, McIntyre, & Flavell, 1973). In a memory task, each participant was given an opportunity to study some of a set of 36 pictures for a retest after learning which pictures had been missed on a previous test.

As Table 13−2 shows, the third graders and college students were more likely than younger children to look at missed rather than remembered items. They also looked for a longer time at those pictures they had missed on the previous test, while the first graders spent equal time looking at both remembered and forgotten pictures.

The Development of Perception

An important first step in solving a problem is noticing its important features or distinctive elements. This is a particularly difficult task for beginning readers, who must distinguish between written symbols, such as M and W or O and Q, that closely resemble each other. Preschoolers tend to perceive objects as similar based on their overall resemblance and hence tend not to notice slight differences (Gibson, Osser, Schiff, & Smith, 1963; Odom, 1978).

During the elementary school years, children become more adept at perceiving subtle details. This developmental change is illustrated in a study by Dirks and Neisser (1977). They showed 24 first, third, and sixth graders as well as a group of 24 adults, toy scenes like the one in Figure 13−2. After each child or adult inspected the scene, two items were removed, two were added, and two were moved to new positions, while the child or adult was told to look away. As Figure 13−3 shows, with increasing age, children became more accurate in noticing these changes. Interestingly, sixth graders did as well as adults in reporting items that had been moved or added.

Developmental changes also take place in the ability to perceive particular dimensions or aspects of objects, such as shape differences. Elementary school-children are more likely than preschoolers to see objects in terms of separable dimensions, and they are less likely to have personal preferences for certain aspects, such as liking green objects (Kemler & Smith, 1978).

Table 13−2

PERCENTAGE OF PREVIOUSLY MISSED ITEMS SELECTED FOR STUDY ON SUBSEQUENT TRIALS OF A MEMORY TASK

Grade Level	Second	Trial Third	Fourth
First grade	53%	67%*	66%
Third grade	85%*	74%*	80%*
College	87%*	85%*	82%*

*Differs significantly from chance level (50%). (From Masur, McIntyre, & Flavell, *Journal of Experimental Child Psychology*, 1973, Vol. 15. Orlando, FL: The Academic Press. Reprinted by permission of author and publisher.)

Figure 13–2

Toy Scene Used in Dirks and Neisser Study

(Adapted from Dirks & Neisser, *Journal of Experimental Child Psychology*, 1977, Vol. 23. Orlando, FL: The Academic Press. Reprinted by permission of author and publisher.)

Why do these changes in perception take place? Piaget argues that maturation and everyday experiences with objects interact to produce these changes. Others point to more specific environmental factors, such as schooling. For example, children learn new perceptual strategies as they acquire reading skills.

Eleanor Gibson (Gibson & Levin, 1975) studied how skilled and unskilled readers differed in their perception of print and found that skilled readers were able to take in seven to ten letter spaces of meaningful prose in a single fixation, while unskilled readers perceived far fewer letters. This meant that unskilled readers had to fixate more frequently and for longer durations to process the same amount of information that skilled readers processed. In addition, Gibson observed that unskilled readers had more backward fixations (in languages written from left to right, looking to the left of the previous fixation), slowing them down even further. Thus, practice and experience in reading can lead to more efficient perceptual strategies for taking in written information.

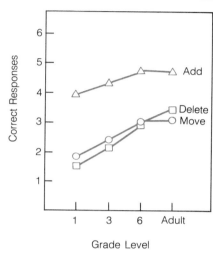

Figure 13–3

Mean Number of Correct Responses Per Subject, for Each Age and Type of Change.

(From Dirks & Neisser, *Journal of Experimental Child Psychology*, 1977, Vol. 23. Orlando, FL: The Academic Press. Reprinted by permission of author and publisher.)

Schooling and other environmental factors affect perception in more subtle ways. For example, at school, children become accustomed to schematic pictures of three-dimensional objects. However, children (and adults) who have not had schooling have difficulty understanding the distance relations implied by visual perspective in Figure 13–4. They tend to see the lines depicting hills as snakes or rivers. Thus, school experiences direct children's perception toward certain aspects of their environment and away from others.

Figure 13–4

Visual Perspective

(From Hudson, *Journal of Social Psychology*, Vol. 52, p. 188, Fig. 3, 1960. Reprinted with permission of the Helen Dwight Reid Educational Foundation, 4000 Albemarle St., N.W., Washington, D.C. 20016. Owner of copyright, 1960, Reid Foundation.)

The Development of Memory

At school, children encounter many memory demands: Learn all the states and their capitals; learn the major exports of Brazil; learn a list of Spanish words and their meanings.

In information processing terms, one can distinguish between the "hardware" of memory—memory storage capacity—and the "software" of memory—the programs or strategies used to put information in and take it out of storage (refer to Chapter 2). Two types of memory storage exist: *short-term* and *long-term*. *Long-term* memory refers to the storage of information for weeks, months, or even years, while *short-term* memory refers to memory "space" or capacity used for current or new information. For this reason, short-term memory is often called "working memory." Although long-term memory has no well-defined limits, short-term or working memory is of limited capacity.

Does short-term *memory span*—how much can be remembered after a brief exposure—increase with development? Older children and adults generally remember more than younger children. For example, if asked to recall ten pictures they have just seen, third graders will do better than kindergarteners, and fifth graders will do better than third graders (Cole, Frankel, & Sharp, 1971). Juan Pascual-Leone (1980) argues that this is because memory capacity improves with changes in brain physiology.

Others (Brown, Bransford, Ferrara, & Campione, 1983; Case, Kurland, & Goldberg, 1982) say that overall memory capacity does not increase with age. However, with development, children learn faster, more efficient memory strategies (better "software"), which free up more of their memory span to store information than is true of younger children.

To demonstrate this, Rob Case and his colleagues compared ten adults and ten six-year-olds on their ability to repeat a list of words, a task called *word span*. When meaningful words were used, adults could repeat more words than could the children. However, when nonsense words were used, the adults' word span (4.36 nonsense words) was no longer than that of the six-year-olds (4.49 meaningful words). Case argued that because nonsense words were unfamiliar to adults, their ability to store these words in memory slowed to the level of six-year-olds (Case, Kurland, & Goldberg, 1982).

The issue of developmental changes in memory capacity cannot be easily resolved. It is impossible to measure directly the "amount" of short-term memory available to children as they develop. As Case points out, the strategies that children use to help them remember appear to be a significant factor in determining how well they do.

During the elementary school years, memory strategies become more frequent, better, and more varied. That is, with age, children increasingly use deliberate strategies for remembering material, they use the strategies more efficiently, and they develop a variety of different techniques suitable for different tasks. This general pattern can be illustrated by examining several of the more commonly used (and studied) strategies (Miller, et al, 1986).

Rehearsal.   As noted in Chapter 9, around age seven, children begin spontaneously rehearsing to-be-remembered items by repeating them silently or aloud. Through middle childhood, rehearsal strategies become increasingly complex (Pressley, Heisel, McCormick, & Nakamura, 1982).

For example, in one study (Ornstein, Naus, & Liberty, 1975), 8-, 11-, and 13-year-olds—56 children at each age level—were asked to rehearse aloud after the presentation of each word on a list they later would be asked to recall. As the responses shown in Table 13–3 indicate, during the pause between each word, the eight-year-olds repeated the item just presented, for example, "Cat, cat, cat." The older children, however, used their rehearsal time to repeat the past few words presented, "desk, man, yard, cat." This more efficient rehearsal strategy of the older children resulted in the recall of more words on the 17-item list, particularly the more difficult-to-remember first items (see Figure 13–5).

Categorization.   When things don't have to be recalled in a specific order, it's helpful to remember items by category, for example, remembering all the animals, all the flowers, and all the colors from the following list: cat, tulip, red, dog, horse, orange, green, lily, rose, grey. Preschool and kindergarten children usually do not use categories, and when they do, they form idiosyncratic categories, like "cat-grey-rose." With age, children use fewer, more stable, and more widely shared categories (Flavell, 1970; Moely, 1977; Corsale & Ornstein, 1980; Ackerman, 1987).

Elaboration.   Another strategy that develops during middle childhood is of particular help in remembering pairs of objects or events that go together, such as U.S. states and their capitals. *Verbal elaboration* is a technique for remembering pairs of words by generating a sentence or phrase that links the two, while *visual elaboration* involves constructing an image linking two ideas. Elaboration works best if the association is active rather than static. For example, suppose I have to remember the pair: LADY–BROOM. The sentence "The LADY flew on a BROOM" (active) or the corresponding mental picture will help me recall these items better than "The LADY has a BROOM" (static) (Siegler, 1983).

In general, older elementary schoolchildren use elaboration more often than younger children, and older children are more apt to use active associations (Pressley, 1982; Paris & Lindauer, 1976; Turnure, Buium, & Thurlow, 1976). However, elaboration is generally more difficult than rehearsal, since the use of elaboration requires the child to form an association among items and store that association in memory along with the individual items to be remembered. For this reason, rehearsal strategies are used spontaneously by most fifth graders, but elaboration strategies are not common until adolescence (Rohwer, 1980; Pressley & Levin, 1977).

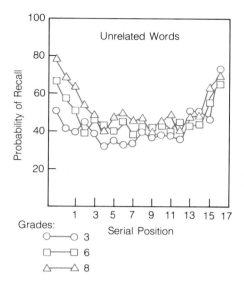

Figure 13–5

Mean Proportion of Unrelated Items Recalled

(From Ornstein et al., *Child Development*, 1975, 26. © The Society for Research in Child Development, Inc. Reprinted by permission of author and publisher.)

Table 13–3

TYPICAL REHEARSAL RESPONSES (UNRELATED WORDS)

| Word Presented | Rehearsal Sets | |
	Eighth-Grade Subject	Third-Grade Subject
1. Yard	Yard, yard, yard	Yard, yard, yard, yard, yard
2. Cat	Cat, yard, yard, cat	Cat, cat, cat, cat, yard
3. Man	Man, cat, yard, man, yard, cat	Man, man, man, man, man
4. Desk	Desk, man, yard, cat, man, desk, cat, yard,	Desk, desk, desk, desk

(From Ornstein et al., *Child Development*, 1975, 26. © The Society for Research in Child Development, Inc. Reprinted by permission of author and publisher.)

Many factors besides the difficulty of the strategy itself affect how children remember. The nature of the task is important. For example, rehearsal will not work if there is no time between the presentation of items. If the facts to be remembered are abstract, complex, or poorly understood, elaboration will be difficult. Many of the ways researchers assess memory employ artificial tasks, such as memorizing a word list. This approach may seriously underestimate children's memory abilities in everyday situations. As an illustration of this, Z. M. Istomina (1975), a Soviet psychologist, showed that children learned approximately twice as many words in a list when it was presented as a shopping list rather than as a laboratory task.

A second important factor, emphasized by learning theorists, is the reinforcement children receive for remembering. Thus, in one study, 72 fourth, sixth, and eighth graders were asked to remember 48 words, each of which was worth one cent, three cents, or five cents for remembering. In general, children remembered more nickel than less "valuable" words (Wilson, Shogren, & Witryol, 1978).

Increasing children's motivation to remember (or pay attention or notice significant details) does not always produce improved performance. A study by Appel, Cooper, McCarrell, Sims-Knight, Yussen, & Flavell, (1972) illustrates this. Twenty preschoolers, 40 first graders, and 40 fifth graders were shown two sets of pictures. For one set, the children in each age group were asked to "look at the pictures," while for the other set, they were instructed to "try to remember the pictures." The results, shown in Table 13–4, indicate that in both the "looking" and "remembering" conditions, older children recalled the pictures better than preschoolers. Variations in the instructions given to the younger children did not affect their performance. However, the fifth graders remembered more when they were instructed to "remember" rather than just "look."

The oldest children in this study seemed to have an awareness of the difference between just looking at something and trying to remember it. Indeed, when the investigators examined what the children actually did under the two conditions, they found that only the fifth graders increased their use of rehearsal and categorization when told to remember than when told to look. These results, and others like them, show that *metamemory*—awareness of one's memory processes—also develops through middle childhood.

Metamemory

Three aspects of metamemory have been studied: awareness of the self as memorizer, awareness of memory strategies, and awareness of how strategies fit different tasks.

Table 13–4

MEAN PERCENTAGE OF ITEMS RECALLED UNDER INSTRUCTIONS TO "LOOK" AND INSTRUCTIONS TO "REMEMBER"

Instructions	Preschool	Grade 1	5
Look	48%	63%	62%
Remember	46%	66%	81%

(From Appel et al., *Child Development*, 1972, *43*. © The Society for Research in Child Development, Inc. Reprinted by permission of author and publisher.)

Awareness of the Self.   During the middle years, children become more realistic and more accurate about their memory capacities. They become better able to predict their short-term memory span and their performance in recalling or recognizing previously seen items (Yussen & Berman, 1981; Yussen & Levy, 1975). In an influential early study of metamemory, children were asked "Do you forget?" (Kreutzer, Leonard, & Flavell, 1975). Almost all the children past first grade said "yes," but many younger children claimed that they never forgot things. In another investigation, when preschoolers were asked how many of ten pictures they would be able to memorize, more than half of them said "all." Very few of the older children thought they would do as well. In reality, although none of the children could remember all the pictures, the older group had significantly better recall than did the preschoolers (Flavell, Friedrichs, & Hoyt, 1970).

Awareness of Strategies.   With age, children become more aware of the different strategies they might employ to remember to take their books in the morning, remember to call home from a friend's house, or remember an important telephone number. In one study, kindergarteners, third graders, and fifth graders were asked what they would do to remember a telephone number. Although 95 percent of the third and fifth graders said it would be best to phone quickly before getting a glass of water, only 40 percent of youngest children agreed with this strategy. Most of the elementary school-age children also indicated that they would write down the number or would rehearse it. However, only 60 percent of the kindergarteners indicated any memory strategy (Kreutzer et al., 1975).

Fitting Strategies to Tasks.   Children need to be able to appraise the difficulty of various learning tasks and to allocate their time and strategies to different problems. There is evidence that preschoolers and kindergarteners are aware that memorizing a long list of words will be more difficult than learning a short list (Wellman et al., 1981) and that recalling information from memory is easier than recognizing previously seen information when it is later presented (Speer & Flavell, 1979).

   Awareness of task difficulty comes earlier than the child's ability to adapt memory strategies to fit differing task demands. This is illustrated in a study by Rogoff, Newcombe, & Kagan (1974) in which four-, six-, and eight-year-olds were told that their recognition of 40 pictures would be tested after a few minutes, one day, or seven days. Only the oldest children studied the pictures longer when anticipating that they would have to remember them for a longer period.

Metamemory and Remembering.   It seems reasonable that becoming aware of how to remember should improve children's actual memory. Although both metamemory and memory performance do increase with age, researchers have found a weak relationship between a child's knowledge about memory and how well that child actually remembers (Siegler, 1983). Knowing about memory strategies does not necessarily mean that a child will use these strategies. Many other factors must be taken into account. The child may not feel confident in performing the strategy or may not believe that the strategy will work, the child may be unmotivated or discouraged, or the task may seem too difficult.

Knowledge and Memory.   What a child already knows influences how easy or difficult it is to learn new material. In fact, some investigators of memory

When children are experts at a task, such as chess, they may remember aspects of the task better than non-expert adults.

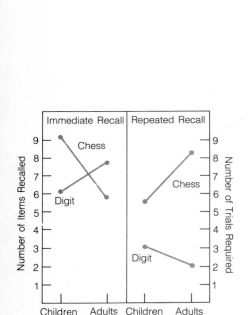

Figure 13—6

The Amount of Recall in Immediate and Repeated Recall Tasks, for Digits and Chess Stimuli

(From Chi, *Children's Thinking: What Develops?* R. Siegler, ed., 1978, p. 83. Hillsdale, NJ: Lawrence Erlbaum Associates. Reprinted by permission of author and publisher.)

development suggest that memory strategies and metamemory may be less important in some situations than the knowledge that an individual has acquired.

An interesting illustration of the contribution of knowledge to memory comes from a study by Michelene Chi (1978), who compared ten-year-olds' memory for chessboards to that of adults. For 10 seconds, Chi displayed an organized arrangement of chess pieces on a chessboard; then she covered the board and asked the child or adult to reproduce the arrangement on a second board. As Figure 13—6 shows, the ten-year-olds were faster and more accurate than the adults.

Why do ten-year-olds outperform adults in this case? The results become less surprising when we learn that the children in this study were chess experts, while the adults were novices at the game. In this situation, the children had more relevant knowledge to bring to the memory task than did the adults and hence performed better. As Figure 13—6 shows, the same children were less able than the adults to memorize a series of numbers, a task called *digit span*. This study illustrates that some of the age changes in memory skill found by researchers can be attributed to increases in knowledge. In cases where children have more knowledge than adolescents or adults, they show better memory performance.

Children's knowledge is closely related to their language development. A child who knows a great deal about chess or dinosaurs or baseball players has a larger vocabulary of terms related to these areas than does a child with other interests. In general, language affects every aspect of information processing.

Language

By the time the average child enters elementary school, he or she has a vocabulary of over 2,000 words (Moskowitz, 1978) and understands and uses complex grammatical forms correctly, such as the passive voice: "The squirrel *was chased* by the dog"; past interrogatives: "When did he do it?"; and irregular verb and noun forms: "We *went* for a walk." (Refer to Chapter 10.)

Although the differences between child language and adult language are less dramatic during middle childhood than during infancy and the preschool years, vocabulary continues to grow, and some aspects of syntax (grammar) continue to be acquired during the elementary school years (Maratsos, 1983).

For example, based on interviews with 40 children, Carol Chomsky (1969) identified several kinds of sentences that posed difficulties for grade-school children (see Table 13—5). The problem in the first sentence—"John is easy to please"—is that John, the subject of the sentence, is also the object of the verb "to please." In Chomsky's experiments, nine-year-olds understood sentences like this correctly, but most of the five-year-olds interpreted the sentence as though John were doing the pleasing, and six- to eight-year-olds showed intermediate levels of understanding.

Although comprehension and use of complex grammatical constructions continue to develop through middle childhood and into adolescence, the basic grammatical structure of adult language has been acquired by the time a child begins school. We can see the level of linguistic competence achieved during middle childhood by looking at children's humor. For example, elementary school-age children delight in tongue twisters, repeated as quickly as possible, such as the following:

Bring a broad-backed black bath brush.
She sold sea shells at the seashore.

This kind of humor indicates that the rules of pronunciation have been mastered. Play languages like *pig latin,* popular in many cultures, are based on an understanding of accepted grammatical rules, with a few added simple rules. This is why elementary school-age children believe that *eakingspay igpay atinlay ancay ebay eryvay umoroushay.* Finally, humorous verse like the following favorite of Russian children indicates an understanding of semantic impossibility (for example, "blind" means "not able to see") (Shultz and Robillard, 1980):

The blind man gazes
The deaf man listens
The cripple runs a race
The mute cries: "Help!"

The consolidation of language skills is evident not only in forms of humor but also in children's developing appreciation for metaphor (figures of speech that imply a likeness between objects or ideas). In one study, children were asked to paraphrase sentences like the following: "After many years of working at the jail, the prison guard had become a hard rock that could not be moved." Six-year-olds understood the sentence literally. For example, one child said that "The king had a magic rock and turned the guard into another rock." Eight-year-olds understood that the guard was like a rock in some way, but

Form	Difficulty	Attained By
"John is easy to see."	Subject of *to see*	5/6—9 years
"John promised Bill to go."	Subject of *to go*	5/6—9 years
"John asked Bill what to do."	Subject of *to do*	9 + years

(From Chomsky, 1969.)

Table 13—5

GRAMMATICAL FORMS ACQUIRED DURING MIDDLE CHILDHOOD

saw the relationship only in physical terms: "The guard had hard, tough muscles." Only by age ten did children capture the psychological connotations of the metaphor. Thus, one ten-year-old answered, "The guard was mean and did not care for the prisoners" (Winner, Rosentstiel, & Gardner, 1976).

These developing language skills affect other aspects of information processing, such as perception, memory, and problem solving.

Language and Perception.   One theory about how language and perception are related was developed by Benjamin Whorf (1956) and Edward Sapir (1958) and is called, not surprisingly, the *Whorf/Sapir hypothesis.* This theory states that the more words we have for different aspects of our environment, the more we are able to perceive these aspects. For example, because the Eskimo language has over a dozen words for various kinds of snow, while English has only a few, Eskimos can perceive finer distinctions when they look at snow than can English speakers. Thus, the Whorf/Sapir hypothesis claims that the language we speak literally determines how we see the world around us.

This view has been challenged by experiments on color perception of adults of different language groups. Basic colors—red, green, yellow, blue—were identified similarly by people from 23 different language groups, including the Dani, a tribe from New Guinea who had only two color terms: *mili* (black) and *mola* (white) (Heider, 1972; Heider & Oliver, 1972; Rosch, 1974, 1977). This suggests that perceptions are universal, but that different languages give us different conceptual tools to understand the environment (Cole & Scribner, 1977).

Language and Attention.   Language has also been shown to be helpful in directing children's attention to certain aspects of a problem. If an adult is helping a child work on a jigsaw puzzle, reminders such as "look for the pale blue piece" or "let's see if we can find a jagged edge piece like this one" will aid the child's performance, provided the child understands the meaning of *jagged* and *pale.* If not, the process of finding pieces that fit the categories of *jagged* and *pale* will aid the child's understanding of the meaning of these words (Bruner, et al, 1966).

Language and Memory.   As we have seen, mnemonic strategies such as rehearsal, categorization, and elaboration involve the use of language as a way of keeping material to be learned in memory. During middle childhood, children more frequently use *verbal mediators*—words to help them remember. When children are given such verbal mediators—"Can you think of any *flowers?*"—their recall of items on a list improves (Kee & Bell, 1981).

Language and Problem Solving.   Before starting out on a problem, it helps to be clear about what needs to be done, to check whether the problem is being correctly understood, and to evaluate how the solution is progressing. The development of such aspects of problem solving, called *metacognition,* is receiving increased attention by researchers (Revelle et al., 1985). Although doing these things doesn't necessarily require language (Flavell, Speer, Green, & August, 1981), problem solvers who can articulate these steps are generally more successful than those who cannot (Wong, 1985; Zabrucky & Ratner, 1986).

An illustration of metacognition comes from a study by Roy Cameron (1984), who taught 154 second, fourth, and sixth graders how to play a pattern-matching game in which the children were shown several complete patterns and one pattern partially hidden behind small windows. Each child

With age, children use increasingly complex rules to solve problems such as those involving a balance scale.

had a number of tries to determine which pattern matched the hidden one. Later, Cameron asked each child to explain the game—"Tell me everything you remember about how to play the game"—and to explain the strategy the child followed during play—"Tell me how you decide which window to open." At each grade level, children who could verbalize the instructions and a relevant strategy were most efficient at solving the problem (that is, they guessed the hidden pattern with fewer tries).

In summary, language plays a role in facilitating perception, attention, memory, and problem solving. However, as noted in Chapter 10, the precise relationship between language and cognition remains a matter of debate. Some see language as an outcome of cognitive growth, while others see language as a means of advancing thought.

Reasoning

When children solve problems, particularly complex ones, more is involved than perception, attention, language, and memory. The information that is acquired through these processes must be integrated in a meaningful way. The child must use reasoning to arrive at a solution and to understand why the solution is correct or incorrect.

According to Robert Siegler (1983), children reason by using rules or hypotheses. Siegler showed that such rules could be discovered by creating problems in which children who use different rules produce different patterns of answers and errors. Siegler presented children with increasingly complex problems involving a balance scale with a lever to keep the arm of the scale motionless (see Figure 13–7). For each problem, the child must guess which side of the scale will go down when the lever is released. Siegler (1976) discovered that the rules children used to solve problems like these become increasingly complex through middle childhood:

Rule I: The side with more weight will go down.
Rule II: If weights are equal, the side whose weight is farthest away from the fulcrum goes down.

Figure 13-7

The Balance Scale

(From Siegler, "Three Aspects of Cognitive Development," *Cognitive Psychology*, 1976, Vol. 8. Orlando, FL: The Academic Press. Reprinted by permission of author and publisher.)

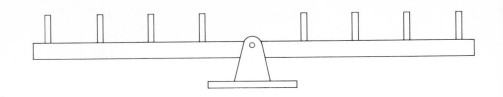

Rule III: If one side has more weight, but the other side has weight farther away from the fulcrum, guess.

Rule IV: Multiply weight times distance from the fulcrum to determine which side goes down (see Table 13–6).

Five-year-olds most often used Rule I and so failed to solve more difficult problems like the conflict-weight one. Nine-year-olds generally used Rule II or III, while 13- and 17-year-olds most often used Rule III. Although the children could not state these rules, they used them to solve the balance scale problems. Even a majority of college students did not use Rule IV.

At this point, let's summarize the development of cognition during the middle years from an information processing perspective. Perception and attention become more selective and more efficient. With age, children can attend to and coordinate multiple aspects of problems. Memory strategies become more deliberate and more complex, with the use of rehearsal, categorization, and elaboration increasing. In addition, children become aware of the demands of different memory tasks and begin to select strategies appropriate to different situations. Children's memory is aided by their developing knowledge and their

Table 13-6

PREDICTIONS FOR PERCENTAGE OF CORRECT ANSWERS AND ERROR PATTERNS FOR CHILDREN USING DIFFERENT RULES

Problem type	Rules				Predicted developmental trend
	I	II	III	IV	
Balance	100	100	100	100	No change—all children at high level
Weight	100	100	100	100	No change—all children at high level
Distance	0 (Should say "balance")	100	100	100	Dramatic improvement with age
Conflict-weight	100	100	33 (Chance responding)	100	Decline with age Possible upturn in oldest group
Conflict-distance	0 (Should say "right down")	0 (Should say "right down")	33 (Chance responding)	100	Improvement with age
Conflict-balance	0 (Should say "right down")	0 (Should say "right down")	33 (Chance responding)	100	Improvement with age

(From Siegler, "Three Aspects of Cognitive Development," *Cognitive Psychology*, 1976, Vol. 8. Orlando, FL: The Academic Press. Reprinted by permission of author and publisher.)

use of language. Finally, children develop increasingly complex rules to integrate information in order to solve problems (Ferretti & Butterfield, 1986).

Limits of the Information Processing Approach

Critics of the information processing approach argue that although the approach describes developmental changes, the reasons for change are not explained (Kail and Bisanz, 1982; Brown, Bransford, Ferrara, and Campione, 1983). For example, why do children use increasingly complex rehearsal strategies? Is it because they are learning such memory skills in school? What role do maturational changes play? The genetic and environmental conditions influencing information processing skills have not been adequately explained to date (Case, 1984).

A second criticism of this approach is that it does not address the role of emotion, personality, or social relations in cognitive development—what some researchers call *hot cognition.* Many of the methods used by investigators have involved laboratory tasks divorced from the real-life activities and concerns of children (Siegler, 1983). Little attention is paid to the social context of learning (Vygotsky, 1978; Rogoff and Wertsch, 1984).

Information processing has also been criticized for presenting a view of cognitive development as a number of fragmented processes without showing how they are combined (Kuhn, 1984; Siegler, 1981; Fischer, 1980). To get a better sense of how the different aspects of information processing work together, let's look at the example of a child reading a story.

As Figure 13–8 shows, during reading, attention is directed to the page; perception involves eye fixations, movement, and the extraction of physical features; and language is used to encode the word and integrate it with the preceding text. Rules are applied to decide where sentences or other meaningful units end. All of these processes are affected by knowledge already stored in working-memory and in long-term memory. At the same time, what the child perceives and encodes is being stored in memory for later use (note the arrows going in both directions into and out of memory).

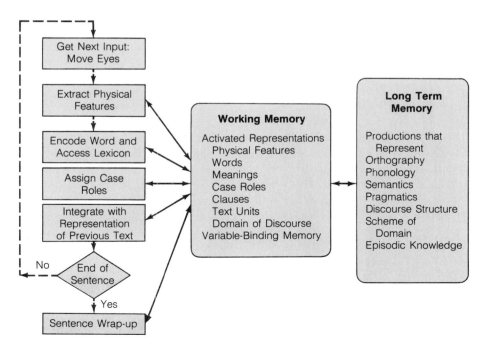

Figure 13—8

Schematic Diagram of the Major Processes and Structures in Reading Comprehension

(From Just & Carpenter, *Psychology Review,* 1980, Vol. 87. Copyright 1980 by the American Psychological Association. Reprinted by permission of the author.)

Learning Problems

Learning disability, or LD, is defined as a "disorder in one or more psychological processes involved in understanding or using language, spoken or written . . . manifested in an imperfect ability to listen, think, speak, read, write, spell or do mathematical calculations. It does not include sensory handicaps, retardation, emotional disturbance or environmental or economic disadvantage" (Public Law (P.L.) 94–142).

Children with learning disabilities are normal in intelligence and often perform as well as their peers in some areas but exhibit specific deficiencies in reading (dyslexia), spelling (dysgraphia), or mathematics (dyscalcula). Approximately two to four percent of all elementary school-age children in the United States are thought to suffer from a learning disability. Such estimates are not precise, because learning disabilities are broadly defined and other terms, such as *learning disorder, minimal brain dysfunction* (MBD), and *hyperactivity* (refer to Chapter 9), are sometimes used to refer to the same or similar problems.

To illustrate what we know about the causes and treatment of learning disabilities, we'll focus on *dyslexia.* Information processing and biological theories have both advanced explanations for this problem.

Information Processing Deficits

Although dyslexics generally do poorly discriminating letters or scanning text, they perform normally on other perceptual discriminations, such as picking out a target shape from a set of unfamiliar shapes (Mason & Katz, 1976) or discriminating a familiar object from a crowded scene (refer to Figure 13–2) (Vellutino, Smith, Steger, & Karman, 1975; Ellis, 1984). However, dyslexics show delayed development of selective attention, do more poorly on tests of memory span (Siegel, 1985; Ellis, 1984) and show less awareness of the cognitive and memory demands of reading tasks (Baker, 1982; Brown et al., 1983) than do normal readers.

Biological Origins

Some researchers believe that the origins of dyslexia are in the brain (hence, the use of the term *minimal brain dysfunction* to refer to the disorder). Dyslexics often show late language development, a tendency to speech errors, and difficulties in object-naming tasks, all activities involving the left hemisphere of the brain. By contrast, they do as well as others on such tasks as picture completion or object assembly which involve the right hemisphere (Ellis, 1984). Moreover, differences in the pattern of electrical activity on the surface of the brain have been detected when dyslexics have been compared with other children (Pirozzolo and Hansch, 1982). Some researchers believe that dyslexic children have disturbances in brain lateralization, with the left, verbal, side of the brain handling spatial reasoning (normally a right-side function), thereby leaving less room for verbal activities, such as reading (refer to Chapter 8) (Wittelson, 1977; Corballis, 1983).

Treatments

Although the origins of dyslexia are still unclear, the importance of literacy skills for adult competence has spurred efforts to treat dyslexics. Since dyslexics have difficulty with printed material and not with other forms of information, they can learn efficiently using other means, such as audio tapes. In addition, some teaching methods directed at improving reading skills have proved effective. Naidoo (1981) has reviewed these methods and has come to the following conclusions regarding successful programs:

1. They directly teach reading, writing, and spelling skills rather than trying to improve perceptual tracking, memory, or coordination.
2. They are highly structured and emphasize cumulative learning, with tasks progressing from simple to increasingly complex.
3. They are based on the phonics method of decoding word sounds from letters rather than recognizing whole words.

Other Factors

Although the definition of learning disabilities such as dyslexia excludes emotional and social factors, in real life such a division is not maintained so easily. Children with learning disabilities who do not receive early diagnosis and treatment often become discouraged about their ability. This leads them to avoid learning situations where they might be embarrassed (for example, volunteering to read aloud) and makes them lack confidence to tolerate mistakes and correct them. They soon define themselves as someone who "can't learn." It's important that those who work with learning disabled children be sensitive to these emotional factors.

Both the Piagetian and the information processing theories examined in this chapter emphasize the developmental patterns common to children during middle childhood. Although these approaches recognize that children of the same age will differ in their attention, perception, memory, language, and reasoning, measuring each child's ability and comparing it to other children of the same age is not of major interest.

Intelligence

During middle childhood, individual differences in cognitive development become more pronounced. By age 12 if not earlier, some children in a classroom will be labeled as "bright," some as "average," and some as "below average." A few may be viewed as learning disabled. Both adults and children apply these labels, which have important consequences for a child's development.

What do "bright," "average," and "below average" mean? What do we mean by "intelligence"? This section considers the meaning and measurement of differences in intelligence.

Defining Intelligence

If you were asked to list behaviors typical of an intelligent person, what behaviors would you name? "Converses easily on a variety of subjects," "makes good decisions," "sizes up situations well," and "displays awareness of the world around him or her" are some common responses (Sternberg, Conway, Ketron, & Bernstein, 1981). The everyday usage of the term *intelligence* is called an *implicit theory* of intelligence (Neisser, 1979; Sternberg, 1985).

Robert Sternberg has questioned experts on intelligence, nonexpert adults, and children of different ages concerning their implicit theories. He finds that being intelligent means different things in different situations. For example, a person who is socially adept cannot be assumed to show equal prowess in solving abstract problems (Sternberg & Powell, 1983). In addition, people's definitions of intelligence are related to age: An intelligent infant might be one who is well coordinated, while an intelligent five-year-old is perhaps described as someone who has a good vocabulary or can solve problems.

Implicit theories of intelligence reveal cultural differences as well. For example, Super (1982) investigated conceptions of intelligence among the Kokwet of western Kenya. They used three different terms to correspond to what we would call "intelligence." *Ngom,* applied only to children, meant being responsible, verbally quick, and interpersonally skilled. *Utat,* used to refer only to adults, suggested inventiveness, cleverness, wisdom, and unselfishness. A third term, *kwelat,* indicated that a person was smart or "sharp." In summary, implicit theories of intelligence are diverse, developmental, and culturally specific. The definition of intelligence used in the development of intelligence tests, called an *explicit theory* of intelligence by Sternberg (1985), is considerably more narrow than everyday conceptions of intelligence.

The Stanford-Binet Intelligence Test

In 1904, the Minister of Public Instruction in Paris asked Alfred Binet and T. Simon to devise a test so that children suspected of retardation could be reliably identified and placed in special classes. Thus, the items selected were designed to predict academic competence at different developmental levels and to distinguish more from less able youngsters (Binet & Simon, 1916). Although these

Alfred Binet

items reflect different kinds of reasoning skills, intelligence is defined in terms of a single global score rather than a set of different abilities.

Lewis Terman, a Stanford University psychologist, modified Binet and Simon's test, and the resulting measure, revised many times since then, became known as the Stanford-Binet Intelligence Test. It has become the most widely used measure of intelligence (Terman & Merrill, 1973).

An individual's score on the test was derived as follows: *Chronological age* (C.A.)—the number of years since birth—is compared to *mental age* (M.A.)—the person's level of performance relative to the "average" score attained by persons of a given age. Thus, a 10-year-old who performs at the level of an average 12-year-old will have an M.A. of 12. The *intelligence quotient*, or IQ, as the final score is known, consisted of the ratio between mental age and chronological age multiplied by 100. In the latest revision, a new method of computing the IQ, called a *deviation IQ*, was introduced. This indicates how far above or below the mean a child's score is compared to same-age children in a comparison group (refer to Chapter 3). Average performance for one's chronological age equals 100, scores above 100 indicate above average IQ, while scores below 100 indicate below average IQ.

The Wechsler Intelligence Scale for Children

The second most commonly used intelligence scale, known as the Wechsler Intelligence Scale for Children-Revised, or WISC-R (Wechsler, 1974), is appropriate for children from ages six to sixteen. As shown in Table 13–7, it consists of 12 subtests (two are optional), half verbal and half performance (activities that do not require verbal answers).

Like the Stanford-Binet, the WISC-R is designed to be administered individually. Children begin with items that are considered easy for their age and progress through increasingly difficult items. The WISC-R differs from the Stanford-Binet in placing less emphasis on verbal responses and in distinguishing between two broad types of intelligence.

Both tests, however, require verbal responses and assume that children share a common knowledge base. Moreover, in both tests, the interpretation of a child's score is based upon a comparison with a large group of other children taking the test. The average score of 100 is derived from *standardizing* the test on large samples of children.

Until the 1970s, minority children were not represented in these standardization samples. Although small numbers of minority children are now included, it is still true that a child's IQ score is based on a largely white standard of comparison. This has led to accusations that IQ tests are culturally biased and unfair.

Influences on IQ Performance

The controversy concerning racial and cultural bias in IQ testing is part of a wider debate about influences on intelligence, at least as defined by an IQ score. For years, this debate has been framed in terms of *nature* versus *nurture*, that is, how much of intelligence is due to heredity versus how much is due to environmental influences (refer to Chapters 1, 2, and 4).

Genetic Influences.   At first glance, it might seem as though the best way to show that intelligence is inherited would be to compare individuals who share similar genes with those who do not. Following this logic, identical, or *mon-*

Table 13–7

SUBSCALES AND EXAMPLES OF
ITEMS FROM WECHSLER
INTELLIGENCE SCALE FOR
CHILDREN—REVISED (WISC–R)

Subscale	Activity	Sample Item
Verbal		
Information	Knowledge about world.	How many wheels does a bicycle have?
Similarities	How two objects are alike.	How are an orange and an apple alike?
Arithmetic	Arithmetic word problems.	Mary had ten pieces of candy. She gave three to Jane. How many does Mary have left?
Vocabulary	Definition of common English words.	What is a peach?
Comprehension	Understand societal customs.	What are libraries used for?
Digit Span (Optional)	Recall digits presented forward and backward.	Repeat these numbers: 7 4 8 9 6 3 2 9
Performance		
Picture Completion	Recognize missing part of a picture of an object.	
Picture Arrangement	Rearrange scrambled set of pictures in sequence so as to tell a coherent story.	
Block Design	Reproduce a picture of a design from a set of red, white, and half-red, half-white blocks.	
Object Assembly	Put together puzzle to form a picture of a common object.	
Coding	Rapidly copy symbols paired with pictures of objects.	
Mazes (Optional)	Trace route through set of mazes from beginning to end.	

Are IQ Tests Culturally Biased?

There is ample evidence that black children generally score lower on IQ tests than do white children. One review of relevant studies concluded that on the average, a 15-point gap exists between the races (Jensen, 1980); when social class is controlled, the white advantage narrows to about 10 points (Blau, 1981). Critics of the IQ test argue that the poorer performance of black children stems from bias in the test contents and administration, while proponents of IQ tests claim that the tests are the least discriminatory and most objective means available to assess individual differences in intelligence. Here, we'll review both sides of this debate and attempt to draw some conclusions.

Language Bias

Because both the Stanford-Binet and WISC-R IQ tests require verbal responses, one way they may be biased is in their reliance on *Standard English*. Some black American children speak *Black English,* which is an alternate form of English with its own grammatical rules (Labov, 1970). For example, "I be goin' home right now" and "Is they gone there?" are Black English for "I am on the way home" and "Have they gone there?" (Foss & Hakes, 1978).

Because expressions that are correct in Black English are labeled as errors in Standard English, many black children may be reluctant to speak freely in front of white adults. Labov (1970) has shown that black children who show poor language skills during testing use sophisticated linguistic codes when talking with their peers. Since Black English is not accepted in school and testing situations, some black children may feel unmotivated, discouraged, and "put down"; these feelings are likely to interfere further with their IQ performance.

Advocates of the use of intelligence tests counter that black children's performance on IQ tests does not differ systematically regardless of whether the tester is white or black. In some situations, black children perform better with white testers, suggesting that fear or suspicion of whites is not a factor in most IQ testing (Bucky & Banta, 1972; Sattler & Gwynne, 1982). Additionally, black children do not in general score lower on verbal items—where language bias would be most evident—than on performance items of the WISC-R (Reynolds and Jensen, 1983). For example, in one study conducted in New York City, black children scored relatively higher on verbal items than they did on items tapping spatial reasoning or mathematical thinking (Lesser, Fifer, & Clark, 1965).

Cultural Bias

Another source of bias may lie in the content of specific items on the test. Black and Hispanic children may be likely to perform more poorly on items that refer to things more familiar to whites. This charge, too, is difficult to document. Efforts to weed out culturally specific items have not eliminated the racial difference in IQ. Moreover, when the responses of black and white children to specific items thought to be most culturally biased are compared, black children do not respond more poorly (Jensen, 1980). Although the matter is still controversial, the evidence for cultural and language bias in IQ tests has not been documented strongly, although it is possible that further research may uncover more subtle sources of bias.

Interpreting Group Differences in IQ

In addition to the black/white difference we have been discussing, other racial and cultural differences in IQ performance have been found. For example, Japanese children score on the average 6 to 11 points higher than whites (Lynn, 1982). And children of all cultural backgrounds who are middle-class score between 10 and 20 points above lower-class children from the same culture. As noted earlier, IQ scores do not tell us about variations in native intelligence or adaptive behavior but help predict how well the child will perform in school. Even here, prediction is far from perfect. The odds of accurately predicting how well a child will do academically in elementary school only from knowing that child's IQ score are only 50-50. The child's motivation to learn, study habits, attitudes about school, general health, and family environment are also important factors (Walden & Ramey, 1983).

It is likely that the environmental stresses and discrimination experienced by many poor, black children adversely affect both their chances of school success and their performance on standardized IQ tests, as we discuss later in this chapter. Similarly, it is likely that Japanese children show enhanced IQ performance because of their culture's emphasis on cognitive skills, longer hours of schooling and homework, and close parental supervision of school work (Stevenson, Stigler, Lee, Lucker, Kitamura, & Hsu, 1985).

Relationship	Median Correlation
Identical twins	+.87
Fraternal twins (same sex)	+.56
Siblings	+.52
Parent (as adults) and child	+.50
Uncle (or aunt) and nephew (or niece)	+.34
Grandparent and grandchild	+.30
First cousins	+.28
Second cousins	+.16
Unrelated persons	−.01

(Adapted from Dworetsky, *Introduction to Child Development*, 1984, Table 12.1. New York: Random House. Reprinted by permission of publisher.)

ozygotic, twins, who developed from the same zygote and hence have the same genetic makeup, should be most alike. (In fact, if IQ score is completely due to one's genes, identical twins should have identical scores.) Fraternal, or *dizygotic,* twins, on the other hand, developed from different zygotes and thus share no more genes than do nontwin sibling pairs. Fraternal twins and siblings should therefore show lower correspondence in IQ than identical twins but should not differ from each other. Thus, the less the shared genetic material between individuals, the less their IQ scores should resemble.

As shown in Table 13–8, the more similar two individuals are genetically, the more similar (more highly correlated) their IQ scores. This evidence would seem to provide powerful ammunition for those who argue that IQ is largely inherited. However, evidence for environmental influences is also strong.

Environmental Influences. We can illustrate how environment operates by looking at Table 13–9, which also shows differences in similarity of IQ, but by shared versus unshared environments. The table shows that when two people are reared together and share similar environmental influences, their IQ scores are more alike. Thus, siblings or identical twins who grow up together are more similar in IQ than are siblings or identical twins who are reared apart.

The influence of the environment probably is stronger than Table 13–9 would suggest. It is not common practice to separate identical twins at birth and rear them in distinctively different environments. Instead, such twins often are separated after living some time together, are generally placed in similar environments, and often have some contact with one another (Farber, 1981; Hoffman, 1985). Because of all these factors, it is now recognized that it is

Relationship	Median Correlation
Identical twins reared together	+.87
Identical twins reared apart	+.75
Siblings reared together	+.52
Siblings reared apart	+.46
Unrelated children reared together	+.20
Unrelated children reared apart	−.01

(Adapted from Dworetsky, *Introduction to Child Development*, 1984, Table 12.1. New York: Random House. Reprinted by permission of publisher.)

impossible to separate genetic from environmental contributions to intelligence even with studies of identical twins. Both genetic and environmental factors account for IQ performance.

Many environmental factors can affect the IQ performance of individuals of varying genetic similarity to one another (see Table 13–10). Engaging in cognitively stimulating activities, usually with another person, is a characteristic common to many of the findings listed in Table 13–10. First-borns and children in smaller families generally get more attention and talk from their parents than do later children and children from large families (Zajonc & Marcus, 1975). Older siblings also may gain intellectually from teaching their younger brothers and sisters (Berbaum & Moreland, 1985). Similarly, special preschool programs and middle-class parents provide more cognitive stimulation (Hess & Shipman, 1967; Streissguth & Bee, 1972). Within middle-class families, stimulating experiences such as travel, movies, or trips to the zoo are associated with children's higher IQ scores (Gottfried & Gottfried, 1984).

The second environmental characteristic repeatedly associated with IQ performance is the warmth and responsiveness of caregivers. This is similar to Vygotsky's (1978) argument that learning takes place in the context of rewarding adult-child relationships. We can see this theme reflected in findings that children score higher on an IQ test when the test is administered by a familiar adult rather than by a stranger (Sachs, 1952), when children are given easy items at first and encouraged to respond (Zigler & Butterfield, 1968), and

Table 13–10

ENVIRONMENTAL INFLUENCES ON IQ

Environmental Factor	Major Finding
Father absence	Lower IQ is associated with father absence (Santrock, 1972).
Family size	Smaller family size is associated with higher IQ (Marjoribanks, etal, 1975).
Birth order	First-borns generally have higher IQs than second-borns, second-borns higher than third-borns (Zajonc & Markus, 1975).
Birth of a sibling	IQ of older sibling decreases temporarily (McCall, 1984).
Style of parenting	More responsive, involved, and non-punitive parents who stress achievement have children with higher IQs (Bradley, Caldwell & Elardo, 1977; Parsons, Adler & Kaczala, 1982).
Institutionalization	Children in institutions lacking in cognitive stimulation have lower IQs (Skeels, 1966).
Nutrition	Inadequate nutrition during early childhood is associated with lower IQ (Barrett, et al, 1982).
Stress	Children who report many stresses have lower IQs (Brown & Rosenbaum, 1983).
Social class	Middle-class children score higher than lower-class children (Scarr, 1981).
Special programs	Preschools and other programs offering social and cognitive stimulation report IQ gains for participants up to 3 yrs. after completing the program (Lazar & Darlington, 1982; Miller & Bizzell, 1983).
Expectations of others	Teachers who expect children to improve in IQ find these expectations confirmed (Rosenthal & Jacobson, 1968).
Testing situation	Amount of stress during test, encouragement by tester, and presentation of easy items first may affect IQ performance (Zigler & Butterfield, 1968).

Educating the Gifted

Although the most common way of identifying giftedness is by IQ score—scoring in the top one or two percent—some children may be exceptionally talented in a particular area, such as playing the piano, doing gymnastics, or performing in leadership roles. In recent years, special programs for gifted children have proliferated. The U.S. Office of Education has supported a wide range of programs, from enrichment experiences in the regular classroom, to special after-school classes, to separate accelerated classrooms within the school. In addition, some gifted children are skipped a grade or two.

Who Is Gifted?

One policy question deals with the definition of a child as gifted and the selection of the child to receive special educational experiences. Using IQ score as the sole criterion of selection may discriminate against children who are lower-class and from cultural or racial minorities. Most school systems place more emphasis on IQ or achievement test scores than on evidence of talents in specific areas when it comes to deciding which children are eligible for gifted children education (Owen, Froman, & Moscow, 1981). Moreover, motivation and creativity are rarely considered as aspects of giftedness. Robert Sternberg (1985) is one of many who argue for a broader view of giftedness:

Many of us are familiar with people who have exceptionally high IQs . . . but who seem to lack insightful or creative ideas. . . . Although they may obtain very high grades in school and be considered to be extremely bright, they lack the spark of originality that distinguishes exceptional people in the arts and sciences. . . . Thus, intellectual giftedness can be of many kinds (p. 291).

Programs

The benefits and drawbacks of different programs for gifted children are also a matter of controversy. Programs that segregate gifted children into separate classrooms have been criticized as weakening regular classrooms by weeding out from them all the best students (Page, 1979). Supporters of special classes for the gifted argue that gifted children will be bored in regular classrooms, and the nongifted may compare themselves unfavorably to their more advanced peers (Stewart, 1981).

Evaluation of enrichment education for gifted children has been mixed (Stanley, 1976, 1979). Some programs simply provide faster learners with extra "busy" work. Others, which may include more interesting experiences such as field trips and projects, have not demonstrated that they are contributing to the gifted child's further cognitive development.

We should not conclude from this that enrichment programs are a failure. More evaluation is needed, and care must be taken that the experiences provided gifted students are meaningful ones, not just extra work to fill their time.

Acceleration allows a student to progress through a curriculum at a faster rate. It may involve studying certain subjects at a higher level (for example, a fourth grader taking sixth-grade math but joining his or her peers for English and social studies), or it may involve moving ahead a grade. Despite popular opinion that children who skip grades are socially maladjusted, the evidence from studies of gifted children does not seem to bear this out (Stanley & Benbow, 1983).

In a famous study of gifted children begun in the 1920s by Lewis Terman, over 1,500 children who had IQs of 140 or higher were identified and followed for 50 years. In general, the "whiz kids" fulfilled their earlier promise in intellectual achievement. When last interviewed, almost a quarter of the 800 men in the study had earned an advanced degree, such as a doctorate, medical, or law degree (Sears, 1977). In addition, they showed evidence of being well-adjusted socially and emotionally. When Terman compared the outcomes experienced by those who had skipped a grade or two with those who had not, he found no signs of maladjustment in most cases (Terman & Oden, 1947).

Parents also can find ways to enrich the development of gifted children. Museums and public libraries offer free programs. Youth groups, such as 4-H, Scouts, YMCA, and YWCA, can provide stimulating experiences to supplement regular education. Of course, such resources are valuable for every child. *Not* stimulating the development of gifted children wastes a precious resource that benefits everyone.

when parents are responsive, involved, and nonpunitive (Bradley & Caldwell, 1976; Ramey, Farren, & Campbell, 1979; Hanson, 1975).

The environmental influences listed in Table 13–10 do not act in isolation. Children growing up in urban poverty are more likely than other children to have absent fathers, harried mothers, inadequate nutrition, and multiple stresses in their lives. These factors cumulatively exert a depressive effect upon IQ.

Continuity of IQ Performance

Because of the many environmental factors that influence IQ, it may not be surprising that IQ scores are not very stable, particularly over long periods of time. Intelligence assessed during infancy is not associated with IQ during the preschool or later periods (Honzik, 1976). In several longitudinal studies, age three IQ was correlated .50 and age six IQ .70 with IQ at age eight (Honzik, 1976). Thus, prediction becomes better the older the child and the closer the interval between tests.

These averages obscure the wide individual variation in stability of IQ. Children in impoverished, isolated environments have shown significant declines in IQ (Kennedy, 1969), while stimulating environments are associated with IQ gains (Gottfried, 1984). Other children may show sudden large spurts in performance. A longitudinal study following 140 children from ages two to seventeen found that the average IQ change was over 28 points, with one in seven shifting more than 40 points (McCall, Appelbaum, & Hogarty, 1973).

Creativity

Individual differences in children exist not only in IQ scores and in specific talents but also in creativity. Suppose you were shown a newspaper and asked to think of all the different things you could do with it. You might say, "Read it" or "Make a paper hat with it" or "Rip it when angry." According to one theory of creativity, the first two responses are conventional and noncreative, while only the third response is a creative one.

Such a conclusion is reached by distinguishing between two basic kinds of thinking: *convergent thinking*—problem solving centered on finding a single correct answer—and *divergent thinking*, which focuses on generating as many novel responses as possible. In the preceding example, "reading a newspaper" and even "making a paper hat out of it" are responses frequently given by children; however, "ripping it while angry" rarely occurs as an answer and hence qualifies as an example of divergent thinking.

T. P. Guilford (1956), who was the first to make this distinction, argued that creativity was synonymous with the ability to generate novel responses to problems and was distinct from IQ performance, which more resembled convergent thinking. He believed that creative thinking included the following:
1. Thinking up unique answers even when not asked specifically to do so.
2. Being able to think of many associations to a single word.
3. Being able to think of many ideas related to a single word or problem.
4. Being able to look at an old problem in a new way.
5. Seeing how common objects can be used for new purposes.

Tests of creativity have been devised based on Guilford's theory. The best known of these, the *Torrance Test of Creative Thinking,* incorporates different tasks to assess divergent thinking. For example, in the Ask and Guess Test, the child is shown a picture and asked to generate as many questions as possible concerning the situation depicted. In the Just Suppose test, the child is shown

Creativity involves the freedom to experiment with materials and to generate novel responses to them.

an unlikely situation, such as a scene with clouds on the ground and water above and asked to tell about all the possible events that could occur in such an event.

The relationship between creativity and intelligence has been of much interest. Does research support Guilford's contention that they are unrelated? Since, as the FOCUS ON POLICY in this chapter shows, most enrichment and acceleration programs use IQ score as their primary criterion for selection, it is important to know whether creative youngsters are failing to be identified and stimulated.

Although creativity and intelligence are separable, some children score high on both divergent and convergent thinking (Wallach & Kogan, 1967; Karkheck & Hogan, 1983). Other children, however, are highly creative and yet of average intelligence. Wallach and Kogan (1967) suggest that such children are most likely to be restless and dissatisfied with school. Some children who are low in creativity but high in IQ tend to do well in school but be rather conformist and fearful of failure. Since creativity and intelligence "mix" differently in each child, school experiences need to be individually tailored.

Evidence also exists that creativity is a fairly stable dimension of individual differences. In one study, both IQ and creativity were assessed on a group of four- and five-year-olds, and the children were followed for seven years. When the children were in the sixth grade, teachers were asked to identify those children who showed creativity. Preschool measures of divergent thinking, but not of IQ, were related to later creativity (Harrington, Block, & Block, 1983).

Developmental influences on creativity have not been studied extensively. Although we are in the realm of speculation here, the kinds of abilities measured in Guilford's concept of divergent thinking suggest that creativity would flourish in environments that encourage a playful, imaginative approach to learning. This would mean feeling free to think of many different possible solutions to a problem, including some that might sound "crazy," rather than searching for *the* right answer.

In summary, intelligence testing has developed as a means of measuring performance in areas related to school achievement. IQ scores provide a way to accurately identify individual differences among children of the same developmental level. Critics of IQ tests, although they have pointed to many possible sources of bias in test construction and administration, have not been able to provide a more objective and fair method. It is likely that teacher impressions or unstructured interviews with children would be susceptible to more bias than the currently used tests.

The intelligence testing approach as a tool for understanding cognitive development in the middle years has serious limitations. Although the IQ score is a developmental index, it does not explain how thinking becomes more abstract and complex with age. It also fails to tap aspects of individual differences, such as creativity, that are likely to affect school performance. Intelligence tests do not allow us to assess how children execute the component processes of thinking (Pellegrino & Glaser, 1979). Does a child perform poorly on an IQ test because he or she has a short attention span, has a poor vocabulary, has difficulty remembering the instructions, or has a perceptual problem and sees letters and figures reversed?

A complete understanding of cognitive development can profit from the following:

1. Piaget's description of the stage of concrete operational thought for understanding the commonalities among children during the middle years.
2. Information processing theory for understanding the development of the component processes of thought.
3. Assessment of individual differences in intelligence and creativity.

Chapter Summary

THE STAGE OF CONCRETE OPERATIONS
□ After a transitional period, called the 5-to-7 shift, children begin to understand such concepts as reversibility, identity, classification, seriation, transitivity, and conservation.
□ The ability to perform logical operations on concrete, everyday objects forms the basis for a child's ability to learn many of the skills taught in the early years of school, such as arithmetic.

INFORMATION PROCESSING APPROACH
□ During the middle years, children become more selective in their attention and less easily distracted.
□ They also use perception more flexibly, noticing the important aspects of a problem.
□ Vocabulary continues to grow, and some complex grammatical forms are mastered.

☐ Memory strategies, such as rehearsal and elaboration, become more deliberate, varied, and successful. Increasing awareness of memory, called *meta-memory,* is found along with awareness of other aspects of cognition (*metacognition*).

INTELLIGENCE

☐ Intelligence tests were devised to measure individual differences in those aspects of thought most closely related to school performance.

☐ The Stanford-Binet and WISC-R IQ tests are the most widely used measures. The former provides a single score that reflects general intelligence, while the WISC-R distinguishes between verbal and performance (nonverbal) aspects.

☐ Both genetic and environmental influences interact to affect IQ scores. Individuals who are genetically similar are also more similar in IQ, but sharing a similar environment also makes IQ scores more alike. Among the many environmental influences shown to affect IQ are social class, family structure and size, birth order, parenting style, nutrition, stress, and cognitively stimulating programs during early childhood.

☐ Racial and cultural differences in IQ scores have been the subject of much controversy. Although bias in test construction and administration cannot be ruled out, it is likely that the differences found reflect racial differences in environmental factors, such as poverty, stress, and the availability of cognitively stimulating experiences.

☐ Another source of individual differences is in creativity, defined as divergent thinking—the generation of many novel responses to a problem—in contrast to convergent thinking, which is centered on finding a single correct answer.

☐ Although creativity and intelligence have been found to be separate, children can both be creative and score high in IQ tests.

☐ Learning disabilities and giftedness are special issues in the areas of intelligence and education.

Recommended Readings

Piaget, J., and Inhelder, B. (1969). *The psychology of the child.* New York: Basic Books. A good overview and integration of Piagetian theory and research.

Sternberg, R. (1985). *Beyond IQ: A triarchic theory of intelligence.* New York: Cambridge University Press. A bit technical in parts, but worth reading for an expanded view of intelligence as encompassing more than IQ performance.

Kail, R. (1979). *The development of memory in children.* San Francisco: Freeman. A comprehensive, well-written account of research and theory on memory development. Clear, simplified figures throughout as illustrations.

CHAPTER 14

Social and Moral Development

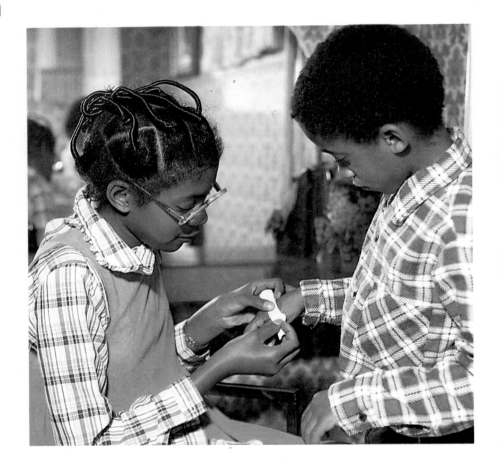

*H*ow is it you can hide the way you feel?
*If he felt real sad and stuff, you put a smile on your face
and you go with everyone else and try to be regular, but sometimes
you can really be sad.*
Is there a kind of inside and outside to a person?
Yes.
What would that mean?
*If there was a brother and a sister, like the brother always says
I can't stand you, but really inside, he really likes her.*
Really deep inside. What is that inside, can you describe it?
Yah, I guess so, really what you really feel about something.
— *Child aged 10 years, 11 months
(Selman, 1980, p. 98)*

During the middle years, children develop an increasingly complex and differentiated concept of self, a private self with emotions that can be hidden from others. They also develop ideas about how they compare to others and what their place in a group is. A very important set of ideas concerns moral understanding, the nature of human relationships, justice, harm, punishment, distribution of resources, and fairness. This chapter describes how these aspects of social understanding develop and traces the links to broader aspects of cognitive development (described in Chapter 13) as well as to the child's experiences with others.

The chapter also explores how changes in social understanding of self and of others are related to how children actually behave in different social situations. The focus is on self-control, self-regulation, moral behavior, and prosocial behavior, because these areas represent the major challenges most children face during the elementary school years, when they have to sit still and focus their energies for longer periods of time, plan and complete longer assignments, deal with issues of fairness and justice towards others, and learn to compete and cooperate in different situations.

Unlike the aspects of cognitive development, these aspects of development are not associated with major theoretical frameworks. Therefore, this chapter draws on cognitive theories, such as Piagetian theory and information processing, as well as learning theory, psychoanalytic theory, and systems theory, where appropriate.

Understanding the Self

Self-Concept Development

During middle childhood, ideas about the self become more psychological, complex, and stable and are based on comparisons with others. Suppose you asked a six-year-old and a twelve-year-old, "Tell me about yourself." The six-year-old might say, "I'm Nancy, I'm six years old, I live at 63 Spruce Street, and I have red hair." The twelve-year-old, on the other hand, would be more likely to say, "I am a human being; I am a friendly person; I am an individual."

From Concrete to Psychological.   Most six-year-olds tend to describe themselves in objective, concrete terms, often citing their appearance and address. By early adolescence, self-descriptions include personal beliefs, characteristics, and motivations (Markus & Nurius, 1984; Damon & Hart, 1982; Livesly & Bromley, 1973). In one study, 262 children from ages 10 to 18 were asked to write down 20 answers to the question, "Who am I?" With advancing age, there were more references to occupational roles (paperboy), beliefs (liberal), a sense of self-determination (ambitious), a sense of personal unity (mixed-up), interpersonal style (shy), and psychological feelings (happy). References to geographical location, possessions, physical characteristics, and body image all declined (Montemayor & Eisen, 1977).

Identity.   Another aspect of self-understanding that becomes well established during the middle years is the concept of an enduring personal identity, a self that continues through time regardless of changes in appearance or behavior (Guardo & Bohan, 1971; Broughton, 1978). Chapter 9 traced the development of gender constancy—the knowledge that one remains a male or female despite changes of appearance or behavior. This aspect of identity is generally achieved by age five or six. However, more abstract aspects of the self—"I'm someone who cares for others"—become seen as enduring parts of the self during middle childhood.

By age eight, most children distinguish between *mind* and *body* and view the mind as that which controls behavior. They become aware of an internal sense of self (*subjective self*) distinguishable from the way others see them (*objective self*). This awareness allows children to understand concepts such as self-deception—that you can talk yourself into saying or doing something while thinking something else (Selman, 1980)—and to begin to look at themselves as others might see them.

A More Complicated Self.   Along with attaining a greater sense of a cohesive personal identity, the self-concept is becoming more differentiated and complex during middle childhood. This can be illustrated by taking a look at a well-respected measure of children's self-concept, Susan Harter's Perceived Competence Scale (see Table 14–1). When self-concept is assessed with this scale, children do not answer similarly to all aspects but distinguish between cognitive, social, and physical competence. For example, a child may feel competent about making friends but not about playing an unfamiliar game. At the same time, use of this measure indicates that children do have global feelings concerning their general self-worth in responding to statements like "I am happy the way I am." Harter argues that within each domain, ideas about the self become increasingly complex and abstract with age (Harter, 1982).

Group Identity.   One reason for this greater complexity of self-identity is the growing realization by the school-age child that individuals belong to different groups in society. This awareness of *social structure* includes understanding social class, ethnic, racial, and religious differences and their meaning in the child's culture. For some children, this leads to recognition of privileged, favored status; "the lower class child [on the other hand] comes to realize that he possesses little of what the culture values" (Kagan, 1978, p. 50).

Why do changes in self-concept occur? Learning theory emphasizes how self-perceptions arise out of rewards and punishments. Consider for example, the possible effects of parents who deal with a child's messy room with comments like, "Why are you such a slob? Can't you do anything right?" or peers

Domain	Item Abbreviation
Cognitive competence	Good at schoolwork.
	Like school, doing well.
	Just as smart as others.
	Can figure out answers.
	Finish schoolwork quickly.
	Remember things easily.
	Understand what read.
Social competence	Have a lot of friends.
	Popular with kids.
	Easy to like.
	Do things with kids.
	Easy to make friends.
	Important to classmates.
	Most kids like me.
Physical competence	Do well at all sports.
	Better at sports.
	Do well at new activity.
	Good enough at sports.
	First chosen for games.
	Play rather than watch.
	Good at new games.
General self-worth	Sure of myself.
	Happy the way I am.
	Feel good/way I act.
	Sure am doing right thing.
	Am a good person.
	Want to stay the same.
	Do things fine.

Table 14—1

HARTER'S PERCEIVED COMPETENCE SCALE FOR CHILDREN

(Adapted from Harter, *Child Development*, 1982, 53, Table 1. © The Society for Research in Child Development, Inc. Reprinted by permission of publisher.)

During the elementary school years, children begin to compare themselves to their peers—who is "on top", who is "on the bottom" in physical, social and intellectual areas of competence.

Focus on Policy

The Development of Attitudes About Race

In the late 1930s, Mamie and Kenneth Clark, two distin-guished black psychologists, conducted a pioneering study of young children's racial preferences. They showed that young black children consistently evaluated the color white and depictions of white persons more positively than the color black and black persons (Clark & Clark, 1939, 1940). These findings led many to conclude that growing up in a segregated society produced a negative self-identity in black children. The justices of the U.S. Supreme Court were influenced by the Clarks' research when, in the historic *Brown* v. *Board of Education* decision of 1954, they found that segregated schooling for blacks and whites was inherently unequal and discriminatory (Powell, 1974).

In the years since the Clarks first reported their findings, other researchers (Brand, Ruiz, & Padilla, 1974; Banks, 1976; Spencer, 1983) have examined the development of racial attitudes among both black and white children. They also have asked how environmental influences such as school and family may affect these attitudes. These studies shed some light on how recent historical changes such as the civil rights movement and racial integration may affect children's self-identity and understanding of society.

Recent studies (Spencer, 1983; Branch & Newcomb, 1986) confirm some of the findings of the Clarks. Among both black and white chil-

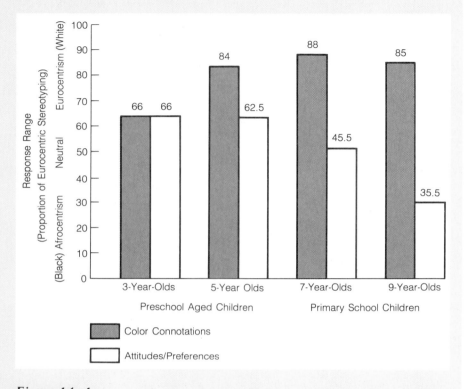

Figure 14—1

Mean Scores for Eurocentric (White) Color Connotations and Racial Attitudes/Preferences

(From Spencer, *Developmental Review*, 1983, Vol. 3, Figure 3. Orlando, FL: The Academic Press. Reprinted by permission of author and Academic Press.)

dren, preference for the color white over the color black increases from age three through nine. Moreover, preschoolers of both races indicate a preference for white children and adults. However, some important differences from the results of the earlier studies were also obtained. As you can see in Figure 14—1, in one investigation (Spencer, 1982) of 384 Southern black children from ages three to nine years, older children, while preferring the color white to the color black, showed either neutral or black racial preferences. Margaret Spencer then conducted interviews with mothers of 45 of the children in this study. She found that

children whose parents taught them about black history, civil rights, and the problems of racial discrimination showed either more neutral attitudes toward black/white differences or displayed more pride in their racial identity (Spencer, 1983).

These findings have implications for social policy. They indicate that young elementary school-age children are sensitive to their own and others' racial identity and to how that identity is valued. Policies that emphasize vigorous enforcement of civil rights for all races along with pride in one's own racial identity appear to promote in children more positive attitudes toward all races.

who respond to a child's shyness with, "What are you, some kind of scaredy cat?"

Cognitive/developmentalists point out that the gains embodied in the stage of concrete operational thought allow children to decenter and hence to see themselves as others might see them. Their understanding of conservation makes it possible for them to grasp that superficial changes in appearance don't change an individual's identity. Their ability to order items in a series—or seriation—enables systematic comparison of the self to others.

Comparing the Self to Others

Compared to preschoolers, children during the middle years spend increasing amounts of time with peers and relatively less time with parents. Both in school and during after-school play, interacting with peers involves comparing and contrasting oneself to others: "Do I run as fast as she can?" "I'm taller than José but shorter than Maria." Furthermore, as children become older, schools place greater emphasis on individual grading, which accentuates the process of comparing the self to others. Thus, environmental experiences emphasize comparisons with others at the same time that the child becomes cognitively capable of understanding them. For example, consider how elementary school-age children develop ideas about how smart they and others are—the dimension of self-concept called cognitive competence by Harter. This is a particularly important aspect of self-concept, since feelings of intellectual incompetence can have long-range negative consequences.

John Nicholls and Arden Miller (1984a; 1984b) have used in-depth interviews with children from ages five to twelve—following the method pioneered by Piaget—to uncover the development of children's reasoning about intellectual competence or "smartness" (as shown in Table 14–2). They found that level I, in which smartness is equated with how hard you tried regardless of how someone else performed at the same task, was characteristic of five-year-olds. By age 12, however, most children were reasoning at level IV, distinguishing effort from ability and using both to assess how smart they and others were. These results, along with others (Ruble et al., 1980), suggest that at the beginning of schooling, most children do not evaluate themselves relative to others, but these social comparison processes appear to become increasingly important with age. (In the absence of longitudinal research following the same

Level	Characteristic	Example
I	Effort = ability	People who try harder are smarter even if they perform more poorly on a test.
II	Effort determines outcome	People perform better on a test because they try harder.
III	Effort and ability partly distinguished	When two people give equal effort, but one performs better, something else is involved.
IV	Ability = capacity	Ability and effort are distinguished. People who achieve more with equal or less effort are seen as having more ability.

(From Nicholls & Miller, 1984a.)

Table 14–2

LEVELS OF REASONING ABOUT INTELLECTUAL COMPETENCE

The Making of a "Dummy"

Some children exhibit self-confidence about their abilities; when confronted with setbacks, they simply redouble their efforts. Sadly, however, other children tend to give up. In fact, their performance deteriorates so badly that they can no longer succeed at tasks they had previously mastered (Dweck & Goetz, 1978). The social comparison processes we've been examining in this chapter, along with a concept called *learned helplessness*, have been used to shed light on this problem (Fincham & Cain, 1985).

An animal researcher named Martin Seligman (Seligman & Maier, 1967) noticed that rats who had been given unavoidable electric shock later made no effort to escape the shock when exits were open. In other words, the animals had learned to be helpless as a result of being in an uncontrollable situation. This pattern, called "learned helplessness," was generalized to human behavior in situations where initial failure leads to subsequent giving up.

Do Children Learn to Be Helpless?

Developmentalists wondered if children who give up after experiencing difficulties on a task are doing so because they see their performance as beyond their control and so feel helpless. By asking children to explain why they succeeded or failed at a task, they discovered that children who persisted in the face of failure explained their performance in terms of motivation and effort. For example, one child was overheard to say, "I missed that one. That means I have to try harder." On the other hand, those children who stopped trying and performed more poorly after an initial setback cited a lack of ability ("I'm not smart enough") (Dweck & Goetz, 1978).

Similar differences have been noted in children's reactions to social situations. For example, when asked, "Suppose you move into a new neighborhood. A girl you meet does not like you very much. Why would this happen to you?", some children cite misunderstandings or other aspects of the situation that could be corrected. Other children, however, say things like, "It happened because I'm no good at making friends" (Dweck & Goetz, 1978). Learned helplessness also appears to have broad effects on children's emotional well-being. In one study (Cain & Fincham, 1985), third graders who showed learned helplessness were more depressed and anxious than were other children.

Helping Children Who Feel Helpless

One explanation for the development of learned helplessness in children is the lack of success experiences that build self-confidence and perseverence. However, attempts to change the performance of learned-helpless children by a steady dose of experimenter-engineered successes have not been successful. Children convinced of their lack of ability discounted their success as just luck; when the next failure came, it confirmed their self-image as "dummies" (Dweck & Goetz, 1978).

A more effective procedure is called *attribution retraining*, which involves teaching the child to respond to failures with statements about effort rather than ability. Each time the child misses at a task, the teacher says something like, "You missed that one; you need to try harder." Gradually, the child learns to spontaneously apply such explanations to his or her own performance. In one study, learned-helpless children who had 25 daily sessions of attribution retraining were later more persistent when solving problems (Dweck & Goetz, 1978).

Although much still needs to be discovered about the origins of learned helplessness and the role that attributions about effort and ability play (Fincham & Cain, in press), existing research suggests that teachers and parents need to be careful not to focus solely on a child's ability when discussing the child's performance (Holloway, 1986). Statements like "You really worked hard on that paper; it shows" are preferable to "You're really good at this kind of math." Many of the gains in understanding made during the middle years—distinguishing effort from ability, comparing the self to others—make some children vulnerable to learned helplessness.

children over time, we have no way of knowing if individual children pass through these stages of reasoning about self-concept.)

To document how social comparison processes affect self-evaluation, Nicholls and Miller (1984b) observed 30 boys and 30 girls at each of three grade levels—second, fifth, and eighth—as they individually worked on some puzzles. Each child then saw a film of another child who they were told did equally well on the puzzles. Half of the filmed children were depicted as working hard, and half were shown "goofing off" during the task. After watching the film, each child was asked, "Is one of you smarter, or are you both the same? How come you both got the same score when you worked hard and the other did not?"

The children's answers were analyzed in terms of the levels of reasoning about self and others shown in Table 14–2. As expected, older children were more likely to reason at higher levels, taking into account both effort and ability, in assessing how smart they were on this task. However, as you can see in Table 14–3, some second graders were beginning to distinguish effort and ability, while a few eighth graders equated smartness with how hard they tried, regardless of how they or someone else performed on the task.

Along with changes in self understanding come feelings about the self, or *self-esteem*. Children who agree with statements like "I'm proud of my schoolwork" and "I'm popular with kids my own age" and disagree with statements like "I find it hard to talk in front of the class" are considered to have high self-esteem (Coopersmith, 1967). Level of self-esteem tends to remain fairly stable throughout middle childhood (Rosenberg, 1979; Coopersmith, 1967), and high self-esteem is linked to authoritative parenting, experiences with success and failure, assertiveness and self-confidence, feelings of personal control, and optimism (Fischer & Leitenberg, 1986; Coopersmith, 1967).

Understanding Others

During middle childhood, the self becomes understood as more complex, abstract, enduring, and relative to the characteristics of others. These changes in self understanding are paralleled by similar changes in understanding other people.

Robert Selman (1980) has presented the most comprehensive theory about how interpersonal understanding develops. Working within a cognitive/developmental framework, Selman developed extended interviews with children of different ages (an excerpt from one interview opens the chapter) to tap children's ideas about other people, friendships, parent-child relations, and peer groups.

To get the flavor of Selman's approach, see Table 14–4, which contains "The Puppy Story" and sample questions used by Selman to uncover children's

Grade	Level of reasoning			
	I	II	III	IV
Second	10	44	6	0
Fifth	4	22	12	22
Eighth	3	5	9	43

(From Nicholls & Miller, *Child Development*, 1984, 55, Table 1. © The Society for Research in Child Development, Inc. Reprinted by permission of author and publisher.)

Table 14–3

NUMBER OF CHILDREN REASONING ABOUT INTELLECTUAL COMPETENCE AT DIFFERENT LEVELS IN GRADES 2, 5, AND 8

Table 14—4

The Puppy Story

Tom has just saved some money to buy Mike Hunter a birthday present. He and his friend Greg go downtown to try to decide what Mike will like. Tom tells Greg that Mike is sad these days because Mike's dog Pepper ran away. They see Mike and decide to try to find out what Mike wants without asking him right off. After talking to Mike for a while the kids realize that Mike is really sad because of his lost dog. When Greg suggests he get a new dog, Mike says he can't just get a new dog and have things be the same. Then Mike leaves to run some errands. As Mike's friends shop some more they see a puppy for sale in the pet store. It is the last one left. The owner says that the puppy will probably be sold by tomorrow. Tom and Greg discuss whether to get Mike the puppy. Tom has to decide right away. What do you think Tom will do?

Questions

* What do you think Tom, the boy who is buying the birthday present, should do? Why? Have you ever known a boy like Mike? What was he like?

* If Mike is smiling, could he still be sad? How is that possible? Could someone look happy on the outside, but be sad on the inside? How is that possible?

* Did he mean what he said? Can someone say something and not mean it? How?

* What kind of person do you think Tom is, the boy who had to decide whether or not to get Mike the puppy?

* What do you think it will take to change the way Mike feels about losing his old dog Pepper? How long will it take him to get over it? Why? What will it take to make him happy again?

(From Selman, *The Growth of Interpersonal Understanding,* © 1980. Orlando, FL: The Academic Press. Reprinted by permission of author and publisher.)

concepts about individuals' characteristics, such as subjectivity, self-awareness, personality, and personality change.

Based on responses to such stories, Selman argues that children pass through a sequence of stages in understanding others. The stages are *invariant*; early stages must precede later ones, and children can't skip any stages (Stone & Selman, 1982). Selman also believes that each stage represents a qualitatively different level of social understanding, providing the child with basic concepts with which to understand many different kinds of social relationships, including friendship, peer groups, and parent-child relations. This is because common issues cut across different relationships, for example, how relationships are formed, how feelings are expressed, how conflict is handled, and how relationships end. Table 14—5 summarizes these issues for the four major areas of interpersonal understanding that Selman has investigated.

The social understanding characteristic of middle childhood in Selman's scheme can be understood best in terms of changes from preschool thinking and differences from adolescent understanding. An overview of Selman's stages (shown in Table 14—6) shows that middle childhood is a period of considerable change in interpersonal understanding. Most children entering first grade are hypothesized to be at stage 0 or 1, while most 12-year-olds have achieved stage 3 understanding. However, age ranges are approximate and overlapping. Thus, some 12-year-olds may exhibit stage 2, 3, or 4 reasoning, although the majority would probably be classified as stage 3.

Certain broad changes in understanding cut across different domains. One such change involves thinking about people and relationships in terms of thoughts and feelings rather than in terms of physical characteristics or behavior. For example, a ten-year-old is more likely than a six-year-old to describe friendship in terms of sharing thoughts and feelings rather than playing together. Another broad change is the tendency to think about relationships as

Individual	Friendship	Peer Group	Parent-child relations
1. *Subjectivity:* covert properties of persons (thoughts, feelings, motives); conflicts between thoughts or feelings within the person	1. *Formation:* why (motives) and how (mechanisms) friendships are made; the ideal friend	1. *Formation:* why (motives) and how (mechanisms) groups are formed; the ideal member	1. *Formation:* motives for having children and why children need parents
2. *Self-awareness:* awareness of the self's ability to observe its own thoughts and actions	2. *Closeness:* types of friendship, ideal friendship, intimacy	2. *Cohesion-loyalty:* group unity	2. *Love and emotional ties:* between parents and children
3. *Personality:* stable or predictive character traits (a shy person, etc.)	3. *Trust:* doing things for friends; reciprocity	3. *Conformity:* range and rationale	3. *Obedience:* why children do as their parents tell them
4. *Personality change:* how and why people change (growing up, etc.)	4. *Jealousy:* feelings about intrusions into new or established friendships	4. *Rules-norms:* types of rules, and reasons for them	4. *Punishment:* the function of punishment from the parent's and the child's perspective
	5. *Conflict resolution:* how friends resolve problems	5. *Decision-making:* setting goals, resolving problems, working together	5. *Conflict resolution:* optimal ways for parents and children to resolve their differences
	6. *Termination:* how friendships break up	6. *Leadership:* qualities, and function to the group	
		7. *Termination:* why groups break up or members are excluded	

(From Selman, *The Growth of Interpersonal Understanding,* © 1980, Table 4.2. Orlando, FL: The Academic Press. Reprinted by permission of author and Academic Press.)

Table 14–5

ISSUES OF INTERPERSONAL UNDERSTANDING RELATED TO CONCEPTS OF THE INDIVIDUAL, CLOSE FRIENDSHIPS, PEER-GROUP, AND PARENT-CHILD RELATIONS

reciprocal rather than one-sided. Note the difference between stage 1 and stage 3 reasoning about the parent-child relationship. In the earlier stage, parents are viewed as taking care of the child and fulfilling the child's needs, while by stage 3, there is recognition that parents too have needs and that the parent-child relationship is (ideally, at least) based on mutual tolerance and respect (Damon & Hart, 1982).

Table 14-6

SUMMARY OF SELMAN'S STAGES
OF INTERPERSONAL
UNDERSTANDING

	Stage 0 (3–6 yrs)	Stage 1 (5–9 yrs)	Stage 2 (7–12 yrs)	Stage 3 (10–15 yrs)	Stage 4 (12–adult)
Individuals	Physical entities	Intentional subjects	Introspective selves	Stable personalities	Complex self-systems
Friendships	Momentary physical interactions	One way assistance	Fair-weather cooperation	Intimate and mutual sharing	Autonomous interdependence
Peer groups	Physical connections	Unilateral relations	Bilateral partnerships	Homogeneous community	Pluralistic organization
Parent-child relationships	Boss-servant	Caretaker-helper	Counselor, need satisfier	Tolerance and respect	Unknown

(From Bee & Mitchell, 1984.)

How accurately does Selman's stage theory fit the way children actually reason about interpersonal relations? A number of cross-sectional and longitudinal investigations provide general support for the hypothesized stages (Gurucharri & Selman, 1982; Cooney & Selman, 1978). For example, in one study, Selman and his colleagues conducted interviews to elicit concepts about individuals, friendships, and groups from three different samples of children ages 6 through 15. The results (see Figure 14–2) show that on the average, higher stage reasoning occurs with advancing age. Note also that throughout middle childhood, reasoning about individuals is slightly more advanced than thinking about friendships, and concepts concerning groups are most difficult. It appears that children form concepts most easily about familiar individuals and then generalize them to one-on-one relationships, such as friendships. Finally, they grasp socially organized experiences, such as group life.

Understanding and Behavior

How stages of interpersonal understanding might be related to social behavior was explored by David Pellegrini (1985), who classified the interpersonal understanding of 100 fourth through seventh graders according to Selman's stages. Teacher and peer ratings were used to assess social behavior, and how well the child solved social problems, such as feeling lonely in a new neighborhood or being rejected by peers, was determined through interviews. The relationships among these measures, summarized in Table 14–7, indicate that children with more advanced interpersonal understanding do better at solving social problems. Such children are viewed more positively by their peers, and teachers see them as more cooperative, less disruptive, and less likely to show poor comprehension or performance anxiety. These results are confirmed in other studies as well; for example, children who have serious problems getting along with their peers score lower in interpersonal understanding than do other children (Selman, Lavin, & Brion-Meisels, 1982).

The size of the relationships reported in Table 14–7 indicates, however, that interpersonal understanding only moderately predicts behavior. (A perfect positive association would be $+1.00$, and a perfect negative association, -1.00.) Many factors intervene between abstract knowledge of what others might be feeling or how conflicts are resolved and actually dealing with others' feelings in a real situation. Motivation, feelings about the specific individuals involved,

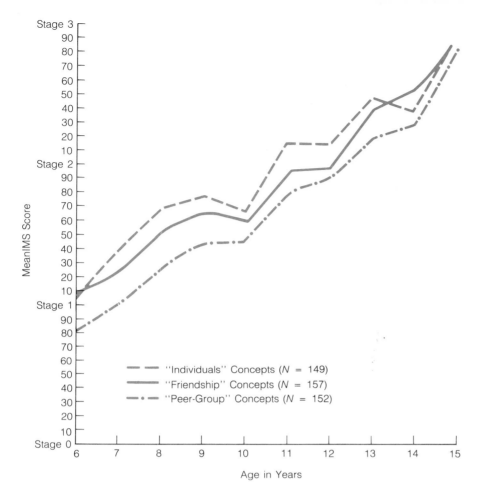

Stage 3
Stage 2
Stage 1
Stage 0

MeanIMS Score

Age in Years

- - - "Individuals" Concepts (*N* = 149)
───── "Friendship" Concepts (*N* = 157)
─·─·─ "Peer-Group" Concepts (*N* = 152)

Figure 14—2

Mean Stage-by-Age Trends in the Development of Individuals, Friendship, and Peer-Group Conceptions

(From Selman, R. *The Growth of Interpersonal Understanding,* © 1980. Orlando, FL: Academic Press. Reprinted by permission of the author and publisher.)

Table 14—7
INTERCORRELATIONS OF VARIABLES IN PELLEGRINI STUDY (1985)

	Interpersonal Understanding	Problem-Solving	Peer: Positive	Peer: Disruptive	Peer: Isolated	Teacher: Disruptive	Teacher: Poor Comprehension	Teacher: Cooperative
Problem-solving	.56*							
Peer: positive	.42*	.56*						
Peer: disruptive	−.05	−.18*	−.21*					
Peer: isolated	−.53*	−.43*	−.42*	−.01				
Teacher: disruptive	−.20*	−.33*	−.42*	.53*	.10			
Teacher: poor comprehension	−.49*	−.52*	−.54*	.05	.50*	.51*		
Teacher: cooperative	.35*	.18*	.23*	.07	−.25*	.12	−.36*	
Teacher: performance anxiety	−.30*	−.23*	−.14	.12	.28*	.39*	.37*	.06

*Statistically significant correlation.
(Adapted from Pellegrini, *Child Development,* 1985, *56,* Table 1. © The Society for Research in Child Development, Inc. Reprinted by permission of author and publisher.)

and stereotypes the child and others might hold are among the factors that should be considered. This is why many studies find that social behavior does not match level of social understanding.

Moral Development

Up until now, we have considered how understanding others develops in a broad sense, covering many different aspects of relationships. Many developmentalists have paid special attention to important moral issues that involve principles of justice, fairness, transgression, and punishment, the "oughts" or "shoulds" of behavior.

Cognitive/Developmental Approaches

Piaget. In Piaget's view, children understand moral issues in ways that are qualitatively different from adolescent or adult understanding. Based on children's responses to stories of moral transgressions, like the one in Table 14–8, Piaget describes a major shift in children's thinking about morality: the shift from *moral realism*, or *heteronomous* moral judgment, to *autonomous* moral judgment. In the stage of moral realism, a child views social rules as fixed and unchangeable, like the laws of nature. The child responds to the letter of the law rather than to the law's spirit and judges acts on the basis of strict conformity, the amount of objective damage done, and whether or not the act was punished. Misfortunes or accidents are viewed as punishment for wrongdoing, an idea Piaget called *immanent justice* (Carroll & Rest, 1982).

With age and cognitive development, a gradual shift takes place toward *autonomous* moral understanding. Piaget believed that through resolving conflicts with peers during play, children gradually learn that social life operates in terms of mutually arrived at agreements that benefit everyone. The child now considers a person's motivations and intentions as well as other extenuating circumstances when determining guilt and punishment. Laws are viewed

Table 14—8

STORIES USED BY PIAGET TO MEASURE MORAL UNDERSTANDING AND SAMPLE ANSWERS

Stories

(1) A little boy named John is in his room. He is called to dinner. He goes into the dining room. But behind the door there was a chair, and on the chair there was a tray with 15 cups on it. John couldn't have known that the tray with the 15 cups was behind the door. He goes in, the door knocks against the tray, bang go the 15 cups and they all get broken.

(2) Once there was a little boy named Henry. One day when his mother was out he tried to get some cookies from a jar in the cupboard. He climbed up on a chair and stretched out his arm. But the cookie jar was too high up and he couldn't reach it to get any. But while he was trying to get it, he knocked over a cup. The cup fell down and broke.

Are these children equally guilty? Which of the two is naughtiest and why?

Sample answers	Level
"John's naughtier; he broke all the cups." "John broke more, so he should be punished more."	Moral realism
"Henry's naughtier; he shouldn't be climbing up." "John didn't mean to do it, so he shouldn't be punished."	Autonomous morality

not as handed down by authority figures to be obeyed without question, but as the product of mutual agreement, constructed by equals to make cooperation possible. Thus, Piaget calls moral realism "the morality of constraint" and autonomous morality "the morality of cooperation."

Piaget did not spell out when this important shift in thinking would take place. He believed, however, that moral judgments of preoperational thinkers would be heteronomous and that the shift to autonomous thinking would take place during the elementary school years.

Limitations of Piaget's Theory. Attempts to test Piaget's ideas have resulted in many modifications and refinements of the moral dilemmas Piaget presented to children (Moran & O'Brien, 1973; Costanzo, Coie, Grumet, & Farnill, 1973). Although the shift from moral realism to autonomous moral understanding has been supported, controversy continues as to when it occurs. Some feel that Piaget underestimated preschoolers' abilities (Lickona, 1976). When the stories are shortened and information about intentions is presented later in the story, preschoolers find it easier to remember the story contents and are more likely to consider the motivations of the story characters (Allen, 1982). More recent research indicates that even five-year-olds assign more moral responsibility and prescribe more punishment for intentional rather than negligent or accidental harm (Shultz, Wright, & Schleifer, 1986).

Moreover, when children's moral understanding is derived from their everyday behavior rather than from responses to hypothetical situations, a more complex picture emerges than Piaget's stages would suggest. Even very young children have been observed to appeal to moral principles, as this four-year-old Kenyan child, J., demonstrates:

> E. (J.'s older brother) pulls J. on a "car" (really a wagon). E. to J.: "Get off. It is the baby's turn." J. does not heed. "Then I won't let you ride again." J. gets off, and E. pulls the infant in the "car." J. to elder E.: "You come and pull me. It's my turn" (Edwards, 1985).

Beginning in the preschool years, children distinguish between situations that involve universal moral principles—causing harm to others—and those that concern social rules, such as using a spoon and fork or being quiet during naptime (Turiel, 1978a, b). Moral rules are viewed as more binding than social rules, and transgressions are judged more severely (Smetana, Kelley, & Twentyman, 1984). These findings suggest that Piaget's theory may not be detailed enough to explain the changes that occur in moral understanding from the preschool years through adolescence.

Kohlberg. A more fine-grained theory of moral understanding is offered by Lawrence Kohlberg. Using a technique similar to that of both Piaget and Selman, Kohlberg presented stories, called "moral dilemmas," to children and analyzed their responses in great detail. (The scoring system has taken 20 years to develop and is over 800 pages long.) Kohlberg uncovered much greater variety in patterns of thinking than had been described by Piaget. As a result, Kohlberg distinguished three broad levels of moral reasoning: *preconventional*, *conventional*, and *postconventional*. Within each level, he identified two stages, making a total of six stages of moral understanding. Table 14–9 presents an example of one of these stories, along with sample responses coded into stages.

Kohlberg's stages bear some resemblance to those of Piaget. For example, stage 1 in Kohlberg's scheme is similar to moral realism, while stage 5 contains many of the same characteristics described by Piaget as autonomous morality.

Lawrence Kohlberg.

Both Piaget and Kohlberg focus on the concept of *justice* as the crux of moral reasoning; in contrast to earlier stages, later stages take into account more factors in determining what is right and fair.

Like both Piaget and Selman, Kohlberg views these stages as invariant. All children begin at stage 1, believing that physical consequences determine whether an action is good or bad, and progress sequentially through higher stages of reasoning. However, advancement from one stage to the next is not inevitable; Kohlberg feels that individuals can get stuck at a particular stage. Therefore, as you'll note in Table 14–9, age levels are not associated with the stage progression. However, Kohlberg believes that stage 1 characterizes most children under age seven, while stage 2 reasoning is most common during the middle years. By the late elementary school period, evidence of stage 3 and stage 4 reasoning can be found in some children (Kohlberg, 1976). Moral reasoning often reflects a mixture of stages rather than "pure" examples of understanding at a particular level.

Developmental change in moral understanding is illustrated in a 20-year longitudinal study of 58 boys, interviewed six times between the ages of 10 and 36 concerning moral dilemmas like the one shown in Table 14–9 (Colby, Kohlberg, Gibbs, & Lieberman, 1983). Following Kohlberg's

Table 14–9

SIX STAGES OF ORIENTATION TO INTENTIONS AND CONSEQUENCES IN RESPONSE TO A MORAL DILEMMA

In Europe, a woman was near death from cancer. One drug might save her, a form of radium that a druggist in the same town had recently discovered. The druggist was charging $2,000, ten times what the drug cost him to make. The sick woman's husband, Heinz, went to everyone he knew to borrow the money, but he could get together only about half of what it cost. He told the druggist that his wife was dying and asked him to sell it cheaper or let him pay later. But the druggist said no. The husband got desperate and broke into the man's store to steal the drug for his wife. Should the husband have done that? Why:

PRECONVENTIONAL:

Stage 1: Motives and need-consequences of act are ignored in judging badness because of focus upon irrelevant physical form of the act (e.g., size of the lie), or of the consequences of the act (e.g., amount of physical damage).
Pro—He should steal the drug. It isn't really bad to take it. It isn't like he didn't ask to pay for it first. The drug he'd take is only worth $200, he's not really taking a $2,000 drug.
Con—He shouldn't steal the drug, it's a big crime. He didn't get permission, he used force and broke and entered. He did a lot of damage, stealing a very expensive drug and breaking up the store, too.

Stage 2: Judgment ignores label or physical consequences of the act because of the instrumental value of the act in serving a need, or because the act doesn't do harm in terms of the need of another. (Differentiates the human need–value of the act from its physical form or consequences.)
Pro—It's all right to steal the drug because she needs it and he wants her to live. It isn't that he wants to steal, but it's the way he has to use to get the drug to save her.
Con—He shouldn't steal it. The druggist isn't wrong or bad, he just wants to make a profit. That's what you're in business for, to make money.

CONVENTIONAL:

Stage 3: Action evaluated according to the type of motive or person likely to perform the act. An act is not bad if it is an expression of a "nice" or altruistic motive or person and it is not good if it is the expression of a "mean" or selfish motive or person. Circumstances may excuse or justify deviant action. (Differentiates good motives to which an act is instrumental from human but selfish need to which it is instrumental.)
Pro—He should steal the drug. He was only doing something that was natural for a good husband to do. You can't blame him for doing something out of love for his wife, you'd blame him if he didn't love his wife enough to save her.
Con—He shouldn't steal. If his wife dies, he can't be blamed. It isn't because he's heartless or that he doesn't love her enough to do everything that he legally can. The druggist is the selfish or heartless one.

prediction, there was a steady increase in level of moral understanding with age: At age ten, 47 percent were reasoning at stages 1 and 2, but only two percent did so by late adolescence. Only five percent of the ten-year-olds showed stage 3 reasoning, but this increased to 16 percent by the time they were 13 to 14 and to 44 percent when they were 16 to 18 years old. Stage 4 reasoning did not appear at all until age 20 (19 percent), and even at age 36 it characterized the reasoning of only 44 percent of the subjects. In about 10 percent of the subjects, postconventional moral understanding (stage 5) appeared when they were in their 30s. None of the subjects skipped a stage, and only four percent showed any evidence of backsliding to an earlier stage.

Influences on Moral Understanding. Kohlberg feels that level of cognitive development makes possible certain kinds of moral understanding. For example, concrete operational thinking (refer to Chapter 13) is considered a prerequisite for Kohlberg's stage 3 moral reasoning, while formal operational thought (see Chapter 16) precedes stage 5 and higher level reasoning (Walker, 1980; Kohlberg & Gilligan, 1971). Another, related influence is the child's level of interpersonal understanding, as reflected in Selman's stages. Children who see relationships as reciprocal and who are aware of the psychological states of others might be expected to employ moral reasoning that takes these

Table 14—9 (continued)

Stage 4: An act is always or categorically wrong, regardless of motives or circumstances, if it violates a rule and does foreseeable harm to others. (Differentiates action out of a sense of obligation to rule from action for generally "nice" or natural motives.)
Pro—You should steal it. If you did nothing you'd be letting your wife die, it's your responsibility if she dies. You have to take it with the idea of paying the druggist.
Con—It is a natural thing for Heinz to want to save his wife but it's still always wrong to steal. He still knows he's stealing and taking a valuable drug from the man who made it.

POSTCONVENTIONAL:

Stage 5: A formal statement that though circumstances or motive modify disapproval, as a general rule the means do not justify the ends. While circumstances justify deviant acts to some extent they do not make it right or lead to suspension of moral categories. (Differentiates moral blame because of the intent behind breaking the rule from the legal or principled necessity not to make exceptions to rules.)
Pro—The law wasn't set up for these circumstances. Taking the drug in this situation isn't really right, but it's justified to do it.
Con—You can't completely blame someone for stealing, but extreme circumstances don't really justify taking the law in your own hands. You can't have everyone stealing whenever they get desperate. The end may be good, but the ends don't justify the means.

Stage 6: Good motives don't make an act right (or not wrong); but if an act follows from a decision to follow general self-chosen principles, it can't be wrong. It may be actually right to deviate from the rules, but only under circumstances forcing a choice between deviation from the rules and concrete violation of a moral principle. (Differentiates good motives of following a moral principle from natural motives as following a rule. Recognizes that moral principles don't allow exceptions any more than do legal rules.)
Pro—This is a situation which forces him to choose between stealing and letting his wife die. In a situation where the choice must be made, it is morally right to steal. He has to act in terms of the principle of preserving and respecting life.
Con—Heinz is faced with the decision of whether to consider the other people who need the drug just as badly as his wife. Heinz ought to act, not according to his particular feelings toward his wife, but considering the value of all the lives involved.

(From Rest, J. *Handbook of Socialization Theory and Research*, David A. Goslin, ed. Boston: Houghton Mifflin, 1969. Reprinted by permission of publisher.)

factors into account. Table 14–10 summarizes the relationship between Piaget's cognitive developmental stages, Selman's development of interpersonal understanding, and Kohlberg's stages of moral reasoning.

Most research supports the view that cognitive development is a necessary but not sufficient condition for advances in moral understanding (Tomlinson-Keasy & Keasy, 1974; Kuhn, Kohlberg, Langer, & Haan, 1977; Rest, 1983).

For example, in a study by Lawrence Walker (1980), 146 children in the fourth through ninth grades were tested for concrete operational thought by a class-inclusion reasoning task and a conservation of weight task (refer to Chapter 9). "The Puppy Story" (refer to Table 14–4) and two other similar stories were used to measure interpersonal understanding, and moral dilemmas were presented to assess moral reasoning.

Table 14–10

PARALLEL STAGES IN COGNITIVE, PERSPECTIVE-TAKING, AND MORAL DEVELOPMENT

Cognitive Stage[a]	Perspective-taking Stage[b]	Moral Stage[c]
Preoperations The "symbolic function" appears but thinking is marked by centration and irreversibility.	*Stage 1 (subjectivity)* There is an understanding of the subjectivity of persons but no realization that persons can consider each other as subjects.	*Stage 1 (heteronomy)* The physical consequences of an action and the dictates of authorities define right and wrong.
Concrete operations The objective characteristics of an object are separated from action relating to it; and classification, seriation, and conservation skills develop.	*Stage 2 (self-reflection)* There is a sequential understanding that the other can view the self as a subject just as the self can view the other as subject.	*Stage 2 (exchange)* Right is defined as serving one's own interests and desires, and cooperative interaction is based on terms of simple exchange.
Beginning formal operations There is development of the coordination of reciprocity with inversion; and propositional logic can be handled.	*Stage 3 (mutual perspectives)* It is realized that the self and the other can view each other as perspective-taking subjects (a generalized perspective).	*Stage 3 (expectations)* Emphasis is on good-person stereotypes and a concern for approval.
Early basic formal operations The hypothetico-deductive approach emerges, involving abilities to develop possible relations among variables and to organize experimental analyses.	*Stage 4 (social and conventional system)* There is a realization that each self can consider the shared point of view of the generalized other (the social system).	*Stage 4 (social system and conscience)* Focus is on the maintenance of the social order by obeying the law and doing one's duty.
Consolidated basic formal operations Operations are now completely exhaustive and systematic.	*Stage 5 (symbolic interaction)* A social system perspective can be understood from a beyond-society point of view.	*Stage 5 (social contract)* Right is defined by mutual standards that have been agreed upon by the whole society.

[a]Adapted from Colby & Kohlberg (Note 1).
[b]Adapted from Selman & Byrne (1974) and Selman (1976).
[c]Adapted from Kohlberg (1976).
(From Walker, *Child Development*, 1980, *51*, Table 1. © The Society for Research in Child Development, Inc. Reprinted by permission of author and publisher.)

Walker found that 47 percent of the children were exactly parallel in the three domains of understanding. For example, these children were concrete operational thinkers, stage 2 (self-reflection) reasoners about interpersonal relations, and stage 2 (exchange) reasoners about moral dilemmas. The remaining children were more advanced in cognitive development than in either interpersonal understanding or moral thinking. Other research also finds a positive relationship between cognitive development and moral reasoning (Keasy, 1975; Krebs & Gallimore, 1982).

A second source of influence on the development of moral reasoning comes from *social experiences*, particularly experiences that challenge the child's existing level of moral reasoning with new ways of thinking. Kohlberg concurs with Piaget that interacting with peers stimulates children to rethink moral issues. He draws on Piaget's concepts of *cognitive disequilibrium* and *assimilation* (refer to Chapters 9 and 13) to explain how social experiences move a child to higher levels of reasoning. When a child is confronted by thinking that utilizes reasoning from a somewhat more advanced stage, new information is introduced that the child must take into account, or assimilate. By upsetting the child's existing mode of thinking about moral issues—or to use Piaget's term, by creating cognitive disequilibrium—new, higher-stage levels of reasoning are made possible.

To demonstrate the role of cognitive disequilibrium in the development of moral understanding, Walker (1982) gave three moral dilemmas, similar to the one shown in Table 14–9, to 101 fifth through seventh graders and analyzed their responses in terms of Kohlberg's stages. He then exposed some of the children to moral reasoning at a level one or two stages higher than their own. (He did this by having them listen to two adults discussing moral issues.) Another group of children heard moral reasoning at the same level as their own, while a third group listened to adults making moral judgments reflecting a lower stage of moral reasoning. Finally, a control group (refer to Chapter 3) received no exposure to adults' moral reasoning.

One week later and again seven weeks later, each child was retested with similar moral dilemmas. As you can see by the results in Table 14–11, children in the control group showed no change in moral reasoning over the seven-week period. Most of those who heard adults reasoning at the child's own level or at a level below also did not change. However, those who were exposed to reasoning at one or two stages beyond their own moved up one stage in moral understanding.

Walker's results also support Kohlberg's contention that the stages of moral reasoning are sequential, with children not skipping any levels. Note too that in this study none of the children backtracked to a lower level of reasoning, even when they heard adults making moral judgments at a lower level than their own. Similarly, none of the children progressed more than one stage in reasoning over the seven-week period, even when they heard reasoning two stages beyond their own.

Piaget's and Kohlberg's emphasis on interacting with peers as a means to stimulate cognitive disequilibrium suggests that discussing moral dilemmas with other children would be a good way to advance moral thinking, and there is evidence to support this (Lawrence, 1980; Higgins, Power, & Kohlberg, 1984). In one study (Damon & Killen, 1982), the moral reasoning of five- to nine-year-old children who discussed issues related to *distributive justice* (what is the right way to distribute resources, such as pieces of cake, among the individuals in a group) in small groups of other children showed

Table 14–11

NUMBER OF CHILDREN SHOWING SAME-, LOWER-, AND HIGHER-LEVEL MORAL REASONING FOLLOWING EXPOSURE TO THE MORAL REASONING OF ADULTS AT DIFFERENT LEVELS

	Change in Moral Reasoning Stage			
Exposure to	Lower	Same	One Stage +	Two Stages +
Lower stage				
Before	....	10	....	....
One week later	....	9	1	....
7 weeks later	....	9	1	....
Same stage				
Before	....	10	....	....
One week later	....	7	3	....
7 weeks later	....	9	1	....
One stage higher				
Before	....	10	....	....
One week later	....	1	9	....
7 weeks later	....	2	8	....
Two stages higher				
Before	....	10	....	....
One week later	....	5	5	....
7 weeks later	....	3	7	....
No exposure (control)				
Before	....	10	....	....
One week later	....	10	....	....
7 weeks later	....	10	....	....

(Adapted from Walker, *Child Development*, 1982, *53*, Table 1. © The Society for Research in Child Development, Inc. Reprinted by permission of author and publisher.)

more advanced understanding than did children who discussed the same issue with an adult.

Limitations of Kohlberg's Theory. Some argue that the stages, developed by administering the measure to groups of white American males, are culturally biased (Simpson, 1974; Edwards, 1977; Baumrind, 1986). Kohlberg's tests have been given in such diverse countries as Mexico, Taiwan, Kenya, India, Israel, New Zealand, and Turkey. In general, this cross-cultural research finds that stages 5 and 6, and in some cases stage 4 as well, are rarely found in non-Western traditional societies, even among adults (Tietjun & Walker, 1985; Edwards, 1982; Kurtines & Grief, 1974). In fact, stage 6 reasoning appears only in the thinking of moral philosophers or exceptional individuals such as Martin Luther King, Jr., or Mahatma Gandhi. As a result, some argue that Kohlberg's stages are not universally applicable (Siegal, 1982).

Findings of sex differences in some studies have tended to reinforce this argument. Suggestions that girls and women tend to reason at stage 3, emphasizing the feelings and needs of others more often than males, have been interpreted as indicating a "lower" level of moral understanding rather than a qualitatively different approach. Critics like Carol Gilligan (1982) argue that men tend to perceive morality in terms of individual rights, while women think more in terms of responsibilities and connections to others. However, Lawrence Walker (1984), in a review of 50 studies of moral reasoning, found no consistent pattern of sex differences. The extent and meaning of sex differences in moral understanding are still being debated (Baumrind, 1986; Walker, 1986).

In addition, Kohlberg's stories have been criticized as not reflecting the real-life concerns of children. Problems with friends and parents tend to be reported most frequently by children over age 10 as situations involving moral issues, while situations involving authority figures and breaking the law (like the story about Heinz in Table 14–9) occur infrequently (Yussen, 1977).

An important limitation of Kohlberg's theory centers around the relationship between moral reasoning and moral behavior. Although Kohlberg focused his theory on the development of moral *reasoning* or *judgment*, not actual behavior, he believes that the way in which children understand moral issues will affect their moral actions. However, the theory tells us little about how children actually behave in situations involving moral issues. Can we know if a child will lie, cheat, feel guilty after wrongdoing, or engage in delinquent behavior in specific situations merely by asking the child to respond to hypothetical moral dilemmas?

Moral Behavior: Learning Theory Approaches

A learning theory orientation to moral development emphasizes situational influences on moral behavior. In this view, children who are taught the "right" way to behave and who are regularly rewarded for appropriate behavior and punished for transgressions will gradually behave in accordance with their experiences. Thus, a child will not necessarily behave consistently in different situations, since he or she may be exposed to differing patterns of reward and punishment.

Martin Luther King, Jr.

Experimental studies have shown that by rewarding children for moral behaviors, the behaviors can be increased, at least in the short run (Peterson, Hartmann, & Gelfand, 1977; Warren, Rogers-Warren, & Baer, 1976). Situational variability also exists; a child's tendency to lie, cheat, or steal is best predicted when situations are similar (e.g., cheating on a test at school and cheating on a game with friends). The more the situations vary (cheating on a test versus stealing from a store), the less the consistency in the child's behavior, particularly among young children (Burton, 1963, 1984).

Reinforcement alone is an unsatisfactory explanation for moral behavior, since the essence of behaving morally is acting according to principles of justice and fairness in the *absence* of external rewards and despite situational pressures. As one writer on moral development put it, "Most people do not go through life viewing society's moral norms (e.g., honesty, justice, fair play) as external, coercively imposed pressures" (Hoffman, 1979, p. 958). Indeed, the behavior of great moral leaders like Martin Luther King, Jr., inspires others precisely because these individuals went against the tide of popular opinion and outside pressure to uphold what is right. Thus, we still need an explanation for how children develop the capacity to resist temptation and regulate their own behavior in accordance with moral principles.

Social learning theory provides one explanation in terms of modeling. When children are exposed to models who exhibit moral action, they will tend to imitate such models. Similarly, they will be affected by observing models who behave immorally. Consistent exposure to positive models, particularly when the child has an emotional bond with the model, should result in *internalization* of moral behavior, resulting in internal standards of conduct.

Proponents of this view (Bandura, 1977; Staub, 1978, 1979) call attention to parenting practices that are associated with the internalization of moral behavior—feelings of guilt after transgressions and resistance to temptations for wrongdoing. Parents who are firm and consistent in enforcing standards of behavior, who use explanation in disciplining their children, who model appropriate behavior themselves, and who are warm and accepting—in short, *authoritative* parents (refer to Chapter 11)—tend to have children who continue to behave morally out of the parents' view (Baumrind, 1975; Walters & Grusec, 1977).

Systems theory emphasizes that cultural differences in moral values result in different moral behaviors. For example, the Israeli kibbutz, a type of collective agricultural settlement, emphasizes the value of distributing resources according to equality or need rather than effort. Its motto "To each according to need; from each according to ability" is communicated daily to children growing up on the kibbutz, through modeling, direct teaching, and rewards and punishments.

To see if kibbutz children would distribute resources in accordance with the principles they had been taught, Mordechai Nisan (1984) gave each of 160 six-year-olds and twelve-year-olds the opportunity to share a large pack of gum with another child as a reward for work they had both done. In some cases, the other child had done less work than the child with the gum; in others, the other child had done more work.

As Table 14—12 shows, compared to Israeli city children, the six- and twelve-year-olds on the kibbutz were more apt to distribute resources according to equality rather than amount of work done. Thus, their moral behavior with respect to *distributive justice* reflected the values of the environment in which they had been reared.

Psychoanalytic Theory

Even more than social learning theory, psychoanalytic theory places primary emphasis on the parent-child relationship as the root of moral (and immoral) behavior. In this view, the process of *identification* with parents results in the formation of a *superego* or conscience, which represents parental standards for conduct internalized within the child. Violating these standards results in feelings of guilt, and to avoid guilt, children form inner controls in the *ego* that enable them to behave morally when parents are absent.

In psychoanalytic theory, such inner controls are called *ego strength* or *ego control* (Block & Block, 1980). This concept includes being able to delay gratifying one's wishes, being oriented toward the future, having a sense of social responsibility, and being reflective rather than impulsive in behavior. Evidence supports the view that ego strength in children is associated with moral behavior. For example, R. L. Krebs (1967) assessed the resistance of a group of sixth graders to cheating. Many of the children subscribed to the moral principle that one should not cheat, but those children with high ego strength were most likely to follow through on their convictions and resist cheating when the temptation arose.

Both the psychoanalytic perspective and the social learning approach suggest that poor parent-child relationships may prevent children from developing moral standards and applying those standards to behavior. Studies of abused children provide support for this idea. Even at an early age, such

Table 14—12

NUMBER OF KIBBUTZ AND CITY CHILDREN WHO DISTRIBUTE REWARDS ACCORDING TO EQUALITY VERSUS OUTPUT

Principle	City	Kibbutz
Six-year-olds		
Equality	21	47
Output	59	33
Twelve-year-olds		
Equality	16	43
Output	64	37

(Adapted from Nisan, *Child Development*, 1984, *55*, Table 2. © The Society for Research in Child Development, Inc. Reprinted by permission of author and publisher.)

children appear less concerned about the feelings of others (Main & George, 1985) than do nonabused children. By the middle years, many abused children show less guilt, self-control, and moral understanding.

Moral Understanding and Moral Behavior: Integrating the Theories

None of the theories of moral development just reviewed provides a completely satisfactory account. The work of cognitive/developmentalists such as Piaget and Kohlberg documents that sequential stages of moral understanding can be identified. However, knowing what is right to do is only one among many influences affecting moral behavior. Learning theories and psychoanalytic theories call attention to the other factors that influence behavior. Experiencing consistent rewards and punishments, observing models behaving morally, and identifying with individuals, particularly parents, who exemplify moral behavior are all important. These factors enhance the child's motivation to behave morally, even in the face of temptation.

The Development of Prosocial Understanding and Behavior

Investigations of both moral understanding and moral behavior focus primarily on certain aspects of morality, such as justice, legitimate authority, and fairness. Another dimension of morality, called *prosocial* or *positive morality*, has received little attention from Piaget, Kohlberg, and others. This refers to situations in which we act to benefit another person through behaviors such as helping, sharing, being generous, and cooperating, often at some personal sacrifice (refer to Chapter 10).

One of the major differences that parents and teachers notice about children in the middle years is a general increase in prosocial behaviors. Although, as we saw in Chapter 10, preschoolers are capable of helping and caring for others, they don't spontaneously exhibit such behaviors in a consistent way. During the middle years—with some important exceptions we'll discuss presently—children are more likely to help someone in trouble, donate to someone in need, and share their possessions with others than they were as preschoolers (Damon, 1983).

Why do these changes occur? Considerable disagreement exists among researchers on this question. Some view children as "naturally" caring creatures and attribute lower levels of prosocial behavior among preschoolers to their cognitive immaturity. Others view self-interest as the natural state of humans; they feel children must be systematically trained to behave prosocially.

Cognitive Approach

The cognitive approach focuses on the characteristics of children's ideas about helping, sharing, being generous, and displaying other prosocial behaviors and how such ideas influence what children are likely to do. The ability to take the perspective of another, called *perspective-taking* or *role-taking skill*, is viewed as a prerequisite for prosocial behavior. When a child can put himself or herself in the shoes of someone else—understanding their pain or need—

the child will want to relieve the other person's distress through acts of kindness or helping (Chapman, et al, 1987).

Cognitive theorists argue that empathy has a cognitive as well as an emotional or affective side (Feshbach, 1977). Feeling another's pain is not enough to stimulate prosocial behaviors; rather, children must also understand how to accurately assess what is needed and how to go about helping. These skills are tied to the stages of cognitive development outlined by Piaget and the stages of interpersonal understanding in Selman's theory. Thus, Martin Hoffman (1979) describes stages in the development of empathy, emphasizing greater role-taking ability with increasing age (Thompson, 1987).

Information processing theorists do not propose stages of cognitive understanding as the underpinnings of prosocial behavior. They stress, however, the cognitive demands of situations calling for prosocial acts. For example, consider the following situation: A seven-year-old sees a friend trying to put together a puzzle. The friend becomes more and more frustrated and, beginning to cry, looks searchingly around the room. To predict whether the child will help the friend, an information processing analysis of this situation would ask the following questions:

1. Is a need for help perceived?
2. Can the child accurately identify the nature of the need?
3. Does the child know how to help?
4. Does the child believe the help will be successful?

Information processing theorists point out that the skills involved in identifying need, assessing competence at helping others, and helping successfully become refined during the middle years. Although even preschoolers understand that it's good to help people in need, they are not as able as older children to identify need (refer to Chapter 10), and it's not until children are about eight to ten years of age that they recognize the role that competence plays in prosocial behavior (Staub, 1978).

This developmental change is demonstrated in a study by Ladd, Lange, and Stremmel (1983) that examined the helping decisions of 72 first and fourth graders. Each child was shown two piles of "work in progress" belonging to two absent peers—for example, sheets of paper, each to be folded into a paper cup, or ropes to be tied into knots—and the child was asked to choose one of the two absent children to assist. (In reality, there were no absent children; the experimenters had provided the paper-folding and rope-tying materials.)

Both first and fourth graders offered to help the child who appeared to need help the most (as indicated by a smaller pile of folded cups or tied ropes), but the older children were more consistent than the younger in recognizing which child was the needier.

Before the experiment began, half the children practiced how to fold a cup from a sheet of paper until they were proficient. Would children who were knowledgeable about the task be more likely to help? The results showed that more than 60 percent of the fourth graders were more likely to offer help when they had relevant expertise, but only 16 percent of the first graders did so.

Other studies also find that cognitive aspects such as perceptions of need and knowledge affect prosocial behaviors such as helping. For example, in another study (Midlarsky & Hannah, 1985), first through tenth graders were interviewed about the reasons they might *not* help a stranger who had fallen down and scraped a knee. Children in the early grades most often cited feelings of incompetence—"I'm too young to help"—while seventh and tenth graders mentioned fear of disapproval or reluctance to embarrass the injured person.

Limits of Cognitive Approach

Although cognitive factors are important, they do not fully explain prosocial behavior. In general, children develop greater understanding of prosocial situations with advancing age and tend to behave more prosocially, but no strong link exists between understanding and behavior for the individual child.

Learning Theory

Although not denying that cognitive processes are important, learning theorists believe that prosocial behaviors are not natural or instinctive but occur as a result of rewards and punishments, exposure to appropriate models, and other forms of adult pressure. In other words, part of rearing children in a society is *teaching* them that it is right to behave prosocially. As B. F. Skinner put it:

> A person does not act for the good of others because of a feeling of belongingness or refuse to act because of feelings of alienation. His behavior depends upon the control exerted by the social environment (1971, p. 105).

A study of children's generosity (Zarbatany, Hartmann, & Gelfand, 1985) illustrates Skinner's view. Classrooms of first-, third- and fifth-grade children were each told that they had a sum of money (the equivalent of $1.00 per child) to spend as they wished. They could split up the money so that each child would have $1.00 (resulting in a generosity score of 0), they could buy something for the class that everyone could use (score of 1), they could buy something for the school (score of 2), or they could give the money to poor children (score of 3).

The children's choices were assessed under five conditions:

1. Secret ballot (a voting booth was set up in the hallway).
2. Peer knowledge (other children from the classroom would know the vote).
3. Experimenter (the experimenter discloses that this is really an experiment on sharing).
4. Experimenter watching (the experimenter goes into the booth with the child and watches while the child votes).
5. Experimenter urges generosity (the experimenter says to the child, "You know it really *is* good to give to poor children").

As you can see from Figure 14–3, third and fifth graders were *not* more generous than first graders when a secret ballot was used. However, as the children's decisions became more public, and especially when the adult urged the child to donate to the poor, older children behaved more generously. Why weren't first and third graders influenced in the same way as fifth graders? A learning theory interpretation might be that the younger children hadn't been exposed to as many years of influence and that adults don't expect as much generosity from younger children. From a cognitive theory point of view, younger children may not have understood exactly what the adult expected of them.

Other studies have moved outside the laboratory experiment and looked at the relation between parental discipline and children's prosocial behavior. These investigations indicate that children whose parents are warm and accepting and discipline them with *induction*—pointing out the consequences of the child's behavior on the actions and feelings of others—are more prosocial than children whose parents use physical punishment and frequent prohibitions and are cold and rejecting (Radke-Yarrow et al., 1983; Staub, 1979; Eisenberg, Lennon, & Roth, 1983).

Children's generosity and charity toward others is affected by many factors: cognitive development, observation of generous models, reinforcement for giving, and societal expectations.

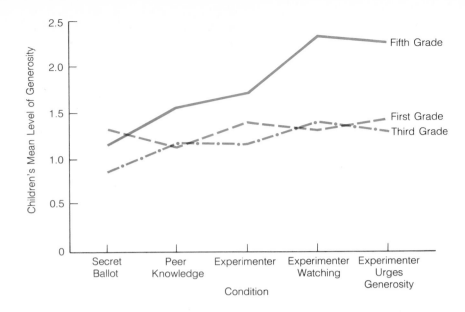

Figure 14—3

Children's Mean Level of Generosity in Five Conditions

(From Zarbatany et al., *Child Development*, 1985, 56, Figure 1. © The Society for Research in Child Development, Inc. Reprinted by permission of author and publisher.)

Television can also have an impact on prosocial behavior. In one study (Freidrich & Stein, 1975), five- and six-year-old children who watched *Mister Roger's Neighborhood*, a program emphasizing kindness, sharing, and cooperation, and who later used hand puppets to review the themes of the program were more likely to help another child. Thus, results from both laboratory experiments as well as studies of parenting and television exposure support the claims of learning theory that environmental pressures are significant influences on prosocial behaviors.

Limits of Learning Theory Explanations

Before you conclude that without adult prodding, children are naturally selfish, take another look at Figure 14—3. On the average, even when decisions were made in secret, most children opted for some form of sharing. These results

Children's educational television programs such as "Sesame Street" can help children learn prosocial behaviors and self-control.

and those from other studies (Radke-Yarrow, Zahn-Waxler, & Cummings, 1983) indicate that sharing is no less common than selfishness, even in first-grade children.

The emphasis on prosocial behavior as a product of adult influence does not tell us anything about the development of *altruism*. Altruistic acts are defined as those performed for intrinsic reasons, not because of self-interest or external pressure. A child who gives money to a needy person to win praise from the teacher or to avoid punishment for being selfish is not acting altruistically, although the child is performing a prosocial act. It is generally recognized that altruistic behavior is the highest form of prosocial responding (Bar-Tal, 1982).

Are children in the middle years altruistic? Although no one would deny that adult influence is important in encouraging children to behave prosocially, altruistic behavior also increases during the middle years. Preschoolers often see the reasons for being prosocial as external—"You'll get a prize if you share." However, by age ten, most children give intrinsic reasons for sharing or helping others—"I'm a kind person"—or refer to norms or values—"You should help someone if you can." By this age, children may actually resist heavy-handed attempts to reward them for behaving prosocially (Lepper, 1981).

As an example, let's look at a study by Daniel Bar-Tal and his colleagues (1980). Pairs of kindergarteners, second graders, and fourth graders—124 in all—played a game: One child in each pair was designated the "winner" and was awarded seven pieces of gum. (To the dismay of dentists, researchers on prosocial behavior seem to love to use sticks of gum as rewards.) When there was no attempt by an adult to influence the children's behavior, 38 percent of the fourth-grade winners shared their gum, while only seven percent of the kindergarten-age children did. However, when an adult told the winner to share and promised the child a big prize in return, 24 percent of the youngest children shared, but only two percent of the oldest children did so. When the children were asked later why they did or did not share, many more of the older children named intrinsic, altruistic reasons. Such internal feelings as motivation for prosocial behavior are emphasized by psychoanalytic theory.

Psychoanalytic Theory

In this view, young children naturally want to gratify their own desires and in the process are likely to ignore others or even harm them. By identifying with parents and wanting to be like them, they gradually curb their impulses, inhibit aggression, and behave more prosocially. Sigmund Freud put it this way:

> Identifications result among other things in a person limiting
> his aggression toward those with whom he has identified himself
> and in his sparing them and giving them help (1953, p. 110).

Evidence supports this view. Interviews with people who have performed dramatic acts of altruism reveal a strong identification with parents who themselves were models of prosocial behavior. For example, in one study (London, 1970), Christians who risked their lives to save Jews from the Nazis during World War II reported a childhood identification with moralistic, highly principled parents. Similarly, interviews with young American adults who were dedicated workers for civil rights during the 1960s showed that they had been deeply affected by parents who were also altruistic. In comparison to youths

The involvement and concern of parents with ethical issues affects children's prosocial development.

who did little in behalf of civil rights, the activists reported that as children they had enjoyed more positive relationships with their parents (Rosenhan, 1969; Clary & Miller, 1986).

It is wise to treat such *retrospective* reports with caution; childhood memories can be easily distorted (refer to Chapter 3). However, other research on the effects of observing adults who model prosocial behavior supports the view that identifying with a prosocial parent is likely to enhance prosocial behavior in children (Radke-Yarrow et al., 1983).

Our overview of prosocial understanding and behavior during the middle years parallels our discussion of moral understanding and behavior in several ways. In both cases, we saw the limits of cognitive explanations for explaining behavior. At the same time, learning theory proved to be too simple an explanation, since it failed to deal with the development of morality and prosocial behavior as internally directed. The issue of how thought and behavior are related is a difficult one for developmentalists to solve.

Cognitive, learning, and psychoanalytic theories each provide a perspective that is helpful in understanding prosocial development; they can be viewed as complementary rather than opposing viewpoints. Level of understanding affects how children will respond to rewards, modeling, or teaching. Thus, giving a prize for sharing may work with a first grader but may backfire when used with a fourth grader who believes that you should share because "it's right" and not to obtain rewards. At the same time, the environment children are exposed to can play an important role in encouraging prosocial behavior. Perhaps the most important environmental experiences are those that call the child's attention to the feelings of others and present prosocial norms. By identifying with prosocial parents, children focus their attention on caring for and benefiting others. When parents or other adults model prosocial behavior, they stimulate the child to think about prosocial issues in a more internal, intrinsic fashion. In this way, understanding and behavior mutually affect one another.

Cooperation and Competition

Is competition a healthy adaptation to our competitive society? Or do children need to be encouraged to be more cooperative? Cooperation occurs when two or more individuals work together to achieve a common goal. Competition can take several forms. Individuals can work separately on their own goals, each trying to do better than the other. Or, an individual can try to prevent others from attaining their goals.

To measure cooperation and competition, Millard Madsen and his co-workers designed an experimental board game to be played by pairs of children. To win this game, the child must "capture" as many marbles as possible in a cup. The game is constructed so that unless the two children cooperate, neither one will be able to win. Among urban North American children playing this game, cooperativeness declines and competition increases during the middle years (Madsen & Shapira, 1977).

Children who grow up in settings where cooperation is emphasized and competitiveness discouraged don't show this pattern. For example, rural children are less competitive at the game than are urban children. Mexican and Israeli children are more cooperative at the game than are children from the United States or Canada.

The results of Madsen's experiments have caused concern not because competition is viewed as always "bad" but because it was chosen as a strategy by many North American children even when it could not bring success. In other words, it appeared that these children did not know how to cooperate, even when working together was needed for success.

Both cooperative and competitive skills are needed in our society, and they often coexist in real-life situations. This occurs when a sports team cooperates to compete successfully against other teams or a classroom works together on a poster to be entered in a citywide competition. Emphasizing competition and neglecting cooperation may make it more difficult for children to develop those cooperative skills needed in many aspects of social life. In addition, evidence exists that when children act competitively, they show less empathy for others (Barnett, Matthews, & Howard, 1979).

Encouraging Cooperation

When children are encouraged to think of themselves as cooperative, working together increases. For example, in one study with seven- to twelve-year-old boys with behavior problems, children who were told statements like "You work well with others" were later more cooperative than children who were told "You're a real winner" (Jensen & Moore, 1977).

We also can learn about ways to encourage cooperation by looking at cultures emphasizing such behavior. For example, in the public schools in Israel, several strategies are used to promote a "we" feeling of group solidarity among children. A classroom of children is kept together as a group throughout the elementary school years, and many educational activities are planned for the group as a whole. The class also plans a series of social events throughout the year. Although individual grades are given to children, creating a positive "group climate" is considered an important aspect of every classroom. When a child has a birthday, the teacher encourages the child to invite the whole class to the party rather than exclude any member of the group. Through such methods, the idea of working together toward common goals gradually becomes second nature.

Of course, methods of fostering cooperation must be adapted to the particular needs of a culture. Nonetheless, along with training children to compete effectively, we can provide opportunities for them to develop the ability to work together.

Thus far, in discussing both moral and prosocial development, we've painted a picture of steady "upward" progress during the middle years, with children showing both more advanced understanding as well as more positive behavior with age. However, some exceptions exist to this pattern; studies of North American youngsters indicate that during the middle years, cooperation declines and competition increases.

Chapter Summary

DEVELOPMENT OF SELF-UNDERSTANDING

☐ During the middle years, ideas about the self become more abstract and complex, containing more psychological attributes and fewer physical characteristics.

☐ Self-identity becomes more stable, with children distinguishing between a subjective and an objective self.

☐ During the elementary school years, children increasingly evaluate themselves relative to others. These processes of social comparison lead some children to be confident about their abilities and others to doubt their self-worth.

UNDERSTANDING OTHERS

☐ According to Selman, stages in the development of interpersonal understanding can be identified; they mark a shift from viewing relationships as unilateral and based on authority to seeing them as reciprocal and based on mutual respect.

☐ Social competence has been moderately associated with level of interpersonal understanding.

MORAL DEVELOPMENT

☐ Piaget describes the development of moral understanding in terms of a shift from moral realism or heteronomous morality to autonomous morality.

☐ Modifications of Piaget's interview stories and evidence from other cultures indicate that Piaget may have underestimated young children's reasoning and failed to account for the complexities of moral development.

☐ Kohlberg's influential six-stage theory of the development of moral understanding describes an invariant progression from preconventional to conventional to postconventional morality. The last is rarely found among adults, and questions concerning the applicability of the theory of all cultures and to both men and women are currently being debated.

☐ Cognitive development, interpersonal understanding, and social experiences all affect level of moral reasoning.

☐ Moral behavior is determined in part by moral understanding but is also affected, as learning theory suggests, by environmental experiences such as reinforcement, models of appropriate morality, and communication of standards of conduct.

DEVELOPMENT OF PROSOCIAL UNDERSTANDING AND BEHAVIOR

☐ Cognitive theories have stressed advances in understanding prosocial situations. With age, children become more able to assess the needs of others, to know how to help, and to feel competent to assist others.

☐ Learning theory emphasizes the conditions that encourage or discourage children to be caring of others, including adult reinforcement and modeling.

☐ Psychoanalytic theory places primary emphasis on the process of identification with parents.

☐ An integration of cognitive, learning, and psychoanalytic theories was viewed as the most complete explanation of the development of prosocial understanding and behavior.

Recommended Readings

Gilligan, C. (1982). *In a different voice*. Cambridge, MA: Harvard University Press (paperback). A provocative and eloquent challenge to Kohlberg's theory of moral development, arguing for qualitative differences between men and women in moral understanding.

Piaget, J. (1932). *The moral judgment of the child*. New York: Harcourt, Brace. A detailed description with sample stories and many illustrative responses of the development of moral reasoning from the stage of moral realism to that of autonomous morality.

Selman, R. (1980). *The growth of interpersonal understanding: Developmental and clinical analyses*. New York: Academic Press. Extensive research and clinical case studies documenting stages in the development of self- and other-understanding as well as the understanding of relationships.

CHAPTER 15

Connecting with Others

W hen the bus was all loaded . . . , one of the boys in the seat behind me tapped me on the shoulder and said, "Hey, shorty, ain't that your mother standin' on the court stoop?"

"Yeah."

He said, "Man, she's cryin'."

I said, "So what?" as if I didn't care. But I cared; I had to care: that was the first time I had seen Mama crying like that. . . . The tears just kept rolling down Mama's face as the bus started to pull away from the curb. I had to care. Those tears shining on Mama's face were falling for me.

— *Brown, 1965, p. 61.*

. . . I used to bother all the girls in the class. Most of them I had beaten up at least once. I didn't like girls much and used to get a lot of fun out of beating them up and chasing them home after school. I chased Grace home one day, but I didn't beat her up. I pulled on her, grabbed her around the neck, and ran with her hat. After a while, I stopped chasing other girls home and only chased Grace home.

— *Brown, 1965, p. 46.*

The quotes that open this chapter are taken from the memoir by Claude Brown of growing up in the slums of Harlem, entitled *Manchild in the Promised Land*. Brown paints a vivid protrait of his relationships with parents, sisters, grandparents, other children, and other adults at home, at school, and on the streets. Though hardly typical of most children, Brown's experiences illustrate the widening world of middle childhood shared by children growing up everywhere.

During the elementary school years, children's social contacts expand beyond the more narrow world of preschoolers and increasingly are chosen by the children themselves rather than by their parents. In industrialized nations, almost all children begin school, at which they establish ties with other children and adults. School-age children explore their neighborhoods and community more widely than do preschoolers, meeting people their parents may not know. Many children begin to participate in after-school activities, both organized and informal. Children exercise more choice in selecting public figures, such as rock stars, as objects of admiration. In these ways, we see in middle childhood the development of children's *construction* of their own social world, a process that will continue throughout their life span.

This chapter examines three aspects of the child's social world during middle childhood: (1) The family, including parent-child and sibling relationships. (2) Peer relations, including how children become part of groups, friendship, and social acceptance and rejection. (3) School, with special attention to the impact of educational philosophy and teacher behaviors on children.

Family

Despite the fact that the social world of children during middle childhood is widening beyond the horizons of the family, parents and siblings—the family system—continue to exert significant influence upon every aspect of the child's development. Moreover, the way the family relates to the other contexts of the child's social world—school and peers, for example—may help determine how the child fares outside the family.

Theories of the Parent-Child Relationship

Psychoanalytic Theory.   *Psychoanalytic theory* views middle childhood as a period of *latency,* when the instinctual urges of infancy and early childhood have been *sublimated* or channeled away from direct expression, freeing energy for task accomplishment and learning. Erikson called this period the stage of *Industry versus Inferiority,* a time when children need to feel industrious, able to accomplish tasks they perceive as worthwhile (Erickson, 1963).

This view of middle childhood suggests that it is a plateau of relative quiet in parent-child relations, between the Oedipal struggles of the preschool period and the hormonal changes during puberty (see Chapter 16). During middle childhood, parents should have less difficulty in securing compliance from their children. Because of the child's identification with the parent and internalization of moral standards, it should not be necessary for the parent to be physically present to enforce proper behavior. Instead, the child should be more *self-regulating* and self-directed than during early childhood.

Cognitive Theories.   Cognitive/developmentalists agree that middle childhood is a period when children show more ability at self-regulation and require less direct monitoring by parents. However, they explain this in terms of cognitive changes that occur from the preschool years through the school years.

Because during middle childhood children become more able to adopt the perspectives of others, or *decenter* in Piaget's terminology, they can respond to explanations from parents about how their behavior might be adversely affecting others. For example, they can understand how their failure to perform requested household chores places an extra burden on the parent. Changes in self-understanding enable children to understand how they are being viewed by others and that they have an identity or self that they can reflect upon (refer to Chapter 14). This means that parents can now appeal to the child's sense of self as a reason for following parental requests, saying things like "You're the kind of person who helps." Such appeals are more likely to make the child self-directed than are demands based only on what the parent wants.

Improved information processing abilities—longer attention span, better memory strategies, and improved problem solving—allow parents to use more reasoning with the elementary school-age child and to monitor the child less closely than in earlier years. Eleanor Maccoby describes the changes occurring during middle childhood as a shift from direct regulation of the child by parents to *co-regulation,* when parents have general supervisory control but the child has moment-to-moment self-regulation (Maccoby, 1984).

Both psychoanalytic and cognitive theories suggest that qualitative differences occur as children move from preschool years into middle childhood. These differences make possible new ways that parents and children can relate to each other. Both theories place an emphasis on changes *within* the child as the source of changes in the parent-child relationship, although the theories differ in the kinds of changes felt to be significant.

Learning Theory.   In contrast, *learning theory,* although recognizing the child's cognitive growth, stresses parental behaviors, such as consistent reinforcement, clear communication of rules, and modeling as leading to acceptance of parental rules and standards by middle childhood. If parents have behaved in a contradictory fashion, often ignoring positive behavior or reacting inconsistently to negative actions, they can reinforce and model undesirable behaviors, which possibly result in an aggressive, out-of-control child or one with other behavior problems.

Learning theory rejects the idea that parent-child relationships change qualitatively during middle childhood. Instead, general principles of reinforcement and observational learning can be used to explain the parent-child relationship, no matter what the age of the child.

Systems Theory.   According to *systems theory*, parent-child relationships during middle childhood will be affected by changes in the family such as the birth and development of siblings, changes in the employment status of parents, changes in the marital relationship, particularly conflict, separation, and divorce, as well as changes in the responsibilities of parents, such as assuming care of an elderly relative (Minuchin, 1985).

With these theories in mind, let's look at research describing first some common themes in parent-child relations during middle childhood and then individual variations on these themes. In doing so, we will evaluate the evidence against the four theoretical frameworks just outlined.

General Characteristics of Parent-Child Relations

Time with Parents.   One of the basic changes occurring in parent-child relationships during middle childhood is that parents and children spend less time together than they did in earlier years. For example, in one study, parents reported spending less than half as much time in caretaking, teaching, reading, talking, and playing with children ages five to twelve years as they did with preschoolers (Hill & Stafford, 1980). This is not surprising, considering some of the characteristics of middle childhood noted earlier: attendance at school for extended periods of the day, after-school play and activities with other children, and independent exploration of the neighborhood. At the same time, parents may use the child's entry into school to make changes in their own responsibilities, such as taking full-time employment. All this decreases the time available for parents and children to be together.

When parents and children are together, however, there is evidence that they devote a greater proportion of their time to social interaction—talking, watching television together, doing activities jointly—than to eating, housework, or child care (dressing/undressing, bathing, etc.).

The findings of one study are shown in Figure 15–1. The child's advances in physical coordination and cognitive development mean that parents need to spend less time helping the child manage daily activities, such as dressing and cleaning up after the child. Many daily routines, like toothbrushing, have become automatic, freeing parent and child to spend time on other activities.

Discipline.   Some of the frequently reported problems that North American parents face with their elementary school-age children are shown in Table 15–1. Many of these issues involve setting standards for the child and monitoring aspects of the child's behavior as the child spends more time in settings outside the parents' direct control. This is an example of parent-child coregulation.

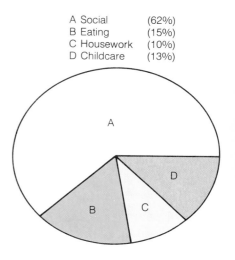

A Social   (62%)
B Eating   (15%)
C Housework   (10%)
D Childcare   (13%)

Figure 15–1

Social Interaction Time among Families of School-Age Children

(From Davey, A. J., and Paolucci, B. 1980. Family interaction: A study of shared time and activities. *Family Relations*, 29, 43–49 National Council on Family Relations.)

Table 15–1

ISSUES FACING PARENTS OF
SCHOOL-AGE CHILDREN

Context	Issue
Family	Should chores be required?
	Should my child be paid for household work?
	Should an allowance be given? How much?
	When can my child be left alone during the day? At night?
	Should my child have responsibility for caring for younger brothers and sisters? How much?
School	What should I do when my child doesn't want to go to school?
	How much and how should I monitor my child's schoolwork?
	How much should I be involved with school problems?
	How should I monitor my child's whereabouts?
	How should I encourage my child's achievement?
	How much should my child be encouraged to do alone, without parental assistance?
Peers	Should I assist my child in making friends and, if so, how?
	Should I encourage or discourage my child from associating with certain children?
	When should my child be ready to spend the night at another child's house?

(From Maccoby, 1984.)

The specific issues that parents and children face during middle childhood will vary by culture. For example, in non-Western rural societies, children ages six to twelve spend most of their time working alongside other family members in household tasks and as apprentices for work roles rather than in school or playing with peers (Weisner, 1984). Yet here too, parents are concerned with setting standards and monitoring behavior.

As children approach middle childhood, parents generally engage in less physical restraint, removal, or punishment. Instead, reasoning with the child,

In problem families, conflict between parents and children tends to escalate in a vicious circle of parental anger and child disobedience.

deprivation of privileges, arousing guilt, appealing to the child's better nature, or reminding the child of rules and responsibilities become more common (Maccoby, 1984). For example, one study assessed childrearing patterns through reports of 111 parents when their children were three years old and again when the children were twelve years of age (Roberts, Block, & Block, 1984). In general, during the second assessment, both mothers and fathers were less likely to report that physical punishment and punishment by isolating the child were used as discipline. Taking away privileges, letting the child know what the parent expects, and the praising the child were viewed as more effective. These changes are consonant with cognitive theory's suggestion that parent-child relations undergo a shift with changes in the child's cognitive development. However, since the reasons for the change were not assessed in this study, the findings also may be explained in terms of the psychoanalytic concept of middle childhood as a latency period.

Other findings of the same study provide evidence of continuity in parenting. On three-fourths of the questions concerning parenting (out of a total of 91 items), mothers responded similarly when their children were preschoolers and when they were 12 years old; half of the fathers gave similar responses at the two time periods (Roberts et al., 1984). For example, parents who reported that they had "strict, well-established rules" for their child or that they "respect the child's opinion" when the child was three years old answered in the same way nine years later. This supports the contention of learning theory that enduring patterns, based on reinforcement, are built up over the years, and these patterns are not easily changed.

Affection. Some changes in the expression of affection between parents and children during middle childhood have been noted. In the same longitudinal study assessing changes in discipline from ages three to twelve, parents reported less physical affection such as hugging and kissing their children as the children became older (Roberts et al., 1984). Other research confirms this finding (Newson & Newson, 1976; Maccoby, 1984).

This does not mean, however, that parents and children are less close during this period than during earlier years; they may express closeness by other, less physical means. Unfortunately, we know relatively little about parent-child attachment during the school years (Maccoby, 1984).

Variations in the Parent-Child Relationship

Parenting Styles. Considerable research has linked variations in parenting to child behaviors, such as aggression, prosocial behavior, moral reasoning, self-esteem, and cognitive competence (Patterson, 1982; Bearison & Cassell, 1975; Saltzstein, 1976; Loeb, Horst, & Horton, 1980). In general, consistent, involved, and firm parents have children who are less likely to be inappropriately aggressive or out of control.

In addition, discipline techniques that combine warmth with an emphasis on the consequences of one's actions, appeals to the self, and explanations based on others' feelings—defined as *induction*—have been associated with the development of conscience and more mature moral judgment as well as prosocial behavior (Saltzstein, 1976; Radke-Yarrow et al., 1983; Maccoby & Martin, 1983). On the other hand, direct physical coercion, or *power assertion*, has been associated with aggression in children, low self-esteem, and less advanced moral and prosocial development.

A caution mentioned before (refer to Chapter 11) needs repeating here. Most of the research relating variations in parenting styles to child behaviors is correlational; it merely shows an association between particular parenting behaviors and certain child behaviors. Developmentalists (Bell, 1968) have pointed out that we cannot conclude from this research that parental behaviors *cause* particular changes in the child. It is just as plausible that variations in the child produce different reactions by parents. For example, children trained to act aggressively in a laboratory situation evoke being restricted, disciplined, and ignored by unrelated adults (Brunk & Henggeler, 1984). Thus, parents who use physical punishment could be reacting to an aggressive child who does not listen to explanations or respond to anything but coercion.

Although almost all developmentalists and parents agree that children make some contribution to the kind of parenting they receive, few would view parents as passive reactors to the child. By the same token, the greater amount of responsibility, authority, and power that parents generally have over children (as compared to children over parents) does not mean that children have little influence over the way they are parented. Rather than asking *which* causes the relationship between parenting and child behaviors—parents or children—developmentalists are currently asking, *How* do parents and children mutually affect one another?

This way of looking at parent-child relationships during middle childhood is nicely illustrated in a study conducted by Gerald Patterson (1980). He observed family interaction patterns in 150 families where an elementary school-age child, usually a boy, had been referred for behavior problems, such as aggression against other children and adults, stealing, truancy, or setting fires.

In these families, mothers engaged in less approval, laughter, and talk with their sons than did mothers of nonproblem boys, while showing more disapproval, yelling, and ignoring. Similarly, the aggressive boys directed more negative behaviors, such as teasing, whining, humiliating, and noncompliance toward their mothers than toward any other member of their family.

The following sequence of interaction often occurred: the aggressive boy would begin to behave negatively toward his mother, perhaps by whining. At first, the mother would ignore the behavior or give in, but as the negative behaviors escalated in frequency and intensity, the mother would finally respond in kind with yelling or physical force. Patterson drew on learning theory to interpret this pattern, which he called a *negative reinforcement trap* (see Figure 15–2). Mothers and their out-of-control sons mutually reinforced each other in a cycle of aggression and coercion. Teaching mothers new forms of parenting—stating clear expectations for the child; monitoring the child's compliance; using firm, consistent, but nonviolent, means of enforcing discipline; and giving praise for good behavior—improved the quality of both parent-child relations within the home and the child's behavior outside the family. These findings suggest that although mutual influence characterizes parent-child relations, it may be easier to change interactions by intervening with the parent, who may have more motivation, cognitive skills, and resources than the child.

Single-Parent Families.   As shown in Table 15–2, the majority of children during middle childhood live in two-parent families. However, substantial minorities of children live in a single-parent household, usually headed by their mother and usually as a result of divorce or marital separation. It is estimated

Behavior:	Time frame 1	Time frame 2	Time frame 3
	Mother ("clean your room") →	Child (whine)	→ Mother (stops asking)

	Short-Term Effect	Long-Term Effect
Mother	The pain (child's whine) stops.	Mother will be more likely to give in when child whines.
Child	The pain (mother nags) stops.	Given a messy room, mother less likely to ask child to clean it up in the future.
Overall	The room was not cleaned.	Child more likely to use whine to turn off future requests to clean room.

(From Patterson, *Monographs of Society for Research in Child Development*, 1980, *45*, Figure 2. © The Society for Research in Child Development, Inc. Reprinted by permission of author and publisher.)

Figure 15—2
Negative Reinforcement Trap

that if current rates persist, 40 percent of all children under 18 years will live in a single-parent household for some period of time (Collins, 1984).

Large ethnic differences exist; as of 1981, black children were six times more likely than white children to live with a mother who is separated from her husband, nine times more likely to live with a widowed mother, and over 18 times more likely to live with a mother who has never been married.

Living with a single parent, if that parent is female, is strongly associated with poverty. As of 1982, 38 percent of white mother-only families lived below the official poverty line, compared with 16 percent of white families with both parents present. Among blacks, 86 percent of the mother-headed families lived in poverty, compared with 46 percent of black two-parent households (Hill, 1983). A study of the impact of divorce on families in California found that on the average, women with children suffered a 73 percent drop in income following divorce, while men (who did not have custody in most cases) increased their income 42 percent (Weitzman, 1985).

Marital Status	White	Black	Total
Married or permanently cohabiting	83.1%	51.3%	79.0%
Father absent; mother present, single, never married	0.8%	15.0%	2.7%
Widowed	0.5%	4.5%	1.0%
Divorced	11.0%	12.7%	11.2%
Separated	2.5%	16.1%	4.3%
Mother absent; father present	2.0%	0.5%	1.8%

(Reprinted from *Development During Middle Childhood: The Years from Six to Twelve*, 1984, with permission of the National Academy Press, Washington, D.C.)

Table 15—2

MARITAL STATUS OF PARENTS OF CHILDREN AGES 6 TO 12, 1981

Some researchers believe that children in single-parent families develop best if reared by a same-sex parent.

Another important characteristic of single-parent families is that they are almost always headed by mothers. Moreover, following divorce or separation, most children lose regular contact with their fathers. For example, in a national survey of children ages seven to eleven years who were living in single-parent or reconstituted (i.e., remarried) families, 49 percent of the children had not seen their fathers during the preceding year, while only one child in six averaged weekly contact or better (Furstenberg & Nord, 1985).

When living in a single-parent household is a result of divorce, the stress of the breakup can have adverse effects on children during middle childhood, just as it can at earlier periods (refer to Chapter 11). Wallerstein and Kelly (1980) examined the reactions of children ages six to twelve to their parents' breakup. They reported that at ages six to eight, grief, fear, and a longing for reconciliation characterized the children's reactions, while those who were nine to twelve years of age reacted with shame, open anger, and rejection of step-parents. Children exhibited more problems at home, showing increased aggression and more childish behavior, as well as problems at school, including difficulties in getting along with other children, keeping up with homework, and relating positively to teachers. Elementary school-age children who experience divorce report it as a shocking, disruptive event that produces insecurity, lowered self-esteem and enduring psychological problems for the child (Plunkett & Kalter, 1984; Kalter & Plunkett, 1984).

The persistence of these effects is not known, since longitudinal research has not followed children who have experienced divorce into adulthood, although some effects persist into late adolescence (see Chapter 17). It's also not clear what the effects of single parenthood are on the child apart from the divorce experience (for example, among never married) and apart from the effects of poverty, which, as we've seen, often coincides with single parenthood (Maccoby, 1984).

We need to know more about differences in parenting behavior that may occur in single-parent rather than dual-parent families. This will tell us about the processes by which family structure may be linked to parent-child interaction patterns. For example, if single mothers are overburdened by the responsibilities of parenting as well as by being the sole economic provider, do they tend to spend less time monitoring their children's behavior or co-regulating their children? Are they less consistent and firm in their discipline? Do they fail to praise the child for good behavior while responding to negative actions with power assertion?

Hetherington's studies of the aftermath of divorce in families with preschool-age children suggest that such parenting patterns do characterize mothers in the year following divorce, but that parent-child interaction significantly improves by the end of the second year (refer to Chapter 11). Although few studies are available that describe single parenting during middle childhood, there is evidence that a similar pattern may characterize families with children during the middle years and adolescence. For example, interviews with over 2,000 children ages seven to eleven found few differences in shared activities, household rules, closeness toward parent, or discipline when intact, single-parent, and reconstituted families were compared (Furstenberg & Nord, 1985).

We should not expect to find uniform patterns characterizing single parents any more than we might expect dual-parent families to be similar in their parent-child interactions. Single parents are a varied group, and many factors might be expected to affect the quality of family relationships, including amount of conflict with former spouse, economic well-being, formation of new intimate relationships by the single parent, and social support by others outside the family (Hetherington et al., 1982; Maccoby, 1984).

Employment Status. Another aspect of family structure—employment status of parents—has been the focus of considerable interest. Table 15–3 shows the variety of employment situations of parents with school-age children. When white or black children live with both parents, dual employment is more likely than the traditional arrangement of a father-breadwinner and mother-homemaker. Substantial ethnic differences also exist. Mothers in Hispanic families are less likely to be in the labor force—whether they are single parents or in dual-parent families—than are mothers in white or black families. And both single and married black mothers are about twice as likely to be unemployed (and searching for work) as are white mothers.

Ethnic differences and family structure interact in complex ways. For example, when white mothers head households, they are much more likely to be employed (63.7 percent) than when they are in married-couple families

Employment Status	White	Black	Hispanic
Married-couple families			
Father unemployed	5.9%	9.3%	9.2%
Mother unemployed	4.4%	8.7%	6.1%
Mother not in labor force	43.5%	32.7%	52.3%
Father & mother unemployed	.1%	2.7%	1.0%
Father & mother employed	46.4%	48.0%	37.5%
Female-headed families			
Mother unemployed	6.6%	11.2%	7.3%
Mother employed	63.7%	43.4%	41.0%
Mother not in labor force	29.7%	45.3%	51.9%

(Based on March 1982 data. Reprinted from *Development During Middle Childhood: The Years from Six to Twelve*, 1984, with permission of the National Academy Press, Washington, D.C.)

Table 15–3

EMPLOYMENT STATUS OF PARENTS OF CHILDREN AGES 6 TO 13

(46.4 percent). This is not true, however, of black mothers, who are somewhat *less* likely to be employed when they are single parents than when they are in dual-parent households. Not all parents are employed full-time. In particular, a substantial portion of mothers may hold part-time jobs, although the statistics were not collected in a manner that allows us to determine this precisely (Collins, 1984).

Because of the central importance of employment as a source of economic resources for the family and as an important source of adult identity for men and women, it is plausible that variations in employment status of parents would have effects upon the parent-child relationship (refer to FOCUS ON ISSUE in Chapter 11).

Glen Elder (1974) (refer to Chapter 2) examined the impact of paternal unemployment and income loss during the economically depressed 1930s on 167 eleven- to fourteen-year-old children, half boys and half girls, living in the Oakland, California, area. Unemployment caused changes in fathers' behaviors, leading them to be more arbitrary, rejecting, and punitive in their relations with their children. Changes in the entire family system also occurred: More responsibility shifted to mothers and older children, children perceived their fathers as less attractive role models, and all family members expressed more uncertainty about their family's social standing.

The effects of such changes on children's development varied depending on characteristics of the child. Both boys and girls reacted to paternal rejection by perceiving their fathers as less attractive role models. However, fathers who had suffered economic losses were most rejecting toward physically unattractive daughters (as rated by the investigators) as compared with attractive daughters or sons in general. The fathers' rejection caused girls but not boys to have lower aspirations and self-esteem and to be more moody and easily hurt. The economic deprivation of the family caused boys to seek out peers for companionship (Elder, Nguyen, & Caspi, 1985). These results indicate that the impact of economic changes on the parent-child relationship is a result of a complex interaction of family characteristics, parent behavior, and child characteristics.

Social Class Differences.   As we've noted, in studying the effects on children of single parenthood, parental employment status, and self-care, it's hard to disentangle the effects of economic well-being or social class differences. *Socioeconomic status,* or *SES,* is a shorthand way of describing variations in income, education, and occupation among families. Using these indexes, families described as middle-class are thought to have more resources and be subject to fewer stresses than those defined as lower-class.

Social class is not defined consistently by all investigators; some use income differences, others use education or occupation, and some combine all three. A family's social class may differ depending on whether the wife's income or education is included along with that of her husband. There is also variation in the number of social class divisions used in research on SES differences in parenting. For example, one study might contrast middle class with lower class, while another study might employ distinctions among upper middle, lower middle, upper lower, and lower lower. Such variations in the "cut-off" points of social classes will affect the range of income, education, and occupational status within a particular class designation (Maccoby, 1984; Hess, 1970; Laosa, 1981).

Latchkey Children: Are They at Risk?

Parental work schedules may make it difficult for parents to be home during the after-school hours to supervise their children. This has led to the phenomenon of so-called latchkey children, who are not under the supervision of an adult for part of the day. For example, in one study of 764 sixth graders, 66 percent of the children whose mothers worked full-time were latchkey, while 20 percent of those with part-time working mothers and 12 percent of those with nonworking mothers were so classified (Medrich, Roizen, & Rubin, 1982).

As of 1974, 1.8 million children between the ages of seven and thirteen regularly spent the after-school hours unsupervised by an adult. With the continuing rise in maternal employment throughout the 1970s and 1980s, the number of such children is projected to increase. Many developmentalists, parents, teachers, and others have expressed concern about latchkey status for the development of children. They worry that school-age children who are home alone after school may become fearful and less confident about themselves and their surroundings (Long & Long, 1982; Turkington, 1983). They are also concerned that latchkey children may not be properly supervised by their parents and hence are more likely to develop behavioral and academic problems (Bronfenbrenner, 1976).

Little research has been conducted to document these presumed effects, however. The studies that do exist challenge some widely held beliefs about the consequences of latchkey status. For example, one study compared fifth and seventh graders who were in latchkey versus adult-supervised arrangements and found no differences in school achievement, fears, or teacher-rated adjustment (Galambos & Garbarino, 1983).

In another investigation (Rodman, Pratto, & Nelson, 1985), 52 fourth graders and 44 seventh graders were studied. Half the children at each grade level regularly cared for themselves at home after school, while half were cared for by an adult. To isolate any possible effects of latchkey status, self-care and adult-care children were carefully matched on sex, race, family composition, and social class.

Each child was interviewed about after-school care arrangements, and measures of self-esteem and locus of control were given. (*Locus of control* refers to the child's perceptions of personal control versus lack of control over positive and negative outcomes.) In addition, each child's teacher rated the child's social and personality adjustment, responding to such questions as, Does this child adapt easily to new situations, feel comfortable in new settings, enter easily into new activities? The results indicated no significant differences on any measures between latchkey and adult-supervised children; both groups scored similarly on self-esteem, locus of control, and adjustment.

The findings of this study as well as that of Galambos and Garbarino (previously cited) suggest that alarm over latchkey status may be premature. Indeed, the researchers argue that the term *latchkey* has negative connotations that are not supported by evidence, and they urge that the more neutral term *self-care* be substituted (Rodman et al., 1985).

Although more research is needed, it appears that after-school care status by itself does not produce clear-cut effects on children. Children who are in self-care after school are likely to vary in many ways. Some are well prepared by their parents who leave instructions for them, maintain frequent contact by telephone, and have contingency plans in case of emergency. Other children home alone after school may not know where their parents are or how to reach them.

How parents structure self-care arrangements in terms of preparation, contact, and instructions may be more important for the child than the care status alone. Characteristics of the child also may be important in determining the effects of after-school care arrangements. Younger school-age children may be more vulnerable to feelings of fear and helplessness than were the fourth and seventh graders studied. Similarly, children experiencing other stresses, such as the aftermath of divorce, may be more adversely affected by self-care. Debate on the effects of self-care continue; additional research is urgently needed, as more children care for themselves after school.

Despite this lack of agreement in the definition and use of SES in research on parent-child relations, consistent class differences in parenting have been found (see Table 15—4). The general picture that emerges from Table 15—4 shows the middle-class parent as more authoritative and less permissive or power-assertive than the lower-class parent. Since, as we've seen, these differences in parenting styles are associated with differences in child behaviors, it is perhaps not surprising that SES differences in child development have also been found. Lower-class school-age children do more poorly in school than middle-class children, feel less self-confident about their abilities, and, in general, feel less in control over their own destiny (a more external rather than internal locus of control) (Bartel, 1971; Maehr, 1974).

It is important to keep in mind that these represent *average* differences and that there is considerable overlap between social classes in parent-child interaction. Moreover, within-class variation—differences between families of the same social class—is usually greater than between-class variation (Maccoby, 1984).

Social class differences by themselves tell us little about the *process* by which families are affected by their social class position. Are lower-class parents subject to many stresses, such as family disorganization or frequent mobility, that interfere with parents' ability to achieve co-regulation with their children? Or do the lack of education and lowered aspirations of lower-class parents lead them to de-emphasize reasoning with their children? Do parents who feel powerless over their environment communicate this sense of helplessness to their children? There is evidence that all of these processes may underlie social class differences in parent-child relations (Rutter, 1983; Hess & Shipman, 1967; Sennett & Cobb, 1982).

Evaluating the Theories

Research on both the general characteristics and individual differences in parent-child relations during middle childhood provide support for elements of each of the theories we have reviewed. The shift from direct regulation to co-

Table 15—4

SOCIAL CLASS DIFFERENCES IN PARENT-CHILD RELATIONS

Dimension of Behavior	Differences Found
Responsiveness to child	Compared to lower-class parents, middle-class parents have higher rates of interaction with children, respond with more information to children's questions, are more likely to know teacher's name and to take child on outings outside home.
Language	Compared to lower-class parents, middle-class parents use longer sentences, include more explanations, issue fewer commands.
Discipline	Compared to lower-class parents, middle-class parents use less physical discipline and more reasoning, call child's attention to consequences of behavior, are more accepting of child's expression of anger toward parent.
Values	Compared to lower-class parents, middle-class parents place less value on obedience and respect for authority and more value on curiosity, maturity, independence, and achievement.
Affection	Higher incidence of hostile or rejecting attitudes toward children among impoverished, multi-problem parents compared to other parents of both low and high income.

(Sources: Maccoby, 1984; Bee, et al., 1969; Hess & Shipman, 1967; Laosa, 1981.)

regulation and the changes in affection and discipline that are characteristic of middle childhood are compatible with both a psychoanalytic and a cognitive orientation. However, at this point, there is no research directly linking children's resolution of the Oedipal/Electra conflict or their level of cognitive reasoning to quality of the parent-child relationship during middle childhood.

We also reviewed evidence that supports the role of parents as reinforcers and models of behavior; however, it appears that both children and parents may reinforce patterns of interacting, as the concept of the negative reinforcement trap illustrates. Finally, studies of the impact of parent employment or marital status on the quality of parent-child relations support a family systems perspective, which emphasizes that changes in any part of the family system may be expected to affect other parts.

Sibling Relations

Unlike parent-child relationships, sibling relations in middle childhood are relatively unexplored terrain. Most major theories of development have focused on parent-child relationships, and only recently has research emerged documenting the importance of siblings for the child's development. As a result, we can identify theoretical perspectives *implied* in this research rather than examine clearly articulated theories.

Theories of Sibling Relations. *Psychoanalytic theory* has paid little attention to the role siblings play in development, emphasizing instead the importance of relations with mother and father for sex-role, moral, and personality development. Cognitive theories have paid more attention to sibling relations. A *cognitive/developmental* perspective emphasizes changes in children's understanding of sibling relations with cognitive development, implying that these changes have implications for sibling behavior. *Learning theory* focuses on siblings as important sources of learning for the child; siblings affect each other by reinforcing each other's behavior and acting as models. *Family systems* theory emphasizes how sibling relations vary as a result of how parents treat each child and family characteristics such as birth order, spacing, and number of children.

General Characteristics. Despite the relative lack of theory and research focused on sibling relations, such relations are very important emotional ties for children, second only to bonds with parents (Lamb & Sutton-Smith, 1982). The beginnings of sibling bonds occur with the birth of a brother or sister and by early childhood are already important (refer to Chapters 7 and 11). During middle childhood, children view their siblings with many and mixed emotions.

In one study, 49 fifth- and sixth-grade children were asked to talk about their relationship with a brother or sister (Furman & Buhrmester, 1985). The different themes mentioned in their responses are shown in Table 15–5. Most of the children spoke of the companionship, intimacy, affection, and prosocial behavior in their sibling relationship, but they also frequently mentioned quarreling and antagonism. Very few children spoke in uniformly positive or negative terms about their sibling.

No research as yet exists exploring developmental changes in cognitions about siblings. However, following cognitive theory, the changes in interpersonal perception described in Chapter 14 make it plausible that between ages six and twelve, children develop more complex ideas about siblings.

Table 15-5

Quality	Percentage of Children
Companionship	93
Antagonism	91
General relationship evaluation	89
Admiration of sibling	81
Quarreling	79
Prosocial behavior	77
Affection	65
Intimacy	55
Nurturance by sibling	48
Similarity	46
Nurturance of sibling	34
Parental partiality	20
Dominance by sibling	18
Competition	10
Admiration by sibling	8
Dominance over sibling	8

(Based on responses of 49 children; from Furman & Buhrmester, *Child Development*, 1985, 56, Table 1. © The Society for Research in Child Development, Inc. Reprinted with permission of author and publisher.)

In addition to the emotional complexity of sibling relations, such bonds also provide frequent learning opportunities, as learning theory suggests. Studies observing sibling pairs during play in their homes find that during both early and middle childhood, older siblings often adopt teacher or "manager" roles, while younger siblings are learners or "managees" (Brody, Stoneman, & MacKinnon, 1982; Stoneman, Brody, & MacKinnon, 1984; Brody, Stoneman, & MacKinnon, 1985). Thus, if two siblings were observed playing a board game, the older sibling would be likely to explain the rules of the game, keep track of the score, and suggest when it was time to play another game. The younger child, on the other hand, would listen to the instructions, ask the older child questions, and let the older sibling keep score (Brody et al., 1982).

Most of the studies observing brothers and sisters together have been conducted in Western industrialized countries where siblings interact together in the context of play. However, in many non-Western rural societies, older children are assigned caretaking responsibility for their younger siblings, a pattern that begins even during early childhood. By the time children are six to seven years old they are beginning to participate more regularly in caretaking tasks under the supervision of their mother and other adults (Weisner, 1984). Observations of sibling caretaking find teacher-learner, manager-managee roles occur here as well as in play situations (Edwards & Whiting, 1980; Edwards, 1985). Second graders with younger siblings are more knowledgeable about babies and infant care than are their classmates who are only or last-born children (Melson, Fogel, & Toda, 1986).

Variations in Sibling Relations.   Although emotional complexity and teacher-learner roles characterize sibling relations in general during middle childhood, great diversity exists in the way brothers and sisters get along. Many factors influence the precise nature of this relationship.

One set of factors includes characteristics such as age spacing between the siblings and sex differences or similarities. Many parents have wondered if their children will get along with each other better if they are close in age or more widely spaced and if they are of the same sex or of different sexes.

When siblings play a game, the older often acts as teacher and leader, while the younger is a learner and follower.

Developmentalists, too, have examined these questions. The answers have turned out to be quite complex. For example, in one study, 73 pairs of siblings were observed in an unstructured situation, working on a cooperative task (wrapping a package together), and playing a competitive game (tossing cards into a basket) (Minnett, Vandell, & Santrock, 1983). One sibling was seven to eight years old, while the other was either older or younger, same-sex or opposite-sex, closely spaced (one to two years) or widely spaced (three to four years). As shown in Table 15–6, the behaviors of these seven- to eight-year-olds differed, depending on many characteristics of their sibling relationship.

Table 15–6

ILLUSTRATED EFFECTS OF BIRTH ORDER, AGE SPACING, AND SEX OF SIBLINGS ON THE BEHAVIOR OF SEVEN- TO EIGHT-YEAR-OLDS WITH THEIR SIBLINGS

Characteristic of Child/Relationship	Behavior
Age relationship	
Younger sibling	More praise, teaching, dominance
Older sibling	More joyful behavior, cooperative work/play, self-criticism
Age spacing	
3 to 4 years	More affection, activity, positive behaviors
1 to 2 years	More aggression
Sex of older sibling	
girl	More praise and teaching
boy	More neutral behaviors and cooperative work/play
Sex composition of pair	
same sex	More negative behaviors, cheating, aggression, dominance
opposite sex	Fewer negative behaviors, less cheating, aggression, dominance
Birth order and age spacing combined	
sibling 3 to 4 years younger	Most positive behavior, teaching, affection, and dominance
sibling 3 to 4 years older	Most self-criticism

(From Minnett et al., 1983.)

To complicate matters further, other studies observing siblings in play situations have found contradictory results. Note that in the results reported in Table 15–6, same-sex sibling pairs showed more negative behaviors, such as cheating and aggression. However, in another observational study of 18 sibling pairs, in which the older child was seven to nine years old and the younger child was $4\frac{1}{2}$ to $6\frac{1}{2}$ years old, sisters showed more positive, prosocial behaviors toward each other than did brothers or brother-sister pairs (Brody, Stoneman, MacKinnon, & MacKinnon, 1985). And in an interview study, children reported feeling more warmth and closeness toward a same-sex than an opposite-sex sibling, but only when they were spaced less than four years apart (Furman & Buhrmester, 1985).

Perhaps clear-cut effects of family structure as sex of siblings and spacing between them will emerge as more research is done on sibling relations during middle childhood. However, there is reason to believe that this will not happen. Family systems theory suggests that how brothers and sisters relate to each other will be affected by parents and their relationships with each child. Thus, birth order, age spacing, sex differences, and other characteristics of children may be interpreted differently by different parents.

Parents often tend to see siblings as being different in personality and temperament from each other, and they contrast first- and second-born children even more than first- and third-borns. This tendency to attribute different characteristics to different siblings is called *sibling deidentification,* and it has been found to occur especially when siblings are of the same sex (Schacter & Stone, 1985).

To the extent that parents tend to treat siblings differently, perhaps seeing one as "Daddy's girl" or "Mamma's boy," the relationship between the siblings also changes (Schacter, 1982). For example, there is evidence that sibling conflict is especially high when a parent shows consistent favoritism toward one child (Bryant & Crockenberg, 1980). And school-age daughters whose mothers are responsive toward them show more prosocial behaviors toward younger sisters than do girls of unresponsive mothers (Bryant & Crockenberg, 1980).

Evaluating the Theories

The emerging research on sibling relations in middle childhood provides support for a cognitive interpretation. Children's understanding of their brothers and sisters becomes more complex during middle childhood. Because siblings frequently take on teacher and learner roles, there may be cognitive benefits for both the older and younger child from sibling interaction. However, this has not yet been demonstrated in research. Learning theory is also supported by evidence that siblings function for one another as models and reinforcers. A family systems perspective is suggested by the fact that the behavior of mothers (and possibly fathers, although research here is lacking) mediates the sibling relationship.

Peers

Although families remain the most important influence upon children's lives during middle childhood, this is a period when children are spending more time away from home with other children. Their relations with other children assume greater importance during these years. Do other kids like me? Who are my friends? Am I part of the group? These are questions that occupy the attention of children during middle childhood.

When children enter elementary school at approximately five to seven years of age—the age of entry varies slightly in different countries—they begin to associate for extended periods of time with peers, or other children of approximately their own age. On the school playground and in the neighborhood, they play with both younger and older children. In cultures where children do not attend school at all or do so only for brief periods, peer interaction may be quite rare. Instead, children of different ages would be found working and playing together, the older ones put in charge of the younger children (Weisner, 1984).

In addition to having variations in the ages of other children, relationships differ in intensity and feeling. Some children interact regularly only as acquaintances, perhaps because they are in the same class at school. Feelings may range from indifference to intense admiration or dislike. Other children become friends, and their friendship may deepen into "best friends" and last over an extended period. Variations in group size and in the extensity of social ties also exist. Some children may spend most of their time with one or two good friends, while others are found mostly in larger groups.

Theories of Peer Relations

The major theoretical positions we have been examining concur that peers are an important influence on children's development during the middle years. From the perspective of *psychoanalytic theory,* the resolution of the Oedipal/ Electra conflict (refer to Chapter 11) frees the school-age child from a preoccupation with parents and allows more energy to be devoted to working and playing with other children. As children channel their energies during this latency period away from sexual urges and into mastering new skills, they spend more time with same-sex peers and even avoid children of the opposite sex. (This also might account for the greater responsiveness of same-sex siblings to one another found in several studies.)

Cognitive theories emphasize the emergence of new cognitive skills rather than the channeling of sexual energy. The same cognitive capacities, such as perspective taking, improved attention and memory, and enhanced problem solving, that enable parents to rely more on reasoning and monitoring make it possible for children to sustain and deepen peer relations, becoming more responsive to one another, more sensitive to subtle social cues, and more enduring in their friendships.

Cognitive changes are predicted to result in changes in the meaning of social relationships such as friendship, and such changes can be expected to influence behavior. Thus, if a twelve-year-old expects that a friend is trustworthy, shares secrets, and cares about one's welfare while a six-year-old feels that a friend is someone who enjoys the same activities, the number, stability, and character of friendships for the two age groups probably would differ. In general, the cognitive perspective emphasizes that how children understand social relationships has an important influence on children's behavior (Hartup, 1984; Rotenberg & Mann, 1986).

Learning theory suggests that children who are experiencing problems getting along with other children or making friends may be exhibiting negatively reinforcing behaviors, such as teasing or hitting. Training that uses models to demonstrate more positive behaviors is suggested to change the reinforcement patterns children are experiencing with one another.

Systems theory places more emphasis on how peer relations and other components of the child's social world fit together. How are peer relations affected by aspects of the home environment, such as parents and siblings? Do parents play a role in how their children get along with peers, for example, by arranging social contacts, helping their children make friends, or teaching them social skills? These are some of the questions a systems perspective poses. To understand peer relations, we need to draw on each of these theories.

General Characteristics

Children ages six to twelve spend more time with other children than do preschool children. Barker and Wright's (1955) observations of children's activities found that for the four-year-olds observed, 20 percent of all social interactions involved other children, while 40 percent of the social contacts of children ages seven to eleven years were with other children. Although many of these contacts were at school, children also got together in their neighborhood and at outdoor public places such as parks.

In Western industrialized societies like the United States, most of these social contacts are with children of the same age, sex, and race (Hartup, 1984). A study by Sagar, Schofield, and Snyder (1983) illustrates this pattern. Observation of 48 black and 44 white sixth graders who were attending the same urban school showed that 88 percent of all social contacts were with the same sex, while 70 percent were with the same race. In fact, 63 percent of all peer contacts were with *both* the same sex and the same race.

This tendency to spend time with similar peers rather than other children is stronger during middle childhood than during earlier years. It peaks at about nine to fourteen years; mixed-sex interactions become more common during the senior high school years (Hartup, 1984).

A similar pattern apparently occurs in other cultures as well. For example, in one study, 152 children ranging from eighteen months to nine years of age from a village in the African country of Kenya were observed as they went about their daily activities (Harkness & Super, 1985). As you can see from Table 15–7, among three- to six-year-olds, boy-boy or girl-girl interactions were not much more likely than boy-girl interactions. However, six- to nine-year-olds spent most of their time relating to children of the same sex.

Why do children during middle childhood gravitate toward same-sex peers? Psychoanalytic theory traces this development to the repression of sexual urges, resulting in avoidance of the opposite sex. Little research supports this view, but some observations of American children at play on school playgrounds and in cafeterias suggest that when cross-sex contacts do occur, there are sometimes sexual overtones, as in games of "kiss and chase" (Thorne, 1986).

Table 15–7

SAME-SEX AND MIXED-SEX INTERACTIONS AMONG CHILDREN FROM A VILLAGE IN KENYA

Age and Sex of Observed Child	Percent Male Peers Interacted With	Percent Female Peers Interacted With
3 to 6 years		
Boys	35	65
Girls	51	49
6 to 9 years		
Boys	72	28
Girls	16	84

(From Harkness & Super, *Child Development*, 1985, 56, Table 1. © The Society for Research in Child Development, Inc. Reprinted with permission of author and publisher.)

Another reason for preferring same-sex peers may arise from *sex-role socialization,* which refers to children's acquisition of behaviors, attitudes, and aspirations considered to be appropriate to their sex. As a result of this sex-role socialization, boys and girls often prefer different activities and are found in different settings. For example, boys are more likely to engage in physically active, outdoor play, such as team sports, while girls prefer more verbal, sedentary activities, often indoors with one or two other girls (Medrich et al., 1982; Hartup, 1984). As a result of these patterns, friendships develop among children, most of them of the same sex.

Friendship

Ideas about Friendship. Although, as we saw in Chapter 11, preschoolers also form friendships, the nature of friendship changes as children develop. The following comments are typical of what friendship means to children during middle childhood:

> Friends don't snatch or act snobby, and they don't argue or disagree. If you're nice to them, they'll be nice to you.—Julie, age 8.
>
> A friend is someone that you can share secrets with at 3 in the morning with Clearasil on your face.—Deborah, age 13.
>
> (Rubin, 1980, p. 31)

In one study (Smollar & Youniss, 1982), children ages six to thirteen years were asked, What do you think might happen to make two children become friends? Not become friends? Become best friends? In their answers, the younger children (six to nine years) answered much like Julie, quoted above, emphasizing spending time together, doing something nice for each other, and engaging in the same activities as ways of becoming friends. They also thought that negative behaviors, like refusing to share, were reasons for friendships to end.

On the other hand, older children (10 to 13 years), like Deborah in the preceding quote, described friendship as a process of getting to know one another and of discovering common interests. As one child put it, "They talk and talk and find out if they like the same things." For them, friendships end when children realize they have little in common. In general, from ages six to twelve, children place increasing emphasis on psychological qualities, such as common interests, mutual understanding, and sharing inner feelings, and less stress on doing the same things as the basis of friendship (Bigelow, 1977; Selman, 1981; Furman & Bierman, 1984).

These changes parallel cognitive gains in self-understanding and in social cognition. Children in middle childhood are more able than in earlier years to infer emotional states of others and understand personality dispositions as enduring despite outward changes of appearance or behavior (refer to Chapter 14). According to cognitive theory, these changes make possible new expectations concerning the nature of friendship.

Keeping Friends. Not only do ideas about friendship change, but friendships themselves become more stable during middle childhood. Berndt & Hoyle (1985) interviewed 49 first graders and 43 fourth graders at the beginning of the school year, asking each child to name their "best friends" and to indicate how much they liked each member of their class. At the end of the school year, the children were reinterviewed. At that time, 54 percent of all the first graders' friends and 76 percent of all the fourth graders' friends were "old" friends, children they had named as friends at the beginning of the year. (Following the pattern of same-sex socializing previously mentioned, all the friendships reported were same-sex.) Interestingly, when the investigators used this interview method with a group of 54 eighth graders, they found the same levels of friendship stability as among fourth graders. This suggests that beyond age ten, friendships may not increase further in stability.

How Friends Behave.   Because friendships change in their meaning and become more stable, it is perhaps not surprising that friends behave differently with one another than do nonfriends. For example, school-age friends have been observed to show more emotion toward each other, share more information, and interact more reciprocally (for example, they do about equal amounts of talking) than do children who are not friends (Newcomb & Brady, 1982). When in competitive situations, like playing a game where only one child can be a winner, friends can display considerable rivalry and conflict (Berndt, 1981a). In some ways, close friends share a relationship similar to that of siblings, one of strong and varied emotional communication. An 11-year-old girl expresses just such a complicated mix of feelings toward her best friend in the following:

> What a wrong day! Lindsey is getting me more and more irritated every day. I think we're both beginning a *bad* relationship. She bothers me a lot. . . . I always have to listen to how she feels but she won't listen to how I feel. I hate her as of the present moment, but I will never take off the bead ring I have that she gave me. I love her alot and never want to part as a friend, but there are times I just can't stand when she does things like that (Rubin, 1980, p. 74).

Impact of Friendship.   Piaget and others, like Harry Stack Sullivan, believed that relations among friends have important consequences for cognitive development. They argued that because friends engage each other intensely, often challenging each other's ideas, they may stimulate increased intellectual growth. Moreover, the supportive atmosphere of friendship—where it's okay to say almost anything—may allow children to more freely explore new ideas.

In a 1985 study Nelson and Aboud illustrate the cognitive consequences of friendship. First they assessed the responses of 192 third and fourth graders to several social and moral dilemmas (for example, "What should you do if a smaller child starts to fight with you?"), and rated their answers in terms of maturity. (An immature answer would be "hit him," while a more mature response was "refuse to fight.") Then half the children discussed the problems with a friend, while the other children discussed the dilemmas with a nonfriend. When the children were questioned again, those who had talked with a friend were more likely to increase the maturity of their answers, but discussions with nonfriends produced no positive results.

How do friends bring about this effect? Nelson and Aboud observed the children's behavior while discussing the problems. Friends gave each other more explanations, made more criticisms, and asked each other for more information than did nonfriends. This more intense involvement, with more conflict and attempts to resolve it, appeared to stimulate the children's thinking.

Isolated or neglected children have difficulty knowing and using appropriate strategies for joining groups of children. The neglected child, who often hovers from a distance, tends to be ignored by the other children.

Because of these cognitive benefits of friendship and because having friends is very important to elementary school-age children, many parents and teachers are concerned when children have difficulty making and keeping friends. Studies of school-age children find that on the average, about three to five "best friends" are reported, and this does not seem to vary much from grades one through eight (Hallinan, 1980; Berndt & Hoyle, 1985). However, wide individual variations exist among children in number of friends. In addition, children differ in how well liked they are by their peers.

Being Liked and Disliked

About two percent of schoolchildren report that they have no friends, and based on the choices of other children in their class, about six to ten percent of children are not chosen by others as a friend (Hallinan, 1980). As noted in Chapter 11, even during the preschool years, children differ in their *social acceptance* by other children. Some children are popular and well liked by their peers, while others are disliked or rejected. Still other children may be ignored as potential playmates or friends. Some children are controversial; they are well liked by some children, but disliked by others (Coie & Dodge, 1983).

These differences in *social status* persist into the elementary school years and indeed become more stable. In one study, 96 third graders and 112 fifth graders were each asked to name three children in their class they "liked most" and three children they "liked least" (Coie & Dodge, 1983). Based on this procedure, about 23 percent of the children were considered *popular*—they were often named as positively liked but seldom considered unliked. Twenty-one percent were *rejected*, receiving few positive mentions but many negative ones. *Neglected* children made up another 20 percent of the children—they were infrequently mentioned at all. *Controversial* children, who received many positive and negative nominations, made up six percent of the group. The remaining children were considered "average" in social status.

To determine how stable social acceptance was, the investigators reassessed the children every year for five years. During this time, the children changed schools, from elementary to junior high, and of course, the peer groups they were part of changed as well. Sixty percent of the children rejected by their peers during the first year of assessment were likely to be rejected or neglected five years later by a different group of children at a different school. Other social statuses showed more change. For example, five years later, only 21 percent of the initially popular children were still popular, and of the initially neglected children, 24 percent had become popular. Thus, even though social status during middle childhood is more stable than during the preschool years, there is evidence of both stability and change in social acceptance. In particular, children rejected by their peers have more difficulty changing their social status than do other children.

There are many reasons for individual differences in social status. As with preschool children, physical attractiveness plays a role (Langlois & Stephan, 1977). And as we've already seen, children express more liking for others who are similar in age, sex, and ethnic background to themselves. More important, however, are differences in social behavior (Reaves & Roberts, 1983). Popular children are viewed by their classmates as cooperative and supportive and as leaders, while rejected children are seen as disruptive and hostile. Neglected children are perceived as shy and controversial children as sometimes cooperative, sometimes aggressive (Coie, Dodge, & Coppotelli, 1982; Coie & Dodge, 1983; Virtue & French, 1984).

When children of different social statuses are observed interacting with other children, including children they have never met before, the same patterns emerge in their actual behavior.

For example, in one study (Dodge, Schlundt, Schocken, & Delugach, 1983), ten popular, ten rejected, and ten neglected kindergarten children—based on their acceptance in their kindergarten class—were each observed as they tried to join a pair of unfamiliar children who were building with blocks. The popular children made more group-oriented statements, such as "That looks like a fun thing you're doing," and the other children responded positively to this, often including the new child. The children who had been rejected in their class were disruptive in their attempts to join the new pair of children, pushing the blocks off the table, for example, and they were usually rebuffed in their attempts to join in play. The neglected children watched, waited, and hovered near the pair; this tactic was usually ignored by the other children.

The results of this study give us a clue as to how social status, particularly among rejected children, may be stable even as children change groups. It appears that rejected children use inappropriate, often aggressive, means of relating to other children, and these means result in their social rejection. With time, such children may acquire a negative reputation, which only worsens the problem (Putallaz & Gottman, 1981).

To summarize the development of peer relations during middle childhood, we have seen that in general children gravitate toward same-sex similar peers. Relationships deepen during this period, ideas about friendship become more complex, and friendship itself becomes more stable. Patterns of peer acceptance and rejection, present in preschool groups, are even more evident during middle childhood. Although social status stems from many factors, differences in social skills are important. In particular, rejected children often misinterpret social situations and act inappropriately toward their peers—problems social skills training has been developed to address.

Helping the Socially Rejected Child

Social rejection appears to pose considerable risks to the developing child. It is clearly a painful experience for any child to be rejected by other children, and as we've seen, social rejection, more than other social statuses, is apt to persist over time, even as the child enters other groups. Thus, problems in getting along with peers is one of the most common reasons parents give for bringing their child for treatment at a mental health clinic (Achenback & Edelbrook, 1981). Furthermore, children who later become delinquents often report that during middle childhood they had been disliked by their peers (West, 1982). Finally, social rejection during childhood is associated with later psychological problems in adolescence and adulthood (Cowen, Pederson, Babijian, Izzo, & Trost, 1973).

Because of these findings, programs have been developed to help rejected children become better accepted by their peers. Some of these programs are derived from cognitive theory, which suggests that rejected children often misinterpret social situations or act inappropriately because they fail to understand what others are communicating to them. It has been found, for example, that boys who are habitually aggressive against other children often misinterpret ambiguous situations—such as someone bumping against them and knocking over their tray of food in the cafeteria—as an intentionally hostile act (Dodge & Frame, 1982).

To counteract these cognitive deficits, programs have been developed to make children more aware of social situations, the intentions of others, and the effects that aggressive or disruptive behavior has on other children. For example, in coaching sessions, children role-play social situations like joining a group of children who are playing a game. They are encouraged to monitor the effects of their actions; the adult coaches call their attention to the negative effects of social strategies like hitting and pushing. This cognitive awareness helps the children modify their behavior (Asher & Renshaw, 1981).

Other approaches are based on a social learning model. Children watch films of peers interacting positively with one another or respond directly to peers chosen for their social skills (Ladd, 1981; Ladd & Mize, 1983). It is hoped that by observing peer models of more effective social strategies, aggressive children will learn new patterns of behavior. These observations also may be accompanied by opportunities to practice new behaviors and direct reinforcement, through teacher praise, for more socially effective behaviors (Mize, 1984).

Programs that combine cognitive, modeling, reinforcement, and practice components appear to be most effective (Ladd & Mize, 1983). Such interventions demonstrate social skills but also call children's attention to those social strategies that are most effective in gaining group acceptance. For example, we know that one way popular children are successful in joining others in play is by using group-oriented statements such as "That looks like fun." Rejected children, on the other hand, often make self-directed statements, such as "I have a puppy dog," in such a situation. Programs have been developed that encourage rejected children to use more effective entry-group strategies by first demonstrating them, then labeling them, and finally having the child practice these new strategies (Mize, 1984).

The real test of social skills training programs is the programs' ability to change rejected children's social status. The results are promising. For example, one program that taught social skills to rejected third and fourth graders succeeded in improving the children's acceptance several months after the training had stopped. Rejected children who had received no treatment did not show any improvement, however (Oden & Asher, 1977).

Many questions remain about helping socially rejected children. We do not know exactly how long social skills training should be or what components of the programs are most effective with which children. The long-term effects on social acceptance are also unclear. Do rejected children who have been coached in social skills improve their acceptance when they join new groups? Despite these questions, social skills training holds promise for helping socially rejected children find a place among their peers.

During the elementary school years, children tend to form same-sex groups, a process called gender segregation.

School

The Physical Setting of the School

Do children fare better in a large school or a small one? What size should a classroom be? Does it make a difference if desks are arranged in rows or if children work in small groups at round tables? These are some of the questions that researchers have asked about how physical aspects of the learning environment might affect children.

Large classes (over 20 students) have been found to contain more cliques, less individualized student activity, more teacher discipline for misbehavior, and more negative student attitudes (Minuchin & Shapiro, 1983). In an early study, Daw (1934) recorded the discussion of kindergarteners in classes ranging in size from 15 to 46 children. As class size increased, the number of children who participated in discussion declined. Moreover, when children did talk, their average amount of participation decreased.

These effects are generally due not to size alone but to how teachers structure their classrooms. For example, in a large class, different small-group activities can be planned that will encourage social interaction among the children and will allow for more individualized learning. In general, aspects of the physical setting of the school are difficult to separate from variations in teacher behavior, curriculum, and other components. When schools are designed to reflect different philosophies of education, all these factors will vary. We can illustrate this by looking at the contrasting philosophies exemplified by *traditional* and *open* education.

Traditional and Open Education

Classrooms organized along traditional versus open education principles differ in many ways. In the traditional classroom, fixed desks are arranged facing the teacher, who usually instructs the class as a whole. In the open classroom, large open areas, activity centers, and work tables are set up to allow the student to move freely about the room and to work together with other children. Along with these physical differences, the two classrooms have different educational goals. In the traditional classroom, the teacher is responsible for setting educational content and ensuring that all children acquire specific skills. In the open classroom, emphasis is placed on independent activity, individu-

Traditional and open classrooms represent differing physical organizations and educational philosophies.

alized learning, and the development of student initiative, curiosity, and responsibility.

Is one educational philosophy better than the other? Evaluation of academic achievement, social relations, and personality adjustment of children in traditional and open classrooms indicate some differences as well as many similarities. For example, in terms of academic achievement, a study of over 7,000 children in traditional and open classrooms at both the elementary and secondary school level concluded: "Students neither gain nor lose in their performance on standardized achievement tests as a consequence of attending open schools" (Epstein & McPartland, 1979). Similarly, there are no systematic differences in students' attitudes about school or their self-esteem as a result of attending a traditional or open classroom (Minuchin & Shapiro, 1983).

Other studies have found some differences in social interaction. For example, patterns of social acceptance and friendship were assessed in 51 classrooms, comprising grades five through eight (Hallinan, 1976). In the traditional classrooms, social status was more rigid and stable than in the open classrooms. That is, in the traditional classrooms there was less disagreement concerning who was popular and who was rejected, and these statuses were less likely to change over time than in the open classrooms. Other studies have found similar patterns. In open classrooms, more children select classmates as best friends and fewer children are rejected (Epstein, 1978). There are also indications that children from open classrooms behave more cooperatively, at least when observed on experimental tasks (Horowitz, 1979).

Some learning style differences have also been found. Since open classrooms are designed to encourage independent mastery, creativity, and curiosity, one might hypothesize that children from these classrooms would show higher levels of such behaviors. In terms of self-directed learning (but not other aspects of learning style), there is support for this prediction. In an extensive review of studies comparing traditional to open education, 78 percent of the 23 studies investigating student independence in learning found results favoring the open classroom (Horowitz, 1979).

In summary, the overall "scoreboard" for traditional versus open education does not indicate a clear victory for either form of instruction. A review of over 200 studies comparing the two philosophies concluded the following:

> The open classroom sometimes has measurable advantages for children, and . . . sometimes appears to make no measurable difference, but . . . rarely appears to produce evidence of measurable harm (Horowitz, 1979).

One possible reason that more marked differences between traditional and open classrooms have not been found is that the philosophical distinction between the two approaches is often blurred in practice. Teachers in an open classroom (as defined by the physical design) may establish traditional rules for behavior, while teachers in traditional schools may modify those spaces to introduce components of open education (Gump, 1975).

Other factors that may be important in terms of impact on the child are the number of years spent in traditional versus open classrooms and the match between the child's educational needs and the orientation of school (Minuchin & Shapiro, 1983). Because public education serves a great variety of students, no single educational philosophy or curriculum will be suitable for everyone.

Bilingual Education

For some educators, parents, and children, bilingual education is an affirmation of cultural diversity enabling children to maintain and even deepen their ethnic heritage through their experiences at school. For others, bilingual education is a slow, costly, and ineffective means of helping children improve their English skills enough to enable them to compete successfully against native English-speaking peers.

Bilingual Education Policy

Current U.S. policy stems from a suit brought by non-English speaking Chinese students against the San Francisco school system in 1971, charging that although most students received no help in acquiring English, they could not graduate from high school without showing English proficiency. The Supreme Court ruled that such treatment unfairly discriminated against non-English speaking students:

> Basic English skills are at the very core of what these public schools teach. Imposition of a requirement that, before a child can effectively participate in the educational program, he must already have acquired those basic skills is to make a mockery of public education. We know that those who do not understand English are certain to find their classroom experiences wholly incomprehensible and in no way meaningful (*Lau v. Nichols,* 1974, p. 3).

To solve this problem, the Court instructed that bilingual educational programs be instituted wherever there are children with limited English skills.

As a result of this decision, the government has issued what are known as Lau Guidelines for school districts to implement bilingual education programs. In addition, bilingual education programs supported by federal and state funds have developed dramatically. For example,

Figure 15—3

Enrichment Model of Bilingual Education

(From Cazden, "Effective Instructional Practices in Bilingual Education," Research Review for the National Institute of Education, July, 1984. ED 249 768.)

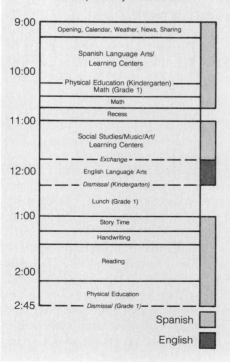

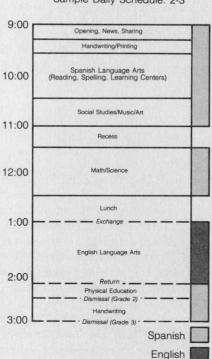

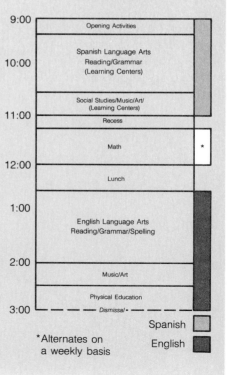

in 1979, federally supported bilingual programs served an estimated 250,000 children in about 70 languages and dialects, with Spanish predominating in 75 percent of the programs (Cervantes, 1981).

What Is Bilingual Education?

The exact nature of bilingual programs varies considerably. In the transitional model, instruction is provided initially in all school subjects by a bilingual teacher in the child's native language. Instruction in English as a second language is also given, and gradually, the child spends increasing amounts of time receiving instruction in English, with instruction in the native language gradually phased out entirely.

In the enrichment model, the goal is to develop and maintain the child's native language along with acquiring proficiency in English. The child's cultural heritage is stressed in the non-English speaking classes, which are maintained throughout the child's education. An example of such a program is shown in Figure 15–3.

In many cases, there are not enough children in a school system speaking a particular language, such as Kurdish, to set up separate classes. In such cases, English as a Second Language (E.S.L.) classes are provided in which teachers focus on the acquisition of basic English speaking, writing, and reading skills, providing translations from the child's native language where possible.

Evaluating Bilingual Education

The success of bilingual education is a controversial issue, largely because considerable disagreement exists about the proper goals. For some, bilingual education should be the shortest and most effective route toward English competency for children who enter the school system with limited skills in that language. Those who favor this goal consider the fact that some children remain in bilingual education programs for many years (see Figure 15–3) as evidence that the programs are a failure.

Proponents of this view advocate *immersion* programs as a substitute for current policy. Based on the highly successful French-English immersion programs in Canada, this approach stresses total and intensive instruction in the to-be-acquired language and culture (Genesee, 1983).

Others argue that Canadian immersion programs cannot be easily transferred to the United States. In the Canadian programs, middle- and upper-class children generally are enrolled, and both French and English are viewed as highly prestigious languages. Most of the children involved in bilingual educational programs in the United States are recent immigrants or members of disadvantaged minorities. Often, low status is accorded their native languages (Cazden, 1984).

Proponents of the enrichment model of bilingual education (Cervantes, 1981) view the multicultural mosaic of American life as an asset to be preserved. They argue that although all children need to be proficient in English, bilingual education should be used as a tool to maintain and enhance competence in the child's native language as well as pride in ethnic heritage.

Because of the differences in basic goals for bilingual education, controversy over these programs is likely to continue.

Teacher-Child Relationship

The teacher-child relationship is expected to differ in important ways from the other social relationships considered in this chapter. Unlike ties with parents or other children, a child's relationship with a teacher is expected to be less intense, personal, or emotional. Teachers are expected to stimulate the learning of all children in their classroom to an equal extent, not to have favorites and not to relate to a child in terms of an emotional bond.

Despite this cultural norm, there is considerable evidence that teachers do not respond to children in the same way and that differences in teacher behavior have impact on both the cognitive and social development of children. Some of this evidence stems from a cognitive theory approach, focusing on how teacher cognitions and expectations about children influence their behavior and affect the child. Other research draws on a learning and social-learning perspective, viewing the teacher as a reinforcing agent and model of desirable behavior.

Teacher Expectations.   During the early weeks of the school year, teachers form impressions of the children in their classrooms and develop expectations of how well each child will do academically. These expectations can become a *self-fulfilling prophecy:* Teachers may behave toward children in such a way as to bring about the outcomes that they expect.

A striking illustration of the self-fulfilling prophecy of teacher expectations occurred in an influential study by Rosenthal and Jacobsen called *Pygmalion in the Classroom* (1968). Elementary school teachers were told that 20 percent of their students were "intellectual bloomers who would show unusual intellectual gains during the academic year" (p. 66). In fact, these children were randomly selected, but at the end of the school year, the first and fifth graders showed a significantly greater increase in IQ than did their classmates who had not been singled out (see Figure 15–4).

In addition to IQ gains, the children whom teachers had been led to perceive as "bloomers" also achieved higher reading scores and higher ratings in intellectual curiosity from their teachers by year's end than did the control children. Children from ethnic minorities, such as Hispanics, who had been identified as intellectually promising made more dramatic gains than did non-minority children so labeled.

The results of the Pygmalion study, as it is called, seemed to show that teacher expectations create either successful or unsuccessful students. However, flaws in the design and execution of the study have been identified, and some attempts to repeat the study have failed to find the same effects (Brophy, 1983; Raudenbush, 1984).

Other evidence, however, confirms that teacher expectations for individual students are formed, but in most cases teachers react to real differences in their students. In contrast to the Pygmalion study, where expectations of student differences were controlled by the experimenters, in the real-life classroom, students themselves contribute to teacher expectations. In general, most teachers appear to develop accurate perceptions of their students and to be receptive to changes in their attitudes and behavior (Brophy, 1983).

Although teacher expectations are based on evidence that students provide, it does appear that teachers may behave in ways that tend to confirm

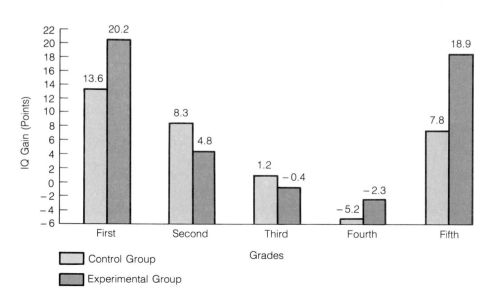

Figure 15–4

Gains in Total IQ in Five Grades after Two Years

(From Rosenthal & Jacobson, *Pygmalion in the Classroom: Teacher Expectation and Pupils' Intellectual Development.* Copyright © 1968 by Holt, Rinehart & Winston, Inc. Reprinted by permission of CBS College Publishing.)

these expectations. Observations of teacher behavior find that students viewed as high-ability often get more attention from the teacher, are called on more often to answer questions, are criticized less often, and are encouraged to rephrase their answers when they respond incorrectly to a question. In contrast, low-ability children are more often ignored by the teacher; when they give a wrong answer, the teacher is more likely to call on another child (Brophy, 1983). This differential treatment tends to encourage the high-ability child and discourage the student viewed as low-ability. Rosenthal and Jacobsen (1968) suggest that such differences in teacher treatment explain the process by which their experiment produced gains for those designated as "bloomers."

Teacher Behaviors Toward Boys and Girls.   Boys and girls get different treatment from teachers. For example, elementary school teachers interact more with boys than with girls, but their contacts with boys more often involve discipline. For example, Meyer and Thompson (1956) observed three sixth-grade classrooms. Although boys received only slightly more approval from their teachers, they were *five times* as likely as girls to be reprimanded and disciplined. Other research suggests that both male and female elementary school teachers prefer behaviors associated with traditional feminine stereotypes—dependency, obedience, and lack of boisterious physical activity (Etaugh & Hughes, 1975).

Based on what we've said about teacher expectancies, you might expect these differences in treatment to result in greater female achievement in school during middle childhood. The evidence here, however, is somewhat contradictory. Although girls outperform boys, on the average, during the earlier elementary school years, by junior high school, girls are falling behind, particularly in science and math. How is it that the more supportive behavior of teachers toward girls does not pay off in their greater achievement?

Some clues can be found in a study by Carol Dweck and her colleagues (Dweck, Davidson, Nelson, & Enna, 1978). They observed teachers' behaviors toward boys and girls in fourth-grade and fifth-grade classrooms. Although they confirmed earlier findings that boys were more often reprimanded, they found that criticism directed toward boys usually focused on the intellectual quality of their work. Moreover, when boys made mistakes, the teachers attributed this to lack of effort, while girls' errors were viewed as lack of ability.

As we saw in Chapter 14, children are more likely to try harder when they see their success or failure as due to effort rather than ability. Thus, the pattern of reinforcement that teachers dispense toward boys versus girls may encourage boys' academic achievement more than that of girls.

In summary, teachers influence children's academic behavior in many ways. Teacher expectations concerning student performance may exert a subtle influence on children's achievement, although there is also evidence that teachers primarily react to pupil differences rather than create them. Differences in behavior toward boys and girls, found among both male and female teachers, tend to reinforce sex differences in achievement. In general, the relationship that a teacher establishes with a child can have wide-ranging effects on the child's school behaviors.

Family and School

The impact of a particular teacher—or any other aspect of the school environment—cannot be considered in isolation from other contexts affecting the child. No matter what kind of educational setting children are exposed to at school, researchers continue to find that the home environment plays an important role in predicting academic achievement and adjustment to school (Epps & Smith, 1984). School-age children whose parents stress academic achievement, speak frequently and in a varied manner to the child, emphasize reading, writing, and good study habits, and closely monitor the child's school activities do better academically (Marjoribanks, 1979; Epps & Smith, 1984; Holloway, 1986).

These correlational findings do not necessarily mean that such parental behavior actually causes children to do better at school. It is possible that parents of particularly bright children respond to them by providing more reading materials, engaging in more conversation, and focusing on achievement (Mercy & Steelman, 1982). It is also possible that because of the genetic similarity in intelligence of parents and children (refer to Chapter 13), bright parents tend to have bright children.

Although such factors must be considered, demonstration programs show some evidence that when parents emphasize achievement-related activities (such as reading) at home, children do better in school as a result. For example, in one British investigation (Tizard, Schofield, & Hewison, 1982) parents were coached to have their seven- to eight-year-olds read aloud to them on a regular basis. At the end of the year, the children who had participated in the program had significantly higher reading scores than did a comparison group of children who had not received the home coaching.

In general, it appears that children benefit when the expectations of home and of school complement rather than conflict with one another (Bronfenbrenner, 1979). For many children who come from impoverished families or whose families speak a different language and share different values from those of the school, severe discontinuities may exist between family and school life. Such children need extra help from schools, which need to be responsive to the broad diversity of family life children experience.

To summarize, we've examined a number of effects of school on children: variations in physical aspects, such as class size, differences in educational philosophy and curriculum design, and teacher expectations and behavior. Although research has focused on each of these aspects separately, it's clear that children experience school as all of a piece. The layout of the classroom, the other children, the curriculum and the books, the schedule, the teacher, all together affect the child. At the same time, these effects vary, depending upon the characteristics of the child. For this reason, few clear-cut effects of school differences have been found.

Chapter Summary

FAMILY

□ A shift in parent-child relations occurs from issues of direct control to co-regulation; the child assumes more independence, but parents monitor the child's actions. Physical affection declines somewhat, and discipline can take advantage of the greater ability of the school-age child to reason, remember, and pay attention.

□ In addition to developmental trends, there is also significant individual variation in how parents and children relate to one another. Social class, single parenthood, and the employment status of parents—particularly unemployment and dual-employment—may be associated with changes in parenting style and child behavior.

□ Sibling relationships also remain important during middle childhood. Cognitive changes permit school-age children to develop more differentiated concepts of siblings than younger children. Observation of siblings indicate that these relationships are often emotionally charged, high in both positive, prosocial behaviors and conflict. Older siblings usually adopt teacher-manager roles, while younger siblings take on the roles of pupil or managee. These roles are often spontaneously adopted during play, but in many parts of the world, parents assign older siblings the teacher-manager role by putting them in charge of younger brothers and sisters.

PEERS

□ While parents and siblings remain important during middle childhood, relations with other children become increasingly significant as children spend more time outside the home. In general, middle childhood is a time of association with same-sex peers.

□ Friendships become more stable than during the preschool years, and children's concept of friendship changes from an emphasis on common activities to a concern with psychological closeness. The developmental benefits of friendships for cognitive and emotional growth have led to concern about children who lack friends.

□ Children also vary in how well they are accepted by groups of peers. Some children are popular, others rejected, neglected, or viewed as controversial. These social statuses tend to become more stable during middle childhood, particularly if the child is rejected by peers. Although many reasons for social rejection and neglect exist, observations of the behavior of children of different social statuses with unfamiliar groups of children indicate that differences in social behaviors are most important. Popular children appear to know and use effective social strategies for entering groups of children and being accepted by them, while rejected children use disruptive, hostile tactics that are ineffective.

SCHOOL

□ Variations in physical setting, such as class size or room organization, have been associated with differences in children's participation in class activities. The open versus traditional classroom reflects not only differences in the physical organization of the classroom but also important differences in educational philosophy, with the open classroom more student-directed and the traditional classroom more teacher-directed. Evaluations of the impact of open versus traditional classrooms find no significant effects on academic achievement, although there are some differences in children's social behavior and learning style. In general, neither open nor traditional classrooms can be considered superior; the match between the student's need and the classroom educational approach is most important.

□ The impact of classroom organization, curriculum, and philosophy is filtered through the teacher. Teacher expectations concerning the academic achievement of students affect children's performance; at the same time, teachers respond to student behavior in developing expectations. When teachers expect much of students, they often behave toward them in ways that encourage academic improvement, and in a self-fulfilling prophecy, students are likely to show some gains.

□ Teachers, male and female, respond to boys and girls differently. Boys receive more criticism and negative attention than do girls, and stereotyped feminine behavior is viewed as more desirable than traditional masculine behavior. Observational studies suggest that teachers may be responding to boys in terms of their intellectual efforts, encouraging them to try harder when they fail. Girls, on the other hand, have been observed to receive more nonintellectual feedback and more suggestions that lack of ability may underlie their academic problems. Such differential behavior by teachers may contribute to sex differences in academic achievement that emerge during the late elementary school years and become more pronounced during adolescence.

☐ The ultimate impact of school, peer group, and family depends not only on the characteristics of each setting as they interact with the child but also on the interrelationships among settings. In general, when the expectations and behaviors at home, at school, and with peers reinforce one another, the child's development is optimized.

Recommended Readings

Zigler, E., Lamb, M., and Child, I. (1982). *Socialization and personality development*. New York: Oxford University Press, (2nd ed.). A book that combines an excellent overview of theory and research on socialization with selected readings. Chapters on child rearing and parenting are especially relevant.

Rosenthal, R., and Jacobson, L. (1968). *Pygmalion in the classroom*. New York: Holt, Rinehart, and Winston. A fascinating account of the influential experiment to change low-achieving children's school performance by manipulating teacher expectations.

Asher, S., and Gottman, J. (eds.) (1981). *The development of children's friendships*. Cambridge: Cambridge University Press. An excellent collection of articles on aspects of children's friendships, including children without friends, social skills training, and children's ideas about friends.

Patterson, G. (1975). *Families: Applications of social learning to family life*. Champaign, IL: Research Press. The researcher whose work with families of out-of-control children discussed in this chapter shows how learning theory principles can help parents establish consistent and firm control.

PART V

Adolescence

Physical and Cognitive Development

: *At what stage in your life do you think you actually will be adult?*

A: 18.

Q: *When, at what point do you think you stopped being a kid or a child?*

A: *(pause) Maybe because, uh, that I'm, 12 or something like that, y'know when I started, stopped playing, y'know, toys and stuff like that.*

Q: *In moving out of the stage of childhood into the stage of teens, what do you think are the most important changes in people that show that they're no longer children?*

A: *Their personality.*

Q: *Go ahead.*

A: *Um, I think they have more responsibility and um they feel different, you know? to different aspects, you know, of like as their, if they were a child, they would think differently than in your teens, you know.*

Q: *Could you give me an example, y'know, of one, some particular aspect where there's a difference that might take place or might be evident?*

A: *Um (pause) ok, let's say that um something of mine gets broken. When I was just a kid, I really, y'know, I really, what you say, like that thing, you know what I mean, but then now as, as a teenager I really don't care, y'know, like it's just a thing. I'm more uh have more feeling to people than y'know just things that I have.*

Q: *What are the best things about being at the age you're at now?*

A: *I guess, um, we're not treated as kids anymore, and uh, we have more responsibility, we don't have, you know, all the troubles that adults have, like um paying bills and all this stuff.*

Q: *What are the worst aspects of being, say, 13?*

A: *Worst aspects? I really wouldn't know, because I've never been an adult. So I wouldn't know, uh, y'know, how good it is being an adult.*

> — *An interview with Graham, a 13-year-old Canadian, from Baker, 1983, pp. 506–507.*

The statements by Graham are typical of many young adolescents in North America. They reflect the adolescent's growing awareness of being somewhere midway between the child of the past and the adult of the future. This ability to view oneself, as if from the outside, marks the beginning of cognitive abilities of abstract thinking that Piaget called formal operations. Graham is aware that he is speaking to an adult. He is careful not to make statements that might conflict with the views of the adult interviewer. He makes clear that he is not yet an adult and that he has limited knowledge of the adult world (Baker, 1982).

This chapter covers the cognitive changes that occur during adolescence and looks at the adolescent's ability to conceptualize the self and others as well as the adolescent's propensity to develop systems of thought about a wide range of topics including religion, morality, creativity, politics, and the meaning and value of life. The chapter also discusses the adolescent's response to the physical changes associated with puberty, including changes in physical size and sexuality, that will affect the adolescent's sense of self, bringing him or her closer to adulthood. Topics related to adolescent health and nutrition are also covered in this chapter.

Physical Changes

As we saw in Chapter 12, middle childhood is a period of relatively slow and even physical growth. Although girls develop skeletal maturity about 20 percent faster than boys during middle childhood, there are few differences between boys and girls in growth rates and physical appearance.

Around the age of 11 years, boys and girls begin developing more rapidly. Adolescence rivals only the prenatal and infancy periods in the rate of skeletal growth increase (refer to Chapter 12, Figure 12–1). In addition, the sexes begin to diverge physically in dramatic ways. Girls begin their adolescent growth spurt several years before boys, and they appear sexually mature at earlier ages than boys.

Physical Growth During Adolescence

One salient feature of the adolescent growth spurt is the rapid increase in height. The average girl gains 28.05 centimeters (about 11 inches) and the average boy, about 30.80 centimeters (about 12 inches) during the adolescent growth spurt. Thus, each sex gains about a foot of height over about a two-year period.

Figure 16–1 shows the rate of change of height, measured in centimeters per year, for two girls. One of the girls—the "early" maturer—has the *onset* of her growth spurt at eight years, the *apex* or peak of the spurt at ten years, and the *end* of the spurt at 11½ years. The "late" maturing girl has her growth spurt onset at about 12 years, after the early maturing girl has completed hers, her apex at 13½, and the end of the spurt at 15.

Now compare the two girls with the data presented in Table 16–1 for boys and girls. Note that the average girl has her growth spurt onset at age 10, the apex at 11½, and the end at 12½. Wide individual differences exist within girls, however, as can be seen in Figure 16–1.

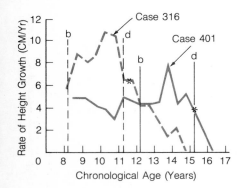

Figure 16–1

Individual Differences in the Adolescent Growth Spurt for Girls

Differences in timing of the pubertal growth period in height. In each example the early-developing girl reached the end (d) of the pubertal period before the late-developing girl reached onset (b). (Stars indicate onset of menarche.)

Table 16–1

THE ADOLESCENT GROWTH SPURT*

	Girls			Boys		
	Onset	Apex	End	Onset	Apex	End
Earliest	7½	9½	10	10	12½	14
Average	10	11½	12½	12½	14	16
Latest	13	15	15½	14	15½	17½

*Ages are given for the onset, apex, and end of the growth spurt for both boys and girls. The earliest and the latest maturing children's ages are given, as well as the average age. These statistics are based on a sample of 94 girls and 67 boys from Oakland, California, and Berkeley, California.
(From Faust, 1977 © *Society for Research in Child Development,* used by permission of publisher and author.)

The average boy, on the other hand, has the growth spurt onset at 12½ years, the apex at 14, and the end at 16. On the average, therefore, boys begin and end their growth spurts about two years later than most girls. Table 16–1 shows that some early maturing boys might have their growth spurts at about the same ages as some late maturing girls.

You might wonder why males, on the average, are taller than females, since there is little difference in height gain between the sexes during adolescence. The answer comes from looking more closely at the timing of the growth spurt for boys and girls.

On the average, girls increase their height at a younger age than boys, and this is the reason girls tend to end up shorter as adults: They spend less time growing before the adolescent growth spurt. The average height attained by males before the onset of the growth spurt is 149 centimeters (about 4 feet, 11 inches), while the average height attained by females before the onset of the growth spurt is 139 centimeters (about 4 feet, 7 inches) (Faust, 1977). The correlation between preadolescent growth and mature stature is .67, while the correlation between adolescent growth and mature stature is only .22 (Tanner, 1974).

Within the United States, large differences exist in height gain during the adolescent years. Although about the same height before the onset of the growth spurt, white boys grow faster and end up taller than black boys. Black girls however, tend to be taller than white girls up to the age of about 15, after which there are no average differences in height for girls (Krogman, 1970). These differences may be due in part to genetic factors and in part to cultural differences in nutrition, exercise, and home conditions.

Although the sexes do not differ much in height gain during adolescence, they do differ in other physical growth characteristics. Boys develop more muscle mass and strength, and girls develop more fatty tissue. While boys increase in shoulder width relative to hips, girls increase in hip width relative to the shoulders.

Other related physical changes—including the development of body hair, breasts, and changes in genital size and shape—mark the beginnings of adult sexual differentiation. The process by which the sexes become physically different and reach mature fertility, is a complex interaction of biological, psychological, and social factors. The next few sections examine these processes.

Puberty

The word *puberty* derives from *pubes,* meaning hair, and the original meaning of puberty referred to the growth of hair in the region of the genitals. Today, *puberty* means the period of sexual maturation of the individual occurring at the time of the adolescent growth spurt. Puberty is part of a longer process of sexual maturation that begins at conception. Both male and female genitals, as well as a lifetime supply of ova for the female, are formed prenatally. At puberty hormone secretion by the *endocrine* (hormone-producing) glands increases dramatically. *Hormones* are chemical substances that "instruct" certain cells of the body to act in specialized ways.

The two basic types of sex-related hormones are *androgens* and *estrogens* and are present in both sexes. Males, however, have higher levels of androgens, while females have more estrogens during and after puberty. These hormones stimulate the development of *secondary sexual characteristics,* such as changes in the size and shape of the genitals, pubic hair development, and breast development in females (see Figure 16–2 and Table 16–2).

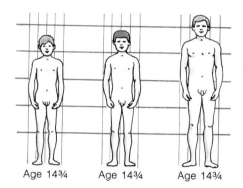

Age 14¾ Age 14¾ Age 14¾

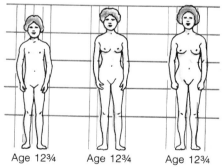

Age 12¾ Age 12¾ Age 12¾

Figure 16–2

Pubertal Development in Boys and Girls

Differing degrees of pubertal development at the same chronological age. Upper row: three boys all age 14¾ years. Lower row: three girls all age 12¾ years. (From Dworetsky, 1985.)

Table 16—2

ADOLESCENT SEXUAL
DEVELOPMENT

STAGE	PUBIC HAIR	MALES	FEMALES
1 Preadolescence	No pubic hair.	Testes, scrotum, and penis same size and shape as early childhood.	Genitals and breasts same size and shape as early childhood.
2 Early adolescence	Long, light-colored slightly curled hair at base of penis and along labia.	Scrotum is slightly larger, skin is red and coarser.	Breast and nipples are elevated (bud stage).
3 Middle adolescence	Hair is darker, more curled, and denser, forming inverse triangle.	Penis lengthens and scrotum and testes enlarge.	Areola and nipple enlarged and elevated, labia enlarged and vaginal secretion becomes acidic.
4 Late adolescence	Adult-type hair but area covered less than in adult.	Further enlargement of penis, skin of scrotum darkens.	Breasts fill out, areola and nipple form secondary mound above contour of breast, menstruation established, clitoris mature.
5 Post-adolescence to adult	Adult quantity and type, spreads to navel in males and along inner surface of thighs.	Adult size and shape.	Breasts fully developed, fertility established.

(From Peterson & Taylor, 1980; Schonfeld, 1969.)

For males, secondary sexual characteristics include hair under the arms (axillary hair) and on the face. Male facial hair does not complete its development until stage 5 (late adolescence) of genital development (Table 16—2). Changes in the pitch of the voice for both sexes and changes in the skin occur. Skin changes include the development of sweat glands and characteristic odors, especially in males, and increased oiliness and skin eruptions (Peterson & Taylor, 1980).

Although these external changes contribute to the development of sexual maturity, the production of spermatozoa in the male and the onset of ovulation in the female are the crucial components, or *primary sexual characteristics.* *Menarche,* or the beginning of a regular monthly cycle of menstrual bleeding, begins on the average about 12 or 13 years of age. Regardless of age, menarche is a relatively late pubertal development, occurring typically during stages 4 and 5 of breast and pubic hair development and after the apex of pubertal height growth (Faust, 1977). Although girls are potentially fertile right after menarche, ovulation occurs irregularly for the first two or three years after menarche (Peterson & Taylor, 1980).

In both girls and boys, the timing of the onset of fertility varies considerably among individuals. The first ejaculation is considered to be the male version of menarche. Like menarche, it is a relatively late pubertal event, occurring after the beginning of accelerated penis growth. Unlike females who develop ova prenatally, the production of spermatozoa begins in boys only after the maturation of the testes. A small percentage of boys can experience ejaculation and nocturnal emission as early as age 10, but they occur in most boys between 12 and 14 years of age (Peterson & Taylor, 1980; Ramsay, 1943).

Each of the physical changes described affects the growing child psychologically. The physical changes and the adolescent's psychological responses can influence other persons, such as family and peers, whose reactions to the adolescent also contribute to the adolescent's growing understanding of self and other.

Theories of Psychological Adaptation to Puberty

Most of the original theories of psychological adaptation to puberty were based on Freud's (1905) psychoanalytic theory, which emphasized the person's psychological adaptation (the ego and superego) to powerful biological urges (the id).

According to psychoanalytic theory (refer to Chapter 2), the ego and superego develop progressively during the oral, anal, and phallic stages. The latency stage of middle childhood is believed to be a period of relative quiet for the id, and the ego and superego do not develop substantially. Thus, the ego is still incomplete when the powerful urges of the genital (or adolescent) stage begin, resulting in the psychological experience of anxiety, conflict about the expression of basic urges and impulses, and greater emotional swings.

Psychoanalytic theory makes the assumption that the hormonal and biological changes have a *direct effect* on psychological outcome, leading the adolescent to an inevitable state of anxiety and conflict (see Figure 16–3). Research evidence for this position is lacking, however (Peterson & Taylor, 1980).

To demonstrate direct effects, the level of hormones present in the body would have to be directly tied to specific psychological states or behavior patterns. Measuring hormonal levels through analysis of blood or urine is difficult and requires expensive and complex medical testing procedures. Furthermore, hormonal levels in the body may not be measurable until hours after they are initially secreted. The human endocrine system is a complex network of many glands and hundreds of different types of hormones that have both specific and general effects. Medical and biological science have only a poor understanding of these hormonal processes.

Another approach is to study people around the time of some physical change that is believed to be directly a result of some hormonal process, such as menarche, or at different phases of the menstrual cycle. Such research has shown that some behavioral changes can be explained partially by physical

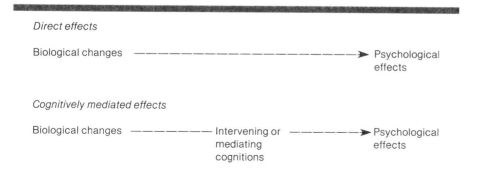

Direct effects

Biological changes ————————————————————→ Psychological effects

Cognitively mediated effects

Biological changes ——————— Intervening or ——————→ Psychological mediating effects cognitions

Figure 16–3

Types of Relationships Between Biological Changes and Psychological Experiences

Adolescent rites of passage, such as the Jewish Bar-Mitzvah, are ways the adult community can formally mark the transition from childhood to adolescence.

changes, but psychological predispositions and cultural factors play a major role in determining how a person responds to physical changes (Melges & Hamburg, 1977).

The cognitive developmental theory suggests that the child's interpretation and evaluation of experience can work to soften the impact of the biological changes for the individual. For example, research has shown that evaluations of the adolescent's changes in positive rather than negative ways by parents and peers can lead to reductions in anxiety and conflict (Clausen, 1975; Schonfeld, 1966). Or, if society as a whole views pubertal changes in an accepting way—through cultural stereotypes or by means of rituals or rites of passage reflecting societal approval of the child's more mature status—children may be more likely to accept, welcome, and positively evaluate their own changes (Christensen & Carpenter, 1972; Ford & Beach, 1951; Mead, 1958). Unfortunately, little systematic research exists to document the specific effects of these broader cultural influences.

Research on Psychological Reactions to Puberty: Effects on Girls. The research in the area of psychological reactions to physical changes has been limited in the past because of society's sensitivity to issues related to sexuality. School boards are not open to studies of sexuality in their students, and those that have been done in the past are confined to changes in height and the onset of menarche (Brooks-Gunn, 1984).

In one research study (Rierdan & Koff, 1981), 94 seventh-grade girls (49 were premenarcheal and 45 were postmenarcheal) were each asked to draw a male and a female human figure. Later, the figures were scored on the child's ability to clearly differentiate the drawings by depicting secondary sexual characteristics. In addition, whether the female figure was drawn first was used as a measure of the girl's identification with her own sex. The drawings of the postmenarcheal girls were scored higher on ability to differentiate the sexes and reflected a clearer identification of the girls with their own sex. This study suggests that menarche brings social maturity. Since drawings are subject to multiple interpretations, however, we can't be sure that other researchers would reach the same conclusions.

Some researchers (Petersen, 1983; Ruble & Brooks-Gunn, 1982) have interviewed girls about their reactions to menarche. Most girls describe the experience with mixed emotions, being both excited and pleased and at the same time scared and upset. Typically, girls do not like to discuss the negative reactions, and there is usually a delay of about six months after menarche until girls feel entirely comfortable talking about it with peers.

Unlike menarche, breast development can be observed by others regardless of the girl's wishes to keep it private. In one research study (Brooks-Gunn & Warren, 1983), 39 fifth-grade and 43 sixth-grade girls were interviewed. Breast development was determined by asking the girls' mothers to rate their children based on schematic drawings of breast development in the five stages of adolescence (refer to Table 16–2).

About half the girls reported being teased about breast development, usually by parents or by female peers. Only 7 percent were teased about not developing breasts, while 38 percent were teased after the breasts had begun to develop. None of the girls liked being teased, but teasing was not related to the girl's psychological adjustment. Indeed, girls with more advanced breast development scored higher on tests of psychological adjustment, had a more positive body image, and had better peer relationships than did girls in earlier stages of development. Like menarche, therefore, breast development seems to contribute to a girl's positive self image and peer status (Aro & Tiapale, 1987).

For girls, then, puberty is generally a positive event, leading to an enhanced self-image and a greater sense of social maturity. These findings support cognitive developmental theory, in which the psychological effects of the biological changes are modulated by social and psychological influences.

Research on Psychological Reactions to Puberty: Effects on Boys. Like menarche for girls, ejaculation is related to sexual maturity for boys. It has been thought to be an upsetting or scary experience at first, leading to the male's feelings of conflict about pubertal changes.

In one of the few studies on boys's reactions to ejaculation, 13 white middle-class boys in eighth, ninth, and tenth grades were interviewed in private with a male interviewer (Gaddis & Brooks-Gunn, 1985). All of the boys knew what an ejaculation was, but only three had been told about it by someone else. Most learned about it through reading, primarily adult magazines rather than books about health and development.

Eleven of the 13 boys had experienced an ejaculation: six through masturbation, four through noctural emission, and one through intercourse. At the time of the interview, 54 percent had had a nocturnal emission, and 72 percent had masturbated, but only one had had intercourse. Most of the boys expressed excitement and pride about their first ejaculation; few reported feeling shame, but most reported feeling "a little scared" when it first happened.

As with girls and menarche, boys report some mixed emotions about their first ejaculation, but most boys felt positively about it. Cultural attitudes toward discussion of these events differ for boys and girls. Although girls will discuss menarche with their peers and parents, boys rarely talk about their own ejaculations with other people, although boys may joke about ejaculation with friends. The researchers speculate that this may be because of the link between ejaculation and masturbation, a link that does not exist for menarche. Studies show that girls are equally reluctant to discuss masturbation experiences (Gaddis & Brooks-Gunn, 1985).

Although boys can hide the experience of ejaculation from others, as girls can with menarche, other physical changes such as height, shoulder width, facial hair growth, and deepening of the voice cannot be hidden. One might expect that these changes, as in girls' breast development, increase the boys' self-esteem and social maturity. Unfortunately, few studies have been done on boys' psychological adjustments to these features.

Several studies have examined the relationship between boys' pubertal changes and adolescent family relationships (Steinberg & Hill, 1978; Steinberg, 1981). These studies show that family interactions change in direct correspondence to pubertal changes and not in relation to cognitive development or age. As adolescent boys mature from the onset to the apex of puberty, boys and their mothers interrupt each other with increasing frequency, boys defer to their mothers less and to their fathers more, and the fathers become more assertive with their sons. After the pubertal apex, mothers interrupt their sons less, and more discussion of issues takes place.

These findings suggest that boys may perceive themselves as stronger and more mature as they develop, which leads them to a greater assertiveness with their mothers. Family systems theory suggests that such assertiveness within one family dyad might be counterbalanced by another dyad within the family. In this case, the father becomes more assertive and the son more submissive with the father. This kind of family dynamics may lead to the adolescent's growing understanding of his own pubertal changes as they affect other people.

Sexuality

Theories of the Development of Sexuality

Freudian psychoanalytic theory, as we saw in the previous section, focuses on the child's response to the biological urges brought about by the hormonal changes of puberty. The adolescent's developmental task, according to this theory, is to find socially appropriate ways to channel or control erotic impulses. One's psychosexual identity is formed by finding an adaptive path between the id's urges and society's regulations.

Cognitive developmental theory as interpreted by Kohlberg (1966) suggests that the adolescent's understanding of sexuality is primarily due to changes in reasoning ability that occur at about the same time as the physical changes of puberty. The major developmental task, according to cognitive theory, is to understand sexuality in relation to other aspects of the self and to integrate that understanding into the adolescent's views of other people and moral principles.

Social learning theory, applied to sexuality by Kinsey (1953), suggests that sexual activity is an inherently reinforcing activity. The pleasure derived from sexual expression is its own motivation. Sexual knowledge and sexual behavior patterns are formed as a result of the person's history of associations between erotic arousal and external events. For example, this view predicts that the images children think about or look at while masturbating will lead to permanent sexual inclinations and expectations.

Little evidence exists that biological urges, logical thinking, or reinforcement taken by themselves can account for the development of sexual knowledge and sexual behavior. Rather, these different perspectives need to be integrated by taking into account both *intrapsychic/personal* aspects of sexuality—erotic arousal, motivation, thought processes—and *interpersonal/social* aspects of sexuality—the immediate context of sexual behavior, the demands and expectations of others, and the cultural ideals and attitudes regarding sexuality (Miller & Simon, 1980). In this view, individuals have both social and personal expectations. An interpersonal expectation, for example, regulates the ways in which the self interacts with other people in seeking information about and engaging in sexual behavior. A personal expectation is one that regulates the level and timing of erotic arousal in relation to specific objects of sexual interest.

This perspective explains some of the issues that adolescents face with regard to the development of sexuality. By following a social expectation related to behavior between the sexes, an adolescent can engage in sexual activity without being highly sexually aroused. For example, a boy or girl may engage in petting because he or she believes it is expected by the partner or because it gives him or her something to brag about with peers. On the other hand, sexual arousal derived from personal expectations may occur in individuals at times and with objects that may be inappropriate. Thus, adolescents may become sexually attracted to teachers and other adults. During adolescence, release of sexual tension seldom occurs while satisfying social expectations, and vice versa.

Expectations and Knowledge of Sexuality

Sources of Erotic Arousal.　　Males more than females are aroused by culturally accepted erotic symbols. Half of college males, but only 14 percent of college females, admit to being sexually aroused by pornographic materials such as books, drawings, and films. More than three-fourths of the males, but only one-fourth of the females, reported that they would be aroused by seeing a nude person of the opposite sex (Miller & Simon, 1980).

When questioned about the kinds of fantasies invoked during masturbation, over 80 percent of both males and females said that the most common fantasy was petting or having intercourse with another person in the context of affection. On the other hand, having sex with a stranger was also highly ranked as an erotic fantasy by males but not by females. These findings suggest that female rejection of pornographic materials may be due to their tendency to value feelings and affection for another as the primary source of erotic arousal, regardless of the presence or absence of explicit sexual symbols, while the opposite may be true for males (Miller & Simon, 1980). It may also be that females report less interest in pornographic materials because the social expectation for some females is violated by admitting to such an interest.

The same research study showed that nonnormative sexual fantasies rarely occurred. For example, homosexual fantasies were reported by only three percent of males and females. About one-fourth of the males and only six percent of the females had fantasized about "forcing someone to do something they did not want to do."

We must be cautious in interpreting the research in which people are asked to give a self report about sensitive material. The responses could be biased in favor of what such people think the examiner wants to hear, or those people may be unwilling to disclose extremely personal information. It is likely, therefore, that the percentages reported here are somewhat low.

Social Expectations and Heterosexual Behavior.   In the 1970s and early 1980s, very few children (about 10 percent to 25 percent) had experienced sexual intercourse before the age of 15 years, or in ninth grade. Estimates of the percentage of premarital coitus among high school students ranged from between 20 percent and 55 percent. Among college students, 70 percent to 80 percent of both sexes reported that they had sexual intercourse (Darling, Kallen, & VanDusen, 1984; Miller & Simon, 1980).

One study compared the reporting rates for sexual intercourse among college-age young people between 1903 and 1980 (Darling et al., 1984). It found steady increases in the rate of reporting over that period, with the fastest increase occurring for females. Before 1970, twice as many college men as college women reported having intercourse. Since 1970, there are equal proportions of men and women reporting. These findings suggest a shift in social attitudes toward sexual activity among college-age youth. Sex is now viewed by a majority of young adults as appropriate in the context of love relationships, without the requirement of progression toward marriage, and is viewed as permissible in casual relationships, so long as no exploitation is involved (Darling et al., 1984).

We can't be sure if the shift in attitudes is associated with a corresponding shift in social and sexual behavior. It could be that although people's ideas about sexuality in general may have become more liberal, people may still behave in more traditional ways.

With respect to the first experience of premarital intercourse, only 31 percent of males, but 59 percent of females, reported that they had been in love with the partner and planned to marry them. For males, the experience of first intercourse has rewards intrinsic to the act itself and has value in the recognition of a certain social status among male peers (Miller & Simon, 1980). White high school males who are the most popular with females had tried more noncoital sexual behaviors and were also more likely to have had intercourse, although no such relationship was found for black high school males (Newcomer, Udry & Cameron, 1983).

For females, on the other hand, the first sexual act occurs in the context of what they view to be a loving relationship leading to conventional goals of a lasting partnership and eventual marriage (Miller & Simon, 1980). Sexual experience does not affect a girl's popularity with the opposite sex, either for black or white female high school students (Newcomer et al., 1983).

Coital relations with the opposite sex, therefore, are infrequent until late adolescence, are reported equally by both sexes, and may derive from different motivations, depending on the sex of the individual. For boys, the sex act has intrinsic value, and boys are likely to have their first orgasms through masturbation. For girls, sex has value in the context of relationships, and a girl is likely to have her first orgasm during sexual intercourse rather than by masturbation (Miller & Simon, 1980).

Reasoning About Contraception.   If adolescents are sexually active, their attitudes toward contraception are related to their reasons for having sex. The issue of contraception is important in light of the current concern about teenage pregnancies in the United States. The issue is also a particularly sensitive one for adolescents, since premarital sexual intercourse is not an activity that is approved by parents or society.

Adolescent male attitudes toward contraception have been studied very little. One research project interviewed 51 males, ages 15 to 17, about their social relationships; history of sex and birth control behavior; level of knowledge about reproduction; and the influence of parents, peers, and girlfriends in making contraceptive decisions (Cohen & Rose, 1984). The major findings of this study, presented in Table 16–3, show that the most effective motivation for birth control is the partner's direct influence. Persons outside the male-female relationship had little impact on the decision to use birth control. In addition, males tend to be inconsistent in their usage of contraceptive methods. When questioned about why they failed to use contraceptives in some situations, the boys said such things as "I forgot," "I didn't know where to get it," "It just happened."

Considerably more research studies have been done on females, and the findings are similar. Partner support is the most effective means of insuring consistent contraceptive use, and a lack of cognitive consistency exists between values and goals on the one hand and sexual behavior on the other. Typically, few differences are found between consistent and inconsistent contraceptive users and between pregnant and nonpregnant girls in their perception of preg-

Table 16–3

MALE ADOLESCENT BIRTH CONTROL KNOWLEDGE AND BEHAVIOR*

Heterosexual and contraceptive behaviors

70% of subjects reported intercourse.

65% were effective contraceptive users at last intercourse.

40% were effective contraceptive users consistently.

They used "male" methods: condom or withdrawal.

Contraceptive used more with casual partner than with girlfriends.

Expectations of others

Partner support for contraception was the most important.

Talk more to peers than to family or adults about birth control and sex.

Relationship decisions viewed as male dominated, while sex and birth control viewed as shared or female dominated.

(Adapted from Cohen & Rose, 1984)

*Subjects were 51 white males from a Northwestern metropolitan area, never married, aged 15 to 17, recruited from a community recreation center, a Lutheran church group, and a Jewish social youth group.

Teenage Pregnancy: An Epidemic?

Risks

Table 16–4 contains some provocative statistics. Forty percent of young girls under the age of 19 will become pregnant each year. Of those, about half will give birth, and of those giving birth, about 40 percent will be single parents. To add to the difficulty, those girls who actually give birth—teenage mothers—are *seven* times as likely to be living in poverty before pregnancy than are mothers who are 20 years or older (Alan Guttmacher Institute, 1981).

Teenage pregnancy puts the adolescent, both the mother and the father, at risk. Still children themselves, with incomplete identities and cognitive inconsistencies, teenage parents must sacrifice some of the time they might have used for their own development in order to meet the more pressing needs of the

fetus and infant. They may drop out of school, lose friends, and lead a relatively isolated existence living alone or with their own mothers (Alan Guttmacher Institute, 1981).

Teenage pregnancy is also a risk for the infant. The death rate for infants born to teenage mothers is twice that of infants born to older mothers, and the incidence of low-birth-weight babies and perinatal complications is also considerably higher. Why does this occur?

Birth complications among adolescent mothers do not appear to be due to inadequacies in the female reproductive system of teenagers. Once fertile, a teenager is just as capable of bringing a baby to term as an older woman. Since teens are physically shorter and weigh less than older women, babies born to teens are proportionately smaller (Garn & Petzhold, 1983). Although babies born to teens are within the normal range of weight and height, the tendency to smallness, combined with other risk factors such as poor prenatal health and nutrition, poverty, or drugs and alcohol

Pregnancy in the teen years may curtail the psychological development of the mother who is still a child herself.

Table 16–4

TEENAGE PREGNANCY: AN EPIDEMIC?

Number of girls under 17 who become pregnant in the USA	¼ million
Percentage of girls under 17 population who become pregnant	10%
Percentage of girls likely to become pregnant before age 19	40%
Of these pregnancies, the result was:	**Percentage**
Out-of-wedlock births	22
Married before the birth	10
Conceived while married	17
Abortion	38
Miscarriage	13
Percentages of pregnancies occurring within:	**Percentage**
one month of first intercourse	20
six months of first intercourse	80

(Adapted from Alan Guttmacher Institute, 1981.)

use during pregnancy, increases the likelihood of having a small, premature, or sick newborn (Zuckerman et al., 1983).

Teenage mothers are at risk because of a loss of social support systems. In a research study comparing pregnant and nonpregnant junior and senior high school girls, pregnant girls reported receiving less affection and more rejection from their mothers than nonpregnant girls (Olson & Worobey, 1984). On the other hand, among pregnant black teenage mothers, those who lived with their parents had higher self-esteem, and their children developed better than those who lived alone (Field, Widmayer, Stinger, & Ignatoff, 1980; Furstenberg & Crawford, 1978).

Interventions

The majority (80 percent) of a sample of 1253 American adults in a recent Louis Harris poll favored television messages about birth control. With the exception of the cable network CNN, major networks have refused to carry advertisements related to birth control because they are too "controversial." On the other hand, television networks seem to have no problem with shows containing sexual subject matter, giving sex an exaggeratedly attractive image (Associated Press, November 5, 1985).

The policy of the Reagan administration is to give federal funds for community programs that advocate sexual abstinence and encourage adolescent mothers to stay in school, get job training, and avoid a second pregnancy. The effectiveness of these programs has yet to be established. Another approach is to establish comprehensive health care clinics in schools that not only provide health-related services and education to disadvantaged youth but also dispense contraceptives without the consent of parents. These programs have seen the adolescent pregnancy rate cut in half within a single year in the most at-risk groups (*New York Times,* June 14, 1985; November 4, 1985).

In addition to prevention efforts, interventions designed to support adolescents after the birth of a child are essential. For the most part, such programs—based in schools, community centers, churches, or even in store fronts—are highly successful in delivering education and services to adolescent mothers. Most provide parent education, self-help skills, job training, encouragement to get teenage fathers involved, and in some cases, medical and financial assistance, especially for low-income mothers.

The success of prevention, education, and assistance programs for teenage pregnancy and sexuality depends upon a complex network of individual needs and goals, family relationships, social institutions and services, and cultural norms and values. Often, little consistency exists between these different systems, leaving teenagers caught in a network of conflicting demands and values (Marecek, 1987).

nancy risk or knowledge about reproduction and fertility (Jones & Philliber, 1983; Smith, Nenney, Weiman, & Mumford, 1982).

Aside from inconsistencies of usage, knowledge of reproductive physiology and contraceptive methods is poor among both male and female teenagers. Seventh and eighth graders indicated that they needed more information on contraceptive methods, venereal disease, abortion, the time of the monthly cycle during which intercourse is most likely to lead to conception, and the kinds of foods and exercise women should have when pregnant (Alexander & Jorgensen, 1983).

Other Types of Sexual Behavior

Masturbation.   Although relatively few in number, studies on the topic of masturbation suggest that the number of adolescents who accept masturbation as normal and who practice it has increased over the past 20 years (Dreyer, 1982). Currently, about 70 percent of boys and 45 percent of girls masturbate by the age of 15. During ongoing sexual relationships, boys masturbate less than usual, but girls masturbate more often, apparently to release sexual tension from sexual activity not resulting in orgasm (Hass, 1979).

Homosexuality. Concurrent with the liberalization of attitudes toward heterosexual relationships and masturbation, there has been a corresponding increase of acceptance in homosexual relationships. About 70 percent of 16- to 19-year-olds hold attitudes generally accepting of homosexual relationships of both sexes. However, less than 15 percent of boys and 10 percent of girls report having a homosexual contact in adolescence, and only 3 percent of boys and 2 percent of girls report ongoing homosexual relationships (Chilman, 1979; Hass, 1979). Thus, although attitudes toward homosexual relationships have become more accepting in the past 20 or 30 years, the number of adolescents participating in such relationships has not changed (Dreyer, 1982).

A number of theories about the origins of homosexual behavior exist. For example, psychoanalytic theory predicts that homosexuality in males will result from having a domineering mother and a weak father who is unable to resolve the child's Oedipal conflicts. Biological approaches suggest that hormonal imbalances lead to homosexual attractions. Social learning theory suggests that previously satisfying encounters with the same sex may lead to homosexual attractions. Such encounters are increased in sex-segregated environments such as schools, summer camps, the military, and prisons. Unfortunately, there is little research. In addition, many heterosexual individuals develop under the same conditions presumed to foster homosexual development (Dreyer, 1982).

Healthful Life Styles in Adolescence

The general lack of knowledge about sexual behavior—both on the part of the individual and in the scientific community—makes the formation of healthy and satisfying sexuality more difficult, particularly for adolescents. This section looks at other health issues such as nutrition, obesity, and alcohol and drug-related problems.

Weight Gain and Eating Disorders

Each child differs in the amount of weight gained during adolescence and in the way in which fat growth occurs. Although the growth of height is continuous and irreversible, the growth of fat is neither. Children put on fat in certain areas of their bodies during the pubertal growth spurt, losing fat in other areas and then later losing fat in some of the areas of initial gain.

Girls' bodies are generally fattier than boys in most areas by the end of adolescence. During adolescence, however, at least half of all boys may temporarily put on fat in the breasts, thighs, and lower trunk, making them look more female and causing self-consciousness about their own bodies (Schonfeld, 1962; Stolz & Stolz, 1951; Tanner, 1970). These temporary fat deposits usually disappear and give way to a more muscular, masculine shape by late adolescence.

The appearance of fatness may depend not only on the proportion of fat tissue in the body but also on the relative size and shape of muscle and bone masses. Some big-boned children will appear overweight even if they have normal amounts of fat. Fat deposits in the cheeks or thighs may contribute to an impression of overweight in an otherwise normal body build. In reality, only 10 percent to 20 percent of adolescents are classified as obese based on the ratio of fat to other body tissue (Cheek, 1968).

To what extent are children sensitive to being overweight? A Canadian study of 97 children from mixed language and ethnic backgrounds tried to answer this question (Mendelson & White, 1985). The children were classified into normal and overweight categories and then given questionnaires asking about their self-esteem (how they feel about their relationships with friends and family, their academic achievement, and themselves in general) and about their body-esteem (how they value their own appearance and how they think others evaluate their looks).

Figure 16—4 shows the mean scores on self-esteem and body-esteem as a function of age, sex, and overweight status. Although there is a general decrease with age in both self-esteem and body-esteem for overweight youngsters, the older overweight boys' self-esteem was no different from non-overweight boys and girls, while the girls' self- and body-esteem was the lowest for the older children.

These results can be explained by different social expectations for male and female bodies. Children are socialized to believe that size is valuable and functional for males, while shapeliness and beauty, defined in terms of thinness, are more valuable for females. In this respect, females are at some risk of developing unrealistic expectations about their own bodies. Cultural conceptions of beauty may override young women's abilities to accept natural differences in body shape, to value differences in size and strength in women, and to develop strong, competent bodies rather than merely decorative ones (Freedman, 1984).

Research has shown that boys may also face health risks due to cultural expectations about body size. A study of food preferences in 78 female and 57 male adolescents ages 14 to 17 years found that boys selected foods high in fat, salt, and sugar more than girls, who chose vegetables more often. Not only taste sensitivity differences but also cultural stereotypes valuing weight gains for males contributed to this finding (George & Krondl, 1983). Given the association between fats and salts and cardiovascular disease (refer to Chapter 12), inappropriate food intake in boys may be a substantial health risk.

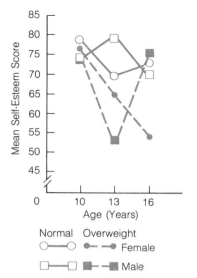

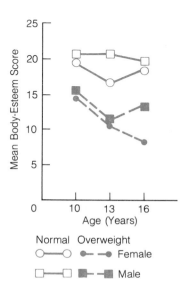

Figure 16—4

The Relationship of Self-Esteem and Overweight

Left: Mean self-esteem score as a function of age for each weight × sex group

Right: Mean body-esteem score as a function of age for each weight × sex group

(From Mendelson & White, *Developmental Psychology,* 1985, Vol. 21, pp. 90—96, Figure 1 and Figure 2, Copyright 1985 by the American Psychological Association. Reprinted by permission of the authors.)

For girls, the desire to be thin may lead to more healthful eating habits in terms of types of food selected, but girls seem to be at risk because of relative irregularity in their eating habits, leading to cycles of overeating at times and dieting at other times. In extreme cases, girls will reduce their eating, putting themselves on a permanent regimen of low food intake. This pattern is called *anorexia nervosa*. In other cases, girls will eat in binges and then purge themselves by self-induced vomiting, a disorder called *bulimia*. These eating disorders occur in about five percent of high school females (Johnson et al., 1984).

In general, inaccurate perception of one's own weight and the tendency toward eating disorders are associated with low self-esteem and depression, but not necessarily with popularity (Forehand, Faust, & Baum, 1985; Johnson et al., 1984). Often, bulimic girls are high in popularity, attractiveness, and achievement and see changes in their appearance as a threat to their social status. They develop bulimia as a means of regulating their weight within acceptable limits.

Alcohol, Cigarettes, and Drugs

Alcohol, cigarettes, and drugs such as marijuana pose serious health risks to young people. Alcohol leads to destructive and delinquent behavior and is the leading factor in fatal and nonfatal traffic accidents among teenage drivers. Each year in the United States, 5,000 young people die in alcohol-related automobile accidents (*New York Times,* November 6, 1985).

The health hazards of smoking have been documented by a considerable number of medical research studies. Cigarette smoking has been called the largest single preventable cause of death in the United States (Barton, Chassin, Presson, & Sherman, 1982). Antismoking campaigns have decreased the incidence of smoking among adults, but there has been considerably less success getting adolescents to stop or preventing them from starting.

Compared to alcohol use, the use of drugs is decreasing. A University of Michigan Institute for Social Research survey found that daily marijuana use fell from 11 percent of high school seniors in 1978 to 5.5 percent in 1983. The percentage of seniors who used marijuana at least once in the year prior to the survey dropped from 51 percent in 1979 to 42 percent in 1983. The

Alcohol and drug abuse by teens and young adults has become a problem of national concern. The leading causes of death among adolescents are alcohol related. Alcohol and automobiles are a particularly fatal combination.

use of amphetamines and barbiturates dropped to five percent, while the use of harder or habit-forming drugs remained the same: 16 percent have used cocaine; 1.2 percent have used heroin. Even with these drops, 63 percent of high school seniors say they have tried some kind of illegal drug, 69 percent have used alcohol, and 21 percent are smokers in 1983. The survey was based on 16,000 seniors in over 160 public and private high schools in the United States (*Science News*, February 18, 1984).

Research on Substance Abuse. The research findings in this area are complex. Parents, peers, and cultural values all contribute to the adolescent's decisions to use substances. In some cases, there are direct modeling effects, and in other cases cognitive influences seem to be at work. For example, direct effects are strongest for coffee, cigarettes, and marijuana. In other words, if a parent uses these substances, a child is likely to take them up during adolescence; conversely, if a parent does not use these substances, the child is not likely to take them up (Fawzy, Coombs, & Gerber, 1983; Newcomb, Huba, & Bentler, 1983).

Low or moderate parental use of alcohol, however, does not affect the adolescent directly. Parents who do not drink or who drink in moderate amounts have nondrinking children only to the extent that the parents are effective in influencing the child's perceptions of other people who drink. In other words, parental modeling of healthful use of alcohol is not enough. The parent must be aware of the child's susceptibility to outside influences, and the parent must work to cast the alcohol use of other young people in a negative light (Newcomb et al., 1983).

In some cases, the parent-child relationship, independent of whether the parent uses substances or not, explains some of the patterns of abuse. Adolescents who report higher levels of parental control and lower levels of parental affection tend to use alcohol and drugs more than children who have more positive views of the parent-child relationship. Of course, adolescent substance abuse could lead to parental control and lowered affection. In addition, if parents are absent from the home, if they do not monitor the adolescent's behavior, or if they fail to influence the adolescent's images of peers who abuse substances, there is a greater likelihood of adolescent abuse (Newcomb et al., 1983).

Cross-cultural studies also reveal that societies in which parents play a more direct role in the decisions of their children are less likely to have substance abuse problems among their adolescents. For example, Israeli children are more likely than middle-class children in the United States to follow their parents' use of alcohol by direct modeling and are more influenced by their parents' opinions of their peers' drinking behavior (Adler & Kandel, 1982). Within the United States, alcohol and drug use is twice as high among American Indians as it is among white youth, which seems to be related to relative lack of parental influence among Indians compared to white groups (Weibel-Orlando, 1984).

Later in adolescence, some individuals "graduate" from trial use to persistent and regular use or from using relatively mild substances such as marijuana and beer to using cocaine and hard liquor. Research has shown that a personality factor called "deviance proneness"—seeing oneself as different from others because of one's substance habits—is more highly correlated with the transition to advanced stages of substance use than is the mere social enhancement of modeling peers (Brook, Whiteman, & Gordon, 1983; Chassin, 1984; Chaisson, Presson, & Sherman, 1984). In other words, adolescents who see themselves as different may continue to use substances to solidify and

The Mass Media and Adolescent Health

Teenagers have health needs that are similar to those of adults. Many teens fail, however, to get their health needs met, in some cases because of the individual's lack of consistency between cognition and behavior leading to a failure to seek help and in other cases because of the relative difficulty teens have in obtaining health services. Not only are medical fees expensive, but medical care often requires the consent of an adult, both of which discourage teens from seeking health information and care.

Parents may not know about some of the health risks of adolescents any more than the adolescents themselves. In some cases, the teenager is reluctant to discuss the problem with the parents or anyone else. For children living in poverty and for handicapped, delinquent, and runaway youth, health care is even more difficult to obtain (Hein, 1982).

Some health problems are experienced immediately by the individual during adolescence. In other cases, unhealthful life styles—such as substance abuse, poor nutrition, and lack of rest—can contribute to diseases and other health problems later in life.

Teenagers have the right to obtain medical care without parental consent, to purchase over-the-counter contraceptives, to get a prescription for contraceptives from a physician, or to terminate a pregnancy. In 1977, the U.S. Supreme Court (*Carey* v. *Population Services International*) ruled that minors have a constitutionally protected right to decide when to bear or conceive a child and the right to privacy about such decisions free from state, school, or parental interference. The Supreme Court has ruled that similar freedoms, guaranteed under the Fourteenth Amendment to the Constitution, apply to all forms of medical care and medicines (Hein, 1982; Pilpel & Paul, 1982).

Teenagers need information about their rights, the types and availability of health care, contraception, fertility, pregnancy testing, and abortion services. Many people think that the broadcasting media— radio and television—can best communicate this information to teenagers. Unfortunately, the broadcasters are doing an inadequate job.

The portrayals of sex in the media are less than realistic. Although sexual intercourse is not shown on TV, sex is mentioned more than 11 times per hour on prime time TV. Extramarital sex is mentioned more often than sex within marriage, and sex is often presented either in a humorous context or in a context of violence such as prostitution, rape, pornography, or striptease. In addition, much of the thematic material of prime time TV is macho and sexist (Gordon, 1982; Sprafkin & Silverman, 1982).

There are exceptions. Some recent TV shows have dealt responsibly with teenage pregnancies, the effect on the family of a homosexual adolescent with AIDS, and honest and accurate portrayals of real male-female relationships. More needs to be done, however. The current network ban on contraceptive advertising should be lifted and may be challenged in court. Table 16–5 lists some other approaches that can be taken by broadcasters who seek to contribute to the health of our teenagers.

Table 16–5

RECOMMENDATIONS TO BROADCASTERS REGARDING TEENAGERS' HEALTH PROBLEMS

Give information about the legal rights of minors for health care and medical services.

Provide education about appropriate medical practices so teenagers can be informed consumers in the search for health care.

Advertise contraceptives, acne preparations, and other teen health products that are safe and effective.

Use fewer stereotypes about health care providers and provider-patient relationships.

Teach about the use of periodic self-examinations and encourage self-inspection of one's own body.

Do not make judgments about health issues. Present the issues and allow the adolescent to work them into his or her own life. Use the results of research to design effective messages that will reach adolescents.

Encourage seeking out local health care resources, including statements of fees, consent, and confidentiality procedures.

(From Hein, 1982, pp. 13–14.)

maintain this difference. Such individuals tend to be more rebellious and have poorer relationships with their families. Long-term smokers in particular tend also to be low in academic achievement (Brunswick & Messeri, 1984).

In summary, then, the use of substances in early and middle adolescence can be explained by a cognitive theory in which the direct modeling of parents must be reinforced by the efforts of parents, teachers, and the media to label smoking, drinking, and drug use as undesirable or less than positive. A recent antismoking advertisement featuring an attractive teenage movie actress who expresses her disgust for people who smoke ("I think people who smoke are real losers") is likely to be more effective for adolescents than an advertisement that merely lists the health risks of smoking.

Cognitive Development in Adolescence

Changes in size, shape, and sexuality are only one aspect of the adolescent experience. The teen years bring significant advances in the child's conceptions of self, other, and environment. The extent to which the physical and hormonal surges of puberty shape the growth of thinking processes is not well understood, and generally, these areas of development are treated separately.

As we have done in the preceding chapters on cognition in children, we shall rely primarily on the work of Jean Piaget, who was one of the first to describe the systematic changes in thinking processes that develop from birth through adolescence. Piaget's theory as applied to adolescence is still the guide used by most researchers in the field.

Piaget's Theory of Adolescent Thinking

The adolescent years correspond to what Piaget has called the period of *formal operations*. Formal operations refer to the ability to think logically about abstract or imagined concepts and situations. While the elementary schoolchild can think logically about a situation that is real and directly present, the adolescent begins to explore the world of ideas, values, and ideologies. According to Keating (1980), adolescent thinking has five important characteristics that distinguish it from earlier forms of thought.

1. *Thinking about possibilities*. Although much of the adolescent's thinking is about situations in the here-and-now, as in the concrete operations period, adolescents can begin to consider possibilities that are not present. Thus, teenagers can think about alternative solutions to a problem and can consider how much solutions might succeed or fail. They can also make more rational decisions by thinking through possible outcomes of their actions. An interest in science fiction—the imaginary world of the possible—is typical of this period.
2. *Thinking through hypotheses*. Adolescents begin to think in ways that typify the scientific methods discussed in Chapter 3. Hypotheses can be tested and proved false. The adolescent, more than the concrete operational child, is willing to generate a series of hypotheses and reject or accept them as best fits the data of experience. When buying an article of clothing, for example, the teenager will be more selective than the younger school-age child, comparing multiple factors such as style, cost, type of fabric, fit, and affordability before making a decision.
3. *Thinking ahead*. Planning ahead is an important strategy in solving problems. Younger children are more apt to approach complex problems one

step at a time, seeking additional information only when it becomes necessary. During adolescence, the ability to think through the whole sequence of steps before attempting to solve a problem and to decide beforehand what information is needed as well as the general form of the solution increases. For example, teens are capable of writing essays for which they must first read a number of different sources and organize their ideas into an outline before they begin to write.

4. *Thinking about thoughts*. During adolescence there is a general increase in metacognitive activity, leading to more efficient thinking and remembering. In addition, adolescents show a tendency to think about their own internal states, often to the point of preoccupation. This introspection leads to increased self-knowledge and self-understanding.

5. *Thinking beyond old limits*. There is a general broadening of the individual's horizons to issues that go beyond immediate situations, including identity, society, existence, religion, morality, and friendship. Each of these topics can be examined in detail to probe their meaning and the place of the self in this complex system of ideas.

Actually, no single element makes up formal operational thinking. Rather, such thinking is the integration of many streams of thought into a growing *system of thought.*

As an example of formal thinking, consider a snail walking along a board, as shown in Figure 16-5. The snail can walk in one direction or the other along the board. If the snail were standing still, someone could make the snail move to the left or to the right by moving the board. Concrete operational children understand that for the snail to return to the same place it started, it has to walk the same distance in each direction, or else the board has to be moved the same distance in each direction.

Assume that the snail's distance of motion to the right is S(r), and its movement to the left is S(l). In addition, let the movement of the board to the right be B(r) and to the left, B(l). The concrete operational child's understanding of getting the snail to return to the same place is represented in Figure 16-5. This equivalence between the left and right movements is called *reversibility* and is the logical basis for the conservation skills described in Chapter 13.

Now let's suppose the snail is walking to the left, and at the same time, someone moves the board to the right at the same speed. In which direction does the snail move? The concrete operational child cannot anticipate that the snail can remain motionless in relation to the surrounding landscape because of the inability to relate one logical relationship with the other.

The formal operational child, beginning about 12 to 14 years of age, can tell you how the movement of the board and the movement of the snail are related. Furthermore, the formal operational child will tell you that the same thing will happen if you move the board to the left while the snail moves to the right, thus finding a general rule that goes beyond the immediate situation (refer to Figure 16-5).

The snail-and-board problem was devised by Piaget to study the differences between concrete and formal operations (Piaget & Inhelder, 1969). Other problems invented by Piaget were designed to test different aspects of formal thinking. An example is the rod flexibility problem. A child is given several different metal rods that can be fastened at one end. By pressing on the other end, the child can judge how flexible the rod is. The rods given to the child are of different lengths and different thicknesses and are made of different kinds of metals. The problem is to determine which of the factors—length, thickness, or material—makes the rod more or less flexible.

$$S(r) = S(l)$$

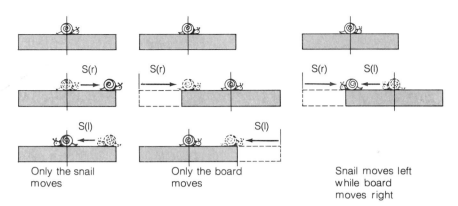

Figure 16—5

The Snail and Board Problem

Concrete operational children will choose one dimension, such as length, and test rods of different length for differences in flexibility. However, they may choose a very thick rod to compare with a very thin rod, without realizing that the thickness makes any difference.

Formal operational children, on the other hand, will list the different factors. They will then test each factor separately, keeping all other factors constant. They will test the length factor, for example, by choosing two rods of different lengths but with the same thickness and of the same material. These children, in testing hypotheses systematically, evidently are thinking about *all* the factors and trying to construct a whole system of thought about the problem (Piaget & Inhelder, 1969).

Alternatives to Piaget's Theory

Piaget assumed that all children would achieve the stage of formal operations with little or no specific training. He believed that there was relatively little impact of the environment on the progress of children through the stages of cognitive development. Although this is generally true up to the stage of concrete operations, it does not appear to happen for formal operations. Some children cannot pass even simple tests of formal operations, even by age 20 (Kuhn, Ho, & Adams, 1979). Evidence suggests that marked differences exist between cultures in the attainment of formal operations favoring complex, technological cultures with formal schooling requirements (Neimark, 1982). One of the reasons for this seems to be that people tend to do better on formal reasoning tasks that are directly relevant to their own culture and their own lives. An example of how this works is shown in Figure 16—6.

This means that the child may have some general ability to think formally, but the nature of the problem and context determines whether or not the child applies formal thinking. Problems that are too difficult, either conceptually or because they cause some negative or conflicting emotions (such as contraceptive use), may be approached by the adolescent from a here-and-now perspective and without critical thought.

Some information processing approaches to adolescent thinking attempt to take account of this process. Although the adolescent has some general capacity to think formally, such thinking must be applied to specific realms of knowledge or particular problems (Case, 1978; Newell & Simon, 1972).

The traditional categories of information processing, such as memory, encoding of knowledge, and mapping knowledge onto mental operations, have

(A) The card problem

Each of the cards shown below has a letter on one side and a number on the other side. Which card or cards need to be turned over in order to discover whether the following rule is true or false: *If there is an A on one side of the card, then there is a 2 on the other side of the card.*

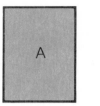 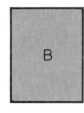  

(B) The drinking age problem

Imagine that you are a police officer responsible for making sure the following regulation is enforced: *If a person is drinking beer, then the person must be over 19.* The cards below represent four people sitting at a table in a bar. On one side of the card is a person's age, and on the other side is what the person is drinking. Which card or cards need to be turned over to determine whether any of these people are violating the regulation?

Answers are given on the next page.

Figure 16—6

Effect of the Problem Context on Formal Thinking

(From Linn, 1983.)

been used to explain individual differences in thinking skills (Sternberg, 1979). Pascual-Leone (1980) divides thinking into components such as information capacity (the amount of information that can be held in short-term memory on any one problem), content knowledge about a particular subject, logical processes that compare elements of knowledge, and contextual factors such as distractions and affective states. Adolescents are more advanced than younger children in each of these areas: greater short-term memory, expanded knowledge, more complex logical processes, and less susceptibility to distraction.

Whatever way we choose to describe adolescent thinking, it is clearly different from cognition in middle childhood. In one study, a group of preadolescents in fourth and fifth grades who failed to pass a test of formal reasoning skills were compared with a group of beginning college students who also failed the same test (Kuhn et al., 1979). The subjects were then given a series of training sessions in which procedures for solving problems such as the one they failed were presented. By the end of the training sessions, the college students were able to pass the formal reasoning test, but the preadolescents were not.

This study suggests that reasoning can be task-specific, as suggested by the information processing theories. It also says that with age, people develop the general skills of formal reasoning in the manner described by Piaget. These general reasoning skills can be applied to specific problems with a small amount of training. With effort, therefore, most college students should be capable of learning the kinds of formal-conceptual skills required in college and university courses.

Knowing how to read a book or solve math problems is not the only form of intelligence. It takes sophisticated problem solving and social relationships skills to organize and carry out a successful hunt. Educators and researchers need to learn more about this and other forms of "practical intelligence."

Thinking and Being: I Think, Therefore I Am

This section personalizes a bit more the general features of adolescent cognitive abilities covered in the previous section. What does the possession of formal thinking skills mean for the adolescent?

How do I know that I exist? What gives me the impression that I am a separate and unique person? How can I know what other people are thinking and feeling? Does the world really exist apart from me? When I close my eyes, does the world disappear?

As intellectual problems, these questions were first taken up by philosophers. In the twentieth century, they are being considered by psychologists and developmentalists. But they also exist as real-life problems, taken up by every generation of adolescents whose minds lead them to contemplate a wider realm of thought and possibility.

A seventeenth-century French philosopher, René Descartes (1596–1650), contemplated similar issues and reached a solution not unlike that held by many adolescents: Existence begins with the individual's mind. Descartes's now famous assertion *Cogito, ergo sum,* "I think, therefore I am," set the stage for the *epistemologies* (theories of knowledge) of Kant and Locke and the twentieth-century cognitive psychologists, including Piaget.

Answers to Figure 16–6: (A) The "A" and the "3" card (B) "Drinking beer" and "Age 16"

Because formal operations allow adolescents to "think about thought," adolescents soon become preoccupied with themselves and their ideas and assume that everyone else is preoccupied with them in the same way. This sense of self-preoccupation is called *adolescent egocentrism*. Developmentalist David Elkind (1980; Elkind & Bowen, 1979) has described this egocentrism of adolescent thinking with two complementary concepts: the imaginary audience and the personal fable.

Since adolescents feel that everyone else is thinking about them, they become worried about how they look in the eyes of others. The *imaginary audience* is the group of people who the adolescent believes constantly monitors the adolescent's appearance, behavior, and action. The imaginary audience leads invariably to a heightened self-consciousness. Young adolescents may spend hours in front of a mirror, become obsessed with clothing and hairstyles, worry about the appropriateness of their actions, and feel that they have to work to hide their innermost desires and fears from the eyes of the watching world.

Because they believe that everyone is watching them, adolescents come to believe that they are really special, and they construct a *personal fable*, a set of ideas about how valuable and important the adolescent is. They believe, for example, that others might die, but they won't; that they are immune from disease or from becoming pregnant; that they will succeed in life, becoming rich and famous, where others will fail. In this sense, adolescents often seem idealistic in their thinking.

Both the imaginary audience and the personal fable remain with the individual in some form throughout adulthood. These ideas about the self are important motivators as one strives to improve and develop. They encourage healthy competition to achieve and win the approval of others, thereby lending support to one's own notion of specialness. The imaginary audience and the personal fable are also important as sources of strength in times of crisis and misfortune (Elkind, 1980).

It seems a bit surprising that formal operational thinking, which has the ultimate goal of widening one's range of thought to encompass the world beyond the self, should lead to a new form of egocentrism. Recent research has shown that adolescent egocentrism actually begins in early adolescence, at the close of the concrete operational period, and declines as the child's ability to think formally increases.

One study examined adolescent egocentrism in a sample of 251 13-year-olds in a rural junior high school (Riley, Adams, & Nielsen, 1984). Each child was given the following tests: The Imaginary Audience Scale (IAS) measures the level of the adolescent's self-consciousness by means of asking about the willingness or unwillingness to expose the self in a variety of interpersonal contexts. The Classroom Test of Formal Operations (CTFO) measures the levels of concrete and formal thinking by asking students to explain in writing how a previously demonstrated complex apparatus works. The Perceived Parental Support scale assesses the child's view of the quality of the relationship with his or her parents. Children with higher levels of formal thinking scored lower on self-consciousness and vice versa. It seems that formal operations allow young people to engage in more social perspective taking and to recognize that their thoughts are not necessarily shared by others.

If the onset of formal operations leads to the decline of adolescent egocentrism in middle adolescence, what, then, accounts for the rise of adolescent egocentrism in early adolescence? Researchers suggest a social-interpersonal

| | Factors Related to Self-Consciousness: | |
	For Boys	For Girls
Father's physical affection	Reduces	Increases
Mother's physical affection	No relation	No relation
Father's emotional support	No relation	Reduces
Mother's emotional support	No relation	Reduces
Father's rejection/control	No relation	Increases
Mother's rejection/control	No relation	No relation

(From Riley, Adams, & Nielson, 1984.)

cause. First of all, as we'll see in Chapter 17, peer pressure and peer group conformity peak in the seventh or eighth grade. Second, the study found positive relationships between a lack of perceived parental support and self-consciousness (see Table 16–6).

It seems that adolescent egocentrism begins as the first glimmers of formal thinking lead the adolescent into wider worlds of consciousness and thus self-consciousness. At that point, increased experience with social perspective taking brought about by supportive family-child relationships and peer group interactions helps the adolescent to more carefully examine the differences in perspectives between self and others and thus to become less egocentric (Gray & Hudson, 1984; Riley et al., 1984).

One area in which formal thinking is needed for daily life is in the ability of adolescents to make legally regulated decisions, such as marriage, consent to medical care, consent to participate in research, and legal responsibilities.

One study investigated 36 subjects in each of three grade levels: seventh, tenth, and twelfth (Lewis, 1981). Subjects were asked to listen to various types of dilemmas involving decision making. One such dilemma is presented in Table 16–7, along with questions that were asked. Subjects' answers were coded for the following:

1. Awareness of the benefits and risks of the situation.
2. Future orientation and the willingness to delay gratification.
3. Advice seeking from others and willingness to comply with advice.
4. Recognition of vested interests in sources of advice.
5. Willingness to check new information with other sources of knowledge.

Table 16–7

DECISION MAKING DILEMMA

Dilemma

I've been thinking about having an operation. It won't make me healthier or anything, but I'd like to have it because it would make me look better since I've always had this ugly thing like a bump on my cheek. I could have an operation to remove it. I'm trying to decide whether to have the operation, and I can't decide. Do you think I should have the operation?

Follow-up questions

How should I decide whether to have the operation?
What different things should I think about to help me decide?
If you were me, would you talk to anyone about the decision, and if so, who?

(From Lewis, 1981, p. 540.)

Creativity in Everyday Life

Creativity was defined in Chapter 13 as *divergent thinking,* or the ability to generate novel responses to a standard situation. In this definition, creativity is measured by whether a person can provide novel solutions to word problems. Adolescence is a time when creativity becomes a central focus of life. Adolescents have to create their own sense of identity, and they must begin to select appropriate career choices. This happens by discovering new possibilities for themselves in the wider world of adults. Creativity also arises in everyday tasks such as cooking, doing school work, and solving difficult interpersonal problems with friends and within the family. How can we explain this kind of creativity?

Researchers have acquired some hints from people who are recognized as creative, such as rock climbers, chess players, dancers, and artists. Regardless of the activity, these people all described a "profound involvement with their activity, which combined a loss of self-consciousness with deep concentration. The experience was subjectively pleasing—compelling enough to inspire rock climbers to risk their lives—and at the same time required highly complex use of mental or physical skills" (Csikszentmihalyi & Larson, 1984, p. 23).

The state of consciousness in which a person is totally involved and committed to the activity is called *flow,* a "condition in which one feels whole and acts with clarity, commitment, and enthusiasm" (Csikszentmihalyi & Larson, 1984, p. 23). A model of the flow experience is presented in Figure 16–7. This model suggests that flow experiences will occur when skills match the challenges of a situation. Thus, high school students enjoy classes in which their effort pays off in mastery and not ones in which they are overwhelmed with work or those that are too boring (Csikszentmihalyi, 1980; Mayers, 1978).

Flow is just as intense and enjoyable at point 'B' (e.g., playing a violin sonata) in Figure 16–7 as in point 'A' (e.g., playing with a kitten). Point 'B' experiences are more complex, however, and may involve greater satisfaction, since they represent the fulfillment of long-term achievements.

In addition, as shown by Figure 16–7, flow experiences are unstable. To recapture the enjoyment of flow, one must continue to formulate new and more complex

Experimenting with new hair and clothing styles, and keeping up with friends in this respect, are typical of the teen years.

goals, face new challenges, and learn new skills.

Defined in this way, creativity takes on a broader meaning than simply insight or resourcefulness. Creativity can apply to the entire life project of an individual: the ability to use internal resources to face challenges, avoid boredom and anxiety, and feel satisfied and happy with one's life. This ability improves with age during the adolescent period. Following is an example from late adolescence:

Your parents can't completely understand you; you gotta understand

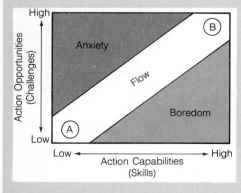

Figure 16–7

Definition of the Flow Experience

where they're coming from. When you have something that goes wrong, getting pressure not just from them but from friends and school, don't take it all out on the family; try to sit down and explain instead of blowing up; try to be more calm (p. 274).

I'm looking at myself more not so much as how other people look at me, I always used to worry about what other people thought and now it doesn't matter because I'm the only one I have to please ... kids in my class might go out and get wild drunk, but that doesn't appeal to me, and I think, heck, if that's what they want to do let them go out and do it ... like some kids wouldn't get caught dead in the kitchen baking a cake, but I enjoy it so I'm gonna do it, who cares? (p. 275). Csikszentmihalyi & Larson, 1982.

Thus, creativity is not reserved for only art projects but is an integral part of making sense of life, becoming an aware and active individual, and creating a sense of meaning and uniqueness about the self's activities. This ability does not develop fully until late in adolescence.

Results show an increase with age in mentioning risks and future consequences of decisions, suggestions to get advice from specialists, and cautious treatment of the vested interest of adult professionals. This study shows that it is not until relatively late in adolescence that independent and informed decision making can be expected. Related research shows that by ninth grade, adolescents can understand the nature of different medical treatments and can make competent decisions about those treatments (Weithorn & Campbell, 1982). Probably because of the complex nature of legally based decisions, it takes a long time to integrate the relevant information into a formal system of thought in which all viewpoints are balanced against each other.

Chapter Summary

PHYSICAL CHANGES
☐ Physical change occurs almost as rapidly in adolescence as in infancy. The adolescent growth spurt is correlated with pubertal changes leading to the development of reproductive fertility.
☐ The psychological response to puberty is generally positive for both boys and girls. Higher levels of self-esteem and body-esteem are associated with family mutuality and respect.

SEXUALITY
☐ Adaptation to sexuality can be explained using personal and social expectations.
☐ Although there are differences between males and females in personal expectation for sexuality (sources of arousal), the 1980s has seen a greater equalization of social expectations (willingness to admit to sexual desire and activity outside of marriage).
☐ Adolescents are generally inconsistent contraceptive users, although mutual communication between partners increases the likelihood of the use of contraceptives.
☐ Masturbation is practiced by the majority of males and females. Homosexuality is rare in the teen population.

HEALTHFUL LIFE STYLES IN ADOLESCENCE
☐ Risks to adolescent health are teenage pregnancy, weight gain and eating disorders, and substance abuse.
☐ Theory and research on substance abuse implicate a complex set of factors including peer, school, and family influences. Health assistance and risk prevention can be encouraged through the mass media.

COGNITIVE DEVELOPMENT IN ADOLESCENCE

□ The nature of adolescent formal operational thinking is the object of research of both Piagetian and information processing perspectives.

□ The role of formal thinking in the teen's sense of self leads to adolescent egocentrism and its decline.

□ Cognition as applied to everyday creativity and decision making is shown to increase during adolescence with the decline of egocentrism.

Recommended Readings

Adelson, J. (1980). *Handbook of adolescent development*. New York: Wiley. One of the most complete sources of current research and knowledge about adolescent development.

Alan Guttmacher Institute (1981). *Teenage pregnancy: The problem that hasn't gone away*. New York: Author. Filled with easy-to-read charts and tables illustrating the rise and importance of the teenage pregnancy problem.

Csikszentmihalyi, M., & Larson, R. (1984). *Being adolescent: Conflict and growth in the teenage years*. New York: Basic Books. An excellent account of everyday life and emotional experience during adolescence.

Mead, M. (1928/1963). *Coming of age in Samoa: A psychological study of primitive youth for western civilization*. New York: Morrow Quill Paperbacks. A classic study of teenage rites of passage in a South Sea island culture.

Social Development in the Wider World

. . . I look back at the past year with gratitude to God and man. But bitter self-reproaches press upon me too. Unkindness, lack of self-control, my unbelief, making fun of the holiest things, exaggerated enthusiasms, and serious offenses against the 4th Commandment. For the New Year, my resolutions are: 1. to stop mockery, even if I unfortunately don't possess a child's faith any more and no other faith has taken its place; 2. to learn to suppress my moods and tempers—to behave equably; 3. to try to fulfill the 4th Commandment at least outwardly. Today I read a book that one should honor one's father not for his personal characteristics but to honor the authority God has vested in him. But it is awfully difficult.

December 31, 1900, at age 15. From The
Adolescent Diaries of Karen Horney
by Karen Horney.
—*Copyright © 1980 by Basic Books, Inc., Publishers.*
Reprinted by permission of the publisher.

. . . I have, as it were, a dual personality. One half embodies my exuberant cheerfulness, making fun of everything, my high-spiritedness, and above all the way I take everything lightly. . . This side is usually lying in wait and pushes away the other, which is much better, deeper and purer. . .

A voice sobs within me: "There you are, that's what's become of you: you're uncharitable, you look supercilious and peevish, people dislike you and all because you won't listen to the advice given to you by your own better half." Oh, I would like to listen, but it doesn't work; if I'm quiet and serious, everyone thinks it's a new comedy and then I have to get out of it by turning it into a joke. . . I can't keep that up: if I'm watched to that extent, I start by getting snappy, then unhappy, and finally I twist my heart round again, so that the bad is on the outside and the good is on the inside and keep on trying to find a way of becoming what I would so like to be, and which I could be, if . . . there weren't any other people living in the world.

August 1, 1944, at age 15. Excerpt from
Anne Frank: The Diary of a Young Girl *by Anne Frank.*
—*Copyright 1952 by Otto H. Frank. Reprinted by
permission of Doubleday and Company, Inc.*

In the paragraphs quoted here, two 15-year-old girls discuss some of the difficulties of growing up. They are both concerned that their outward behavior does not reflect what they are really feeling and thinking. It is as if they are fighting a constant battle to keep each of the two "parts" of the self under control and have a lingering fear that the inner self will become exposed.

These teenagers were in the process of forming a sense of personal identity when they wrote these entries in their diaries. *Identity* is a "self-structure—an internal, self-constructed, dynamic organization of drives, abilities, beliefs, and individual history. The better developed this structure is, the more aware individuals appear to be of their own uniqueness and similarity to others and of their own strengths and weaknesses in making their way in the world" (Marcia, 1980, p. 159).

These diaries are also historical documents. As discussed in Chapter 1, diaries are firsthand accounts of how children grow up and experience the world. When it comes to the personal struggles leading to identity formation, little has changed for adolescents in the past century.

The similarity of these accounts is especially striking when one considers the great differences in the social contexts for these two girls. Both were from Germany, but the similarity ends there. Karen was the child of a wealthy commodore in German shipping. She traveled widely as a child, had many social contacts, went to medical school, and eventually became a well-known psychoanalyst. Anne's Jewish family went into hiding in the top floor of the home of a Dutch family in Amsterdam soon after the Germans began their campaign to kill all Jews and other "undesirables." At the age of 15, Anne had been living in the space of a few small rooms for three years with only her family and a few others. The hiding place was discovered by the Germans shortly before the end of World War II, and Anne perished in the Bergen-Belsen concentration camp only weeks before the Germans surrendered to the Allies.

This chapter begins with a review of research on the development of personal identity: When do children begin to think about these issues, and when do they achieve a mature sense of self? Related to identity is the development of values and morals and the regulation of emotions. A major issue of this chapter is the adolescent's relationships with others: through the family, the peer group, and the school. The chapter concludes with a discussion of adolescents' growing awareness of the adult world and adolescents' views on work, marriage, and politics.

The Development of a Personal Identity

Almost all adolescents go through the kind of questioning and uncertainty described by Karen Horney and Anne Frank. Questions like "Who am I?" "Where am I going?" "Am I the same or different from parents and friends?" are raised repeatedly throughout the adolescent years and beyond.

Conflict or Calm?

Developmentalists have differed about how much of a disruption such questions cause for the individual. Recall from Chapters 1 and 2 G. Stanley Hall's (1904) characterization of adolescence as a period of "storm and stress" and Erik Erikson's view of the adolescent "identity crisis."

If adolescence is a period of "storm and stress" or "crisis," the individual's self-concept should change in discontinuous or unstable ways. *Discontinuity* implies that the individual's self-concept may fluctuate over the adolescent period, with wild swings from positive to negative feelings about the self.

Instability means that there is no way to predict a person's ultimate self-concept at the end of adolescence from how that person felt about the self at the beginning of adolescence.

Contrary to this expectation, research has found that self-concept over the adolescent years is both continuous and stable. In one major study (Dusek & Flaherty, 1981), the self-concepts of over 1700 fifth-grade through tenth-grade children were tested. The study combined both longitudinal and cross-sectional samples and tested for cohort effects by collecting different sets of data beginning in three successive years: 1975, 1976, and 1977.

Each child was given 21 pairs of adjectives, as shown in Table 17–1. For each pair, the child was asked to assign a number from "1" to "7." A "7" was related to the positive end of the scale and a "1" to the negative end of the scale. These ratings were correlated across subjects using a method called *factor analysis,* which isolates groups of variables (in this case, the ratings on each adjective pair) that are correlated with each other. Each cluster of variables that are correlated with each other is called a "factor." Different factors that emerge in such an analysis are uncorrelated.

As shown in Table 17–1, four factors emerged from the entire sample of subjects. Factor 1 consisted of the positive adjectives, for example, "relaxed," "steady," "happy," "stable." Thus, people who rated themselves highly "relaxed" were also likely to label themselves as very "steady" and "happy." This factor was given the name *adjustment.*

Factor 2, consisting of adjectives like "smart" and "success," was labeled *achievement/leadership.* Factor 3, including "nice" and "friendly," was called *congeniality/sociability.* Factor 4, including "rugged" and "strong," was labeled *masculinity.* Since each factor is uncorrelated with the others, ratings on adjectives within the congeniality/sociability factor did not predict ratings on the other factors, and so forth.

The same factors emerged for all the ages studied when the factor analysis was done on each age separately, suggesting that self-concept is highly continuous over time. There was high stability in the individual's own self-concept for those children who were tested longitudinally. For example, fifth-grade children who saw themselves as low on achievement/leadership continued to feel the same way when they were in the tenth grade.

Similarly, Offer (1969), studying adolescent boys, and Douvan and Adleson (1966), studying girls, found that most children negotiated adolescence

Factor 1 Adjustment	Factor 2 Achievement/ leadership	Factor 3 Congeniality/ sociability	Factor 4 Masculinity
relaxed/nervous	smart/dumb	nice/awful	rugged/delicate
steady/shaky	success/failure	kind/cruel	hard/soft
refreshed/tired	superior/inferior	friendly/unfriendly	strong/weak
stable/unstable	sharp/dull	good/bad	
healthy/sick	valuable/worthless		
happy/sad	confident/unsure		
satisfied/ dissatisfied	leader/follower		

Table 17–1

RESULTS OF FACTOR ANALYSIS OF SELF-CONCEPT DATA

(From Dusek & Flaherty, *Mong. Soc. Res. Child Devel.,* 1981, Vol. 46. © The Society for Research in Child Development, Inc. Reprinted by permission of author and publisher.)

continuously and without major crises. These studies suggest that even though adolescents may experience their own development with some degree of struggle and conflict, it does not necessarily lead them into crisis and rebellion. The quotes from Karen Horney's and Anne Frank's diaries show that adolescents make active attempts to continue to conform to other's expectations, even though inwardly they may be questioning the appropriateness of those expectations.

Theories of Identity Formation

The term *identity* was first used in the context of Erikson's psychoanalytic theory of human development. According to Erikson (refer to Chapter 2), human life is made up of psychosocial stages, which represent a series of life goals and are characterized by Erikson as having a bipolar quality. During adolescence, the life goal is the formation of *identity:* who one is and how one fits into role relationships with others. The polar opposite of identity is *role confusion,* being unable to fit into society and feeling rebellious and alienated.

According to Erikson, the stage of identity versus role confusion involves a crisis in self-definition, and the end result should be to find a role and commit oneself to that role. Role commitment involves taking on the values and attitudes that are consistent with that role (Lerner & Shea, 1982). One acquires an identity, according to Erikson, by getting information about role expectations during social interaction.

In a series of research studies, James Marcia (1966) developed a more detailed analysis of one's progress toward role commitment. Each level of commitment is called an *ego identity status.* Definitions of each of the four ego identity statuses are given in Table 17–2. In studies using Marcia's definitions of ego identity statuses, adolescents are given an open-ended interview in which they are asked about their levels of commitment to various occupational, political, and religious attitudes. This research has found a general increase in commitment to ideals over the adolescent period.

Table 17–2

EGO IDENTITY STATUSES

Identity Diffusion	No commitment has been made and no attempt to explore or question values. Person has no idea about occupational future, politics, or religion. Child may show knowledge of a content area, may work or be politically involved, but without a sense of personal commitment.
Foreclosure	Strong commitments are made but without active questioning of those commitments. These commitments are usually a direct extension of the values of parents and teachers. Child may want the same career as parent but without seriously having considered alternatives. Such commitments appear premature and developmentally unsophisticated.
Moratorium	The individual is in the process of actively seeking information but without making a decision. Conflicts between current experiences and past beliefs and values may arise, leading the person to read more, talk to others, or more deeply reflect on feelings. This is the period that comes closest to the notion of "identity crisis."
Identity Achievement	The individual has experienced moratorium and is currently active in implementing a commitment. Examples are the resolution of a sex-role identity, choice of a college or a program of study, and choice of a career goal, all of which are based on a prior period of active value exploration and discussion.

(From Archer & Waterman, 1983; Marcia, 1966.)

In the sixth through the tenth grades, over 90 percent of children are in the *diffusion* and *foreclosure* statuses. During the high school years, there is a slight shift to the *moratorium* and *achievement* statuses, but not much change takes place over this period, and only 20 percent of college freshmen were rated as identity *achievers*. The college years seem to be the time during which most individuals make the transition to achievement status (Adams & Jones, 1983; Archer & Waterman, 1983).

Cognitive developmental theory suggests that the formation of identity in adolescence depends upon formal operational thinking applied to the entire system of attitudes, beliefs, and values developed in the child's own personal history integrated with the new set of attitudes, beliefs, and values to which the adolescent becomes exposed from the wider world.

The psychoanalytic perspective of Erikson is consistent with the cognitive perspective, since formal operational thinking is required to integrate the perspectives of other people into a consistent role identity for the individual. Systems theory attempts to bring both social influences and cognitive interpretations together, suggesting that the child is embedded in a context of social relationships. These social relationships not only are direct causes of the adolescent's changes but also may serve to mediate indirectly the impact of physical and emotional changes on the adolescent. The family, for example, can function as a buffer to ease the child's transition into adult values and roles (refer to Chapter 16)(Lerner & Shea, 1982).

Research on Individual Differences in Identity Status

We might expect, then, that the child's achievement of a given identity status (Table 17–2) would depend on such factors as the level of formal operational thinking, the quality of the parent-child and peer social relationships, and the cultural norms for early identity achievement. One study that is representative of research in this area was done with 107 high school girls (Adams & Jones, 1983). In addition to measuring each girl's identity status according to Marcia's formulation, the researchers collected data on the girls' impressions of their relationship to their parents. The students were asked to rate how often the parents try to control or regulate their lives, and how often the parents express approval or praise as well as how often the parents express warmth and affection.

Female adolescents who were assessed to be in the identity achievement or moratorium (questioning and searching) statuses perceived their mothers as low on control and regulation and high on encouragement of independence. They perceived their fathers as low on praise but high on fairness of punishment.

Females who had relatively low identity statuses perceived their parents in somewhat contradictory ways. They viewed their mothers as controlling but as encouraging independence. They viewed their fathers as offering lots of praise but as being unfair in punishment. These extremes of parental behavior, at least as perceived by the adolescent, may lead to inconsistencies in parenting that may not encourage the child toward independence and identity formation. On the other hand, the findings could be explained by a parental response to the child's low level of personal maturity.

Other studies have found that low levels of parental restrictiveness combined with high levels of parent-child communication and a willingness to discuss problems are related to higher levels of identity status (LaVoie, 1976; Marcia, 1983; Matteson, 1975; Waterman & Waterman, 1971). All of these studies, however, measure the adolescent's perception of the parent-child interaction and thus tell us little about what actually happens in that interaction.

What do I want to be? How do I want to look? While these questions continue throughout the life span, they begin to be asked in the teen years.

Grotevant and Cooper (1985) made direct observations of parent-child communication patterns using 84 Caucasian, middle-class, two-parent families with a child who was a senior in high school. The family was asked to plan together a fictional two-week vacation. This interaction was coded for self-assertion (expressing directly one's point of view), separateness (distinguishing views of the self from those of others), mutuality (indirectly expressing one's views, stating others' feelings, compromising), and permeability (asking others' views, agreeing, complying with requests).

Ego identity was assessed using Marcia's open-ended interview asking about attitudes toward occupational roles, religion, politics, dating, and sex roles. It was scored differently, however. Rather than rate the level of commitment to values, this study rated the level of willingness to explore values, looking for consideration of a variety of options for the self and a clear understanding of each option. The results are shown in Table 17—3. The findings support systems theory and show that families are effective mediators of adolescent identity status and identity exploration. Adolescents who are able to communicate openly with their parents and who are given opportunities to express independent views and actions are more likely to explore a wide range of values and commit themselves to particular value orientations.

Values and Morality

As we saw in the previous section, identity formation brings increases in commitment to and exploration of values. The specific values that adolescents explore and adopt depend upon socialization experiences in the family, the

Table 17—3

IDENTITY EXPLORATION AND PARENT-CHILD COMMUNICATION

Higher levels of identity exploration are associated with:

Fathers		Mothers	
Sons	**Daughters**	**Sons**	**Daughters**
Self-assertion(A)	Mutuality(A)	No relation	Mutuality(A)
Separateness(A)	Permeability(P)		Self-assertion(P)
Mutuality(P)	Separateness(P)		

A = adolescent, P = parent

Summary for Males

Higher scoring sons expressed disagreements and made direct suggestions to their fathers, while their fathers accepted the suggestions and made few direct suggestions of their own, thus encouraging the sons' assertiveness in this task.

Males appear more direct and assertive. Communication is maintained with them by fathers who are willing to compromise and accept the sons' ideas.

Summary for Females

Higher scoring daughters expressed their suggestions indirectly to both mother and father. Their fathers made relevant comments and disagreements but few suggestions, while their mothers made more direct suggestions.

Females are more indirect in their suggestions and are willing to compromise. Their fathers maintain communication by asking the daughters for more information and clarifying the daughters' perspectives as distinct from others. Their mothers maintain communication by making more direct suggestions to their daughters.

(From Grotevant & Cooper, 1985.)

Individual Differences in Values

A series of major studies of values was done in the late 1960s and early 1970s using the Rokeach Value Survey. Teenagers were given a list of values and asked to rank them in order of importance. *Terminal values* are those concerned with positive end-states of life, or things that are meaningful and worth striving for. Teenagers in both New York City and Adelaide, Australia, ranked most highly the terminal values of peace, freedom, family security, and equality. *Instrumental values* are seen as means to an end or modes of conduct in the present. The same group of children placed honesty, loving, responsibility, and ambition at the top of their instrumental value list (Beech & Schoeppe, 1974; Feather, 1975). There were differences, however, between larger countries and smaller ones. Israel and Papua New Guinea, small countries beset by struggles with their neighbors, ranked "a world at peace" and "national security" in the top 4, while students from the other countries ranked these values in the lowest 4 (Feather, 1980).

Although relatively few national differences in values have been found, consistent sex differences have been found in each nation. When describing themselves, male adolescents from Norway, Sweden, Denmark, Finland, England, and the United States tend to use adjectives such as practical, assertive, competitive, and ambitious, while females tend to use words like loving, sympathetic, generous, and sensitive (Block, 1973). This male value pattern of competence-effectiveness has been called *agency,* while the female pattern of warmth-expressiveness has been called *communion.* (Refer to Table 17–1 for similar sex differences in identity factors.) These differences have been found even in a culture such as Japan, which emphasizes cooperative values for both sexes. A study of Japanese high school students found that although both boys and girls ranked cooperative values above competitive values, boys ranked competitive values higher than girls did (Shwalb & Shwalb, 1985).

Many studies of adolescent behavior do not find sex differences in agency versus communion. However, when a sex difference is found, such as in the study previously described, it almost always reflects the male-agency, female-communion parallel (Lerner & Spanier, 1980).

Related to the issue of sex differences in general values is sex differences in perception of a value as being "male" or "female." What does each sex think about the other? To what extent do adolescents hold traditional sex role stereotypes?

Under age 16, children describe the achievement of both sexes as due to effort. After this age, female ability and effort are generally undervalued compared with ability and effort of males. For example, higher achievements in sports by females were explained as due to luck by both boys and girls 16 and 18 years of age. The same level of achievement for males was explained as due to effort. In general, by late adolescence, both males and females become biased against females (Deaux & Emswiller, 1974).

Culture, values, and identity formation are all related in complex ways. The dominant and male values of Western society define mature identity as being independent, assertive, and successful. According to Erikson's view of identity, the "mature" state is one in which the person makes an independent commitment to his or her values.

Some authors have suggested that there may be a contradiction between certain kinds of values related to cooperation and affiliation and the notion

Fitting-in. School uniforms worn by these Japanese girls help to preserve sex-role differences that define both self and others.

of independent commitment (Gilligan, 1982; Sampson, 1985). Women, black Americans, and some Oriental societies (refer to Chapter 1) all tend to place a high value on affiliation. If there is to be commitment, affiliative value orientations suggest that it should arise as part of a group process rather than in taking a stand independent of the group.

Moral Development in Adolescence

The reasoning process that people experience in relation to the formation of and commitment to values is called *morality*. Moral development was discussed extensively in Chapter 14. Here we will apply those ideas to changes that occur during the adolescent years. Adolescence marks the transition from *conventional* to *postconventional* morality, and most adolescents are in stages 4 and 5 of Kohlberg's theory of moral development (refer to Chapter 14, Tables 14–8 and 14–9).

Conventional reasoning justifies actions on the basis of authority, doing one's duty, and conforming to expectations without questioning the rules. *Postconventional* reasoning involves the recognition that such rules are sometimes arbitrary and unjust but that the preservation of social order requires that conflicts between the individual and the law should be decided in favor of the law. At the highest level of postconventional reasoning, unjust laws may be seen as subordinate to universal moral principles (refer to Chapter 14).

According to cognitive developmental theory, moral development should be correlated with changes in cognitive development. Some studies have found that children at higher levels of formal thinking also tended to be higher in moral reasoning (Tomlinson-Keasey & Keasey, 1974). Consistent with systems theory, on the other hand, is the fact that many children who have reached formal levels of reasoning do not progress into postconventional morality. This appears to be because of the mediating factors of culture and family.

Research by Haan, Smith, and Block (1968) has shown that college students who were conventional reasoners were more likely to be politically conservative and inactive in campus issues and to hold values that were consistent with typical cultural norms for men and women. The postconventional reasoners were more likely to live off campus, be involved with more organizations, be more politically active, and value individual self-expression and freedom regardless of sex-role stereotypes. This suggests that active social and political participation may enhance moral reasoning, or that higher levels of moral reasoning may lead to greater political activism.

More recently, Haan (1985) has studied the impact of peer group discussions on the child's level of moral reasoning. She found that discussion and involvement in moral issues enhanced moral development independent of cognitive level. Mere group discussion of the typical moral dilemmas was not enough to enhance moral reasoning. Students who participated in a role-playing "game"—such as pretending to be members of the last group of survivors after world disaster or ghetto citizens confronting a slum landlord, or competing among poor countries to acquire the resources to feed their citizens—were more likely to show increases in moral reasoning levels.

Systems theory suggests that adolescents from different cultures should have different modes of reasoning about moral issues. This has been confirmed in a study of 92 adolescents ranging in age from 12 to 17 years living in Israeli kibbutzim (Snarey, Reimer, & Kohlberg, 1985). Standard moral dilemmas were presented to the subjects, who were then asked about how they might resolve the dilemmas. Their answers were coded using the Kohlberg scoring manual (refer to Chapter 14).

The sequence of developmental progression and the age norms for attainment of each of Kohlberg's moral stages was almost identical to those found in the United States. Nevertheless, cultural differences emerged in types of reasons kibbutz adolescents gave to justify their decisions compared to reasons given by North American children.

In one of the standard dilemmas, a man's wife is likely to die if she does not get a particular drug. The man has no money to purchase the drug. Should he steal the drug to save his wife? The responses of two kibbutz members to this dilemma are given in Table 17–4.

According to the Kohlberg scoring manual (refer to Chapter 14), these responses should be scored as stage 4, or conventional. This is because the subjects seem to be justifying their response (to steal the drug) on the basis of an unquestioning acceptance of the existing kibbutz social system in which everyone has a basic right to medical care and happiness.

On the other hand, these subjects do not seem to be conforming blindly to the equality of the kibbutz system. They clearly recognize the limits of kibbutz society—that not everyone is treated as equal—and they envision a world in which everyone has equal opportunity. They see morality not as blind conformity to the rules of utopian society but rather as a collective commitment of people who actively work to achieve these ideals rather than of a society based on power.

The researchers conclude that the Kohlberg manual reflects a Western ideal of society as a collection of individuals governed by laws. Societies in which the law is formed on the basis of collective benefit (no one person should have happiness or privilege unless all have those rights) require a different type of moral reasoning.

Our discussion of values and morality as well as the review of belief systems about children and childbearing in Chapter 1 shows that at least two distinct forms of social organizations exist in the world today: the individualistic and the collective. Male-agency and female-communion, and Western

Table 17—4

KIBBUTZNIK'S RESPONSES TO
THE "LIFE VS. STEALING"
DILEMMA

Excerpt 1 (Kibbutz female):

Q. It is against the law for Moshe to steal the drug. Does that make it morally wrong?

A. It will be illegal or against the formal law, but not against the law which is the moral law. Again, if we were in a utopian society, my hierarchy of values, and the hierarchy of others through consensus, would be realized.

Q. What are those values?

A. Socialism! But (laughter) don't ask me to explain it.

Q. What is wrong with a nonsocialistic society that makes it unjust?

A. In a utopia there will be all the things I believe in. There would not be murder, robbery, and everyone will be equal. In this society, the greatest value, the value of life, is perfectly held. Disvaluing life is forbidden. It is like our dream, our ideal. In one way it is ridiculous since this utopia will never be achieved, of course. You can even observe children in the kindergarten; they can be very nasty and cruel to each other.

Q. Should people still do everything they can to obey the law in an imperfect world?

A. Yes, unless it will endanger or hurt another important value. . . . But generally speaking, people should obey the law. The law was created in order to protect . . . from killing, robbery, and other unjust uses of power. . . . I believe everyone has the right to self-growth and the right to reach happiness. . . . People are not born equally genetically, and it is not fair that one who is stronger physically should reach his happiness by whatever means at the expense of one who is weaker, because the right to happiness is a basic human right of every person and equal to all. A nonkibbutz society that is based on power negates the right and possibility of those who are weaker to get their happiness.

Excerpt 2 (Kibbutz male):

Q. Should Moshe steal the drug? Why or why not?

A. Yes. . . . I think that the community should be responsible for controlling this kind of situation. The medicine should be made available to all in need; the druggist should not have the right to decide on his own . . . the whole community or society should have the control of the drug.

Q. Is it important for people to do everything they can to save another's life? Why or why not?

A. If I want to create a better community, a nice and beautiful one, an ideal world, the only way we can do it is by cooperation between people. . . . We need this cooperation among ourselves in order to achieve this better world. . . . The happiness . . . principle underlies this cooperation—the greatest happiness for the greatest number of people in the society.

Q. Should people try to do everything they can to obey the law?

A. In principle, yes. It is impossible to have any kind of state, country, society without laws. [Otherwise], it will be completely anarchy and those who have the power will dominate the weaker.

Q. Why is that wrong?

A. I am [not] strong. [Laughter]. But really, you can see in the totalitarian countries today in contrast to, for example, the kibbutz. You damage the principal of democracy and, most importantly, you destroy the principle of equality. Which is why I [have chosen to] live on a kibbutz.

(From Snarey, Reimer, & Kohlberg, *Developmental Psychology*, 1985, Vol. 21 p. 14. Reprinted by permission of author.)

individual fulfillment and Eastern interpersonal harmony, are examples. Those who work with young people need to be attuned to such differences in value orientation.

Emotional Issues Facing Adolescents

One of the characteristics of adolescent experience is the occurrence of relatively frequent and wide swings of emotion and mood. A young person can

Juvenile Delinquency: Courts and Corrections

Serious transgressions of society's laws can be seen in a small group of adolescents called juvenile delinquents. The causes of juvenile delinquency are not well understood. Theories of delinquency point to a number of factors that might be relevant. These theories fall into two groups: individual causes and social causes (Sametz, 1983–1984).

Theories that focus on the individual see delinquent acts as resulting from either frustration or alienation. Youths who see themselves as failures become frustrated in their attempts to achieve goals and commit crimes as a way of obtaining those goals. Some young people affirm their identity by breaking ties with others and violating values rather than adopting those values as their own.

Theories of social causes of delinquency attribute deviant behavior to the adolescent's association with a deviant subculture within the family, peer group, or neighborhood. The deviancy is thus seen as a product of the child's social network, and the child may not even be aware of the deviant nature of his or her behavior.

Some empirical justification exists for both the individual and social explanations of delinquency (Sametz, 1983–1984). Unfortunately, the tendency to resort to individual-oriented correctional approaches to delinquency has continued to grow within the juvenile justice system since its beginnings, in spite of the changes in legal rights of minors such as those reviewed in Chapter 1. In the United States, almost one million children are admitted to some kind of detention facility each year, and on any given day, 12,000 children are being held in over 300 detention centers nationwide (Pabon, 1983).

It is handcuffs from court to facility and a strip-search upon admission. It is lack of freedom, choice and spontaneity. It is separation from familiar surroundings, parents, siblings and friends. It is stale air and limited access to the outdoors, regulations, regimentation and routine. It is enforced passivity and boredom, the lack of variety in places, faces and activities. Detention is temporariness, the limbo of not knowing, of living with anxiety and uncertainty about what will happen next, of being outside one's world (Pabon, 1983, p. 42).

Most young people are arrested and brought into the juvenile justice system for *status offenses,* offenses that would not be crimes if committed by an adult. Status offenses include disobeying parents, promiscuity, and running away from home. Although many would argue that serious crimes committed by juveniles require incarceration, there is little justification for jailing status offenders, even overnight (Pabon, 1983; Sametz, 1983–1984; Huntington, 1982).

The tragedy of the status offender is that in many cases the criminal acts are those committed by families from whom the child is running: neglect, sexual abuse, and physical abuse. The problem is particularly acute for girls. Nine of every ten girls arrested are status offenders; girls are held for longer periods than boys; and girls are more likely than boys to come from problem families.

A girl might be sexually abused by her father or uncle. She runs away, becomes a prostitute, and later gets arrested. She is jailed and given therapy for her promiscuity. While in jail she is more likely than a boy to suffer sexual abuse by law enforcement and corrections personnel, and she is likely to remain in prison longer than a boy will. Because no one wants them and they are exploited by sexual inequality, these girls may spend a significant portion of their youth in an institution (Huntington, 1982).

Alternatives to detention in correctional facilities are presented in Table 17–5. A wide variety of options is available, depending upon the type and age of the child and nature of the offense, as well as on the availability of community resources.

Do alternatives to detention really work? The research is unclear on this point. Alternative methods may be abused by offenders who should have been assigned to more secure care. In addition, some alternative foster homes and group homes may be just as restrictive of the child's personal freedoms and just as prone to neglect and maltreatment of the children as was the jail or the family of origin (Reamer & Shireman, 1981).

Nevertheless, the research shows that return to delinquent behavior after release is no higher for alternative programs than for detention programs (Reamer & Shireman, 1981), and some programs are

Table 17–5

ALTERNATIVES TO DETENTION FOR JUVENILE OFFENDERS

Family-based alternatives

Consent decree	Child is given supportive help without the need of a formal hearing or a court record, including counseling for child and family.
Community probation	Child's behavior is monitored by regular contacts with court-appointed probation officer.
Home detention	Monitored by youth worker, teachers, and parents. Includes rules for regular school attendance, curfews, avoidance of drugs and alcohol, notification of adults of whereabouts.
Restitution	Rehabilitation of offender by correcting the wrongs against the victim. Includes payment of fines and restoration of damaged property.
Community service	Community work without pay for a limited duration. Teaches appreciation for the work of others and creates a sense of responsibility.
Outpatient psychotherapy	Court-ordered psychotherapy and participation in drug and alcohol abuse treatment programs.

Non-family-based alternatives

Detention and incarceration	Imprisonment focusing on improvements in self-control, decision making, self-image, goal setting, academic, and vocational skills.
Group homes	Includes group living detention as well as homes for runaways and abused children.
Foster home placement	When detention is not necessary but the family is a poor environment.

Prevention alternatives

Community youth services	Community involvement for at-risk youth. Youth involvement programs run by community service organizations such as summer camps, Big Brother/Big Sister programs.
School-based services	Expansion of special educational alternatives to children at risk for delinquency, particularly in elementary school, such as programs for hyperactivity and learning disabilities.
Early intervention	Preschool programs such as Head Start and parent education programs play a role in primary prevention of learning difficulties and family problems.

(From Haynes & Moore, 1983; Pabon, 1983; Sametz, 1983–1984.)

highly successful in integrating youth into family and community life (Henggeler, 1986). In addition, those who receive kinder treatment at times when they are developmentally vulnerable may be better able to learn constructive coping skills in later life (Sametz, 1983–1984; Sweet, 1985).

Adolescent Suicide and Depression

To many people, an adolescent suicide seems unexpected. While those who contemplate killing themselves give warning signs to others, such signs may be more difficult to read in an adolescent than in an adult. Psychiatrist John Mack (1980) lists a few warning signs: suicidal talk, extreme moodiness and deep depression, sudden loss of self-esteem, withdrawing from parents and friends, failure in school, increased substance abuse, promiscuity, loss of interest in hobbies, giving away prized possessions, and a preoccupation with death. Such signs are often ignored, because some are part of normal adolescent development. In addition, parents are highly resistant to the idea that their own child might be suicidal.

Mack traces such symptoms in the suicide of a 14-year-old girl, Vivienne, who hung herself in her mother's silversmithing studio (Mack & Hickler, 1980). Vivienne's letters to a friend and to a former teacher and her personal poetry mark a growing sense of desperation, a willingness to take risks, and a fascination with death. After one of several unsuccessful suicide attempts, Vivienne wrote to her friend:

> Last Thursday night I sort of snapped. I mean, I became disgusted with *everything,* and for the first time in a really long time I got a really selfish streak. In the afternoon Laurel and I had a terrible fight. Her friends . . . were here, but I didn't care. It was all about how my problems couldn't be Laurel's, as she had to have her own life, but I said that I needed her right now, and couldn't she help me? She said that [a boy] . . . needed her too. I said who was more important? I was irrational and so was she. In the end, I said "OK, have another evening, with [your boyfriend]. You *may* see me whenever you get in." (She was eating out with [the boy] and then spending the evening with him where he was staying.) Then I walked into the bathroom, spotted some cold pills (prescription) which were fairly powerful, and swallowed about four. Then I took the bottle with the remaining pills (about twelve left) and shut the door behind me in my room. Laurel stood outside justifying herself to [her girl friends] and nobody was paying the slightest attention to me, so I took a few more pills. I sat there and told myself that I just couldn't handle all of Mummy's problems (which she invariably brings to me now), Daddy's problems, Laurel's problems, and most of all my problems. I said, damn the family. I've carried them long enough, now I'll do something for myself.

(From VIVIENNE: *The Life and Suicide of an Adolescent Girl* by John E. Mack and Holly Hickler. Letter copyright © 1981 by David Loomis and Paulette Loomis. By permission of Little, Brown and Company.)

This is not an isolated case. In the United States every day, 13 people between the ages of 15 and 24 kill themselves. The suicide rate for this age group has tripled in the past 30 years, and suicide is now the third leading cause of death for this age group (*Science News*, October 27, 1984). Every year over 2,000 teens will kill themselves, and somewhere between 20,000 and 40,000 will try. Suicide rates for different countries are given in Table 17–6.

It seems odd that the countries with the highest suicide rates for males—Austria and Switzerland, mountainous countries in the beautiful Alps—are among the most picturesque in the world. Indeed, no clear reason exists for the differences in suicide rates between countries and sexes.

Among the risk factors associated with suicide attempts are displaying impulsive behavior, being a victim of child abuse, having a family history of suicide, having a close friend who commits suicide, having psychiatric disorders, especially extreme depression, and having a perception of being unwanted and unloved by family and friends (*Science News,* October 27, 1984; Triolo, McKenry, Tishler, & Blyth, 1984; Weiner, 1980). These findings suggest that withdrawal, alienation, and depression are the most common symptoms of adolescents who attempt suicide.

One of the problems in recognizing symptoms of suicide is that depression in adolescence is marked not by introspective preoccupation of the type seen in adults but by some of the following symptoms: extreme fatigue, substance abuse, lack of concentration, restlessness, a constant need for change to avoid thinking about the self, running away from difficult situations to relieve fears of being rejected, and appealing for attention through antisocial, rebellious, or delinquent acts (Weiner, 1980).

It is better to assume the worst if you suspect someone might be suicidal. Psychologists have found that

Table 17–6

INCIDENCE OF SUICIDE IN
INDUSTRIALIZED NATIONS
FOR AGES 15 TO 24 YEARS,
BASED ON 1981 STATISTICS

Country	Males	(per 100,000) Females
Austria	33.6	6.8
Switzerland	33.5	10.2
Denmark	17.1	5.0
West Germany	21.1	6.4
Sweden	14.3	4.1
France	14.6	5.0
Poland	19.5	4.3
Japan	14.8	6.4
UNITED STATES	19.7	4.6
Norway	20.2	3.3
Australia	17.6	4.5
United Kingdom	7.0	2.1
Israel	10.8	1.2

(From *The 1986 Information Please Almanac*, p. 133.)

the likelihood of a second suicide attempt is significantly reduced if parents and friends can help by being supportive, listening to problems without making judgments, asking questions, and talking openly about the person's depression and thoughts about suicide. Responding to the person with anger, scorn, or lack of interest increases the likelihood of further attempts (Weiner, 1980). One can also help a friend find professional counseling and therapy. Greater understanding of suicide and willingness to recognize that a close friend or relative may feel suicidal is the best prevention.

go from wide-eyed enthusiasm to the depths of despair in a relatively short time. Even though, as we found earlier in this chapter, identity and values remain relatively stable over the adolescent years negating the "storm and stress" idea for most adolescents, the individual may still experience a variety of "small" highs and lows in the course of everyday experience. The fluctuations of good and bad feelings seem to occur more often during adolescence than during other times in the life cycle. In a small number of cases, these emotional swings can lead to depression and suicide.

According to Csikszentmihalyi and Larson (1984), whose theory of creativity was reviewed in Chapter 16, adolescents struggle to find order in their emotional lives. The adolescent is more cognitively aware than the younger child of the role of society in shaping behavior, such as attending school, performing chores, or conforming to social standards. Conflicts between goals and rules often lead to negative emotions. These negative emotions, listed in Table 17–7, are experienced as disorder, as a loss of control, or as an unpleasant state. Subsequent to this experience of disorder, the adolescent tries actively to regain a sense of psychic order, a sense of feeling in control or of feeling good.

Csikzentmihalyi and Larson (1984) studied the daily life and experience of a large number of adolescents. Their study was unique, since it did not use questionnaires, subjects' responses to standard dilemmas, or even direct observation of subjects under controlled conditions.

Their method is called the *Experience Sampling Method* (ESM). Each member of a randomly selected group of adolescents was given an electronic pager, similar to the kind that doctors carry, and a pad of self-report forms.

Table 17—7

THE ADOLESCENT'S
EMOTIONAL WORLD

Negative Emotions

Bad moods	Sadness, loneliness, anger, irritability, frustration, anxiety, guilt, alienation, e.g., refusing to do an assignment because of anger at a teacher.
Tired	Passivity, vegetating, boredom, e.g., staying up late followed by a week of exhaustion.
Loss of motivation	Goal confusion, conflict, inability to do a required task if a more desirable activity is unable to be performed, e.g., inability to do homework if forced to stay home while friends go out.
Unfocused attention	E.g., unable to do homework because of being "madly in love."

Positive Emotions

Positive feelings	Happiness, friendliness, good cheer, commitment, enthusiasm, e.g., a smile or wink from the opposite sex.
Psychological activation	Energy, competence, acting without hesitation, e.g., cooking, games, sports.
Intrinsic motivation	Identification with activity, e.g., going out on a date.
Effective concentration	Absorbed in activity with full concentration and clarity, e.g., doing math, music, or sports.

(From Csikszentmihalyi & Larson, 1984, pp. 19–25.)

At a random moment within every two-hour waking period, the pager was signaled and the adolescent was asked to write down what he or she was doing and feeling at that moment.

The method captured the subjects in all kinds of activities, and because an observer was not immediately present and the responses were confidential, the subjects were extremely honest and open about their activities and emotions. As a result, this study is one of the most comprehensive sources of data about the day-to-day experiences of the normal adolescent.

Participation in athletics makes high school males more popular.

513

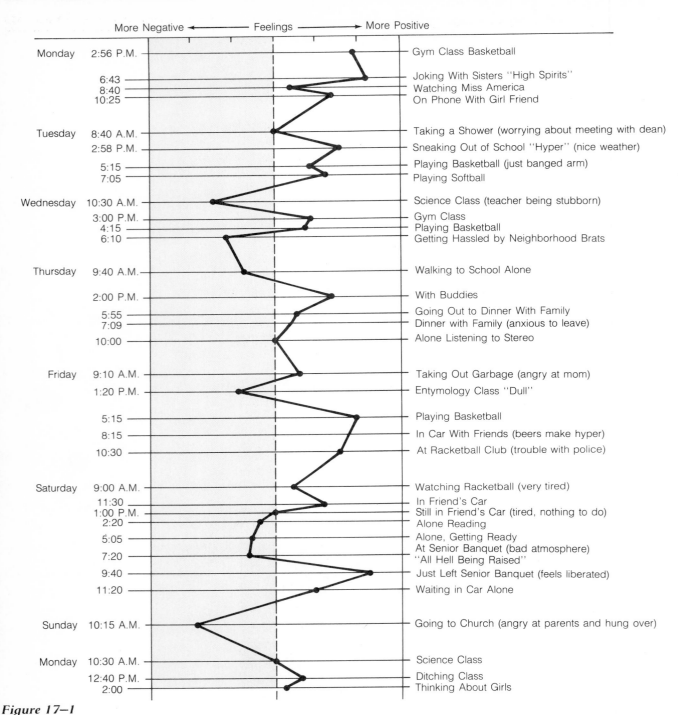

Figure 17—1

A Week in the Life of Jerzy Madigan: Aged 17, Football Star at Belmont High, Average Student

(From *Being Adolescent: Conflict and Growth in the Teenage Years* by Mihaly Csikszentmihalyi and Reed Larson. Copyright © 1984 by Basic Books, Inc., Publishers. Reprinted by permission of the publisher.)

Figure 17—1 shows the activities and emotional states of one week in the life of Jerzy Madigan. It clearly documents the wide emotional swings of his daily life. The low points of negative emotion are usually generated by some external event that inhibits other desires or goals. Disappointments, lack of experience in handling certain situations, and the boredom of everyday events are the sources of psychic disorder.

Adolescents' emotions occur in the contexts of peer group, family, and school. The next sections of this chapter take a closer look at these contexts during the adolescent years.

The Peer Group

During adolescence, the social world of the child expands dramatically. A good deal of this change comes about because of the move from elementary to junior and senior high school. Instead of sitting in the same classroom and having only a few teachers, the junior high school student moves between classes and may have as many as seven or eight teachers. In addition, most junior highs are bigger than elementary schools, exposing children to a wider variety of peers.

Informal activities also increase. School clubs, sports, organizations such as the YMCA and YWCA, part-time jobs, and social activities such as parties and school dances contribute to the diversity of the adolescent's social experiences.

In senior high, the school may become the center of the adolescent's world. Adolescents develop peer relationships that satisfy mutual needs leading to the formation of gangs, crowds, and cliques. High school students have a great deal of control over their social life, with the freedom to select activities, friends, and dates. This freedom is enhanced if the individual is earning money independent of his or her parents (Higgins & Parsons, 1984).

Most high school students do not have total freedom, however. They are not permitted to be self-supporting, cannot vote or buy alcoholic beverages, and are not permitted to marry without adult consent. In addition, recent research shows that parents still play a major role in how both high school and college students respond to the freedoms and responsibilities of their expanding social world.

Family Versus Peer Relationships

Some theories of socialization tend to portray the peer group as a source of developmental change that is independent of the family. It has been thought that the peer group is where the child learns autonomy from the family, brought about by the increased conformity of the adolescent with the norms of the peer group.

Peers are thought to influence dress and life styles, while parents influence career choices. Peers are thought to share intimate feelings that could never be shared between children and parents, and peer friendships are considered to be buffers to alleviate parent-child conflict. In sum, peer friendships are considered to be *egalitarian*, while the parent-child relationship is considered to be *hierarchical* (Hartup, 1979; 1983).

The view that parent-child and peer relationships constitute separate and independent social worlds has received little support from research studies. Peer *conformity*—defined as the susceptibility to peer influence over one's own perceptions—has been shown to increase and peak during early adolescence and to decline thereafter (Costanzo, 1970). Thus, conformity to peer norms is a rather short-lived phenomenon.

When adolescents are asked to decide between conforming to the values of parents and conforming to the values of peers, they are just as likely to take the parents' view as the peers', and in many instances there is little or no conflict between the parents' and peers' values (Coleman, 1980). These findings suggest that adolescents tend to choose friends who share the values of their families.

In addition, parents exert indirect influence over the kinds of peers with whom their children are likely to contact through their choice of neighborhood, school, and church and exert direct influence by approval or disapproval of friendship choices (Rubin & Sloman, 1984). In an interview study of parents' roles in the formation of peer relationships, parents with children in early adolescence report coaching their children about peer relationship problems or recommending strategies for mediating disputes or for dealing with shyness (Rubin & Sloman, 1984; Steinberg, 1987).

Parent-child and peer relationships are thus not independent but rather, overlap. In addition, during adolescence, parent-child relationships shift from hierarchical to egalitarian. We have already reviewed research showing that higher levels of parent-child mutuality are associated with adolescent identity formation (Grotevant & Cooper, 1985). It may be that parent-child mutuality trains children in perspective-taking skills that enhance both parent-child and peer relationships (Cooper & Ayers-Lopez, 1985).

Intimacy in friendship is an essential part of the adolescent experience; the ability to share one's deepest feelings in the context of a trusting relationship.

Peer Friendships and Intimacy

What about the hypothesis that peer relationships in adolescence are egalitarian and marked by mutuality and social support? Although children develop stable friendships during the preschool and middle childhood years, the nature of the friend relationship and the things friends do with and say to each other change over time. Early adolescence seems to mark an increase in intimacy between friends. *Intimacy* is the willingness to share inner thoughts and feelings through self-disclosure.

While elementary schoolchildren tend to value helping, acceptance, and common interests, children beginning in the sixth grade seek out friends who will be loyal, open, and honest and with whom they can share intimate feelings (Bigelow & LaGaipa, 1975). Between fifth and twelfth grade there is a steady increase in ratings of agreement with statements about intimacy with friends, such as "I feel free to talk with him (her) about almost everything" and "I know how he (she) feels about things without his (her) having to tell me" and "I speak up to defend him (her) when other kids say bad things about him (her)" (Sharabany, Gershoni, & Hofman, 1981). In addition to agreeing with these statements, junior high school students have more knowledge of the intimate details of their friends' lives than do elementary school students (Diaz & Berndt, 1982).

In yet another type of study, pairs of children are given tasks on which they can work either competitively or cooperatively to get small sums of money. They could work to get the most money for themselves, or they could pool their efforts and share the money. Eighth graders were more willing than fourth or sixth graders to cooperate and share (Berndt, 1985).

Sex Differences in Intimacy.   Because of girls' tendency to value "commun-ion" and boys' tendency to value "agency," we might expect girls to show more intimacy in peer relationships than boys; this has been found to be the case. Girls are more likely to describe intimate conversations between friends and express greater concern about friends' faithfulness and rejection, perhaps because of fears that former friends may tell others about their intimate secrets (Berndt, 1982).

On the other hand, boys seem to know just as much as girls about intimate details of their friends, suggesting that although girls share and acquire intimate information through long conversations, boys may have other means to gain such knowledge (Berndt, 1982). Although little research is available, one study found that while girls self-disclose emotions in intimate one-to-one relationships, boys share actions and experiences in group activities such as sports (Camarena, 1985).

Cross-Sex Friendships

In a Midwestern city, about one-fourth of the children in grades six through eight reported dating and having an opposite-sex girlfriend or boyfriend. However, 50 percent of sixth graders and 70 percent of eighth graders reported social telephone calls with members of the opposite sex. Thus, even though very few children said they had an intimate friend of the opposite sex, a quarter had started dating, and most were talking regularly with the opposite sex showing the beginnings of a shift in attention to the opposite sex beginning as early as the sixth grade (Crockett, Losoff, & Petersen, 1984).

By high school, adolescents report similar levels of intimacy between opposite-sex friends as they had for same-sex friends in junior high school (Sharabany et al., 1981). The incidence of exclusive opposite-sex relationships—"going steady—also increases during the high school years. Not all "steadies" plan to marry, however. Those twelfth graders who plan to marry their current steady tend to be white females without college plans who come from a relatively low social class family (Gordon & Miller, 1984).

In many cases, both same-sex and opposite-sex friendships in adolescence are not exclusive relationships. Young people tend to do things in groups of varying sizes that are composed of individuals who are all close friends.

Peer Friendships and Groups

Adolescent groups fall into two categories: cliques and crowds. *Cliques* are smaller groups than crowds. They involve intimate relationships in which friends go places and do things together. They tend to be closed to outsiders. Cliques are unisexual during early adolescence and may become heterosexual during middle and late adolescence (Coleman, 1980).

Research shows that cliques usually have less than six members. Members tend to be from the same social and economic background, are in the same grade, and have the same values and tastes, thus enhancing the sense of being different from others (Coleman, 1980). Adolescents tend to spend over 80 percent of their free time in groups rather than alone or with only one other person, and by eighth grade, most children feel positively toward cliquishness (Crockett et al., 1984).

Crowds tend to be associations of cliques. Although cliques tend to operate on weekdays, crowds come together on weekends. Cliques are preoccupied with conversation and communication, while crowds are concerned with organized social activities such as parties, dances, and sporting events (Coleman, 1980).

Cliques are believed to enhance the formation of identity, since the members are similar to each other and different from nonclique members. The clique's intimacy and mutuality may function as a kind of surrogate family in the promotion of self-esteem and reasoning about identity.

Crowds, on the other hand, are thought to facilitate heterosexual relationships by bringing together cliques of different sexes in the context of social activities. In the crowd, individuals can practice new social roles, especially heterosexual roles, under the watchfulness and "protection" of other members of the clique (Dunphy, 1963). There are too few research studies in this area, however, to establish with certainty the processes of group dynamics and to ascertain the contribution peer groups make to individual development. The existing research also has failed to examine peer relationships in a variety of social status, ethnic, and racial groups.

Popularity in the Peer Group. Some children participate more in groups and get more out of them than other children. What makes an adolescent popular or lonely? Although most peer interactions center around school, studies have shown that academic competence is definitely not a factor in determining popularity among adolescents. By middle adolescence, a girl's popularity is determined by physical appearance and social skills or personality, while boys become popular primarily for their athletic achievement (Coleman, 1960; Crockett et al., 1984).

The research in this area is controversial, however, since the relationship between popularity and these factors holds primarily for the individuals in the extremes. The most attractive and least attractive girls will likely be the most and least popular. For the vast majority of girls who fall somewhere in the middle range of physical attractiveness, however, physical attractiveness does not seem to relate to popularity in any predictable ways (Cavior & Dokecki, 1973).

In addition, settings other than school tend to yield different indicators of popularity. For example, in a summer camp setting of 16- and 17-year-old females, both interpersonal skills and athletic ability were associated with popularity (Paikoff & Savin-Williams, 1983). Thus, while the heterosexual and achievement-oriented environment of the school popularizes traditional female traits of interpersonal skills and attractiveness, in the all-female summer camp, athletic ability replaces physical attractiveness in popularity ratings.

Loneliness and Alienation. It is difficult to specify why certain children are less liked and more withdrawn than others. Loneliness in adolescence is associated with depression, self-consciousness, feelings of inferiority, anxiety about social encounters, unwillingness to take social risks, and self-reported low physical attractiveness (Goswick & Jones, 1982; Moore & Schultz, 1983). Loneliness is the opposite end of the social scale from popularity, since popular children have high interpersonal skills while lonely children have poor interpersonal skills (Marcoen & Brumagne, 1985).

Alienation—a rejection of the values of the school and peer group—leads often to being alone but is not the same as loneliness. Lonely adolescents feel sad and depressed about their loneliness, while alienation is a more active rejection of the adolescent culture that is associated with the individual's identity. Alienation, like poor identity formation, is associated with deviance-proneness and aggressive behavior, including negative attitudes toward the school (Kulka, Kahle, & Klingel, 1982). In addition, there are significantly higher rates of alienation among lower social class, lower social status adolescents, suggesting that alienation is related to sociocultural attitudes toward certain groups (Holmgren, Fitzgerald, & Carman, 1983).

Children cope with loneliness and alienation in different ways. Although feelings of alienation often lead to rebellious, delinquent, or antisocial behavior, loneliness leads to increases in solitary activities such as watching TV or listening to music (Moore & Schultz, 1983). These findings suggest that interventions directed toward these difficulties should be different.

Adolescent alienation may be helped by changing the individual's attitudes toward the school or by offering special programs in the school to reach out to these children. Their families, who are typically low on parent-child mutuality or who may come from social and cultural groups that themselves are alienated from the mainstream of society, need to be approached and empowered as equal partners in the educational task (Cervantes, 1982; Kulka et al., 1982).

Loneliness deprives adolescents of a sense of belonging, closes off participation in social activities, and makes the individual feel in limbo. Although a certain amount of time spent alone is normal and adaptive for adolescents (Csikszentmihalyi & Larson, 1984), excessive time alone leads to boredom and other negative emotions. Parents can help by facilitating relationships and offering new ways in which the adolescent can participate in social activities with a minimum of social risk taking (Moore & Schultz, 1983).

The Family

As we've seen in this and the previous chapter, the family plays an extremely important role in adolescent development. Just at the time when the adolescent is attempting to break out of the family patterns of middle childhood to achieve an identity, the family's response to the adolescent is more crucial than even the peer group in this developmental process.

The Adolescent's Perception of Family Conflicts

We saw in the last section that the peer group does not replace the family in the adolescent's social world. Research on the adolescent's perception of the family shows that there are fewer conflicts over less serious issues than one might imagine.

Jerzy Madigan, whose week was illustrated in Figure 17–1, had this to say when he was paged at 10:15 AM on a Sunday morning:

> I never want to go to church, but I'll go. Finally I get a Sunday off; I don't have to work, so I can sleep a little later. But now I've got to go to church. I've got to wake up earlier than if I'd had to go to work.
>
> They always wake you up, and they're always cheerful, and you go "oh, no!." They act cheerful, but they are really hostile if you don't want to go.
>
> Right then I'd just asked them to turn the channel. They were listening to some opera stuff. They just ignored me; you know, because we were parking and everything. Still, they could have acknowledged me. That's why I was so upset. I went, "Jesus Christ, at least they could answer me."
>
> (Csikszentmihalyi & Larson, 1984, p. 141.)

This kind of attitude is typical of parent-child conflict during the adolescent years. In one study, 150 tenth graders from intact families with an average of 3.8 siblings were interviewed over the telephone on three randomly

Even though the school and peer group occupy a good deal of the adolescent's time, the family remains an important source of support for most teens.

selected evenings at about one-week intervals. They were asked if they had interactions with parents or siblings that resulted in a conflict.

It was found that adolescents had conflicts with their siblings about as much as with their parents. In addition, conflicts tended to be over interpersonal issues such as teasing, annoying behavior, whose turn it was to do a certain chore, or being courteous (Montmayor & Hanson, 1985).

In general, parents and adolescents rarely argue over difficult topics such as drugs, sex, politics, religion, or identity struggles but rather about day-to-day annoyances produced when people of different personalities live under the same roof. Adolescent complaints that "my parents don't understand me" more often revolve around such day-to-day issues than around larger issues of values and beliefs. This has been consistently found in research studies going back to 1929. Even during the 1960s, the civil rights movement, the Vietnam war, and college student protests did not surface as major sources of parent-child conflict (Montmayor, 1983).

Some studies have found that adolescent annoyance with parental criticism may not be entirely unfounded. Parents' criticisms often reflect actual undesirable behavior of the child but may also reflect the parents' own preconceived notions of what the child should be or do.

In a study of 883 high school students asking them about the kinds of criticisms they received from parents, boys were more often criticized for being disobedient, not applying themselves, being impulsive, and having undesirable friends, while girls felt criticized for being foolish, unappreciative, quarrelsome, and stubborn. Sons, therefore, are criticized for not being goal-oriented and achievement-minded and daughters for not being affectionate and sensitive (Harris & Howard, 1984). Thus, parental sex-role stereotypes—males should be breadwinners, females should be social and nurturant—are embedded in day-to-day socialization practices.

Some adolescents complain that their parents are "unfair" in their treatment of them compared to their brothers and sisters. This perception, too, has

Are Long-Term Effects of Divorce During Early Childhood Felt During Adolescence?

Divorce and reconstitution of families is more common today than ever before. Because of the importance of peers in identity formation and the tendency of adolescents to select peers with similar family backgrounds and values, one might think that the sharing of experiences between adolescents of divorced parents would lessen the long-term impact of divorce.

Until recently, most studies of divorce focused on the short-term effects of divorce and of living in a single-parent, or father-absent, family. This research on short-term (one to four years after the divorce) effects has shown that the age at which the divorce occurs is a significant factor in how the divorce will affect the children.

Preschool children show disruptions of behavior such as eating and sleeping problems, tantrums, and sullenness, five- to eight-year-olds suffer feelings of rejection and sadness, and nine- to twelve-year-olds are frightened and worry about how it will affect their transition to puberty and adolescence. Adolescents whose parents divorce are concerned about their own ability to form a successful marriage. Some may show signs of depression, substance abuse, and suicide attempts, while others may feel angry and sad that they have lost their home. In general, adolescents find it more difficult to make the transition to an effective stepparent-child relationship than do younger children (Cox & Cox, 1984; Farber, Primavera, & Felner, 1983).

The negative effects of divorce during the adolescent years may often persist into the college years. Young people whose parents had divorced five to seven years before still had negative views of marriage and felt dissatisfied with their heterosexual relationships (Kelly, 1981). Even though teenagers would rather live in a one-parent home than a two-parent home that is full of parental conflict (McLoughlin & Whitfield, 1984), teens living in single-parent homes have a lower self-concept (Rosenthal, Peng, & McMillan, 1980) and show more deviant behavior than do children living in intact families (Dornbusch et al., 1985; Steinberg, 1987).

In a study comparing freshman college students whose parents had divorced before they were 11 years old with students from intact families, the students from divorced families described their relationships with their parents as more distant, less affectionate and warm, and less communicative (Fine, Moreland, & Schwebel, 1983). This same study found, however, that certain conditions alleviated the negative impact of the divorce. For example, among students coming from divorced families, a higher quality of current father-child relations was associated with perceptions of a positive predivorce family life and with parents who had more frequent contact after the divorce.

More positive current perceptions of the mother-child relationship were correlated with more positive predivorce mother-child ties, better adjustment of the teenager to the single-mother family at the time of divorce (92 percent of this sample were in the custody of the mothers), and a higher quality postdivorce relationship between the parents.

Thus, the relationship of the noncustodial father with the children and mother following divorce is a crucial element in the children's adjustment. Continuing arguments between parents and mothers who shut out the children's father or make noncustodial visits difficult or infrequent do damage to the children's relationship not only with the father but also with the mother.

some element of truth to it. A study of 348 families with more than one child (232 Caucasian, 116 minority, mostly black) interviewed adolescents and their parents about parent-child closeness, expectations, and conflicts. The results showed that the sibling in the family who is better adjusted (less emotional distress, more obedient, and more satisfied with life and the family) also experiences more maternal closeness, more sibling and peer friendliness, more say in family decision making, and more parental chore expectations than the other, less well-adjusted sibling (Daniels, Dunn, Furstenberg, & Plomin, 1985).

Even considering the sometimes arbitrary and prejudicial way in which parents may sometimes behave with their adolescents, 40 percent of middle-class junior high school students in another study attended religious services with the family, and one-third participated on a weekly basis in family outings, projects, chores, and entertainment such as visiting relatives, playing games, and watching TV together. On a daily basis, 85 percent to 90 percent of a sample of 335 sixth, seventh, and eighth graders from middle-class Caucasian families ate with and talked to their parents, while 50 percent reported watching TV with parents on a daily basis (Richardson, Galambos, Schulenberg, & Petersen, 1984).

Toward the Future: The School and the Wider World

The final section of this chapter looks at areas that will lead the adolescent into his or her future life. In particular this section considers attitudes toward school achievement and adolescents' ideas about and expectations for future families and occupations.

Perceptions of the School Experience

Many teachers and parents believe that most junior and senior high school students care little about academic achievement. Is this really true? Two major studies of teenagers' attitudes toward school suggest that it is not the case. One study interviewed 335 middle-class Caucasian junior high school students (Schulenberg, Asp, & Petersen, 1984) and found that far more students aspired to be a "straight-A student" than to be either a "star athlete" or "most popular." In addition, the survey found that the primary causes of worry (in response to the question, What are your main concerns in life right now?) were grades and homework.

Surprisingly, this study found that math and science classes were most often chosen as the favorite class for both boys and girls; girls, however, tended to receive higher grades than boys. In terms of extracurricular activities, both sexes most often participated first in athletics and next in music.

The study of high school students by Csikszentmihalyi and Larson (1984) has similar findings. When paged during class, students reported that 78 percent of the classtime was taken up with academic activity such as listening, discussing, or doing classwork. However, their reported moods during class were more negative than positive. The students described active struggles with boredom, irritability, fatigue, concentration, and desire to be elsewhere. On the other hand, many managed to control these negative states to tune into the classwork for a sufficient amount of time.

Contrary to the findings for the junior high students, high school students are more likely to report positive feelings in classes that require other than academic skills such as industrial arts, physical education, and music. Negative feelings were associated with math, foreign languages, and English. This may be due to the greater difficulty of concentration in the more academic subjects. Teachers who were the most successful at maintaining positive emotions during class were those who were the best entertainers and who could help the students pull the material into their lives in a meaningful way.

In general, students at both junior and senior high school levels view academic achievement as important and are more concerned about grades than about social events. This pattern continues into college, where worries about studying and grades make up over 50 percent of the students' requests for counseling and psychotherapy (Blaine & McArthur, 1971). This reflects a good deal of future orientation on the part of those adolescents who are college oriented, although we can't say much about those who are not college oriented.

For most adolescents, it seems, school can be a positive and academically rewarding experience. School is viewed by many teens as their "job" at this time in their lives and as a preparation for future advancement, and as such it is approached seriously and with some measure of commitment.

Problems with the School Experience

Underachievement and school failures are often caused by too much pressure for achievement from home. Students can "get back" at their parents by doing less well in school and thereby defeating their parents' dreams and purposes. Other students hold back so as not to draw attention to themselves or not to "show up" their friends, siblings, or parents' past performance. Still others may let their school performance slip while keeping up with intellectually challenging extracurricular areas such as current events or computers (Weiner, 1980).

Other problems—extreme dislike of school and anxiety about school attendance, called *school phobia*—may have little to do with feelings about academic achievement but affect achievement nevertheless. School phobia has been associated with having overprotective parents and thus a difficulty separating from the family, discomfort with pubertal changes and the fear of humiliation during gym class, and social concerns such as the fear of rejection by peers (Weiner, 1980).

Moving Toward Adulthood

The age at which people make the transition from childhood to adulthood depends primarily on social and cultural conditions. As we saw in Chapter 16, initiation into adulthood and the termination of adolescence are due partly to cultural beliefs. They may also be due to the occurrence of unexpected events—such as natural disasters, epidemics, wars, and famine—that change society and make demands for adultlike behavior from people younger than what is typical for that society (Foner & Kertzer, 1979).

In North America, individuals are not expected to act or think like adults until relatively late in adolescence, and the research suggests that few adolescents have mature concepts of marriage or work roles. We can think of adolescence as a period in the life cycle when the individual begins to explore adult role concepts but is still far from attaining a set life plan(Csikszentmihalyi & Larson, 1984).

Concepts about Marriage and Family. As we saw earlier, dating does not usually begin until middle adolescence, and the vast majority of high school graduates are not yet ready for marriage. Most college freshmen express rather idealized and unrealistic expectations about marriage, suggesting that marriage before the age of 20 years is likely to pose significant risks for later separation and divorce (Robson, 1983).

Most adolescents in fact seem to be aware of this risk. In a sample of 557 teenage women (25.7 percent white, 43 percent black, 17.6 percent Hispanic, 8.4 percent Asian, and 5.3 percent other), the group as a whole rated a good education and financial independence over a good marriage as a life goal. Being a mother and childrearing was ranked seventh and eighth in importance, suggesting an awareness that motherhood was not in their best interests.

Research on adolescents' responsiveness to babies tend to confirm this pattern. Responsiveness to babies was measured by reactions to photos of babies and to live babies with and without an adult present. In high school, males are considerably less interested in and responsive to babies than females. In college, however, there are no sex differences in responsiveness to babies. These results are due partly to differential sex-role expectations for adolescent boys and girls and partly to a greater receptivity to marriage and family life of older males (Feldman & Nash, 1979).

Individual differences exist between girls, however, in the life path they see for themselves. Using longitudinal data collected in the 1930s, the high school career and family aspirations of girls were found to be related to girls' future life course. Girls who were most concerned with having a good marriage and family while in high school were most preoccupied with boys and dating and tended to bear more children in their adult years. Girls who sought a good education and a career were more preoccupied with academics, grades, and issues other than boy-girl relationships. As adults, these women married after finishing school and started having children at a later age (Elder & MacInnis, 1983).

Vocational Role Development.   Attitudes toward marriage and family are closely bound with attitudes toward vocational goals, since most people must struggle to balance work with family. As with marriage concepts and expectations, vocational role choices during adolescence are relatively undeveloped.

The period between 15 and 24 years has been called the exploration phase of vocational development and has three substages: tentative, transition, and trial (Super, 1953). During the tentative stage, between 15 and 17 years, vocational choices are made in fantasy and proposed to parents and peers. During the transition stage, between approximately 18 and 21 years, the individual becomes committed to some form of professional training leading to an intended career goal. During the trial phase, from 22 to 24 years, the career choice is tried out in an appropriate job. Empirical research, though sparse, tends to confirm that vocational commitment and stability do not occur until the late 20s or later (Vondracek & Lerner, 1982). The research has been, however, limited mostly to middle-income groups.

What careers do high school students fantasize for themselves? Most studies find clear and consistent sex differences in career choices. Junior high students of both sexes selected arts and entertainment careers (artist, actor, athlete, musician) more than any other. Boys ranked technological (engineer, mechanic, air traffic controller) and outdoor (forest ranger, surveyor, heavy machinery operator) careers higher than did girls. Girls preferred careers involving service (social worker, police officer), general culture (teacher, lawyer), organization (bank teller, computer programmer), science, and sales (Erb, 1983).

Differences in career choices may be due to social role expectations for males and females. On the other hand, they may be due to the individual's own identity orientations. For example, Stake (1978) found that college females wanted jobs with greater intrinsic work enjoyment and fewer financial re-

Part-time jobs may help teens make the transition to the responsibility required in work roles, so long as the job does not detract from the individual's school and social life.

sponsibilities than did males. Jobs with higher financial responsibilities and work time commitments were viewed negatively by some females because of possible conflicts with future family life (McLure & Piel, 1978).

Career orientations are influenced by a complex network of relationships best described by ecological systems theory (Young, 1983). Within the microsystem, family influences derive from parent-child interaction, identification with parental values, parental support, and differential sex-role socialization practices. Other microsystems that contribute to career choices are the school, peer group, and work place.

Work experience during the adolescent years has not been found to contribute effectively either to vocational role choice or to short-term goals such as enhancing self-management, taking responsibility, or being exposed to the world of adults. This is because the kind of work usually available to adolescents does not make cognitive demands or lead to subsequent employment. Most adolescent work is in unskilled jobs doing routine tasks. In addition, adolescents who never have such jobs are just as likely to assume adult work roles as are those who do (Steinberg, 1982). Furthermore, such jobs may have a negative effect on teenagers. Since the labor force continues to shift to white-collar and professional jobs, the best training for such work is academic success in schools and universities. Extensive work time in unskilled positions leads to spending less time with family and school and may lower the adolescent's chances for academic success (Greenberger & Steinberg, 1981; Steinberg, 1982).

Other aspects of ecological system have not been as well researched. The mesosystem involves the relationships between the family or school and the work place. More research is needed to determine the effect on adolescent development of field trips, work experience programs as part of the curriculum, and bringing professionals into the school environment (Young, 1983).

The exosystem influence on career development involves social contexts in which the child does not directly participate. Such contexts include social class, maternal employment, the mass media, the family's social network, and public policy, including child labor laws and legislation that increases the opportunities for disadvantaged youths and provides financial aid for higher education. Chapter 1 reviewed some of the historical changes in exosystem factors that affected children's entrance into the work force, and Chapter 11 reviewed the effects of maternal employment on children.

The macrosystem influences include the role of women, the culture's attitudes toward work, achievement, and education, and technological change. Although these are all potential contributors to adolescent career development, there is little research on their effects (Young, 1983).

The research on both marriage and family and on vocational role development seems to suggest that better paying careers in our increasingly technological society are those that are attained through academic achievement during late adolescence. Early marriage as well as early work experience is not necessarily conducive to white-collar and professional employment goals. This means that for many older teenagers in advanced nations, school is their work, and financial dependence on the family of origin extends well into young adulthood.

The relatively underdeveloped concepts of marriage, family, and work roles—and the highly developed commitment to academic achievement—for adolescents in complex societies may reflect the demands such societies place on higher levels of technological attainment through schooling. The end result is that the demands of the exosystem and macrosystem have extended the period of adolescence by delaying young people's entry into adulthood until their vocational training is completed.

Chapter Summary

THE DEVELOPMENT OF A PERSONAL IDENTITY
□ Although adolescents experience some emotional conflict, most children negotiate adolescence without major crises.
□ Research on identity shows an increasing amount of role commitment to occupational, political, and religious ideals during the adolescent years. Mature identity is achieved sometime during the college years.

□ Families play an important role in the achievement of higher levels of commitment and identity. Adolescents who are able to communicate openly and express independent views with parents reach higher levels of identity status.

VALUES AND MORALITY
□ Consistent sex differences in values are found across cultures, with males valuing agency and females valuing communion.
□ Adolescents acquire the values of the family and of the culture in which they live.
□ Family and culture, as well as level of cognitive development, contribute to the formation of postconventional moral reasoning.
□ Advances in moral reasoning are due to active participation in social groups—peer and family groups.

EMOTIONAL ISSUES FACING ADOLESCENTS
□ Adolescents are subject to wide swings from positive to negative emotions.
□ Most adolescents become increasingly able to turn negative emotions into positive ones to maintain psychological order.

THE PEER GROUP
□ Entry into junior and senior high school expands the adolescents' contact with peers.
□ Parents affect the kinds of friends adolescents make, through supervision, advice, and establishment of parent-child mutuality.
□ Peer conformity peaks in early adolescence and declines thereafter.
□ Intimacy in peer friendships increases with age for both boys and girls.
□ During early and middle adolescence, intimate friendships are same-sex. Cross-sex intimate friendships increase significantly during the high school and college years.
□ Cliques contribute to adolescent identity formation.
□ Popularity of the individual depends on the context and on a wide variety of individual factors. No one factor determines popularity.

THE FAMILY
□ Parents and adolescents seldom come into conflict over difficult topics such as religion and drugs. Most parent-child conflict is over day-to-day matters stemming from living under the same roof.
□ Families can be important sources of support for adolescents, and family rituals provide important sources of positive attachments to the family.

TOWARD THE FUTURE: THE SCHOOL AND THE WIDER WORLD
□ Most adolescents take seriously their academic achievement.
□ School problems may have to do with conflicts over identity, achievement, or family problems.
□ Marriage before the age of 20 may pose risks for later separation and divorce due to idealized and unrealistic expectations for marriage and low male responsiveness to babies before this age.
□ Commitment to vocational roles is not generally complete until the early to mid-twenties.
□ Work experience during adolescence may detract from rather than enhance future vocational goals, since the best training for higher level jobs is to be found in schools and colleges.
□ The period of adolescence, including financial dependency on the family of origin and lack of commitment to adult roles, is longer in complex technological societies than in simpler ones.

Recommended Readings

Erikson, E. (1950). *Childhood and society.* New York: Norton. Refers to the adolescent identity crisis and suggests other works by Erikson that deal with youth, change, and crisis.

Frank, A. (1952). *The diary of a young girl* (trans. B. M. Mooyaart-Doubleday). New York: Doubleday. A touching and engaging journey through adolescence, written as a diary while hiding from the Nazis during World War II.

Mack, J. E., and Hickler, H. (1981). *Vivienne: The life and suicide of an adolescent girl.* New York: New American Library. The history of a suicide as told by a psychiatrist and as expressed in the letters and poems of Vivienne herself.

GLOSSARY

Accommodation The changes that occur in existing skills in the process of meeting new challenges from the environment.

Actometer Automatic recording device for measuring a child's activity level.

Adaptation The process by which individuals adjust their behavior to enhance their ability to survive in a particular environment.

Adiposity Proportion of fat cells (or *adipose* cells) in the body.

Adolescent egocentrism A preoccupation about the self, and the assumption that everyone else is also preoccupied with him or her.

Agency Typically male value orientation including competence, assertiveness, ambition, and effectiveness.

Age norm The percentage of infants of a particular age that are able to pass an item on an assessment test.

Alienation An active rejection of the values of the school, family and/or peer group, leading to a self-imposed separateness from others.

Allele A gene whose action depends upon at least one other gene, its allellic counterpart, to determine the phenotype. Usually, alleles are found at the same location on each chromosome of a paired set.

Allergen Substance to which individual is allergic.

Altruism Behavior motivated by the desire to benefit another, even at a cost of oneself.

Amniocentesis A test for birth defects in which a small portion of amniotic fluid is extracted for testing of genetic and chromosomal disorders.

Amniotic fluid A watery substance that surrounds the embryo and fetus.

Amniotic sac A membrane that encloses the embryo and fetus containing amniotic fluid in which the fetus floats. It provides a natural cushion against abrupt movements of the mother's body.

Anal stage Psychoanalytic stage in which the child becomes interested in the body's waste products, self-control and autonomy.

Analgesia Drugs used for relief of pain.

Androgens Male hormones, including *testosterone*, that help create secondary sexual characteristics.

Androgyny Identification of the self as both masculine and feminine.

Anesthesia Blocking of nerve pathways to cut off pain sensation.

Animism The tendency to ascribe feelings and motivations to natural phenomena, such as snow, inanimate objects, such as rocks, and mechanical devices, such as telephones. According to Piaget, characteristic of preoperational thought.

Anorexia nervosa An eating disorder characterized by self-starvation and an unjustified perception of the self as overweight.

Apneic pauses Brief periods, lasting up to 30 seconds, in which an infant's breathing is temporarily suspended; occurring normally in most infants.

Appraisal The ability to cognitively assess a situation in order to regulate one's emotional expressions.

Apprenticeship Period of infant social development, beginning at about 6 months, in which the infant learns social skills by participating in social routines structured by an adult.

Artificial insemination Injecting spermatozoa from a male donor into the uterus of a potential mother.

Artificial intelligence The collaboration of psychologists and computer scientists working to develop machines that have the ability to develop new control strategies that are similar to the process of human thought.

Artificialism The belief that everything that exists has been created by humans or by divine plan. According to Piaget, characteristic of preoperational thought.

Asphyxia Loss of oxygen, especially that which occurs during birth and delivery of the newborn.

Assimilation The process of acting on the environment with skills that are directly suited to the environmental demands.

Associative play Term used by Parten for play in which children adapt their behavior to each other but do not assume complementary roles.

Asthma Chronic disease characterized by episodes of wheezing and shortness of breath.

Asynchronous growth Growth of different parts of the body or different aspects of the individual at different rates.

Atheoretical Not based on or derived from any theory.

Atherosclerosis Hardening of the arteries.

Attachment The emotional bond, including feelings of affection and desire to remain in close proximity, between two people.

Attachment behavior Overt signals such as crying and following that bring the parent and the child into close physical proximity.

Attachment system The set of beliefs, feelings and thoughts about one's object of attachment.

Attention   Focusing the sensory systems on a particular stimulus.

Attention Deficit Disorder with Hyperactivity (ADD/H)   The technical term used to refer to hyperactivity.

Attributions   Explanations for characteristics or actions of self or others: for example, "She got an A because she's smart."

Attribution retraining   Teaching an individual to make different self-statements in order to aid problem-solving: for example, saying "I am someone who needs to try harder" instead of "I'm just too dumb to solve this problem."

Attrition   The loss of subjects over time in longitudinal research studies.

Authoritarian parenting   Parental behavior characterized by high control and demands, low warmth, and poor communication.

Authoritative parenting   Parental behavior characterized by a combination of warmth, firm control, clear communication, and encouragement of independence.

Automatic recording   Electronic and mechanical devices to record motor and physiological activity in the body.

Autonomous moral judgment   According to Piaget, the stage of moral understanding in which motivations and intentions are considered in judging wrongdoing and in which moral rules are viewed as humanly constructed in order to make cooperation possible. Also called *the morality of cooperation.*

Autism   A communication disorder of early childhood in which children fail to develop language, avoid contact with others, and display rhythmical stereotypes.

Axon   The "tail" of the nerve cell that extends out to connect with other nerve cells.

Babbling   The production of syllables containing vowel and consonant sounds, made for the purpose of vocal play, beginning about 5 or 6 months of age.

Baby biography   A written detailed observation of the day-to-day changes in the behavior of a single infant. This was one of the first forms of scientific observation of children's behavior.

Baby talk   Adult speech to young infants consisting of marked changes in pitch, short bursts of sound, and a high rate of repetition.

Babyishness   The characteristic physical appearance of infants compared to adults of the same species.

Basic theory and research   Scientific investigation having the goal of discovering the universal processes of human behavior and development, without regard to applied issues.

Behavioral assessment   Testing of the newborn for responsiveness to external stimulation such as sound, light, and movement.

Behavioral system   An interdependent set of behavioral responses between two or more people that regulate interpersonal exchange so that the behavior of one individual leads to the response of the other, and so on.

Behavior setting   The social rules and physical characteristics that pertain to a particular physical location in which behavior takes place, for example, the living room vs. the dining room, the school vs. the playground.

Behavior modification   Techniques to change behavior through the use of reward and punishment.

Belief system   The set of ideas a person has about something. In this text we study childrearing belief systems, which include ideas about childhood, childrearing and parent-child relationships.

Bias   Unintended effects resulting from the procedures of a research study that may influence the outcome of the study.

Bilingual education   Programs involving instruction in a student's native language as well as a to-be-acquired language.

Bilingualism   The speaking and understanding of two languages.

Black English   Form of English characterized by its own grammatical rules spoken by some Black children and adults in North America.

Blastocyst   A fertilized ovum during the first two weeks of cell division.

Blended family   A family created by the union of adults and their offspring from prior relationships (also called *reconstituted family*).

Bone-age   Skeletal maturity.

Botulism   A disease affecting the nervous system caused by a toxin found on some fruits and vegetables, and in honey.

Brain hemisphere   The right or left side of the brain.

Brain lateralization   Specialization of functions in the left or right side of the brain.

Braxton-Hicks contractions   Gentle contraction and relaxation cycles occurring the last month of pregnancy, also called "false labor."

Breech birth   When the fetus is oriented with its buttocks toward the cervix.

Bulimia   An eating disorder characterized by "binges" of excessive eating, followed by "purges" of self-induced vomiting.

Canalization   The tendency for a phenotypic characteristic to be expressed in a similar way across all individuals, and within different environments.

Carrier   A person who has a recessive gene for a genetic disorder, but who does not show any symptom of the disorder.

Case study   A research design in which a single subject is observed on multiple occasions.

Castration anxiety   According to psychoanalytic theory, the fear felt by a male child that he will be punished by his father by castration for desiring to possess his mother exclusively.

Catch-up growth Acceleration of physical growth after a disturbance in normal growth patterns due to disease, malnutrition, or other factors.

Category A mental grouping of objects that share similar properties.

Categorical reasoning Use of categories to organize information and solve problems.

Categorization The use of group labels or categories as an aid in remembering information.

Centration Concentration or attention to only one aspect of a situation or object.

Cephalocaudal direction of growth Growth proceeding from top of the body to the bottom.

Cervix The aperture connecting the uterus to the vagina.

Cesarean section Delivery of an infant through a surgical opening in the abdominal wall of the mother.

Chaining The linking together of already learned behavior units into the proper sequence.

Child-life specialist Hospital staff professional who helps children and families adjust to hospitalization.

Chorion The membrane that separates the placenta from the amnionic sac and the fetus.

Chorionic Villi Sampling A test for birth defects in which a small amount of chorionic tissue is sampled to check for genetic and chromosomal defects.

Chromosome Chains of genes that are found in a cell nucleus. They are the basic reproducing structures that are formed during meiosis and mitosis.

Chronological Age (C.A.) The number of years since birth.

Classical conditioning The process by which a conditioned stimulus becomes associated with a conditioned response by repeated exposure of the individual to the simultaneous pairing of the stimulus and response.

Classification Grouping of objects, people or events by some criterion.

Clinical interview An interview technique in which the researcher probes the child's level of knowledge about something as part of a naturalistic conversation.

Clique A small group of intimate friends.

Clustering A means of sorting and organizing information as an aid to memory or problem-solving.

Code-switching Ability to modify language to adjust to the perceived needs of different listeners.

Coefficient of correlation A measure of the degree of relationship between two variables.

Cognitive developmental theory A stage theory of the development of intelligence, based on the theory of Jean Piaget.

Cognitive style Individual variation in how information is typically processed.

Cognitive training methods Ways of helping children modify their behavior by making them more aware of how they perceive, use and remember information.

Cohort effect Differences between groups of people of the same age that occur as a result of the time and place in which the group was born and lived.

Colostrum The yellowish fluid excreted by the breasts late in pregnancy and during the first few days after the birth, containing digestive and immunizing agents.

Communicative competence The effective use of language as a tool for social communication.

Communion Typically female value orientation including warmth, expressiveness, affiliation, and sensitivity to others.

Comparative terms Words that compare two or more objects or events. (Ex. "older", "younger")

Compensation Environmental factors that assist developmentally delayed children to catch up to normal children.

Compliance Responsiveness of child to requests made by others.

Comprehension The "input" side of language, the extent to which language is understood by the listener (see *production*).

Comprehension monitoring Behaviors related to successful problem-solving by checking the progress of one's understanding of a problem.

Conception The fertilization of an ovum with a spermatazoon.

Concrete-logical stage A stage of reasoning about illness in which factors within and outside the body are distinguished.

Concrete operations Piaget's stage of cognitive development between the ages about 6 to 12 years in which children can think logically about concrete and observable concepts.

Conformity The susceptibility to other's influence over one's actions or perceptions.

Conjugate reinforcement A consequence in which the amount of reinforcement is directly proportional to the amount of effort expended by the individual.

Conservation The ability to understand the invariance of certain properties, such as number, length, volume, and weight in spite of apparent changes in objects.

Constructivist The view of perceptual development that perception develops slowly from sensation as a result of the child's experiences with the environment (see *ecological perception*).

Co-regulation Form of child-rearing in which adult has supervisory control but child has moment-to-moment independence.

Conscious According to Freud, the part of the mind about which the individual is aware (see also *unconscious*).

Consequences of behavior The response of the environment that immediately follows an emitted behavior.

Contagion A stage of thinking about health and illness characterized by the belief that illness is caused by physical proximity, for example, getting measles by being close to someone with the disease. Also characterized by confusion between the causes of accidents and causes of illnesses.

Contamination A stage of thinking about health and illness characterized by the belief that physical contact of a source of infection with the surface of the body causes illness.

Continuity Steady increases or decreases over time in some developmental variable, no abrupt changes.

Continuous reinforcement schedule A schedule in which reinforcement is provided each time a child emits a desired behavior (see also *schedule of reinforcement* and *partial reinforcement schedule*).

Control group A group used in experimental studies that does not experience the intervention received by the experimental group.

Control strategies Decision points in the information processing system that monitor the flow of information from one processing step to the next.

Control techniques Efforts made by adults to foster compliance in children.

Conventional morality Justification of action based on authority, without questioning the rules.

Conventional words Those that are used and shared by the speakers of a language.

Convergent thinking Problem-solving centered on finding a single correct answer to a problem.

Cooing Sing-song production of vowel sounds beginning about the 2nd or 3rd month of life.

Cooperative play Games in which both partners work to achieve the same goal, such as a pretend tea party.

Corpus Callosum Membrane separating the two halves or hemispheres of the brain.

Couvade The acting out by a male of the postures and behaviors of women during pregnancy and childbirth.

Crèche Lit. cradle in French. French term for nursery school or preschool.

Criterion measure A standard and accepted measure of a concept or variable, used in the determination of *validity*.

Cross-cultural research Comparing people of different cultures in order to test the universality of developmental theories, to increase the range of knowledge about variations in human behavior.

Cross-sectional research A research design in which age differences are studied using different groups of people at each age.

Cross-sequential study A study in which a number of cohorts of subjects, born in different years, are followed longitudinally so that both longitudinal and cross-sectional comparisons can be made.

Crowd An association of cliques for the purpose of social activity.

Data The set of observed facts about children's development.

Day care services Child care provided outside the home for children who live in their own homes.

Decalage Term used by Piaget to refer to chronological variation in the emergence of different conservation abilities.

Deciduous teeth Also called "baby teeth". Set of teeth that erupt in infancy and begin to loosen at age 5-6 years.

Defense mechanisms Mental processes that protect the individual from understanding the true nature of his actions or intentions.

Deferred imitation The ability to imitate an absent model.

Demand characteristics The subject's psychological reaction to the research procedures and settings, which may contribute to unintended *bias*.

Dendrites Nerve cell endings which receive impulses from adjacent cells.

Dependent variable The outcome variable in a research study; that which is hypothesized to depend on the influence of the *independent variable*.

Detour ability The ability to retrieve an object from behind a barrier, especially a transparent barrier.

Developmental theory A theory that explains how individuals change over time.

Diabetes A disease in which the pancreas does not produce insulin, a substance essential in breaking down food into energy the body can use.

Diagnostic test Assessments of infant growth and development for the purpose of detecting risk.

Dichotic listening Presentation of material to the right or left ear to determine degree of brain lateralization.

Differentiation The process of becoming distinct from others.

Direct effect When a biological event such as hormonal secretion has a one-to-one correspondence with a psychological state (see *mediated effects*).

Discontinuity Developmental change that is abrupt rather than smooth and steady (see *continuity*).

Discrepancy The perceived difference between two stimuli.

Disequilibrium The experience of an individual when encountering a situation in which existing schemes are not appropriate or are incomplete to meet the environmental demands.

Distribution A graph showing the number of subjects as a function of the value each obtained on some variable.

Distributive justice Issues concerning the right way to divide resources among a group of individuals.

Divergent thinking Problem-solving focussed on generating as many novel responses as possible. Considered indicative of creativity.

Diversion Programs that remove the child from the formal system of juvenile justice at the time of arrest.

Dizygotic Twins that are produced when two ova are released and fertilized in the same cycle. The twins are genetically unique.

Dominant allele An allelle that will be expressed whenever it appears in the genotype.

Dose response relationship A relationship between a drug dosage and the drug's effect in which increasing dosages lead to stronger effects.

Double blind study A study in which the experimenters and the subjects are both unaware of the hypotheses of the study and the group to which the subjects have been assigned.

Down's syndrome A *trisomy* of the 21st pair of chromosomes causing short stature, flabbiness, cardiac and glandular abnormalities, a small mouth, mental retardation, and folds of skin over the eyes.

Echolalia A speech disorder characterized by repetition of speech sounds.

Ecological factors Aspects of the physical environment, such as climate, physical dangers, etc., that may influence child or parent behavior.

Ecological perception The view of perceptual development that pure sensation does not exist, and that there are innate perceptual categories (see *constructivist*).

Ecological theory (Also referred to as *ecological systems perspective* and *ecological approach to human development*) The point of view that child development and behavior is determined by a complex system of environmental factors including family, school, laws and culture.

Ectoderm One of the cell layers of the embryonic disk that will become the central nervous system, brain, sense organs, skin, hair, nails and teeth (see *endoderm* and *mesoderm*).

Effector The muscles, bones and joints responsible for making a movement (see *receptor*).

Egalitarian interaction Characteristics of peer relationships in early childhood, and parent-child relationships in late adolescence, in which both partners have more or less equal status.

Ego The ability to tolerate strong emotions and stress without being overwhelmed; a synonym is *self-regulation*.

Ego control Ability to delay immediate gratification of wishes, being oriented toward the future, being socially responsible and being more reflective than impulsive in behavior. Also called *Ego strength*.

Ego identity status Based on Marcia's theory of identity formation, each level reflects the individual's commitment to the values and actions of a particular role.

Egocentrism Term used by Piaget to refer to the preoperational thinker's inability to understand another's point of view.

Elaborated language Speech (to young children) characterized by relatively long, complex sentences, explanations, and references to internal states. Contrasted with *restricted language*.

Elaboration A memory aid, which involves the association of one bit of information with another in a phrase or sentence (*verbal elaboration*) or a visual image (*visual elaboration*).

Electra conflict According to psychoanalytic theory, a young girl's feelings of rivalry with her mother and desire to possess her father.

Embryonic disk A layer of cells in the blastocyst that will eventually become the embryo's body.

Embryo The period of pre-natal development beginning at the implantation of the zygote in the uterine wall and ending when the major organ systems are formed, about 8 weeks gestation.

Embryo transfer The process by which an embryo that has been conceived in one woman's body is removed and placed into another woman's uterus.

Emitted behavior Behavior that occurs in the absence of an eliciting stimulus; spontaneous behavior.

Emotional expression Feelings children have in relation to events, persons, or ideas.

Empathy The vicarious sharing of another's emotion.

Empiricists Nineteenth century thinkers who developed the idea that knowledge is derived from direct sensation, and that human problems could be solved using logical reasoning.

Encoding The placing of information into memory.

Encoding shift hypothesis A change in thinking believed to occur around age seven when children shift from storing information primarily in terms of visual images to storing information primarily in terms of words. See also *Five-to-seven shift*.

Endocrine Hormonal system that induces the development of the reproductive organs and sexual behavior, includes androgens and estrogens.

Endoderm A layer of cells in the embryonic disk that will become the digestive, urinary and respiratory systems.

Environmental factors Those aspects of the social and physical setting that contribute to the development of individual uniqueness.

Environmental specificity The environment does not act in a global fashion; specific aspects of the environment are more likely to affect certain types of children, or specific aspects of developmental change.

Epiphyses Growth regions within bones.

Episiotomy The surgical cutting of the perineum (the tissue between the vagina and the anus) that helps to prevent it from tearing during birth.

Epistemology The study of the origins and structure of knowledge and thinking.

Erogenous zone A region of the body that creates pleasurable feelings when stimulated.

Estrogen Hormone leading to the development of female secondary sexual characteristics.

Ethological theory A point of view that explains child behavior and development on the basis of biological processes, some of which are specific to each species, and others of which are universal for all species.

Euthanasia The act of putting to death painlessly a person suffering from an incurable disease.

Event recorder A device used to keep track of the time of occurrence of behavioral events.

Exosystem The social institutions—such as the work place, the media, and the government—that affect children, but in which children are not involved directly.

Experience Sampling Method An event sampling observational approach in which subjects describe their behavior and experience when they are signalled by an electronic pager.

Experiment A research design in which the independent variables are manipulated by the researcher by performing some controlled intervention on the subjects.

Experimental group The group of subject in a between subjects experimental research design who receive the experimental intervention (see *control group* and *experiment*).

Explicit theory of intelligence Definition of intelligence used in intelligence tests.

Exploration play Play in which the infant or child uses different sensory modalities in a systematic way to obtain information about the properties of objects (also called *Exploration*).

Expression of fluids Refers to the technique of sucking used by infants in which the nipple is pressed against the roof of the mouth to squeeze the milk out.

Expressive speech Use of social control language, in interpersonal situations, usually poorly articulated in infants.

Extinction The elimination, by instrumental conditioning, of an individual's emitted behavior.

Factor analysis A method of isolating groups of variables called factors that are intercorrelated with each other; between factors, variables are uncorrelated.

Family structure The positions, roles, and relationships defining the family.

Federal Interagency Day Care Requirements A set of regulations designed to control the quality of publicly funded day care, but never officially implemented or enforced.

Fertilization The process by which the ovum becomes impregnated with a single spermatozoon, initiating cell division.

Fetal alcohol syndrome A combination of symptoms—including low birth weight, learning problems, small head, abnormally spaced eyes, underdeveloped jaw, and a flattened nose—believed to be caused by pre-natal alcohol consumption by the mother.

Fetal distress Rapidly fluctuating or diminishing of fetal life signs, such as heart rate and respiration.

Fetal medicine The field of medicine leading to the treatment and prevention of disorders occurring during pre-natal development.

Fetus The period of pre-natal development from the time of completion of the organ systems (about 8 weeks gestation) until birth.

Field independence-dependence cognitive style The ease (field independence) or difficulty (field dependence) with which a person can perceive a part as separate from a complex whole in which it is embedded.

Finalism The belief that every event must have a specifiable cause. According to Piaget, characteristic of preoperational thought.

Five-to-seven shift A gradual change in children's thinking occurring between ages five and seven years. Characterized by gradually increasing ability to organize information logically, coordinate information from several sources, and use verbal rather than visual images in problem-solving. (See also *Encoding shift hypothesis*.)

Fixation time The duration of continuous looking at a stimulus.

Flow A psychological state in which one feels whole and acts with clarity, commitment and enthusiasm.

Fontanels Fissures in the infant's skull that allow for brain growth during the first years of life.

Formal operations The ability to think logically about abstract or imagined situations, and to think about the process of reasoning.

Formal-logical stage A stage of reasoning about illness in which multiple causes of illness are recognized and internal body functioning is understood. Thought to coincide with the stage of Formal Operations (see above).

Free association Spontaneous insights derived during psychoanalysis as one's mind wanders freely.

Friendship Feelings of mutual preference between individuals.

Function of behavior The contribution of a particular behavior to making one better suited, or adapted, to a situation.

Full-term A baby that is born after 37 weeks of gestation, plus or minus two weeks.

Full-term birth Birth that occurs at 38 plus or minus 2 weeks gestational age.

Gametes The sexual reproductive cells: spermatozoa and ova.

Gender Identity as a biological male or female.

Gender constancy The realization that one's sex cannot be changed by changes in outward appearance.

Gender labelling Identifying the self as male or female.

Gender stability The realization that one was in the past and will remain over time a male, or female.

Gender understanding Knowledge concerning one's identity as male or female.

Gene The basic unit of hereditary information.

Geneology Patterns of inheritance over many generations within a family.

Generalization   The process by which learning in one situation is extended to other related situations.

Generalized event structure   Sequence of actions that make up a familiar event: for example, the actions of ordering food, eating, and paying involved in going to a restaurant. (Also called *script*).

Generativity   The adult's need to extend his or her influence beyond one's lifetime, usually satisfied by having and raising children.

Genetic counseling   Assessment of a family's likelihood of producing a child with genetic or chromosomal abnormalities in which geneologies and fetal testing are used.

Genetic engineering   Using modular biology to alter the genetic structure of an organism or individual.

Genital stage   The stage of psychoanalytic theory associated with pubertal changes at the time of adolescence.

Genotype   The set of chemical "messages" contained in DNA that direct the formation of specific proteins within a cell.

Gestation   The period from conception to birth.

Gestational age   The age of the infant from the time of conception.

GOBI   A health education program for underdeveloped nations, standing for *G*rowth charts, *O*ral rehydration, *B*reast feeding, and *I*mmunization.

Habituation   The gradual decrease in fixation time occurring when an infant is presented repeatedly with the same stimulus.

Handedness   Preferential use of one hand over another in motor tasks.

Harmony   A concept derived from Confucianism, meaning that one should live with due respect for the powers and processes of the natural world, and that in interpersonal relationships one should respect the individuality and needs of the other person.

Harmonious parenting   A style characterized by high agreement and cooperation between parent and child, with issues of control rarely arising.

Hawthorne effect   Unintended bias due to the subject's awareness of being in an experimental study, creating a *demand characteristic* leading to artificial behavior patterns.

Hemophilia   A genetic disorder leading to a failure of the blood to clot properly, causing excessive bleeding even for small cuts.

Heteronomous morality   According to Piaget, stage of reasoning about morality, in which rules are viewed as inflexible and guilt is assessed by the consequences of wrongdoing, not the intentions (cf. *Moral realism*).

Hierarchical interactions   Social relationships in which one partner has more power or resources than another (see *egalitarian interactions*).

Hormones   Chemical substances that instruct certain cells of the body to act in specific ways.

Hostile aggression   Behaviors directed at harming others.

Human chorionic gonadotrophin   A hormone secreted by the placenta after a zygote has been implanted that causes menstruation to cease.

Hyperactivity   Chronic inability to sustain attention and inhibit impulsiveness.

Hypertension   High blood pressure.

Hypoglycemia   Loss of blood sugar.

Hypotheses (1)   A specific statement, derived from theory, that relates two or more observable entities to each other.

Hypotheses (2)   Refers to infant's interest in objects due to raising of questions about the nature of the object (see also *discrepancy*).

Id   The set of biological impulses, or drives, including hunger, fatigue and sex, that were thought by Freud to motivate behavior.

Identification   The process whereby children take on the attitudes, values, and behaviors of another person, usually a parent.

Identity (1)   An internal, self-constructed, dynamic organization of drives, abilities, beliefs, and individual history.

Identity (2)   Understanding that an object is "the same" despite changes in outward appearance.

Identity crisis   The discovery of one's own potentialities and limitations that occurs during the adolescent years.

Idiosyncratic words   Words and gestures invented by the infant, that do not correspond to adult usage.

Ikonic stage   Term used by Bruner for the period of cognitive development, from approximately ages 2 to 7 years, when thought is dominated by images (e.g. ikons).

Imaginary audience   Part of *adolescent egocentrism;* feeling that others are watching leading to a heightened self-consciousness about appearance and behavior.

Immanent justice   The view that accidents are punishment for wrongdoing. Thought to be characteristic of the stage of moral realism.

Immersion   Program of language learning involving total and intensive instruction in the to-be-acquired language.

Implicit theory of intelligence   The everyday meaning of the term "intelligence."

Imprinting   The learning of a preference for one object during a relatively brief period in the life cycle of the individual.

In vitro fertilization   Removing an ovum from the mother for fertilization outside of her body, and later transplantation into her uterus.

Incidental learning   Acquiring a behavior by observing it performed by someone else. The learner need not imitate the behavior immediately, nor does the behavior need to be reinforced at the time of learning.

Independent variable   A variable that is hypothesized to be the causal or controlling factor determining the *dependent variable*.

Individuation The process of developing a personal sense of self.

Induction The use of reasoning and explanations to secure cooperation from a child.

Industry vs. inferiority According to Erikson, the stage of development occurring after the stage of *initiative vs. guilt* and characterized by the need to engage in productive work and develop a sense of accomplishment.

Inferential reasoning Problem-solving that requires one to infer information.

Inflections Word endings such as *-ing*, *-'s*, and *-ed*.

Information processing theory The point of view that human thinking is analogous to the working of a computer; that perception, awareness, comparison, integration and memory are separate steps in the flow of information through the brain.

Informed consent The principle that participation of human subjects in research should be voluntary consent based on a complete description of the procedures involved in the research.

Initiative vs. guilt According to Erikson, stage of development usually occurring from ages 3-6, in which child can experience sense of mastery over accomplishments.

Insecure-avoidant attachment Infants who are not upset when left in strange settings and who avoid caregivers upon reunion.

Insecure- resistant attachment Infants who feel uncomfortable in strange settings, and who show ambivalent responses to caregivers upon reunion.

Instability The inability to predict a person's ranking in a group at some point in development on the basis of knowing the person's ranking at an earlier point in development.

Instrumental aggression Quarrels over objects, privileges, or territory.

Instrumental competence Term used by Baumrind to refer to the ability to successfully achieve goals through social cooperation, independence, problem-solving, and assertiveness.

Instrumental conditioning The process by which the frequency of emission of particular behaviors is either increased or decreased, depending on the consequences of the behavior, that is, whether the behavior is followed by a positive or by a negative reinforcer.

Instrumental values Values that are the means to an end, or that regulate here-and-now action including honesty, loving, obedience, and cleanliness (see *terminal values*).

Insulin Substance normally produced by the body that is essential in breaking down food into energy the body can use. Deficiency in the production of insulin is characteristic of the disease *diabetes*.

Intelligence Quotient (I.Q.) Intelligence test score originally derived by dividing Mental Age (M.A.) by Chronological Age (C.A.) and multiplying by 100. More recently derived by determining how far above or below the mean of a group of same-age children an individual child's score is (called a *deviation IQ score*) above or below.

Intentionality Goal seeking behavior.

Interest centers Sections of an open area classroom with resources and suggested activities where children may pursue varied interests.

Internalization (1) The adoption of characteristics and standards of another as one's own internal guide to behavior.

Internalization (2) Stage of thinking about health and illness characterized by the belief that contaminants must be taken inside the body for illness to occur.

Interobserver reliability The extent to which two or more independent observers agree on the occurrence of a particular behavior.

Interpersonal aspects of sexuality The individual's perceptions and actions regarding the context of sexual activity, the expectations of others, and the cultural ideals about sexuality (see *intrapsychic aspects*).

Intersensory percept The ability to coordinate information coming from more than one sensory modality.

Intervention strategies The therapeutic and educational curricula designed to improve the lives of children and families at risk.

Intimacy The sharing of inner thoughts and feelings through self-disclosure to others.

Intrapsychic aspects of sexuality Personal aspects of sexuality including sources of erotic arousal, and the motivations and justifications involved in sexual behavior (see *interpersonal aspects*).

Juvenile-onset diabetes A disease beginning in childhood, which is characterized by a deficiency in the production of insulin.

Karotyping Arranging a microphotograph of a cell's chromosomes in order to show the relationships between pairs.

Kibbutz (pl:Kibbutzim) Israeli collective settlement, in which children are reared with peers.

Kwashiorkor African term for severe protein-calorie malnutrition.

Labor The series of muscular contractions leading to the birth of the infant.

Lamaze method A set of breathing patterns and posture changes to help muscles relax and to relieve pain during childbirth.

Language Acquisition Device (LAD) A hypothetical information processing system designed specifically for the learning of a first language.

Lanugo The fine hair that covers the fetus during the 2nd and 3rd trimesters of gestation.

Latch-key children Also referred to as *self-care*. Children who are home without an adult present during part or all of the day.

Latency According to psychoanalytic theory, the period following the resolution of the Oedipal conflict; characterized by the sublimation of sexual urges.

Learned helplessness The tendency for individuals who experience initial failure subsequently to give up in future problem-solving situations. May underlie some children's learning problems.

Learning disability (LD) A disorder in one or more psychological processes involved in understanding or using language, spoken or written; excludes sensory handicaps, retardation, emotional disturbance or environmental disadvantage. Also called *Minimal Brain Dysfunction.*

Learning theory The explanation of behavior change on the basis of associations between the subject's actions and an environmental event, and by the environmental consequences of the subject's actions.

Let-down response Stimulated by sucking, it allows milk to be released from the breast.

Linguistic universals The subject-action-object structure of language, independent of word meaning and word order that is specific to individual languages.

Locus of control The degree to which one feels a sense of personal control over outcomes (*internal locus of control*) or a sense of personal helplessness (*external locus of control*).

Long-term memory Storage of information in memory for weeks, months or even years.

Longitudinal study A research design in which developmental changes are studied by following the same individuals over time.

Love withdrawal A technique to secure cooperation from a child by appealing to the parent-child relationship.

Lymph system A network of vessels in the body that carry lymph or tissue fluid from tissues into veins.

Macrosystem The set of values, beliefs and rules that regulate behavior in a society; equivalent to culture.

Marasmus An illness afflicting infants under one year of age as a result of severe protein-calorie malnutrition.

Mainstreaming Integration of handicapped children into regular classrooms with their non-handicapped peers.

Marfan's syndrome A disorder caused by a single defective gene that may cause a weakened heart, mild bone structure deformities, long fingers and eye lens disorders.

Matrilineal The tracing of descent through the maternal line.

Matrilocal The tendency for couples to establish residence with the family of the wife.

Maturation Developmental change that is controlled by hereditary timing mechanisms, and in which the change points are highly *canalized.*

Mean The sum of scores in a sample, divided by the total number of subjects.

Mean Length of Utterance (MLU) Average number of morphemes a child produces. Used as an index of language development.

Meconium The substance contained in the newborn's bowels at birth.

Median The score that falls exactly in the middle of a sample's distribution.

Mediated effects The ways in which a particular kind of organismic factor influences the infant's responsiveness to certain kinds of environmental factors (see also *environmental specificity*).

Meiosis The cell division process that produces gametes, each containing only half the usual number of chromosomes.

Memory span Amount of information that can be remembered immediately after seeing or hearing the information.

Menarche The onset of menstruation in the adolescent female.

Mental Age (M.A.) Level of performance on an I.Q. test indicating performance in relation to average score attained by persons of a given chronological age. Example: A seven year old who performs at the level of an average nine year old has a M.A. of 9.

Mesoderm A layer of cells in the embryonic disk that leads to the development of muscles, bones, circulatory and reproductive systems (see *endoderm* and *ectoderm*).

Mesosystem Encompasses the relationships between the *microsystems* of which the child is a member; for example, the transactions between the school and the home.

Metacognition The awareness of one's own cognitive processes.

Metamemory Awareness of one's own memory processes.

Microsystem The interactions between the child and the immediate environmental setting; for example, the family, school and peer group.

Minimal Brain Dysfunction (MBD) Term sometimes used for learning disability.

Minimally sufficient control The use of just enough control to bring about a response.

Miscarriage The birth of a fetus before it can survive apart from the mother.

Mission-oriented theory The application of developmental theory to real-world problems and issues.

Mitosis Normal cell division in which all chromosomes in the cell are copied and passed on to the two daughter cells.

Mnemonics Aids to memory.

Mode The score that is obtained by the largest number of subjects in a sample.

Monolingualism The ability to speak and understand only one language.

Monosomy An error of meiosis in which one chromosome is missing from the gamete, producing, if fertilized, a zygote with one non-paired chromosome.

Monozygotic A set of twins created by the splitting of the zygote, so that each individual has the same genotype.

Morality The reasoning process that people experience in relation to the formation of and commitment to values.

Morpheme A meaningful unit of language.

Mortality rate The number of deaths as a ratio of the number of births.

Moral realism According to Piaget, stage in the development of moral understanding, when children view rules as inflexible and judge wrongdoing by damage done, not by intentions. (also called *heteronomous morality* and the *morality of constraint*).

Moral understanding Judgments about right and wrong.

Motherese Characteristic speech style to infants and toddlers used by adults and children, as well as mothers. (also called *baby talk*).

Motor coordination Skills involved in coordinating physical movements.

Multiple sclerosis A degenerative disease in which myelin sheaths around nerves disintegrate, causing motor and sensory impairments.

Myelin A protective protein coating of nerve conduction pathways.

Myelinization The process by which myelin coatings or sheaths are formed around nerves.

Natural selection The theory of evolution of species, proposed by Charles Darwin, in which genetic change is explained by differential survival of offspring who have characteristics that are well suited to the environment.

Nature Refers to the belief that behavior and development are controlled primarily by hereditary influences (see *nurture*).

Negative correlation Indicates an inverse relationship between two variables; larger scores for one variable tend to be associated with smaller scores for the other variable.

Negative reinforcement A consequence of an action that reduces the frequency of that action in the future (see *positive reinforcement*).

Negative reinforcement trap Term used by Gerald Patterson to refer to patterns of interaction in which physical coercion of one individual and aggression of another are mutually maintained.

Neolocal The tendency for couples to establish independent residence after marriage.

Neurological assessment Test of newborn reflexes to reveal underlying abnormalities in the brain and nervous system.

Neurons Nerve cells, including cell body, axons, dendrites and synapses.

Neurotransmitters Chemical substances that are secreted from nerve cells at their juncture with other cells and that allow nerve cells to communicate.

Non-verbal communication Interpersonal exchanges that are mediated by gestures and facial expressions, as opposed to verbalization.

Normal physiological jaundice Slight yellowish coloring of the newborn's skin that lasts for several days.

Normative sample The group of infants on which an assessment test was standardized.

Norm-referenced test An assessment procedure in which a subject's score is compared to the scores obtained by other people within the same reference group.

Nurture Refers to the belief that behavior and development are controlled by environmental influences, including the physical and social environment (see *nature*).

Object fantasy play Play in which the child uses play materials to represent an imaginary thing.

Object permanence The ability to search for hidden objects, reflecting an awareness of the existence of objects, even when out of sight or hearing range.

Objective self The way the self is viewed by others, the "me."

Obligatory attention The inability to look away from an attractive stimulus, occurring between 1 and 3 months of age.

Observational learning Learning by watching another person's behavior, and imitating that behavior.

Observational methods Assessment procedures in which direct recording and rating of ongoing behavior is used.

Obstetrician/gynecologist Physicians who care for mothers during pregnancy and delivery of the baby (see *Pediatrician*).

Oedipal conflict According to Freud, period during which young boy experiences rivalry with his father and desires to possess his mother exclusively. (cf. *Electra complex*)

Ontogeny The development of the individual from conception to death.

Open education Principles of education emphasizing student decision-making, individualized learning, and the development of initiative, curiosity, and self-motivation.

Open-ended interview A interview in which subjects are allowed to respond freely to questions.

Operant conditioning Controlling the consequences of an action so as to change the frequency of occurrence of that action in the future.

Organismic factors Properties of the individual child such as sex and temperament, that mediate the effect of the environment on developmental change.

Ossification Hardening of the bones.

Overextension The use of a word to apply to instances not typically included in the adult's definition.

Overregularization Application of regular grammatical rules to irregular cases. Ex.: "He goed."

Ovum The female gamete.

Parallel play Term used by Parten to refer to activities in which children play near each other and are aware of each other's presence, but do not interact.

Parens patriae As derived from English common law, this means that parents have the ultimate authority over their children. In modern times it means that the state can only intervene in the affairs of the family if the parents fail to behave responsibly to their children.

Parent education programs Programs that share information with parents or prospective parents concerning aspects of child-rearing or child development.

Parenting techniques The tendency to behave in consistent fashion in disciplining or relating to the child (also called *parenting styles*).

Partial reinforcement schedule A schedule of reinforcement in which the child is sometimes reinforced and sometimes not reinforced following a desired behavior (see *schedule of reinforcement* and *continuous reinforcement schedule*).

Patrilineal The tracing of descent through male descendants.

Patrilocal The tendency for couples to establish residence in the household of the husband's family.

Pediatrician A physician specializing in the care of infants and children (see *Obstetrician/gynecologist*).

Percentile A number that divides a series into 100 equal groups. For example, a score at the 75th percentile means that it is higher than 75% of all other scores in the group and lower than 25% of all other scores in the group.

Perception The meaningful interpretation of sensory information.

Perinatal period The time from two weeks before, until two weeks after delivery.

Perinatal factors Events that occur during the two weeks before and after birth.

Permissive parenting The tendency to combine warmth with low control and few demands on the child.

Personal fable An aspect of *adolescent egocentrism;* the ideal person that the adolescent believes him/herself to be, one who will be successful and who is invulnerable.

Personality The relatively consistent and enduring unique manner in which an individual behaves, thinks and feels.

Perspective-taking ability Ability to take the view or perspective of another when it is different from one's own. (Also called *role-taking ability*).

Phallic stage Stage of psychoanalytic theory in which the child becomes interested in the genitals, gender identity, and identification with same-sex parent.

Phenomism Stage of thinking about health and illness characterized by the belief that illness is caused by a single dramatic event associated with it, for example, a strong wind making an individual sick.

Phenotype The functioning organism (see *genotype*).

Phenylketonuria A genetic disease marked by a deficiency of an enzyme needed to digest certain kinds of foods, which, if eaten, will lead to brain damage.

Phylogeny The gradual change in the genetic structure of a species, occurring through the process of natural selection, and taking place over millions of years.

Physiological stage Stage of thinking about health and illness in which illness is explained in terms of physiological mechanisms, for example, the blockage of a heart valve causing a heart attack.

Phoneme The basic sound units of a language.

Play therapy The use of play to help distressed young children express their feelings to a psychotherapist.

Pleasure principle The urge to meet one's needs without delay.

Plietropy Inheritance pattern in which multiple phenotypes are caused by a single gene.

Polygenic Inheritance pattern in which several genes are responsible for a single phenotypic characteristic.

Polygynous Family structure in which husbands may have more than one wife at a time.

Positive correlation Indicates a direct relationship between two variables; larger scores for one variable tend to be associated with larger scores for the other variable.

Positive reinforcement A consequence of an action that increases the frequency of that action in the future (see *negative reinforcement*).

Post-conventional morality Recognition of accepted laws and rules as arbitrary and possibly unjust, but as needing to be obeyed nevertheless (see *conventional morality*).

Post partum blues Brief episodes of unexpected crying following childbirth, typically due to stress and fatigue.

Power assertion A disciplinary technique emphasizing commands, threats, and punishment.

Practice play Term used by Piaget for play that perfects and practices a motor skill.

Preconventional morality One of three broad stages of moral reasoning according to Kohlberg. Characterized by moral judgments based on avoiding punishment and obeying and pleasing authority.

Preoperational thought One of the four broad stages of cognitive development described by Piaget. Occuring approximately between the ages of two and six or seven, it is characterized by the ability to use symbols and language, but the inability to understand logical operations such as reversibility.

Pre-term Infants born before 35 weeks gestational age.

Primary circular reaction   Refers to the second stage of Piaget's sensorimotor period, in which infants repeat actions of their own bodies that are discovered by chance.

Primary sexual characteristics   The reproductive organs and the production of *gametes*.

Primary sources   Historical documents that are written by individuals about their own lives.

Production   The "output" of language: speech and other vocal expressions (see *comprehension*).

Productive vocabulary   The number of words a child can use.

Productivity   The property of a language to express multiple meanings by recombining a small number of words.

Project Head Start   A federally funded preschool program to provide compensatory early education for disadvantaged children.

Project Follow-Through   A federally funded program designed to maintain the gains of "graduates" of Project Head Start by providing enrichment experiences to disadvantaged elementary schoolage children as well as social, medical and nutritional services to their families.

Projection   Denial of one's own feeling or thought by assuming that someone else has that same feeling or thought.

Prosocial behavior   Sharing, helping, donating, cooperating and other behaviors that aid or benefit others. (also called *prosocial morality*).

Protective service   A social service for children who are abused, neglected or exploited, usually administered by a child welfare agency.

Pseudoconservation   The ability to give correct responses to conservation problems without understanding the logical principles underlying them.

Psychoanalysis   A method of psychotherapy that relies on *free associations* and explanation of current conflicts by reference to events during childhood.

Psychoanalytic theory   The view that development is the product of the interaction of the child's natural urges with the influences of the socializing environment.

Psychophysiological stage   Stage of reasoning about health and illness that is characterized by recognition that multiple factors may be involved in causing illness.

Puberty   Literally, the growth of hair; more generally, the time during which secondary sexual characteristics and reproductive fertility become mature.

Punishment   A consequence that decreases the frequency of the behavior that it follows.

Quality of attachment   The extent to which infants feel secure vs. insecure in the company of their attachment object.

Quasi-experimental study   A study in which the experimenter does not manipulate the independent variables, but takes advantages of natural variations in the environment.

Random assignment   A procedure in which subjects are placed into experimental and control groups by the flip of a coin, or some other non-biased method.

Reaction time   Speed of response to a stimulus.

Readiness   The idea that environmental challenges should be adjusted to the developmental level of the child; that is, the child can only *accommodate* that which can be partially *assimilated*.

Reality principle   Meeting needs by evaluating alternative courses of action and selecting the one that is most adaptive under the circumstances.

Recall memory   The ability to generate previously seen or heard information.

Receptor   The sensory organs and perceptual processing that lead up to and control eventual *effector* outputs.

Receptive vocabulary   The number of words a child can understand.

Recessive allele   An allele for which two are required in order for the gene to be expressed.

Recognition memory   The ability to determine if a currently seen object or currently experienced event is novel or familiar.

Reconstituted family   (also called *blended family*). The family formed by remarriage, usually including children of previous marriages.

Recovery   Increase in fixation time due to dishabituation.

Referential speech   Speech about objects and their properties, usually simple, clear and direct.

Reflection-impulsivity cognitive style   Also called *Cognitive tempo* or *conceptual tempo*. The extent to which a person delays responding while searching for the correct alternative in a context of response uncertainty.

Reflex   Spontaneous response of the newborn to specific types of stimulation.

Regression   A temporary developmental reversal.

Rehearsal   The use of repetition to help in remembering information.

Reinforcement   The use of rewards and punishments to increase or decrease the likelihood of a response.

Relational play   The ability to combine objects that functionally go together, such as cups and saucers (see also *exploratory play*).

Reliability   The extent to which multiple observers agree about the coding of ongoing behavior, or the extent to which repeated administrations of the same test will give similar results.

Replication   The repetition of a research study in order to verify the original results on a new sample of subjects.

Representation   The mental or motor construction of an object or a relationship between objects.

Representativeness   The extent to which a research sample reflects the characteristics of the larger population.

Repression The placement of a conscious thought or memory into the unconscious.

Research The process by which predictions made from theory are verified in situation involving real children.

Research design The consideration of the methods of assessment, setting, ages and characteristics of subjects, and the number of subjects used in a research study.

Retrieval The ability to take information out of memory for current use.

Retrospective reports Information derived from recalling memories of past events, usually by adults of their childhoods.

Reversibility A mental operation in which equal but opposite effects cancel each other out.

Role confusion The inability to establish a cohesive *identity* during the adolescent years, and a lack of commitment to a consistent set of values.

Role overload The feeling of having too many (and conflicting) duties and obligations. (Also termed *Task overload*)

Romantics Nineteenth century thinkers who believed that children are inherently good and have the ability to develop successfully with minimal guidance.

Rooting A reflex turning of the head to the side on which the cheek is stroked.

Rough and tumble A type of vigorous play involving running, chasing, and mock fighting.

Rubella A type of measles that has been shown to have adverse effects on the fetus if contracted by a pregnant mother.

Rule of One-to-One Correspondence Rule that in counting objects, one must count each object once and only once and that no objects in the group can be skipped.

Sample The group of subjects selected to participate in a research study (see *representativeness*).

Scaffolding The adult's ability to create social situations that take advantage of the infant's limited ability to interact.

Schedule of reinforcement The pattern of relationship between emitted behavior and its consequences (see *continuous reinforcement schedule* and *partial reinforcement schedule*).

Schemes The thought and action patterns that the individual develops to operate on the environment in adaptive ways to meet specific goals.

School phobia Fear of attending school due to academic concerns, self-consciousness, or family problems.

Screening assessments Tests that give an indication of the newborn's ability to survive.

Script A conceptual framework that contains a set of specific events in their usual sequence, has "slots" for the introduction of new information, and designates appropriate roles and behaviors.

Search (of memory) Techniques used to scan memory to find information.

Secondary circular reactions The repetition of a chance discovery about the relationship of one's own movements to some effect on the environment.

Secondary sexual characteristics Physical characteristics typically associated with males or females, but not related to the reproductive organs (see *primary sexual characteristics*).

Secondary sources Works of literature, art, medicine or religion that interpret the meaning of life. The way individuals view their own lives, as seen in *primary sources*, may be quite different.

Secular trends Changes in the average value of a variable (e.g., height) of a population over a number of years.

Secure attachment Type of relationship between adult and infant in which the infant feels comfortable in unfamiliar settings when the adult is present, and is able to approach the adult for comfort when needed.

Secure base The infant's use of an adult as a checkpoint during exploration of an unfamiliar environment.

Selective attention Taking notice of only specific aspects of complex objects or events.

Self-awareness Knowledge of the self's internal states and external appearance.

Self-concept Ideas about the self.

Self-control The ability to regulate behavior to achieve adaptive goals.

Self-esteem Feelings one has about oneself and one's self-worth.

Self-fulfilling prophecy The tendency to behave toward others in ways that tend to confirm their expectations.

Self-regulation The ability to control one's own behavior.

Self-righting The ability of the organism to maintain normal developmental progress in spite of minor or temporary fluctuations in the quality of environmental stimulation.

Sensation The ability of each sense organ to detect information (see *perception*).

Sensitive period A period in the life cycle in which an individual is particularly susceptible to acquiring experiences leading to a developmental change.

Sensorimotor intelligence The use of motor skills to meet adaptive goals, to remember and to organize the environment.

Seriation Ordering items in a series along a dimension. For example, a group of children from shortest to tallest.

Sex-linked Inheritance related to the genes appearing on the 23rd pair of chromosomes, the "sex" chromosomes.

Sex ratio The proportion of males to females in the population at any given age.

Sex-role behaviors Behaviors that are believed to be characteristic of males or females in a particular culture. (also called *sex-typed behaviors*).

Sex-role concepts Ideas about the ways males and females are thought to differ in behavior, appearance, and thought.

Sex-role socialization The child's acquisition of behaviors, attitudes and aspirations considered appropriate to one's gender.

Sexual dimorphism Physical and behavioral differences between individuals of different sexes.

Shaping A technique of behavior modification, whereby successive approximations to a desired behavior are rewarded.

Short-term memory Memory capacity or "space" used for current or new information. Also called *working memory*.

Sibling deidentification Tendency of some parents with more than one child to attribute contrasting characteristics to each of their children.

Sickle-cell anemia A genetic disorder of the red blood cells that may cause retarded growth, neurological disorders, and heart and kidney failure.

Sign Arbitrary notation signifying some object or event; bears no resemblance to its referent. Example: "cat" as sign for the corresponding animal.

Situational constraints Aspects of the environment that affect relationships between individuals, especially peers, such as familiarity and prior experience with others.

Skeletal maturity Also called *Bone age*. Measure of physical growth in terms of degree of ossification or hardening of the bones.

Small-for-gestational-age An infant that weighs less than the norm for a given gestational age.

Social acceptance The degree to which a person is liked by others.

Social cognition Knowledge about other people and relationships.

Social fantasy play "Make believe" play characterized by the adoption and coordination of different roles. Also known as *social role-taking*.

Social impact The degree to which a child is noticed, positively or negatively, by peers.

Social learning theory The variant of *learning theory* in which consequences of action seen as information rather than as reinforcers, and in which the child is seen as an active evaluator of experiences; learning can occur by conditioning or by imitation.

Social policy Using theory and research to influence laws and social structures that affect children and families.

Social preference How liked a child is by peers. (see *social acceptance*).

Social referencing Using the facial expressions of another person to regulate one's own emotions.

Social structure The social class, ethnic, racial and religious distinctions within a society and the distribution of power and resources among these groups.

Social support Individuals that a person can turn to for various kinds of assistance.

Socialization The transmission of attitudes, values, and behaviors from one individual to another.

Sociocultural risk Dangers to growth and development due to social problems such as poverty, disease, death, divorce, and abuse.

Sociodramatic play Fantasy or make-believe that involves several children and the coordination of different roles.

Socioeconomic status (or *SES*) An index of social class position in terms of one or more of the following: income, education, and occupation.

Sociometric status A measure of social acceptance by members of a group. (See also *social acceptance*)

Solitary play Child plays alone.

Species specific innate behavior Behavior pattern that occurs only in one species and is the result of evolution by natural selection.

Spermatozoon The male gamete.

Spontaneous abortion The involuntary expulsion of the zygote or embryo.

Stability The extent to which an individual maintains the same ranking within the reference group at different ages.

Stages of development Periods of relatively slow change that come between more rapid growth spurts.

Standard English Form of English taught in schools and used as standard in texts and on ability and achievement tests.

Standardized test Assessment procedures that are identical for every subject in the sample, and which have been designed to be valid and reliable measures of a particular psychological or behavioral construct.

Stanford-Binet Intelligence Test Most commonly used test of intelligence. Developed by Alfred Binet of France and adapted for use in North America by Lewis Terman of Stanford University.

State dependent Behavior that can only occur during a particular state of arousal.

State of arousal Organized system of physical and physiological responding of the newborn that is related to the internal level of arousal or activation, from sleep to crying.

Statistics Summary scores that reveal how the "average" subject performed in a research study.

Status offense A reason for detaining a juvenile that would not be considered a crime if commited by an adult, for example, running away from home.

Strategy Decisions affecting the flow of information in the cognitive system, for example, whether to store information in short or long-term memory.

Subjective self The internal, psychological sense of self, the "I". (see *objective self*).

Sublimation   The channeling of sexual urges into more socially accepted behaviors.

Sudden infant death syndrome (SIDS)   The unexpected death of an infant from unknown causes.

Superego   The ability to distinguish right from wrong, the sense or morality.

Symbol   Bears some resemblance to thing signified. For example, a road sign with a curved line indicates a curve in the road.

Symbolic mode   According to Bruner, the stage of thinking beginning around age 7 when the child stores information primarily in terms of verbal symbols rather than visual images. (contrast to *Ikonic mode*)

Symbolic play   Also called *Fantasy play*. Activities in which objects, people, and events are represented in fantasy.

Symbolic representation   A representation of an object by another related object.

Synapse   Connecting link between two neurons.

Syncretic reasoning   The use of shifting and inconsistent categories to group information.

Syntax   The rules of word ordering, the grammar of a language.

System of thought   A view of the self and the world in which all ideas are logically connected (see *belief system*).

Systems theory   The view that the child develops as part of an interdependent set of environmental components exerting mutual influences over each other.

Tabula rasa   Literally, a "blank sheet of paper." The concept expresses the view that the child is shaped by *nurture,* that is, by the influences found in the environment after birth.

Tay-Sachs disease   A genetic enzyme deficiency leading to a deterioration of mental and physical abilities, and death before the age of 5 years.

Telegraphic speech   Speech in which articles, and word endings are left off; the first stage of speaking in sentences.

Temperament   Persistent patterns of individual reactivity to the environment.

Teratogen   An environmental factor that causes birth defects.

Teratology   The study of birth defects.

Terminal values   Values related to the end states of life, or to things that are worth striving for, such as peace, freedom and family security.

Tertiary circular reaction   Corresponds to sub-stage V in Piaget's sensorimotor period characterized by the repetition of actions on the environment in which each action is slightly different from the preceding one and related to each other by some patterns of systematic experimentation, also called *trial-and-error learning.*

Testosterone   A hormone responsible for the creation of male sex characteristics.

Test-retest reliability   The extent to which an assessment procedure yields similar results over repeated administrations.

Thalidomide   A tranquilizer that causes birth defects when taken during the first trimester of pregnancy.

Theme-and-variation format   Repetition with minor variations seen in adult speech to infants (see *baby talk*).

Theory   Belief system that explains some features of the observable world with structures, processes or mechanisms that are presumed to exist but cannot be observed directly.

Thyroid   A hormone essential for normal physical growth.

Time of measurement effect   Occurs when the results of a research study become biased because of special conditions occurring only at the time when the subjects are assessed, and not before or after.

Time sampling   A method of direct observation in which all events occurring within a pre-set time interval are recorded without noting the exact time of onset and offset.

Torrance Test of Creative Thinking   Well known test of creative thought; consists of subtests in which children are asked to generate as many novel responses as possible.

Traditional education   Principles of instruction emphasizing teacher-directed learning and the step-by-step acquisition of material by students.

Trait rating   A summary judgement about a child's level of performance made after observing the child in a particular situation.

Transductive reasoning   The linking together in a cause-effect sequence of two events which occur close together in time but are otherwise unrelated.

Trial-and-error learning   See *tertiary circular reactions.*

Triceps skinfold   Skin and underlying fat layer on the back of the arm muscle, midway between the elbow and the shoulder. Thickness of the triceps skinfold is the most accurate measure of obesity.

Trimester   One-third of a normal pregnancy, about three months.

Trisomy   An error of meiosis in which one too many chromosomes are included in a gamete, which, if fertilized, will lead to a chromosome triplet in the zygote.

Turn-taking   The exchange of turns in conversation or in play.

Type A behavior pattern   Also called *Coronary- prone behavior pattern*. The tendency to exhibit extreme competitiveness, hostility, impatience, time urgency, and striving for achievement. In adults, this pattern is associated with increased risk of heart disease.

Ultrasound   A method of "viewing" the fetus by using reflected sound waves.

Unconscious   A protective mechanism by which painful or difficult memories remain hidden outside of the person's awareness.

Universal education   Equal access and opportunity in education for all people, regardless of sex, race, ethnicity or religion.

Validity   The extent to which assessment procedures accurately measure the concept underlying the variable.

Variable   An attribute of the child or environment that can be expected to vary between children, or within the child over time.

Verbal organizers   The use of words to coordinate and regulate behavior.

Vernix caseosa   A white, cheesy coating over the fetal skin.

Vestibular-proprioceptive stimulation   The stimulation of the infant caused by physical movement of the infant's body.

Viability   The individual's ability to survive without external life support systems.

Visual object constancy   The ability to recognize the same object from different perspectives and distances from the viewer.

Visual preference test   Allowing the infant to choose, by preferential looking time, between two or more objects. Consistent preference of one over another object shows that infants can perceptually discriminate between the objects.

Wechsler Intelligence Scale for Children (WISC-R)   Widely used I.Q. test for children aged 6 to 16 years. Contains 12 subtests and yields two scores, one for verbal intelligence and one for "performance" or nonverbal intelligence.

Whorf-Sapir hypothesis   View that perception and language are related; that is, the more words for a particular phenomenon exist in a language the more perceptual distinctions speakers of that language can make.

Word span   The number of words from a list that can be remembered immediately after seeing or hearing the list.

Yolk sac   A region of cells in the blastocyst that will eventually become the embryonic blood supply and internal organs.

Zero correlation   Indicates no relationship between two variables.

Zygote   The fertilized ovum.

Aberle, D. F. & Naegele, K. D. (1962). Middle class fathers' occupational role and attitudes toward children. *American Journal of Orthopsychiatry, 22,* 366–378.

Abraham, S., Collins, G., & Nordsieck, M. (1971). Relationship of childhood weight status to morbidity in adults. *Public Health Reports, 86,* 273–284.

Abraham, S., & Nordsieck, M. (1960). Relationship of excess weight in children and adults. *Public Health Reports, 25,* 263–273.

Abramovitch, R., Corter, C., & Landau, B. (1979). Sibling interaction in the home. *Child Development, 50,* 997–1003.

Abramovitch, R., & Grusec, J. E. (1978). Peer imitation in a natural setting. *Child Development, 49,* 60–65.

ABT Associates (1979). *Children at the center: Final report on the national day care study* (Executive summary). Washington, D.C.: Department of Health, Education and Welfare.

Achenbach, T. M. (1978). *Research in developmental psychology: Concepts, strategies and methods.* New York: The Free Press.

Achenbach, T. M., & Edelbrock, C. S. (1981). Behavior problems and competencies reported by parents of normal and disturbed children aged 4 to 16. *Monograph of the Society for Research in Child Development, 46,* (No. 188).

Ackerman, B. (1987). Developmental differences in episodic retrieval: The role of differences in concept representation in semantic memory. *Developmental Psychology, 23,* 31–38.

Acredolo, C. & Acredolo, L. P. (1979). Identity, compensation and conservation. *Child Development, 50,* 524–535.

Acredolo, C., & Horobin, K. (1987). Development of relational reasoning and avoidance of premature closure. *Developmental Psychology, 23,* 13–21.

Adams, G. R., & Jones, R. M. (1983). Female adolescent development: Age comparisons and perceived child-rearing experience. *Developmental Psychology, 19,* 249–256.

Adelson, J., & Doehrman, M. J. (1980). The psychodynamic approach to adolescence. In J. Adelson (Ed.), *Handbook of adolescent psychology* (pp. 99–116). New York: Wiley.

Affonso, D. (1977). "Missing pieces": A study of postpartum feelings. *Birth and the Family Journal, 4,* 158–164.

Ainsworth, M. (1979). Attachment as related to mother-infant interaction. In R. Hinde & J. Rosenblatt (Eds.), *Advances in the study of behavior.* New York: Academic Press.

Ainsworth, M. D. S., & Bell, S. M. (1970). Attachment, exploration, and separation: Illustrated by the behavior of one-year-olds in a strange situation. *Child Development, 41,* 49–67.

Ainsworth, M., Bell, S., & Stayton, D. (1971). Individual differences in strange situation behavior of one-year-olds. In H. R. Schaffer (Ed.), *The origins of human social relations.* London: Academic Press.

Ainsworth, M., Blehar, M. C., Waters, E., & Wall, S. (1978). *Patterns of attachment: A psychological study of the strange situation.* Hillsdale, NJ: Erlbaum.

Alexander, S. J., & Jorgensen, S. R. (1983). Sex education for early adolescents: A study of parents and students. *Journal of early adolescence, 3,* 315–325.

Allen, D. A., Affleck, G., McGrade, B. J., & McQueeney, M. (1984). Effects of single-parent status on mothers and their high-risk infants. *Infant Behavior and Development, 7,* 347–359.

Allen, J. E. (1982). *The assessment of moral reasoning in preschool children and the relationship between moral reasoning and peer interaction.* Unpublished Ph.D. dissertation, Purdue University.

Alley, T. R. (1983). Infantile head shape as an elicitor of adult protection. *Merrill-Palmer Quarterly, 29,* 411–427.

American Psychiatric Association (1980). *Diagnostic and statistical manual of mental disorders.* (3rd Ed.). Washington, D.C.: American Psychiatric Association.

Ames, G. & Murray, F. B. (1982). When two wrongs make a right: Promoting cognitive change by social conflict. *Developmental Psychology, 18,* 892–895.

Anderson, D. R., Alwitt, L. F., Lorch, E. P. and Levin, S. R. (1979). Watching children watch television. In G. A. Hale and M. Lewis (Eds.), *Attention and cognitive development.* New York: Plenum Press.

Anderson, G. C., Burroughs, A. K., Measel, C. P. (1983). Nonnutritive sucking opportunities: A safe and effective treatment for preterm neonates. In T. Field & A. Sostek (Eds.), *Infants born at risk.* New York: Grune & Stratton.

Apgar, V. (1953). A proposal for a new method of evaluation in the newborn infant. *Current Research in Anesthesia and Analgesia, 32,* 260.

Appel, L. F., Copper, R. G., McCarrell, N., Sims-Knight, J., Yussen, S. R., & Flavell, J. H. (1972). The development of the distinction between perceiving and memorizing. *Child Development, 43,* 1365–1381.

Archer, S. L., & Waterman, A. S. (1983). Identity in early adolescence: A developmental perspective. *Journal of Early Adolescence, 3,* 203–214.

Arehart-Treichel, J. (1979). Down's syndrome: the father's role. *Science News,* December 1, 381–382.

Arend, R., Gove, F. L., & Sroufe, L. A. (1979). Continuity of individual adaptation from infancy to kindergarten: A predictive study of ego resiliency and curiosity in preschoolers. *Child Development, 50,* 950–959.

Aries, P. (1962). *Centuries of childhood.* New York: Vintage (trans. R. Baldick).

Aro, H., & Tiapale, V. (1987). The impact of timing of puberty on psychosomatic symptoms among fourteen- to sixteen-year-old Finnish girls. *Child Development, 58,* 261–268.

Aronfreed, J. (1968). *Conduct and conscience: The socialization of internalized control over behavior*. NY: Academic Press.

Aronfreed, J. (1970). The socialization of altruism and sympathetic behavior: Some theoretical and experimental analyses. In J. Macaulay & L. Berkowitz (Eds.), *Altruism and helping behavior*. NY: Academic Press.

Aschkenasy, J. R. and Odom, R. D. (1982). Classification and perceptual development: Exploring issues about integrality and differential sensitivity. *Journal of Experimental Child Psychology, 34*, 435–448.

Asher, S. R., & Renshaw, P. D. (1981). Children without friends: Social knowledge and social skill training. In S. R. Asher & J. M. Gottman (Eds.), *The development of children's friendships*. London: Cambridge University Press.

Asher, S. R., Singleton, L. C., Tinsley, B. R., & Hymel, S. (1979). A reliable sociometric measure for preschool children. *Developmental Psychology, 15*, 443–444.

Azarnoff, P., & Woody, P. (1981). Preparation of children for hospitalization in acute care hospitals in the United States. *Pediatrics, 68*, 361–368.

Bach, G. F. (1946). Father-fantasies and father typing in father-separated children. *Child Development, 17*, 63–80.

Baer, J. (1984). Personal communication.

Bakeman, R., & Adamson, L. B. (1984). Coordinating attention to people and objects in mother-infant and peer-infant interaction. *Child Development, 55*, 1278–1289.

Baker, C. D. (1982). The adolescent as theorist: An interpretive view. *Journal of Youth and Adolescence, 11*, 167–181.

Baker, C. D. (1983). A "second look" at interviews with adolescents. *Journal of Youth and Adolescence, 12*, 501–519.

Baker, L. (1982). An evaluation of the role of metacognitive deficits in learning disability. *Topics in Learning and Learning Disability, 2*, 27–35.

Balamore, U. & Wozniak, R. H. (1984). Speech-action coordination in young children. *Developmental Psychology, 20*, 850–858.

Bandura, A. L. (1969). Social learning theory of identificatory processes. In D. A. Goslin (Ed.), *Handbook of social theory and research*. New York: Rand-McNally.

Bandura, A. L. (1971). Analysis of modeling processes. In A. L. Bandura (Ed.), *Psychological modeling*. Chicago: Aldine-Atherton.

Bandura, A. L. (1977). *Social learning theory*. Englewood Cliffs, N.J.: Prentice-Hall.

Bandura, A. L., Ross, D., & Ross, S. A. (1963). A comparative test of the status envy, social power and secondary reinforcement theories of identificatory learning. *Journal of Abnormal and Social Psychology, 67*, 527–534.

Banks, W. C. (1976). White preference in blacks: A paradigm in search of a phenomenon. *Psychological Bulletin, 83*, 1179–1186.

Bannister, D., & Agnew, J. (1977). The child's constancy of self. In J. Cole (Ed.), *Nebraska symposium on motivation*. Lincoln: University of Nebraska Press.

Banta, H. D. (1981, October). *The risks and benefits of episiotomy*. Paper presented at the conference on "Obstetrical management and infant outcome 1981: Implications for future mental and physical development," sponsored by the American Foundation for Maternal and Child Health, Inc., New York.

Barker, R. G., & Wright, H. F. (1955). *Midwest and its children: The psychological ecology of an American town*. Evanston, Il.: Row-Peterson.

Barnard, K. E., Bee, H. L., & Hammond, M. A. (1984). Developmental changes in maternal interactions with term and pre-term infants. *Infant Behavior and Development, 7*, 101–113.

Barnett, M. A., Matthews, K. A., & Howard, J. A. (1979). The relationship between competence and empathy in six and seven year olds. *Developmental Psychology, 15*, 221–222.

Barney, G. O. (1980). *The global 2000 report to the President*. Washington, D.C.: Government Printing Office.

Barrera, M. E., & Maurer, D. (1981). Recognition of mother's photographed face by the three-month-old. *Child Development, 52*, 714–716.

Barrett, D. E., (1979). A naturalistic study of sex differences in children's aggression. *Merrill-Palmer Quarterly, 25*, 193–203.

Barrett, D. E., Radke-Yarrow, M. & Klein, R. E. (1982). Chronic malnutrition and child behavior: effects of early caloric supplementation on social and emotional functioning at school age. *Developmental Psychology, 18*, 541–556.

Barstis, S. W. & Ford, L. H. Jr. (1977). Reflection-impulsivity, conservation, and the development of ability to control cognitive tempo. *Child Development, 48*, 953–959.

Bar-Tal, D. (1976). *Prosocial behavior: Theory and research*. Washington, D.C.: Hemisphere Pub. Co.

Bar-Tal, D. (1982). The sequential development of helping behavior: A cognitive-learning approach.

Bar-Tal, D., Raviv, A., & Goldberg, M. (1982). Helping behavior among preschool children: an observational study. *Child Development, 53*, 396–402.

Bar-Tal, D., Raviv, A., & Leiser, T. (1980). The development of altruistic behavior: Empirical evidence. *Developmental Psychology, 16*, 516–525.

Bartel, N. R. (1971). Locus of control and achievement in middle- and lower-class children. *Child Development, 42*, 1099–1107.

Barton, J., Chassin, L., Presson, C. C., & Sherman, S. J. (1982). Social image factors as motivators of smoking initiation in early and middle adolescence. *Child Development, 53*, 1499–1511.

Bates, E. (1979). *The emergence of symbols*. New York: Academic Press.

Baumrind, D. (1967). Child-care practices anteceding three patterns of preschool behavior. *Genetic Psychology Monographs, 75*, 43–88.

Baumrind, D. (1973). The development of instrumental competence through socialization. In A. D. Pick (Ed.), *Minnesota symposium on child psychology*. (Vol. 7). Minneapolis: University of Minnesota Press.

Baumrind, D. (1975). *Early parenting socialization and the discipline controversy.* Morristown, NJ: General Learning Press.

Baumrind, D. (1977). *Socialization determinants of personal agency.* Paper presented to biennial meeting of the Society for Research in Child Development, New Orleans.

Baumrind, D. (1982). Are androgynous individuals more effective persons and parents? *Child Development, 53,* 44–75.

Baumrind, D. (1986). Sex differences in moral reasoning: response to Walker's (1984) conclusion that there are none. *Child Development, 57,* 511–521.

Bayley, N. (1969). *Manual for the Bayley scales of infant development.* New York: Psychological Corporation.

Bearison, D. J. & Cassell, T. Z. (1975). Cognitive decentering and social codes: Communicative effectiveness in young children from differing family contexts. *Developmental Psychology, 11,* 29–36.

Becker, W. C. (1964). Consequences of different kinds of parental discipline. In M. L. Hoffman & L. W. Hoffman (Eds.), *Review of child development research* (Vol. 1). New York: Russell Sage Foundation.

Bee, H. L., Disbrow, M. A., Johnson-Crowley, N., & Barnard, K. (1981). *Parent-child interaction during teaching in abusing and non-abusing families.* Paper presented to the biennial meeting of the Society for Research in Child Development, Boston.

Bee, H. L., VanEgeren, L. F., Streissguth, L. F., Nyman, A. P., Barry, A., & Leckie, M. S. (1969). Social class differences in maternal teaching strategies and speech patterns. *Developmental Psychology, 1,* 726–734.

Beech, R. P., & Schoeppe, A. (1974). Development of value systems in adolescents. *Developmental Psychology, 10,* 644–656.

Bell, R. Q. (1968). A reinterpretation of the direction of effect in studies of socialization. *Psychological Review, 75,* 81–95.

Bell, R. Q. (1979). Parent, child and reciprocal influences. *American Psychologist, 34,* 821–826.

Bell, R. Q., & Harper, L. V. (1977). *Child effects on adults.* Hillsdale, NJ: Erlbaum.

Bell, R. Q., Weller, G., & Waldrop, M. (1971). Newborn and preschooler: Organization of behavior and relation between periods. *Monographs of the Society for Research in Child Development, 36,* (Serial no. 142).

Bellugi, U. (1964). *The emergence of inflections and negation systems in the speech of two children.* Paper presented at New England Psychological Association meetings.

Bellugi, U. (1971). Simplification in children's language. In R. Huxley & E. Ingram (Eds.), *Methods and models in language acquisition.* NY: Academic Press.

Belsky, J. (1980). Child maltreatment: An ecological approach. *American Psychologist, 35,* 320–335.

Belsky, J. (1981). Early human experience: A family perspective. *Developmental Psychology, 17,* 3–23.

Belsky, J. (1984). The determinants of parenting: A process model. *Child Development, 55,* 83–96.

Belsky, J., Gilstrap, B., & Rovine, M. (1984). The Pennsylvania infant and family project, I: Stability and change in mother-infant and father-infant interaction in a family setting at one, three, and nine months. *Child Development, 55,* 692–705.

Belsky, J., Lerner, R. M. and Spanier, G. (1984). *The child in the family.* Reading, MA: Addison-Wesley Publishing Co.

Belsky, J., Rovine, M., & Taylor, D. G. (1984). The Pennsylvania infant and family development project, III: The origins of individual differences in infant-mother attachment: Maternal and infant contributions. *Child Development, 55,* 718–728.

Benson, J. B., & Uzgiris, J. C. (1985). Effect of self-initiated locomotion on infant search activity. *Developmental Psychology, 21,* 923–931.

Berbaum, M. L., & Moreland, R. L. (1985). Intellectual development within transracial adoptive families: Retesting the confluence model. *Child Development, 56,* 207–216.

Berenson, G., Frank, G., Hunter, S., Srinivasan, S., Voors, A., & Webber, L. (1982). Cardiovascular risk factors in children: should they concern the pediatrician? *American Journal of Diseases of Children, 136,* 855–862.

Berger, J., & Cunningham, C. C. (1983). Development of early vocal behaviors and interactions in Down's syndrome and nonhandicapped infant mother-pairs. *Developmental Psychology, 19,* 322–331.

Bergman, C. (1976). Interference vs. independent development in infant bilingualism. In G. D. Keller, R. V. Taescher & S. Viera, (Eds.), *Bilingualism in the bicentennial and beyond.* New York: Bilingual Press.

Berko-Gleason, J. (1958). The child's learning of English morphology. *Word, 14,* 150–177.

Berndt, T. J. (1981). Age changes and changes over time in prosocial intentions and behavior between friends. *Developmental Psychology, 17,* 408–416.

Berndt, T. J. (1982). The features and effects of friendships in early adolescence. *Child Development, 53,* 1447–1460.

Berndt, T. J. (1985). Prosocial behavior between friends in middle childhood and early adolescence. *Journal of Early Adolescence, 5,* 307–318.

Berndt, T. J., & Hoyle, S. G. (1985). Stability and change in childhood and adolescent friendships. *Developmental Psychology, 21,* 1007–1015.

Berrueta-Clement, J. R., Schweinhart, L. J., Barnett, W. S., Epstein, A. S., & Weikart, D. P. (1984). *Changed lives: The effects of the Perry Preschool Program on youths through age 19.* Ypsilanti, MI: Monograph of the High Scope/Educational Research Foundation, No. 8.

Bettleheim, B. (1969). *The children of the dream.* New York: MacMillan.

Bibace, R., & Walsh, M. E. (1980). Development of children's concepts of illness. *Pediatrics, 66,* 913–917.

Bibace, R., & Walsh, M. E. (1981). Children's conceptions of illness. In R. Bibace & M. E. Walsh (Eds.), *New directions for child development.* Vol. 14 (pp. 31–48) San Francisco: Jossey-Bass.

Bigelow, B. J. (1977). Children's friendship expectations: A cognitive developmental study. *Child Development, 48,* 246–253.

Bigelow, B. J., & LaGaipa, J. J. (1975). Children's written descriptions of friendship. *Developmental Psychology, 11,* 857–858.

Bijou, S. W. (1984). Behaviorism—history and educational applications. In T. Husen & T. N. Postlethwaite (Eds.), *International encyclopedia of education.* Oxford: Pergammon Press.

Bijou, S. W., & Baer, D. M. (1965). *Child development.* Vol. 2, *Universal stages of infancy.* New York: Appleton-Century-Crofts.

Biller, H. B. (1969). Father-absence, maternal encouragement and sex-role development in kindergarten-age boys. *Child Development, 40,* 539–546.

Biller, H.B. (1981). The father and sex role development. In M. E. Lamb (Ed.), *The role of the father in child development.* New York: Wiley.

Biller, H. B., & Bahm, R. M. (1971). Father-absence, perceived maternal behavior and masculinity of self-concept among junior high boys. *Developmental Psychology, 4,* 178–181.

Binet, A., & Simon, T. (1916). *The development of intelligence in children.* (E. S. Kite, trans.). Baltimore: Williams & Wilkins.

Bingham-Newman, A. M., Saunders, R. A. & Hooper, F. H. (1976). *Logical operations in the preschool: The contributions of Piagetian theory to early childhood education.* Technical Report No. 354. Madison, Wis: Wisconsin Research and Development Center for Cognitive Learning.

Birch, L. L. & Billman, J. (1986). Preschool children's food sharing with friends and acquaintances. *Child Development, 57,* 387–395.

Birnholz, J. C., & Farrell, E. E. (1984). Ultrasound images of human fetal development. *American Scientist, 72,* 608–614.

Birns, B., & Golden, M. (1972). Prediction of intellectual performance at 3 years from intelligence tests and personality measures. *Merrill-Palmer Quarterly, 18,* 53–58.

Black, H. K. (1974). Physical attractiveness and similarity of attitude in interpersonal attraction. *Psychological Reports, 35,* 403–406.

Black, L., Steinschneider, A., & Sheehe, P. R. (1979). Neonatal respiratory instability and infant development. *Child Development, 50,* 561–564.

Blaikie, P. M. (1975). *Family planning in India.* New York: Holmes & Meier.

Blake, A., Stewart, A., & Turcan, D. (1975). Parents of babies of very low birth weight: long-term follow-up. In Ciba Foundation (Ed.), *Parent-infant interaction.* NY: Elsevier.

Blank, M., & Klig, S. (1982). The child and the school experience. In C. B. Kopp & J. B. Krakow (Eds.), *The child: Development in a social context* (pp. 456–513). Reading, MA: Addison-Wesley.

Blau, Z. S. (1981). *Black children/white children.* New York: Free Press.

Blehar, M. C., Lieberman, A., & Ainsworth, M. (1977). Early face-to-face interaction and its relation to later mother-infant attachment. *Child Development, 48,* 182–194.

Block, J., Block, J. H. & Harrington, D. M. (1974). Some misgivings about the Matching Familiar Figures Test as a measure of reflection-impulsivity. *Developmental Psychology, 10,* 611–632.

Block, J. H. (1973). Conceptions of sex role: Some cross-cultural and longitudinal perspectives. *American Psychologist, 28,* 512–526.

Block, J. H. (1983). Differential premises arising from differential socialization of the sexes: some conjectures. *Child Development, 54,* 1335–1354.

Block, J. H., & Block, J. (1980). The role of ego-control and ego-resiliency in the organization of behavior. In W. A. Collins (Ed.), *Development of cognition, affect and social relations: The Minnesota symposium on child psychology* (Vol. 13). Hillsdale, NJ: Erlbaum (pp. 39–101).

Block, J. H., Block, J. & Harrington, D. M. (1974). *The relation of parental teaching strategies to ego-resiliency in preschool children.* Paper presented to the Western Psychological Association meeting, San Francisco.

Bloom, L., Rocissano, L., & Hood, L. (1976). Adult-child discourse: developmental interaction between information-processing and linguistic knowledge. *Cognitive Psychology, 8,* 521–552.

Blos, P. (1962). *On adolescence.* New York: Free Press.

Blurton-Jones, N. (Ed.) (1972). *Ethological studies of child behavior.* Cambridge: Cambridge University Press.

Borke, H. (1975). Piaget's mountains revisited: changes in the egocentric landscape. *Developmental Psychology, 11,* 240–243.

Bornstein, M. H. (1976). Infants are trichromats. *Journal of Experimental Child Psychology, 21,* 425–445.

Bortner, R. W., & Rosenman, R. H. (1967). The measurement of pattern A behavior. *Journal of Chronic Diseases, 20,* 525–533.

Bower, T. G. R., Broughton, J., & Moore, M. (1970). The coordination of vision and touch in infancy. *Perception and Psychophysics, 8,* 51–53.

Bower, T. G. R. (1974). *Development in infancy.* San Francisco: Freeman.

Bowlby, J. (1969). *Attachment.* New York: Basic Books.

Boyce, W. T., Jensen, E. W., Cassel, J. C., Collier, A. M., Smith, A. H., & Ramey, C. T. (1977). Influence of life events and family routines on children's respiratory tract illness. *Pediatrics, 60,* 609–615.

Brackbill, Y. (1970). Acoustic variation and arousal level in infants. *Psychophysiology, 6,* 517–526.

Brackbill, Y. (1975). Continuous stimulation and arousal levels in infancy: Effects of stimulus intensity and stress. *Child Development, 46,* 364–369.

Brackbill, Y. (1979). Obstetrical medication and infant behavior. In J. Osofsky (Ed.), *Handbook of infant development.* New York: Wiley.

Bradley, R. H. & Caldwell, B. M. (1976). The relation of infants' home environments to mental test performance at fifty-four months: a follow-up study. *Child Development, 47,* 1172–1174.

Bradley, R. H., Caldwell, B. M. & Elardo, R. (1977). Home environment, social status and mental test performance. *Journal of Educational Psychology, 69,* 697–701.

Bradley, R. H., Caldwell, B. M., & Elardo, R. (1979). Home environment and cognitive development in the first two years: A cross-lagged panel analysis. *Developmental Psychology, 15,* 246–250.

Braine, M. D. S. (1976). Children's first word combination. *Monographs of the Society for Research in Child Development, 164* (Serial No. 164).

Brainerd, C. J. (1978). *Piaget's theory of intelligence.* Englewood Cliffs, NJ: Prentice-Hall.

Brainerd, C. J. & Brainerd, S. H. (1972). Order of acquisition of number and liquid quantity conservation. *Child Development, 43,* 1401–1405.

Branch, C. W. & Newcomb, N. (1986). Racial attitude development among young black children as a function of parental attitudes: A longitudinal and cross-sectional study. *Child Development, 57,* 712–721.

Branchfeld, S., Goldberg, S., & Sloman, J. (1980). Parent-infant interaction in free play at 8 and 12 months: Effects of prematurity and immaturity. *Infant Behavior and Development, 3,* 289–306.

Brand, E. S., Ruiz, R. A., & Padilla, A. M. (1974). Ethnic identification and preference behavior: A review. *Psychological Bulletin, 81,* 860–890.

Brazelton, T. B. (1972). Implications of infant development among the Mayan Indians of Mexico. *Human Development, 15,* 9–11.

Brazelton, T. B., Koslowski, B., & Main, M. (1974). The origins of reciprocity. In M. Lewis & L. Rosenblum (Eds.), *The effect of the infant on its caregiver.* New York: Wiley.

Bretherton, I. (1985). Attachment theory: Retrospect and prospect. *Monographs of the Society for Research in Child Development, 50,* (Serial No. 209), 3–38.

Bretherton, I., McNew, S., & Beeghly-Smith, M. (1981). Early person knowledge as expressed in gestural and verbal communications: When do infant acquire a "theory of mind"? In M. Lamb & L. Sherrod (Eds.), *Infant social cognition.* Hillsdale, NJ: Erlbaum.

Brody, G. H., Stoneman, Z., & MacKinnon, C. E. (1982). Role asymmetry in interactions among school-age children, their younger siblings and their friends. *Child Development, 53,* 1364–1370.

Brody, G. H., Stoneman, Z., MacKinnon, C. E., & MacKinnon, R. (1985). Role relations and behavior between preschool-aged and school-aged sibling pairs. *Developmental Psychology, 21,* 124–129.

Brody, J. (1985). *New York Times,* Nov. 7.

Brodzinsky, D. M. (1979). Sex differences in children's expression and control of fantasy and overt aggression, *Child Development, 50,* pg. 372–379.

Brodzinsky, D. M. (1980). Cognitive style differences in children's spatial perspective taking. *Developmental Psychology, 16,* 151–152.

Brodzinsky, D. M. (1982). Relation between cognitive style and cognitive development: A two-year longitudinal study. *Developmental Psychology, 18,* 617–626.

Brodzinsky, D. M., Singer, L. M., & Braff, A. M. (1984). Children's understanding of adoption. *Child Development, 55,* 869–878.

Bronfenbrenner, U. (1976). Who cares for America's children? In V. C. Vaughn III & T. B. Brazelton (Eds.), *The family: Can it be saved?* (pp. 3–20) Chicago: Yearbook Medical Publishers.

Bronfenbrenner, U. (1979). *The ecology of human development: Experiments by nature and design.* Cambridge, MA: Harvard University Press.

Bronson, G. W. (1972). Infant's reactions to unfamiliar persons and novel objects. *Monographs of the Society for Research in Child Development, 47,* (Serial no. 148).

Brook, J. S., Whiteman, M., & Gordon, A. S. (1983). Stages in drug use in adolescence: Personality, peer, and family correlates. *Developmental Psychology, 19,* 269–277.

Brookhart, J., & Hock, E. (1976). The effects of experimental context and experiential background on infant's behavior toward their mother and a stranger. *Child Development, 47,* 333–340.

Brooks, J., & Lewis, M. (1976). Infants' responses to strangers: midget, adult, and child. *Child Development, 47,* 323–332.

Brooks, M., & Knowles, D. (1982). Parents' views of children's imaginary companions. *Child Welfare, 61,* 25–33.

Brooks-Gunn, J. (1984). The psychological significance of different pubertal events to young girls. *Journal of Early Adolescence, 4,* 315–327.

Brooks-Gunn, J., & Furstenberg, F. (1986). Antecedents and consequences of parenting: The case of adolescent motherhood. In A. Fogel & G. F. Melson (Eds.), *Origins of nurturance.* Hillsdale, NJ: Erlbaum.

Brooks-Gunn, J., & Lewis, M. (1979). "Why momma and papa?" The development of social labels. *Child Development, 50,* 1203–1206.

Brooks-Gunn, J., & Lewis, M. (1982). Affective exchanges between normal and handicapped infants and their mothers. In T. Field and A. Fogel (Eds.), *Emotion and early interaction.* Hillsdale, NJ: Erlbaum.

Brooks-Gunn, J., & Warren, M. P. (1983). *Psychological functioning and pubertal status: The effects of different maturational indices.* Paper presented at American Psychological Association meetings, Anaheim, CA.

Brophy, J. E. (1983). Research on the self-fulfilling prophecy and teacher expectations. *Journal of Educational Psychology, 75,* 631–661.

Broughton, J. (1978). Development of concepts of self, mind, reality, and knowledge. *New Directions for Child Development, 1,* 75–100.

Brown, A. L., Bransford, J. D., Ferrara, R. A., & Campione, J. C. (1983). Learning, remembering and understanding. In J. H. Flavell & E. M. Markman (Eds.), *The Handbook of Child Psychology* (Vol. 3). New York: Wiley.

Brown, B., & Rosenbaum, L. (1983). *Stress and IQ*. Paper presented to American Association for the Advancement of Science, Detroit, MI.

Brown, C. (1965). *Manchild in the promised land*. NY: New American library.

Brown, J., Bakeman, R., Snyder, P., Fredrickson, W., Morgan, S., & Hepler, R. (1975). Interactions of black inner-city mothers with their newborn infants. *Child Development, 46,* 677–686.

Brown, R. (1966). Organ weight in malnutrition with special reference to brain weight. *Developmental Medicine and Child Neurology, 8,* 512–522.

Brown, R. (1973). *The first language: The early stages*. Cambridge, MA: Harvard University Press.

Brown, R., Cazden, C. & Bellugi-Klima, U. (1969). The child's grammar from I to III. In J. P. Hill (Ed.), *Minnesota Symposium of Child Psychology*. Vol. 2. University of Minnesota Press.

Browne, A. & Finkelhor, D. (1986). Impact of child sexual abuse: A review of the research. *Psychological Bulletin, 99,* 66–77.

Bruch, H. (1973). *Eating disorders: Obesity, anorexia nervosa and the person within*. New York: Basic Books.

Bruner, J. (1964). The course of cognitive growth. *American Psychologist, 19,* 1–15.

Bruner, J. (1972). The nature and uses of immaturity. *American Psychologist, 27,* 687–708.

Bruner, J. (1975). The ontogenesis of speech acts. *Journal of Child Language, 2,* 1–19.

Bruner, J., Olver, R. R. and Greenfield, P. M. (1966). *Studies in cognitive growth*. New York: Wiley.

Brunk, M. A. & Henggeler, S. W. (1984). Child influences on adult controls: An experimental investigation. *Developmental Psychology, 20,* 1074–1081.

Brunswick, A. F., & Messeri, P. A. (1984). Origins of cigarette smoking in academic achievement, stress and social expectations: Does gender make a difference? *Journal of Early Adolescence, 4,* 353–370.

Bryant, B. & Crockenberg, S. (1980). Correlates and dimensions of prosocial behavior: A study of female siblings with their mothers. *Child Development, 51,* 529–544.

Bryant, P. E. & Trabasso, T. (1971). Transitive inferences and memory in young children. *Nature, 232,* 456–458.

Bryden, M. P. (1982). *Laterality*. NY: Academic Press.

Bryden, M. P. & Saxby, L. (1985). Developmental aspects of cerebral lateralization. In J. E. Obrzat & G. W. Hynd (Eds.), *Child neuropsychology. Vol. I. Theory and research*. NY: Academic Press.

Bucky, S. F. & Banta, T. J. (1972). Racial factors in test performance. *Developmental Psychology, 6,* 7–13.

Burns, S. M. & Brainerd, C. (1979). Effects of constructive and dramatic play on perspective taking in very young children. *Developmental Psychology, 15,* 512–521.

Burgess, A. W., Groth, A. N., Holmstrom, L. L. & Sgroi, S. M. (1978). *Sexual assault of children and adolescents*. Lexington, MA: Lexington Books.

Burton, R. V. (1963). The generality of honesty reconsidered. *Psychological Review, 70,* 481–499.

Burton, R. V. (1984). A paradox in theories and research in moral development. In W. M. Kurtines & J. L. Gerwirtz (Eds.), *Morality, moral behavior, and moral development*. NY: Wiley.

Buss, D. M., Block, J. H. & Block, J. (1980). Preschool activity level: personality correlates and developmental implications. *Child Development, 51,* 401–408.

Bussis, A. M., & Chittenden, E. A. (1970). *Analysis of an approach to open education*. Princeton, NJ: Educational Testing Service.

Buster, J. E. (1984). Embryo transfer. *Science News,* February 11, p. 85.

Butler, J. A., Starfield, B., & Stenmark, S. (1984). Child health policy. In H. W. Stevenson & A. E. Siegel (Eds), *Child development research and social policy* (pp. 110–188). Chicago: University of Chicago Press.

Butler, N. (1974). Late postnatal consequences of fetal malnutrition. In M. Winick (Ed.), *Nutrition and fetal development*. New York: Wiley.

Butler, N. (1980). Child health and education in the 70's: Some results on the five-year followup of the 1970 British birth cohort. *Health Visitor, 35,* 81–82.

Byrne, J. M., & Horowitz, F. D. (1979). Rocking as a soothing intervention: The influence of direction and type of movement. *Infant Behavior and Development, 2,* 209–214.

Cain, K. M., & Fincham, F. D. (1985). *Learned helplessness and mastery orientation in third-grade children*. Paper presented at the biennial meetings of the Society for Research in Child Development, Toronto, Canada.

Cain, L. P., Kelly, D. H., & Shannon, D. C. (1980). Parents' perceptions of the psychological and social impact of home monitoring. *Pediatrics, 66,* 37–41.

Cairns, R. (1979). *Social development: The origins and plasticity of interchanges*. San Francisco: Freeman.

Caldeyro-Barcia, R. (1981, October). *The scientific bases for preserving the normal physiology of labor and birth through non-intervention*. Paper presented at the Conference on Obstetrical Management and Infant Outcome, New York.

Callaghan, J. W. (1981). A comparison of Anglo, Hopi, and Navaho mothers and infants. In T. Field, A. Sostek, P. Vietze, & P. Leiderman (Eds.), *Culture and early interactions*. Hillsdale, NJ: Erlbaum.

Calnan, M., & Peckham, C. S. (1977). Incidence of insulin-dependent diabetes in the first 16 years of life. *Lancet, 1,* 589–590.

Calvert, S. C., Huston, A. C., Watkins, B. A., & Wright, J. C. (1981). *The effects of selective attention to television forms on children's comprehension of content*. Paper presented to the biennial meeting of the Society for Research in Child Development meetings, Boston, M.A.

Camerena, P. (1985). *Intimacy in early adolescence*. Paper presented at American Psychological Association meetings, Los Angeles, CA.

Cameron, R. (1984). Problem-solving inefficiency and conceptual tempo: A task analysis of underlying factors. *Child Development, 55,* 2031–2041.

Campbell, S. B. (1973). Cognitive styles in reflective, impulsive and hyperactive boys and their mothers. *Perceptual and Motor Skills, 36,* 747–775.

Campos, J. J., Hiatt, S., Ramsay, D., Henderson, C., & Svejda, M. (1978). The emergence of fear on the visual cliff. In M. Lewis & L. Rosenblum (Eds.), *The origins of affect.* New York: Plenum.

Campos, J. J., Langer, A., & Krowitz, A. (1970). Cardiac responses on the visual cliff in prelocomotor human infants. *Science, 170,* 196–197.

Campos, R. J., & Sternberg, C. R. (1981). Perception, appraisal and emotion: The onset of social referencing. In M. Lamb & L. Sherrod (Eds.). *Infant social cognition.* Hillsdale, NJ: Erlbaum.

Caplan, P. J., & Kinsbourne, M. (1976). Baby drops the rattle: Asymmetry of duration of grasp by infants. *Child Development, 47,* 532–534.

Carew, J. V. (1980). Experience and the development of young children at home and in day care. *Monographs of the Society for Research in Child Development, 187,* (Serial no. 187).

Carey, S. (1977). The child as word learner. In M. Halle, J. Bresman & G. A. Miller (Eds.), *Linguistic theory and psychological reality.* Cambridge, MA: MIT Press.

Carr, K. (1980). Obstetric practices which protect against neonatal morbidity: Focus on maternal position in labor and birth. *Birth and the Family Journal, 7,* 249–254.

Carroll, J. J. & Steward, M. S. (1984). The role of cognitive development in children's understanding of their feelings. *Child Development, 55,* 1486–1492.

Carroll, J. L., & Rest, J. R. (1982). Moral development. In B. B. Wolman (Ed.), *Handbook of developmental psychology.* Englewood Cliffs, NJ: Prentice-Hall (pp. 434–451).

Carter, G. L. & Kinsbourne, M. (1979). The ontogeny of right cerebral lateralization of spatial mental set. *Developmental Psychology, 15,* 241–245.

Carver, C. S., Coleman, A. E., & Glass, D. C. (1976). The coronary-prone behavior pattern and the suppression of fatigue on a treadmill task. *Journal of Personality and Social Psychology, 33,* 361–366.

Cashion, B. (1982). Female-headed families: Effects on children and clinical implications. *Journal of Marriage and Family Therapy, 8,* 77–85.

Case, R. (1978). Intellectual development from birth to adulthood: A neo-Piagetian perspective. In R. S. Siegler (Ed.), *Children's thinking: What develops?* (pp. 37–72). Hillsdale, NJ: Erlbaum.

Case, R. (1984). The process of stage transition: A Neo-Piagetian view. In R. Sternberg (Ed.), *Mechanisms of cognitive development.* NY: Freeman.

Case, R., Kurland, D. M., & Goldberg, J. (1982). Operational efficiency and the growth of shortterm memory span. *Journal of Experimental Child Psychology, 33,* 386–404.

Cassileth, B. R. (1980). Informed consent—why are its goals so imperfectly realized? *New England Journal of Medicine, 302,* 896–900.

Cavallaro, S. A. & Porter, R. H. (1980). Peer preference of at-risk and normally developing children in preschool mainstream classrooms. *American Journal of Mental Deficiency, 84,* 357–366.

Cavior, N., & Dokecki, P. R. (1973). Physical attractiveness, perceived attitude similarity, and academic achievement as contributors to interpersonal attraction among adolescents. *Developmental Psychology, 9,* 44–54.

Cazden, C. (1974). Play with language and metalinguistic awareness: One dimension of language experience. *Urban Review, 7,* 23–39.

Cazden, C. (1984). *Effective instructional practices in bilingual education.* Research Review for the National Institutes of Education, Washington, D.C. (ED 249768)

Cernoch, J. M., & Porter, R. H. (1985). Recognition of maternal axillary odors by infants: *Child Development, 56,* 1593–1598.

Cervantes, R. A. (1982). Bilingual education: The best of times, the worst of times. In K. Cirincione-Coles (Ed.), *The future of education* (pp. 81–109). Sage Publications.

Chacon, M. A., & Tildon, J. T. (1981). Elevated values of triiodothyronine in victims of sudden infant death syndrome. *Journal of Pediatrics, 99,* 758–760.

Chang, H., & Trehub, S. E. (1977). Infant's perception of temporal grouping in auditory patterns. *Child Development, 48,* 1666–1670.

Chapman, M., Zahn-Waxler, C., Cooperman, G., & Ianotti, R. (1987). Empathy and responsibility in the motivation of children's helping. *Developmental Psychology, 23,* 140-145.

Chapman, R. S. (1981). Cognitive development and language comprehension in 10-to-21-month-olds. In R. Start (Ed.), *Language behavior in infancy and early childhood.* New York: Elsevier.

Charlesworth, W. (1979). Ethology: Understanding the other half of intelligence. In M. von Cranach, K. Foppa, W. Lepenies, & D. Ploog (Eds.), *Human ethology: Claims and limits of a new discipline.* Cambridge: Cambridge University Press.

Charlesworth, W., & Kreutzer, M. (1973). Facial expressions of infants and children. In P. Ekman (Ed.), *Darwin and facial expression.* New York: Academic Press.

Chassin, L. (1984). Adolescent substance use and abuse. *Advances in Child Behavioral Analysis and Therapy, 3,* 99–152.

Chassin, L., Presson, C. C., & Sherman, S. J. (1984). Cigarette smoking and adolescent psychosocial development. *Basic and Applied Social Psychology, 5,* 295–315.

Cheek, D. B. (1968). *Human growth.* Philadelphia: Lea & Febiger.

Chi, M. T. H. (1978). Knowledge structures and knowledge development. In R. S. Siegler (Ed.), *Children's thinking: What develops?* Hillsdale, NJ: Erlbaum.

Chilman, C. (1979). *Adolescent sexuality in a changing American society: Social and psychological perspectives.* Washington, D.C.: U.S. Government Printing Office.

Chisholm, J. S. (1981). Residence patterns and the environment of mother-infant interaction among the Navaho. In T. Field, A. Sostek, P. Vietze, & P. Leiderman (Eds.), *Culture and early interactions*. Hillsdale, NJ: Erlbaum.

Chomsky, C. (1969). *The acquisition of syntax in children from five to ten*. Cambridge, MA: MIT Press.

Chomsky, N. (1975). *Reflections on language*. New York: Pantheon.

Christensen, H. T., & Carpenter, G. (1972). Value-behavior discrepancies regarding premarital coitus in three western cultures. *American Sociological Review, 27,* 66–74.

Chukovsky, K. (1963). *From two to five*. Berkeley, CA: University of California Press.

Cicirelli, V. (1969). *The impact of Head Start: An evaluation of the effects of Head Start on children's cognitive and affect development*. Washington, D.C.: National Bureau of Standards Institute of Applied Technology.

Claeys, W. & DeBoeck, P. (1976). The influence of some parental characteristics on children's primary abilities and field independence: A study of adopted children. *Child Development, 47,* 842–845.

Clark, E. V. (1971). On the acquisition of the meaning of *before* and *after. Journal of Verbal Learning and Verbal Behavior, 10,* 266–275.

Clark, H. H. & Clark, E. V. (1977). *Psychology and language: An introduction to psycholinguistics*. NY: Harcourt, Brace, Jovanovich.

Clark, K. B., & Clark, M. P. (1939). The development of consciousness of self and the emergence of racial identity in Negro preschool children. *Journal of Social Psychology, 10,* 591–599.

Clark, K. B., & Clark, M. P. (1940). Skin color as a factor in racial identification and preference in Negro preschool children. *Journal of Social Psychology, 11,* 156–169.

Clarke-Stewart, K. A. (1978). And daddy makes three: The father's impact on mother and young child. *Child Development, 49,* 466–478.

Clarke-Stewart, K. A. (1982). *Day care*. Cambridge: Harvard University Press.

Clarke-Stewart, K. A. & Hevey, C. M. (1981). Longitudinal relations in repeated observations of mother-child interaction from 1 to 2 1/2 years. *Developmental Psychology, 17,* 127–145.

Clarke-Stewart, K. A., VanderStoep, L. P., & Killian, G. A. (1979). Analysis and replication of mother-child relations at two years of age. *Child Development, 50,* 777–793.

Clarkson, M. G., & Berg, W. K. (1983). Cardiac orienting and vowel discrimination in newborns: Crucial stimulus parameters. *Child Development, 54,* 162–171.

Clary, E.G., & Miller, J. (1986). Socialization and situational influences on sustained altruism. *Child Development, 57,* 1358–1369.

Clausen, J. A. (1975). The meaning of differential physical and sexual maturation. In S. E. Dragastin & G. H. Elder, Jr. (Eds.), *Adolescence in the life cycle*. New York: Halsted.

Coates, S., Lord, M. & Jakabovics, E. (1975). Field independence-dependence, social-nonsocial play, and sex differences in preschool children. *Perceptual and Motor Skills, 40,* 195–202.

Coddington, R. D. (1972). The significance of life events as etiologic factors in the diseases of children. *Journal of Psychosomatic Research, 16,* 7–18.

Cohen, D. D., & Rose, R. D. (1984). Male adolescent birth control behavior: The importance of developmental factors and sex differences. *Journal of Youth and Adolescence, 13,* 239–251.

Cohen, L. B., & Strauss, M. S. (1979). Concept acquisition in the human infant. *Child Development, 50,* 419–424.

Cohen, S. E., & Beckwith, L. (1979). Preterm infant intervention with the caregiver in the first year of life and competence at age two. *Child Development, 50,* 767–776.

Cohn, A. (1983). *An approach to preventing child abuse*. Chicago: National Committee for Prevention of Child Abuse.

Cohn, J. F., & Tronick, E. Z. (1987). Mother-infant face-to-face interaction: The sequence of dyadic states at 3, 6, and 9 months. *Developmental Psychology, 23,* 68–77.

Coie, J. D. & Dodge, K. A. (1983). Continuities and changes in children's social status: A five year longitudinal study. *Merrill-Palmer Quarterly, 29,* 261–282.

Coie, J. D., Dodge, K. A., & Coppotelli, H. (1982). Dimensions and types of social status: A cross-age perspective. *Developmental Psychology, 18,* 557–570.

Colby, A., Kohlberg, L., Gibbs, J., & Lieberman, M. (1983). A longitudinal study of moral judgment. *Monograph of the Society for Research in Child Development, 48,* No. 200.

Cole, M., Frankel, F., & Sharp, D. (1971). Development of free recall in children. *Developmental Psychology, 4,* 109–123.

Cole, M., Gay, J., Glick, J. A. & Sharp, D. W. (1971). *The cultural context of learning and thinking*. New York: Basic Books.

Cole, M. & Scribner, S. (1977). Cross-cultural studies of memory and cognition. In R. V. Kail & J. W. Hagen (Eds.), *Perspectives on the development of memory and cognition*. Hillsdale, NJ: Erlbaum Publishers.

Cole, P. M. (1986). Children's spontaneous control of facial expression. *Child Development, 57,* 1309–1321.

Coleman, J. C. (1980). Friendship and the peer group in adolescence. In J. Adelson (Ed.), *Handbook of adolescent psychology* (pp. 408–431). New York: Wiley.

Coleman, J. S. (1960). The adolescent sub-culture and academic achievement. *American Journal of Sociology, 65,* 337–347.

Coleman, M., & Rimland, B. (1976). Familial autism. In M. Coleman, (Ed.), *The autistic syndromes*. New York: American Elsevier Publishing Co.

Collins, W. A. (1983). Social antecedents, cognitive processing and comprehension on social portrayals on television. In E. T. Higgins, D. N. Ruble & W. W. Hartup (Eds.), *Social cognition and social development*. NY: Cambridge University Press.

Collins, W. A. (1984). Introduction. In W. A. Collins (Ed.), *Development during middle childhood: The years from six to twelve*. Washington, D.C.: National Academy Press.

Collins, W. A., Sobol, B. L., & Westby, S. (1981). Effects of adult commentary on children's comprehension and inferences about a televised aggressive portrayal. *Child Development, 52,* 158–163.

Collis, G. (1977). Visual co-orientation and maternal speech. In H. R. Schaffer (Ed.), *Studies in mother-infant interaction.* London: Academic Press.

Committee on nutrition, American Academy of Pediatrics (1981). On the feeding of solid food to infants. *Pediatrics, 68,* 435–443.

Condry, J. C., & Ross, D. F. (1985). Sex and aggression: The influence of gender label on the perception of aggression in children. *Child Development, 56,* 225–233.

Connolly, J. A., & Doyle, A. (1984). Relation of social fantasy play to social competence in preschoolers. *Developmental Psychology, 20,* 797–806.

Connolly, K. & Elliott, J. (1972). The evolution and ontogeny of hand function. In N. Blurton-Jones (Ed.), *Ethological studies of child behavior.* Cambridge: Cambridge University Press.

Cook, T. (1983). *Testimony before the Subcommittee on Crime of the House Committee on Judiciary.* Washington, D.C., April 13.

Cooney, E. W. & Selman, R. L. (1978). Children's use of social conceptions: Toward a dynamic model of social cognition. In W. Damon (Ed.), *New directions for child development: Social cognition.* No. 1. San Francisco: CA: Jossey-Bass.

Cooper, C. R., & Ayers-Lopez, S. (1985). Family and peer systems in early adolescence: New models of the role of relationships in development. *Journal of Early Adolescence, 5,* 9–21.

Coopersmith, S. (1967). *The antecedents of self-esteem.* San Francisco: CA: W. H. Freeman.

Corballis, M. C. (1983). *Human laterality.* NY: Academic Press.

Corrigan, R. (1978). Language development as related to stage of object permanence development. *Journal of Child Language, 5,* 173–190.

Corsale, K., & Ornstein, P. A. (1980). Developmental changes in children's use of semantic information in recall. *Journal of Experimental Child Psychology, 30,* 213–245.

Corter, C. (1977). Brief separation and communication between infant and mother. In T. Alloway, P. Pliner, & L. Krames (Eds.), *Attachment behavior.* New York: Plenum.

Costanzo, P. R. (1970). Conformity development as a function of self-blame. *Journal of Personality and Social Psychology, 14,* 366–374.

Costanzo, P. R., Coie, J. D., Grumet, J. F., & Farnill, D. (1973). A re-examination of intentions and consequences in children's moral judgments. *Child Development, 44,* 154–161.

Cowen, E. L., Pederson, A., Babijian, H., Izzo, L. D. & Trost, M. A. (1973). Long-term followup of early detected vulnerable children. *Journal of Consulting & Clinical Psychology, 41,* 438–446.

Cox, R. D., & Cox, M. J. (1984). Children in contemporary families: Divorce and remarriage. *Advances in Developmental and Behavioral Pediatrics, 5,* 1–31.

Cratty, B. J. (1979). *Perceptual and motor development in infancy and childhood* (2nd Ed.). Englewood Cliffs, NJ: Prentice-Hall.

Cravioto, J. (1968). Nutritional deficiencies and mental performance in childhood. In D. Glass (Ed.), *Environmental influences.* New York: Rockefeller University Press.

Crawford, J. W. (1982). Mother-infant interaction in premature and full-term infants. *Child Development, 53,* 957–962.

Crittenden, P. (1985). Social networks, quality of child rearing and child development. *Child Development, 56,* 1299–1313.

Crockenberg, S. B. (1981). Infant irritability, mother responsiveness, and social support influences on the security of infant-mother attachment. *Child Development, 52,* 857–865.

Crockett, L., Losoff, M., & Petersen, A. C. (1984). Perceptions of the peer group and friendship in early adolescence. *Journal of Early Adolescence, 4,* 155–181.

Crook, C. K. (1978). Taste perception in the newborn infant. *Infant Behavior and Development, 1,* 52–69.

Crook, C. K., & Lipsitt, L. P. (1976). Neonatal nutritive sucking: Effects of taste stimulation upon sucking rhythm and heart rate. *Child Development, 47,* 518–522.

Crowley, P. H., Gulati, D. K., Hayden, T. L., Lopez, P., & Dyer, R. A. (1979). A chiasma-hormonal hypothesis relating Down's syndrome and maternal age. *Nature, 280,* 417–419.

Csikszentmihalyi, M. (1978). Intrinsic rewards and emergent motivation. In M. R. Lepper & D. Greene (Eds.), *The hidden costs of reward* (pp. 205–216). Hillsdale, NJ: Erlbaum.

Csikszentmihalyi, M., & Larson, R. (1984). *Being adolescent: Conflict and growth in the teenage years.* New York: Basic Books.

Curnutte, M. (Oct. 18, 1985). "The quest to compete" and "Researchers are studying kids' minds and bodies". *Associated Press.*

Curry, M. (1979). Contact during the first hour with the wrapped or naked newborn: Effect on maternal attachment at 36 hours and three months. *Birth and the Family Journal, 6,* 227–235.

Dale, P. S. (1976). *Language development: Structure and function* (2nd Edition). New York: Holt, Rinehart & Winston.

Damon, W. (1977). *The social world of the child.* San Francisco: Jossey Bass.

Damon, W. (1983). *Social and personality development: Infancy through adolescence.* New York: W. W. Norton.

Damon, W. & Hart, D. (1982). The development of self-understanding from infancy through adolescence. *Child Development, 53,* 841–864.

Damon, W. & Killen, M. (1982). Peer interaction and the process of change in children's moral reasoning. *Merrill-Palmer Quarterly, 28,* 347–367.

Danforth, D. N. (1977). *Obstetrics and gynecology,* 3rd Edition. New York: Holt, Rinehart and Winston.

Daniels, D., Dunn, J., Furstenberg, F. F., & Plomin, R. (1985). Environmental differences within the family and adjustment differences within pairs of adolescent siblings. *Child Development, 56,* 764–774.

Daniels, D., Plomin, R., & Greenhalgh, J. (1984). Correlates of difficult temperament in infancy. *Child Development, 55,* 1184–1194.

Dansky, J. L., & Silverman, I. W. (1973). Effects of play on associative fluency in preschool aged children. *Developmental Psychology, 9,* 44–54.

Dansky, J. L. & Silverman, I. W. (1975). Play: A general facilitation of associative fluency in preschool aged children. *Developmental Psychology, 11,* 104–114.

Darling, C. A., & Hicks, M. W. (1982). Parental influences on adolescent sexuality: Implications for parents as educators. *Journal of Youth and Adolescence, 11,* 231–245.

Darling, C. A., Kallen, D. J., & VanDusen, J. E. (1984). Sex in transition, 1900–1980. *Journal of Youth and Adolescence, 13,* 385–399.

Darwin, C. (1859). *The origins of species.* New York: Modern Library.

Darwin, C. (1877). A biographical sketch of an infant. *Mind, 2,* 285–294.

Dasen, P. R. (1977). *Piagetian psychology: Cross-cultural contributions.* New York: Gardner Press.

Davenport-Slack, B., & Boylan, C. H. (1974). Psychological correlates of childbirth pain. *Psychosomatic Medicine, 36,* 215–223.

Davidson, E. S., Yasuma, A. & Tower, A. (1979). The effect of television cartoons on sex-role stereotyping in young girls. *Child Development, 50,* 597–600.

Davie, R., Butler, N. & Goldstein, H. (1972). *From birth to seven: The second report of the National Child Development Study.* London: Longmara.

Davis, H. (1978). A description of aspects of mother-infant vocal interaction. *Journal of Child Psychology and Psychiatry, 19,* 379–386.

Dawe, H. C. (1934). The influence of size of kindergarten group upon performance. *Child Development, 5,*295–303.

Dawson, G., Finley, C., Phillips, S., & Galpert, L. (1986). Hemispheric specialization and the language ability of autistic children. *Child Development, 57,* 1440–1453.

DeCasper, A. J., & Fifer, W. P. (1980). Of human bonding: Newborns prefer their mother's voices. *Science, 208,* 1174–1176.

DeCasper, A. J., & Sigafoos, A. D. (1983). The intrauterine heartbeat: A potent reinforcer for newborns. *Infant Behavior and Development, 6,* 19–26.

DeLissovoy, V. (1973). Child care by adolescent parents. *Children Today, 14,* 22.

DeMause, L. (1974). The evolution of children. In L. DeMause (Ed.), *The history of childhood.* New York: Psychohistory Press.

Demos, V. (1982). Facial expressions in young children: A descriptive analysis. In T. Field & A. Fogel (Eds.), *Emotion and early interaction.* Hillsdale, N.J.: Erlbaum.

Denckla, M. B. (1984). Developmental dyspraxia: the clumsy child. In M. D. Levine & P. Satz (Eds.), *Middle childhood: Development and dysfunction* (pp. 245–260). Baltimore: University Park Press.

Denham, S. (1986). Social cognition, prosocial behavior and emotion in preschoolers: contextual validation. *Child Development, 57,* 194–201.

Dennis, W. (1960). Causes of retardation among institutional children: Iran. *Journal of Genetic Psychology, 96,* 46–60.

Dennis, W., & Sayegh, Y. (1965). The effects of supplementary experiences on the behavioral development of infants in institutions. *Child Development, 36,* 81–90.

deVilliers, J. G. & deVilliers, P. A. (1973). A cross-sectional study of the development of grammatical morphemes in child speech. *Journal of Psycholinguistic Research, 2,* 267–278.

DeVries, R. (1969). Constancy of generic identity in the years three to six. *Monograph of the Society for Research in Child Development, 34,* No. 127.

Diaz, R. M., & Berndt, T. J. (1982). Children's knowledge of a best friend: Fact or fancy? *Developmental Psychology, 18,* 787–794.

Dickerson, J. W., Merat, A., & Yusuf, H. K. (1982). Effects of malnutrition on brain growth and development. In J. W. Dickerson & H. McGurk (Eds.), *Brain and behavioral development* (pp. 77–108). London: Surrey University Press.

DiPietro, J. A. (1981). Rough and tumble play: a function of gender. *Developmental Psychology, 17,* 50–58.

Dirks, J., & Neisser, U. (1977). Memory for objects in real scenes: The development of recognition and recall. *Journal of Experimental Child Psychology, 23,* 315–328.

Dix, T., & Grusec, J. E. (1983). Parental influence techniques: an attributional analysis. *Child Development, 54,* 645–652.

Dodge, K. A. (1980). Social cognition and children's aggressive behavior. *Child Development, 57,* 162–170.

Dodge, K. A. (1982). Social information-processing variables in the development of aggression and altruism in children. In C. Zahn-Waxler, M. Cummings & M. Radke-Yarrow (Eds.), *The development of altruism and aggression: Social and sociobiological origins.* NY: Cambridge University Press.

Dodge, K. A., & Frame, C. L. (1982). Social cognitive biases and deficits in aggressive boys. *Child Development, 53,* 620–635.

Dodge, K. A., Schlundt, D. C., Schocken, I., & Delugach, J. D. (1983). Social competence and children's sociometric status: The role of peer group entry strategies. *Merrill-Palmer Quarterly, 29,* 309–336.

Doland, D. M., & Adelberg, K. (1967). The learning of sharing behavior. *Child Development, 38,* 695–700.

Dornbusch, S. M., Carlsmith, J. M., Bushwall, S. J., Ritter, P. L., Leiderman, H., Hastorf, A. H., & Gross, R. T. (1985). Single parents, extended households, and the control of adolescents. *Child Development, 56,* 326–341.

Douglas, V. I., Parry, P., Marton, P. & Gaston, C. (1976). Assessment of a cognitive training program for hyperactive children. *Journal of Abnormal Child Psychology, 4,* 389–410.

Douglas, V. I., & Peters, K. G. (1979). Toward a clearer definition of the attention deficit of hyperactive children. In G. A. Hale and M. Lewis (Eds.), *Attention and cognitive development.* New York: Plenum Press.

Douvan, E., & Adelson, J. (1966). *The adolescent experience.* New York: Wiley.

Doyle, A. B., Champagne, M. & Segalowitz, N. (1978). Some issues on the assessment of linguistic consequences of early bilingualism. In M. Paradis (Ed.), *Aspects of bilingualism.* Columbia, NC: Hornbeam Press.

Drabble, M. (1982). With all my love, (signed) mama. In S. Cahill (Ed.), *Motherhood: A reader for men and women* (p. 6). New York: Avon.

Draper, T. W., & James, R. S. (1983). *Preschool fears: longitudinal sequence and cohort changes.* Paper presented to the biennial meeting of the Society for Research in Child Development meetings, Detroit, MI.

Dreyer, P. H. (1982). Sexuality during adolescence. In B. B. Wolman (Ed.), *Handbook of developmental psychology* (pp. 559–600). Englewood Cliffs, NJ: Prentice-Hall.

Drotar, D., & Irvin, N. (1979). Disturbed maternal bereavement following infant death. *Childcare, Health and Development, 5,* 239–247.

Dunn, J. (1983). Sibling relations in early childhood. *Child Development, 54,* 787–811.

Dunn, J., Bretherton, I., & Munn, P. (1987). Conversations about feeling states between mothers and their young children. *Developmental Psychology, 23,* 132–139.

Dunn, J., & Kendrick, C. (1981). Interaction between young siblings: Association with the interaction between mother and firstborn child. *Developmental Psychology, 17,* 336–343.(a)

Dunn, J., & Kendrick, C. (1981). Social behavior of young siblings in the family context: Differences between same-sex and different-sex dyads. *Child Development, 52,* 1265–1273. (b)

Dunn, J., & Kendrick, C. (1982). *Siblings: Love, envy, and understanding.* Cambridge, MA: Harvard University Press.

Dunn, J., & Munn, P. (1985). Becoming a family member: family conflict and the development of social understanding in the second year. *Child Development, 56,* 480–492.

Dunphy, D. C. (1963). The social structure of urban adolescent peer groups. *Sociometry, 26,* 230–246.

Durant, W. (1961). *The story of philosophy.* New York: Washington Square Press.

Durrett, M. E., Otaki, M., & Richards, P. (1984). Attachment and the mother's perception of support from the father. *International Journal of Behavioral Development, 7,* 167–176.

Dusek, J. B., & Flaherty, J. F. (1981). The development of self-concept during the adolescent years. *Monographs of the Society for Research on Child Development, 46,* (Serial No. 191).

Dweck, C. S., & Goetz, T. E. (1978). Attributions and learned helplessness. In J. Harvey, W. Ickes & R. Kidd (Eds.), *New directions in attribution research.* Vol. 2. Hillsdale, NJ: Erlbaum (pp. 157–179).

Dweck, C. S., Davidson, W., Nelson, S., & Enna, B. (1978). Sex differences in learned helplessness:II. Contingencies of evaluative feedback in the classroom and III. An experimental analysis. *Developmental Psychology, 14,* 268–276.

Dyk, R. B. & Witkin, H. A. (1965). Family experiences related to the development of differentiation in children. *Child Development, 36,* 21–55.

Dyson, S. E. & Jones, D. G. (1976). Undernutrition and the developing nervous system. *Progress in Neurobiology, 7,* 171–196.

Easterbrooks, M. A., & Goldberg, W. A. (1984). Toddler development in the family: impact of father involvement and parenting characteristics. *Child Development, 55,* 740–752.

Eaton, W. O. (1983). Measuring activity level with actometers: reliability, validity and arm length. *Child Development, 54,* 720–726.

Eaton, W. O. & Enns, L. R. (1983). *Review of sex differences in activity level.* Paper presented at the bienniel meeting of the Society for Research in Child Development, Detroit.

Eaton, W. O. & Enns, L. R. (1986). Sex differences in human motor activity level. *Psychological Bulletin, 100,* 19–28.

Eaton, W. O. & Keats, J. G. (1982). Peer presence, stress and sex differences in the motor activity levels of preschoolers. *Developmental Psychology, 18,* 534–540.

Eckerman, C. O., & Whately, J. L. (1975). Infants' reactions to unfamiliar adults varying in novelty. *Developmental Psychology, 11,* 562–566.

Eckerman, C. O., & Whately, J. L. (1977). Toys and social interaction between infant peers. *Child Development, 48,* 1645–1656.

Eder, D., & Hallinan, M. T. (1978). Sex differences in children's friendships. *American Sociological Review, 43,* 237–250.

Edwards, C. P. (1977). The comparative study of the development of moral judgment and reasoning. In R. Monroe, R. Monroe & B. B. Whiting (Eds.), *Handbook of cross-cultural human development.* NY: Garland.

Edwards, C. P. (1982). Moral development in comparative cross-cultural perspective. In D. A. Wagner & H. W. Stevenson (Eds.), *Cultural perspectives on child development.* San Francisco, CA: W. H. Freeman.

Edwards, C. P. (1984). The age group labels and categories of preschool children. *Child Development, 55,* 440–452.

Edwards, C. P. (1986). Another style of competence: the caregiving child. In A. Fogel & G. F. Melson (Eds.), *Origins of Nurturance: Developmental, biological and cultural perspectives on caregiving.* Hillsdale, NJ: Lawrence Erlbaum.

Edwards, C. P. & Whiting, B. B. (1980). Differential socialization of girls and boys in light of cross-cultural research. In C. M. Super & S. Harkness (Eds.), *Anthropological perspectives on child development.* (New Directions for Child Development, No. 8). San Francisco: Jossey-Bass.

Egeland, B., Breitenbucher, M. & Rosenberg, D. (1980). Prospective study of the significance of life stress in the etiology of child abuse. *Journal of Consulting and Clinical Psychology, 48,* 195–205.

Egeland, B., & Farber, E. A. (1984). Infant-mother attachment: factors related to its development and changes over time. *Child Development, 55,* 753–771.

Eichorn, D. (1970). Physiological development. In P. Mussen (Ed.), *Carmichael's manual of child psychology,* Vol. I, 3rd Edition. New York: Wiley.

Eichorn, D. (1979). Physical development: Current foci of research. In J. Osofsky (Ed.), *Handbook of infant development* (pp. 253–282). New York: Wiley.

Eilers, R. E., & Gavin, W. J. (1981). The evaluation of infant speech perception skills: Statistical techniques and theory development. In R. Stark (Ed.), *Language behavior in infancy and early childhood.* New York: Elsevier.

Eilers, R. E., Gavin, W. J., & Wilson, W. R. (1979). Linguistic experience and phonemic perception in infancy: A cross-linguistic study. *Child Development, 50,* 14–18.

Eimas, P. D., Siqueland, E. R., Jusczyk, P., & Vigorito, J. (1971). Speech perception in infants. *Science, 171,* 303–306.

Eisenberg, N. & Hand, M. (1979). The relationship of preschoolers' reasoning about prosocial moral conflicts to prosocial behavior. *Child Development, 50,* 356–363.

Eisenberg, N. & Lennon, R. (1983). Sex differences in empathy and related capacities. *Psychological Bulletin, 94,* 100–131.

Eisenberg, N., Lennon, R., & Roth, K. (1983). Prosocial development: A longitudinal study. *Developmental Psychology, 19,* 846–855.

Eisenberg, N., & Miller, P. A. (1987). The relation of empathy to prosocial and related behaviors. *Psychological Bulletin, 101,* 91–119.

Eisenberg, N., Pasternak, J. F., Cameron, E., & Tryon, K. (1984). The relationship of quantity and mode of prosocial behavior to moral cognition and social style. *Child Development, 55,* 1479–1485.

Eisenberg, N., Tryon, K., & Cameron, E. (1984). The relation of preschoolers' peer interaction to their sex-typed toy choices. *Child Development, 55,* 1044–1050.

Eisenberg, R. B. (1976). *Auditory competence in early life.* Baltimore: University Park Press.

Eiser, C. (1985). *The psychology of childhood illness.* New York: Springer-Verlag.

Eiser, C., & Patterson, D. (1983). "Slugs and snails and puppy dog tails": Children's ideas about the insides of their bodies. *Child: Care, Health and Development, 9,* 233–240.

Eiser, C., Patterson, D., & Eiser, J. R. (1983). Children's knowledge of health and illness: Implications for health education. *Child: Care, Health and Development, 9,* 285–292.

Ekman, P. (1973). Darwin and facial expression. In P. Ekman (Ed.), *Studies in nonverbal behavior.* NY: Academic Press.

Ekman, P., Friesen, W. & Ellsworth, P. (1972). *Emotion in the human face.* New York: Pergamon Press.

Elardo, R. & Bradley, R. (1981). The Home Observation for Measurement of the Environment (HOME) scale: A review of research. *Developmental Review, 1,* 113–145.

Elder, G. H., (1974). *Children of the great depression.* Chicago: University of Chicago Press.

Elder, G. H., & MacInnis, D. J. (1983). Achievement imagery in women's lives from adolescence to adulthood. *Journal of Personality and Social Psychology, 45,* 394–404.

Elder, G. H., Nguyen, T. V., & Caspi, A. (1985). Linking family hardship to children's lives. *Child Development, 56,* 361–375.

Elkind, D. (1967). Egocentrism in adolescence. *Child Development, 38,* 1025–1034.

Elkind, D. (1967). Piaget's conservation problems. *Child Development, 38,* 15–27.

Elkind, D. (1976). *Child development and education.* New York: Oxford University Press.

Elkind, D. (1980). Strategic interactions in early adolescence. In J. Adelson (Ed.), *Handbook of adolescent psychology* (pp. 432–444). New York: Wiley.

Elkind, D. (1981). *The hurried child: Growing up too fast too soon.* Reading, MA: Addison-Wesley.

Elkind, D., & Bowen, R. (1979). Imaginary audience behavior in children and adolescents. *Developmental Psychology, 15,* 38–44.

Elkind, D. & Schoenfeld, E. (1972). Identity and equivalence conservation at two age levels. *Developmental Psychology, 6,* 529–533.

Ellis, A. W. (1984). *Reading, writing and dyslexia: A cognitive analysis.* Hillsdale, NJ: Erlbaum.

Emler, N. P. & Rushton, J. P. (1974). Cognitive-developmental factors in children's generosity. *British Journal of Social and Clinical Psychology, 13,* 277–281.

Epps, E. G., & Smith, S. F. (1984). School and children: The middle childhood years. In W. A. Collins (Ed.), *Development during middle childhood: The years from six to twelve.* Washington, D.C.: National Academy Press.

Epstein, A. S. & Radin, N. (1975). Motivational components related to father behavior and cognitive functioning in preschoolers. *Child Development, 46,* 831–839.

Epstein, H. T. (1978). Growth spurts during brain development: implications for educational policy and practice. In J. S. Chall and A. F. Mirsky (Eds.), *National society for the study of education yearbook.* Chicago, IL: University of Chicago Press.

Epstein, J. L. (1978). *Friends in school: Patterns of selection and influence in secondary schools* (Report No. 266) Baltimore, MD: Johns Hopkins University Center for the Social Organization of Schools.

Epstein, J. L. (1983). Selection of friends in differently organized schools and classrooms. In J. L. Epstein & N. Karenweit (Eds.), *Friends in school: Patterns of selection and influence in secondary schools.* New York: Academic Press.

Epstein, J. L., & McPartland, J. M. (1979). Authority structures. In H. J. Walberg (Ed.), *Educational environments and effects.* Berkeley, CA: McCutchan.

Erb, T. O. (1983). Career preferences of early adolescents: Age and sex differences. *Journal of Early Adolescence, 3,* 349–359.

Erikson, E. (1963). *Childhood and society.* New York: Norton (2nd Ed.)

Eron, L. (1980). Prescription for reduction of aggression. *American Psychologist, 35,* 244–252.

Eron, L. & Huesmann, L. R. (1984). Television violence and aggressive behavior. In B. B. Lahey & A. E. Kazdin (Eds.), *Advances in clinical child psychology.* (Vol. 7). NY: Plenum Press.

Eron, L., Walder, L. O. & Lefkowitz, M. M. (1971). *Learning of aggression in children.* Boston, MA: Little, Brown.

Ervin-Tripp, S. (1970). Discourse agreement: How children answer questions. In J. R. Hayes (Ed.), *Cognition and the development of language*. NY: John Wiley.

Escalona, S. K., & Corman, H. H. (1968). *Albert Einstein scales of sensori-motor development*. Unpublished manuscript.

Etaugh, C. & Hughes, V. (1975). Teachers' evaluations of sex-typed behaviors in children: the role of teacher sex and school setting. *Developmental Psychology, 11,* 394–395.

Fagot, B. I. (1977). Consequences of moderate cross-gender behavior in preschool children. *Child Development, 48,* 902–907.

Falbo, T. (1979). Only children, stereotypes and research. In M. Lewis & L. A. Rosenblum (Eds.), *The child and its family*. NY: Plenum.

Falbo, T. (1984). Only children: A review. In T. Falbo (Ed.), *The single child family*. NY: Guilford.

Fantz, R. L. (1963). Pattern vision in newborn infants. *Science, 140,* 296–297.

Farber, S. L. (1981). *Identical twins reared apart*. New York: Basic Books.

Farber, S. S., Primavera, J., & Felner, R. D. (1983). Older adolescents and parental divorce: Adjustment problems and mediators of coping. *Journal of Divorce, 7,* 59–75.

Faust, M. S. (1977). Somatic development of adolescent girls. *Monographs of the Society for Research in Child Development, 42* (Serial no. 169).

Fawzy, F. I., Coombs, R. H., & Gerber, B. (1983). Generational continuity in the use of substances: The impact of parental substance use on adolescent substance use. *Addictive Behaviors, 8,* 109–114.

Feather, N. T. (1980). Values in adolescence. In J. Adelson (Ed.), *Handbook of adolescent psychology* (pp. 247–294). New York: Wiley.

Fein, G., Schwartz, P., Jacobson, S. & Jacobson, J. (1983). Environmental toxins and behavioral development. *American Psychologist, 38,* 1188–1197.

Fein, R. (1976). The first weeks of fathering: The importance of choices and supports for new parents. *Birth and the Family Journal, 3,* 53–58.

Feingold, B. (1974). *Why your child is hyperactive*. New York: Random House.

Feiring, C., & Lewis, M. (1981). *The birth of a sibling: Its effect on the mother-firstborn child interaction*. Paper presented at the meeting of the Society for Research in Child Development, Boston.

Feldman, A., & Acredolo, L. (1979). The effect of active versus passive exploration on memory for spatial location in children. *Child Development, 50,* 698–704.

Feldman, J. F., Brody, N., & Miller, S. H. (1980). Sex differences in non-elicited neonatal behavior. *Merrill-Palmer Quarterly, 26,* 63–73.

Feldman, S. S., & Nash, S. C. (1979). Changes in responsiveness to babies during adolescence. *Child Development, 50,* 942–949.

Feldman, S. S., & Nash, S. C. (1986). Antecedents of early parenting. In A. Fogel & G. F. Melson (Eds.), *Origins of nurturance*. Hillsdale, NJ: Erlbaum.

Feldman, S. S., Nash, S. C., & Aschenbrenner, B. G. (1983). Antecedents of fathering. *Child Development, 54,* 1628–1636.

Fenson, C., Kagan, J., Kearsley, R. B., & Zelazo, P. R. (1976). The developmental progression of manipulative play in the first two years. *Child Development, 47,* 232–236.

Ferguson, C. A., & Farwell, C. (1975). Words and sound in early language acquisition: English consonants in the first 50 words. *Language, 51,* 419–439.

Ferretti, R. P. & Butterfield, E. C. (1986). Are children's rule-assessment classifications invariant across instances of problem types? *Child Development, 57,* 1419–1428.

Feshback, N. D. (1977). Studies on the empathic behavior of children. In B. A. Maher (Ed.), *Progress in Experimental Personality Research*. (Vol. 8), NY: Academic Press.

Field, D. (1981). Can preschool children really learn to conserve? *Child Development, 52,* 326–334.

Field, T. M. (1978). Interaction patterns of primary vs. secondary caretaker fathers. *Developmental Psychology, 14,* 183–184.

Field, T. M. (1979). Differential behavior and cardiac responses of 3-month-old infants to a mirror and a peer. *Infant Behavior and Development, 2,* 179–184. (a)

Field, T. M. (1979). Infant behaviors directed toward peers and adults in the presence and absence of mother. *Infant Behavior and Development, 2,* 47–54. (b)

Field, T. M. (1982). Affective and physiological changes during manipulated interactions of high-risk infants. In T. Field & A. Fogel (Eds.), *Emotion and early interaction*. Hillsdale, NJ: Erlbaum.

Field, T. M., DeStefano, L. & Koewler, J. H. III (1982). Fantasy play of toddlers and preschoolers. *Developmental Psychology, 18,* 503–508.

Field, T. M., Gewirtz, J. L., Cohen, D., Garcia, R., Greenberg, R., & Collins, K. (1984). Leave-takings and reunions of infants, toddlers, preschoolers, and their parents. *Child Development, 55,* 628–635.

Field, T. M., & Sostek, A. (1983). *Infants born at risk: Physiological, perceptual and loginive processes*. New York: Grune & Stratton.

Field, T. M., Vega-Lahr, N., & Jagadish, S. (1984). Separation stress of nursery school infants and toddlers graduating to new classes. *Infant Behavior and Development, 7,* 277–284.

Field, T. M., & Widmayer, S. M. (1982). Motherhood. In B. B. Wolman (Ed.), *Handbook of developmental psychology*. Englewood Cliffs, N.J.: Prentice-Hall.

Field, T. M., Widmayer, S., Stringer, S., & Ignatoff, E. (1980). Teenage, lower-class black mothers and their preterm infants: An intervention and developmental follow-up. *Child Development, 51,* 426–436.

Fincham, F. D., & Cain,, K. M. (1985). *The role of attributions in learned helplessness*. Paper presented to the biennial meetings of the Society for Research in Child Development, Toronto, Canada.

Fincham, F. D., & Cain, K. M. (in press). Learned helplessness in humans: A developmental analysis. *Developmental Review*.

Fine, M. A., Moreland, J. R., & Schwebel, A. F. (1983). Long-term effects of divorce on parent-child relationships. *Developmental Psychology, 19*, 703–713.

Fine, P., Thomas, C. W., Subs, R. H., Cohnberg, R. I. & Flasher, B. A. (1972). Pediatric blood lead levels. *Journal of the American Medical Association, 221*, 1475–1479.

Fischer, K. W. (1980). A theory of cognitive development: the control and construction of hierarchies of skills. *Psychological Review, 87*, 477–531.

Fischer, K. W., & Bullock, D. (1984). Cognitive development in school-age children: conclusions and new directions. In W. A. Collins (Ed.), *Development during middle childhood: The years from six to twelve*. Washington, D.C.: National Academy Press.

Fischer, M., & Leitenberg, H. (1986). Optimism and pessimism in elementary school-aged children. *Child Development, 57*, 241–248.

Flannery, R. C. & Balling, J. D. (1979). Developmental changes in hemispherical specialization for tactile spatial ability. *Developmental Psychology, 15*, 364–372.

Flavell, J. H. (1970). Developmental studies of mediated memory. In H. W. Reese & L. P. Lipsitt (Eds.), *Advances in child development and behavior* (Vol. 5). New York: Academic Press.

Flavell, J. H. (1977). *Cognitive development*. Englewood Cliffs, NJ: Prentice-Hall.

Flavell, J. H. (1982). On cognitive development. *Child Development, 53*, 1–10.

Flavell, J. H., Beach, D. R. & Chinsky, J. M. (1966). Spontaneous verbal rehearsal in a memory task as a function of age. *Child Development, 37*, 283–299.

Flavell, J. H., Friedrichs, A. G., & Hoyt, J. D. (1970). Developmental changes in memorization processes. *Cognitive Psychology, 1*, 324–340.

Flavell, J. H., Shipstead, S. G. & Croft, K. (1978). Young children's knowledge about visual perception: hiding objects from others. *Child Development, 49*, 1208–1211.

Flavell, J. H., Speer, J. R., Green, F. L., & August, D. L. (1981). The development of comprehension monitoring and knowledge about communication. *Monographs of the Society for Research in Child Development, 46*, No. 192.

Fogel, A. (1979). Peer vs. mother directed behavior in 1- to 3-months-old infants. *Infant Behavior and Development, 2*, 215–226.

Fogel, A. (1980). The effect of brief separations on 2-month-old infants. *Infant Behavior and Development, 3*, 315–330.

Fogel, A. (1980). The role of emotion in early childhood education. *Current Topics in Early Childhood Education, 3*, 1–14.

Fogel, A. (1981). The ontogeny of gestural communication: The first six months. In R. Stark (Ed.), *Language behavior in infancy and early childhood*. New York: Elsevier.

Fogel, A. (1982). Emotional development. In H. E. Mitzel (Ed.), *Encyclopedia of educational research* (5th Ed.) Vol. 2. Glencoe, Ill: The Free Press, Macmillan.

Fogel, A. (1982). Affect dynamics in early infancy: Affective tolerance. In T. Field & A. Fogel (Eds.), *Emotion and early interaction*. Hillsdale, NJ: Erlbaum.

Fogel, A. (1984). *Infancy: Infant, family, and society*. St. Paul, MN: West.

Fogel, A. (1985). Coordinative structures in the development of expressive behavior in early infancy. In G. Zivin (Ed.), *The development of expressive behavior: Biology-environment interactions*. New York: Academic Press.

Fogel, A., & Hannan, T. E. (1985). Manual actions of nine-to-fifteen-week-old human infants during face-to-face interaction with their mothers. *Child Development, 56*, 1271–1279.

Fogel, A., & Melson, G. (1986). Conceptualizing the determinants of nurturance: A reconsideration of sex differences. In A. Fogel, & G. Melson (Eds.), *Origins of nurturance*. Hillsdale, NJ: Erlbaum.

Fogel, A. & Thelen, E. (in press). The development of expressive and communicative action in the first year, *Developmental Psychology*.

Foley, M. A., Johnson, M. K. & Raye, C. L. (1983). Age-related changes in confusion between memories for thoughts and memories for speech. *Child Development, 54*, 51–60.

Foner, A., & Kertzer, D. I. (1979). Intrinsic and extrinsic sources of changes in life-course transitions. In M. W. Riley (Ed.), *Aging from birth to death: Interdisciplinary perspectives*. Boulder, CO: Westview Press.

Ford, C. S., & Beach, F. A. (1951). *Patterns of sexual behavior*. New York: Harper & Row.

Forehand, R., Faust, J., & Baum, C. G. (1985). Accuracy of weight perception among young adolescent girls: An examination of personal and interpersonal correlates. *Journal of Early Adolescence, 5*, 239–245.

Fosberg, S., & Abt Associates (1981). *Family day care in the United States: Summary of findings*. Vol. 1. Washington, D.C.: Department of Health and Human Services.

Foss, D. J., & Hakes, D. T. (1978). *Psycholinguistics: An introduction to the psychology of language*. Englewood Cliffs, NJ: Prentice-Hall.

Fox, N. (1977). Attachment of kibbutz infants to mother and metapelet. *Child Development, 48*, 1228–1239.

Fox, N. A., & Porges, S. W. (1985). The relation between neonatal heart period patterns & developmental outcome. *Child Development, 56*, 28–37.

Fraiberg, S. (1977). *Every child's birthright: In defense of mothering*. NY: Basic Books.

Fraiberg, S. (1977). *Insights from the blind*. NY: Basic Books.

Frank, A. (1952). *The diary of a young girl* (trans. B. M. Mooyaart-Doubleday). New York: Doubleday.

Frankenburg, W. K., Dodd, J. B., Fandal, A. W., Kuzuk, E., & Cohrs, M. (1975). *Denver Developmental Screening Test: Reference manual* (Rev. ed.) Denver: Ladoka Project and Publication Foundation.

Frederickson, W. T., & Brown, J. V. (1975). Posture as a determinant of visual behavior in newborns. *Child Development, 46,* 579–582.

Freedman, D. G. (1974). *Human infancy: An evolutionary perspective.* Hillsdale, NJ: Erlbaum.

Freedman, R. J. (1984). Reflections on beauty as it relates to health in adolescent females. *Women & Health, 9,* 29–45.

Freeman, N. H. (1980). *Strategies of representation in young children: Analysis of spatial skill and drawing processes.* London: Academic Press.

Freud, S. (1905/1953). The transformation of puberty. In J. Strachey (Ed.), *The standard edition of the complete psychological works of Sigmund Freud,* Vol. 7. London: Hogarth Press.

Freud, S. (1949). *An outline of psychoanalysis.* New York: Norton.

Freud, S. (1933/1964). New introductory lectures on psychoanalysis. In J. Strachey (Ed.), *The standard edition of the complete psychological works of Sigmund Freud,* Vol. 22, London: Hogarth Press.

Freud, S. (1953). *Group psychology and the analysis of the ego.* In J. Strachey (Ed.), *The standard edition of the complete psychological works of Sigmund Freud,* Vol. 18. London: Hogarth Press.

Friedman, M., & Rosenman, P. H. (1959). Association of specific overt behavior patterns with blood and cardiovascular findings. *Journal of the American Medical Association, 169,* 205–210.

Friedman, S. L., & Jacobs, B. S. (1981). Sex differences in neonates, behavioral responsiveness to repeated auditory stimulation. *Infant Behavior and Development, 4,* 175–183.

Friedrich, L. K. & Stein, A. H. (1975). Prosocial television and young children: the effects of verbal labeling and role playing on learning and behavior. *Child Development, 46,* 27–36.

Fullard, W., & Reiling, A. M. (1976). An investigation of Lorenz's "babyishness". *Child Development, 47,* 1191–1193.

Furman, W., & Bierman, K. L. (1983). Developmental changes in young children's conceptions of friendship. *Child Development, 54,* 549–556.

Furman, W., & Bierman, K. L. (1984). Children's conceptions of friendship: A multimethod study of developmental changes. *Developmental Psychology, 20,* 925–931.

Furman, W., & Buhrmester, D. (1985). Children's perceptions of the qualities of sibling relations. *Child Development, 56,* 448–461.

Furman, W., & Masters, J. (1980). Peer interaction, sociometric status and resistance to deviation in young children. *Developmental Psychology, 16,* 229–236.

Furman, W., Rahe, D. F., & Hartup, W. W. (1979). Rehabilitation of socially withdrawn preschool children through mixed-age and same-age socialization. *Child Development, 50,* 915–922.

Furstenberg, F. F. (1985). Sociological ventures in child development. *Child Development, 56,* 281–288.

Furstenberg, F. F., & Crawford, A. G. (1981). Family support: Helping teenage mothers to cope. In F. F. Furstenberg, R. Lincoln, & J. Menken (Eds.), *Teenage sexuality, pregnancy and childbearing.* Philadelphia: University of Pennsylvania Press.

Fustenberg, F. F., & Nord, C. W., (1985). Parenting apart: Patterns of child-rearing after marital disruption. *Journal of Marriage and the Family, 47,* 893–904.

Gaddis, A., & Brooks-Gunn, J. (1985). The male experience of pubertal change. *Journal of Youth and Adolescence, 14,* 61–69.

Galambos, N. L., & Garbarino, J. (1983). Identifying the missing links in the study of latchkey children. *Children Today* (July-August), 2–4, 40–41.

Galler, J. R., Ramsey, F., Solimano, G., Kucharski, L. T. & Harrison, R. (1984). The influence of early malnutrition on subsequent behavioral development. IV. Soft neurological signs. *Pediatric Research, 18,* 826–832.

Ganchrow, J. R., Steiner, J. E., & Daher, M. (1983). Neonatal facial expressions in response to different qualities and intersites of gustutary stimuli. *Infant Behavior and Development, 6,* 189–200.

Garbarino, J. (1982). *Children and families in the social environment.* Chicago: Aldine.

Garbarino, J. (1985). *Prospects for reducing child abuse by 20% in 1990: Issues in policy, programming and research.* Chicago: National Committee for Prevention of Child Abuse.

Garbarino, J. & Sherman, D. (1980). High-risk neighborhoods and high-risk families: The human ecology of maltreatment. *Child Development, 51,* 188–198.

Garcia-Coll, C., Kagan, J., & Reznick, J. S. (1984). Behavioral inhibition in young children. *Child Development, 55,* 1005–1019.

Garmezy, N. (1983). Stressors of childhood. In N. Garmezy & M. Rutter (Eds.), *Stress, coping and development in children.* NY: McGraw-Hill.

Garmezy, N., & Rutter, M. (1983). *Stress, coping and development in children.* NY: McGraw-Hill.

Garn, S. B. (1966). Body size and its implications. In L. W. Hoffman & M. L. Hoffman (Eds.), *Review of child development research.* New York: Sage.

Garn, S. B., Clark, D. C., & Guire, K. E. (1975). Growth, body composition and development of obese and lean children. In M. Winick (Ed.), *Childhood obesity.* New York: John Wiley.

Garn, S. B., & Petzold, A. S. (1983). Characteristics of the mother and child in teenage pregnancy. *American Journal of Disabled Children, 137,* 365–368.

Garner, A. M., & Thompson, C. W. (1974). Factors in the management of juvenile diabetes. *Pediatric Psychology, 2,* 6–7.

Garvey, C. (1974). Some properties of social play. *Merrill-Palmer Quarterly, 20,* 163–180.

Garvey, C. (1975). Requests and responses in children's speech. *Journal of Child Language, 2,* 41–64.

Garvey, C. (1977). *Play.* Cambridge, MA: Harvard University Press.

Garvey, C. (1977). The contingent query: A dependent act in conversation. In M. Lewis & L. A. Rosenblum (Eds.), *Interaction, conversation and the development of language.* New York: Wiley.

Garvey, C. (1984). *Children's talk.* Cambridge, MA: Harvard Univ. Press.

Garvey, C., & Hogan, R. (1973). Social speech and social interaction: egocentrism revisited. *Child Development, 44,* 562–568.

Gaull, G. E., Jensen, R. G., Rassin, D. K., & Malloy, M. H. (1981). Human milk as food. In A. Milunsky, E. A. Friedman, & L. Gluck (Eds.), *Advances in perinatal medicine* (Vol. 2). New York: Plenum.

Gellert, E. (1958). Reducing the emotional stresses of hospitalization for children. *American Journal of Occupational Therapy, 12,* 125–129.

Gelles, R. (1978). Violence toward children in the United States. *American Journal of Orthopsychiatry, 48,* 580–592.

Gelman, R. (1969). Conservation acquisition: a problem of learning to attend to relevant attributes. *Journal of Experimental Child Psychology, 7,* 167–187.

Gelman, R. & Baillargeon, R. (1983). A review of some Piagetian concepts. In J. H. Flavell & E. M. Markman (Eds.), *Handbook of Child Psychology.* Vol. 3, NY: Wiley.

Gelman, S. A., Collman, P. & Maccoby, E. E. (1986). Inferring properties from categories vs inferring categories from properties: The case of gender. *Child Development, 57,* 396–404.

Genesee, F. (1983). Bilingual education of majority-language children: the immersion experiments in review. *Applied Psycholinguistics, 4,* 1–46.

George, R. S., & Krondl, M. (1983). Perceptions and food use of adolescent boys and girls. *Nutrition and Behavior, 1,* 115–125.

Gerbner, G. & Gross, L. (1976). Living with television: the violence profile. *Journal of Communication, 26,* 173–199.

Gerbner, G., Gross, L., Morgan, M. & Signorelli, N. (1980). The mainstreaming of America. *Journal of Communication, 30,* 12–29.

Gesell, A. (1925). *The mental growth of the preschool child.* New York: MacMillan.

Gewirtz, J. L. (1972). *Attachment and dependency.* New York: Halsted Press, 1972.

Gianconia, R. M., & Hedges, L. V. (1982). Identifying features of effective open education. *Review of Educational Research, 52,* 579–602.

Gibbs, J. C., Arnold, K. D. & Burkhart, J. (1984). Sex differences in the expression of moral judgment. *Child Development, 55,* 1040–1043.

Gibson, E. J. & Levin, H. (1975). *The psychology of reading.* Cambridge, MA: MIT Press.

Gibson, E. J., Osser, H., Schiff, W., & Smith, J. (1963). An analysis of critical features of letters tested by a confusion matrix. In *Final report on a basic research program on reading,* No. 639. Cornell University and the U.S. Office of Education.

Gibson, E. J. & Spelke, E. S. (1983). The development of perception. In J. H. Flavell and E. M. Markman (Eds.) Vol. III, *Handbook of Child Psychology* (P. Mussen, General Editor). New York: John Wiley.

Gibson, E. J., & Walk, R. D. (1960). The "visual cliff." *Scientific American, 202,* 64–71.

Gibson, J. J. (1966). *The senses considered as perceptual systems.* Boston: Houghton Mifflin.

Gil, D. G. (1970). *Violence against children: Physical abuse in the United States.* Cambridge, MA: Harvard University Press.

Gil, D. G. (1971). Violence against children. *Journal of Marriage and the Family, 33,* 637–648.

Gill, T. J., Repetti, C. S., Metlay, L. A., Rabin, B. S., Taylor, F. H., Thompson, D. S., & Cortese, A. L. (1983). Transplacental immunization of the human fetus to tetanus by immunization of the mother. *Journal of Clinical Investigation, 72,* 987–996.

Gilligan, C. (1982). *In a different voice: Psychological theory and women's development.* Cambridge, MA: Harvard University Press.

Ginzburg, H. J., & Miller, S. M. (1982). Sex differences in children's risk-taking behavior. *Child Development, 53,* 426–428.

Ginzburg, H. J., Pollman, V. A., & Wauson, M. S. (1977). An ethological analysis of nonverbal inhibitors of aggressive behavior in male elementary school children. *Developmental Psychology, 13,* 417–418.

Gleason, J. B. (1973). Code-switching in children's language. In T. E. Moore (Ed.), *Cognitive development and the acquisition of language.* New York: Academic Press.

Gleason, J. B., & Weintraub, S. (1978). Input language and the acquisition of communication competence. In K. E. Nelson (Ed.), *Children's language.* Vol. 1. NY: Gardner Press.

Glick, P. G., & Norton, A. J. (1978). Marrying, divorcing and living together in the U.S. today. *Population Bulletin, 32,* 3–38.

Gnepp, J. & Gould, M. E. (1985). The development of personalized inferences: understanding other people's emotional reactions in light of their prior experiences. *Child Development, 56,* 1455–1464.

Gnepp, J., McKee, E., & Domanic, J. A. (1987). Children's use of situational information to infer emotion: Understanding emotionally equivocal situations. *Developmental Psychology, 23,* 114–123.

Goldberg, W. A., & Easterbrooks, M. A. (1984). Role of marital quality in toddler development. *Developmental Psychology, 20,* 504–514.

Goldfarb, W., Levy, D., & Meyers, D. (1972). The mother speaks to her schizophrenic child: language in childhood schizophrenia. *Psychiatry, 35,* 217–226.

Goldsmith, H. H., & Gottesman, I. I. (1981). Origins of variations in behavioral style: A longitudinal study of temperament in young twins. *Child Development, 52,* 91–103.

Golnikoff, R. M., & Ames, G. J. (1979). A comparison of fathers' and mothers' speech with their young children. *Child Development, 50,* 28–32.

Golomb, C. (1974). *Young children's sculpture and drawing: A study in representation development.* Cambridge, MA: Harvard University Press.

Golomb, C. & Cornelius, C. B. (1977). Symbolic play and its cognitive significance. *Developmental Psychology, 13,* 246–252.

Gomez, F., Ramox-Galvan, R., Frenk, S., Craivoto, M. Jr., Chavex, R., & Vasques, J. (1956). Mortality in second and third degree malnutrition. *Journal of Tropical Pediatrics, 2,* 77–83.

Goodnow, J. (1977). *Children drawing.* Cambridge, MA: Harvard University Press.

Gordon, A. M. (1984). Adequacy of responses given by low-income and middle-income kindergarten children in structured adult-child conversation. *Developmental Psychology, 20,* 881–892.

Gordon, M. & Miller, R. L. (1984). Going steady in the 1980s: Exclusive relationships in six Connecticut high schools. *Sociology and Social Research, 68,* 463–479.

Gordon, S. (1982). Teenage sexuality. In M. Schwarz (Ed.), *TV and teens* (pp. 136–138). Reading, MA: Addison-Wesley.

Goswick, R. A., & Jones, W. H. (1982). Components of loneliness during adolescence. *Journal of Youth and Adolescence, 11,* 373–383.

Gottfried, A. W. & Gottfried, A. E. (1984). Home environment and cognitive development in young children of middle SES families. In A. W. Gottfried (Ed.), *Home environment and early cognitive development: longitudinal research.* New York: Academic Press.

Gottman, J. M. (1983). How children become friends. *Monographs of the Society for Research in Child Development, 48,* No. 3.

Gottman, J. M., & Parkhurst, J. T. (1980). A developmental theory of friendship and acquaintance processes. In A. Collins (Ed.), *Minnesota symposium on child psychology* (Vol. 13). Hillsdale, NJ: Erlbaum.

Gouze, K. & Nadelman, L. (1980). Constancy of gender identity for self and others in children between ages three and seven. *Child Development, 51,* 275–278.

Gray, W. M., & Hudson, L. M. (1984). Formal operations and the imaginary audience. *Developmental Psychology, 20,* 619–627.

Greenberg, M. T., Siegel, J. M., & Letich, C. J. (1983). The nature and importance of attachment relationships to parents and peers during adolescence. *Journal of Youth and Adolescence, 12,* 373–386.

Greenberger, E., & Steinberg, L. (1981). The workplace as a context for the socialization of youth. *Journal of Youth and Adolescence, 10,* 185–210.

Greenleaf, P. (1978), *Children through the ages: A history of childhood.* New York: Barnes & Noble.

Gregg, C. L., Haffner, M. E., & Korner, A. F. (1976). The relative efficacy of vestibular-proprioceptive stimulation and the upright position in enhancing visual pursuit in neonates. *Child Development, 47,* 309–314.

Griffore, R. J., & Schweitzer, J. H. (1983). Child-parent racial attitude relationships. *Psychology: A Quarterly Journal of Human Behavior, 20,* 9–13.

Grigoroiu-Serbanescu, M. (1981). Intellectual and emotional development in premature children from 1 to 5 years. *International Journal of Behavioral Development, 4,* 183–200.

Groffman, K. J. (1970). Life-span developmental psychology in Europe: Past and present. In L. R. Goulet & P. B. Baltes (Eds.), *Life-span developmental psychology: Research and theory.* New York: Academic Press.

Grosjean, F. (1982). *Life with two languages: An introduction to bilingualism.* Cambridge, MA: Harvard University Press.

Grossmann, K., Grossmann, K. E., Spangler, G., Suess, G., & Unzer, L. (1985). Maternal sensitivity and newborn's orientation responses as related to quality of attachment in Northern Germany. *Monographs of the Society for Research in Child Development, 50,* (Serial No. 209), 233–256.

Grotevant, H. D., & Cooper, C. R. (1985). Patterns of interaction in family relationships and the development of identity exploration in adolescence. *Child Development, 56,* 415–428.

Grubb, W. N., & Lazerson, M. (1982). *Broken promises.* New York: Basic Books.

Gruen, G. E., & Vore, D. A. (1972). Development of conservation in normal and retarded children. *Development Psychology, 6,* 146–157.

Gruendel, J. M. (1977). Referential extension in early language development. *Child Development, 48,* 1567–1576.

Grunewaldt, E., Bates, T., & Guthrie, D. (1960). The onset of sleeping through the night in infancy. *Pediatrics, 26,* 667–668.

Grusec, J. E., & Kuczynski, L. (1980). Direction of effect in socialization: A comparison of the parent's vs. the child's behavior as determinant of discipline technique. *Developmental Psychology, 16,* 1–9.

Guardo, C., & Bohan, J. B. (1971). The development of a sense of self-identity in children. *Child Development, 42,* 1909–1921.

Guilford, J. P. (1956). The structure of intelligence. *Psychological Bulletin, 52,* 267–293.

Gump, P. V. (1975). Ecological psychology and children. In E. M. Hetherington (Ed.), *Review of Child Development Research* (Vol. 5). Chicago: University of Chicago Press.

Gunter, N., & LaBarba, R. (1980). The consequences of adolescent childbearing on postnatal development. *International Journal of Behavioral Development, 3,* 191–214.

Gurucharri, C. & Selman, R. L. (1982). The development of interpersonal understanding during childhood, preadolescence and adolescence: A longitudinal followup study. *Child Development, 53,* 924–927.

Gussow, J. (1972). Counternutritional messages of television ads aimed at children. *Journal of Nutrition Education, 4,* 48–54.

Gustafson, G. E., Green, J. A., & West, M. J. (1979). The infant's changing role in mother-infant games: The growth of social skills. *Infant Behavior and Development, 2,* 301–308.

Guthrie, H. A. (1979). *Introduction to nutrition.* St. Louis: Mosby.

Guttmacher, A. (1973). *Pregnancy, birth and family planning: A guide for expectant parents in the 1970's.* New York: Viking Press.

Guttmacher, A. (1981). *Teenage pregnancy: The problem that hasn't gone away.* New York: Author.

Guttmacher, A., & Kaiser, I. H. (1986). *Pregnancy, birth & family planning: The definitive work.* New York: E. P. Dutton.

Gzesh, S. M. & Surber, C. F. (1985). Visual perspective-taking skills in children. *Child Development, 56,* 1204–1213.

Hakuta, K. (1982). Interaction between particles and word order in the comprehension and production of simple sentences in Japanese children. *Developmental Psychology, 18,* 62–76.

Halford, G. S. & Boyle, F. M. (1985). Do young children understand conservation of number? *Child Development, 56,* 165–176.

Hall, E. G., & Lee, A. M. (1984). Sex differences in motor performance of young children: fact or fiction? *Sex Roles, 10,* 217–230.

Hall, G. S. (1904). *Adolescence.* New York: Appleton-Century-Crofts.

Hall, W. M., & Cairns, R. B. (1984). Aggressive behavior in children: An outcome of modeling or social reciprocity? *Developmental Psychology, 20,* 739–745.

Hallahan, D. P. & Kaufman, J. M. (1977). *Introduction to learning disabilities: A psychobehavioral approach.* Englewood Cliffs, NJ: Prentice-Hall.

Halliday, M. A. K. (1979). One child's protolanguage. In M. Bullowa (Ed.) *Before speech.* New York: Cambridge University Press.

Hallinan, M. T. (1976). Friendship patterns in open and traditional classrooms. *Sociology of Education, 49,* 254–265.

Hallinan, M. T. (1980). Patterns of cliquing among youth. In H. C. Foot, A. J. Chapman & J. R. Smith (Eds.), *Friendship and peer relations in childhood.* New York: John Wiley.

Halonen, J. S., & Passman, R. (1978). Pacifier's effects on play and separations from the mother for the one-year-old in a novel environment. *Infant Behavior and Development, 1,* 70–78.

Halverson, C. F. & Waldrop, M. F. (1973). The relation of mechanically recorded activity level to varieties of preschool play behavior. *Child Development, 44,* 678–681.

Hamburg, D., Elliott, G., & Parron, D. (Eds.) (1982). *Health and behavior: Frontiers of research in the biobehavioral sciences.* Report of a study from the Institutes of Medicine. Washington, D.C.: National Academy Press.

Hannan, T. E. (1982). Young infant's hand and finger expression: An analysis of category reliability. In T. Field & A. Fogel (Eds.), *Emotion and early interaction.* Hillsdale, NJ: Erlbaum.

Hanson, R. A. (1975). Consistency and stability of home environment measures related to IQ. *Child Development, 46,* 470–480.

Hardwick, D. A., McIntyre, C. W. & Pick, H. L. Jr. (1976). The content and manipulation of cognitive maps in children and adults. *Monographs of the Society for Research in Child Development, 41,* No. 166.

Hardyck, C. & Petrinovich, L. F. (1977). Left-handedness. *Psychological Bulletin, 84,* 385–404.

Harkness, S., & Super, C. M. (1985). The cultural context of gender segregation in children's peer groups. *Child Development, 56,* 219–224.

Harlow, H., & Harlow, M. (1965). The affectional systems. A. Schrier, H. Harlow, & F. Stollnitz (Eds.), *Behavior of non-human primates.* Vol. 2. New York: Academic Press.

Harrington, D. M., Block, J. H., & Block, J. (1983). Predicting creativity in preadolescence from divergent thinking in early childhood. *Journal of Personality and Social Psychology, 45,* 609–623.

Harris, I. D., & Howard, K. I. (1984). Parental criticism and the adolescent experience. *Journal of Youth and Adolescence, 13,* 113–121.

Harter, S. (1982). The perceived competence scale for children. *Child Development, 53,* 87–97.

Harter, S. (1983). Developmental perspectives on the self-system. In M. Hetherington, (Ed.), *Handbook of child psychology,* Vol. IV (4th Ed.). New York: John Wiley.

Harter, S., & Buddin, B. (1983). *Children's understanding of the simultaneity of two emotions: a developmental acquisition sequence.* Paper presented to the Society for Research in Child Development meetings, Detroit, MI.

Hartup, W. W. (1974). Aggression in childhood: developmental perspectives. *American Psychologist, 29,* 336–341.

Hartup, W. W. (1979). The social worlds of childhood. *American Psychologist, 34,* 949–950.

Hartup, W. W. (1983). Peer relations. In P. H. Mussen (Ed.), *Handbook of child psychology* (4th Ed.), pp. 103–196.

Hartup, W. W. (1984). The peer context in middle childhood. In W. A. Collins (Ed.), *Development during middle childhood: The years from six to twelve* (pp. 240–282). Washington, D.C.: National Academy Press.

Hartup, W. W. & Coates, B. (1967). Imitation of a peer as a function of reinforcement from the peer group and rewardingness of the model. *Child Development, 38,* 1003–1016.

Harvey, P. G. (1984). Lead and children's health: recent research and future questions. *Journal of Child Psychology and Psychiatry, 25,* 517–522.

Hass, A. (1979). *Teenage sexuality, a survey of teenage sexual behavior.* New York: MacMillan.

Hatcher, S. (1973). The adolescent experience of pregnancy and abortion: A developmental analysis. *Journal of Youth and Adolescence, 2,* 53–102.

Haviland, J. M., & Lelwica, M. (1987). The induced affect response: 10-week-old infants' response to three emotion expressions. *Developmental Psychology, 23,* 97–104.

Hay, D. F. (1979). Cooperative interactions and sharing between very young children and their parents. *Developmental Psychology, 15,* 647–653.

Hay, D. F. (1980). Multiple functions of proximity seeking in infancy. *Child Development, 51,* 636–645.

Hayes, D. S. (1978). Cognitive bases for liking and disliking among preschool children. *Child Development, 49,* 906–909.

Hayghe, H. (1979). Working wives' contributions to family income in 1977. *Monthly Labor Review, 102,* 62–64.

Haynes, J. P., & Moore, E. A. (1983). Particular dispositions. *Journal and Family Court Journal,* May, 41–48.

Hazelwood, V. (1977). The role of auditory stimuli in crying inhibition in the neonate. *Journal of Auditory Research, 17,* 225–240.

Hazen, N. (1982). Spatial exploration and spatial knowledge: Individual and developmental differences in very young children. *Child Development, 53,* 826–833.

Hebb, D. O. (1949). *The organization of behavior.* New York: Wiley.

Heider, E. R. (1972). Universals in color naming and memory. *Journal of Experimental Psychology, 93,* 10–20.

Heider, E. R. & Olivier, D. (1972). The structure of the color space in naming and memory for two languages. *Cognitive Psychology, 3,* 337–354.

Hein, K. (1982). Promoting teenage health care. In M. Schwarz (Ed.), *TV and teens.* Reading, MA: Addison-Wesley.

Heinicke, C. M. (1984). Impact of prebirth parent personality and marital functioning on family development: A framework and suggestions for further study. *Developmental Psychology, 20,* 1044–1053.

Heinonen, O., Sloane, D., Shapiro, S. (1976). *Birth defects and drugs in pregnancy.* Littleton, Mass.: Publishing Sciences Group.

Held, R., & Hein, A. (1963). Movement-produced stimulation in the development of visually guided behavior. *Journal of Comparative and Physiological Psychology, 56,* 872–876.

Helmrath, T., & Steinitz, E. (1978). Death of an infant: Parental grieving and the failure of social support. *Journal of Family Practice, 6,* 785–790.

Hendrick, J. (1975). *The whole child: New trends in early education.* St. Louis, MO: C. V. Mosby.

Henggeler, S. W., Rodick, J. D., Borduin, C. M., Hanson, C. L., Watson, S. M., & Urey, J. R. (1986). Multisystemic treatment of juvenile offenders: Effects on adolescent behavior and family interaction. *Developmental Psychology, 22,* 132–141.

Hess, E. H. (1970). Ethology and developmental psychology. In P. H. Mussen (Ed.), *Charmichael's manual of child psychology,* 3rd Edition, New York: Wiley.

Hess, R. D. (1970). Social class and ethnic influence on socialization. In P. H. Mussen (Ed.), *Carmichael's manual of child psychology* Vol. II. New York: Wiley.

Hess, R. D., & Shipman, V. C. (1967). Cognitive elements in maternal behavior. In J. P. Hill (Ed.), *Minnesota symposium on child psychology.* Vol. I. Minnesota: University of Minnesota Press.

Hess, R. D., & Shipman, V. C. (1967). Parents as teachers: How lower and middle class mothers teach. In C. S. Lavatelli & F. Stendler (Eds.), *Readings in child behavior and development.* (3rd Ed.) NY: Harcourt, Brace, Jovanovich.

Hetherington, E. M. (1965). A developmental study of the effects of sex of dominant parent on sex-role preference, identification and imitation in children. *Journal of Personality and Social Psychology. 2,* 188–194.

Hetherington, E. M. (1967). The effects of familial variations on sex-typing, on parent-child similarity and on imitation in childhood. In J. P. Hill (Ed.), *Minnesota symposium on child psychology.* New York: McGraw-Hill.

Hetherington, E. M., Cox, M. & Cox, R. (1978). The aftermath of divorce. In J. H. Stevens, Jr. & M. Matthews (Eds.), *Mother-child, father-child relations.* Washington, D.C.: National Association for the Education of Young Children.

Hetherington, E. M., Cox, M. & Cox, R. (1979). Family interaction and the social-emotional and cognitive development of children following divorce. In V. Vaughn & T. B. Brazelton (Eds.), *The family: Setting priorities.* New York: Science and Medicine Publishing Co. (a)

Hetherington, E. M., Cox, M. & Cox, R. (1979). Play and social interaction in children following divorce. *Journal of Social Issues, 35,* 26–49. (b)

Hetherington, E. M., Cox, M. & Cox, R. (1982). Effects of divorce on parents and children. In M. Lamb (Ed.), *Nontraditional families: Parenting and child development.* Hillsdale, NJ: Erlbaum.

Higgins, A., Power, C. & Kohlberg, L. (1984). The relation of moral atmosphere to judgments of responsibility. In W. M. Kurtines & J. L. Gewirtz (Eds.), *Morality, moral behavior and moral development.* NY: Wiley.

Higgins, A. T., & Turnure, J. E. (1984). Distractibility and concentration of attention in children's development. *Child Development, 55,* 1799–1810.

Higgins, E. T., & Parsons, J. E. (1984). Social cognition and the social life of the child: Stages as sub-cultures. In E. T. Higgins, D. N. Ruble & W. W. Hartup (Eds.), *Social cognition and social development* (pp. 15–62). New York: Cambridge University Press.

Hildebrandt, K. A., & Fitzgerald, H. E. (1979). Facial feature determinants and perceived infant attractiveness. *Infant Behavior and Development, 2,* 329–340.

Hill, C. R., & Stafford, F. P. (1980). Parental care of children: Time diary estimates of quantity, predictability and variety. *Journal of Human Resources, 15,* 219–239.

Hill, M. S. (1983). Trends in the economic situation of U.S. families and children. In R. Nelson & F. Skidmore (Eds.), *American families and the economy.* Washington, D.C.: National Academy Press.

Hinde, R. A. (1974). *Biological bases of human social behavior.* New York: McGraw-Hill.

Hirsch, J. (1975). Cell number and size as determinant of subsequent obesity. In M. Winick (Ed.), *Childhood obesity.* NY: Wiley.

Hobson, R. P. (1982). The question of childhood egocentrism: The coordination of perspectives in relation to operational thinking. *Journal of Child Psychology and Psychiatry, 23,* 43–60.

Hoff-Ginsberg, E. (1986). Function and structure in maternal speech: Their relation to the child's development of syntax. *Developmental Psychology, 22,* 155–163.

Hoffman, L. W. (1977). Changes in family roles, socialization and sex differences. *American Psychologist, 32,* 644–657.

Hoffman, L. W. (1979). Maternal employment: 1979. *American Psychologist, 34,* 859–865.

Hoffman, L. W. (1985). The changing genetics/socialization balance. *Journal of Social Issues, 41,* 127–148.

Hoffman, M. L. (1975). Altruistic behavior and the parent-child relationship. *Journal of Personality and Social Psychology, 31,* 937–943.

Hoffman, M. L. (1978). Towards a theory of empathic arousal and development. In M. Lewis & L. A. Rosenblum (Eds.), *The Development of Affect.* New York: Plenum Press.

Hoffman, M. L. (1979). Development of moral thought, feeling and behavior. *American Psychologist, 34,* 958–966.

Hoffman, M. L. (1980). Moral development in adolescence. In J. Adelson (Ed.), *Handbook of adolescent psychology* (pp. 295–343). New York: Wiley.

Hoffman, M. L. (1984). Empathy, its limitations and its role in a comprehensive moral theory. In W. M. Kurtines & J. L. Gewirtz (Eds.), *Morality, moral behavior and moral development.* NY: Wiley.

Holden, G. W. (1983). Avoiding conflict: Mothers as tacticians in the supermarket. *Child Development, 54,* 233–240.

Hollenbeck, A. R., Gewirtz, J. L., Seloris, S. L., & Scanlon, J. W. (1984). Labor and delivery medication influences parent-infant interaction in the first post-partum month. *Infant Behavior & Development, 7,* 201–210.

Holloway, S. D. (1986). The relation of mother's beliefs to children's math achievement: Some effects of sex differences. *Merrill-Palmer Quarterly, 32,* 231–250.

Holmgren, C., Fitzgerald, B. J., & Carman, R. S. (1983). Alienation and alcohol use by American Indian and Caucasian high school students. *Journal of Social Psychology, 120,* 139–140.

Holmes, T., & Rahe, R. (1967). The social readjustment rating scale. *Journal of Psychosomatic Research, 11.*

Homans, G. C. (1958). Group factors in worker productivity. In E. E. Maccoby, T. M. Newcomb, & E. L. Hartley (Eds.). *Readings in social psychology.* New York: Holt, Rinehart, & Winston.

Hong, K., & Townes, B. (1976). Infants' attachment to inanimate objects: A cross-cultural study. *Journal of the American Academy of Child Psychiatry, 15,* 49–61.

Honzik, M. P. (1976). Value and limitations of infant tests: An overview. In M. Lewis (Ed.), *Origins of intelligence.* NY: Plenum.

Hooker, D. (1952). *The prenatal origins of behavior.* Lawrence: University of Kansas Press.

Hooper, F. H., Sipple, T. S., Goldman, J. A. & Swinton, S. (1974). *A cross-sectional investigation of children's classification abilities.* Technical Report No. 295. Madison, WI: Research and Development Center for Cognitive Learning.

Hormann, E. (1977). Breast feeding the adopted baby. *Birth and the Family Journal, 4,* 165–173.

Horney, K. (1980). *The adolescent diaries of Karen Horney.* New York: Basic Books.

Horowitz, R. (1979). Psychological effects of the "open classroom". *Review of Educational Research, 49,* 71–86.

Howes, C. (1983). Patterns of friendship. *Child Development, 54,* 1041–1053.

Hubert, N. C., Wachs, T. D., Peters-Martin, P., & Gandour, M. J. (1982). The study of early temperament: Measurement and conceptual issues. *Child Development, 53,* 571–600.

Hudson, W. (1960). Pictorial depth perception in subcultural groups in Africa. *Journal of Social Psychology, 52,* 183–208.

Huesmann, L. R. (1982). Television violence and aggressive behavior. In D. Pearl, L. Bouthilet & J. Lazar, (Eds.) *Television and behavior: Ten years of scientific progress and implications for the eighties: Vol. 2 Technical reviews* (pps. 126–137). Washington, D.C.: U.S. Government Printing Office.

Huesmann, L. R., Eron, L. D., Klein, R., Brice, R. & Fischer, P. (1983). Mitigating the imitation of aggressive behaviors by changing children's attitudes about media and violence. *Journal of Personality and Social Psychology, 44,* 899–910.

Huesmann, L. R., Eron, L. D., Lefkowitz, M. M., & Walder, L. O. (1984). Stability of aggression over time and generation. *Developmental Psychology, 20,* 1120–1134.

Huntington, J. F. (1982). Powerless and vulnerable: The social experiences of imprisoned girls. *Juvenile and Family Court Journal,* May, 33–44.

Huntington, L., Zeskind, P. S., & Weiseman, J. R. (1985). Spontaneous startle activity in newborn infants. *Infant Behavior & Development, 8,* 301–308.

Huston, A. C. (1983). Sex-typing. In E. M. Hetherington (Ed.), *Handbook of child psychology. Vol. 4: Socialization, personality and social development.* NY: Wiley.

Hutt, C. (1979). Exploration and play. In B. Sutton-Smith (Ed.), *Play and learning.* NY: Gardner Press.

Huttenlocher, J. & Presson, C. C. (1979). The coding and transformation of spatial information. *Cognitive Psychology, 11,* 375–394.

Huxley, A. (1932). *Brave New World.* New York: Doubleday.

Hyde, J. S. (1984). How large are gender differences in aggression? A developmental meta-analysis. *Developmental Psychology, 20,* 722–736.

Hymes, D. (1971). Competence and performance in linguistic theory. In R. Huxley & E. Ingram (Eds.), *Language acquisition: models and methods.* London: Academic Press.

Ilg, F. L. & Ames, L. B. (1965). *School readiness: Behavioral tests used at the Gesell Institute.* NY: Harper & Row.

Information Please Almanac (1986). Boston: Houghton-Mifflin.

Information Please Almanac (1987). Boston: Houghton-Mifflin.

Ingram, D. (1976). *Phonological disabilities in children. (Studies in language disability and remediation, Vol. 2).* London: Ed. Arnold.

Inhelder, B., & Piaget, J. (1964). *The growth of logical thinking from childhood to adolescence.* New York: Basic Books.

Isabella, R. A., Ward, M. J., & Belsky, J. (1985). Convergence of multiple sources of information on infant individuality: Neonatal behavior, infant behavior, & temperament reports. *Infant Behavior and Development, 8,* 283–292.

Istomina, Z. M. (1975). The development of voluntary memory in preschoolage children. *Soviet Psychology, 13,* 5–64.

Izard, C. (1971). *The face of emotion.* New York: Appleton-Century-Crofts.

Izard, C. (1977). *Human emotions.* New York: Plenum Press.

Izard, C. (1981). *The primacy of emotion in human development.* Paper presented at Society for Research in Child Development, Boston.

Izard, C. E., Hembree, E. A., & Huebner, R. R. (1987). Infants' emotion expressions to acute pain: Developmental change and stability of individual differences. *Developmental Psychology, 23,* 105–113.

Jacklin, C. N., & Maccoby, E. E. (1978). Social behavior at 33 months in same-sex and mixed-sex dyads. *Child Development, 49,* 557–569.

Jacklin, C. N., Snow, M. E., & Maccoby, E. E. (1981). Tactile sensitivity and muscle strength in newborn boys and girls. *Infant Behavior and Development, 4,* 261–269.

Jacobson, J. L. (1981). The role of inanimate objects in early peer interaction. *Child Development, 52,* 618–626.

Jacobson, J. L., Jacobson, S. W., Fein, G. G., Schwartz, P. M., & Dowler, J. K. (1984). Prenatal exposure to an environmental toxin: A test of the multiple effects model. *Developmental Psychology, 20,* 523–532.

Jennings, K. (1975). People versus object orientation, social behavior, and intellectual abilities in preschool children. *Developmental Psychology, 11,* 511–519.

Jensen, A. R. (1980). *Bias in mental testing.* New York: Free Press.

Jensen, R., & Moore, S. G. (1977). The effect of attribute statements on cooperation and competition in schoolage boys. *Child Development, 48,* 305–307.

Jersild, A. T., & Holmes, F. (1935). Children's fears. *Child Development Monographs,* No. 20.

Jiao, S., Ji, G. & Jing, Q. (1986). Comparative study of behavioral qualities of only children and sibling children. *Child Development, 57,* 357–361.

Johnson, C. F. (1971). Hyperactivity and the machine: the actometer. *Child Development, 42,* 2105–2110.

Johnson, C., Lewis, C., Love, S., Lewis, L. & Stuckey, M. (1984). Incidence and correlates of bulimic behavior in a female high school population. *Journal of Youth and Adolescence, 13,* 15–26.

Johnson, C. N., & Wellman, H. M. (1982). Children's developing conceptions of the mind and brain. *Child Development, 53,* 222–234.

Johnson, J. E. & Ershler, J. (1981). Developmental trends in preschool play as a function of classroom programs and child gender. *Child Development, 52,* 995–1004.

Jones, J. B., & Philliber, S. (1983). Sexually active but not pregnant: A comparison of teens who risk and teens who plan. *Journal of Youth and Adolescence, 12,* 235–251.

Jones, K. L. (1975). The fetal alcohol syndrome. In R. D. Haribson (Ed.), *Perinatal addiction.* New York: Halsted Press.

Jones, O. (1977). Mother-child communication with prelinguistic Down's syndrome and normal infants. In H. R. Schaffer (Ed.), *Studies in mother-infant interaction.* London: Academic Press.

Jones, W. R. (1960). A critical study of bilingualism and nonverbal intelligence. *British Journal of Educational Psychology, 30,* 71–76.

Jordan, M. K., & O'Grady, D. J. (1982). Children's health beliefs and concepts: Implications for child health care. In P. Karoly, J. J. Steffen & D. J. O'Grady (Eds.), *Child health psychology: Concepts and issues.* New York: Pergamon Press.

Just, M. A. & Carpenter, R. A. (1980). A theory of reading: From eye fixations to comprehension. *Psychological Review, 87,* 329–354.

Kaffman, M. (1979). Adolescent rebellion in the kibbutz. *Annual Progress in Child Psychiatry and Child Development,* 635–645.

Kagan, J. (1965). Impulsive and reflective children: significance of conceptual tempo. In J. D. Krumboltz (Ed.), *Learning and the educational process.* Chicago: Rand McNally.

Kagan, J. (1971). *Change and continuity in infancy.* New York: Wiley.

Kagan, J. (1978). The child in the family. In A. S. Rossi, J. Kagan, & T. K. Hareven (Eds.), *The family.* NY: W. W. Norton (pp. 33–56).

Kagan, J., Kearsley, R. & Zelazo, P. (1978). *Infancy: Its place in human development.* Cambridge, MA: Harvard University Press.

Kagan, J. & Kogan, N. (1970). Individual variation in cognitive processes. In P. Mussen (Ed.), *Carmichael's Manual of Child Psychology.* Vol. I. NY: Wiley.

Kagan, J., & Moss, H. A. (1959). Parental correlates of a child's IQ and height: A cross-validation of the Berkeley Growth Study results. *Child Development, 30,* 325–340.

Kail, R. (1979). *The development of memory in children.* San Francisco: W. H. Freeman & Co.

Kail, R., & Bisanz, J. (1982). Cognitive development: An information-processing perspective. In R. Vasta, (Ed.), *Strategies and techniques of child study.* New York: Academic Press.

Kail, R. & Hagen, J. W. (1982). Memory in childhood. In B. B. Wolman (Ed.), *Handbook of developmental psychology.* Englewood Cliffs, NJ: Prentice-Hall.

Kaltenbach, K., Weinraub, M., & Fullard, W. (1980). Infant wariness toward strangers reconsidered: Infant's and mother's reactions to unfamiliar persons. *Child Development, 51,* 1197–1202.

Kalter, N., & Plunkett, J. W. (1984). Children's perceptions of the causes and consequences of divorce. *Journal of the American Academy of Child Psychiatry, 23,*326–334.

Kamerman, S. B., & Kahn, A. J. (1981). *Child care, family benefits and working parents: A study in comparative policy.* Columbia University: Columbia University Press.

Kamii, C. & DeVries, R. (1974). Piaget for early education. In R. K. Parker (Ed.), *The preschool in action* (2nd Ed.), Boston: Allyn & Bacon.

Karkheck, R. H. & Hogan, J. D. (1983). Relationship of selected variables to improvement of children's problem-solving abilities. *Perceptual and Motor Skills, 57,* 961–962.

Karmel, M. (1959). *Painless childbirth: Thank you Dr. Lamaze.* Philadelphia: Lippincott.

Katz, P. (1979). The development of female identity. *Sex Roles, 5,* 155–178.

Kanner, L. (1943). Autistic disturbances of affective contact. *Nervous Child, 2,* 217–250.

Kauffman, J. M. & Hallahan, D. P. (1979). Learning disabilities and hyperactivity (with comments on minimal brain dysfunction). In B. B. Lahey & A. E. Kazdin (Eds.), *Advances in clinical child psychology.* Vol. 2. NY: Plenum.

Kaufman, A. S., Zalma, R. & Kaufman, N. L. (1978). The relation between hand dominance to the motor coordination, mental ability and right-left awareness of young normal children. *Child Development, 49,* 885–888.

Kaye, K. (1977). Toward the origin of dialogue. In H. R. Schaffer (Ed.). *Studies in mother-infant interaction.* London: Academic Press.

Kaye, K. (1982). *The mental and social life of babies.* Chicago: University of Chicago Press.

Kaye, K., & Fogel, A. (1980). The temporal structure of face-to-face communication between mothers and infants. *Developmental Psychology, 16,* 454–464.

Kaye, K., & Wells, A. J. (1980). Mother's jiggling and the burst-pause pattern of neonatal feeding. *Infant Behavior and Development, 3,* 29–46.

Keasy, C. B. (1975). Implications of cognitive development for moral reasoning. In D. J. DePalma & J. M. Foley (Eds.), *Moral development: current theory and research.* Hillsdale, NJ: Erlbaum.

Keating, D. P. (1980). Thinking processes in adolescence. In J. Adelson (Ed.) *Handbook of adolescent psychology* (pp. 211–246). New York: Wiley.

Kee, D. W. & Bell, T. S. (1981). The development of organizational strategies in the storage and retrieval of categorical items in free-recall learning. *Child Development, 52,* 1163–1171.

Keeney, T. J., Cannizzo, S. R. & Flavell, J. H. (1967). Spontaneous and induced verbal rehearsal in a recall task. *Child Development, 38,* 953–966.

Keith-Spiegel, P. (1983). Children and consent to participate in research. In G. B. Melton, G. P. Koocher, & M. J. Saks

(Eds.), *Children's competence to consent* (pp. 179–211). New York: Plenum.

Keller, A., Ford, L. H., & Meacham, J. A. (1978). Dimensions of self-concept in preschool children. *Developmental Psychology, 14,* 483–489.

Kellogg, R. (1969). *Analyzing children's art.* Palo Alto, CA: National Press.

Kellogg, R. (1979). *Children's drawings, children's minds.* NY: Avon Books.

Kelly, J. B. (1982). Divorce: The adult perspective. In B. B. Wolman (Ed.), *Handbook of developmental psychology.* Englewood Cliffs, NJ: Prentice-Hall.

Kempe, H. C. & Helfer, R. E. (Eds.) (1972). *Helping the battered child and his family.* Philadelphia: Lippincott.

Kendrick, C., & Dunn, J. (1980). Caring for a second baby: effects on interaction between mother and firstborn. *Developmental Psychology, 16,* 303–311.

Kendrick, C. & Dunn, J. (1982). Protest or pleasure? The response of first-born children to interactions between their mothers and infant siblings. *Journal of Child Psychiatry and Psychology, 23,* 117–129.

Kennedy, W. A. (1969). A follow-up normative study of Negro intelligence and achievement. *Monograph of the Society for Research in Child Development, 34,* No. 126.

Kent, R. D. (1981). Articulatory-acoustic perspectives on speech development. In R. Stark (Ed.), *Language behavior in infancy and early childhood.* New York: Elsevier.

Keppel, F. (1968). Food for thought. In N. S. Scrimshaw & J. E. Gordon (Eds.), *Malnutrition, learning and behavior.* Cambridge, MA: MIT press.

Kessen, W. (1965). *The Child.* New York: Wiley.

Kessen, W., Haith, M., & Salapatek, P. (1970). Human infancy: A bibliography and guide. In P. H. Mussen (Ed.), *Carmichael's manual of child psychology* (3rd ed.). New York: Wiley.

Kilbride, H. W., Johnson, D. & Streissguth, A. P. (1977). Social class, birth order and newborn experience. *Child Development, 48,* 1686–1688.

Kipnis, D. (1987). Psychology and behavioral technology. *American Psychologist, 42,* 30–36.

Klahr, D., & Wallace, J. G. (1976). *Cognitive development: An information processing view.* Hillsdale, NJ: Erlbaum.

Klaus, M. H., Jerauld, R., Kreger, N. C., McAlpine, W., Steffa, M. & Kennell, J. H. (1972). Maternal attachment importance of the first few post-partum days. *New England Journal of Medicine, 46,* 187–192.

Klein, R. P. (1985). Caregiving arrangements by employed women with children under 1 year of age. *Developmental Psychology, 21,* No. 3, 403–406.

Klima, E. S. & Bellugi, U. (1966). Syntactic regularities in the speech of children. In T. Lyons & R. Wales (Eds.), *Psycholinguistic papers.* Edinburgh: Edinburgh University Press.

Klinnert, M. D. (1981). *Infant's use of mother's facial expressions for regulating their own behavior.* Paper presented at meeting of the Society for Research in Child Development, Boston.

Kogan, N. (1976). *Cognitive styles in infancy and early childhood.* Hillsdale, NJ: Erlbaum.

Kogan, N. (1983). Stylistic variation in childhood and adolescence: creativity, metaphor and cognitive style. In J. H. Flavell and E. Markman (Eds.), *Cognitive Development,* Vol. III. *Handbook of Child Psychology.* NY: Wiley.

Kohlberg, L. (1966). A cognitive-developmental analysis of children's sex-role concepts and attitudes. In E. Maccoby (Ed.), *The development of sex differences.* Stanford, CA: Stanford University Press.

Kohlberg, L. (1976). Moral stages and moralization: The cognitive/developmental approach. In T. Lickona (Ed.), *Moral development and behavior.* NY: Holt, Rinehart & Winston.

Kohlberg, L. & Gilligan, C. (1971). The adolescent as philosopher: the discovery of the self in a postconventional world. *Daedalus, 100,* 1051–1086.

Kojima, H. (1986). The history of child development in Japan. In H. Azuma & H. Stevenson (Eds.), *Child Development and Education in Japan.* New York: Academic Press.

Kojima, H. (1986). Becoming nurturant in Japan. In A. Fogel & G. Melson (Eds.), *Origins of nurturance.* Hillsdale, NJ: Erlbaum.

Konner, M. (1975). Relations among infants and juveniles in comparative perspective. In M. Lewis & L. Rosenblum (Eds.), *Friendship and peer relations.* New York: Wiley.

Kopf, K. E. (1970). Family variables and school adjustment of eighth grade father-absent boys. *Family Coordinator, 19,* 145–150.

Kopp, C. B. (1982). Antecedents of self-regulation: A developmental perspective. *Developmental Psychology, 18,* 199–214.

Kopp, C. B., & Parmelee, A. (1979). Prenatal and perinatal influences on infant behavior. In J. Osofsky (Ed.) *Handbook of infant development.* New York: Wiley.

Korn, S. J., Chess, S., & Fernandez, P. (1978). The impact of children's physical handicaps on marital quality and family interaction. In R. M. Lerner & G. B. Spanier (Eds.) *Child influences on marital and family interaction.* New York: Academic Press.

Korner, A. (1969). Neonatal startles, erections and reflex sucks as related to sex, reflex state and individuality. *Child Development, 40,* 1039–1053.

Korner, A. (1979). Maternal rhythms and water beds: A form of intervention with premature infants. In E. Thoman (Ed.) *Origins of the infant's social responsiveness.* Hillsdale, NJ: Erlbaum.

Korner, A., Kraemer, H., Haffner, M., & Thoman, E. (1974). Characteristics of crying and non-crying activity of full-term neonates. *Child Development, 45,* 953–958.

Korner, A., & Thoman, E. (1970). Visual alertness in neonates as evoked by maternal care. *Journal of Experimental Child Psychology, 10,* 67–78.

Korner, A., Zeanah, C. H., Linden, J., Berkowitz, R. I., Kraener, H. C., & Agras, N. S. (1985). The relation between neonatal and later activity & temperament. *Child Development, 56,* 38–42.

Koski, M. L. (1969). The coping processes in childhood diabetes. *Acta Paediatrica Scandinavia, 198,* 7–56.

Kovar, M. G., & Meny, D. J. (1981). A statistical profile. In the Report of the Select Panel for the Promotion of Child Health, *Better health for our children: A national strategy* (Vol. 3) (DHHSPHS, Pub. No. 79–55071). Washington, D.C.: Government Printing Office.

Krasnor, L. R. & Pepler, D. J. (1980). The study of children's play: Some suggested future directions. In K. H. Rubin (Ed.), *Children's Play.* San Francisco: Jossey-Bass.

Krebs, D. & Gillmore, J. (1982). The relation among the first stages of cognitive development, role-taking abilities and moral development. *Child Development, 53,* 877–886.

Krebs, R. L. (1967). *Some relations between moral judgment, attention, and resistance to temptation.* Unpublished Ph.d. dissertation, University of Chicago.

Kreutzer, M. A., Leonard, C. & Flavell, J. H. (1975). An interview study of children's knowledge about memory. *Monographs of the Society for Research in Child Development, 40,* No. 159.

Kreppner, K., Paulsen, S., & Schuetze, Y. (1981). *Infant and family development: from triads to tetrads.* Paper presented at the meeting of the International Society for the Study of Behavioral Development, Toronto.

Krogman, W. M. (1970). Growth of head, face, trunk and limbs in Philadelphia white and Negro children of elementary and high school age. *Monographs of the Society for Research in Child Development, 35* (Serial no. 136).

Kropp, J. P., & Haynes, O. M. (1987). Abusive and non-abusive mothers' ability to identify general and specific emotion signals of infants. *Child Development, 58,* 187–190.

Kuczynski, L. (1984). Socialization goals and mother-child interaction: strategies for long-term and short-term compliance. *Developmental Psychology, 20,* 1061–1073.

Kuhl, P. K. (1981). Auditory category formation and developmental speech perception. In R. Stark (Ed.). *Language behavior in infancy and early childhood.* New York: Elsevier.

Kuhn, D. (1984). Cognitive development. In M. H. Bornstein & M. E. Lamb (Eds.), *Developmental psychology: An advanced textbook.* Hillsdale, NJ: Erlbaum.

Kuhn, D., Ho, V. & Adams, C. (1979). Formal reasoning among pre- and late adolescents. *Child Development, 50,* 1128–1135.

Kuhn, D., Kohlberg, L., Langer, J. & Haan, N. (1977). The development of formal operations in logical and moral judgment. *Genetic Psychology Monographs, 95,* 97–188.

Kuhn, D., Nash, S. C. & Brucken, L. (1978). Sex role concepts of two- and three-year-olds. *Child Development, 49,* 445–451.

Kulka, R. A., Kahle, L. R., & Klingel, D. M. (1982). Aggression, deviance, and personality adaptation as antecedents and consequences of alienation and involvement in high school. *Journal of Youth and Adolescence, 11,* 261–277.

Kurtines, W. & Grief, E. B. (1974). The development of moral thought: Review and evaluation of Kohlberg's approach. *Psychological Bulletin, 81,* 453–470.

Kuzemko, J. A. (Ed.) (1980). *Asthma in children.* Turnbridge Wells: Pitman Medical.

Labov, W. (1970). The logic of nonstandard English. In F. Williams (Ed.), *Language and poverty*. Chicago: Markham.

Ladd, G. W. (1981). Effectiveness of a social learning method for enhancing children's social interaction and peer acceptance. *Child Development, 52,* 171–178.

Ladd, G. W., Lange, G., & Stremmel, A. (1983). Personal and situational influences on children's helping behavior: Factors that mediate compliant helping. *Child Development, 54,* 488–501.

Ladd, G. W., & Mize, J. (1983). A cognitive-social learning model of social skill training. *Psychological Review, 90,* 127–157.

LaFreniere, P., Strayer, F. F., & Gauthier, R. (1984). The emergence of same-sex affiliative preferences among preschool peers: a developmental/ethological perspective. *Child Development, 55,* 1958–1965.

Lamb, M. E. (1977). Father-infant and mother-infant interaction in the first year of life. *Child Development, 48,* 167–181.

Lamb, M. E. (1978). Interactions between eighteen-month-olds and their preschoolaged siblings. *Child Development, 49,* 51–59. (a)

Lamb, M. E. (1978). Qualitative aspects of mother-and father-infant attachments. *Infant Behavior and Development, 1,* 265–277. (b)

Lamb, M. E. (1981). (Ed.) *The role of the father in child development*. New York: Wiley.

Lamb, M. E., Easterbrooks, M. A., & Holden, G. W. (1980). Reinforcement and punishment among preschoolers: characteristics, effects and correlates. *Child Development, 51,* 1230–1236.

Lamb, M. E., & Roopnarine, J. L. (1979). Peer influences on sex-role development in preschoolers. *Child Development, 50,* 1219–1222.

Lamb, M. E., & Sutton-Smith, B. (1982). *Sibling relations: Their nature and significance across the life-span*. Hillsdale, NJ: Erlbaum.

Lane, D. M. & Pearson, D. A. (1982). The development of selective attention. *Merrill-Palmer Quarterly, 28,* 317–337.

Lange, G. W. (1979). Organization-related processes in children's recall. In P. A. Ornstein (Ed.), *Memory organization and structure*. NY: Academic Press.

Langlois, J. & Downs, C. (1979). Peer relations as a function of physical attractiveness: the eye of the beholder or behavioral reality? *Child Development, 50,* 409–418.

Langlois, J. H. & Downs, A. C. (1980). Mothers, fathers and peers as socialization agents of sex-typed play behaviors in young children. *Child Development, 51,* 1237–1247.

Langlois, J. H., Gottfried, N. W., & Seay, B. (1973). The influence of sex of peer on the social behavior of preschool children. *Developmental Psychology, 8,* 93–98.

Langlois, J. H., & Stephan, C. (1977). The effects of physical attraction and ethnicity on children's behavioral attributions and peer preferences. *Child Development, 48,* 1694–1698.

Langlois, J. H. & Stephan, C. W. (1981). Beauty and the beast: The role of physical attractiveness in the development of peer relations and social behavior. In S. S. Brehm, S. M. Kassin & F. X. Gibbons (Eds.), *Developmental social psychology: Theory and research*. NY: Oxford University Press.

Langlois, J. H. & Vaughn, B. E. (1982). A longitudinal study of the relation between physical attractiveness and sociometric status in preschool children. Unpublished manuscript.

Laosa, L. M. (1980). Maternal teaching strategies and cognitive styles in Chicano families. *Journal of Educational Psychology, 72,* 45–54.

Laosa, L. M. (1981). Maternal behavior: Sociocultural diversity in modes of family interaction. In R. W. Henderson (Ed.), *Parent-child interaction: Theory, research and prospects*. New York: Academic Press.

Laosa, L. M. (1984). Social policies toward children of diverse ethnic, racial, and language groups in the United States. In H. W. Stevenson & A. E. Siegel (Eds.), *Child development research and social policy*. Chicago: University of Chicago Press.

Larsen, G. W. (1977). Methodology in developmental psychology: an examination of research on Piagetian theory. *Child Development, 48,* 1160–1166.

Larson, R., & McMahan, R. (1966). The epiphyses of the childhood athlete. *Journal of the American Medical Association, 196,* 607–612.

Lavatelli, C. S. (1977). Environment, experience and equilibration. In M. H. Appel & L. S. Goldberg (Eds.), *Topics in cognitive development*. Vol. 1. NY: Plenum Press.

LaVoie, J. C. (1976). Ego identity formation in middle adolescence. *Journal of Youth and Adolescence, 5,* 371–385.

Lawler, K. A., & Allen, M. T. (1984). The type A behavior pattern in children and adolescents. In W. J. Burns & J. V. Lavigne (Eds.), *Progress in pediatric psychology*. New York: Grune & Stratton (pp. 135–162).

Lawler, K. A., Allen, M. T., Critcher, E. C., & Standard, B. A. (1981). The relationship of physiological responses to the coronary-prone behavior pattern in children. *Journal of Behavioral Medicine, 4,* 203–216.

Lawrence, J. A. (1980). Moral judgment intervention studies using the Defining Issues Test. *Journal of Moral Education, 7,* 178–191.

Lawson, A., & Ingleby, J. D. (1974). Daily routines of preschool children: effects of age, birth order, sex and social class, and developmental correlates. *Psychological Medicine, 4,* 399–415.

Lawson, K. R., & Turkewitz, G. (1980). Intersensory functioning in newborns: Effect of sound on visual performance. *Child Development, 51,* 1295–1298.

Lawton, J. T. & Hooper, F. H. (1978). Piagetian theory and early childhood education. In L. S. Siegel & C. J. Brainerd (Eds.), *Alternatives to Piaget: Critical essays on the theory*. NY: Academic Press.

Lazar, I., & Darlington, R. (1982). Lasting effects of early education: A report from the Consortium for Longitudinal

Studies. *Monographs of the Society for Research in Child Development, 47,* No. 195, pgs. 1–151.

LeBow, M. D. (1984). *Child obesity: A new frontier of behavior therapy.* NY: Springer Pub. Co.

Leboyer, F. (1975). *Birth without violence.* New York: Knopf.

Lefkowitz, M. M., Eron, L. D., Walder, L. O. & Huesmann, L. R. (1977). *Growing up to be violent: A longitudinal study of the development of aggression.* NY: Pergamon Press.

Legg, C., Sherick, I., & Wadland, W. (1975). Reactions of preschool children to the birth of a sibling. *Child Psychiatry and Human Development, 5,* 5–39.

Leifer, M. (1980). *Psychological effects of motherhood: A study of first pregnancy.* New York: Praeger.

Lein, L. (1979). Working couples as parents. In E. Corfman (Ed.), *Families today.* (Vol. I) Bethesda, MD: National Institutes of Mental Health.

Lempers, J. D., Flavell, E. R. & Flavell, J. H. (1977). The development in very young children of tacit knowledge concerning visual perception. *Genetic Psychology Monographs, 95,* 3–53.

Lennard, H., Bealieu, M., & Embry, M. (1965). Interaction in families with a schizophrenic child. *Archives of General Psychiatry, 12,* 166–183.

Lenneberg, E. H. (1969). On explaining language. *Science, 164,* 635–643.

Lenneberg, E. H. (1967). *Biological foundations of language.* NY: Wiley.

Leopold, W. F. (1949). *Speech development of a bilingual child,* (Vol. 4). Evanston, Ill. Northwestern University Press.

Lepper, M. R. (1981). Intrinsic and extrinsic motivation in children: Detrimental effects of superfluous social controls. In W. A. Collins (Ed.), *Aspects of the development of competence: The Minnesota symposium on child psychology* Vol. 14. Hillsdale, NJ: Erlbaum.

Lepper, M. R. (1982). Social control processes, attributions of motivation and the internalization of social values. In E. T. Higgins, D. N. Ruble & W. W. Hartup (Eds.), *Social cognition and social behavior: Developmental perspectives.* Cambridge: Cambridge University Press.

Lerner, R. M., & Shea, J. A. (1982). Social behavior in adolescence. In B. B. Wolman (Ed.), *Handbook of developmental psychology* (pp. 503–525). Englewood Cliffs, NJ: Prentice-Hall.

Lerner, R. M., & Spanier, G. B. (1978). (Eds.), *Child influences on marital and family interaction.* New York: Academic Press.

Lerner, R. M., & Spanier, G. B. (1980). *Adolescent development: A life-span perspective.* New York: McGraw Hill.

Lesser, G., Fifer, G., & Clark, D. (1965). Mental abilities of children from different social classes and cultural groups. *Monographs of the Society for Research in Child Development, 30,* No. 102.

Lester, B. M. (1979). A synergistic process approach to the study of prenatal malnutrition. *International Journal of Behavioral Development, 2,* 377–394.

LeVine, R. A. (1977). Child-rearing as cultural adaptation. In P. H. Leiderman, S. R. Tolkin & A. Rosenfeld (Eds.), *Culture and infancy.* New York: Academic Press.

Levine, L. E. (1983). Mine: Self-definition in 2-year old boys. *Developmental Psychology, 19,* 544–549.

Levy, H. L., Karolkewicz, V., Houghton, S. A., & MacCready, R. A. (1970). Screening the "normal" population in Massachusetts for phenylketonuria. *New England Journal of Medicine, 282,* 1455–1458.

Lewin, K. (1942). Field theory and learning. In *Forty-first year book, National society for the study of education.* Part II. Bloomington, IL: Public School Publishing.

Lewis, C. C. (1981). How adolescents approach decisions: Changes over grades seven to twelve and policy implications. *Child Development, 52,* 538–544.

Lewis, M., & Brooks-Gunn, J. (1979). *Social cognition and the acquisition of self.* New York: Plenum.

Lewis, M., & Michaelson, L. (1983). *Children's emotions and moods.* New York: Plenum Press.

Lewis, M., & Weinraub, M. (1974). Sex of parent X sex of child: Socioemotional development. In R. Richart, R. Friedman, R. VandeWiele (Eds.), *Sex differences in behavior.* New York: Wiley.

Lewis, M., Young, G., Brooks, J., & Michalson, L. (1975). The beginning of friendship. In M. Lewis & L. Rosenblum (Eds.), *Friendship and peer relations.* New York: Wiley.

Liben, L. S. (1978). Perspective-taking in young children: seeing the world through rose-colored glasses. *Developmental Psychology, 14,* 87–92.

Lickona, T. (1976). Research on Piaget's theory of moral development. In T. Lickona (Ed.), *Moral development and behavior: Theory, research and social issues.* NY: Holt, Rinehart & Winston.

Lieberman, A. F. (1977). Preschoolers' competence with a peer: Relations with attachment and peer experience. *Child Development, 48,* 1277–1287.

Lindholm, K. J. (1980). Bilingual children: some interpretations of linguistic development. In K. Nelson (Ed.), *Children's language.* Vol. II. New York: Gardner Press.

Linn, M. C. (1983). Content, context, and process in reasoning during adolescence: Selecting a model. *Journal of Early Adolescence, 3,* 63–82.

Lipsitt, L. P. (1979). Infants at risk: Perinatal and neonatal factors. *Infant Behavior and Development, 2,* 23–42.

Lipsitt, L. P., Engen, T., & Kaye, H. (1963). Developmental changes in the olfactory threshold of the neonate. *Child Development, 34,* 371–376.

Lively, W. J. & Bromley, D. B. (1973). *Person perception in children and adolescents.* London: Wiley.

Lockman, J. J. (1984). The development of detour ability during infancy. *Child Development, 55,* 482–491.

Loeb, R. B., Horst, L. & Horton, P. J. (1980). Family interaction patterns associated with self-esteem in preadolescent girls and boys. *Merrill-Palmer Quarterly, 26,* 203–217.

Loewe, M. (1966). *Imperial China: The historical background to the modern age*. New York: Praeger.

London, P. (1970). The rescuers: Motivational hypotheses about Christians who saved Jews from the Nazis. In J. R. Macaulay & L. Berkowitz (Eds.), *Altruism and helping behavior*. NY: Academic.

Long, R. T., Lamont, J. E., Whipple, B., Bandler, L., Blom, G. E., Burgin, L., & Jessner, L. (1958). A psychosomatic study of allergic and emotional factors in children with asthma. *American Journal of Psychiatry, 114,* 890–899.

Long, T. J., & Long, L. (1982). *Latchkey children: The child's view of self-care*. Washington, D.C.: Catholic University of America (ERIC Document Reproduction Service, No. ED 211229).

Longen, K. (1981). *Domestic food programs: An overview*. (U.S. Dept. of Agriculture, Economics, Statistics and Cooperative Services, ESCS81). Washington, D.C.: Government Printing Office.

Lorenz, K. Z. (1952). *King Solomon's ring*. New York: Crowell.

Lounsbury, M. L., & Bates, J. E. (1982). The cries of infants of differing levels of temperamental difficultness: Acoustic properties and effects on listeners. *Child Development, 53,* 677–686.

Lovaas, O. I. (1977). *The autistic child: Language development through behavior modification*. New York: Irvington Publishers.

Lowry, G. H. (1978). *Growth and development of children*. (7th Ed.) Chicago: Yearbook Medical Pubs.

Luria, A. R. (1980). *Higher cortical functions in man*. (3rd Ed.) NY: Basic Books.

Lynn, D. B. (1976). Fathers and sex-role development. *Family Coordinator, 25,* 403–409.

Lynn, D. B., & Sawrey, W. L. (1959). The effects of father-absence on Norwegian boys and girls. *Journal of Abnormal and Social Psychology, 59,* 258–262.

Lynn, R. (1982). IQ in Japan and the U.S. shows a growing disparity. *Nature, 297,* 222–223.

Maccoby, E. E. (1980). *Social development*. NY: Harcourt, Brace, Jovanovich.

Maccoby, E. E. (1984). Middle childhood in the context of the family. In W. A. Collins (Ed.), *Development during middle childhood: The years from six to twelve*. Washington, D.C.: National Academy Press.

Maccoby, E. E., & Jacklin, C. N. (1974). *The psychology of sex differences*. Stanford, CA: Stanford University Press.

Maccoby, E. E., & Martin, J. A. (1983). Socialization in the context of the family: parent-child interaction. In P. H. Mussen (Ed.), *Handbook of child psychology* (Vol. IV) 4th Ed. NY: Wiley.

Mack, J. E., & Hickler, H. (1981). *Vivienne: The life and suicide of an adolescent girl*. New York: New American Library.

Mack, J. E., & Webster, C. D. (1980). The family phenomenon. In C. D. Webster, M. M. Konstantareas, J. Oxman & J. E. Mack (Eds.), *Autism: New directions in research and education* (pgs. 31–40). New York: Pergamon Press.

MacLean, P. (1984). Brain evolution: The origins of social and cognitive behaviors. In M. Frank (Ed.), *A Child's brain* (pp. 9–24). New York: Haworth Press.

Madsen, M. C., & Shapira, A. (1977). Cooperation and challenge in four cultures. *Journal of Social Psychology, 102,* 189–195.

Maehr, M. L. (1974). Culture and achievement motivation. *American Psychologist, 29,* 887–896.

Mahaffy, P. (1965). The effects of hospitalization on children admitted for tonsillectomy and adenoidectomy. *Nursing Research, 14,* 12–19.

Mahler, M., Pine, F., & Bergman, A. (1975). *The psychological birth of the human infant*. New York: Basic.

Main, M. (1981). Avoidance in the service of attachment: A working paper. In K. Immelmann, G. Barlow, L. Petrinovich, & M. Main (Eds.), *Behavioral development: The Bielefeld interdisciplinary project*. New York: Cambridge University Press.

Main, M., & George, C. (1985). Responses of abused and disadvantaged toddlers to distress in agemates: A study in the day care setting. *Developmental Psychology, 21,* 407–412.

Main, M., & Weston, D. R. (1981). The quality of the toddler's relationship to mother and father: Relation to conflict behavior and readiness to establish new relationships. *Child Development, 52,* 932–940.

Malina, R. M. (1982). Motor development in the early years. In S. G. Moore & C. R. Cooper (Eds.), *The young child: Reviews of research*. (Vol. 3) Washington, D.C.: National Association for the Education of Young Children.

Mannheimer, D. L. & Mellinger, G. D. (1967). Personality characteristics of the child accident reporter. *Child Development, 38,* 491–513.

Maracek, J. (1987). Counseling adolescents with problem pregnancies. *American Psychologist, 42,* 89–93.

Maratsos, M. (1983). Some current issues in the study of the acquisition of grammar. In P. H. Mussen (Ed.), *Handbook of child psychology*. (Vol. 3). NY: Wiley.

Marcia, J. E. (1966). Development and validation of ego identity status. *Journal of Personality and Social Psychology, 3,* 551–558.

Marcia, J. E. (1983). Some directions for the investigation of ego development in early adolescence. *Journal of Early Adolescence, 3,* 215–223.

Marcoen, A., & Brumagne, M. (1985). Loneliness among children and young adolescents. *Developmental Psychology, 21,* 1025–1031.

Marcus, D. E., & Overton, W. F. (1978). The development of cognitive gender constancy and sex-role preferences. *Child Development, 49,* 434–444.

Markus, H. J., & Nurius, P. S. (1984). Self-understanding and self-regulation in middle childhood. In W. A. Collins (Ed.), *Development during middle childhood: The years from 6 to 12*. Washington, D.C.: National Academy Press.

Marjoribanks, K. (1979). Family environments. In H. Walberg (Ed.), *Educational environments and effects*. Berkeley, CA: McCutchan.

Majoribanks, K. (1984). Aspirations: sibling and family environmental correlates. *Genetic Psychology Monographs, 110,* 3–20.

Majoribanks, K., Walberg, H. S., & Bargen, M. (1975). Mental abilities: Sibling constellations and social class correlates. *British Journal of Social and Clinical Psychology, 14,* 104–116.

Markman, E. M. (1973). The facilitation of part-whole comparisons by use of the collective noun "family". *Child Development, 44,* 837–840.

Markman, E. M. & Siebert, J. (1976). Classes and collections: internal organization and resulting wholistic properties. *Cognitive Psychology, 8,* 561–577.

Markusen, E., Owen, G., Fulton, R., & Bendiksen, R. (1977). SIDS: Survivor as victim. *Omega, 8,* 277–284.

Marshall, R. E., Stratton, W. C., Moore, J. A., & Boxerman, S. B. (1980). Circumcision: The effect upon newborn behavior. *Infant Behavior and Development, 3,* 1–14.

Martens, R. (1978). *Joy and sadness in children's sports.* Champaign, IL: Human Kinetics Pubs.

Martens, R. (1986). Youth sports in the USA. In M. Weiss & D. Gould (Eds.), *Competitive sport for children and youth.* Champaign, IL: Human Kinetics Pubs.

Martin, B. (1975). Parent-child relations. In F. D. Horowitz (Ed.), *Review of child development research.* (Vol. IV). Chicago: University of Chicago Press.

Martini, M., & Kirkpatrick, J. (1981). Early interactions in the Marquesas Islands. In T. Field, J. M. Sostek, P. Vietze, & P. Leiderman (Eds.), *Culture and early interactions.* Hillsdale, NJ: Erlbaum.

Marx, J. L. (1978). Botulism in infants: A cause of sudden death? *Science, 201,* 799–801.

Mason, M., & Katz, L. (1976). Visual processing of nonlinguistic strings: redundancy effects and reading disability. *Journal of Experimental Psychology: General, 105,* 338–348.

Masters, J. C., & Furman, W. (1981). Popularity, individual friendship selection and specific peer interaction among children. *Developmental Psychology, 17,* 344–350.

Masur, E. F., McIntyre, C. W., & Flavell, J. H. (1973). Developmental changes in apportionment of a study time among items in a multitrial free recall task. *Journal of Experimental Child Psychology, 15,* 237–246.

Matteson, D. R. (1975). *Adolescence today: Sex roles and the search for identity.* Homewood, IL: Dorsey.

Matteson, M. T., & Ivancevich, J. M. (1980). The coronary-prone behavior pattern: A review and appraisal. *Social Science and Medicine, 14,* 337–351.

Matthews, K. A., & Angulo, J. (1980). Measurement of the Type A behavior pattern in children: Assessment of children's competence, impatience-anger, and aggression. *Child Development, 51,* 466–475.

Matthews, K. A., & Avis, N. E. (1983). Stability of overt Type A behaviors in children: Results from a one-year longitudinal study. *Child Development, 54,* 1507–1512.

Matthews, K. A., & Siegel, J. M. (1983). Type A behaviors by children, social comparison, and standards for self-evaluation. *Developmental Psychology, 19,* 135–140.

Maurer, D., & Heroux, L. (1980). *The perception of faces by three-month-old infants.* Paper presented at the International Conference on Infant Studies, New Haven.

Maurer, D., & Salapatek, P. (1976). Developmental changes in the scanning of face by young infants. *Child Development, 47,* 523–527.

Mayer, J. (1968). *Overweight: Causes, cost and control.* Englewood Cliffs, NJ: Prentice-Hall.

Mayer, J. (1975). Obesity during childhood. In M. Winick (Ed.), *Childhood Obesity.* NY: Wiley.

Mayers, P. (1978). *Flow in adolescence and its relation to school experience.* PhD Dissertation, University of Chicago.

McBride, A. B. (1973). *The growth and development of mothers.* New York: Harper & Row.

McCall, R. B. (1984). Developmental changes in mental performance: The effect of birth of a sibling. *Child Development, 55,* 1317–1321.

McCall, R. B., Appelbaum, M. I., & Hogarty, P. S. (1973). Developmental changes in mental performance. *Monographs of the Society for Research in Child Development, 38,* No. 150.

McCartney, K. (1984). Effect of quality of day care environment on children's language development. *Developmental Psychology, 20,* 244–261.

McCartney, K. & Nelson, K. (1981). Children's use of scripts in story recall. *Discourse Processes, 4,* 59–70.

McClearn, G. E. (1970). Genetic influences on behavior and development. In P. H. Mussen (Ed.), *Carmichael's Manual of Child Psychology,* Vol. I. 3rd Edition. New York: Wiley.

McDonald, D. (1978). Paternal behavior at first contact with the newborn in a birth environment without intrusions. *Birth and the Family Journal, 5,* 123–132.

McGarrigle, J., Grieve, R. & Hughes, M. (1978). Interpreting inclusion: A contribution to the study of the child's cognitive and linguistic development. *Journal of Experimental Child Psychology, 26,* 528–550.

McHale, S. M., & Huston, T. L. (1984). Men and women as parents: Sex-role orientations, employment, and parental roles with infants. *Child Development, 55,* 1349–1361.

McIntosh, K. (1984). Viral infections of the fetus and newborn. In M. E. Avery & H. W. Taeusch, Jr. (Eds.), *Schaffer's diseases of the newborn* (5th Ed.), Philadelphia: Saunders.

McLaughlin, B. (1977). Second-language learning in children. *Psychological Bulletin, 84,* 438–459.

McLaughlin, B. (1978). *Second-language acquisition in children.* Hillsdale, NJ: Erlbaum.

McLaughlin, B. (1983). Child compliance to parental control techniques. *Developmental Psychology, 19,* 667–673.

McLaughlin, M. (1976). Survivors and surrogates: Children and parents from the ninth to the thirteenth centuries. In L. deMause (Ed.), *The history of childhood.* London: Souvenir Press.

McLoughlin, D., & Whitfield, R. (1984). Adolescents and their experience of parental divorce. *Journal of Adolescence, 7,* 155–170.

McLure, G. T. & Piel, E. (1978). College bound girls and science careers: Perception of barriers and facilitating factors. *Journal of Vocational Behavior, 12,* 172–183.

McMillen, M. M. (1979). Differential mortality by sex in fetal and neonatal deaths. *Science, 204,* 89–91.

McNeill, D. (1968). What does a child mean when he says "No"? In E. M. Zale (Ed.), *Proceedings of the conference on language and language behavior.* NY: Appleton-Century-Crofts.

McNeill, D. (1970). *The acquisition of language.* New York: Harper and Row.

Mead, M. (1958). Adolescence in primitive and modern society. In G. E. Swanson, T. E. Newcomb & E. K. Hartley (Eds.), *Readings in social psychology.* New York: Holt.

Meares, R., Grimwalde, J., & Woods, C. (1976). A possible relationship between anxiety in pregnancy and puerperal depression. *Journal of Psychosomatic Research, 20,* 605–610.

Mechanic, D. (1980). Education, parental interest and health perceptions and behavior. *Inquiry, 17,* 331–338.

Medrich, E. A., Roizen, J., & Rubin, V. (1982). *The serious business of growing up.* Berkeley, CA: University of California Press.

Melges, F. T., & Hamburg, D. A. (1977). Psychological effects of hormonal changes in women. In F. A. Beach (Ed.), *Human sexuality in four perspectives.* Baltimore: The Johns Hopkins University Press.

Melson, G. F. (1980). *Family and environment: An ecosystem perspective.* Minneapolis, MN: Burgess.

Melson, G. F., & Fogel, A. (1982). Young children's interest in unfamiliar infants. *Child Development, 53,* 693–700.

Melson, G. F., Fogel, A. & Toda, S. (1986). Children's ideas about infants and their care. *Child Development, 57,* 519–527.

Melton, G. B., & Russo, N. F. (1987). Adolescent abortion: Psychological perspectives on public policy. *American Psychologist, 42,* 69–72.

Mendelson, B. K., & White, D. R. (1985). Development of self-body-esteem in overweight youngsters. *Developmental Psychology, 21,* 90–96.

Menyuk, P., & Bernholtz, N. (1969). Prosodic features of children's language production. *MIT Research Laboratory of Electronics Quarterly Progress Reports, 93,* 216–219.

Mercy, J. A., & Steelman, L. C. (1982). Familial influence on the intellectual attainment of children. *American Sociological Review, 47,* 532–542.

Meredith, H. (1963). Changes in the stature and body weight of North American boys during the last 80 years. *Advances in Child Development and Behavior, 1,* 69–114.

Meredith, H. (1976). Findings from Asia, Australia, Europe and North America on secular change in mean height of children, youths, and young adults. *American Journal of Physical Anthropology, 44,* 315–326.

Meredith, H. (1978). Research between 1960 and 1970 on standing height of young children in different parts of the world. In H. Reese & L. P. Lipsitt (Eds.), *Advances in child development and behavior,* Vol. 12. NY: Academic Press.

Messer, S. B. (1970). The effect of anxiety over intellectual performance on reflectivity-impulsivity in children. *Child Development, 41,* 723–735.

Messer, S. B. (1976). Reflection-impulsivity: A review. *Psychological Bulletin, 83,* 1026–1052.

Messer, S. B. & Brodzinsky, D. M. (1981). Three year stability of reflection-impulsivity in young adolescents. *Developmental Psychology, 17,* 848–850.

Meyer, W. J., & Thompson, G. G. (1956). Sex differences in the distribution of teacher approval and disapproval among sixth grade children. *Journal of Educational Psychology, 47,* 385–396.

Midlarsky, E., & Hannah, M. E. (1985). Competence, reticence and helping by children and adolescents. *Developmental Psychology, 21,* 534–541.

Mill, J. G. (1960). *Autobiography of John Stuart Mill.* NY: Columbia Univ. Press.

Miller, N. & Maruyama, G. (1976). Ordinal position and peer popularity. *Journal of Personality and Social Psychology, 33,* 123–131.

Miller, P. H. (1983). *Theories of developmental psychology.* San Francisco: W. H. Freeman.

Miller, P. H., Haynes, V. F., DeMarie-Dreblow, D., & Woody-Ramsey, J. (1986). Children's strategies for gathering information in three tasks. *Child Development, 57,* 1429–1439.

Miller, P. Y., & Simon, H. (1980). The development of sexuality in adolescence. In J. Adelson (Ed.), *Handbook of adolescent psychology* (pp. 383–407). New York: Wiley.

Minnett, A. M., Vandell, D. L., & Santrock, J. W. (1983). The effects of sibling status on sibling interaction: Influence of birth order, age spacing, sex of child and sex of sibling. *Child Development, 54,* 1064–1072.

Minuchin, P. P. (1985). Families and individual development: Provocations from the field of family therapy. *Child Development, 56,* 289–302.

Minuchin, P. P., & Shapiro, E. K. (1983). The school as a context for social development. In P. H. Mussen (Ed.), *Handbook of child psychology* (Vol. 4) E. M. Hetherington (Vol. Ed.). New York: Wiley.

Minuchin, S., Baker, L., Rosman, B., Leibman, R., Milman, L., & Todd, T. (1975). A conceptual model of psychosomatic illness in children. *Archives of General Psychiatry, 32,* 1031–1038.

Mischel, H. N., & Mischel, W. (1983). Development of children's knowledge of self-control strategies. *Child Development, 54,* 603–619.

Mischel, W. (1974). Processes in the delay of gratification. In L. Berkowitz (Ed.), *Advances in experimental social psychology,* (Vol. 7). New York: Academic Press.

Mischel, W., & Mischel, H. N. (1975). *A cognitive-social-learning analysis of moral development.* Paper presented to the biennial meeting of the Society for Research in Child Development, Denver, CO.

Mistry, J. (1983). *Children's organization and recall of information in scripted narratives.* Unpublished Ph.d. dissertation, Purdue University.

Mitchell, D. C. (1982). *The process of reading: A cognitive analysis of fluent reading and learning to read.* NY: John Wiley.

Mitchell, G. (1981). *Human sex differences: A primatologist's perspective.* New York: Van Nostrand Reinbold.

Mize, J. (1984). *Social skills training for rejected and isolated preschool children.* Unpublished Ph.d. dissertation. Purdue University.

Moely, B. E. (1977). Organizational factors in the development of memory. In R. Kail & J. W. Hagen (Eds.), *Perspectives on the development of memory and cognition.* Hillsdale, NJ: Erlbaum.

Moely, B. E., Olson, F. A., Halwes, T. G. & Flavell, J. H. (1969). Production efficiency in young children's clustered recall. *Developmental Psychology, 1,* 26–34.

Molfese, V. S., & Thomson, B. (1985). Optimizer vs. complications: Assessing productive values of perinatal states. *Child Development, 56,* 810–823.

Money, J. (1968). *Sex errors of the body: Dilemmas, education, counselling.* Baltimore: Johns Hopkins University Press.

Montemayor, R. (1982). The relationship between parent-adolescent conflict and the amount of time adolescents spend alone and with parents and peers. *Child Development, 53,* 1512–1519.

Montemayor, R. (1983). Parents and adolescents in conflict: All families some of the time and some families most of the time. *Journal of Early Adolescence, 3,* 83–103.

Montemayor, R., & Eisen, M. (1977). The development of self-conceptions from childhood to adolescence. *Developmental Psychology, 13,* 314–319.

Montemayor, R., & Hanson, E. (1985). A naturalistic view of conflict between adolescents and their parents and siblings. *Journal of Early Adolescence, 5,* 23–30.

Moore, D., & Schultz, N. R. (1983). Loneliness at adolescence: Correlates, attributions, and coping. *Journal of Youth and Adolescence, 12,* 95–100.

Moore, J. W., Hauck, W. E., & Deene, T. C. (1984). Racial prejudice, interracial contact and personality variables. *Journal of Experimental Education, 52,* 168–173.

Moore, N., Everson, C. & Brophy, J. (1974). Solitary play: Some functional reconsiderations. *Developmental Psychology, 10,* 830–836.

Moran, J. D., & O'Brien, G. (1983). The development of intention-based moral judgments in three- and four-year-old children. *Journal of Genetic Psychology, 143,* 175–179.

Morgan, G. (1983). Child daycare policy in chaos. In E. F. Zigler, S. L. Kagan, & E. Klugman (Eds.), *Children, families and government: Perspectives on American social policy.* Cambridge University Press.

Morrison, D. M. (1985). Adolescent contraceptive behavior: A review. *Psychological Bulletin, 98,* 538–568.

Morrison, H., & Kuhn, D. (1983). Cognitive aspects of preschoolers' peer imitation in a play situation. *Child Development, 54,* 1041–1053.

Moskowitz, B. A. (1978). The acquisition of language. *Scientific American, 239,* 92–108.

Moskowitz, D. S., Dreyer, A. S. & Kronsberg, S. (1981). Preschool children's field independence: prediction from antecedent and concurrent maternal and child behavior. *Perceptual and Motor Skills, 52,* 607–616.

Mossler, D. G., Marvin, R. S. & Greenberg, M. T. (1976). Conceptual perspective-taking in 2- to 6-year-old children. *Developmental Psychology, 12,* 85–86.

Mueller, E., & Brenner, J. (1977). The growth of social interaction in a toddler play group: The role of peer experience. *Child Development, 48,* 854–861.

Muir, D., & Field, J. (1979). Newborn infants orient to sounds. *Child Development, 50,* 431–436.

Munroe, R. H., & Munroe, R. L. (1971). Household density and infant care in East African society. *Journal of Social Psychology, 83,* 3–13.

Munroe, R. H., Shuimin, H. S., & Munroe, R. L. (1984). Gender understanding and sex-role preference in four cultures. *Developmental Psychology, 20,* 673–682.

Murai, N., Murai, N., & Takahashi, I. (1978). A study of moods in postpartum women. *Tohuku Psychologica Ioliak, 37,* 32–40.

Murdock, G. P. (1959). *Africa: Its people and their culture and history.* NY: McGraw Hill.

Murphy, C. M. (1978). Pointing in the context of a shared activity. *Child Development, 49,* 371–380.

Murray, F. B. (1983). Equilibration as cognitive conflict. *Developmental Review, 3,* 54–61.

Murray, F. B., Ames, G. & Botvin, G. (1977). The acquisition of conservation through cognitive dissonance. *Journal of Educational Psychology, 69,* 519–527.

Mussen, P., & Eisenberg-Berg, N. (1977). *Roots of caring, sharing, and helping: the development of prosocial behaviors in childhood.* San Francisco: W. H. Freeman.

Nadelman, L., & Begun, A. (1981). *The effect of the newborn on the older sibling.* Paper presented at the Society for Research in Child Development, Boston.

Naeye, R., Diener, M., & Dellinger, W. (1969). Urban poverty: Effects of prenatal nutrition, *Science, 166,* 1206.

Naidoo, S. (1981). Teaching methods and their rationale. In G. T. Pavlidis & T. R. Miles (Eds.), *Dyslexia research and its application to education.* New York: Wiley.

National Science Foundation (1977). *Research on the effects of television advertising on children: A review of the literature and recommendations for future research.* Washington, D.C.: National Science Foundation.

Needleman, H. L. (1984). Neurotoxins: An ignored source of perturbed development. In M. D. Levine & P. Satz (Eds.), *Middle childhood: development and dysfunction.* Baltimore, MD: University Park Press.

Needleman, H. L., Gunnoe, C., Leviton, A., Reed, R., Peresie, H., Maher, C. & Barrett, P. (1979). Deficits in psychological and classroom performance of children with elevated dentine lead levels. *New England Journal of Medicine, 300,* 689–695.

Neimark, E. D. (1982). Adolescent thought: transition to formal operations. In B. B. Wolman (Ed.), *Handbook of developmental psychology* (pp. 486–502). New York: Wiley.

Neisser, U. (1979). The concept of intelligence. In R. J. Sternberg & D. K. Detterman (Eds.), *Human intelligence: perspectives on its theory and measurement.* Norwood, NJ: Ablex.

Nelson, C. A., & Horowitz, F. D. (1983). The perception of facial expressions and stimulus motion by two- and five-month-old infants using holographic stimuli. *Child Development, 54,* 868–877.

Nelson, J., & Aboud, F. E. (1985). The resolution of social conflict between friends. *Child Development, 56,* 1009–1017.

Nelson, J. R., Jr. (1982). The politics of federal daycare regulations. In E. Sigler & E. Gordon (Eds.), *Day care: Scientific and social policy issues.* Boston: Auburn House.

Nelson, K. (1973). Structure and strategy in learning to talk. *Monographs of the Society for Research in Child Development, 38* (Serial no. 149).

Nelson, K. (1978). How children represent knowledge of their world in and out of language: A preliminary report. In R. S. Siegler (Ed.), *Children's thinking: What develops?* Hillsdale, NJ: Erlbaum.

Nelson, K. (1981). Individual differences in language development: Implication for development and language. *Developmental Psychology, 17,* 170–187.

Nelson, K., Rescorla, L., Gruendel, J., & Benedict, H. (1978). Early lexicons: What do they mean? *Child Development, 49,* 960–968.

Nettlebladt, P., Fagerstrom, C., & Udderberg, M. (1976). The significance of reported childbirth pain. *Journal of Psychosomatic Research, 20,* 215–221.

Neumann, C. G. (1977). Obesity in pediatric practice: Obesity in the preschool and schoolage child. *Pediatric Clinics of North America, 24,* 117–122.

Newcomb, A. F., & Brady, J. E. (1982). Mutuality in boys' friendship relations. *Child Development, 53,* 392–395.

Newcomb, M. D., Huba, G. J., & Bentler, P. M. (1983). Mother's influence on the drug use of their children: Confirmatory tests of direct modeling and mediational theories. *Developmental Psychology, 19,* 714–726.

Newcomer, S. F., Udry, J. R., & Cameron, F. (1983). Adolescent sexual behavior and popularity. *Adolescence, 18,* 515–522.

Newell, A., & Simon, H. (1972). *Human problem solving.* Englewood Cliffs, NJ: Prentice-Hall.

Newson, J., & Newson, E. (1968). *Four years old in an urban community.* Chicago: Aldine.

Newson, J., & Newson, E. (1976). *Seven years old in the home environment.* New York: Wiley.

Newton, N. (1972). Childbearing in broad perspective. In Boston Children's Medical Center (Ed.), *Pregnancy, birth, and the newborn.* Boston: Delacorte Press.

Neyzi, O., Saner, G., Alp, H., Binyildiz, P., Yazicioghu, S., Emre, S. & Gurson, C. T. (1976). Relations between body weight in infancy and weight in later childhood and adolescence. In Z. Laron (Ed.), *The adipose child.* NY: Karger.

Nicholls, J. G., & Miller, A. T. (1984). Development and its discontents: The differentiation of the concept of ability. In J. G. Nicholls (Ed.), *The development of achievement motivation.* Greenwich, Conn: JAI. (a)

Nicholls, J. G., & Miller, A. T. (1984). Reasoning about the ability of self and others: A developmental study. *Child Development, 55,* 1990–1999. (b)

Nicholls, J. G., & Miller, A. T. (1985). Differentiation of the concepts of luck and skill. *Developmental Psychology, 21,* 76–82.

Ninio, A. (1979). A naive theory of the infant and other maternal attitudes in two subgroups in Israel. *Child Development, 50,* 976–980.

Ninio, A. (1980). Picture-book reading in mother-infant dyads belonging to two subgroups in Israel. *Child Development, 51,* 587–590.

Ninio, A. (1983). Joint book reading as a multiple vocabulary acquisition device. *Developmental Psychology, 19,* 445–451.

Nisan, M. (1984). Distributive justice and social norms. *Child Development, 55,* 1020–1029.

Nora, J., & Fraser, C. (1974). *Medical genetics: Principles and practice.* Philadelphia: Lea & Febiger.

Norton, A. J., and Moorman, J. E. (1987). Current trends in marriage and divorce among American women. *Journal of Marriage and the Family, 49,* 3–14.

O'Brien, M., Huston, A. C. & Risley, T. (1983). Sex-typed play of toddlers in a day-care center. *Journal of Applied Developmental Psychology, 4,* 1–9.

O'Brien, T., & McManus, C. (1978). Drugs and the fetus: A consumer's guide by generic and brand name. *Birth and the Family Journal, 5,* 58–86.

O'Bryan, K. G., & Boersma, F. J. (1971). Eye movements, perceptual activity and conservation development. *Journal of Experimental Child Psychology, 12,* 157–169.

Oden, S., & Asher, S. R. (1977). Coaching children in social skills for friendship making. *Child Development, 48,* 495–506.

Odom, R. D. (1978). A perceptual salience account of decalage relations and developmental change. In L. S. Siegel & C. J. Brainerd (Eds.), *Alternatives to Piaget: Critical essays on the theory.* New York: Academic Press.

Odom, S. L., Jenkins, J. R., Speltz, M. L. & Deklyen, M. (1982). Promoting social integration of young children at risk for learning disabilities. *Learning Disability Quarterly, 5,* 349–387.

Offer, D. (1969). *The psychological world of the teenager.* New York: Basic Books.

Olson, C. F., & Woroby, J. (1984). Perceived mother-daughter relations in a pregnant and non-pregnant adolescent sample. *Adolescence, 19,* 781–794.

Orlick, T., & Botterill, C. (1975). *Every kid can win.* Chicago: Nelson-Hall.

Ornstein, P. A., Naus, J. J., & Liberty, C. (1975). Rehearsal and organization processes in children's memory. *Child Development, 26,* 818–830.

Osofsky, J. D., & O'Connel, E. J. (1977). Patterning of newborn behavior in an urban population. *Child Development, 48,* 532–536.

Oviatt, S. L. (1978). *Qualitative change in the language comprehension of 9- to 17-month-old infants: An experimental approach.* Paper presented at International Conference on Infant Studies, Providence, RI.

Owen, S. V., Froman, R. D., & Moscow, H. (1981). *Educational psychology.* Boston: Little, Brown.

Owen, G. & Lippman, G. (1977). Nutritional status of infants and young children: USA. *Pediatric Clinics of North America, 24,* 211–227.

Pabon, E. (1983). The case for alternatives to detention. *Juvenile and Family Court Journal, 34,* 37–45.

Page, E. G. (1979). Acceleration vs. enrichment: theoretical perspectives. In W. C. George, S. J. Cohn & J. C. Stanley (Eds.), *Educating the gifted: acceleration and enrichment.* Baltimore: Johns Hopkins University Press.

Paikoff, R. L., & Savin-Williams, R. C. (1983). An exploratory study of dominance interactions among adolescent females at a summer camp. *Journal of Youth and Adolescence, 12,* 419–433.

Palkovitz, R. (1984). Parental attitude and fathers' interactions with their 5-month-old infants. *Developmental Psychology, 20,* 1054–1060.

Palkovitz, R. (1985). Fathers' birth attendance, early contact, and extended contact with their newborns: A critical review. *Child Development, 56,* 392–408.

Panneton, R. K., & DeCasper, A. J. (1986). *Newborns' postnatal preference for a prenatally experienced melody.* Paper presented at International conference on Infant Studies, Los Angeles.

Parfitt, R. R. (1977). *The birth primer.* Philadelphia: The Running Press.

Paris, S. C., & Lindauer, B. K. (1976). The role of inference in children's comprehension and memory for sentences. *Cognitive Psychology, 8,* 217–227.

Parke, R. D., & Collmer, C. W. (1975). Child abuse: An interdisciplinary analysis. In E. M. Hetherington (Ed.), *Review of child development research.* (Vol. V). Chicago: University of Chicago Press.

Parke, R. D., & Slaby, R. G. (1983). The development of aggression. In E. M. Hetherington (Ed.), *Handbook of child psychology* (Vol. 4). NY: John Wiley.

Parmelee, A. H. (1986). Children's illnesses: their beneficial effects on behavioral development. *Child Development, 57,* 1–10.

Parpal, M. & Maccoby, E. E. (1985). Maternal responsiveness and subsequent child compliance. *Child Development, 56,* 1326–1334.

Parsons, J. E., Adler, T. J. & Kaczala, C. M. (1982). Socialization of achievement attitudes and beliefs: parental influences. *Child Development, 53,* 310–321.

Parten, M. (1932). Social participation among preschool children. *Journal of Abnormal Psychology, 27,* 243–269.

Parten, M. (1933). Social play among preschool children. *Journal of Abnormal and Social Psychology, 28,* 136–147.

Pascual-Leone, J. (1980). Constructive problems for constructive theories: The current relation of Piaget's work and a critique of information-processing simulation psychology. In R. H. Kluwe & H. Spada (Eds.), *Developmental models of thinking.* New York: Academic Press.

Pastor, D. L. (1981). The quality of mother-infant attachment and its relationship to toddler's initial sociability with peers. *Developmental Psychology, 17,* 326–335.

Patterson, G. R. (1982). Mothers: The unacknowledged victims. *Monographs of the Society for Research in Child Development, 45,* No. 186.

Pellegrini, D. (1985). Social cognition and competence in middle childhood. *Child Development, 56,* 253–264.

Pederson, F. A., Anderson, B. T., & Cain, R. L. (1977). *An approach to understanding linkages between the parent-infant and spouse relationships.* Paper presented to the biennial meeting of the Society for Research in Child Development, New Orleans.

Pedersen, P. E., Williams, C. L., & Blass, E. M. (1982). Activation and odor conditioning of suckling behavior in three day old albino rats. *Journal of Experimental Psychology: Animal Behaviors Processes, 8,* 329–341.

Peery, J. C. (1979). Popular, amiable, isolated, rejected: A reconceptualization of sociometric status in preschool children. *Child Development, 50,* 1231–1234.

Pellegrino, J. W. & Glaser, R. (1979). Cognitive correlates and components in the analysis of individual differences. In R. J. Sternberg & D. K. Detterman (Eds.), *Human intelligence: perspectives on its theory and measurement.* Norwood, NJ: Ablex.

Pepler, D. (1981). *Naturalistic observations of teaching and modeling between siblings.* Paper presented at the biennial meeting of the Society for Research in Child Development, Boston.

Petersen, A. C. (1983). Menarche: Meaning of measures and measuring meaning. In S. Golub (Ed.), *Menarche.* Lexington, MA: Lexington Books.

Petersen, A. C., & Taylor, B. (1980). The biological approach to adolescence. In J. Adelson (Ed.), *Handbook of adolescent development* (pp. 117–158). New York: Wiley.

Peters-Martin, P., & Wachs, T. D. (1984). A longitudinal study of temperament and its correlates in the first 12 months. *Infant Behavior and Development, 7,* 285–289.

Peterson, L., Hartmann, D. P., & Gelfand, D. M. (1977). Developmental changes in the effects of dependency rates and reciprocity cues on children's moral judgments and donation rates. *Child Development, 48,* 1331–1339.

Peterson, N. L. & Haralick, J. G. (1977). Integration of handicapped and nonhandicapped preschoolers: An analysis of play behavior and social interaction. *Education and Training of the Mentally Retarded, 12,* 235–245.

Peterson, P. E., Jeffrey, D. B., Bridgwater, C. A. & Dawson, B. (1984). How pronutrition television programming affects children's dietary habits. *Developmental Psychology, 20,* 55–63.

Phillips, D. (1984). Day care: Promoting collaboration between research and policymaking. *Journal of Applied Developmental Psychology, 5,* 91–113.

Phillips, S., King, S., & DuBois, L. (1978). Spontaneous activities of female vs. male newborns. *Child Development, 49,* 590–597.

Phipps-Yonas, S. (1980). Teenage pregnancy and motherhood: A review of the literature. *American Journal of Orthopsychiatry, 50,* 403–431.

Piaget, J. (1950). *The psychology of intelligence.* New York: Harcourt Brace.

Piaget, J. (1952). *The child's conception of number.* NY: Humanities Press.

Piaget, J. (1952). *The origins of intelligence in children.* NY: International Universities Press.

Piaget, J. (1960). *The child's conception of the world.* London: Routledge.

Piaget, J. (1963). *Play, dreams and imitation in childhood.* New York: Norton.

Piaget, J. (1964). Development and learning. In R. Ripple & V. Rockcastle (Eds.), *Piaget Rediscovered.* Ithaca, NY: Cornell University Press.

Piaget, J. (1965). *The moral judgment of the child.* New York: Free Press.

Piaget, J. (1967). *Six psychological studies.* NY: Random House.

Piaget, J. (1972). Problems of equilibration. In C. Nodine, J. Gallagher & R. Humphrey (Eds.), *Piaget and Inhelder on equilibration.* Philadelphia, PA: Jean Piaget Society.

Piaget, J. (1977). Piaget on Piaget. Film.

Piaget, J., & Inhelder, B. (1969). *The psychology of the child.* New York: Basic Books.

Piaget, J. & Inhelder, B. (1973). *Memory and intelligence.* NY: Basic Books.

Pihl, R. O. & Parkes, M. (1977). Hair element content in learning disabled children. *Science, 198,* 203–206.

Pilpel, H. F., & Paul, E. W. (1982). Contraceptive advertising. In M. Schwarz (Ed.) *TV and teens.* Reading, MA: Addison-Wesley.

Pinard, A. (1981). *The conservation of conservation: The child's acquisition of a fundamental concept.* Chicago: University of Chicago Press.

Piotrkowski, C. S. (1984). Living with preschool children: The Bernard family. In R. LaRossa (Ed.), *Family case studies: A sociological perspective.* New York: The Free Press.

Pipp, S., Fischer, K. W., & Jennings, S. (1987). Acquisition of self-and mother knowledge in infancy. *Developmental Psychology, 23,* 86–96.

Pipp, S. L., & Giffen, K. V. (1981). *Parameters of scanning in the first three months of life.* Paper presented at the meeting of the Society for Research on Child Development, Boston.

Pirozzolo, F. J., & Hansch, E. C. (1982). The neurobiology of developmental reading disorders. In R. N. Malatesha &

P. G. Aaron (Eds.), *Reading disorders: Varieties and treatments.* New York: Academic Press.

Pleck, J. (1977). The work-family role system. *Social Problems, 24,* 417–427.

Pleck, J., & Rustad, M. (1980). *Husbands' and wives' time in family work and paid work in 1975–1976 study of time use.* Unpublished paper. Wellesley College Center for Research on Women.

Plionis, E. M. (1977). Family functioning and childhood accident occurrence. *American Journal of Orthopsychiatry, 47,* 250–263.

Plunkett, J. W., & Kalter, N. (1984). Children's beliefs about reactions to parental divorce. *Journal of the American Academy of Child Psychiatry, 23,* 616–621.

Pollack, L. A. (1983). *Forgotten children.* London: Cambridge University Press.

Pollitt, E., Garza, C., & Leibel, R. L. (1984). Nutrition and public policy. In H. W. Stevenson & A. E. Siegel (Eds.), *Child development research and social policy.* (pp. 421–470) Chicago: University of Chicago Press.

Pollitt, E. & Thomson, C. (1977). Protein-calorie malnutrition and behavior: a view from psychology. In R. J. Wurtman & J. J. Wurtman (Eds.), *Nutrition and the brain* (Vol. 2). NY: Basic Books.

Porac, C. & Coren, S. (1981). *Lateral preferences and human behavior.* NY: Springer-Verlag.

Porter, R. H., Cernoch, J. M., & McLaughlin, F. J. (1983). Maternal recognition of neonates through olfactory cues. *Physiology and Behavior, 30,* 151–154.

Porter, R. H., Ramsey, B., Tremblay, A., Iaccobo, M. & Crawley, S. (1978). Social interactions in heterogeneous groups of retarded and normally developing children: an observational study. In G. P. Sackett (Ed.), *Observing behavior. Vol. I: Theory and applications in mental retardation.* Baltimore, MD: University Park Press.

Portnoy, A., & Simmons, C. H. (1978). Day care and attachment. *Child Development, 49,* 239–242.

Powell, D. (1984). Enhancing the effectiveness of parent education: An analysis of program assumptions. *Current Topics in Early Childhood Education, 5,* 121–139.

Powell, G. (1974). *Black Monday's children.* NY: Appleton-Century-Croft.

Power, T. G. (1985). Mother- and father-infant play: A developmental analysis. *Child Development, 56,* 1514–1524.

Power, T. G. & Parke, R. D. (1980). Play as a context for early learning: Lab and home analyses. In I. E. Sigel & L. J. Laosa (Eds.), *The family as a learning environment.* NY: Plenum Press.

Prader, A., Tanner, J. M. & VonHarnack, G. A. (1963). Catch-up growth following illness or starvation: an example of developmental canalization in man. *Journal of Pediatrics, 62,* 646–659.

Pratt, L. (1973). Child-rearing methods and children's health behavior. *Journal of Health and Social Behavior, 14,* 61–69.

Pratt, M. W., Golding, G. & Hunter, W. J. (1984). Does morality have a gender? Sex, sex role and moral judgment relations across the adult life span. *Merrill-Palmer Quarterly, 30,* 321–340.

President's Council on Physical Fitness and Sports (1977). *The physically underdeveloped child.* Washington, D.C.: Government Printing Office.

Pressley, M. (1982). Elaboration and memory development. *Child Development, 53,* 296–309.

Pressley, M., Heisel, B. E., McCormick, C. B. & Nakamura, G. V. (1982). Memory strategy instruction with children. In C. J. Brainerd & M. Pressley (Eds.), *Verbal processes in children.* NY: Sprenger-Verlag.

Pressley, M. & Levin, J. R. (1977). Developmental differences in subjects' associative learning strategies and performance: assessing a hypothesis. *Journal of Experimental Child Psychology, 24,* 431–439.

Pulaski, M. (1970). Play as a function of toy structure and fantasy predisposition. *Child Development, 41,* 531–537.

Putallaz, M., & Gottman, J. M. (1981). An interactional model of children's entry into peer groups. *Child Development, 52,* 986–994.

Quienan, J. T. (1980). *A new life: Pregnancy, birth and your child's first year.* New York: Van Nostrand Reinbold.

Radin, N. (1971). Maternal warmth, achievement motivation and cognitive functioning in lower-class preschool children. *Child Development, 42,* 1560–1565.

Radin, N. (1981). The role of the father in cognitive, academic and intellectual development. In M. Lamb (Ed.), *The role of the father in child development* (2nd Ed.), NY: Wiley.

Radke-Yarrow, M., Zahn-Waxler, C. & Chapman, M. (1983). Children's prosocial dispositions and behavior. In P. H. Mussen (Ed.), *Handbook of child psychology.* (4th Ed.) Vol. IV. New York: Wiley.

Ragozin, A. S. (1980). Attachment behavior of day-care children: Naturalistic and laboratory observations. *Child Development, 51,* 409–415.

Ramey, C. T., Farran, D. C. & Campbell, F. A. (1979). Predicting IQ from mother-infant interactions. *Child Development, 50,* 804–814.

Ramsay, G. V. (1943). The sexual development of boys. *American Journal of Psychology, 56,* 217–233.

Rapaport, R., Rapaport, R. N., & Strelitz, Z. (1977). *Fathers, mothers, and society: Toward new alliances.* New York: Basic Books.

Raudenbusch, S. W. (1984). Magnitude of teacher expectancy effects on pupil IQ gain as a function of the credibility of expectancy induction: A synthesis of findings from 18 experiments. *Journal of Experimental Psychology, 76,* 85–97.

Reamer, F. G., & Shireman, C. H. (1981). Alternatives to the juvenile justice system: Their development and the current "state of the art". *Juvenile and Family Court Journal, 32,* 17–32.

Reaves, J. Y., & Roberts, A. (1983). The effect of type of information on children's attraction to peers. *Child Development, 54,* 1024–1031.

Reisinger, K. S., & Williams, A. F. (1982). Evaluation of programs designed to increase the protection of infants in cars. *Pediatrics, 68,* 280–287.

Remmers, H. H. (1954). *Four years of New York television: 1951–1954.* Urbana: National Association of Educational Broadcasters.

Rest, J. R. (1983). Morality. In J. Flavell & E. M. Markman (Eds.), *Cognitive Development. Vol. III. Handbook of Child Psychology.* NY: Wiley.

Revelle, G. L., Wellman, H. M. & Karabenick, J. D. (1985). Comprehension monitoring in preschool children. *Child Development, 56,* 654–663.

Reynolds, C. R. & Jensen, A. R. (1983). WISC-R subscale patterns of abilities of blacks and whites matched on full scale IQ. *Journal of Educational Psychology, 75,* 207–214.

Rheingold, H. L. & Cook, K. V. (1975). The contents of boys' and girls' rooms as an index of parents' behavior. *Child Development, 46,* 459–463.

Rheingold, H. L., Cook, K. V., & Kolowitz, V. (1987). Commands activate the behavior and pleasure of 2-year-old children. *Developmental Psychology, 23,* 146–151.

Riccuiti, H. N. (1974). Fear and the development of social attachments in the first year of life. In M. Lewis & L. Rosenblum (Eds.) *Origins of fear.* New York: Wiley.

Richards, M. P. M. (1977). An ecological study of infant development in urban Britain. In P. Leiderman, S. Tulkin, and A. Rosenfeld (Eds.), *Culture and infancy: Variations in the human experience.* New York: Academic Press.

Richardson, R. A., Galambos, N. L., Schulenberg, J. E., & Petersen, A. C. (1984). Young adolescents' perceptions of the family environment. *Journal of Early Adolescence, 4,* 131–154.

Richardson, S. A. (1969). The effect of physical disability on the socialization of a child. In D. A. Goslin (Ed.), *Handbook of socialization theory and research.* (pp. 1047–1063). Chicago: Rand McNally.

Richardson, S. A., Hastorf, A. H., & Dornbusch, S. M. (1964). Effects of physical disability on a child's description of himself. *Child Development, 35,* 893–907.

Richardson, S. A., Goodman, N., Hastorf, A. H. & Dornbusch, S. M. (1961). Cultural uniformity in reaction to physical disabilities. *American Sociological Review, 26,* 241–247.

Rienert, G. (1979). Prolegomena to a history of life-span developmental psychology. In P. B. Baltes & O. G. Brim (Eds.), *Life-Span development and behavior* (Vol. 2) New York: Academic Press.

Rierdan, J., & Koff, E. (1981). The psychological impact of menarche: Integrative versus disruptive changes. *Annual Progress in Child Psychiatry and Child Development,* 483–493.

Riley, C. A. & Trabasso, T. (1974). Comparatives, logical structures, and encoding in a transitive inference task. *Journal of Experimental Psychology, 17,* 187–203.

Riley, T., Adams, G., & Nielsen, E. (1984). Adolescent egocentrism: The association among imaginary audience behavior, cognitive development, and parental support and rejection. *Journal of Youth and Adolescence, 13,* 401–417.

Ritvo, E. R. (1976). *Autism: Diagnosis, current research and management.* New York: Wiley.

Rivara, F. P. (1982). Epidemiology of childhood injuries. In *Preventing childhood injuries.* Columbus, OH: Ross Labs.

Roberts, C., & Lowe, C. (1975). Where have all the conceptions gone? *Lancet, 1,* 498–499.

Roberts, G. C., Block, J. H., & Block, J. (1984). Continuity and change in parents' child-rearing practices. *Child Development, 55,* 586–597.

Robertson, J., & Robertson, J. (1971). Young children in brief separation: A fresh look. *Psychoanalytic Study of the Child, 26,* 264–315.

Robson, B. E. (1983). And they lived happily ever after: Marriage concepts of older adolescents. *Canadian Journal of Psychiatry, 28,* 646–649.

Rochat, P. (1983). Oral touch in young infants: Response to variations of nipple characteristics in the first months of life. *International Journal of Behavioral Development, 6,* 123–134.

Roche, A. F. (Ed.) (1979). Secular trends in human growth, maturation and development. *Monographs of the Society for Research in Child Development, 44,* No. 179.

Roche, A. F. (1981). The adipocyte-number hypothesis. *Child Development, 52,* 31–43.

Rodholm, M., & Larsson, K. (1978). Father-infant interaction at the first contact after delivery. *Early Human Development, 3,* 21–27.

Rodman, H., Pratto, D. J., & Nelson, R. S. (1985). Child care arrangements and children's functioning: A comparison of self-care and adult-care children. *Developmental Psychology, 21,* 413–418.

Rogoff, B. (1982). Integrating context and cognitive development. In M. E. Lamb & A. L. Brown (Eds.), *Advances in developmental psychology.* Vol. 2. Hillsdale, NJ: Erlbaum.

Rogoff, B., Gauvain, M., & Ellis, S. (1984). Development viewed in its cultural context. In M. H. Bornstein & M. E. Lamb (Eds.), *Developmental psychology: An advanced textbook.* Hillsdale, NJ: Erlbaum.

Rogoff, B., Newcombe, N., & Kagan, J. (1974). Planfulness and recognition memory. *Child Development, 45,* 972–977.

Rogoff, B., & Wertsch, J. V. (1984). (Eds.), *Children's learning in the "zone of proximal development".* New Directions for Child Development. No. 23. San Francisco: Jossey-Bass.

Rohwer, W. D. (1980). An elaborative conception of learner differences. In R. E. Snow, P. A. Frederico & W. E. Montague (Eds.), *Aptitude, learning and instruction.* (Vol. 2) Hillsdale, NJ: Erlbaum.

Roopnarine, J. L. (1984). Sex-typed socialization in mixed-age classrooms. *Child Development, 55,* 1078–1084.

Rosch, E. R. (1974). Linguistic relations. In A. Silverstein (Ed.), *Human Communication: theoretical perspectives.* NY: Halsted Press.

Rosch, E. R. (1977). Human categorization. In N. Warren (Ed.), *Advances in cross-cultural psychology* (Vol. 1). NY: Academic Press.

Rosch, E. R., Mervis, C. B., Gray, W. D., Johnson, D. M. & Boyes-Braem, P. (1976). Basic objects in natural categories. *Cognitive Psychology, 8,* 382–439.

Rosenberg, M. (1979). *Conceiving the self.* NY: Basic Books.

Rosenblatt, J. S. (1972). Learning in newborn kittens. *Scientific American, 277,* 18–25.

Rosenblith, J. F., & Sims-Knight, J. E. (1985). *In the beginning: Development in the first two years.* Belmont, Ca: Brooks-Cole.

Rosenhan, D. L. (1969). Some origins of concern for others. In P. H. Mussen, J. Langer & M. Covington (Eds.), *Trends and issues in developmental psychology.* NY: Holt, Rinehart & Winston.

Rosenthal, D. M., Peng, C. J., & McMillan, J. M. (1980). Relationship of adolescent self-concept to perceptions of parents in single- and two-parent families. *International Journal of Behavioral Development, 3,* 441–453.

Rosenthal, R., & Jacobsen, L. (1966). Teachers' expectancies: determinants of pupils' IQ gains. *Psychological Reports, 19,* 115–118.

Rosenthal, R., & Jacobsen, L. (1968). *Pygmalion in the classroom.* New York: Holt, Rinehart & Winston.

Ross, C. J. (1982). Of children and liberty: An historian's view. *American Journal of Orthopsychiatry, 52,* 470–480.

Ross, H. S., & Goldman, B. D. (1977). Establishing new social relationships in infancy. In T. Alloway, P. Pliner, & L. Krames (Eds.), *Attachment behavior.* New York: Plenum.

Ross, D. M. & Ross, S. A. (1982). *Hyperactivity: research, theory and action.* NY: Wiley. (2nd Ed.)

Rossi, A. (1968). Transition to parenthood. *Journal of Marriage and the Family, 30,* 26–39.

Rotenberg, K., & Mann, L. (1986). The development of the norm of reciprocity of self-disclosure and its function in children's attraction to peers. *Child Development, 57,* 1349–1357.

Rothbart, M. K., & Hanson, M. J. (1983). A caregiver report comparison of temperamental characteristics of Down's Syndrome and normal infants. *Developmental Psychology, 19,* 766–769.

Rubenstein, J. L., Howes, C., & Boyle, P. C. (1981). A two-year follow-up of infants in community based infant day care. *Journal of Child Psychology and Psychiatry, 22,* 209–218.

Rubenstein, J., Howes, C., & Pedersen, F. A. (1982). Second-order effects of peers on mother-toddler interaction. *Infant Behavior and Development, 5,* 185–194.

Rubin, K. H. (1982). Non-social play in early childhood: necessarily evil? *Child Development, 53,* 651–658.

Rubin, K. H., Fein, G. G., Vandenberg, B. (1983). Play. In E. M. Hetherington (Ed.), *Handbook of Child Psychology,* (Vol. 4). New York: Wiley.

Rubin, K. H., & Maioni, T. L. (1975). Play preference and its relation to egocentrism, popularity, and classification skills in preschoolers. *Merrill-Palmer Quarterly, 21,* 171–178.

Rubin, K. H., & Pepler, D. J. (1980). The relation of children's play to social-cognitive growth and development. In H. Foot, J. Smith & T. Chapman (Eds.), *Friendship and childhood relations.* NY: Wiley.

Rubin, K. H. & Schneider, F. W. (1973). The relation between moral judgment, egocentrism and altruistic behavior. *Child Development, 44*, 661–665.

Rubin, Z. (1980). *Children's friendships.* Cambridge, MA: Harvard University Press.

Rubin, Z., & Sloman, J. (1984). How parents influence their children's friendship. In M. Lewis (Ed.), *Beyond the dyad.* New York: Plenum.

Ruble, D. N., Boggiano, A. K., Feldman, N. S., & Loebl, J. H. (1980). Developmental analysis of the role of social comparison in self-evaluation. *Developmental Psychology, 16*, 105–115.

Ruble, D. N., & Brooks-Gunn, J. (1982). The experience of menarche. *Child Development, 53*, 1557–1566.

Ruff, H. A. (1978). Infant recognition of invariant forms of objects. *Child Development, 49*, 293–306.

Ruff, H. A. (1984). Infants' manipulative exploration of objects: Effects of age and object characteristics. *Developmental Psychology, 20*, 9–20.

Ruopp, R. R., & Travers, J. (1982). Janus faces of day care: Perspectives on quality and cost. In E. Zigler, & E. Gordon (Eds.), *Day care: Scientific and social policy issues.* Boston: Auburn House.

Rushton, J. P. (1975). Generosity in children: immediate and long-term effects of modeling, preaching and moral judgment. *Journal of Personality and Social Psychology, 31*, 459–466.

Russell, B. (1945). *A history of western philosophy.* New York: Simon & Schuster.

Russell, M. J. (1976). Human olfactory communication. *Nature, 260*, 520–522.

Rutherford, E. & Mussen, P. H. (1968). Generosity in nursery school boys. *Child Development, 39*, 755–765.

Rutter, D. R., & Durkin, K. (1987). Turn-taking in mother-infant interaction: An examination of vocalization and gaze. *Developmental Psychology, 23*, 54–61.

Rutter, M. (1983). Stress, coping and development: Some issues and some questions. In N. Garmezy & M. Rutter (Eds.), *Stress, coping and development in children.* New York: McGraw-Hill.

Sackin, S., & Thelen, E. (1984). An ethological study of peaceful associative outcomes to conflict in preschool children. *Child Development, 55*, 1098–1102.

Sachs, E. (1952). Intelligence scores as a function of experimentally established social relations between child and examiner. *Journal of Abnormal and Social Psychology, 46*, 354–358.

Sachs, J., & Devin, J. (1976). Young children's use of age-appropriate speech styles in social interaction and role-playing. *Journal of Child Language, 3*, 81–98.

Sagar, H. A., Schofield, J. W., & Snyder, H. N. (1983). Race and gender barriers: Preadolescent peer behavior in academic classrooms. *Child Development, 54*, 1032–1040.

Sagi, A., Lamb, M. E., Lewkowicz, K. S., Shoham, R., Dvir, R., & Estes, D. (1985). Security in infant-mother, -father, and -metapelet attachments among kibbutz-reared Israeli children. *Monographs of the Society for Research in Child Development, 50*, (Serial No. 209) 257–275.

Sahlins, M. D. (1968). *Tribesmen.* Englewood Cliffs, NJ: Prentice-Hall.

Salkind, N. J. & Nelson, C. F. (1980). A note on the developmental nature of reflection-impulsivity. *Developmental Psychology, 16*, 237–238.

Saltzstein, H. D. (1976). Social influence and moral development: A perspective on the role of parents and peers. In T. Lickona (Ed.), *Moral development and behavior: Theory, research and social issues.* New York: Holt, Rinehart & Winston.

Sameroff, A., & Chandler, M. (1975). Reproductive risk and the continuum of caretaking casualty. In F. Horowitz (Ed.), *Review of Child Development Research.* Chicago: University of Chicago Press.

Sameroff, A. (1978). Organization and stability of newborn behavior: A commentary on the Brazelton Neonatal Assessment Scale. *Monographs of the Society for Research in Child Development, 177* (Serial No. 177).

Sameroff, A. J., & Seifer, R. (1983). Familial risk and child competence. *Child Development, 54*, 1254–1268.

Sametz, L. (1983/84). Revamping the adolescent's justice system to serve the needs of the very young offender. *Juvenile and Family Court Journal, 21*–30.

Sampson, E. E. (1985). The decentralization of identity: Toward a revised concept of personal and social order. *American Psychologist, 40*, 1203–1211.

Sander, L. W. (1962). Issues in early mother-infant interaction. *Journal of the American Academy of Child Psychiatry, 1*, 141–166.

Sanders, K. M. & Harper, L. V. (1976). Free play fantasy behavior in preschool children: relations among gender, age, season and location. *Child Development, 47*, 1182–1185.

Sandoval, J., Lambert, N. & Sassone, D. (1980). The identification and labeling of hyperactivity in children: an interactive model. In C. K. Whalen & B. Henker (Eds.), *Hyperactive children: the social ecology of identification and treatment.* NY: Academic Press.

Santrock, J. W. (1972). The relationships of onset and type of father absence to cognitive development. *Child Development, 43*, 455–469.

Santrock, J. W., Warshak, R. A., & Elliott, G. L. (1982). Social development and parent-child interaction in father-custody and stepmother families. In M. E. Lamb (Ed.), *Non-traditional families: Parenting and child development.* Hillsdale, NJ: Erlbaum. (pgs. 289–314).

Sapir, E. (1958). Language and environment. In D. G. Mandelbaum (Ed.), *Selected writings of Edward Sapir in language, culture and perception.* Berkeley, CA: University of California Press.

Sartre, J. P. (1964). *The Words.* NY: Vintage Books.

Sattler, J. M., & Gwynne, J. (1982). White examiners generally do not impede the intelligence performance of black children: To debunk a myth. *Journal of Consulting and Clinical Psychology, 50*, 196–208.

Saxby, L. & Bryden, M. P. (1984). Left-ear superiority in children for processing auditory emotional material. *Developmental Psychology, 20*, 72–80.

Saxby, L. & Bryden, M. P. (1985). Left visual-field advantage in children for processing visual emotional stimuli. *Developmental Psychology, 21*, 253–261.

Scanlan, T. C., & Passer, M. W. (1978). Anxiety inducing factors in competitive youth sports. In F. L. Smoll & R. E. Smith (Eds.), *Psychological perspectives in youth sports* (pp. 107–122). Washington, D.C.: Hemisphere Publishing Company.

Schachter, F. F. (1982). Sibling deidentification and split-family identification: A family tetrad. In M. E. Lamb & B. Sutton-Smith (Eds.), *Sibling relations: Their nature and significance across the life-span*. Hillsdale, NJ: Erlbaum.

Schachter, F. F., Gilutz, G., Shore, E., & Adler, M. (1978). Sibling deidentification judged by mothers: cross-validation and developmental studies. *Child Development, 49*, 543–546.

Schachter, F. F., Shore, E., Feldman-Rotman, S., Marquis, R. E., & Campbell, S. (1976). Sibling deidentification. *Developmental Psychology, 12*, 418–427.

Schachter, F. F., & Stone, R. K. (1985). Difficult sibling, easy sibling: temperament and the within-family environment. *Child Development, 56*, 1335–1344.

Schaefer, E. S. (1959). A circumplex model for maternal behavior. *Journal of Abnormal and Social Psychology, 59*, 226–235.

Schaffer, H. R., & Crook, C. K. (1979). Maternal control techniques in a directed play situation. *Child Development, 50*, 989–996.

Schaffer, H. R., & Crook, C. K. (1980). Child compliance and maternal control techniques. *Developmental Psychology, 16*, 54–56.

Schaffer, H. R., & Emerson, P. (1964). Patterns of response to physical contact in early human development. *Journal of Child Psychiatry and Psychology, 5*, 1–13.

Schaller, J., Carlsson, S. G., & Larsson, K. (1979). Effects of extended post-partum mother-child contact on the mother's behavior during nursing. *Infant Behavior and Development, 2*, 319–324.

Schank, R. C. & Abelson, R. (1977). *Scripts, plans, goals and understanding*. NY: Erlbaum.

Schleifer, M., Weiss, G., Cohen, N., Elman, M., Dvejec, H. & Kruger, E. (1975). Hyperactivity in preschoolers and the effect of methylphenidate. *American Journal of Orthopsychiatry, 45*, 38–50.

Schonfeld, W. (1966). Body image disturbances in adolescents: Influences of family attitudes and psychopathology. *Archives of General Psychiatry, 15*, 16–21.

Schreiber, J. (1977). Birth, the family and the community: A Southern Italian example. *Birth and the Family Journal, 4*, 153–157.

Schreibman, L., & Koegel, R. L. (1982). Multiple-cue responding in autistic children. In Steffen, J. J. & Karoly, P. (Eds.), *Autism and severe psychopathology. Vol. 2: Advances in child behavior analysis and therapy.* (pgs. 81–102) Lexington, MA: Lexington Books.

Schroeder, C., Teplin, S. & Schroeder, S. (1982). An overview of common medical problems encountered in schools. In C. R. Reynolds & T. B. Gutkin (Eds.), *Handbook of school psychology*. NY: Wiley.

Schulenberg, J. E., Asp, C. E., & Petersen, A. C. (1984). School from the young adolescent's perspective: A descriptive report. *Journal of Early Adolescence, 4*, 107–130.

Schwartz, A., Campos, J., & Baisel, E. (1973). The visual cliff: cardiac and behavioral correlates on the deep and shallow sides at 5 and 9 months of age. *Journal of Experimental Child Psychology, 15*, 85–99.

Schwarz, J. (1979). Childhood origins of psychopathology. *American Psychologist, 34*, 879–885.

Schweinhart, L. J., & Weikart, D. P. (1979). *Perry preschool effects in adolescence*. Paper presented to the biennial meeting of the Society for Research in Child Development, San Francisco.

Sears, P. S. (1951). Doll-play aggression in normal young children: influence of sex, age, sibling status, father's absence. *Psychological Monographs, 65*, No. 6.

Sears, R. (1977). Sources of life satisfactions of the Terman gifted men. *American Psychologist, 32*, 119–128.

Secord, P. & Peevers, B. H. (1974). The development and attribution of person concepts. In T. Mischel (Ed.), *Understanding other persons*. Totowa, NJ: Rowman & Littlefield.

Seefeldt, V. in Curnutte, M. (Oct. 18, 1985). "The quest to compete" and "Researchers are studying kids' minds and bodies." *Associated Press*.

Seefeldt, V., & Gould, D. (1980). *Physical and psychological effects of athletic competition on children and youth*. Washington, D.C.: ERIC Clearinghouse on Teacher Education.

Segalowitz, N. S. (1981). Issues in the cross-cultural study of bilingual development. In H. C. Triandic & A. Heron (Eds.), *Handbook of cross-cultural psychology* (Vol. 4). Boston: Allyn & Bacon.

Select Panel for the Promotion of Child Health (1981). *Better health for our children: A national strategy*. DHHS(PHS) Pub. No. 79–55071. Washington, D.C.: U.S. Dept. of Health and Human Services.

Self, P., & Horowitz, F. D. (1979). Assessment of the newborn infant. In J. Osofsky (Ed.), *Handbook on infant development*. New York: Wiley.

Seligman, M. E. P., & Maier, S. (1967). Failure to escape traumatic shock. *Journal of Experimental Psychology, 74*, 1–9.

Selman, R. L. (1976). The development of social-cognitive understanding: a guide to educational and clinical practice. In T. Lickona (Ed.), *Morality: theory, research, and social issues*. NY: Holt, Rinehart & Winston.

Selman, R. L. (1980). *The growth of interpersonal understanding: Developmental and clinical analyses*. NY: Academic Press.

Selman, R. L. (1981). The child as a friendship philosopher: A case study in the growth of interpersonal understanding. In S. R. Asher & J. M. Gottman (Eds.), *The development of children's friendships*. Cambridge: Cambridge University Press.

Selman, R. L., Lavin, D., & Brion-Meisels, S. (1982). Troubled children's use of self-reflection. In P. Serafica (Ed.), *Social-cognitive development in context*. NY: Guilford (pp. 62–99).

Sennett, R., & Cobb, J. (1982). *The hidden injuries of class*. New York: Random House.

Serifica, F. C. (1978). The development of attachment behaviors: An organismic-developmental perspective. *Human Development, 21*, 119–140.

Shaheen, S. J. (1984). Neuromaturation and behavioral development: the case of childhood lead poisoning. *Developmental Psychology, 20*, 542–550.

Shank, R. (1970). A chink in our armor. *Nutrition Today, 5*, 2–11.

Shantz, D. W. (1986). Conflict, aggression and peer status: An observational study. *Child Development, 57*, 1322–1332.

Sharabany, R., Gershoni, R., & Hofman, J. E. (1981). Girlfriend, boyfriend: Age and sex differences in intimate friendships. *Developmental Psychology, 17*, 800–808.

Shatz, M., & Gelman, R. (1973). The development of communication skills: Modifications in the speech of young children as a function of listener. *Monographs of the Society for Research in Child Development, 38*, No. 152.

Sheehan, R. (1982). Infant assessment: A review and identification of emergent trends. In D. Bricker (Ed.), *Intervention with at-risk and handicapped infants: From research to application*. Baltimore: University Park Press.

Shepp, B. E. & Swartz, K. B. (1976). Selective attention and the processing of integral and nonintegral dimensions: a developmental study. *Journal of Experimental Child Psychology, 22*, 73–85.

Sheppard, J. J., & Mysak, E. D. (1984). Ontogeny of infantile oral reflexes and emerging chewing. *Child Development, 55*, 831–843.

Sherrod, K. B., Crawley, S., Petersen, G., & Bennett, P. (1978). Maternal language to prelinguistic infants: Semantic aspects. *Infant Behavior and Development, 1*, 335–346.

Sherrod, L. R. (1979). Issues in cognitive and perceptual development: The special case of social stimuli. In M. E. Lamb & L. R. Sherrod (Eds.), *Infant social cognition*. Hillsdale, NJ: Erlbaum.

Shonkoff, J. P. (1984). The biological substrate and physical health in middle childhood. In W. A. Collins (Ed.), *Development during middle childhood: The years from six to twelve*. Washington, D.C.: National Academy Press.

Shultz, T. R., & Horibe, F. (1974). Development of the appreciation of verbal jokes. *Developmental Psychology, 10*, 13–20.

Shultz, T. R., & Robillard, J. (1980). The development of linguistic humor in children: incongruity through rule violation. In P. E. McGhee & H. J. Chapman (Eds.), *Children's Humour*. New York: Wiley.

Shultz, T. R., Wright, K. & Schleifer, M. (1986). Assignment of moral responsibility and punishment. *Child Development, 57*, 177–184.

Shwalb, D. W., & Schwalb, B. J. (1985). Japanese cooperative and competitive attitudes: Age and gender effects. *International Journal of Behavioral Development, 8*, 313–328.

Siegal, L. S., McCabe, A. E., Brand, J. & Matthews, J. (1978). Evidence for the understanding of class inclusion reasoning in preschool children: linguistic factors and training effects. *Child Development, 49*, 688–693.

Siegal, M. (1980). Kohlberg vs. Piaget: to what extent has one theory eclipsed the other? *Merrill-Palmer Quarterly, 26*, 285–297.

Siegel, L. S. (1978). The relationship of language and thought in the preoperational child: a reconsideration of nonverbal alternatives in Piagetian tasks. In L. S. Siegel & C. J. Brainerd (Eds.), *Alternatives to Piaget: Critical essays on the theory*. NY: Academic Press.

Siegel, L. S. (1985). Psycholinguistic aspects of reading disability. In L. S. Siegel & F. J. Morrison (Eds.), *Cognitive development in atypical children: Progress in cognitive developmental research*. New York: Springer-Verlag.

Siegler, R. S. (1976). Three aspects of cognitive development. *Cognitive Psychology, 8*, 481–520.

Siegler, R. S. (1981). Developmental sequences within and between concepts. *Monographs of the Society for Research in Child Development, 46*, No. 189.

Siegler, R. S. (1983). Information-processing approaches to development. In W. Kessen (Ed.), *Handbook of Child Psychology* (Vol. 1). New York: Wiley.

Sigel, I. E., Roeper, A. & Hooper, F. H. (1968). A training procedure for the acquisition of Piaget's conservation of quantity: A pilot study and its replication. In I. E. Sigel & F. H. Hooper (Eds.), *Logical thinking in children: research based on Piaget's theory*. NY: Holt, Rinehart & Winston.

Silver, M. (1985). Life after tay-sachs. *Jewish Monthly, 99*, 14–23.

Silverman, I. W. & Stone, J. M. (1972). Modifying cognitive functioning through participation in a problem-solving group. *Journal of Educational Psychology, 63*, 603–608.

Simons, J. A. & Marteus, R. (1979). Children's anxiety in sport and nonsport evaluative activities. *Journal of Sport Psychology, 1*, 160–169.

Sims, L., & Morris, P. (1974). Nutritional status of preschoolers. *Journal of the American Dietetic Association, 64*, 492–499.

Simpson, E. L. (1974). Moral development research: a case study of scientific cultural bias. *Human Development, 17*, 81–106.

Sinclair, D. (1978). *Human growth after birth* (3rd Ed.). London: Oxford University Press.

Singer, J. L. & Singer, D. G. (1981). *Television, imagination and aggression: a study of preschoolers*. Hillsdale, NJ: Erlbaum.

Singer, L. M., Brodzinsky, D. M., Ramsay, D., Steir, M., & Waters, E. (1985). Mother-infant attachment in adoptive families. *Child Development, 56*, 1543–1551.

Singleton, L. C., & Asher, S. R. (1979). Racial integration and children's peer preferences: An investigation of developmental and cohort differences. *Child Development, 47*, 1159–1165.

Skarin, K. (1977). Cognitive and contextual determinants of stranger fear in six- and eleven-month-old infants. *Child Development, 48,* 537–544.

Skeels, H. (1966). Adult status of children with contrasting early life experiences. *Monographs of the Society for Research in Child Development, 31,* No. 105.

Skinner, B. F. (1969). *Contingencies of reinforcement: A theoretical analysis.* Englewood Cliffs, NJ: Prentice-Hall.

Skinner, B. F. (1971). *Beyond freedom and dignity.* NY: Knopf.

Slaby, R. G., & Frey, K. S. (1975). Development of gender constancy and selective attention to same-sex models. *Child Development, 46,* 849–856.

Slade, A. (1987). Quality of attachment and early symbolic play. *Developmental Psychology, 23,* 78–85.

Slaughter, D. T. (1980). Social policy issues affecting infants. In D. Weissbourd, & J. Musick (Eds.), *Infants: Their social environments.* National Association for the Education of Young Children.

Slobin, D. (1970). Universals of grammatical development in children. In G. B. Flores d'Arcais & W. J. M. Levelt (Eds.), *Advances in psycholinguistics.* Amsterdam: North-Holland.

Slobin, D. & Bever, T. A. (1982). A cross-linguistic study of sentence comprehension. *Cognition, 12,* 229–265.

Slobin, D. & Welsh, C. A. (1973). Elicited imitation as a research tool in developmental psycholinguistics. In C. A. Ferguson & D. I. Slobin (Eds.), *Studies of childhood language development.* NY: Holt, Rinehart & Winston.

Smetana, J., Kelley, M., & Twentyman, C. T. (1984). Abused, neglected, and nonmaltreated children's conceptions of moral and socio-conventional transgressions. *Child Development, 55,* 277–287.

Smetana, J., & Letoureau, K. J. (1984). Development of gender constancy and children's sex-typed free play behavior. *Developmental Psychology, 20,* 691–696.

Smith, L. B. & Kemler, D. G. (1977). Developmental trends in free classification: evidence for a new conceptualization of perceptual development. *Journal of Experimental Child Psychology, 24,* 279–298.

Smith, L. B., Kemler, D. G. & Aronfreed, J. (1975). Developmental trends in voluntary selective attention: differential effects of source distinctiveness. *Journal of Experimental Child Psychology, 20,* 352–365.

Smith, N. V. (1973). *The acquisition of phonology: A case study.* Cambridge: Cambridge University Press.

Smith, P., & Connolly, K. (1972). Patterns of play and social interaction in preschool children. In N. B. Jones (Ed.), *Ethological studies of child behavior.* Cambridge: Cambridge University Press.

Smith, P. B., Nenney, S. W., Weiman, M. L., & Mumford, D. M. (1982). Factors affecting perception of pregnancy risk in the adolescent. *Journal of Youth and Adolescence, 11,* 207–215.

Smith, P. K. (1983). Differences or deficits? The significance of pretend and sociodramatic play. *Developmental Review, 3,* 6–10.

Smith, P. K. & Connolly, K. J. (1976). Social and aggressive behavior in preschool children as a function of crowding. *Social Science Information, 16,* 601–620.

Smith, P. K., & Whitney, S. (1987). Play and associative fluency: Experimenter effects maybe responsible for previous positive findings. *Developmental Psychology, 23,* 49–53.

Smith, R. J. (1978). Agency drags its feet on warning to pregnant women. *Science, 199,* 748–749.

Smollar, J., & Youniss, J. (1982). Social development through friendship. In K. H. Rubin & H. S. Ross (Eds.), *Peer relations and social skills in children.* New York: Springer-Verlag.

Snarey, J. R., Reimer, J., & Kohlberg, L. (1985). Development of social-moral reasoning among Kibbutz adolescents: A longitudinal cross-cultural study. *Developmental Psychology, 21,* 3–17.

Snow, C. E., DeBlauw, A., & VanRoosmalen, G. (1979). Talking and playing with babies: The role of ideologies in child-rearing. In M. Bullowa (Ed.) *Before Speech.* Cambridge University Press.

Speece, M. W., & Brent, S. B. (1984). Children's understanding of death: A review of three components of a death concept. *Child Development, 55,* 1671–1686.

Speer, J. R. & Flavell, J. H. (1979). Young children's knowledge of the relative difficulty of recognition and recall memory tasks. *Developmental Psychology, 15,* 214–217.

Spemann, H. (1938). *Embryonic development and induction.* New Haven: Yale University Press.

Spencer, M. B. (1982). Personal and group identity of black children: An alternative synthesis. *Genetic Psychology Monographs, 106,* 59–84.

Spencer, M. B. (1983). Children's cultural values and parental child-rearing strategies. *Developmental Review, 3,* 351–370.

Sponseller, D. & Jaworski, A. (1979). *Social and cognitive complexity in young children's play: A longitudinal analysis.* Paper presented to the annual meeting of the American Educational Research Association, San Francisco.

Sprafkin, J. N., Liebert, R. M. & Poulos, R. W. (1975). Effects of a prosocial televised example on children's helping. *Journal of Experimental Child Psychology, 20,* 119–126.

Sprafkin, J., & Silverman, T. (1982). Sex on prime time. In M. Schwarz (Ed.), *TV and teens* (pp. 130–135). Reading, MA: Addison-Wesley.

Sroufe, L. A., & Waters, E. (1976). The ontogenesis of smiling and laughter. *Psychological Review, 83,* 173–189.

Sroufe, L. A. (1979). Socioemotional development. In J. Osofsky (Ed.), *Handbook of infant development.* New York: Wiley.

Staffieri, J. R. (1967). A study of social stereotype of body image in children. *Journal of Personality and Social Psychology, 7,* 101–104.

Stake, J. E. (1978). Motive for occupational goal setting among male and female college students. *Journal of Applied Psychology, 63,* 617–622.

Stallings, J. (1974). *Follow-through classroom observation evaluation 1972–73: Executive Summary,* Menlo Park, CA: Stanford Research Institute.

Stanley, J. C. (1976). Concern for intellectually talented youths: how it originated and fluctuated. *Journal of Clinical Child Psychology, 5,* 38–42.

Stanley, J. C. (1979). Identifying and nurturing the intellectually gifted. In W. C. George, S. J. Cohn & J. C. Stanley (Eds.), *Educating the gifted: acceleration and enrichment.* Baltimore: Johns Hopkins Press.

Stanley, J. C. & Benbow, C. P. (1983). SMPY's first decade: Ten years of posing problems and solving them. *Journal of Special Education, 17,* 11–25.

Stanton, A. N., Scott, D. J., & Downham, M. A. (1980). Is overheating a factor in some unexpected infant deaths? *Lancet,* 1054–1057.

Stark, R. E. (1978). Features of infant sounds: The emergence of cooing. *Journal of Child Language, 3,* 379–390.

Staub, E. (1971). Helping a person in distress: the influence of implicit and explicit "rules" of conduct on children and adults. *Journal of Personality and Social Psychology, 17,* 137–144.

Staub, E. (1974). Helping a distressed person. In L. Berkowitz (Ed.), *Advances in experimental social psychology.* (Vol. 7). NY: Academic Press.

Staub, E. (1979). *Positive social behavior and morality.* Vol. 2. New York: Academic Press.

Stayton, D. J., Ainsworth, M. D. S., & Main, M. B. (1973). The development of separation behavior in the first year of life: Protest, following, greeting. *Developmental Psychology, 9,* 213–225.

Steele, B. F., & Pollack, D. (1968). A psychiatric study of parents who abuse infants and young children. In R. E. Helfer & C. H. Kempe (Eds.), *The battered child.* Chicago: University of Chicago Press.

Stein, A. H., & Friedrich, L. K. (1972). Television content and young children's behavior. In J. P. Murray, E. A. Rubinstein & G. A. Comstock (Eds.), *Television and social behavior.* Vol. 2: Television and social learning. Washington, D.C.: Government Printing Office.

Stein, B. S., Bransford, J. D., Franks, J. J., Owings, R. A., Vye, M. J. & McGraw, W. (1982). Differences in the precision of self-generated elaborations. *Journal of Experimental Psychology: General, 11,* 399–405.

Steinberg, L. D. (1981). Transformations in family relations at puberty. *Developmental Psychology, 17,* 833–840.

Steinberg, L. D. (1982). Jumping off the work experience bandwagon. *Journal of Youth and Adolescence, 11,* 183–204.

Steinberg, L. D. (1987). Single parents, stepparents and the susceptibility of adolescents to antisocial peer pressure. *Child Development, 58,* 269–275.

Steinberg, L. D., & Hill, J. (1978). Patterns of family interaction as a function of the age, the onset of puberty, and formal thinking. *Developmental Psychology, 14,* 680–684.

Steinmetz, S. K., & Straus, M. A. (1974). *Violence in the family.* NY: Harper & Row.

Stephan, C. W. & Langlois, J. H. (1984). Baby beautiful: adult attributions of infant competence as a function of infant attractiveness. *Child Development, 55,* 576–585.

Stern, D. N. (1974). Mother and infant at play: The dyadic interaction involving facial, vocal and gaze behaviors. In M. Lewis & L. Rosenblum (Eds.), *The effect of the infant on its caregivers.* New York: Wiley.

Stern, D. N., Beebe, B., Jaffee, J., & Bennett, S. (1977). The infant's stimulus world during social interaction. In H. R. Schaffer (Ed.), *Studies in mother-infant interaction.* London: Academic Press.

Stern, D. N., Spieker, S., & MacKain, K. (1982). Intonation contours as signals in maternal speech to pre-linguistic infants. *Developmental Psychology, 18,* 727–735.

Sternberg, R. J. (1982). A componential approach to intellectual development. In R. J. Sternberg (Ed.), *Advances in the psychology of human intelligence* (Vol. 1, pp. 413–463). Hillsdale, NJ: Erlbaum.

Sternberg, R. J. (1985). *Beyond IQ: A triarchic theory of human intelligence.* New York: Cambridge University Press.

Sternberg, R. J., Conway, B. E., Ketron, J. L., & Bernstein, M. (1981). People's conceptions of intelligence. *Journal of Personality and Social Psychology: Attitudes and Social Cognition, 41,* 37–55.

Sternberg, R. J., & Powell, J. S. (1983). The development of intelligence. In J. H. Flavell & E. M. Markman (Eds.), *Handbook of Child Psychology* (Vol. 3). New York: Wiley.

Stevens, J. H. (1984). Black grandmothers' and black adolescent mothers' knowledge about parenting. *Developmental Psychology, 20,* 1017–1025.

Stevenson, H. W. (1954). Latent learning in children. *Journal of Experimental Psychology, 47,* 17–21.

Stevenson, H. W. (1965). Social reinforcement of children's behavior. In L. P. Lipsitt & C. C. Spiker (Eds.), *Advances in child development and behavior* (Vol. II). New York: Academic Press.

Stevenson, H. W., Stigler, J. W., Lee, S., Lucker, G. W., Kitamura, S., & Hsu, C. (1985). Cognitive performance and academic achievement of Japanese, Chinese, and American children. *Child Development, 56,* 718–734.

Stewart, E. D. (1981). Learning styles among gifted/talented students: instructional technique preferences. *Exceptional children, 48,* 134–138.

Stewart, R. B. (1983). Sibling attachment relations: child-infant interaction in the Strange Situation. *Developmental Psychology, 19,* 192–199.

Stith, S. M., & Davis, A. J. (1984). Employed mothers and family daycare substitute caregivers: A comparative analysis of infant care. *Child Development, 55,* 1340–1348.

Stolz, H. R., & Stolz, L. M. (1951). *Somatic development of adolescent boys.* New York: MacMillan.

Stone, C. R., & Selman, R. L. (1982). A structural approach to research on the development of interpersonal behavior among grade school children. In K. Rubin & H. S. Ross (Eds.), *Peer relations and social skills in childhood*. NY: Springer-Verlag.

Stone, L. (1977). *The family, sex and marriage in England: 1500–1800*. London: Weidenfeld & Nicolson.

Stoneman, Z., Brody, G. H., & MacKinnon, C. E. (1984). Naturalistic observation of children's activities and roles while playing with their siblings and friends. *Child Development, 55*, 617–627.

Strayer, F. F. (1980). Social ecology of the preschool peer group. In W. A. Collins (Ed.), *Development of cognition, affect, and social relations*. Hillsdale, NJ: Erlbaum.

Strayer, F. F., & Strayer, J. (1976). An ethological analysis of social agonism and dominance relations among pre-school children. *Child Development, 47*, 980–999.

Streissguth, A. P. & Bee, H. L. (1972). Mother-child interactions and cognitive development in children. In W. W. Hartup (Ed.), *The young child: reviews of research*. Washington, D.C.: NAEYC.

Streissguth, A. P., Martin, D. C., Barr, H. M., Sandman, B. M., Kirchner, G. L., & Darby, B. L. (1984). Intrauterine alcohol & nicotine exposure. Attention and reaction time in 4-year-old children. *Developmental Psychology, 20*, 533–541.

Stunkard, A. J., Sorensen, T. I. A., Harris, C., Teasdale, T. W., Chakraborty, R., Schull, W. J. & Schulsinger, F. (1986). An adoption study of human obesity. *New England Journal of Medicine, 314*, 193–197.

Subirana, A. (1969). Handedness and cerebral dominance. In P. J. Vinken & G. W. Bruyn (Eds.), *Handbook of clinical neurology*, Vol. 4. Amsterdam: North-Holland Press.

Sullivan, M. W., Rovee-Collier, C. K., & Tynes, D. M. (1979). A conditioning analysis of infant long-term memory. *Child Development, 50*, 152–162.

Suomi, S. J., Mineka, S., & Delizio, R. D. (1983). Short- and long-term effects of repetitive mother-infant separations on social development in rhesus monkeys. *Developmental Psychology, 19*, 770–786.

Super, C. (1982). Application of multi-dimensional scaling techniques to the estimation of children's ages in field research. Unpublished manuscript. Cited in Sternberg, R. (1985).

Super, D. E. (1953). A theory of vocational development. *American Psychologist, 8*, 185–190.

Supreme Court of the United States. (1974). Decision in Lau v. Nichols, 414 U.S. 563.

Suransky, V. P. (1982). *The erosion of childhood*. Chicago: University of Chicago Press.

Surgeon General. (1979). *Report on health promotion and disease prevention*. Washington, D.C.: Government Printing Office.

Suwalsky, J. T., & Klein, R. P. (1980). Effects of naturally-occurring nontraumatic separations for mother. *Infant Mental Health Journal, 1*, 196–201.

Swanson, J. M. & Kinsbourne, M. (1979). The cognitive effects of stimulant drugs on hyperactive children. In G. A. Hale & M. Lewis (Eds.), *Attention and cognitive development*. NY: Plenum Press.

Sweet, J. (1985). Probation as therapy. *Corrections Today, 89–90*.

Sylva, K., Bruner, J. & Genova, P. (1976). The role of play in the problem-solving of children 3–5 yrs. old. In J. Bruner, A. Jolly, & K. Sylva (Eds.). *Play*. NY: Basic Books.

Taeuber, I. B., & Orleans, L. A. (1965). Mainland China. In B. Berelson (Ed.), *Family planning and population programs*. Chicago: University of Chicago Press.

Takahashi, K. (1986). Examining the strange-situation procedure with Japanese mothers and 12-month-old infants. *Developmental Psychology, 22*, 265–270.

Tan, L. E. (1985). Laterality and motor skills in four-year-olds. *Child Development, 56*, 119–124.

Tanner, J. M. (1968). Earlier maturation in man. *Scientific American, 218*, 21–27.

Tanner, J. M. (1970). Physical growth. In P. H. Mussen (Ed.), *Manual of child psychology* (3rd ed.) (pp. 77–156). New York: Wiley.

Tanner, J. M. (1978). *Foetus into man: physical growth from conception to maturity*. London: Open Books.

Taub, H. B., Goldstein, K. M., & Caputo, D. V. (1977). Indices of neonatal prematurity as discriminators of development in middle childhood. *Child Development, 48*, 797–805.

Television and behavior: Ten years of scientific progress and implications for the eighties (1982). Vol. 4: Summary report. Washington, D.C.: U.S. Department of Health and Human Services.

Ten-State Nutrition Survey: 1968–1970. IV. Biochemical (1972). Atlanta, GA: Dept. of HEW, Health Services and Mental Health Administration, Center for Disease Control, DHEW Pub. No. HSM 72–8132.

Terman, L. M., & Merrill, M. A. (1973). *Stanford-Binet intelligence scale: Manual for third revision form L-M*. Boston: Houghton-Mifflin.

Terman, L. M., & Oden, M. H. (1947). *Genetic studies of genius: The gifted child grows up* (Vol. 4). Palo Alto: Stanford University Press.

Teyler, T. J., & Chiaia, N. (1984). Brain structure and development. In M. Frank (Ed.) *A child's brain* (pp. 23–44). New York: Haworth Press.

Thelen, E. & Fisher, D. M. (1982). Newborn stepping: An explanation for the "disappearing reflex." *Developmental Psychology, 18*, 760–775.

Thelen, E., Fisher, D. M., & Ridley-Johnson, R. (1984). The relationship between physical growth and a newborn reflex. *Infant Behavior and Development, 7*, 479–493.

Thomas, B. & Chess, S. (1968). *Temperament and behavior disorders in children*. NY: NYU Press.

Thomas, G., Lee, P., Franks, P., & Paffenbarger, R. (Eds.) (1981). *Exercise and health: The evidence and the implications*. Cambridge, England: Oelgeschlager, Gunn & Hain.

Thomas, R. M. (1985). *Comparing theories of child development* (2nd edition). Belmont, CA: Wadsworth.

Thompson, R. A. (1987). Development of children's inferences of the emotions of others. *Developmental Psychology, 23,* 124–131.

Thompson, S. K. (1975). Gender labels and early sex-role development. *Child Development, 46,* 339–347.

Thomson, C. A. & Pollitt, E. (1977). Effects of severe protein-calorie malnutrition on behavior in human populations. In L. S. Greene (Ed.), *Malnutrition, behavior and social organization.* NY: Academic Press.

Thorne, B. (1986). Girls and boys together . . . but mostly apart: Gender arrangements in elementary schools. In W. W. Hartup & Z. Rubin (Eds.). *Relationships and development.* Hillsdale, NJ: Erlbaum.

Tieger, T. (1980). On the biological basis of sex differences in aggression. *Child Development, 51,* 943–963.

Tietjen, A. M. & Walker, L. J. (1985). Moral reasoning and leadership among men in a Papua New Guinea society. *Developmental Psychology, 21,* 982–992.

Tinsley, V. S. & Waters, H. S. (1982). The development of verbal control over motor behavior: a replication and extension of Luria's findings. *Child Development, 53,* 746–753.

Tizard, B., Philps, J. & Plewis, I. (1976). Play in preschool centers. I. Play measures and their relation to age, sex, and I.Q. *Journal of Child Psychology and Psychiatry, 17,* 251–264.

Tizard, J., Schofield, W. N., & Hewison, J. (1982). Collaboration between teachers and parents assisting children's reading. *British Journal of Educational Psychology, 52,* 1–15.

Todd, C. & Perlmutter, M. (1980). Reality recalled by preschool children. In M. Perlmutter (Ed.), *Children's Memory.* San Francisco: Jossey-Bass.

Tomlinson-Keasey, C., & Keasey, C. B. (1974). The mediating role of cognitive development and moral judgment. *Child Development, 45,* 291–298.

Tompkins, S. (1962). *Affect, imagery and consciousness.* Vol. 1. New York: Springer.

Trause, M. A. (1977). Stranger responses: Effects of familiarity, stranger's approach and sex of infant. *Child Development, 48,* 1657–1661.

Trehub, S. E., Bull, D., & Thorpe, L. A. (1984). Infant's perception of melodies: The role of melodic contour. *Child Development, 55,* 821–830.

Trevarthen, C. (1973). Behavioral embryology. In E. C. Carteretteaud & M. P. Friedman (Eds.), *Handbook of perception.* New York: Academic Press.

Trevarthen, C. (1977). Descriptive analysis of infant communicative behavior. In H. R. Schaffer (Ed.), *Studies in mother-infant interaction.* London: Academic Press.

Trevarthen, C. (1980). Neurological development and the growth of psychological functions. In J. Sants (Ed.), *Developmental Psychology & Society.* London: MacMillen.

Triolo, S. J., McKenry, P. C., Tishler, C. L., & Blyth, D. A. (1984). Social and psychological discriminants of adolescent suicide: Age and sex differences. *Journal of Early Adolescence, 4,* 239–251.

Tucker, M. J. (1976). The child as beginning and end: Fifteenth- and seventeenth-century English childhood. In L. deMause (Ed.), *The history of childhood.* London: Souvenir Press.

Turiel, E. (1978). The development of concepts of social structure: Social convention. In J. Glick & K. A. Clarke-Stewart (Eds.), *The development of social understanding.* New York: Gardner Press. (a)

Turiel, E. (1978). Social convention and morality: Two distinct conceptual and developmental systems. In C. B. Keasy (Ed.), *Nebraska symposium on motivation: Social-cognitive development.* Vol. 25. Lincoln, Neb: University of Nebraska Press. (b)

Turkington, C. (1983). Lifetime of fear may be legacy of latchkey children. *APA Monitor,* Nov., p. 19.

Turnbull, A. P. (1982). Preschool mainstreaming: A policy and implementation analysis. *Educational Evaluation and Policy Analysis, 4,* 281–291.

Turnure, J., Buium, N., & Thurlow, M. (1976). The effectiveness of interrogatives for promoting verbal elaboration productivity in children. *Child Development, 47,* 851–855.

U.S. Bureau of the Census. (1981). *Child support and alimony: 1978* (Series P–23, No. 112). Washington, D.C.: U.S. Government Printing Office.

U.S. Select Committee on Nutrition and Human Needs. (1977). *Dietary goals for the U.S.* (2nd Ed.). Washington, D.C.: Government Printing Office.

United Nations Department of Economic and Social Affairs. (1980). *Demographic Yearbook,* New York: United Nations.

United Nations Department of Economic and Social Affairs. (1984). *Demographic Yearbook.* New York: United Nations.

Urbain, E. S. & Kendall, P. C. (1980). Review of social-cognitive problem-solving intervention with children. *Psychological Bulletin, 88,* 109–143.

Uzigiris, I. C. (1964). Situational generality of conservation. *Child Development, 35,* 831–841.

Vadham, V. P. & Smothergill, D. W. (1977). Attention and cognition. *Cognition, 5,* 251–263.

Vandell, D. (1979). Effects of playgroup experience on mother-son and father-son interaction. *Developmental Psychology, 15,* 379–385.

Vandell, D. (1980). Sociability with peer and mother during the first year. *Developmental Psychology, 16,* 355–361.

Vandell, D. L., & Wilson, K. S. (1987). Infants' interactions with mother, sibling and peer: Contrasts and relations between interaction systems. *Child Development, 58,* 176–186.

Vandenberg, B. (1980). Play, problem-solving & creativity. In K. Rubin (Ed.) *Children's Play. New Directions for Child Development, 9,* 49–68.

Vaughn, B. E., Bradley, C. F., Joffe, L. S., Seifer, R., & Barglow, P. (1987). Maternal characteristics measured prenatally are predictive of ratings of temperamental "difficulty" on the Carey Infant Temperament Questionnaire. *Developmental Psychology, 23,* 152–161.

Vaughn, B., Egeland, B., Sroufe, L. A., & Waters, E. (1979). Individual differences in infant-mother attachment at twelve and eighteen months: Stability and change in families under stress. *Child Development, 50*, 971–975.

Vaughan, B. & Langlois, J. (1983). Physical attractiveness as a correlate of peer status and social competence in preschool children. *Developmental Psychology, 19*, 561–567.

Vega-Lahr, N., & Field, T. (1986). Type A behavior in preschool children. *Child Development, 57*, 1333–1348.

Vellutino, F. R., Smith, H., Steger, J. A., & Karman, M. (1975). Reading disability: Age differences and the perceptual-deficit hypothesis. *Child Development, 46*, 487–493.

Virtue, M. S. & French, D. C. (1984). Peer and teacher ratings of socially neglected and rejected 4th & 5th grade boys. *Journal of Applied Developmental Psychology, 5*, 13–22.

Vondracek, F. W., & Lerner, R. M. (1982). Vocational role development in adolescence. In B. B. Wolman (Ed.), *Handbook of developmental psychology* (pp. 602–615). Englewood Cliffs, NJ: Prentice-Hall.

Vurpillot, E. (1968). The development of scanning strategies and their relation to visual differentiation. *Journal of Child Psychology, 6*, 632–650.

Vurpillot, E. & Ball, W. A. (1979). The concept of identity and children's selective attention. In G. A. Hale & M. Lewis (Eds.), *Attention and cognitive development*. NY: Plenum.

Vygotsky, L. S. (1962). *Thought and language*. Cambridge, MA: MIT Press.

Vygotsky, L. S. (1978). *Mind in society*. Cambridge, MA: Harvard University Press.

Wachs, T. E., & Gruen, G. E. (1982). *Early experience and human development*. New York: Plenum.

Wagner, D. A. (1981). Culture and memory development. In H. C. Triandis & A. Heron (Eds.), *Handbook of cross-cultural psychology* (Vol. 4). Boston: Allyn & Bacon.

Walden, T. A. & Ramey, C. T. (1983). Locus of control and academic achievement: Results from a preschool intervention program. *Journal of Educational Psychology, 75*, 347–358.

Walker, L. J. (1980). Cognitive and perspective-taking prerequisites for moral development. *Child Development, 51*, 131–139.

Walker, L. J. (1982). The sequentiality of Kohlberg's stages of moral development. *Child Development, 53*, 1330–1336.

Walker, L. J. (1984). Sex differences in the development of moral reasoning: a critical review. *Child Development, 55*, 677–691.

Walker, L. J. (1986). Sex differences in the development of moral reasoning: a rejoinder to Baumrind. *Child Development, 57*, 522–526.

Wallach, M. A. & Kogan, N. (1965). *Modes of Thinking in Young Children*. New York: Holt, Rinehart & Winston.

Wallander, J. L. & Hubert, N. C. (1985). Long-term prognosis for children with attention deficit disorder with hyperactivity (ADD/H). In B. B. Lahey & A. E. Kazdin (Eds.), *Advances in clinical child psychology*. (Vol. 8). NY: Plenum Press.

Wallerstein, J. S., & Kelly, J. B. (1980). *Surviving the breakup: How children and parents cope with divorce*. New York: Basic Books.

Walters, G. C. & Grusec, J. E. (1977). *Punishment*. San Francisco: W. H. Freeman & Co.

Wapner, J. G., & Connor, K. (1986). The role of defensiveness in cognitive impulsivity. *Child Development, 57*, 1370–1374.

Ward, S., Wackman, D. & Wartella, E. (1977). *How children learn to buy*. Beverly Hills, CA: Sage Publications.

Ward, T. B. (1980). Separable and integral responding by adults and children to the dimensions of length and density. *Child Development, 50*, 109–124.

Warren, S. F., Rogers-Warren, A., & Baer, D. M. (1976). The role of offer rates in controlling sharing by young children. *Journal of Applied Behavior Analysis, 9*, 491–497.

Warshak, R. & Santrock, J. W. (1979). *The effects of father and mother-custody on children's social development*. Paper presented at the biennial meeting of the Society for Research on Child Development, San Francisco.

Waterman, A. S., & Waterman, C. K. (1971). A longitudinal study of change in ego identity status during the freshman year at college. *Developmental Psychology, 5*, 167–173.

Waters, E. (1983). The stability of individual differences in infant attachment: Comments on the Thompson, Lamb, and Estes contributions. *Child Development, 54*, 516–520.

Waters, E., Vaughn, B., & Egeland, B. (1980). Individual differences in infant-mother attachment relationships at age one: Antecedents in neonatal behavior in an urban, economically disadvantaged sample. *Child Development, 51*, 208–216.

Waters, E., Wippman, J., & Sroufe, L. A. (1979). Attachment, positive affect, and competence in the peer group: Two studies of construct validation. *Child Development, 50*, 821–829.

Watson, J. B. (1928). *Psychological care of infant and child*. New York: Norton.

Watson, J. S. (1973). Smiling, cooing and "the game." *Merrill-Palmer Quarterly, 18*, 323–339.

Watson, M. W. (1981). The development of social roles: A sequence of social-cognitive development. In K. W. Fischer (Ed.), *Cognitive Development*. New Direction for Child Development (No. 12). San Francisco: Jossey-Bass.

Wechsler, D. (1974). *Manual for the Wechsler Intelligence Scale for Children-Revised*. New York: Psychology Corp.

Wehren, A., & DeLisi, R. (1983). The development of gender understanding: judgments and explanations. *Child Development, 54*, 1568–1578.

Weibel-Orlando, J. (1984). Substance abuse among American Indian youth: A continuing crisis. *Journal of Drug Issues, 14*, 313–335.

Weikart, D. P. (1978). Development of effective preschool programs: A report on the results of the High/Scope-Ypsilanti preschool projects. Unpublished report, cited in Lawton & Hooper, op cit.

Weiner, I. B. (1980). Psychopathology in adolescence. In J. Adelson (Ed.), *Handbook of adolescent psychology* (pp. 447–471). New York: Wiley.

Weinraub, M., Clemens, L. P., Sockloff, A., Ethridge, T., Gracely, E., & Myers, B. (1984). The development of sex role stereotypes in the third year: relations to gender labelling, sex-typed toy preference and family characteristics. *Child Development, 55,* 1493–1503.

Weinraub, M., & Frankel, J. (1977). Sex differences in parent-infant interactions during free play, departure and separation. *Child Development, 48,* 1240–1249.

Weinraub, M., & Lewis, M. (1977). The determinants of children's responses to separation. *Monographs of the Society for Research in Child Development, 42,* (Serial no. 172).

Weinraub, M., & Putney, E. (1978). The effect of height on infant's social responses to unfamiliar persons. *Child Development, 49,* 598–603.

Weir, R. H. (1962). *Language in the crib.* The Hague: Mouton Pubs.

Weir, R. H. (1966). Questions on the learning of phonology. In F. Smith & G. A. Miller (Eds.), *The genesis of language: a psycholinguistic approach.* Cambridge, MA: MIT Press.

Weir, R., & Feldman, W. (1975). A study of infant feeding practices. *Birth and the Family Journal, 2,* 63–64.

Weisner, T. (1982). Sibling interdependence and child caretaking: A cross-cultural view. In M. Lamb & B. Sutton-Smith (Eds.), *Sibling relations: Their nature and significance across the life-span.* Hillsdale, NJ: Erlbaum.

Weisner, T. (1984). Ecocultural niches of middle childhood: A cross-cultural perspective. In W. A. Collins (Ed.), *Development during middle childhood: The years from six to twelve* (pp. 335–369). Washington, D.C.: National Academy Press.

Weisner, T., & Gallimore, R. (1977). My brother's keeper: Child and sibling caretaking. *Current Anthropology, 18,* 169–190.

Weiss, B. (1982). Food additives and environmental chemicals as sources of childhood behavior disorder. *Journal of the American Academy of Child Psychiatry, 21,* 144–152.

Weithorn, L. A., & Campbell, S. B. (1982). The competency of children and adolescents to make informed treatment decisions. *Child Development, 53,* 1589–1598.

Weitzman, L. J. (1985). *The divorce revolution: The unexpected social and economic consequences for women and children in America.* New York: Free Press.

Wellman, H. M. (1977). Preschoolers' understanding of memory-related variables. *Child Development, 48,* 1720–1723.

Wellman, H. M. (1978). Knowledge of the interaction of memory variables: A developmental study of metamemory. *Developmental Psychology, 14,* 24–29.

Wellman, H. M., Collins, J. & Glieberman, J. (1981). Understanding the combination of memory variables: developmental considerations of memory limitations. *Child Development, 52,* 1313–1317.

Wenckstern, S., Weizmann, F., & Leenaars, A. A. (1984). Temperament and tempo of play in eight-month-old infants. *Child Development, 55,* 1195–1199.

Wente, A., & Crockenberg, S. (1976). Transition to fatherhood: Pre-natal Lamaze preparation, adjustment difficulty and the adult husband-wife relationship. *Family Coordinator, 25,* 351–357.

Werker, J. F., & Tees, R. C. (1984). Cross-language speech perception: evidence for perceptual reorganization during the first year of life. *Infant Behavior and Development, 7,* 49–63.

Werner, E. (1979). *Cross-cultural child development.* Monterey, Calif: Brooks-Cole.

Werner, E. (1986). The infant's view of planet earth. Paper presented at International Conference on Infant Studies, Los Angeles.

Werner, E., Bierman, J., & French, F. (1971). *The children of Kauai.* Honolulu: University of Hawaii Press.

West, D. J. (1982). *Delinquency: Its roots, careers and prospects.* Cambridge: Harvard Univ. Press.

West, M. J., & Rheingold, H. L. (1978). Infant stimulation of maternal instruction. *Infant Behavior and Development, 1,* 205–215.

Westbrook, M. (1978). Analyzing affective responses to past events: Women's reaction to a childbearing year. *Journal of Clinical Psychology, 34,* 967–971.

White, B. L. (1975). *The first three years of life.* Englewood Cliffs, NJ: Prentice-Hall.

White, B. L., & Castle, P. W. (1964). Visual and exploratory behavior following post-natal handling of human infants. *Perceptual and Motor Skills, 18,* 497–502.

White, S. H. (1965). Evidence for a hierarchical arrangement of learning processes. In L. P. Lipsitt & C. C. Spiker (Eds.), *Advances in child development and behavior* (Vol. 2). New York: Academic Press.

Whiting, B. B. (1974). Folk wisdom and child-rearing. *Merrill-Palmer Quarterly, 20,* 9–19.

Whiting, B. B. & Edwards, C. P. (1973). A cross-cultural analysis of sex differences in the behavior of children aged 3 through 11. *Journal of Social Psychology, 91,* 171–188.

Whiting, B. B., & Whiting, J. W. M. (1975). *Children of six cultures: a psychocultural analysis.* Cambridge, MA: Harvard University Press.

Whiting, J. W. M. (1981). Environmental constraints on infant care practices. In R. Monroe, R. Monroe, & B. Whiting (Eds.), *Handbook of cross-cultural development.* New York: Garland.

Whorf, B. (1956). *Language, thought and reality.* New York: Wiley.

Williams, J. W., & Stith, M. (1980). *Middle childhood: Behavior and development.* New York: Macmillan.

Wills, D. M. (1972). Problems of play and mastery in the blind child. In E. P. Trapp & P. Himelstein (Eds.), *Readings on the exceptional child.* NY: Appleton-Century-Crofts.

Wilson, E. (1975). *Sociobiology.* New York: Wiley.

Wilson, R. S. & Harpring, E. B. (1972). Mental and motor development in infant twins. *Developmental Psychology, 7,* 277–287.

Wilson, W. P., Shogren, R. E., & Witryol, S. L. (1978). Storage in children's word recognition as a function of incentives. *Journal of Genetic Psychology, 132,* 137–147.

Winick, M. (1975) (Ed.), *Childhood obesity.* NY: Wiley.

Winick, M. (1976) *Malnutrition and brain development.* NY: Oxford University Press.

Winner, E., Rosenstiel, A. K., & Gardner, H. (1976). The development of metaphoric understanding. *Developmental Psychology, 12,* 289–297.

Witkin, H. A., Dyk, R. B., Paterson, H. F., Goodenough, D. R. & Karp, S. A. (1962). *Psychological differentiation.* NY: Wiley.

Wittelson, S. F. (1977). Developmental dyslexia: Two right hemispheres and none left. *Science, 195,* 309–311.

Wolf, T. M., Sklov, M. C., Wenzl, P. A., Hunter, S., & Berenson, G. S. (1982). Validation of a measure of Type A behavior pattern in children: Bogalusa Heart study. *Child Development, 53,* 126–135.

Wolff, P. H. (1966). The causes, controls and organization of behavior in the neonate. *Psychological Issues, 5,* 1–105.

Wolman, R., Lewis, W., & King, M. (1971). The development of the language of emotions: Conditions of emotional arousal. *Child Development, 42,* 1288–1293.

Wong, B. Y. L. (1985). Metacognition and learning disability. In D. L. Forrest-Pressley, G. E. MacKinnon & T. G. Waller (Eds.). *Metacognition, cognition and human performance. Vol. 2: Instructional practices.* NY: Academic Press.

Woodson, R., Drinkwin, J., & Hamilton, C. (1985). Effects of nonnutritive sucking on state and activity: Term and preterm comparisons. *Infant Behavior and Development, 8,* 435–442.

World Health Organization. (1963). *Malnutrition and disease.* Geneva: WHO.

Yang, R. K. (1979). Early infant assessment: An overview. In J. Osofsky (Ed.), *Handbook of infant development.* New York: Wiley.

Yawkey, T. D. (1980). *The self-concept of the child.* Salt Lake City, UT: Brigham Young University Press.

Yogman, M. W., Dixon, S., Tronick, E., Als, H., Adamson, L., Lester, B., & Brazelton, T. B. (1977). *The goals and structure of face-to-face interaction between infants and fathers.* Paper presented at the meeting of the Society for Research in Child Development, New Orleans.

Yonas, A., Bechtold, A., Frankel, D., Gordon, F., McRoberts, G., Norcia, A., & Sternfels, D. (1977). Development of sensitivity to information for impending collision. *Perception and Psychophysics, 21,* 97–104.

Young, R. A. (1983). Career development of adolescents: An ecological perspective. *Journal of Youth and Adolescence, 12,* 401–417.

Yussen, S. R. (1977). Characteristics of moral dilemmas written by adolescents. *Developmental Psychology, 13,* 162–163.

Yussen, S. R. & Berman, L. (1981). Memory predictions for recall and recognition in first, third and fifth grade children. *Developmental Psychology, 17,* 224–229.

Yussen, S. R. & Levy, V. M. (1975). Developmental changes in predicting one's own span of short-term memory. *Journal of Experimental Child Psychology, 19,* 502–508.

Zabrucky, K. & Ratner, H. H. (1986). Children's comprehension monitoring and recall of inconsistent stories. *Child Development, 57,* 1401–1418.

Zack, P. M., Harlan, W. R., Leaverton, P. E. & Cornoni-Huntley, J. (1979). A longitudinal study of body fatness in childhood and adolescence. *Journal of Pediatrics, 95,* 126–130.

Zahn-Waxler, C., Iannotti, R., & Chapman, M. (1982). Peers and prosocial development. In K. H. Rubin & H. S. Ross (Eds.), *Peer relations and social skills in childhood.* NY: Springer-Verlag.

Zajonc, R. B., & Marcus, G. B. (1975). Birth order and intellectual development. *Psychological Review, 82,* 74–88.

Zakin, D. F., Blyth, D. A., & Simmons, R. G. (1984). Physical attractiveness as a mediator of the impact of early pubertal changes for girls. *Journal of Youth and Adolescence, 13,* 439–451.

Zarbatany, L., Hartmann, D. P., & Gelfand, D. M. (1985). Why does children's generosity increase with age: susceptibility to experimenter influence or altruism? *Child Development, 56,* 746–756.

Zeitz, D. (1969). *Child welfare: Services and perspectives.* New York: Wiley.

Zelnicker, T. & Jeffrey, W. E. (1976). Reflective and impulsive children: strategies of information-processing underlying differences in problem-solving. *Monographs of the Society for Research in Child Development, 41,* No. 168.

Zeskind, P. S., & Iacino, R. (1984). Effects of maternal visitation to preterm infants in the neonatal intensive care unit. *Child Development, 55,* 1887–1893.

Zeskind, P. S., & Lester, B. M. (1978). Acoustic features of auditory perceptions of the cries of newborns with prenatal and perinatal complications. *Child Development, 49,* 580–589.

Zeskind, P. S. & Lester, B. M. (1981). Analysis of cry features of newborns with differential fetal growth. *Child Development, 52,* 207–212.

Zeskind, P. S., Sale, J., Maio, M. L., Huntington, L., & Weiseman J. R. (1985). Adult perceptions of pain and hunger cries: A synchrony of arousal. *Child Development, 56,* 549–554.

Zigler, E. & Butterfield, E. C. (1968). Motivational aspects of changes in IQ test performance of culturally deprived nursery school children. *Child Development, 39,* 1–14.

Zill, N. (1983). *Happy, healthy and insecure.* New York: Cambridge University Press.

Zimmerman, B. J. & Lanaro, P. (1974). Acquisition and retaining conservation of length through modeling and reversibility cues. *Merrill-Palmer Quarterly, 20,* 145–161.

Zimmerman, M. (1981). The Home Observation for Measurement of the Environment: A comment on Elardo and Bradley's review. *Developmental Review, 1,* 301–313.

Zlatin, M. A. (1973). Explorative mapping of the vocal tract and primitive syllabification in infancy: The first six months. *Purdue University Contributed Papers,* Fall.

Zuckerman, B., Alpert, J., Dooling, E., Hingson, R., Kayne, H., Morelock, S., & Oppenheimer, E. (1983). Neonatal outcome: Is adolescent pregnancy a risk factor? *Pediatrics, 71,* 489–493.

Photo Credits

1 Alec Duncan/Taurus Photos, 2 Used with permission of Grandma Moses Properties, Inc., and The White House Collections., 6 Elizabeth Crews, 12 The Bettman Archive, Inc., 14 The Bettmann Archive Inc., 15 Alan Fogel, 19 The Bettmann Archive Inc., 21 The Bettmann Archive Inc., 21 The Bettmann Archive Inc., 22 Historical Pictures Service Inc., 26 Blair Seitz/Photo Researchers, 29 Lenore Weber/ Taurus Photos, 32 The Bettmann Archive Inc., 35 Michael Plack/Berg & Associates, 38 UPI/Bettmann Newsphotos, 38 The Bettmann Archive Inc., 44 James Holland/Stock, Boston, 47 Berg & Associates, 54 Purdue University, West Lafayette, Indiana, 56 K. Gross/Historical Pictures Service Inc., 57 Steve Hansen/Stock, Boston, 64 Peter Menzel/Stock, Boston, 65 Michael Weisbrot/Stock, Boston, 70 Purdue University, West Lafayette, Indiana, 72 Charles Nelson, Institute of Child Development, University of Minnesota, 78 Jerry Howard/Stock, Boston, 82 Stu Rosner/Stock, Boston, 84 Peter Menzel/Stock, Boston, 90 Harold M. Lambert Studios, 95 (top)Martin Ratker/Taurus Photos, 95 (bottom)Donald Yeager/ Camera M.D., 96 Donald Yeager/Camera M.D., 104 Elizabeth Crews/Stock, Boston, 110 Jerry Howard/Stock, Boston, 114 Jeff Grosscup, 116 Jeff Grosscup, 123 Frederick Bodin/Stock, Boston, 125 (left)James Holland/Stock, Boston, 125 (right)George Malare/ Stock, Boston, 132 (left)Julia Oesterle, 132 (middle)Ellis Herwig/ Stock, Boston, 132(right) Elizabeth Crews/Stock, Boston, 137 George Adams/Frederic Lewis Inc., 145 Peter Vandermark/Stock, Boston, 146 Alan Fogel, 151 Dagmar Fabricius/Stock, Boston, 153 Frederic Lewis Inc., 157 Courtesy of Richard Walk, 161 Susan Lapides/Design Conceptions, 164 Peter Vandermark/Stock, Boston, 173 Elizabeth Crews/Stock, Boston, 182 Alan Carey/The Image Works, 184 Jean-Claude Lejeune/Stock, Boston, 191 Martin Rogers/Stock, Boston, 192 Michael Plack/Berg & Associates, 197 Betsy Lee/Taurus Photos, 200 Laimute Druskis/Taurus Photos, 205 Elizabeth Crews, 208 George Bellerose/Stock, Boston, 212 Joel Gordon, 215 Peter Vandermark/ Stock, Boston, 216 Michael Hayman/Stock, Boston, 220 Natalie Leimkuhler, 226 Phil Mezey/Taurus Photos, 231 Jeff Albertson/Stock, Boston, 232 (both)Natalie Leimkuhler, 234 Owen Franken/Stock, Boston, 237 Jeffry Meyers/Stock, Boston, 242 Joe Skymba/Berg & Associates, 244 Laimute Druskis/Taurus Photos, 255 Lenore Weber/ Taurus Photos, 257 David Stone/Berg & Associates, 262 L.L.T. Rhodes/Taurus Photos, 265 Edith Hawn/Stock, Boston, 272 Ruth Silverman/Stock, Boston, 276 Susan Lapides/Design Conceptions, 281 Michael Weisbrot/Stock, Boston, 293 Elizabeth Crews/Stock, Boston, 294 Mary Schiller, 297 Gail Melson, 299 Ira Kirschenbaum/Stock, Boston, 306 Lenore Weber/Taurus Photos, 310 Owen Franken/Stock, Boston, 312 Alec Duncan/Taurus Photos, 318 Steve Maines/Stock, Boston, 320 David Woo/Stock, Boston, 325 Alan Fogel, 330 Jerry Berndt/Stock, Boston, 334 Elizabeth Hamlin/Stock, Boston, 339 Miro Vintoniv/Stock, Boston, 340 Mike Mazzaschi/Stock, Boston, 344 PHOTRI, 345 Charles Gupton/Stock, Boston, 347 Julia Oesterle, 356 Billy Barnes/Stock, Boston, 357 Joel Gordon, 361 Joel Gordon, 364 Frank Siteman/Taurus Photos, 370 Chris Grajczyk, 372 Natalie Leimkuhler, 375 Michael Weisbrot/Stock, Boston, 384 Susan Lapides/ Design Conceptions, 387 Natalie Leimkuhler, 391 Historical Pictures Service Inc., 399 George Bellerose/Stock, Boston, 402 Pam Hasegawa/ Taurus Photos, 405 Stan Goldblatt/Photo Researchers, 415 Historical Pictures Service Inc., 421 Historical Pictures Service Inc., 425 Ellis Herwig/Stock, Boston, 426 Children's Television Workshop, 428 James Holland/Stock, Boston, 432 Jim Caccavo/Stock, Boston, 436 Pam Hasegawa/Taurus Photos, 440 Liane Enkelis/Stock, Boston, 447 Charles Schmidt/Taurus Photos, 453 Leonard Freed/Magnum, 456 Steve Hansen/Stock, Boston, 457 (top)Natalie Leimkuhler, 457 (bottom)Bohdan Hrynewych/Stock, Boston, 467 Willie Hill, Jr./Stock, Boston, 468 Gail Melson, 474 Peter Southwick/Stock, Boston, 480 Jeff Grosscup, 484 Charles Gatewood/Stock, Boston, 491 David Austen/Stock, Boston, 494 Natalie Leimkuhler, 498 Natalie Leimkuhler, 503 Herb Snitzer/Stock, Boston, 506 Alan Fogel, 513 John Running/Stock, Boston, 516 Charles Gupton/Stock, Boston, 520 Billy Barnes/Stock, Boston, 525 Steve Hansen/Stock, Boston,